THE PROCESS OF MODERNIZATION

An Annotated Bibliography
on the Sociocultural Aspects of Development

Written under the auspices of

The Center for International Affairs

Harvard University

THE PROCESS OF MODERNIZATION

An Annotated Bibliography
on the Sociocultural Aspects of Development

BY JOHN BRODE

Foreword by Alex Inkeles

HARVARD UNIVERSITY PRESS

Cambridge, Massachusetts

FOREWORD

by

Alex Inkeles

Some of my less sanguine colleagues advised me that to undertake a
compilation of a discriminating bibliography on the social and cultural
aspects of economic development and modernization was to entangle oneself in
a very sticky business. Indeed, it seemed to them to be courting an academic
disaster. The factual basis for their anxiety is not hard to discern,
because it is obviously extremely difficult to decide what can safely be ex-
cluded from a bibliography on so broad a subject. The nations now in various
stages of development are, of course, the essential focus of attention. But
we must also include the already developed countries, because they provide
the presumed model for the process we are studying. And we cannot omit the
peoples who have not yet begun to modernize, because their failure to do so
is an obvious challenge to whatever theory of development we may hold. We
may not neglect the past, because it presumably foreshadows the development
of nations in the future. And how are we to decide what to omit among all the
myriad aspects of social structure which enter into the process of social
change we call "modernization"--themes political, administrative, linguistic,
familial, economic, those touching on social stratification and communica-
tions, those bearing on religion, on law, on education, and so forth.

Obviously some principle is needed to focus and refine the search for
relevant materials. In the case of Mr. Brode, who compiled this bibliography,
his assignment was to assemble materials that would be peculiarly relevant to
the work of the Harvard Project on the Sociocultural Aspects of Development.

The basic objective of the project is to understand more fully the
role of the common man in the process of industrialization, and particularly
to enrich our understanding of the process by which the "traditional" man of
village and farm is transformed into the "modern" man of city and factory.
An initial survey of studies of development complete and in progress
convinced us of the relative neglect of the ordinary man who for the first
time enters modern productive enterprises in developing countries. Our survey
revealed that significant studies have been made of entrepreneurship and conditions conducive to it; of institutional and structural sources of resistance
to modernization; and of the disruption or disorganization of traditional culture so often accompanying the development process. However, previous
research appears to neglect the common man relative to the elite, the factory
and town relative to the farm and village, and the learning of new skills and
adaptive values relative to the loss of traditional activities and social
ties.

Sustained development seems to depend on the wide diffusion through the population of certain attitudes, values, dispositions to act, and habits of doing things which, in combination, characterize the "industrial man" and differentiate him from the man of tradition who makes up the great bulk of the population in most underdeveloped countries. The working assumption of our research is that experience in a modern industrial enterprise will induce changed attitudes which, on the whole, will make men better adapted and more effective citizens of a modern society. In our view, the factory is not only a productive enterprise but also a school, imparting certain more general lessons whose significance will be felt far beyond the confines of the factory compound.

Since the concept of modernization plays so central a role in our research, and therefore was a key in Mr. Brode's approach to the literature, we should make clear how we have used the term. The term "modern" has so many meanings and is surrounded by so much feeling that it might be best if we did not need to use it at all. Since that does not seem feasible, we should make our position as unambiguous as possible.

To begin with, we should stress that we are not making value judgments in using the term "modern" as against "traditional." We do not regard traditional relations--however these may be defined for a given culture--as necessarily inferior to those likely to be imported from outside.

Neither do we assume that traditional practices--that is, common and standard culturally routine ways of doing things in a given population--are necessarily better or more sacred than those brought from outside or newly developed. In addition, we do not assume that the traditional is uniform. For example, the traditional culture of the Maya reflects a very keen sense of time, perhaps more "modern" than that of many New Yorkers, whereas among the Chilean peasants the sense of time may be quite different.

We do not use the term "modern" to mean everything contemporaneous. And we hope we are not using the term simply to disguise the diffusion of certain values, such as individualism as against collectivism, which have a history in Western culture long antedating industrial development.

We use the term "modern" much in the sense that Weber used the term "rational" as a way of characterizing the predominant tone or ethos of relations in the contemporary industrial world. We designate an enterprise as modern to the degree that certain patterns of relations predominate in it, especially in the treatment of workers by foremen and management. We term a factory more modern to the extent that it uses advanced technology, seeks to maximize rationality in its organization, shows awareness of and respect for the worker's sense of dignity, facilitates his understanding of the tasks he is to perform, provides opportunity for advancement through the acquisition of industrial skills, encourages him to hold opinions about his work and respects those he expresses, and permits him to have his own more or less autonomous representative organizations.

The object of the research is to find out whether (and if so, how) employment in modern factories or similar enterprises changes attitudes, values, and habits in the ways which are relevant to the individual's adjustment in and contribution to a modern or modernizing society. The matters to be investigated include orientations to time, technical competence, efficacy or mastery, trust, dignity, planning, particularism-universalism, new experience, and opinion. We also deal with educational aspirations and attitudes toward education; aspirations for advancement for self, children, community, and nation; readiness for change and mobility; political orientations, attitudes, and activities; use of modern and traditional information media; attitudes about family size and planning, women's rights, and kinship obligations; religious orientations and behavior; and social-class attitudes and consumption behavior.

The answers to the questions raised by our research are being sought mainly through a large-scale program of field work which the project is carrying out, with the aid of local collaborators, in six developing countries--Argentina and Chile, India and Pakistan, Nigeria and Israel. In each we are conducting over a thousand detailed interviews on the attitudes, life experiences, and work history of farmers, workers, and urban nonindustrial employees. To provide a firm foundation for the special type of investigation we were undertaking, we needed to know the experience and the ideas of others who had attempted both similar and methodologically different studies in other places and times while yet dealing with approximately the same type of man and situation with which our research dealt.

This, then, largely set the limits of the task Mr. Brode faced: to find studies of village communities that highlighted the elements of stability, innovation, and change; those that threw light on why rural people left the village community in search of new opportunities in factories and urban centers; studies that exposed the problems industry and urban centers have in absorbing and adjusting to the new industrial worker; and particularly those studies that gauge the impact on the new industrial worker of his first experiences in the modern milieu. Mr. Brode, in his Introduction, explains in detail how he fulfilled his assignment and indicates some of the limits of his accomplishment. While these limits are real and substantial, I feel he has provided a most useful addition to the resources of everyone struggling to understand better the momentous process of sociocultural change the world is now experiencing.

CONTENTS

THE PROCESS OF MODERNIZATION

An Annotated Bibliography
on the Sociocultural Aspects of Development

INTRODUCTION

        This bibliography is one product of a large research effort: the Har-
vard Project on the Sociocultural Aspects of Development, conceived and
directed by Professor Alex Inkeles; but of course it is not designed only for
the researchers connected with that project. Rather, it is offered as a tool
by which scholars the world over may sort out for their respective purposes
the vast literature dealing with various aspects of a central theme, "Modernization."

        As defined by Professor Inkeles in his Foreword, "modernization" is a
term for "characterizing the predominant tone or ethos of relations in the
contemporary industrial world." Modernity in this sense manifests itself
through goal-directed behavior that required cognizance of the milieu in
which the intermediate steps toward the goal take place. In other words, it
is the recognition that action at an intermediate level will have indirect
repercussions on the goal. For example, industrialists have come to realize
that they must not only tell a worker what to do; but they must also take care
that he is receptive to the order. An unreceptive worker will obey but not
fulfill: an order is not independent of its context, and in this context, the
order may have indirect and undesirable repercussions on the goal. "Modernization" is thus a rationalization, an attempt to maximize the net or final
achievement of the goal, namely, the achievement left after the effects of all
the repercussions have been deducted.

        Maximization of the net rather than the direct effect is not typical
of all industrialization. Neither the English nor the Russian industrial
revolution proceeded on this basis. Influential groups in both countries
were too intent on achieving certain goals to be concerned with the efficiency
of the approach. These groups tended to the shortsighted belief that the
maximization of profits or achievement in the present is the equivalent of
maximization over a longer time span. In recent years, however, waste has
become intolerable in modern industry, sometimes because any wastage would
reduce the net effect below the lowest useful minimum; in other cases because
the indirect effects had become too expensive to ignore. For these reasons,
industries have developed modern practices of industrial management in an
attempt to rationalize the production process to the fullest.

        In the broad sense, Professor Inkeles and his colleagues are investi-
gating the manner in which a worker's contact with the modern aspects of
industrialization changes his outlook and personality. As is normally the
case, this contact is best studied at the edge of its initial impact, where
a series of examples before, during, and after can be taken from a fairly
homogeneous population. Such edges of impact are to be found throughout the
world, in the developed as well as the developing nations. However, in the
developed nations, the edges of impact are marginal. There may also be a
saturation effect once modernization has been implanted in the greater part
of a society. In other words, past a certain point, modernization with or

without direct contact may become part of the individual's culture. Both
these factors make the study of the process of modernization in a developed
nation considerably more complicated than in a developing nation. Thus the
Harvard Project has turned to the developing nations for source material,
deeming this the most rewarding approach.

At first, material was gathered on primitive groups. In some cases,
these studies dealt with the process of contact with the modern world. Others
were concerned only with the group itself, and they have not been included in
this bibliography. (In all, there were approximately 150 such works, the
largest subgroup being the series of tribal studies covering the African
continent that the International African Institute has sponsored.) Of course,
they do provide a picture of premodern life, but, without at least some sign
of change, these studies are not of immediate use in investigating the process
of modernization. If and when they do become useful, I have no fear that they
will be cited as needed; thus there is no need to give them here.

Since one function of this bibliography is to provide a means for
comparing the findings of the Project, particular emphasis has been placed on
reports of direct field work bearing on the process of modernization. The
process rather than the state of modernization is also stressed. Thus items
have been annotated with an eye only to what they can contribute to an understanding of the process: descriptions of social change under the impact of
some modern factor are noted; other sociological conclusions are ignored.
Annotation does not indicate the over-all worth of the item but only signals
its pertinence to the theme of modernization.

Modernization may be thought of in three categories: the direct impact
of a rationalized, large-scale production process on the individual (industrialization); the indirect effects of modernization induced by the increasing
communication between the developed and developing communities when individuals
confront the elements of modernization (urbanization); and the indirect effects
of modernization when these elements go to the individuals (rural modernization).
In addition to the category "General," these are the three divisions of this
bibliography.

The entries have been gathered from a number of sources. Chief among
these are the International Bibliographies of Sociology and of Social and
Cultural Anthropology published under the auspices of UNESCO. These have been
consulted through 1964. The other bibliographies cited have also been consulted, largely as a check on coverage. Of these, the UNESCO Southern Asia
Social Science Bibliographies and those of the American Association of Asian
Studies are particularly important. Therefore we believe there is relatively
little pertinent material inadvertently left out.

Language forms another factor of selection. Works in the Slavic
language have been left out because the East Europeans have not been carrying
on field work outside their national boundaries. A few studies in Arabic or
Indonesian have been omitted, however pertinent, because of my inability to
read them. Most citations are in English or French; some are in Spanish or
Japanese; and a few are in the other West European languages or in Chinese.

There are three major levels of classification, and many items find
a place in all three. The first level, which applies to all entries, refers
to the four major categories, "General," "Industrialization," "Urbanization,"
and "Rural Modernization." On the second level (except for "General" with
only four sections) each major category is divided into at least five

subsections: "Theory," "Case Studies," "General Studies," "Socioeconomic Studies," and "Bibliographies." (The main category "General" contains no case studies because of the obvious contradiction in terms.) Collections of basic data on social or economic happenings are grouped as "Socioeconomic Studies."

The third level of classification concerns only the case studies. These have been categorized partly because of a predetermined structure, partly because of frequency, and partly because of practicality. Whenever called for case studies have been further subdivided under such headings as "Villages" or "Tribal Factors." Both these subsections happen to include case studies that are specific, but at the same time global. To have subdivided them yet further would give excessive repetition and therefore a certain artificiality. "Community Development" became the fifth subdivision in Part IV because of the very large number of items under this heading. Otherwise they might have been placed in the second subdivision, "Modernization of the Rural Sector." The other subsections are justifiable because of structure.

All case studies dealing with industrialization (the first phase of modernization) are grouped under three headings: "The Impact of Industry," covering urban areas, and "Rural Industry" list those works treating the effect of modern industry on the surrounding community. The effects of industry on individuals, though not covered very extensively, have been placed in a separate subsection, "The Industrial Worker."

Parts III and IV, "Urbanization" and "Rural Modernization," deal with the process of modernization from the viewpoint of the initiated rather than that of the initiator. Family studies form a section under each of these Parts. Further divisions were not made in the category "Urbanization." Studies of urbanizing areas tend to be along geographical rather than topical lines. Urban economic and political structures are already modernized to a considerable degree, whereas our interest is in the process of modernization itself. The items under "Rural Modernization" are more pertinent to the purpose of the bibliography, for rural economic studies usually describe process, and are therefore included along with studies of rural leadership (section 5). "Industrial Agriculture" (section 3) finds a place as a rational, modern approach to production outside a factory environment.

To clarify the classification scheme, let us look at one example, R. E. Phillips, The Bantu in the City (Lovedale, South Africa: Lovedale Press, 1938. 452 pp.). It has been entered in Part III, "Urbanization," section 2, "Urban Problems." The case studies in Part III are so numerous that they form two groupings, subsection 2:B and subsection 3:B. Since this entry has no annotation, it appears in alphabetical order under "Other Case Studies." In short, the categories descend from Part to section to subsection, and according to the nature of the material, to further subordinate groupings. The sequence and numbering of all entries are explained on pages 36-37.

The scope of the annotation was limited in two ways. First, a very few books were not available for consultation. Nevertheless, they have been included because of faith in the bibliographer who originally cited them. Second, and far more importantly, only a few periodical articles were consulted. The reason was a purely technical one. At best, it is often very difficult to locate specific numbers of a given periodical; and many of the periodicals cited here have a very limited circulation. In short, the return to be had from an extensive annotation of articles was not great enough to justify the expense in both time and money that would have been involved.

[3]

The annotations do not try to describe fully either a given work or its
results. On the contrary, they attempt only to indicate the cause of the
change that has occurred and its effects. If an analysis of this process
gives any conclusions, these have been transcribed. If no conclusions are
given, then the item in question does not give any. This does not imply that
conclusions could not be derived from the material contained in that study.
Even a study listed under the category "General," that is, a study of a
particular case but in quite general terms usually not based on detailed field
work, may contain sufficient material to support an analysis, especially when
compared with other studies.

The annotated items have been further rated by the addition of one,
two, or three stars--to be interpreted just as are the well-known étoiles of
the Guides Michelin. The three-star entries are listed in Recommended Readings (p. 23), for in my judgment they are the truly remarkable works in this
field. As these few superb citations do not represent a balanced picture of
what is important, a few items from the sections on theory and general works
have been included with them. It should not be thought that a one-starred
or an unstarred item is not a good book or article. The evaluation in this
bibliography is based only on the relevance of the work to our understanding
of the process of modernization as explained in the Introduction.

At the end of the bibliography there are two indices, one by author,
and another by area. Further information about these, as well as about
recommended readings, about periodicals, about the system of abbreviation,
and about how to use the bibliography is given before the bibliography itself
begins.

Immediately following this Introduction comes a brief survey of the
social science literature bearing on "modernization." Three aspects are
stressed: the methodology used in the research; the tendency of the approach
to vary with the area of the world covered; and the integration of economics
into this part of sociology. This is not an attempt to reiterate conclusions
or to furnish theories, but rather, it is hoped, to indicate to the reader
what to expect from previous research.

My indebtedness runs to great lengths. Foremost is my debt to
Professor Alex Inkeles, under whose able guidance this work was carried to
completion. At a later stage I profited from the acute comments of Professor
Sydney Mintz of Yale University. As with all bibliographical work, the
present compilation made great demands on library staff, in particular on the
former Assistant Librarian of the Center for International Affairs, Miss Nancy
Barber. She was admirably patient as I devoured an endless series of books.
Her successor, Mrs. Dimity Berkner, was equally helpful. I must likewise
thank Miss Margaret Currier, Head Librarian of the Peabody Museum of Archae-
ology and Ethnology, and Mmes Lacoin, de Thomas, and Leurmeusse of the Library
of the Fondation Nationale des Sciences Politiques in Paris. Special thanks
are due to Mrs. Katharine Strelsky, Editor of Publications at the Center for
International Affairs, who is responsible for the clarity and the consistency
of the Bibliography, and to Mrs. Lillian Christmas, Secretary of Publications,
for her undying patience in the preparation of the final manuscript.

A BRIEF SURVEY OF THE LITERATURE

The study of the sociological effects of industrialization, whether modern or not, is of very recent origin. Industrialization dates back nearly two centuries and studies of its impact well into the early part of the nineteenth century. Marx and his followers, but also Saint-Simon, Cobden, and others, were greatly preoccupied with this impact. However, for them it was to be measured in economic or philosophical terms--pauperization or alienation. Comte, Spencer, Sombart, and Weber turned to the theory of the historical development of societies--including the industrialized--but still did not touch on the sociological effects of this process on the people involved.

Sociological studies based on intensive field work were first undertaken at the end of the nineteenth century, and most of them were limited to attitudes or themes. Not until the 1930's did studies of whole communities emerge. Middletown by the Lynds (1937) and Tepoztlán by Robert Redfield (1930; RUR 8077), are landmarks.* Of course, ethnology and anthropology date back much further. But these disciplines are concentrated on cultures, not on groups within a culture. Recently, as we shall see, ethnological and anthropological studies have begun to treat the process of change as part of their domain, thus coming closer to sociology. Margaret Mead's The Changing Culture of an Indian Tribe (1932) is one of the earliest studies of this kind.

Nevertheless, studies of the worker and of urbanization in the developing world are scarce even today, not because of a lack of interest but because of the problems posed by this type of research. It is obvious at first glance that a village or tribal study presents the advantage of a small, mor or less delimited group. With good reason, the researcher can assume this group to be a valid sociological unit and on this basis proceed to investigate it. In the modern industrial-urban setting, groups are far less clearly defined. Indeed, some research has dealt solely with the delimitation of urban social groups. In short, different techniques of research are needed. These have not been immediately available to the postwar student of industrialization.

As with any new field, experts from more or less closely related disciplines were asked to move in and fill the void. Unfortunately, these experts by and large seem to have done no more than the one study each was brought in to conduct. Thus there has been a lack of continuity. This is the danger in using outside experts: coming from outside and already having

---

*Letters and numerals in parentheses following the mention of a work--in the above case RUR 8077--constitute the number assigned to that work in the bibliography. The numbering system is explained on pp. 36-37.

established certain patterns of thought, they do not tend to absorb the ideas already current in the field; nor do they stay long enough to expose their own approach in more than the barest detail. However, this situation is changing considerably. There is now a very solid kernel of specialists in the sociological problems of development and the beginnings of substantial theoretical work.

There is still another facet of the newness of the interest in this subject. Many of the works presented here are the first efforts of young aspirants--doctoral theses, first reports of field work, etc. The subject is new and much talked of; it is not difficult to find a topic not previously treated; particularly for village studies, the topics can be made small so as to fit into the time span of a fellowship and the desire to travel abroad. Unfortunately, initial studies are seldom mature and profound. They often lack the depth of perception and judgment needed for analysis. Usually, these first studies are descriptive or are simply collections of data vaguely arranged. Yet they are a mine of valuable information that has yet to be seriously used.

At this point, it is well to consider the methods of research that have been applied to the problems of economic growth. The oldest of these methods is the anthropological study, which covers a multitude of different, even opposing, ideas. Nevertheless, it has certain well-defined characteristics that distinguish it from other approaches to the study of economic growth. Most importantly, it is a study of a culture, and thus is little adapted to the study of the parts of a culture when these are in the process of change.

Either because these anthropological studies described relatively isolated cultures--the South Seas, or African tribes--or because of the nature of the discipline, they tended to be timeless. In part, the attempt to describe the culture under study led the anthropologist to codify it. As is often the case, those informants who were best able to present a coherent picture of their culture were the more tradition-oriented elements. Thus the picture they presented was often an idealized conception of what the culture was supposed to be. Those elements of the culture in the process of change or those provoking the change are normally less visible and thus less communicable. An evolving society is never completely or coherently codified.

The results obtained by the anthropologists, particularly before World War II, reflect the techniques used to gather their information. The researchers relied very largely on informants to furnish the basic material from which the culture would be codified. These informants (members of the culture being studied) would recount the myths or explain the life cycle of their society. Of course, what they said they did and what they did were not necessarily the same, particularly in a changing culture. Some anthropologists were not insensitive to this dilemma. Margaret Mead in her studies of the South Seas and Clyde Kluckhohn in his study of American Indians began to turn away from the codification of a society to a more direct attempt to describe the dynamics of culture.

After the war, the approach of the anthropologist changed considerably: the concept of change was in the air; a sudden expansion of the possibilities of communication and transport brought change or modernization to most parts of the world; and for the first time anthropologists were able to revisit a culture: societies were no longer viewed as static formations but were found to have a dynamic status. This is particularly true of studies of the South

Seas, where war had a profound effect on the natives: Richard F. Salisbury's From Stone to Steel (RUR 6048), for example, or Cyril S. Belshaw's The Great Village (RUR 8016) and In Search of Wealth (RUR 6005).

The British school of anthropology, however, is somewhat of an exception to what has been said above. The influence of A. R. Radcliffe-Brown's functionalism has caused this school to become more interested in the economic and political structure of a society--the economic and the political so obviously serve a function--and thus more involved in dynamic processes. Even more importantly, the function of an act is not ahistorical--it can change independently of the act itself. Thus in the 1930's the British did considerable work on the then current economic structure of the African native. The best of these works--Max Gluckman's Analysis of a Social Situation in Modern Zululand (RUR 2398), Monica Hunter's Reaction to Conquest (RUR 2022), and especially Ellen Hellmann's Rooiyard (URB 2019)--are outstanding examples of an explanation of behavior in terms of the current environment. Unfortunately, "functionalism" has been less successful in the postwar period. Since every act was to be explained in terms of the current environment, no attempt was made to integrate the theory derived from one case study into that of the next. Cases were dealt with rather than processes.

In many ways, the functionalist approach of the British resembles what the Americans call sociology. The approach of the British, however, is much larger, extending often into the field of economics. In recent years, Karl Polanyi and his disciples (see GEN 1442) have attempted to pursue this avenue even further. Basically, Polanyi postulated that an economic "act" could only be understood in its context--that is, that there are no universal economic constructs that can help us understand an economic act apart from its environment. As detailed below, this line of reasoning has led to a number of studies of markets in non-Western economies.

The second method that has traditionally been applied to the study of the social structure of the developing world is the village study. This method does not try to study a culture or society--it is limited to a fairly well-defined subunit. The peasant village of forty years ago was not only small enough but isolated enough, so it was thought, to form a coherent unit of study. Whether this isolation was indeed present is a moot question. In any case, the spirit of the times placed the peasant culture in another world far from the world of the modern city, particularly until the work of Redfield in the late 1920's. There were village studies before Redfield, for example, H. H. Mann's work in India (RUR 8464, RUR 8465), but these were largely collections of socioeconomic data.

Redfield's contribution was to bring the peasant back into the world. Yet in so doing, he too opposed the peasant and his society to the city or the modern world. Redfield maintained that between these two poles there was a "continuum": the peasant did not jump from his background into the modern world; he moved slowly in many stages. Yet, as Oscar Lewis pointed out in his follow-up of Redfield's study of Tepoztlán (RUR 8059), one is not justified in thinking that the peasant world itself does not change. Some peasants do adopt the urban world, but at the same time so does their society. In short, by concentrating on the process of change (primarily that in the individual), Redfield failed to bring out the functionalism of the peasant society. As the economy develops, so must the functional relations of the peasant society.

Since the early 1950's, Polanyi and others (see GEN 1442 inter alia) have tended to recreate Redfield's continuum in the sphere of economics.

[7]

Polanyi considered that economies were of two distinct types: primitive-sub-sistence and market. The former were considered to be multicentric and the latter, unicentric. In applying these types to markets in Africa, Paul Bohannan and George Dalton (GEN 4312) postulated essentially a continuum of multicentric economies in the process of becoming unicentric. Unlike Red-field's theory, however, this approach to the study of primitive-peasant society sins in its overemphasis on functionalism. By postulating a complete dichotomy between the nonmarket and the market economies, the substantivist school, as Polanyi and his followers have been called, maintains that economic incentives are subordinated to the economic structure within which they occur. The individual as such is thought not to respond, except as pertinent to this context. Thus change in the context entrains an automatic change in the individual. If Redfield has shown anything, it is that such automatic change does not occur.

The most recent approach is to consider the entire society in the process of change. Obviously, the urban areas are likely to be in the fore-front of this change. And though the rural sectors may be influenced by the city, they do not become cities but instead alter their own basic structures. From this standpoint, rural change must be studied for its own patterns. There are advantages in studying rural patterns. A village is small enough to allow the researcher to come to grips with a coherent whole, and the rural village faced with the modern world has a longer path to go to meet this new situation: change in the rural sector is likely to be more obvious.

More recent village studies have tended to pursue one of three approaches: some have remained descriptive, but now they describe the changing patterns of communication or power within the village; others have turned to an analysis of the village's reaction to the challenge and the demands of the modern market; still others have tried to isolate the component parts of rural change.

The first of these three orientations has tended to concentrate on the structural relations within the village. These are analyzed from the stand-point not only of their form but also of their origin and growth. The village is not considered static, though it is treated as an identifiable whole, that is, a unit, elements of which can be isolated and thus studied. This is not to say that the influence of the outside world is ignored. On the contrary, the growth and mutation of the structural relations of a village will be a function of outside influences. Still, as the village is considered an integral unit, these outside influences are simply the cause of the change and do not tend to be treated as part of the study at hand. The village has been opened to the outside world without becoming part of it.

In a sense, this new emphasis emerged as the social scientist became aware that decisions within a village were as much a function of the personal-ities involved as of the traditional structure of the society. The social scientist of prewar years, and many still today, have tended to see the decision-making process as one set by tradition. The individual has not been considered to be an element of change. The postwar sociologist, however, has tended to focus on the relations between individuals as the foundation for the process which decisions are made and enforced. The individuals involved remold the decision-making process handed down to them to make it fit their own needs and purposes. We are very close here to the view that tradition does not even serve as a porte-manteau. Structural relations are formed by the individuals involved on the basis of elements common to all human beings. In the works listed in this bibliography, however, this tendency of modern

social science is scarcely evident. After all, if human beings are every-
where similar, why go abroad to study them?

The other two directions that sociologists have taken in the study of
the impact of industrialization are not confined to the village. Both are
very specifically postwar phenomena. Attitudes toward what are now called
the underdeveloped parts of the world have changed enormously since before
World War II. Even during the war, when economists spoke about the underdeveloped parts of the world, they were often referring to Eastern Europe
and not to Asia and Africa. In the immediate postwar years, this situation
changed very rapidly, until now the problems of the underdeveloped countries
have become one of the central concerns of the entire world.

As interest in the economic status of the non-Western societies has
grown since the war, more attention has been paid to the modalities of
economic growth. What has caused some countries to grow while others seem
to have stagnated? Economists in studying the blocks to economic growth
have come to realize that one of the most important factors is the sociological milieu in which the economy has to grow. Thus, there directly
emerges the second research orientation: how do people react to the pressures
and demands of the market in a non-Western society? Indirectly, we come to
the third orientation. For, in trying to determine how people react to the
market, we must be able to isolate the functioning of change itself. A further orientation, one beyond the strict confines of the village, has been the
study of nonlocal functional groups, for example, the studies of peasant
markets by Sidney Mintz (RUR 6040 and RUR 6417-6423). This orientation is
similar to the "functionalism" of Radcliffe-Brown, but it is quite different
in its tendency to derive general theory from the isolated case.

Bohannan and Dalton's book on markets in Africa (GEN 4312) presents
an extensive treatment of markets ranging from the quite primitive to those
thoroughly commercialized. M. Sahlins in two works (RUR 6047 and RUR 6452)
presents a considerable theoretic structure of exchange. His work tends to
be dominated by Polanyi's antimarket bias. Nevertheless, Sahlins' critique
of the static, purely material nature of much of economic thought is
extremely pertinent. Some of the most promising work has been done on West
African cattle markets (Hill, RUR 6381, and Temple, RUR 6473). Both studies
attempt to bring out the interplay between the social structure of the
traders and the economic forces at work.

The second orientation requires a firmer integration of economics
into modern sociology, while the third entails an application of the modern
techniques of sociological analysis to the problems of change. Both have a
promising future, but neither can offer a well-stocked past.

By modern techniques of sociological analysis, I mean quite simply
the use of tests, questionnaires, and the like. These methods require an
approach that differs from that used in descriptive studies. A descriptive
study need only set out the material that has been gathered; order and
structure come from the society itself. Tests and questionnaires imply a
hypothesis that the researcher is trying to vindicate. For the case at hand,
this means a theory of change, or, looking at the problem from a slightly
different angle, a theory of modernization.

As already mentioned, few of the studies in the bibliography use these
techniques of analysis. The principal center for the use of this direction
seems to have been the Cornell Cross-Cultural Methodology Program. R. K.

Goldsen (RUR 2016), Robert Textor (IND 2035), and others began to use these techniques in the mid-1950's. Because of lack of funds the studies were not followed up, or in some cases were even terminated before completion. The British Africanists centered at the Rhodes-Livingstone Institute in Northern Rhodesia as well as others have touched on these techniques, but they often tend to use them simply for the collection of data.

The socioeconomic survey is worthy of mention in its own right. In the sense meant here, this term is of Indian origin. It is used to describe the collection of demographic, economic, ecological, and related statistics. These surveys are a form of census in the broadest meaning of the term. They seldom offer any analysis but are a reservoir of untapped background material.

The integration of economics and sociology has tempted more than one author--Weber, Sombart, Tawney, Polanyi (GEN 1442), and Parsons and Smelser, to name only a few. Much progress has been made in this matter, although the greater part is of such recent vintage that most of the works contained in this bibliography have not profited from it. Much of the recent discussion focuses on a somewhat fruitless effort by Polanyi and his followers (especially Dalton) to deny the pertinence of modern economic analysis to the study of primitive economics. Unfortunately, this school does not seem to have kept up with the study of economics beyond the 1920's, so that many of the reasons it gives for the inapplicability of modern economics to primitive societies apply with equal force to the applicability of economics to modern societies. On the more positive side, this school has generated considerable interest in markets in nonmodern contexts. Mintz's work on Haiti (for example, RUR 6039 and RUR 6040) is one of the more outstanding examples of this feature.

Some recent studies of primitive economies (see Leopold Pospisil, RUR 6445, Richard F. Salisbury, RUR 6048, or Raymond Firth, RUR 6017 and RUR 6018) lend support to the universality of economic concepts. The indications of this field work have yet to be formalized in a theoretical construct. (Cyril S. Belshaw [GEN 1320] presents many interesting ideas but is essentially an introductory work.) Far more study is necessary to determine the essentials of the dynamics of exchange. The manner in which conflicting wants and availabilities are balanced is the heart of economics. This management or resolution of tension may take many different forms, but it is universally present. By introducing new availabilities, modernization induces new wants. A new resolution of tensions is then called for. How a society achieves this new resolution needed to handle new economic forms has been too little studied as yet.

Georges Balandier, Bert F. Hoselitz, and Wilbert E. Moore are undoubtedly the three most important theoreticians who have dealt with the process of absorbing modern economic forms into a traditional society. All three began their work shortly after the end of the war--Balandier and Moore in the field, the former in Central Africa, the latter in Mexico. Moore (IND 2022) studied the problems of labor in the process of industrialization; Balandier (RUR 9002) investigated social change among two African tribes. Moore posed the problem in very specific terms: he studied the workers in two factories which drew labor from two nearby mountain villages. Balandier's approach was much more general, as the subject of his study indicates. But he was a product of French sociology which, under the influence of Marxism and the very grave economic problems of the immediate postwar years, had crystallized its theoretical thought around the supposedly necessary liaison

[10]

between social and economic happenings. The French sociologists paid particular attention to the condition and nature of the working class. In his study on social change in Africa, Balandier is no exception. Social change in Central Africa was thought to come from the impact of Western economic structures on the native system. To study this change, Balandier sought to determine the reaction of the working-class family to this new situation. Thus, although more broadly based, Balandier's study like Moore's focused on the new industrial worker.

Since these first studies conducted in the late 1940's, both authors have continued their empirical and theoretical work on the problems of industrialization, in particular, the reactions of the worker to the exigencies of the modern factory or of the modern market--Balandier placing somewhat greater emphasis on the social context (class structure) through which these exigencies are felt (see RUR 8006). Great as has been the contribution of these two sociologists, they seem to have treated only one side of the integration of economics into sociology. In a sense, what they have studied is the second step in the process of industrialization or modernization: the reaction to industry after it has been installed. The first is the response, whether that of the entrepreneur or the individual buyer, to economic stimuli as expressed in the modern market.

This first step in the process of industrialization is portrayed most clearly in the work of R. F. Salisbury, From Stone to Steel (RUR 6048). By treating a social system that did not use money, he was able to isolate the basic pattern of response to technological change--in this case, the replacement of stone axes by steel ones. This change enabled the farmer to produce subsistence goods with greater ease. However, every family in the society produced its own supply of subsistence goods, and there was no market for the surplus. Thus the first effect of this technological change was to increase the time available to produce prestige or luxury items. The consequent increase in the production of these elements of wealth led to a general increase in capital. In turn, this increase upset the previous social equilibrium. People were generally richer than they would have expected from their role in society, and on the other hand the distribution of wealth was altered. Gradually the social system changed to achieve a new equilibrium with a higher level of demand for subsistence goods and different hierarchical values and structure.

There have been two other key studies that have attempted to analyze this first stage of reaction: Claude Tardits' study on Porto-Novo, 1958 (URB 2043), and Trude S. Epstein's study on South India, 1962 (RUR 8030). Tardits' work is based on the results of a questionnaire. The society he chose to study was and still is a particularly competitive one. This fact has enabled Tardits to focus on the interaction between the new stimuli presented by the European economy and the individuals of this society. This interaction has changed the structure of the society. In Porto-Novo the individual is not just a worker--Tardits shows him choosing between employed work and commerce. In the tension of this choice, we see not only the adaptation of the individual to the new circumstances but also the society's use of these new circumstances to reformulate its equilibrium.

Epstein's book focuses even more directly on this interaction between economic stimuli and the society. Having been trained in both economics and sociology, she designed a project that would highlight their interaction. In an area of India that was first irrigated some fifteen years previous to her study, she chose two villages for closer examination, one irrigated, the

[11]

other just above the level of the water in the irrigation system and thus dry. With irrigation came sugar mills offering cash for cane. The response of the irrigated village was direct and immediate. But because the cultivation of sugar cane fitted into the traditional pattern of agriculture, the village society was left nearly unchanged, though richer. The response of the dry village was of course indirect, for it could not grow the cane the mills would buy so readily. Witnessing the prosperity brought about by the modern economy, the village set about to integrate itself into this economy. In due time, the village turned to milling and light industry, using its own funds to bring electricity into the village. As the author brings out, this village was not just responding within the scope of tradition but was changing its own structure in order to use to better advantage the stimuli of the modern market. Other social scientists have treated this interaction more or less explicitly; Clifford Geertz (RUR 2014), James B. Hendry (RUR 8048), and Manning Nash (IND 4007) are examples. Yet such studies are not numerous, especially when compared to the number of descriptive works on villages or tribes that have come out since the end of the war.

An outstanding exception is the series of articles edited by Firth and Yamey (GEN 4324) on capital and saving in peasant societies. Of particular interest are the works of Firth (RUR 6018), Epstein (RUR 6016), and Belshaw (RUR 6006). The common theme of these three authors is the importance of credit and the credit mechanisms in determining a society's response to new economic stimuli.

Still, there seems to have been little attempt as yet to formulate the theory of the total reaction of a society to economic stimuli, as these are understood by an economist. By economic stimuli I mean the response of supply to an increase in demand such that, temporarily, demand exceeds supply. This is not the same situation as when new techniques are introduced, which the Westerner (an expert in the matter) assures the native are better than the indigenous methods. Unfortunately, here "better" means more "Western" and may or may not bring about a greater material profit. In addition to a few studies of the economic side of this process (studies of market and saving), there have been a number of studies of what might be called the passive reaction to economic stimuli: a direct acceptance or rejection of the opportunities offered, without the society's trying to adapt itself to take advantage of or even to create these opportunities. This passive reaction is to be opposed to the active response just described, in which the society changes in order to fit into the modern economy that confronts it.

A yet unpublished work by Joel Halpern on what he calls the village revolution is a hopeful shift in direction. The rural revolution is caused primarily by the change in possibilities brought about by modern transport. People and goods can effectively and profitably leave and enter the village. For the first time, economic incentives, political changes, and countrywide social factors can play a role within the village.

The studies of the passive reaction usually examine some aspects of the following phenomena: the introduction of innovations, work in a factory, and life in a city. The most common study in fact embraces a combination of these three--the study of the impact of the modern world on a particular village. An excellent study of this sort, dealing with a Colombian village, is The People of Aritama (RUR 8078), by the Reichel-Dolmatoffs. Their work focuses on the cultural response of the Mestizo village to the attractions of the very materialistic life of the nearby towns and cities. The key element is the factor of prestige thought to reside in the urban way of life. Unfortunately, the study is not complete. The shift from subsistence farming to the cultivation of cash crops is mentioned; thus there are economic stimuli; but there is no analysis of the interactions between these stimuli and the cultural change taking place. Indeed, the same criticism could be made of most of these studies.

Prime among the studies of the effect of innovation have been the numerous examinations of community development projects. Such is the case in India in particular, but also in Africa, Southeast Asia, and the Pacific Islands. The usefulness of these studies for our purposes, however, is often limited by the researcher's failure to distinguish between economic and noneconomic stimuli. The failure of a peasant to adopt a new method or type of cultivation may come from the realization that he cannot sell the additional or the new produce. If this is the case, his refusal is not a sign of traditionalism or a block to economic development--quite the contrary, it is an indication of a very modern commercial attitude. This distinction is seldom made in community development studies. Expert advice is taken for economic forces actually present.

The classic study of community development is that by Shyama Charan Dube, India's Changing Villages (RUR 4002). He attempted to get at the "response to change" of the villagers. By change, he means modernization or, specifically, the ideas put forth by the community development leaders. He does not consider those factors of change that are independent of these leaders, that is, the workings of the market. In short, his study explores the villagers' reaction to an imposed development rather than to a modernizing economy. As an example of a tendency I just noted, the author gives economic advantage as a reason for adopting an innovation but nowhere does he cite economic disadvantage as an obstacle to such adoption. "Suspicion of officials" is so cited by Dube, and he gives what is virtually a justification of this attitude on the part of the peasant. In this case, the peasants were urged to adopt a new technique that demanded a commercial fertilizer in order to be profitably used. The government assured the peasants that this fertilizer would be available at a price which would make its use profitable. But when the peasants adopted the new technique, the fertilizer was not to be had. The entire affair was a financial disaster for those who tried the new method. The conclusion should be that the peasants are better economists (in the modern sense) than the government. It is to Dube's merit that he has brought out the opposition of feeling between the peasant and the government. Still, it would have been of greater interest if he had focused on the interaction between the modern economy and the traditional society, instead of on the interaction between the government (containing both traditional and modern aspects) and the peasant.

Studies of industrialization and urbanization are more directly pertinent to the problem of the adaptation of a member of a traditional society to the exigencies of the modern economy. Yet, as is apparent from the proportions of this bibliography, studies of the impact of industry and the urban center on non-Western societies are far less numerous than are those studies concerned only with rural areas. A lack of theory is also apparent in these broader studies. Many of them tend to be descriptive and not analytic. Other than the work of Moore on labor, few of the sociological works have tackled more than the particular case chosen for the purposes of the research. This is inevitable, for one does not have the same grasp of the larger-scale problems of the effects of industrialization and

[13]

urbanization as one does for, the modernization of a rural sector. Whereas one can take a village as the societal unit for purposes of research on the rural world, the student of industrialization or urbanization must take a region or nation. This area is too large to study as a whole at once, and there seems to be some doubt as to what aspects should be examined first. Some investigators seem simply to have collected data, others to have confined their efforts to a very specific component of these subjects.

Study of the industrial worker seems far less hampered by the lack of theory relating economics to sociology. Factory studies are usually of groups of power structures--matters equally present in the West and treated there at great length. The novelty, however, is in the application of these hypotheses to a non-Western group. There is some excellent early work, in particular, Shih Kuo-heng (IND 2030) and Fei Hsiao-t'ung (IND 4003 and IND 4004) in China just before World War II. This line was carried on in the postwar period--Ellen Hellmann (IND 2072) in South Africa, Manning Nash (IND 4007) in Guatemala, Albert K. Rice (IND 2028), and Richard Lambert (IND 2019 and IND 2020) in India, Charles H. Savage (IND 2029) in Peru, and various works by the Japanese (excellent but unfortunately in Japanese) (e.g., IND 2017). The harvest is good in quality but very meager. However, when it comes to integrating the study of the factory into the wider context of social change, the yield is even scarcer--Nash and above all the Japanese. As the problem here is one of effort and not theory, the future should bring vast improvements.

The future of the study of urbanization seems less hopeful. Ellen Hellmann's 1935 study of Johannesburg (URB 2019) has yet to be surpassed. The Belgians in the Congo (Louis Baeck, URB 2002, Robert Dethier, URB 2012 and URB 2013, V. G. Pons, URB 2033, and others) made great headway, but Congolese independence has put a stop to this effort. Some very good work has been done by the British in West and Central Africa, but outside of Africa there would appear to be little of note. I am not surprised; it is no easy matter to grasp the essence of so large a movement as urbanization, especially in a foreign country. Outside of Japan and India, few of the countries included in this bibliography have trained native sociologists to conduct urban studies. Even where available, as in India, the resources and the inclination have been missing.

As I have tried to make clear, the principal lacuna in most of the work cited in this bibliography is precisely the failure to project the case under examination onto a larger horizon. The horizon that seems of the greatest interest at present is the integration of economics into sociology, in order to explain the problems of economic development in the non-Western world. Part of the problem seems to reside in the lack of a theoretical structure into which the isolated case could be set. This is particularly true of the many doctoral theses written on subjects in this field. A student cannot be expected to erect a base of the dimensions needed in what is usually his first independent work.

This lack of a theoretical structure, however, is only part of the problem. Equally grave is the widespread lack of background in economics, whether on the level of business accounting or of an economic variable. A researcher must know what an economic incentive is if he is to examine how it functions. This does not demand much--cost-benefit analysis, input-output analysis, location theory--but this little is not immediately obvious to the uninitiated. The distinction between an economic stimulus and reaction and an economic impediment must be posed in general economic terms and not, as is usually the case, in terms of what the West or the city dweller may happen to think.

In effect, there seems to be considerable confusion as to whether one is investigating Westernization or industrialization: the two are not identical. To study either of these two is legitimate, provided the researcher is clear as to the distinction. Nevertheless, the latter would seem to be not only more important but also more interesting. Westernization is the transfer of one culture into the milieu of another--one movement among many similar cultural transfers. Industrialization on the other hand, is the motive force behind the material success of Westernization. Economic development, as we think of it today, is a unique experience. To explain it is to explain the basic, nonrepetitive structure of world-wide growth.

A BRIEF SURVEY OF REGIONAL STUDIES

There would seem to be a greater difference between studies of
different parts of the world than between the various types of studies just
discussed. For this reason, a brief description of the sort of work that
has already been carried out in each of the regions of the world is given
here.

Africa

Leaving North Africa aside to be included with the Middle East,
Black Africa can be neatly divided into two parts, the Anglophone and the
Francophone. The difference has little to do with the nature of the areas
involved, as can be seen. With very few exceptions, these studies have been
conducted by whites from the European country that is governing (or was
formerly governing) the area studied.

The British were the first to get started, with the foundation of the
Rhodes-Livingstone Institute located at Livingstone in what is now Zambia.
Beginning in the late 1930's, this Institute encouraged studies of the tribes
in East and Central Africa. This tribal basis for the study of Africa has
remained typical of English work despite titles that are often misleading.
Ellen Hellmann's work on South Africa and Kenneth L. Little's studies of West
Africa are two of the few exceptions to this rule. More typical are the
series of tribe-by-tribe ethnologies sponsored by the International African
Institute in London.

The reasons for this tribal orientation of British African studies
would seem to be twofold: tribes are pervasive in East, Central, and South
Africa; and the theoretical base of British anthropology was inclined toward
the particular rather than the general. "Functionalism" was mentioned
briefly, and it may be well to deepen our comments here. Roughly speaking,
this theory held that every social act served a function in the particular
society in question. In his famous study, Analysis of a Social Situation in
Modern Zululand (1940; RUR 1337), Max Gluckman begins with a ceremony (the
opening of a bridge) and, by explaining its function in Zulu society, tries
to situate that society. This sort of analysis is common to most of the
British Africanists; the function of an event is explained by reference to
the tribe. Even studies of urban events have tended to situate the event
with regard to the tribe more than to the city. While tribal affiliations
are certainly extremely important in this part of Africa, the particularist
bent of "functionalism" has not encouraged any cross-tribal generalization
leading to conclusions about the nature of urban society per se.

Although the French have also been engaged in a good bit of work with
the tribe as a base, they have tended to be far more interested in the
problems of the city and of industrialization. Georges Balandier and Claude

[16]

Tardits in particular have contributed to this line of study. Both authors have stressed economic adaptation and the problems facing the worker. This economic and urban orientation is to be found even among the Belgians, who have spent much of their time studying the social groups that have replaced the tribes in the cities of the Congo. There is a very interesting article by V. G. Pons (URB 2033) on social groups, one which should be followed up. The same can be said of the efforts of Louis Baeck (e.g., GEN 2311) to define certain key economic variables in their Congolese context. Unfortunately, unlike the French who have continued their work in Africa, the Belgians' studies came to an end with the granting of independence to the Congo.

The Middle East

Outside of the French areas of influence in North Africa, no consistent line of inquiry has been followed in this part of the world. The few studies that are available are but random efforts and cannot be easily set into an over-all picture.

The French work on North Africa, however, is quite a different matter. As with the French work on the rest of Africa, these studies have concentrated on the problems of the worker and of the city-dweller. The direction is similar, but the depth is quite different. These studies have tended to be more all-inclusive. In addition, sociologists have also investigated the rise of the middle class. This work is still going on and should yield interesting results.

The Pacific Islands

Studies on Polynesia and Melanesia are largely the result of the interest of Anglo-Americans and reflect the nature of their first work in the area. This has been an area of predilection for the Anglo-American anthropologist, beginning in the 1920's and carrying on to the present day. These studies would be of little interest to the student of industrialization or modernization if it were not for World War II. The brutal injection of modern armed forces into this region in the early 1940's brought many of these islands out of the stone age into modern life. This is undoubtedly the only region in which the introduction of the modern world has been so sudden. Here, there is truly a "before" and "after," although it is difficult to distinguish those reactions of the natives that are caused by shock from other reactions that reflect a more normal adaptation to a different culture. This has been done, however, in the excellent study by R. K. Salisbury (RUR 6048) on the impact of the introduction of steel axes into a stone-age culture (RUR 6048, From Stone to Steel).

As for prewar studies of the area, both Bronislaw Malinowski (RUR 6034) and W. E. Armstrong (RUR 6306) have attempted to describe the structure and function of economic activities in certain societies of the Pacific area. Both their studies are more descriptive than analytic: pages are devoted to minute details concerning the form of shell money or the flows of trade. To some extent, Malinowski has tried to integrate the patterns of trade into the social system. His solution, however, is to subordinate trading to the dictates of the social system. He has little or nothing to say about the economic content of these trade patterns. Firth's work is of quite a different sort, one that has been discussed above.

[17]

We are fortunate in having a number of postwar studies by this same author (for example, RUR 6017). In particular, he has restudied the same village as was described in his prewar work (RUR 8032). This is the only case in which there is an adequate study of a tribe in its primitive context and also after it has made contact with a modern market economy. In all these works Firth has attempted to integrate both the economic function and the social meaning of an act. He treats social meaning or tradition as a modulator on the apperception of, and reaction to, economic stimuli. Underneath this traditional veneer, however, Firth finds primitive man to be as "realistic" as any modern man.

Latin America

Until fairly recently most of the work on this region was done by the Americans. As described earlier, the first modern village studies (those of Robert Redfield, e.g., RUR 8077) were located in Mexico. Most of the earlier studies were purely descriptive. During and after the war, however, greater attention was paid to the process of change. A few scholars--Oscar Lewis (RUR 8059 and RUR 8060), Sol Tax (RUR 8089), and later, Manning Nash (IND 4007) and Emilio Willems (RUR 8093 and RUR 8094)--were interested in the place of economic factors in this change. In recent years, this tendency has been pushed further, as exemplified in the work of the Reichel-Dolmatoffs (RUR 8078) mentioned earlier. In fact, South America has been a proving ground for the development of the theory of rural change. This search for an ever deeper understanding has produced many excellent studies, but it has also meant that few of these studies are comparable, since the perspective of the reporters changes from one study to another.

In the last few years the Latin Americans themselves (for example, Gino Germani, URB 2015, and Orlando Fals-Borda, RUR 8031) have begun to investigate the sociology of their countries. Unlike the Americans, they have been more interested in the cities and the problems of large-scale industrialization; in this, they are closer to the French.

Southeast Asia

Diverse tendencies are to be found in this part of the world. The British have done few studies in Malaya, and the Dutch, a fair number in Indonesia. The Dutch studies were seconded by the Americans in the 1950's. Together, the Dutch and the Americans produced a number of works on the plantations and on the rise of a commercial class among the natives. The most interesting work, however, was done by the Cornell and Michigan university study groups. The interest of their work lies in the attempt to apply the methodology of the modern survey to the study of the underdeveloped countries. An initial probing application of the questionnaires and other techniques to be used was made, but, unfortunately, political troubles did not permit the completion of the work.

East Asia

There are three rather distinct areas in this region, China, the Philippines, and Japan. Some of the earliest sociological work available on non-Western villages and cities was done in China starting in the early 1920's. With the studies of Fei Hsiao-t'ung (IND 4003 and IND 4004), and

Shih Kuo-heng (IND 2030) in the late 1930's and early 1940's, the Chinese initiated the study of the non-Western worker, for the first time engaged with the tools of sociology. Unfortunately, the Chinese revolution stopped this very promising line of work in the mid-1940's. China could have provided a very fruitful comparison with Japan.

The remaining two areas in this region present very hopeful prospects for the study in depth of the problems of development. With the sole exception of India (Latin America has only a few isolated sociologists, particularly in Brazil, Mexico, and Argentina, though this is likely to change in the near future), the Philippines and Japan are the only non-Western societies studying themselves. This does not imply better work but tends to assure the continuity often lacking elsewhere.

It is recognized that Japan is not an underdeveloped country; nevertheless, it has been included in this bibliography for several reasons. Japan is the only case of the successful industrialization of a non-Western country; its sociologists are among the best in the world (Fukutake, RUR 8036 and RUR 8037, in particular). There has been a good bit of work on change in the rural sector, where modernization is after all a relatively recent phenomenon. Village studies in Japan date back to the 1930's, to the excellent work of J. F. Embree (RUR 8029). In a country in which industrialization could not be taken for granted, he could not avoid dealing with economic factors (as was also the case in China but not so of the American work in Mexico). Emphasis on economic factors was even more pronounced in the work by the Japanese themselves, but their prewar studies are highly colored by a dogmatic Marxism applied helter-skelter in a non-European context. As in many other fields, the American occupation after the war radically changed the orientation of the Japanese sociologists. From then on they were well-trained and creative appliers of modern methodology. Writing mostly in Japanese, they have done a good deal on the problem of integrating rural change and economic growth: Furushima (IND 1006) on the introduction of mechanized sericulture into a hitherto isolated village; Fukutake (RUR 8037) on the contrast between an industrialized village and a nearby mountain village; the study by the Japan Culture Science Society (IND 2017) of the impact of large-scale water-resource projects or area development programs on nearby villages and towns.

Philippine studies have delved into the topic of induced change in the rural sector, primarily in the rural aspects of communication, acculturation, and political power. There are quite a few articles and books. Few of them, however, deal with the problems posed by the introduction of economic stimuli. Some Americans have carried out inquiries along much the same lines as the Philippine sociologists.

India and Pakistan

It is almost an understatement to say that sociological work in India is extensive and extremely good. Socioeconomic surveys date back to World War I and have been accumulating ever since. After World War II, sociology in India moved into high gear with studies by the Indians, British, Americans, and lately by the Japanese. Outside of Japan, this is the only non-Western country that has a full complement of first-rate studies on rural change, urbanization, and industrialization. However, it must also be said that India is so vast that studies are often spread very thinly over any single cultural area. Certain regions have been especially favored: Uttar Pradesh

[19]

(New Delhi and the upper Ganges plain), Maharashtra (Bombay-Poona), Madras, and the Calcutta-Dacca area.

The sociological work on India is far too rich to be easily classified. Some has been done on community development (Shyama Charan Dube, Oscar Lewis, and many others) as described earlier. Lewis (RUR 8061) has used his Indian experience to compare rural change there with rural change in Mexico. This is virtually the only cross-cultural study based on field experiences. More work should be done along this line so that the basic elements of the process of rural change could be isolated. This comment applies equally well to the fields of urbanization and industrialization. In these latter categories, however, there are more studies that have dealt with these subjects on a multicultural basis--for example, the work of Wilbert E. Moore and the current research of Alex Inkeles.

Frederick G. Bailey's studies on Orissa (for example, RUR 8005) have been concerned with tribes in the British African tradition, but with greater emphasis on the impact of commercial opportunities. Trude Epstein (RUR 8030), also British, in her excellent study previously described deals solely with a location (in this case, two adjacent villages). The Americans for their part have been engaged in everything from anthropology, with an accent on change induced by economic growth, through village studies, to the study of the efficiency of factory workers. The investigations of Albert K. Rice (IND 2028), Arthur and Juanita Niehoff (RUR 2031), and Richard Lambert (IND 2019 and IND 2020) are virtually the only studies available on workers in an underdeveloped country. The Indians themselves, however, have begun to inquire into the psychology of the worker (see Ganguli, IND 2009). As just mentioned, the research by Inkeles will enhance this effort greatly, not only in India but in five or ten other countries as well. We have here the two most promising prospects for future work, studies on India and cross-cultural analysis.

RECOMMENDED READINGS

AND

THE MOST IMPORTANT CURRENT PERIODICALS

     Having discussed the approach toward "modernization" taken by the Harvard Project on the Sociocultural Aspects of Development, and having surveyed previous published research on the subject, I now venture to suggest a basic reading list. Not only are the following thirty-one books (including all eleven of the three-star items in the bibliography) especially germane by Project criteria, but also in my opinion they are fundamental for any serious student of the sociological effects of industrialization.

General

GEN 1391   Hoselitz, Bert F., Sociological Aspects of Economic Growth (1960).

GEN 1395   Hoselitz, Bert F., and Wilbert E. More (eds.), Industrialization and Society (1963).

GEN 1425   Moore, Wilbert E., Social Change (1963).

GEN 4302   Balandier, Georges, Economic Development and Its Social Implications: Technological Change and Industrialization (1962).

GEN 4312   Bohannan, Paul J., and George Dalton, Markets in Africa (1962).

GEN 4324   Firth, Raymond W., and B. S. Yamey, Capital, Saving and Credit in Peasant Societies: Studies from Asia, Oceania, the Caribbean, and Middle America (1964).

GEN 4356   Meynaud, Jean, Social Change and Economic Development (1963).

Industrialization[†]

**IND 2017   Japan Cultural Science Society, Sakuma Dam (1958). (In Japanese; see IND 2016 for a summary in English.)

[†]There are no three-star items.

**IND 2020   Lambert, Richard D., Workers, Factories, and Social Change in India (1963).

IND 2028   **Rice, Albert K., Productivity and Social Organization: The Ahmedabad Experiment (1958).

**IND 2029   Savage, Charles H., Jr., Social Reorganization in a Factory in the Andes (1964).

**IND 2030   Shih Kuo-heng, China Enters the Machine Age (1944).

**IND 4003   Fei Hsiao-t'ung, Peasant Life in China: A Field Study of Country Life in the Yangtze Valley (1939).

**IND 4007   Nash, Manning, Machine Age Maya: The Industrialization of a Guatemalan Community (1958).

**IND 4009   Salz, Beate R., "The Human Element in Industrialization: A Hypothetical Case Study of Ecuadorean Indians" (1955).

Urbanization

***URB 2013   Dethier, Robert, Une famille de citadins du Katanga (1961).

***URB 2020   Hellmann, Ellen P., Rooiyard: A Sociological Survey of an Urban Slum Yard (1948).

***URB 2033   Pons, V. G., "Two Small Groups in Avenue 21: Some Aspects of the System of Social Relations in a Remote Corner of Stanleyville, Belgian Congo," in GEN 4384 (1961).

***URB 2043   Tardits, Claude, Porto-Novo: Les nouvelles générations africaines entre leurs traditions et l'Occident (1958).

**URB 3010   Marris, Peter, Family and Social Change in an African City: A Study of Rehousing in Lagos (1961).

Rural Modernization

**RUR 2023   Jayawardena, C., Conflict and Solidarity in a Guianese Plantation (1963).

**RUR 2025   Maher, Robert F., New Men of Papua: A Study in Cultural Change (1961).

***RUR 3009   Norbeck, Edward, Pineapple Town, Hawaii (1959).

***RUR 4016   Weingrod, Alex, Reluctant Pioneers: Village Development in Israel (1966).

**RUR 5003   Béteille, André, <u>Caste, Class and Power: Changing Patterns of Stratification in a Tanjore Village</u> (1965).

**RUR 6006   Belshaw, Cyril S., <u>Under the Ivy Tree: Society and Economic Growth in Rural Fiji</u> (1964).

***RUR 6048   Salisbury, Richard F., <u>From Stone to Steel: Economic Consequences of a Technological Change in New Guinea</u> (1962).

***RUR 8007   Banfield, Edward C., <u>The Moral Basis of a Backward Society</u> (1958).

***RUR 8030   Epstein, Trude S., <u>Economic Development and Social Change in South India</u> (1962).

***RUR 8033   Fraser, T. M., <u>Rusembilan: A Malay Fishing Village in Southern Thailand</u> (1960).

***RUR 8078   Reichel-Dolmatoff, Gerardo, and Alicia Reichel-Dolmatoff, <u>The People of Aritama: The Cultural Personality of a Colombian Mestizo Village</u> (1961).

Among current periodicals, the sixteen listed below appear to me consistently to publish work of greatest interest on the sociocultural aspects of development.

American Anthropologist
Bijdragen Tot de Taal-, Land- en Volkenkunde
Cahiers Internationaux de Sociologie
Eastern Anthropologist
Economic Development and Cultural Change
Economic Weekly
L'Homme. Revue Française d'Anthropologie
Human Organization
Human Problems in Central Africa
International Development Review
International Journal of Comparative Sociology
International Review of Community Development
International Social Sciences Journal
Journal of Asian and African Studies
Man in India
Sociologus

ABBREVIATIONS FOR PERIODICALS CITED

The system of abbreviations for journals employed in this bibliography is derived from the World List of Scientific Periodicals. It is easily adaptable to bibliographies in all disciplines, and is preferred by librarians. The rules are simple: nouns are capitalized; adjectives (with few exceptions) are not; articles, conjunctions, adverbs, etc., are dropped; one-word titles are spelled out in full; accents on capital letters are dropped; if place names are used as adjectives, they are usually abbreviated. Examples:

Acta am.	Acta Americana
Am. econ. Rev.	American Economic Review
Amér. indíg.	América Indígena
Etud. rur.	Etudes Rurales
J. soc. Res.	Journal of Social Research
J. sociol. Issues	Journal of Sociological Issues
Rev. Econ.	Revista de Economía
Rev. écon.	Revue Economique
Sociologia	Sociologia

In this bibliography the circumflex and the bar are used interchangeably in Japanese titles having accents. In a few cases the place of publication of a journal could not be found, and in some the volume number or the pagination is not known.

Acta am.	Acta Americana (Los Angeles)
Acta trop.	Acta Tropica (Basel)
Actual. d'outre-mer	Actualités d'Outre-Mer (Paris)
Admve. Sci. Quart.	Administrative Science Quarterly (Ithaca, N.Y.)
Africa	Africa (London)
Afr. Aff.	African Affairs (London) (formerly African Society Journal, then Journal of the Royal African Society)
Afr. Asie	Afrique et Asie (Paris)
Afr. Docums.	Afrique Documents (Dakar)
Afr. J. Econ.	African Journal of Economics
Afrika Kenkyû	Afrika Kenkyû (Tokyo)
Afr. Stud.	African Studies (Johannesburg)
Afr. Wld.	African World (London)
Afr. Women	African Women (London)
Agra Univ. J. Res.	Agra University Journal of Research (Agra, India)
Aichi Daigaku Kiyô	Aichi Daigaku Kokusai Mondai Kenkyujo Kiyô (Toyohashi, Japan)
Aichidaigaku Ronsô	Aichi Daigaku Bungaku Ronsô (Toyohashi, Japan)
All India Congr. Comm. econ. Rev.	All India Congress Committee Economic Review (New Delhi)
Am. Anthrop.	American Anthropologist (New York)

Am. behavl. Scient.	American Behavioral Scientist (Princeton, N.J.)
Am. econ. Rev.	American Economic Review (Menasha, Wis.)
Am. J. Econ. Sociol.	American Journal of Economics and Sociology (Lancaster, Pa.)
Am. J. Sociol.	American Journal of Sociology (Chicago)
Am. polit. Sci. Rev.	American Political Science Review (Washington, D.C.)
Am. sociol. Rev.	American Sociological Review (New York)
Am. Univ. Field Staff	American Universities Field Staff. Reports from Foreign Countries: South America (New York)
Amér. indíg.	América Indígena (Mexico City)
Amér. lat.	América Latina (Rio de Janeiro)
Análise soc.	Análise Social (Lisbon)
Ann. Am. Acad. polit. soc. Sci.	Annals of the American Academy of Political and Social Science (Philadelphia)
Ann. Géogr.	Annales de Géographie (Paris)
Ann. Inst. Statist. math.	Annales de l'Institut de Statistique Mathématique (Paris)
Ann. lateran.	Annali Lateranensi (Rome)
Ann. N.Y. Acad. Sci.	Annals of the New York Academy of Sciences (New York)
Annls. Univ. Paris	Annales de l'Université de Paris (Paris)
Anthrop. Forum	Anthropological Forum (Perth, Australia)
Anthrop. Quart.	Anthropological Quarterly (Washington, D.C.)
Anthropologica	Anthropologica (Ottawa)
Anthropology	Anthropology (London)
Anthropos	Anthropos (Freiburg, W. Germany)
Arbeitzphysiologie	Arbeitzphysiologie (Heidelberg, W. Germany)
Arch. Rechts- Soz.	Archiv für Rechts- und Sozialphilosophie (Berlin)
Archs. int. Sociol. Coop.	Archives Internationales de Sociologie de la Coopération (Gif-sur-Yvette, France)
Arctic Anthrop.	Arctic Anthropology (Madison, Wis.)
Arid Zone	Arid Zone (UNESCO, Paris)
Artha Vijnana	Artha Vijnana (Bombay)
Asia Keizai	Asia Keizai (Tokyo)
Asian Aff.	Asian Affairs (Tokyo)
Asian Cult.	Asian Culture (Saigon)
Asian Cult. Stud.	Asian Culture Studies (Tokyo)
Asian econ. Rev.	Asian Economic Review (Hyderabad, India)
Asian Surv.	Asian Survey (Berkeley, Calif.)
Ass. Cadres dir. Ind. B.	Association de Cadres Dirigeants de l'Industrie pour le Progrès Social et Economique. Bulletin (Paris)
Austr. Geogr.	Australian Geographer (Sydney)
Austr. J. agric. Econ.	Australian Journal of Agricultural Economics (Sydney)
Austr. Territ.	Australian Territories (Canberra)
Baessler-Arch.	Baessler-Archiv. Beiträge zur Völkerkunde (Berlin)
Bantu Stud.	Bantu Studies (Johannesburg)
Behavl. Sci.	Behavioral Science (Ann Arbor, Mich.)
Bijdr. Taal- Land- Volk.	Bijdragen Tot de Taal-, Land- en Völkenkunde van Nederlandsch-Indie (The Hague)
Bol. cult. Guiné port.	Boletim Cultural da Guiné Portuguesa (Bissau, Portuguese Guinea)
Bol. geral Ultramar	Boletim Geral Ultramar (Lisbon)
Bol. Soc. Estud. Moçambique	Boletim da Sociedade de Estudos de Moçambique (Lourenço-Marques, Mozambique)

Br. J. Sociol.   British Journal of Sociology (London)
Bull. Amér. lat.   Bulletin de l'Amérique Latine (Port-au-Prince, Haiti)
Bull. écon. Afr.   Bulletin Economique pour l'Afrique (Addis Ababa, Ethiopia)
Bull. écon. soc. Maroc   Bulletin Economique et Social du Maroc (Rabat)
Bull. écon. soc. Tunisie   Bulletin Economique et Social de Tunisie (Tunis)
Bull. Inst. fr. Afr. noire   Bulletin de l'Institut Français d'Afrique Noire (Dakar, Senegal)
Bull. Inst. Stud. centrafr.   Bulletin de l'Institut d'Etudes Centrafricaines (Brazzaville, Congo)
Bull. Res. écon. soc. Univ.   Bulletin de l'Institut de Recherches Economiques et Sociales de l'Université (Louvain)
Bull. Inst. tradit. Cult.   Bulletin of the Institute of Traditional Culture (Madras, India)
Bull. Mém. Soc. Anthrop. Paris   Bulletin et Mémoires de la Société d'Anthropologie de Paris
Bull. Res. Grp. Migration Probl.   Bulletin of the Research Group for European Migration Problems (The Hague)
Bull. tribal Res. Inst.   Bulletin of the Tribal Research Institute (Chhindwara, India)
Bull. trimest. Cent. Etud. Probl.   Bulletin Trimestriel du Centre d'Etudes des Problèmes Sociaux Indigènes (Elizabethville, Congo)

C. r. mens. Séanc. Acad. Sci. d'Outre-Mer   Comptes Rendus Mensuels des Séances de l'Académie des Sciences d'Outre-Mer (Paris)
Cah. Bruges   Cahiers de Bruges (Bruges)
Cah. d'outre-mer   Cahiers d'Outre-Mer (Paris)
Cah. Etud. afr.   Cahiers d'Etudes Africaines
Cah. Inst. Sci. écon.   Cahiers de l'Institut de Science Economique Appliquée (Paris)
Cah. int. Sociol.   Cahiers Internationaux de Sociologie (Paris)
Cah. Sociol. écon.   Cahiers de Sociologie Economique (Le Havre)
Cah. Tunisie   Chaiers de Tunisie (Tunis)
Calcutta Statist. Ass. Bull.   Calcutta Statistics Association Bulletin (Calcutta)
Can. Rev. Sociol. Anthrop.   Canadian Review of Sociology and Anthropology (Calgary, Alta.)
Cent. Asian Rev.   Central Asian Review (London)
Centro escolar Univ.   Centro Escolar. University Graduate and Faculty Studies (Philippines)
Ceylon J. hist. soc. Stud.   Ceylon Journal of Historical and Social Studies (Peradeniya, Ceylon)
Cienc. polít. soc.   Ciencias Políticas y Sociales (Mexico City)
Civilisations   Civilisations (Brussels)
Communautés et Continents   Communautés et Continents (Paris)
Comm. Dev. Bull.   Community Development Bulletin (Washington, D.C.)
Comp. Stud. Soc. Hist.   Comparative Studies in Society and History (The Hague)
Confluence   Confluence (Amsterdam)
Conspectus   Conspectus (New Delhi)

Contemp. Rev.	Contemporary Review (London)
Contemp. Stud.	Contemporary Studies (Manila)
Corona Libr.	Corona Library (London)
Cuad. Estud. afr.	Cuadernos de Estudios Africanos (Madrid)
Curr. Anthrop.	Current Anthropology (Chicago)
Curr. Sociol.	Current Sociology (Oxford, England)
Def. Sci. J.	Defence Science Journal (New Delhi)
Dév. Civilis.	Développement et Civilisations (Paris)
Dev. Econ.	The Developing Economies (Tokyo)
Diogène	Diogène (Paris)
E. Afr. econ. Rev.	East African Economic Review (Nairobi, Kenya)
E. Asian cult. Stud.	East Asian Cultural Studies (Tokyo)
East. Anthrop.	Eastern Anthropologist (Lucknow, India)
Econ. Aff.	Economic Affairs (Calcutta)
Econ. Busin. Bull.	Economics and Business Bulletin (Philadelphia)
Econ. Comm. Asia Far E. Tsûshin (ECAFE)	Economic Commission for Asia and the Far East Tsûshin (Tokyo)
Econ. Dev. cult. Change	Economic Development and Cultural Change (Chicago)
Econ. Geogr.	Economic Geography (Worcester, Mass.)
Econ. int.	Economia Internazionale (Genoa)
Econ. J.	Economic Journal (London)
Econ. Pap.	Economic Papers (Patna, India)
Econ. soc. Tijdschr.	Economisch en Sociaal Tijdschrift (Antwerp)
Econ. Wkly.	Economic Weekly (Bombay)
Economía	Economía (Santiago de Chile)
Educ. Ciênc. soc.	Educação e Ciências Sociaias (Rio de Janeiro)
Educ. Psychol.	Education and Psychology (Delhi)
Egypte contemp.	Egypte Contemporaine (Cairo)
Ekon. Keuangan Indonesia	Ekonomia Keuangan Indonesia (Djakarta)
Encycl. mens. d'outre-mer	Encyclopédie Mensuelle d'Outre-Mer (Paris)
Estud. etnogr.	Estudos Etnograficos (Luanda, Angola)
Estud. polít. soc.	Estudos Políticos e Sociais (Lisbon)
Estud. soc.	Estudios Sociales (Buenos Aires)
Estud. ultramarinos	Estudos Ultramarinos (Lisbon)
Ethnology	Ethnology (Pittsburgh, Pa.)
Etud. éburn.	Etudes Eburnéennes (Ibadjan, Ivory Coast)
Etud. guiné.	Etudes Guinéennes (Conakry, Guinea)
Etud. mélanés.	Etudes Mélanésiennes (Noumea, N. Caledonia)
Etud. rur.	Etudes Rurales (Paris)
Etud. Tiers-Monde	Etudes Tiers-Monde (Paris)
Eur. J. Sociol.	European Journal of Sociology (Paris)
Fam. Monde	Familles dans le Monde (Paris)
Far E. econ. Rev.	Far Eastern Economic Review (Hong Kong)
Folk	Folk (Copenhagen)
Foro int.	Foro Internacional (Mexico City)
Forschn. Fortschr.	Forschungen und Fortschritte (Berlin)
Fundl. Educ. adult Educ.	Fundakental Education and Adult Education (Paris)

Geogr. J.	Geographical Journal (London)
Geogr. Rev.	Geographical Review (New York)
Geogr. Rev. India	Geographical Review of India (Calcutta)
Geogr. Tidsskr.	Geografisk Tidsskrift (Copenhagen)
Gids maatsch. Gebied	Gids op Maatschappelijk Gebied (Brussels)
Heerbaan	De Heerbaan (Amsterdam)
Hekichi Kyoiku Kenkyû	Hekichi Kyoiku Kenkyû
Hesperis	Hesperis (Rabat, Morocco)
Hitotsubashi Ronsô	Hitotsubashi Ronsô (Tokyo)
Hôgaku Kenkyû	Hôgaku Kenkyû
Hôgaku Shimpô	Hôgaku Shimpô (Tokyo
Hôkeikai Ronsô	Hôkeikai Ronsô
Hokkaidô Gakugei Daigaku Kiyô	Hokkaidô Gakugei Daigaku Kiyô (Sapporo, Japan)
Homme (L')	L'Homme. Revue Française d'Anthropologie (Paris)
Homme d'outre-mer	Homme d'Outre-Mer (Paris)
Howard Univ. Mag.	Howard University Magazine (Washington, D.C.)
Hum. Organiz.	Human Organization (New York)
Hum. Probl. B.C.A.	Human Problems in British Central Africa (Lusaka, Uganda)
Hum. Relat.	Human Relations (London)
Ibadan	Ibadan (Ibadan, Nigeria)
India Quart.	India Quarterly (New Delhi)
Indian coop. Rev.	Indian Cooperative Review (Delhi)
Indian econ. Rev.	Indian Economic Review (New Delhi)
Indian J. adult Educ.	Indian Journal of Adult Education (New Delhi)
Indian J. agric. Econ.	Indian Journal of Agricultural Economics (Bombay)
Indian J. Labour Econ.	Indian Journal of Labour Economics (Lucknow)
Indian J. Psychol.	Indian Journal of Psychology (Calcutta)
Indian J. pub. Adm.	Indian Journal of Public Administration (New Delhi)
Indian J. soc. Res.	Indian Journal of Social Research (Baraut)
Indian J. soc. Wk.	Indian Journal of Social Work (Bombay)
Indian Labour J.	Indian Labour Journal (Delhi)
Indian Sociol.	Indian Sociologist (Indora)
Indian sociol. Bull.	Indian Sociological Bulletin (Ghaziabad)
Indo-Asian Cult.	Indo-Asian Culture (New Delhi)
Indonesië	Indonesië (The Hague)
Indust. Labor Rel. Rev.	Industrial and Labor Relations Review (New York)
Indust. Relat.	Industrial Relations (Berkeley, Calif.)
Industrie	Industrie (Brussels)
Inform. Birispt	Inform. Birispt (Paris)
Inform. ISSC	Informations. International Social Sciences Council (Paris)
Inform. Sci. soc.	Information sur les Sciences Sociales (Paris)
Inform. Svimez	Inform. Svimez (Rome)
Inst. belles Lettres arabes	Institut des Belles Lettres Arabes (Tunis)

Int. Dev. Rev.	International Development Review (Washington, D.C.)
Int. econ. Rev.	International Economic Review (Osaka, Japan)
Int. J. comp. Sociol.	International Journal of Comparative Sociology (Dharwar, India)
Int. J. Sociom. Sociat.	International Journal of Sociometry and Sociatry (Beacon, N.Y.)
Int. Labour Rev.	International Labour Review (Geneva)
Int. Rev. Comm. Dev.	International Review of Community Development (Rome)
Int. Rev. Missions	International Review of Missions (Geneva)
Int. Rev. Service	International Review of Service (New York)
Int. soc. Sci. Bull. (J.)	International Social Sciences Bulletin (later Journal) (New York)
Int. soc. Wk.	International Social Work (New York)
Inter-Am. econ. Aff.	Inter-American Economic Affairs (Washington
Items	Items (New York)

J. aero-med. Soc.	Journal of the Aero-Medical Society (New Delhi)
J. afr. Adm.	Journal of African Administration (London)
J. afr. Hist.	Journal of African History (London)
J. afr. Law	Journal of African Law (London)
J. Ala. Acad. Sci.	Journal of the Alabama Academy of Sciences (Auburn)
J. Am. Folkl.	Journal of American Folklore (New York)
J. appl. Psychol.	Journal of Applied Psychology (Washington
J. Arctic Inst. No. Am.	Journal of the Arctic Institute of North America (Montreal)
J. Asian afr. Stud.	Journal of Asian and African Studies (Leiden)
J. Asian Stud.	Journal of Asian Studies (Ann Arbor, Mich.)
J. Burma Res. Soc.	Journal of the Burma Research Society (Rangoon)
J. China Soc.	Journal of the China Society (T'aipei, T'aiwan)
J. E. Asiat. Stud.	Journal of East Asiatic Studies (Manila)
J. econ. Hist.	Journal of Economic History (New York)
J. Educ. Psychol.	Journal of Education and Psychology (Baroda, India)
J. Gujarat Res. Soc.	Journal of the Gujarat Research Society (Bombay)
J. Inst. Engng.	Journal of the Institute of Engineering (Dacca, E. Pakistan)
J. Karnatak Univ. (Hum.)	Journal of Karnatak University (Humanities) (Dharwar, India)
J. local Adm. Overseas	Journal of Local Administration Overseas (London)
J. Maharaja Sayajirao Univ.	Journal of the Maharaja Sayajirao University (Baroda, India)
J. Marketing	Journal of Marketing (Chicago)
J. Marr. Fam. Living	Journal of Marriage and Family Living (Minneapolis)
J. mod. afr. Stud.	Journal of Modern African Studies (Cambridge, England)
J. nat. Acad. Adm.	Journal of the National Academy of Administration (Mussorie, India)
J. Pakistan Acad. Vill. Dev.	Journal of the Pakistan Academy of Village Development (Comilla, E. Pakistan)
J. Polynesian Soc.	Journal of Polynesian Society (Wellington, New Zealand)
J. racial Aff.	Journal of Racial Affairs (Stellenbosch, South Africa)
J. Rhodes-Livingst. Inst.	Journal of the Rhodes-Livingstone Institute (Livingstone, Zambia)

J. roy. afr. Soc.	Journal of the Royal African Society (London) (see African Affairs)
J. roy. anthrop. Inst. Gt. Br. Ir.	Journal of the Royal Anthropological Institute of Great Britain and Ireland (London)
J. roy. asiat. Soc. (Malayan)	Journal of the Royal Asiatic Society, Malayan Branch (Singapore)
J. roy. Soc. Arts	Journal of the Royal Society of the Arts (London)
J. S. E. Asian Hist.	Journal of South East Asian History (Singapore)
J. Soc. Afric.	Journal de la Société des Africanistes (Paris)
J. Soc. Amér.	Journal de la Société des Américanistes (Paris)
J. soc. Issues	Journal of Social Issues (Ann Arbor, Mich.)
J. Soc. Océanist.	Journal de la Société des Océanistes (Paris)
J. soc. Psychol.	Journal of Social Psychology (Provincetown, Mass.)
J. soc. Res.	Journal of Social Research (Ranchi, India)
J. soc. Sci.	Journal of the Social Sciences (Agra, India)
J. Univ. Bombay	Journal of the University of Bombay (Bombay)
Jinbun Chiri	Jinbun Chiri (Tokyo)
Jinbun Gakuhô	Jinbun Gakuhô (Kyoto)
Jinbun Kagaku Kenkyû	Jinbun Kagaku Kenkyû (Niigata, Japan)
Jinrui Kagaku	Jinrui Kagaku (Tokyo)
Jinruigaku Zasshi	Jinruigaku Zasshi (Tokyo)
Kagoshima Hôkoku	Kagoshima Hôkoku (Kagoshima, Japan)
Kaigaijijô Kenkyûsho Hôkoku	Kaigaijijô Kenkyûsho Hôkoku (Tokyo)
Kaiho	Kaiho (Tokyo)
Kajian Ekonomi Malaysia	Kajian Ekonomi Malaysia (Kuala Lumpur)
Keiô Daigaku Kiyô	Keiô Daigaku Kiyô (Tokyo)
Kenkyû	Kenkyû (Kobe)
Kenkyû Nempô	Kenkyû Nempô (Kobe)
Kenkyû Tsûshin	Kenkyû Tsûshin (Tokyo)
Kôbe Hôgaku	Kôbe Hôgaku Zasshi (Kobe)
Kôbe Jyogakuin Daigaku Ronshû	Kôbe Jyogakuin Daigaku Ronshû (Kobe)
Kölner Z. Soziol. Sozialps.	Kölner Zeitschrift für Soziologie und Sozialpsychologie (Cologne, W. Germany)
Kroeber anthrop. Soc. Pap.	Kroeber Anthropological Society Papers (Berkeley, Calif.)
Kula	Kula (Baarn, Netherlands)
Kyklos	Kyklos (Berne, Switzerland)
Kyôdôtai No Hikaku Kenkyû	Kyôdôtai No Hikaku Kenkyû (Tokyo)
Kyoto Gakujitsu Hôkoku	Kyoto Gakujitsu Hôkoku (Kyoto)
Kyûshû Daigaku Ronbunshû	Kyûshû Daigaku Ronbunshû (Fukuoka, Japan)
Malay. J. tropic. Geogr.	Malayan Journal of Tropical Geography (Singapore)
Man	Man (London)
Man Art	Man Art (India)
Man in India	Man in India (Ranchi, India)
Mankind	Mankind (Sydney, Australia)
Méditerranée	Méditerranée (Aix-en-Province, France)

Meiji Gakuin Ronsô   Meiji Gakuin Ronsô (Tokyo)
Mém. Inst. sci.   Mémoires de l'Institut de Science de Madagascar
    Madagascar   (Tanarive, Malagasy Republic)
Mens en Maatschappij   Mens en Maatschappij (Amsterdam)
Mid. E. J.   Middle East Journal (Washington, D.C.)
Minzokugaku Kenkyû   Minzokugaku Kenkyû (Tokyo)
Mitt. anthrop. Ges.   Mitteilungen der Anthropologischen Gesellschaft in
    Wien   Wien (Vienna)
Mod. Rev.   Modern Review (Calcutta)
Monogr. Inst. natn.   Monographies de l'Institut National d'Hygiène
    Hyg.   (Paris)

Nagpur agric. Col.   Nagpur Agriculture College Magazine (Nagpur, India)
    Mag.
Nat. Life S. E. Asia   Nature and Life in Southeast Asia (Kyoto)
Neues Afr.   Neues Afrika (Munich)
New Outlook   New Outlook (Tel-Aviv)
Nieuw-Guinea Stud.   Nieuw-Guinea Studien (The Hague)
Niger. geogr. J.   Nigerian Geographical Journal (Ibadan)
Nigeria   Nigeria (Lagos, Nigeria)
Nihon Minzokugaku   Nihon Minzokugaku (Tokyo)
Nôgyo Gijitsu Kenkyû   Nôgyo Gijitsu Kenkyû (Tokyo)
Nôgyo Sôgô Kenkyû   Nôgyo Sôgô Kenkyû (Tokyo)
Notes afr.   Notes Africaines (Dakar, Senegal)
Notes maroc.   Notes Marocaines (Rabat)
Nuovo Oss.   Nuovo Osservatore (Rome)

Occup. Psychol.   Occupational Psychology (London)
Oceania   Oceania (Sydney, Australia)
Okayama Shûruku   Okayama Shûruku (Okayama, Japan)
Orient. Geogr.   Oriental Geographer (Dacca, E. Pakistan)
Orient/West   Orient/West (Paris)
Orio Koto Gakko Kiyô   Orio Koto Gakko Kiyô (Japan)
Oversea Educ.   Oversea Education. Journal of Educational Experiment
       and Research in Tropical and Subtropical Areas
       (London)
Oversea Quart.   Oversea Quarterly (London)

Pacif. Aff.   Pacific Affairs (New York; and Vancouver, B.C.)
Pacif. Spectator   Pacific Spectator (Stanford, Calif.)
Pacif. Viewpoint   Pacific Viewpoint (Wellington, New Zealand)
Paideuma   Paideuma (Wiesbaden, W. Germany)
Pakist. Dev. Rev.   Pakistan Development Review (Karachi, W. Pakistan)
Pakist. econ. J.   Pakistan Economic Journal (Dacca, E. Pakistan)
Pakist. Labour Gaz.   Pakistan Labour Gazette (Karachi, W. Pakistan)
Panorama   Panorama (Buenos Aires)
Patna Univ. J.   Patna University Journal (Patna, India)
Personnel Psychol.   Personnel Psychology (Baltimore, Md.)
Peru indíg.   Peru Indígena (Lima)
Philipp. econ. Bull.   Philippine Economic Bulletin (Manila)
Philipp. econ. J.   Philippine Economic Journal (Manila)
Philipp. educ. Forum   Philippine Educational Forum (Manila)
Philipp. J. pub. Adm.   Philippine Journal of Public Administration (Manila)

[31]

Philipp. sociol. Rev.	Philippine Sociological Review (Quezon City)
Philipp. Stat.	Philippine Statistics (Manila)
Philipp. Stud.	Philippine Studies (Manila)
Phylon	Phylon (Atlanta, Ga.)
Polit. étrang.	Politique Etrangère (Paris)
Polynesian Soc. Mem.	Polynesian Society Memoirs (Wellington, New Zealand)
Population	Population (Paris)
Popul. Stud.	Population Studies (London)
Pract. Anthrop.	Practical Anthropology (Tarrytown, N.Y.)
Présence afr.	Présence Africaine (Paris)
Preuves	Preuves (Paris)
Probl. Afr. cent.	Problèmes d'Afrique Centrale (Brussels)
Proc. Am. ethnol. Soc.	Proceedings of the American Ethnology Society (Seattle, Wash.)
Prod. fr.	Productivité Française (Paris)
Progr. soc.	Progrès Social (Liège, Belgium)
Psychol. afr.	Psychologia Africana (Johannesburg)
Psychol. Stud.	Psychological Studies (Mysore, India)
Pub. Adm.	Public Administration (Sydney, Australia)
Pub. Am. Archeol. Ethnogr.	Publications in American Archeology and Ethnography (Berkeley, Calif.)
Pub. Opin. Q.	Public Opinion Quarterly (Princeton, N.J.)
Quad. Azione soc.	Quaderni di Azione Sociale (Rome)
Quad. Sociol.	Quaderni di Sociologia (Turin)
Race	Race (London)
Race Relat.	Race Relations (Johannesburg)
Razón y Fe	Razón y Fe (Madrid)
Rech. Débats	Recherches et Débats (Paris)
Remp. B.	Remp. B. (The Hague)
Res. Stud.	Research Studies (Pullman, Wash.)
Rev. Action pop.	Revue de l'Action Populaire (Paris)
Rev. afr.	Revue Africaine (Algiers, Algeria)
Rev. algér. tunis. maroc.	Revue Algérienne, Tunisienne, et Marocaine (Algiers, Algeria)
Rev. Antrop.	Revista di Antropologia (São Paulo, Brazil)
Rev. bras. Ciênc. soc.	Revista Brasileira de Ciências Sociais (Belo Horizonte, Brazil)
Rev. bras. Geogr.	Revista Brasileira de Geografia (Rio de Janeiro)
Rev. Campanha nac. Educ. rur.	Revista de Campanha Nacional de Educação Rural (Rio de Janeiro)
Rev. Chambre Comm. Marseille	Revue de la Chambre de Commerce de Marseille (Marseille)
Rev. Cienc. soc.	Revista de Ciencias Sociales (San Juan, Puerto Rico)
Rev. colomb. Antrop.	Revista Colombiana de Antropologia (Bogotá)
Rev. colomb. Folkl.	Revista Colombiana de Folklore (Bogotá)
Rev. Déf. natn.	Revue de Défense Nationale (Paris)
Rev. Econ.	Revista de Economía (Mexico City)
Rev. écon.	Revue Economique (Paris)
Rev. Fac. Cienc. econ. coml.	Revista de la Facultad de Ciencias Económicas y Comerciales (Lima, Peru)
Rev. fr. Sociol.	Revue Française de Sociologie (Paris)
Rev. Géogr. Lyon	Revue de Géographie de Lyon (Lyon, France)
Rev. Géogr. maroc.	Revue de Géographie Marocaine (Casablanca, Morocco)

Rev. Inst. Sociol.	Revue de l'Institut de Sociologie (Brussels)
Rev. int. Ethnopsy-chol.	Revue Internationale d'Ethnopsychologie Normale et Pathologie (Tangier, Morocco)
Rev. interamer. Cienc. soc.	Revista Interamericana de Ciencias Sociales (Washington, D.C.)
Rev. int. Travail	Revue Internationale du Travail (Paris)
Rev. mex. Sociol.	Revista Mexicana de Sociologia (Mexico City)
Rev. Mus. nac.	Revista del Museo Nacional (Lima, Peru)
Rev. Psychol. Peuples	Revue de Psychologie des Peuples (Le Havre)
Rev. Soc. haïtienne Géogr.	Revue de la Societe Haïtienne de Géographie (Port-au-Prince, Haiti)
Rev. Sud-Est asiat.	Revue du Sud-Est Asiatique (Brussels)
Rev. Trav. Acad. Sci. mor. polit.	Revue des Travaux de l'Académie des Sciences Morales et Politiques (Paris)
Rev. Univ. Bruxelles	Revue de l'Université de Bruxelles (Brussels)
Rhod. Sci. Ass.	Rhodesia Science Association (Salisbury, S. Rhodesia)
Riv. int. Sci. soc.	Rivista Internazionale di Scienzi Sociali (Milan)
Riv. Sociol.	Rivista de Sociologia (Rome)
Rur. India	Rural India (Bombay)
Rur. Sociol.	Rural Sociology (Lexington, Ky.)
S. Afr. J. Econ.	South African Journal of Economics (Johannesburg)
S. Afr. J. Sci.	South African Journal of Science (Johannesburg)
S. Afr. Outlook	South African Outlook (Lovedale, South Africa)
S. Pacif.	South Pacific (Sydney, Australia)
S. Pacif. Comm. quart. Bull.	South Pacific Commission Quarterly Bulletin (Noumea, N. Caledonia)
Sankhya	Sankhya: Indian Journal of Statistics (Calcutta)
Sci. Am.	Scientific American (New York)
Sci. Mon.	Scientific Monthly (New York)
Sci. Rev.	Science Review (Manila)
Sci. Soc.	Science and Society (New York)
Science	Science (Washington, D.C.)
Sekai	Sekai (Tokyo)
Seminar	Seminar (Bombay)
Shakai Kagaku Kenkyû	Shakai Kagaku Kenkyû (Tokyo)
Shakai Kagaku Tôkyû	Shakai Kagaku Tôkyû (Tokyo)
Shakai Kyôiku Kenkyujo	Shakai Kyôiku Kenkyujo (Tokyo)
Shakaigaku Hyôron	Shakaigaku Hyôron (Tokyo)
Shehui K'ohsueh Luents'ung	Shehui K'ohsueh Luents'ung (T'aipei, T'aiwan)
Shien	Shien (Tokyo)
Shimane Daigaku Ronshû	Shimane Daigaku Ronshû (Matsue, Japan)
Shimane Kiyô	Shimane Kiyô (Matsue, Japan)
Shiron	Shiron (Kyoto)
Shisô	Shisô (Tokyo)
Silliman J.	Silliman Journal (Dumaguete City, Philipp.)
Soc. Action	Social Action (New Delhi)
Soc. econ. Stud.	Social and Economic Studies (Kingston, Jamaica)
Soc. Forces	Social Forces (Chapel Hill, N.C.)
Soc. indust. Rev.	Social and Industrial Review (Pretoria, South Africa)
Soc. Order	Social Order (St. Louis, Mo.)
Soc. Probl.	Social Problems (New York)
Soc. Psychol.	(see Journal of Social Psychology)

Soc. Res.	Social Research (New York)
Sochioroji	Sochioroji (Tokyo)
Sociol. Bull.	Sociological Bulletin (Bombay)
Sociol. Meddr.	Sociologisk Meddelelser (Copenhagen)
Sociol. Rev.	Sociological Review (Keele, England)
Sociol. soc. Res.	Sociology and Social Research (Los Angeles)
Sociol. Trav.	Sociologie du Travail (Paris)
Sociologia	Sociologia (São Paulo, Brazil)
Sociologus	Sociologus (Berlin)
Sociometry	Sociometry (New York)
Sols afr.	Sols Africains (Paris)
Sthwest. J. Anthrop.	Southwestern Journal of Anthropology (Albuquerque, N.M.)
Sthwest. soc. Sci. Quart.	Southwestern Social Sciences Quarterly (Baton Rouge, La.)
Stud. gen.	Studium Generale (Berlin)
Sudan Notes	Sudan Notes (Khartoum, Sudan)
Synthèses	Synthèses (Brussels)
T'aiwan Chih-Hsueh	T'aiwan Chih-Hsueh (T'aipei, T'aiwan)
Tamil Cult.	Tamil Culture (Madras, India)
Tempi mod.	Tempi Moderni (Rome)
Tiers-Monde	Tiers-Monde (Paris)
Tijdschr. econ. soc. Geogr.	Tijdschrift voor Economische en Sociale Geographie (Rotterdam)
Tijdschr. Maat. Navors	Tijdschrift Maat. Navors
Tijdschr. soc. Wet.	Tijdschrift voor Sociale Wetenschappen (Ghent)
Tochiseido Shigaku	Tochiseido Shigaku (Tokyo)
Toshi Mondai Kenkyû	Toshi Mondai Kenkyû (Tokyo)
Tottori Kenkyukohoku	Tottori Kenkyukohoku (Tottori, Japan)
Trans. N.Y. Acad. Sci.	Transactions of the New York Academy of Sciences (New York)
Trav. hum.	Travail Humain (Paris)
Trav. Inst. Rech. saharéennes	Travaux de l'Institut de Recherches Saharéennes (Algiers, Algeria)
Uebersee-Rdsch.	Uebersee-Rundschau (Hamburg)
Uganda J.	Uganda Journal (Kampala)
Unit. Asia	United Asia (Bombay)
Universo	Universo (Florence, Italy)
Urban rur. Plann. Thought	Urban and Rural Planning Thought (New Delhi)
Vanyajati	Vanyajati (Delhi)
Vie urb.	Vie Urbaine (Paris)
Waseda Daigaku Kiyô	Waseda Daigaku Kiyô (Tokyo)
Way Forum	Way Forum (Brussels)
Weltwirtsch. Arch.	Weltwirtschaftliches Archiv (Kiel University, Hamburg)
Wirtschaftdienst	Wirtschaftdienst (Bad Wörishofen, W. Germany)
Wld. Islam	World of Islam (Leiden, Netherlands)
Wld. Polit.	World Politics (Princeton, N.J.)

[34]

Yale Univ. Pub. Anthrop.	Yale University Publications in Anthropology (New Haven)
Yb. wld. Aff.	Yearbook of World Affairs (London)
Z. Agrargesch. Agrarsoziol.	Zeitschrift für Agrargeschichte und Agrarsoziologie (Frankfurt-am-Main)
Z. Ethnol.	Zeitschrift für Ethnologie (Braunschweig, W. Germany)
Z. ges. Stattswiss.	Zeitschrift für die gesamte Staatswissenschaft (Tübingen, W. Germany)
Zaïre	Zaïre (Brussels)

HOW TO USE THE BIBLIOGRAPHY

As indicated in the Introduction, the entries in this bibliography
are divided into four parts:

I.   General (GEN), covering works on general theory or de-
     scription.

II. Industrialization (IND), citing works specifically on
     the social impact of industrialization.

III. Urbanization (URB), including works dealing especially
     with the problems of urbanization.

IV. Rural Modernization (RUR), listing works that treat
     the various aspects of modernization in rural areas.

The three letters given in parentheses after the title of each part
are the code name for that part. The code is combined with the number
assigned to each book or article.

Each of these four parts is, in turn, split into a number of sections. The first section in each part comprises theoretical works. An
entry in a theory section will be listed under a number from 1001 to 1999.
In every section, the units, tens, and hundreds are used to number serially
the books within the section. The thousands and tens of thousands are
reserved for the serial number of the section within its part as given in
the Table of Contents. Thus a book in a section on theory will always begin
with a "1" followed by three more digits. Throughout, the numbers from 001
to 299 have been set aside for annotated works. Non-annotated works are
given numbers from 301 to 999. Since none of the theoretical works is
annotated, the first entry in a theory section will be numbered 1301.

With regard to numbering, each section is self-contained in that the
units, tens, and hundreds begin anew. The parts are similarly self-contained
in that the thousands and ten thousands (if any) begin again. Thus the whole
code is necessary to indicate an entry's location. In the Introduction, I
used R. E. Phillips' The Bantu in the City as an example of classification.
The code number for that book is URB 2420, which places it in Part III
(Urbanization), section 2 (Urban Problems), 120th in the unannotated subdivision (in which the numbering begins with 301). By contrast, IND 3120
would designate an annotated entry (annotations take nos. 001-299) in section
3 of the part on Industrialization. In the Indices, as an additional aid,
the last two digits of the year of publication have been given in parentheses
following the last code digit. Thus for The Bantu in the City, published in
1938, the Author Index entry reads:

Phillips, R. E.
    URB 2420 ('38).

Subject matter that has more than one part or that does not seem to justify a more detailed classification has been placed in Part I in the section entitled, "General Descriptions of Social Change."

As the reader will appreciate, the sections interposed between "Theory" and "General Studies" in Parts II-IV form the core of this bibliography. Only the items of these sections have been annotated, and only the annotated works have been rated with stars: one star for the work that is above average, two stars for the excellent work, and three for the truly outstanding study. As has been explained in the Introduction, limitations of time and space have prevented any systematic reading of the items in periodicals. Some articles have been annotated, but for the most part only books have been consistently analyzed. For this reason the reader will find many outstanding articles in periodicals that have not been annotated or rated.

A certain number of general decisions have been made with regard to alphabetizing. The particles attached to surnames, such as "de," "von," and so forth, are considered as an integral part of the surname and therefore govern the position of the entry in the alphabet. Mc and St. are treated as if spelled out in full: Mac and Saint. The works by a single author are cited alphabetically by title before the works he has done in collaboration with others. For members of those cultures that do not use surnames (for example, the Indonesian or Ethiopian) the given name has been treated as a surname. If more than one word forms the surname, these are treated in their natural order as a compound; for example: Gutierrez de Pineda, V. The first author of a work with coauthors is cited in directory style, while his coauthors are cited with the first name followed by his others. This order has been followed even for those cultures such as the Japanese or Chinese, in which the surname commonly precedes the given name.

Periodicals are cited first by the abbreviated name of the journal, followed by the volume, number, month, year, and pages, if all these data are known, as: Am. Anthrop. 61:2 (Apr. 1959), 185-199. When only one number follows the title of the journal, it is either the volume (the issue being unknown) or the issue, if the periodical is not issued in volumes. In a few cases some element of the full citation was not obtainable. As is usual, "n.d." indicates that the date is not known. Titles of dissertations are placed within quotation marks, as are titles of articles in periodicals.

PART I.   GENERAL (GEN)

1301-4402

1.   General Theory

1301   Aguirre Beltrán, Gonzalo, El proceso de aculturación [The accultura-
        tion process].   Mexico City: Universidad Nacional Autónoma de México,
        Dirección General de Publicaciones, 1957.   269 pp.

1302   Arensberg, Conrad M., and Arthur H. Niehoff, Introducing Social
        Change.   Chicago: Aldine, 1964.   214 pp.

1303   Bailey, Frederick George, The Margins of Social Anthropology.
        Berkeley: Center for South Asia Studies, 1964.   26 mim. pp.

1304   Balandier, Georges, "Comparative Study of Economic Motivations and
        Incentives in a Traditional and in a Modern Environment," in GEN 4356
        (1963), 25-40.

1305   ------ "Le contexte socio-culturel et le coût social du progrès" [The
        sociocultural context and the social cost of progress], in GEN 4304
        (1956), 289-303.

1306   ------ "Déséquilibres socio-culturels et modernisation des pays sous-
        développes" [Sociocultural disequilibrium and modernization of the
        underdeveloped countries], Cah. int. Sociol. 3:20 (1956), 30-44.

1307   ------ "Introduction," in GEN 4302 (1962), 5-27.

1308   ------ Les pays "sous-développés": Aspects et perspectives [The "under-
        developed" countries: Aspects and perspectives].   2 vols.   Paris: Les
        Cours de droit, 1959.   286 pp.

1309   ------ "Phénomènes sociaux totaux et dynamique sociale" [Total social
        phenomena and social dynamics], Cah. int. Sociol. 30 (Jan.-June 1961),
        23-25.

1310   ------ Sociologie actuelle de l'Afrique noire: Dynamique sociale en
        Afrique Centrale [Present-day sociology of Black Africa: The social
        dynamics of central Africa].   2nd rev. ed.   Paris: Presses Universi-
        taires de France, 1963.

1311   ------ "Sociologie des régions sous-développées" [Sociology of the
         underdeveloped regions], in GEN 4331 (1962), 332-344.

1312   Balkrishna, R., "Social Implications Impeding Economic Progress,"
         Bull. Inst. tradit. Cult. 2 (1960), 244-276.

1313   Banks, J. A., "Social Implications of Technological Change," in GEN
         4302 (1962), 61-106, bibl.

1314   Barnett, H. G., Innovation: The Basis of Cultural Change. New York:
         McGraw-Hill, 1953. 462 pp.

1315   Beaglehole, E., "Cultural Factors in Economic and Social Change," S.
         Pacif. 8:2 (Jan.-Feb. 1955), 14-20.

1316   Beattie, John H. M., "Ritual and Social Change," Man 1:1 (March 1966),
         60-74.

1317   Bellah, Robert N., "Religious Aspects of Modernization in Turkey and
         Japan," Am. J. Sociol. 64:1 (July 1958), 1-5, bibl.

1318   Belshaw, Cyril S., Changing Melanesia: Social Economics of Culture
         Contact. Melbourne: Oxford University Press, 1954. 197 pp.

1319   ------ "La structure sociale et les valeurs culturelles dans leurs
         rapports avec la croissance économique" [The relationship of social
         structure and cultural values with economic growth], Riv. int. Sci.
         soc. 16:2 (1964), 236-249.

1320   ------ Traditional Exchange and Modern Markets. Englewood Cliffs,
         N.J.: Prentice-Hall, 1965. 146 pp.

1321   Berliner, J. S., "The Feet of the Natives Are Large: An Essay on
         Anthropology by an Economist," Curr. Anthrop. 3:1 (Feb. 1962), 47-61.
         See Cardoso de Oliveira in GEN 1328 (1962).

1322   Bernard, S., Les conséquences sociales du progrès technique [The
         social consequences of technical progress]. Brussels: Institut de
         Sociologie Solvay, 1956. 217 pp.

1323   Bertolino, A., "Aree depresse e cultura sociale" [Depressed areas and
         social culture], Econ. int. 10:4 (1957), 625-646.

1324   Bičanić, R., "Le passage du seuil de développement économique: Con-
         ditions préalables et effets ultérieurs sur le plan social" [Beginning
         economic development: Preconditions and aftereffects on the social
         level], Int. soc. Sci. Bull.(J.) 16:2 (1964), 299-309.

1325   Boskoff, A., "Social Indecision: A Dysfunctional Focus of Transi-
         tional Society," Soc. Forces 37 (May 1959), 305-311, bibl.

1326   Brozen, Y., "Social Implications of Technological Change," Items 3:3
         (1949), 31-34.

1327   Burling, R., "Maximization Theories and the Study of Economic Anthro-
         pology," Am. Anthrop. 64:4 (Aug. 1962), 802-821.

1328   Cardoso de Oliveira, Roberto, "Combinatorial Analysis," Curr. Anthrop.
        5:2 (Apr. 1964), 104-105. A reply to J. S. Berliner, in GEN 1321
        (1962).

1329   Centro Latino-americano de Pesquisas em Ciências Sociais, Resistências
        à mudança: Fatôres que impedem ou dificultam o desenvolvimento.
        Anais do Seminário Internacional, reunido no Rio de Janeiro, em
        Outubro de 1959 [Resistance to change: Factors that impede or slow
        down development. Annals of the International Seminar held in Rio de
        Janeiro in October 1959]. Rio de Janeiro: Centro Latino-americano
        de Pesquisas em Ciências Sociais, 1960. 349 pp.

1330   Chowdhury, J. K., "Resistance to Change," East. Anthrop. 13:3 (Mar.-
        May 1960), 75-83.

1331   "Les conséquences sociales de l'industrialisation rapide des pays
        insuffisamment dévéloppés" [The social consequences of the rapid
        industrialization of insufficiently developed countries], Prog. Soc.
        56 (July 1958), 3-48.

1332   Costa Pinto, L. A., Sociología e desenvolvimento: Temas e problemas
        de nosso tempo [Sociology and development: Themes and problems of a
        new age]. Rio de Janeiro: Editôra Civilização Brasileira, 1963.
        314 pp.

1333   Crespi, P., Analisi sociologica e sottosviluppo economico [Sociologi-
        cal analysis and economic underdevelopment]. Milan: Giuffrè, 1963.
        266 pp.

1334   Crockett, Harry, "Psychological Origins of Mobility," in GEN 4381
        (1966), 280-309.

1335   Dalton, G., "Economic Theory and Primitive Society," Am. Anthrop.
        63:1 (Feb. 1961), 1-25.

1336   Danziger, K., "Ideology and Utopia in South Africa: A Methodological
        Contribution to the Sociology of Knowledge," Br. J. Sociol. 14:1
        (Mar. 1963), 59-76.

1337   Deutsch, Karl W., "Some Quantitative Constraints on Value Allocation
        in Society and Politics," Behavl. Sci. 11:4 (Oct. 1966), 245-252.

1338   Doob, L. W., Communication in Africa: A Search for Boundaries. New
        Haven: Yale University Press, 1961. 406 pp.

1339   Duncan, Otis Dudley, "Methodological Issues in the Analysis of Social
        Mobility," in GEN 4381 (1966), 51-97.

1340   Du Toit, B. M., "Substitution: A Process in Culture Change," Hum.
        Organiz. 23:1 (Spring 1964), 16-23.

1341   Eggan, F., "Cultural Drift and Social Change," Curr. Anthrop. 4:4
        (Oct. 1963), 347-355.

1342   Ehrenfels, U. R., "Example and Responsibility: Two Acculturation
        Problems," Indian J. soc. Wk. 19:2 (Sept. 1958), 143-149.

1343   Eisenstadt, S. N., The Absorption of Immigrants. London: Routledge
        & Kegan Paul, 1954. 225 pp. [Israel]

1344   ------ "Breakdowns of Modernization," Econ. Dev. cult. Change 12:4
        (July 1964), 345-367.

1345   ------ Essays on Comparative Institutions. New York: Wiley, 1965.
        376 pp.

1346   ------ From Generation to Generation. Glencoe, Ill.: Free Press,
        1956. 357 pp. [Israel]

1347   ------ "Institutionalization and Change," Am. soc. Rev. 29:2 (Apr.
        1964), 235-247.

1348   ------ "Modernization and Conditions of Sustained Growth," Wld.
        Polit. 16:4 (July 1964), 576-594.

1349   ------ Modernization: Growth and Diversity. Bloomington: Department
        of Government, Indiana University, 1963. 26 pp.

1350   ------ "Modernisation: Growth and Diversity," Amér. lat. 9:1 (1966),
        34-58.

1351   ------ "Modernizzazione: Sviluppo e diversità" [Modernization:
        Development and diversity], Quad. Sociol. 13:2 (Apr.-June 1964),
        147-175.

1352   ------ "Social Change, Differentiation and Evolution," Am. soc. Rev.
        29:3 (June 1964), 375-386.

1353   ------ "Social Change and Modernization in African Societies South
        of the Sahara," Cah. Etud. afr. 5:3 (1965), 453-471.

1354   Epstein, T. Scarlett, "Social Structure and Entrepreneurship," Int.
        J. comp. Sociol. 5:2 (Sept. 1964), 162-165. [South India]

1355   Fallers, Lloyd A., "Social Stratification and Economic Processes,"
        in GEN 4336 (1964), 113-130. [Africa]

1356   Firth, Raymond William, Essays on Social Organization and Values.
        London: Athlone Press of the University of London, 1964. 326 pp.

1357   Firth, R. W., F. J. Fisher, and D. G. MacRae, "Social Implications
        of Technological Change as Regards Patterns and Models," in GEN
        4303 (1958), 261-293.

1358   Foster, George M., Traditional Cultures and the Impact of Techno-
        logical Change. New York: Harper, 1962. 292 pp.

1359   Frankel, S. H., "Some Conceptual Aspects of Technical Change," in
        GEN 4356 (1963), 53-62.

1360   Fraser, T. M., "Sociocultural Parameters in Directed Change," Hum.
        Organiz. 22:1 (Spring 1963), 95-104. [India]

1361   Fried, Morton H., "Ideology, Social Organization, and Economic
        Development in China: A Living Test of Theories," in GEN 4351
        (1964), 47-62.

1362   Friedmann, F. G., "Thé Impact of Technically Advanced Civilizations
        on Underdeveloped Areas," Confluence 4:4 (Jan. 1956), 391-406.

1363   Fukutake, Tadashi, Man and Society in Japan. Tokyo: Tokyo University
        Press, 1962. 241 pp.

1364   Germani, Gino, Política y sociedad en una época de transición: De
        la sociedad tradicional a la sociedad de masas [Politics and society
        in a transitional epoch: From traditional society to mass society].
        Buenos Aires: Editorial Paidos, 1963. 266 pp.

1365   ------ "Social and Political Consequences of Mobility," in GEN 4381
        (1966), 364-394.

1366   Ghosh, D., "Social Implications of Technological Change," Indian J.
        soc. Res. 1:1 (July 1960), 93-97.

1367   Girod, Roger, "Sous-développement, stratification sociale et évolution
        politique" [Underdevelopment, social stratification, and political
        evolution], Rev. Inst. Sociol.   (1959), 7-14.

1368   Godelier, Maurice, "Objets et méthodes de l'anthropologie économique"
        [Objects and methods of economic anthropology], Homme 5:2 (Apr.-June
        1965), 32-91.

1369   Goldschmidt, W. W., "The Interrelations between Cultural Factors and
        the Acquisition of New Technical Skills," in GEN 4340 (1952), 135-151.

1370   Goode, William J., World Revolution and Family Patterns. New York:
        Free Press of Glencoe, 1963. 432 pp.

1371   Goodfellow, D. M., Principles of Economic Sociology as Illustrated
        from the Bantu Peoples. London: Routledge, 1939. 289 pp. [South
        and East Africa]

1372   Gras, N. S. B., "Anthropology and Economics," in GEN 4362 (1927),
        10-23.

1373   Groenman, S., "External and Internal Casualty in Cultural Change,"
        Int. J. comp. Sociol. 1:1 (Mar. 1960), 103-108.

1374   Hagen, Everett E., On the Theory of Social Change: How Economic
        Growth Begins. Homewood, Ill.: Dorsey, 1962. 557 pp. [Japan;
        Colombia]

1375   Hawley, Amos H., Human Ecology. New York: Ronald Press, 1950. 456
        pp.

1376   Hays, H. R., From Ape to Angel: An Informal History of Social
        Anthropology. New York: Knopf, 1958. 440 pp.

1377   Hegba, M., "Aspects sociologiques du développement économique" [Sociological aspects of economic development], Afr. Docums. 72 (1964), 3-26.

1378   Herskovits, Melville J., Cultural Dynamics. Abridged ed. New York: Knopf, 1964. 260 pp.

1379   ------ "Economic Change and Cultural Dynamics," in GEN 4314 (1961), 114-138.

1380   ------ "Motivation and Cultural Patterns in Technological Change," Int. soc. Sci. Bull.(J.) 6:3 (Fall 1954), 388-399. See GEN 4301.

1381   ------ "Motivation and Culture-Pattern in Technological Change," in GEN 4356 (1963), 41-52.

1382   Hoselitz, Bert F., "Economic Development and Change in Social Values and Thought Patterns," in GEN 4402 (1964), 673-697.

1383   ------ "Interaction Between Industrial and Pre-Industrial Stratification Systems," in GEN 4381 (1966), 177-193.

1384   ------ "Nationalism, Economic Development and Democracy," Ann. Am. Acad. polit. soc. Sci. 305 (May 1956), 1-11.

1385   ------ "Non-Economic Barriers to Economic Development," Econ. Dev. cult. Change 1:1 (Mar. 1952), 8-21.

1386   ------ "Noneconomic Factors in Economic Development," Am. econ. Rev. 47:2 (May 1957), 28-41.

1387   ------ "Population Pressure, Industrialization and Social Mobility," Popul. Stud. 11:2 (Nov. 1957), 123-135.

1388   ------ "Problems of Adapting and Communicating Modern Techniques to Less Developed Areas," Econ. Dev. soc. Change 2:4 (Feb. 1954), 249-268.

1389   ------ "Social Implications of Economic Growth," in GEN 4359 (1963), 78-94.

1390   ------ "Social Structure and Economic Growth," Econ. int. 6:3 (Aug. 1953), 52-77.

1391   ------ Sociological Aspects of Economic Growth. Glencoe, Ill.: Free Press, 1960. 250 pp.

1392   ------ "Some Potentialities and Limitations of Research on Social Implications of Technical Change," Civilisations 6:2 (Apr.-June 1956), 157-178.

1393   ------ "Some Reflections on the Social and Cultural Conditions of Economic Productivity," Civilisations 12:4 (Oct. 1962), 489-498.

1394   ------ "Tradition and Economic Growth," in GEN 4314 (1961), 83-113.

1395   Hoselitz, Bert F., and Wilbert E. Moore (eds.), Industrialization and Society. Paris: Mouton, 1963. 437 pp.

1396   Hoyt, E. E., "Culture Change and Integration: Thesis, Antithesis, Synthesis," Anthrop. Forum 1:1 (July 1963), 122-134.

1397   Hsu, Francis L. K., "Cultural Factors," in GEN 4316 (1954), 318-364.

1398   Inkeles, Alex, "The Modernization of Man," in GEN 4397 (1966), 138-150.

1399   Janne, H., and S. Bernard, "Analyse critique de concepts relatifs aux implications sociales du progrès technique" [A critical analysis of concepts relating to the social implications of technical progress], in GEN 4303 (1958), 21-150.

1400   Jones, William O., "Environment, Technical Knowledge, and Economic Development," in GEN 4315 (1965), 29-48.

1401   Kahl, Joseph A., "Some Social Concomitants of Industrialization and Urbanization," Hum. Organiz. 18:2 (Summer 1959), 53-75. [Mexico]

1402   Kaplan, B. A., "Social and Technical Change." Ph.D. dissertation, University of Chicago, 1953. Mim.

1403   Karve, D. G., "Some Sociological Implications of Planned Development," East. Anthrop. 13:3 (Mar.-May 1960), 64-74.

1404   Katz, E., "Social Itinerary of Technical Change: Two Studies on the Diffusion of Innovation," Hum. Organiz. 20:2 (Summer 1961), 70-82.

1405   Kindermann, G. K., Kulturen im Umbruch. Studien zur Problematik und Analyse des Kulturwandels in Entwicklungsländern [Studies on the problems and analysis of the cultural change in developing countries]. Freiburg, W. Germany: Rombach, 1962. 422 pp.

1406   Kuhne, O., "El progreso técnico y el progreso social" [Technical and social progress], Rev. méx. Sociol. 22:3 (Sept.-Dec. 1960), 823-846.

1407   Kuznets, S., "Measurement of Social Implications of Technological Change," in GEN 4302 (1959), 151-192.

1408   LaPiere, Richard T., Social Change. New York: McGraw-Hill, 1965. 556 pp.

1409   Lebret, L. J., Dynamique concrète du développement [The real dynamics of development]. Paris: Les Editions Ouvrières, 1961. 551 pp.

1410   LeClair, E. E., Jr., "Economic Theory and Economic Anthropology," Am. Anthrop. 64:6 (Dec. 1962), 1179-1203.

1411   Lévi-Strauss, C., "Les discontinuités culturelles et le développement économique et social" [Cultural discontinuities and economic and social development], Inform. Sci. soc. 2:2 (July 1963), 7-15.

1412   Levy, Marion J., Jr., "Some Aspects of 'Individualism' and the Problem

[45]

of Modernization in China and Japan," Econ. Dev. soc. Change 10:3
(Apr. 1962), 225-240.

1413   ------ "Some Sources of the Vulnerability of the Structures of Rela-
          tively Non-Industrialized Societies to those of Highly Industrialized
          Societies," in GEN 4340 (1952), 113-125.

1414   Linton, R., "Cultural and Personality Factors Affecting Economic
          Growth," in GEN 4340 (1952), 73-88.

1415   Lipset, Seymour Martin, "Problèmes posés par les recherches compara-
          tives sur la mobilité et le développement" [Problems of comparative
          research on mobility and development], Riv. int. Sci. soc. 16:1 (1964),
          39-54.

1416   Locher, G. W., "Nieuwe perspectieven in de studie van de acculturatie"
          [New perspectives in the study of acculturation], Bijdr. Taal-Land-
          Volk. 119:1 (1963), 122-139.

1417   Mair, Lucy, An Introduction to Social Anthropology. London: Claren-
          don Press, 1965.   283 pp.

1418   Marroquin, A. D., "Factor económico y cambio social" [The economic
          factor and social change], Amér. indíg. 15:3 (1955), 215-226.

1419   Martín de Nicolás, J., "Análisis de la dinámica social de Puerto-
          Rico" [Analysis of the social dynamics of Puerto Rico], Razón y Fe
          168:786-787 (July-Aug. 1963), 79-94.

1420   Mead, Margaret, Continuities in Cultural Evolution. New Haven:
          Yale University Press, 1964.   471 pp.

1421   Mezerik, A. G., "Social Factors in Economic Development of Under-
          developed Countries," Int. Rev. Service 5:54 (June 1959), 1-24.

1422   Mookherjee, Debnath, "Cultural Lag or Adjustmental Delay: A Note,"
          Mod. Rev. 116 (Oct. 1964), 275-277.

1423   Moore, Wilbert E., "Changes in Occupational Structures," in GEN
          4381 (1966), 194-212.

1424   ------ "Measurement of Organizational and Institutional Implications
          of Changes in Productive Technology," in GEN 4303 (1958), 229-259.

1425   ------ Social Change. Englewood Cliffs, N.J.: Prentice-Hall, 1963.
          120 pp.

1426   ------ "Social Consequences of Technical Change from the Sociological
          Standpoint," Int. soc. Sci. Bull.(J.) 4:2 (Summer 1952), 280-288.

1427   ------ "The Social Framework of Economic Development," in GEN 4314
          (1961), 57-82.

1428   Morgan, James N., "The Achievement Motive and Economic Behavior,"
          Econ. Dev. soc. Change 12:3 (Apr. 1964), 243-267.

1429   Murdock, Peter George, Culture and Society. Pittsburgh: University
        of Pittsburgh Press, 1965. 359 pp.

1430   Naroll, R., "A Preliminary Index of Social Development," Am. Anthrop.
        58:4 (Aug. 1956), 687-715.

1431   Nash, Manning, "Some Social and Cultural Aspects of Economic Develop-
        ment," Econ. Dev. soc. Change 7:2 (Jan. 1959), 137-150.

1432   Nettl, J. P., and R. Robertson, "Industrialization, Development or
        Modernization," Br. J. Soc. 17:3 (Sept. 1966), 274-291.

1433   Nicolai, André, Comportement économique et structures sociales [Eco-
        nomic activity and social structures]. Paris: Presses Universi-
        taires de France, 1960. 322 pp.

1434   Niehoff, Arthur H., and J. Charnel Anderson, "The Process of Cross-
        Cultural Innovation: Positive, Negative, and Neutral Factors," Int.
        Dev. Rev. 6:2 (June 1964).

1435   Nimkoff, M. F., and R. Middleton, "Types of Family and Types of
        Economy," Am. J. Sociol. 66:3 (Nov. 1960), 215-225.

1436   Novack, D. E., and R. Lekachman (eds.), Development and Society:
        The Dynamics of Economic Change. New York: St. Martin's, 1964.
        433 pp.

1437   Orans, Martin, "Surplus," Hum. Organiz. 25:1 (Spring 1966), 24-32.
        [Polynesia; Melanesia]

1438   Parkinson, F., "Social Dynamics of Underdeveloped Countries," Yb.
        wld. Aff. 14 (1960), 207-235.

1439   Pastore, J., "As funções da educação numa sociedade em mudança" [The
        function of education in a changing society], Sociologia 26:1 (Mar.
        1964), 20-31. [Brazil]

1440   Piatier, A., Equilibre entre développement économique et développement
        social [Balance between economic and social development]. Paris:
        Editions Genin, 1962. 181 pp.

1441   Pimpley, P. N., "Integration and Conflict: A Sociological Analysis,"
        Sociol. Bull. 13:2 (Sept. 1964), 67-72.

1442   Polanyi, Karl, Conrad M. Arensberg, and Harry W. Pearson, Trade and
        Market in the Early Empires: Economies in History and Theory.
        Glencoe, Ill.: Free Press, 1957. 382 pp. [India; North Africa; Near
        East; Mexico; Dahomey]

1443   Pouwer, Jan, "A Social System in the Star Mountains: Toward a
        Reorientation of the Study of Social Systems," Am. Anthrop. 66:4,
        Pt. 2 (Aug. 1964), 133-161. [Indonesia]

1444   Pullman, D. R., "Social Change in Economic Development Theory," Can.
        Rev. Sociol. Anthrop. 3:1 (Feb. 1966), 9-22.

1445   Reader, D. H., "Models in Social Change, with Special Reference to
        Southern Africa," Afr. Stud. 23:1 (Mar. 1964), 11-34.

1446   Riggs, F. W., "The Bazaar-Canteen Model: Economic Aspects of the
        Prismatic Society," Philipp. sociol. Rev. 6:3-4 (July-Oct. 1958),
        6-59.

1447   Rogers, Everett M., "A Conceptual Variable Analysis of Technological
        Change," Rur. Sociol. 23:2 (June 1958), 136-145.

1448   ------ Diffusion of Innovations. New York: Free Press of Glencoe,
        1962. 367 pp.

1449   Rosenberg, Nathan, "Neglected Dimensions in the Analysis of Economic
        Change," in GEN 4402 (1964) 651-672.

1450   Sahlins, Marshall D., and Elman R. Service, Evolution and Culture.
        Ann Arbor: University of Michigan Press, 1960. 131 pp.

1451   Sapir, Edward, "Anthropology and Sociology," in GEN 4362 (1927), 97-
        113.

1452   Sjoberg, Gideon, "Rural-Urban Balance and Models of Economic Develop-
        ment," in GEN 4381 (1966), 235-261.

1453   Smelser, Neil J., "The Modernization of Social Relations," in GEN
        4397 (1966), 110-121.

1454   ------ The Sociology of Economic Life. Englewood Cliffs, N.J.:
        Prentice-Hall, 1963. 667 pp.

1455   ------ "Toward a Theory of Modernization," in GEN 4319 (1967), 29-48.

1456   Smelser, Neil J., and Seymour M. Lipset, "Social Structure, Mobility
        and Development," in GEN 4381 (1966), 1-50.

1457   Smith, David Horton and Alex Inkeles, "The OM Scale: A Comparative
        Measure of Individual Modernity," Sociometry 29:4 (Dec. 1966), 353-
        377.

1458   Smith, Michael G., "Pre-Industrial Stratification Systems," in GEN
        4381 (1966), 141-176.

1459   Smith, Robert J., "Comparative Studies in Anthropology of the Inter-
        relations between Social and Technological Change," Hum. Organiz.
        16:1 (Spring 1957), 30-36.

1460   Takasu, Y., "Kōshin Chiiki no Shakai Kōzō" [Social structure in
        underdeveloped areas], Econ. Comm. Asia Far E. Tsushin 182 (1959),
        1-20.

1461   Tax, Sol, "Acculturation," in GEN 4395 (1960), 192-201.

1462   Thompson, Laura, "Applied Anthropology, Community Welfare, and Human
        Conservation," in GEN 4395 (1960), 769-774.

1463   Thorsrud, E., "The Social Consequences of Technical Change from the
        Psychological Standpoint," Int. soc. Sci. Bull. (J.) 4:2 (Summer 1952),
        300-309.

1464   Van der Kroef, Justin M. A., Indonesian Social Evolution: Some
        Psychological Considerations. Amsterdam: van der Peet, 1958.
        189 pp.

1465   ------ "A Social Psychological Approach to Problem Areas in Indo-
        nesia," Am. behavl. Scient. 5:10 (June 1962), 19-22.

1466   Vellas, P., "Connaissance du milieu social et développement éco-
        nomique" [Understanding of the social structure and economic develop-
        ment], Rev. Inst. Sociol. 2 (1964), 239-250.

1467   Vilakazi, A. L., "Social Research and Problems of African Economic and
        Social Development," in GEN 4313 (1964), 184-189.

1468   Wertheim, Willem F., Proeve van een Sociaalwetenschappelijke Bena-
        dering der Achtergebleven Gebieden [Toward a sociological compre-
        hension of backward areas]. Amsterdam: Sociologisch-Historisch
        Seminarium voor Zuidoost Azie, University of Amsterdam, 1961. 34 pp.

1469   ------ "Sociologishe Aspecter der Achtergebleven Gebieden" [Socio-
        logical aspects of backward regions], Mens en Maatschappij 35:5
        (Sept.-Oct. 1960), 346-358.

1470   Wilensky, Harold L., "Measures and Effects of Mobility," in GEN
        4381 (1966), 98-140.

1471   Wilson, Godfrey, and Monica Hunter Wilson, The Analysis of Social
        Change. London: Cambridge University Press, 1945. 177 pp.
        [Southern Rhodesia]

1472   ------ The Study of African Society. The Rhodes-Livingstone Papers,
        No. 2. Lovedale, South Africa: The Lovedale Press, 1939. 20 pp.

1473   Wolf, Eric R., "Kinship, Friendship, and Patron-Client Relations in
        Complex Societies," in GEN 4305 (1966), 1-22.

1474   Wolfe, A. B., "Sociology and Economics," in GEN 4362 (1927), 299-310.

2.   General Descriptions of Social Change

2301   Adjari, A., "Influence des valeurs traditionnelles sur la mentalité
        économique dans les pays islamiques du Moyen Orient" [Influence of
        traditional values on economic thinking in the Islamic countries of
        the Middle East], Dév. Civilis. 10 (Apr.-June 1962), 55-79.

2302   Ahumada, J., "El desarrollo económico y los problemas del cambio social en América Latina" [Economic development and problems of social change in Latin America], Rev. brasil. Ciênc. Soc. 2:2 (July 1962), 53-101.

2303   Almond, Gabriel A., and Sidney Verba, The Civil Culture: Political Attitudes and Democracy in Five Nations. Princeton: Princeton University Press, 1963. 562 pp. [Mexico]

2304   Ames, Michael, "Ideological and Social Change in Ceylon," Hum. Organiz. 22:1 (Spring 1963), 45-53.

2305   Apter, D. E., The Gold Coast in Transition. Princeton: Princeton University Press, 1955. 355 pp. [Ghana]

2306   Arasteh, Josephine D., "Iranian Family Life in a Changing Society." Microfilm 6757 HN, Ph.D. dissertation, University of Chicago, 1960.

2307   Arens, R., "Religious Rituals and Their Implications for Economic Development," Philipp. sociol. Rev. :1-2 (June 1959), 34-45. [Philippines]

2308   Arensberg, Conrad M., and Arthur H. Niehoff, Introducing Social Change. Chicago: Aldine, 1964. 214 pp.

2309   "Aspects sociaux du développement économique" [Social aspects of economic development], Bull. écon. Afr. 2:2 (June 1962), 105-115.

2310   Baeck, Louis, "Le changement social en Afrique centrale" [Social change in Central Africa], Bull. Res. écon. soc. Univ. 25:8 (Dec. 1959), 729-768.

2311   ------ Economische Ontwikkeling en Sociale Structuur in Belgisch-Kongo [Economic development and social structure in the Belgian Congo]. Louvain: Catholic University of Louvain, 1959. 332 pp.

2312   Balandier, Georges, "Africanism Confronted with Problems of Political Anthropology and Political Sociology," in GEN 4313 (1964), 267-271.

2313   ------ Afrique ambiguë [Ambiguous Africa]. Paris: Plon, 1957. 291 pp.

2314   ------ "L'anthropologie et l'Afrique noire" [Anthropology and Black Africa], Synthèses 6:65 (Oct. 1951), 170-178.

2315   ------ "Les modifications dans les structures sociales" [Modifications in the social structure], Preuves, 88 Suppl. (June 1958).

2316   ------ "Sociologie dynamique et historique à partir de faits africains" [A dynamic and historical sociology with African facts as the point of departure], Cah. int. Sociol. 10:34 (Jan.-June 1963), 3-12.

2317   ------ Structures sociales traditionnelles et problèmes du développement [Traditional social structures and development problems]. Paris: Université de Paris, 1958. 37 mim. pp.

2318   Banton, M. P., and D. G. M. Dosser, "The Balance between Social and
        Economic Development in Africa South of the Sahara," Inform. ISSC 27
        (June 1961), 5-20.

2319   Barbosa da Silva, J. F., "Organização social de Juázeiro e tensões
        entre litoral e interior" [Social organization of Juázeiro and
        tensions between coast and interior], Sociologia 24:3 (Sept. 1962),
        181-194. [Brazil]

2320   Bastide, Roger, "The Development of Race Relations in Brazil," in
        GEN 4341 (1965), 9-29.

2321   Batten, T. R., Problems of African Development. 3rd ed. London:
        Oxford University Press, 1960. Pt. 1, 140 pp.; Pt. 2, 152 pp.

2322   Baumann, H., "Grundeinsichten der Ethnologie in die neuen afrikanis-
        chen Entwicklungen" [Principle insights of ethnology in new African
        developments], Z. Ethnol. 87:2 (1962), 250-263.

2323   Beaglehole, E., "Social and Political Changes in the Cook Islands,"
        Pacif. Aff. 21 (1948), 383-398. [Polynesia]

2324   Beck, D. F., "Changing Moslem Family of the Middle East," J. Marr.
        Fam. Living 19 (Nov. 1957), 340-347.

2325   Bellah, Robert N., "Values and Social Change in Modern Japan," Asian
        cult. Stud. 3 (1962), 13-56.

2326   Belshaw, Cyril S., Changing Melanesia: Social Economics of Culture
        Contact. Melbourne: Oxford University Press, 1954. 197 pp.

2327   Bendix, Reinhard, "A Case Study in Cultural and Educational Mobility:
        Japan and the Protestant Ethic," in GEN 4381 (1966), 262-279.

2328   Bennabi, M., "Sous-développement en civilisation" [Cultural under-
        development], Confluence 44 (Oct. 1964), 725-741. [Algeria]

2329   Berque, J., et al., La réforme agraire au Maghreb [Agrarian reform
        in the Maghreb]. Paris: F. Maspero, 1963. 160 pp. [North Africa]

2330   Beteille, André, "Family and Social Change in India and Other South
        Asian Countries," Econ. Wkly. 16:5-7 (Feb. 1964), 237-244.

2331   Biebuyck, Daniel, "Land Holding and Social Organization," in GEN
        4336 (1964), 99-113.

2332   Blair, A. P., "The Experience of Expatriate Industrial Enterprise,"
        in GEN 4341 (1965), 201-219.

2333   Blair, R. V. V., Africa: A Market Profile. New York: Praeger,
        1965. 260 pp.

2334   Borghuis, F., "Sociale Gevolgen van de Technologische Ontwikkeling:
        Een Terreinverkenning" [Social consequences of technical development:
        A field study], Mens en Maatschappij 33:3 (May-June 1958), 161-169.

2335   Braithwaite, L. E., "Race Relations and Industrialisation in the
        Caribbean," in GEN 4341 (1965), 30-45.

2336   Brausch, G. E. J. B., "Applied Anthropology in the Belgian Terri-
        tories in Africa: An Experience of Integration of the Tribal
        Institutions into the Pattern of the New Social Action in Central
        Africa," in GEN 4395 (1960), 755-763.

2337   Carreira, A., "Organização social e econômica dos provos da Guiné
        Portuguese" [The Social and economic organization of the people of
        Portuguese Guinea], Bol. cult. Guiné port. 16:64 (Oct. 1962), 641-
        736.

2338   Carstairs, G. M., This Island Now: The Surge of Social Change in
        the Twentieth Century. New York: Basic Books, 1963. 102 pp.

2339   Casanova, P. G., "Sociedad plural y desarrollo: El caso de México"
        [Plural society and development: The case of Mexico], Amér. lat.
        5:4 (Oct.-Dec. 1962), 31-49.

2340   Centro Latino-americano de Pesquisas em Ciências Sociais, Situação
        social da América Latina [Social situation of Latin America]. Rio
        de Janeiro: Centro Latino-americano de Pesquisas em Ciências
        Sociais, 1964. 467 pp.

2341   Centro per gli Studi sullo Sviluppo Economico, L'evoluzione del
        comportamento in un processo di sviluppo [The evolution of behavior
        in a process of development]. Milan: Giuffrè, 1964. 500 pp.

2342   Chen, Cheng-Siang, "The Changing Economy of T'aiwan," Pacif. View-
        point 6:2 (Sept. 1965), 179-190.

2343   Chen, Shao-Hsing, "Social Change in Taiwan," T'aiwan Chih-Hsueh
        1:1 (1956), 1-19. In Chinese.

2344   Christensen, J. B., "Problems of a Society in Transition," Unit.
        Asia 9:1 (Feb. 1957), 15-22.

2345   Clemens, R., "Changes in Social and Legal Systems in the Near and
        Middle East as a Result of Technological Development," Int. soc.
        Sci. Bull. (J.) 5:4 (Winter 1953), 766-785.

2346   Colson, E., "Family Change in Contemporary Africa," Ann. N.Y. Acad.
        Sci. 96:2 (20 Jan. 1962), 641-652.

2347   Costa Pinto, L. A., and W. Bazzanella, "Economic Development, Social
        Change and Population Problems in Brazil," Ann. Am. Acad. polit. soc.
        Sci. 316 (Mar. 1958), 121-126.

2348   Crane, R. I., "Strata Disruption and Social Change in South Asia,"
        Unit. Asia 6 (1954), 228-235.

2349   Curle, A., "Tradition, Development and Planning," Soc. Res. 8:2
        (Dec. 1960), 223-238. [Pakistan]

2350   Dalton, G., "Le développement des économies de subsistance et des économies paysannes en Afrique" [Development of subsistence and peasant economies in Africa], Riv. int. Sci. soc. 16:3 (1964), 409-422.

2351   D'Arboussier, G. E., "Le facteur humain: Frein et moteur du développement économique" [The human factor: The brake and motor of economic development], Rev. Chambre Comm. Marseille 51:757 (Aug. 1964), 478-488.

2352   Davin, L., "Phénomènes de polarisation: Seuils de croissance et expansion économique en Afrique Centrale" [Phenomena of polarization, thresholds of growth, and economic expansion in Central Africa], Cah. Inst. Sci. écon. 5:5 (Nov. 1962), 7-60.

2353   De Azevedo, A., "Educação em África" [Education in Africa], Estud. ultramarinos 3 (1962), 19-161. [Portuguese Guinea; Angola; Mozambique]

2354   DeLannoy, J. L., Los niveles de vida en América Latina [Living standards in Latin America]. Bogotá: Centro de Investigaciones Sociales de Fédération Européenne de Recherches Economiques et Sociales, 1963. 235 pp.

2355   Desanti, Dominique, Côte d'Ivoire [The Ivory Coast]. Lausanne: Editions Rencontre, 1962. 291 pp.

2356   De Sousa, A., "Economia e sociedade em África: Evolução actual" [Economy and society in Africa: Present evolution], Análise soc. 2:6 (Apr. 1964), 248-295.

2357   ------ "Estruturas socio-económicas e dialéctica de Culturas em Africa" [Socioeconomic structures and dialectics of cultures in Africa], Análise soc. 1:3 (July 1963), 423-458.

2358   De Vries, Egbert, and José M. Echavarria, Social Aspects of Economic Development in Latin America. Vol. I: Papers Submitted to the Expert Working Group on Social Aspects of Economic Development in Latin America, Mexico City, 12-21 December 1960. Paris: UNESCO, 1963. 401 pp.

2359   Dez, V., "Développement économique et tradition à Madagascar" [Economic development and tradition in Madagascar], Cah. Inst. Sci. econ. Series 5:4 (Sept. 1962), 79-108.

2360   D'Haucourt, Genevieve M., "De quelques difficultés dues aux différence de cultures rencontrées dans les missions d'assistance technique" [On some difficulties due to cultural differences encountered by technical assistance missions], in GEN 4395 (1960), 764-768.

2361   Doucy, A., "Sociologie coloniale et réformes de structure au Congo belge" [The sociology of colonial territories and structural reforms in the Belgian Congo], Rev. Univ. Bruxelles 2:3 (1957).

2362   Drogat, N., Les pays de la faim [Lands of hunger]. Paris: Flammarion, 1963. 221 pp.

2363   D'Souza, Victor S., "Social Grading of Occupation in India," <u>Sociol</u>.
        <u>Rev</u>. 10:2 (July 1962), 145-159.

2364   Dube, S. C., "Cultural Problems in the Economic Development of India,"
        in GEN 4308 (1965), 43-55.

2365   Eisenstadt, S. N., <u>The Absorption of Immigrants</u>. London: Routledge
        & Kegan Paul, 1954. 275 pp. [Israel]

2366   ------ "Social Transformation in Modernization," <u>Am. soc. Rev</u>. 30:5
        (Oct. 1965), 659-673. [Israel]

2367   Etzioni, Amitai, and Eva Etzioni (eds.), <u>Social Change: Sources</u>,
        <u>Patterns, and Consequences</u>. New York: Basic Books, 1964. 503 pp.

2368   Fallers, Lloyd A., "Social Stratification and Economic Processes," in
        GEN 4336 (1964), 113-133.

2369   Fals-Borda, Orlando, <u>La educación en Colombia: Bases para su inter</u>-
        <u>pretación sociológica</u> [Education in Colombia: Bases for its socio-
        logical interpretation]. Bogotá: Universidad Nacional de Colombia,
        Facultad de Sociología, 1962. 37 pp.

2370   ------ <u>La teoria y la realidad del cambio sociocultural en Colombia</u>
        [The theory and the reality of sociocultural change in Colombia].
        Bogotá: Universidad Nacional de Colombia, 1959. 44 pp.

2371   ------ <u>La trasformación de la America latina y sus implicaciones</u>
        <u>sociales y económicas</u> [The transformation of Latin America and its
        social and economic implications]. Bogotá: Universidad Nacional
        de Colombia, 1961. 21 pp.

2372   Fillol, Tomás Roberto, <u>Social Factors in Economic Development: The</u>
        <u>Argentine Case</u>. Cambridge, Mass.: M.I.T. Press, 1961. 118 pp.

2373   Firth, Raymond W., "Social Changes in the Western Pacific," <u>J. roy</u>.
        <u>Soc. Arts</u> 101:4909 (Nov. 1953), 803-819. [Micronesia]

2374   Fonsecca, M. B., "Family Disorganisation and Divorce in Indian
        Communities," <u>Sociol. Bull</u>. 12:2 (Sept. 1963), 14-33.

2375   Forde, Daryll, "The Conditions of Social Development in West Africa:
        Retrospect and Prospect," <u>Civilisations</u> 3:4 (Oct. 1953), 471-489.

2376   Franzoi, A., <u>Continente Nero</u> [Black continent]. Novara, Italy:
        Istituto Geografico De Agostini, 1961. 253 pp.

2377   Freeman, M., "The Growth of a Plural Society in Malaya," in GEN 4396
        (1966), 278-289.

2378   Friedlander, Stanley L., <u>Labor Migration and Economic Growth</u>. Cam-
        bridge, Mass.: M.I.T. Press, 1965. 181 pp.

2379   Froehlich, J.-C., <u>Les Musulmans d'Afrique noire</u> [The Muslims of
        Black Africa]. Paris: Editions de l'Orante, 1962. 408 pp.

2380   ------, P. Alexandre, and R. Cornevin, Les populations du Nord-Togo
        [The populations of North Togo]. Paris: Presses Universitaires de
        France, 1963. 200 pp. [West Africa]

2381   Furnivall, J. S., Netherlands India: A Study of Plural Economics.
        London: Cambridge University Press, 1939. 502 pp. [Indonesia]

2382   García-Figueras, T., "The Participation of the Native in the Evolution
        of His Country," Civilisations 6:2 (Apr.-June 1956), 193-206.
        [Morocco]

2383   Geertz, Clifford, The Development of the Javanese Economy: A Socio-
        Cultural Approach. Cambridge, Mass.: Center for International
        Studies, Massachusetts Institute of Technology, 1956. 130 pp.
        [Indonesia]

2384   ------ "Modernization in a Muslim Society: The Indonesian Case," in
        GEN 4308 (1965), 93-108.

2385   ------ (ed.), Old Societies and New States: The Quest for Modernity
        in Asia and Africa. New York: Free Press of Glencoe, 1963. 310 pp.

2386   Gendarme, R., "La résistance des facteurs socio-culturels au développe-
        ment économique: L'example de l'Islam en Algérie" [The resistance of
        sociocultural factors to economic development: The example of Islam in
        Algeria], Rev. Econ. 10:2 (Mar. 1959), 237-267.

2387   Germani, Gino, Política y sociedad en una época de transición de la
        sociedad tradicional a la sociedad de masas. [Politics and society
        in a period of transition from a traditional society to a mass
        society]. Buenos Aires: Paidos, 1962. 266 pp.

2388   ------ "Social and Political Consequences of Mobility," in GEN 4381
        (1966), 364-394.

2389   Glade, William, "Social Backwardness, Social Reform, and Productivity
        in Latin America," Inter-Am. econ. Aff. 15:3 (Winter 1961), 3-32.

2390   Gray, R. F., "Political Parties in New African Nations: An Anthro-
        pological View," Comp. Stud. Soc. Hist. 5:4 (July 1963), 449-461.

2391   Green, T. L., "Technology and Education in South-East Asia," Oversea
        Educ. 26:2 (July 1954), 70-74.

2392   Halperin, M., "La América Latina en transición" [Latin America in
        transition], Ciênc. polít. soc. 1:2 (Oct.-Dec. 1955), 77-89.

2393   Halpern, Joel M., Economy and Society of Laos: A Brief Survey. New
        Haven: Southeast Asia Studies, Yale University, 1964. 180 pp.

2394   ------ The Rural and Urban Economies. Los Angeles: Department of
        Anthropology, University of California, n.d. 178 mim. pp. [Lacs]

2395   Harwitz, Mitchell, "Subsaharan Africa as a Growing Economic System,"
        in GEN 4336 (1964), 15-53.

2396   Herskovits, Melville J., "Africa and the Problems of Economic Growth," in GEN 4336 (1964), 3-15.

2397   ------ Economic Anthropology: A Study in Comparative Economy. New York: Knopf, 1952. 547 pp.

2398   ------ The Human Factor in Changing Africa. New York: Knopf, 1962. 500 pp.

2399   Hirsch, Anne-Rose, "The Development and Organization of Commerce in the Ivory Coast and Senegal," Pacif. Viewpoint 6:2 (Sept. 1965), 167-178.

2400   Hsu, Francis L. K., Clan, Caste, and Club. Princeton: Van Nostrand, 1963. 335 pp. [Tai'wan]

2401   Hunt, Chester L., "Changing Social Patterns in the Philippines," Silliman J. 9 (1962), 32-43.

2402   ------ Social Aspects of Economic Development. New York: McGraw-Hill, 1966. 255 pp.

2403   Hunter, George, The New Societies of Tropical Africa. London: Oxford University Press, 1962. 376 pp.

2404   Husain, I. Z., "Social Forces and Economic Change," All India Congr. Comm. econ. Rev. 15 (9 Jan. 1964), 157-161.

2405   Izumi, S. (ed.), Black Africa no Shakai Keizai Henyo [Social and economic changes in Black Africa]. Tokyo: Institute of Asian Economic Affairs, 1964. 215 pp.

2406   Jantzen, G., "Emanzipation und Einordnung Afrikanischer Bevölkerungen Südlich der Sahara" [Emancipation and integration of African populations south of the Sahara], Stud. gen. 15:8 (1962), 529-536.

2407   Johnson, G., "Health Conditions in Rural and Urban Areas of Developing Countries," Popul. Stud. 17:3 (Mar. 1964), 293-310.

2408   Kagaya, H., "Black Africa shakai no kindaika to Islam" [Modernization of Black African societies and Islam], Afrika Kenkyū 1:1 (1964), 17-31.

2409   Kapadia, K. M., "Changing Patterns of Hindu Marriage and Family," Sociol. Bull. 3:1 (Mar. 1954), 61-87; 3:2 (Sept. 1954), 131-157; 4:2 (Sept. 1955), 161-192. [India]

2410   ------ Marriage and Family in India. 2nd ed. London: Oxford University Press, 1958. 286 pp.

2411   ------ "Perspective Necessary for the Study of Social Change in India," Sociol. Bull. 6:1 (Mar. 1957), 43-60.

2412   Kaplan, D., "City and Countryside in Mexican History," Amér. indíg. 24:1 (1st Quarter 1964), 59-69.

2413   Karim, A. K. N., <u>Changing Society in India and Pakistan: A Study in
        Social Change and Social Stratification</u>. Dacca: Oxford University
        Press, 1956. 173 pp.

2414   Katz, E., "Social Itinerary of Technical Change: Two Studies on the
        Diffusion of Innovation," <u>Hum. Organiz</u>. 20:2 (Summer 1961), 70-82.

2415   Katzin, Margaret, "The Role of the Small Entrepreneur," in GEN 4336
        (1964), 179-199.

2416   Khatri, A. A., "Social Change in the Caste Hindu Family and Its
        Possible Impact on Personality and Mental Health," <u>Sociol. Bull</u>. 11:2
        (Oct. 1961), 146-165. [India]

2417   Kubik, G., "Traditions- und Akkulturationselemente in der materiellen
        Kultur Ostafrikas" [Traditional and acculturational elements in the
        material culture of East Africa], <u>Mitt. anthrop. Ges. Wien</u> 92 (1962),
        317-321.

2418   Lambert, Richard D., and Bert F. Hoselitz, "Western Societies," in
        GEN 4350 (1963), 9-43.

2419   Lerner, Daniel, "Changing Social Structure and Economic Development:
        Reflections on a Decade of International Experience," in GEN 4322
        (1964), 1-16.

2420   ------ <u>The Passing of Traditional Society: Modernizing the Middle
        East</u>. Glencoe, Ill.: Free Press, 1958. 466 pp.

2421   Levine, Donald N., <u>Wax and Gold: Tradition and Innovation in Ethio-
        pian Culture</u>. Chicago: University of Chicago Press, 1965. 315 pp.

2422   Levy, Marion J., Jr., "El análisis historico comparativo como base de
        los descubrimientos sociológicos: China, Japan y la modernización"
        [Comparative historical analysis as the basis for sociological discov-
        eries: China, Japan, and modernization], <u>Rev. méx. Sociol</u>. 24 (1962),
        471-495.

2423   ------ <u>Modernization and the Structure of Societies: A Setting for
        International Affairs</u>. 2 vols. Princeton: Princeton University
        Press, 1966. 855 pp.

2424   Lewis, W. Arthur, "Some Economic and Social Problems of Transition to
        an Industrial Economy," in GEN 4338 (1957), 89-96.

2425   Little, Kenneth L., "The Study of 'Social Change' in British West
        Africa," <u>Africa</u> 23:4 (Oct. 1953), 274-284.

2426   McWilliam, M. D., "Economic Viability and the Race Factor in Kenya,"
        <u>Econ. Dev. cult. Change</u> 12:1 (Oct. 1963), 55-69.

2427   Madigan, F. C., "Some Filipino Population Characteristics and Their
        Relation to Economic Development," <u>Philipp. Sociol. Rev</u>. 7:1-2 (Jan.-
        Apr. 1959), 16-26.

2428   Makere College, <u>Seminar on Social Problems of East Africa, Feb.-Apr.</u>

1956. Religion and Social Change in Modern East Africa. Kampala, Uganda: Makere College, 1956. 100 pp.

2429   Mamoria, C. B., Social Problems and Social Disorganization in India. Allahabad, India: Kitab Mahal, 1960. 432 pp.

2430   Manglapus, Raul S., "Philippine Culture and Modernization," in GEN 4308 (1965), 30-42.

2431   Manis, J. G., "Philippine Culture in Transition," Silliman J. 7:2 (Apr.-June 1960), 105-133.

2432   Manndorff, Hans, "Probleme des Sozialen Wandels in Indien" [The problem of social change in India], Z. Ethnol. 87 (1962), 209-216.

2433   Maquet, J. J., "Schwarz-Afrika im Zeitalter der Industrialisierung. Sechs grosse Kulturkreise; Behauptung der Tradition" [Black Africa in the age of industrialization: Six great culture areas; The persistence of tradition], Neues Afr. 5:5 (May 1963), 180-185.

2434   Mathur, A. S., and B. L. Gupta, "Social Welfare in Uttar Pradesh," Agra Univ. J. Res. 12 (Jan. 1964), 107-121. [India]

2435   Matiba, J. I., "Les valeurs permanentes de la civilisation africaine" [The permanent values of African civilization], Dév. Civilis. 13 (Mar. 1963), 92-103.

2436   Matos-Mar, J., "Consideraciones sobre la situación social del Perú" [Reflections on the social situation in Peru], Amér. lat. 7:1 (Jan.-Mar. 1964), 57-70.

2437   Mehta, Aban B., The Domestic Servant Class. Bombay: Popular Book Depot, 1960. 324 pp. [India]

2438   Molnos, Angela, Die sozialwissenschaftliche Erforschung Ostafrikas 1954-1963: Kenya, Tanganyika-Sansibar, Uganda [The sociological study of East Africa, 1954-1963: Kenya, Tanganyika-Zanzibar, Uganda]. Berlin: Springer-Verlag, 1965. 304 pp.

2439   Moore, Wilbert E., "Changes in Occupational Structures," in GEN 4381 (1966), 194-212.

2440   Moreira, J. R., Educação e desenvolvimento no Brasil [Education and development in Brazil]. Rio de Janeiro: Centro Latino-americano de Pesquisas em Ciências Sociais, 1960. 298 pp.

2441   Moribura, M., "India no Kēzai Hatten ni okeru Chiiki to Caste no Yōin" [Regional and caste factors in India's development], Econ. Comm. Asia Far E. Tsūshin 258 (1963), 49-63.

2442   Mukerjee, Radhakamal, "Ways of Dwelling in the Communities of India," in GEN 4390 (1961), 390-401.

2443   Mukherjee, R., "Indian Tradition and Social Change," Patna Univ. J. 20 (Jan. 1965), 56-80.

2444   ------ The Problem of Uganda: A Study in Acculturation. Berlin:
        Akademie Verlag, 1956. 281 pp.

2445   ------ "Sociologists and Social Change in India Today," Sociol. Bull.
        11:1 (Oct. 1962), 4-13.

2446   Mya Maung, "Cultural Values and Economic Changes in Burma," Asian
        Surv. 4:3 (Mar. 1964), 757-764.

2447   Naraghi, E., "Conséquences sociales de développement économique et
        technique en Iran" [Social consequences of economic and technological
        development in Iran], Inform. ISSC 20 (Apr. 1959), 1-13.

2448   Nash, Manning, "The Multiple Society in Economic Development: Mexico
        and Guatemala," Am. Anthrop. 59:5 (Oct. 1957), 825-833.

2449   ------ "Social Prerequisites to Economic Growth in Latin America and
        Southeast Asia," Econ. Dev. cult. Change 12:3 (Apr. 1964), 225-242.

2450   ------, and R. Chin, "Psycho-Cultural Factors in Asian Economic
        Growth," J. sociol. Issues 19:1 (Jan. 1963), 1-87.

2451   Nelson, Lowry, Charles E. Ramsey, and Coolie Verner, Community Struc-
        ture and Change. New York: Macmillan, 1960. 455 pp.

2452   Norbeck, Edward, "Economic Change and Japanese Social Organization,"
        in GEN 4321 (1960), 337-353.

2453   Novak, D. E., and R. Lekachman (eds.), Development and Society: The
        Dynamics of Economic Change. New York: St. Martin's, 1964. 433 pp.

2454   Otani, Y., "Africa ni okeru Shakai Hendo to nationalism" [Social
        change and nationalism in Africa], Tottori Kenkyûkohoku 14 (1964),
        95-110.

2455   Palmier, Leslie H., Social Status and Power in Java. London: Athlone,
        1960. 171 pp.

2456   Panchanadikar, K. C., "Determinants of Social Structure and Social
        Change in India," Sociol. Bull. 11:1 (Oct. 1962), 14-35.

2457   Parker, F., African Development and Education in Southern Rhodesia.
        Columbus: Ohio State University Press, 1960. 165 pp.

2458   Passin, H., and K. A. B. Jones-Quartey, Africa: The Dynamics of
        Change. Ibadan, Nigeria: University Press, 1963. 262 pp.

2459   Patai, Raphael, Golden River to Golden Road: Society, Culture and
        Change in the Middle East. Philadelphia: University of Pennsylvania
        Press, 1962. 422 pp.

2460   Radcliffe-Brown, A. R., and Daryll Forde (eds.), African Systems of
        Kinship and Marriage. London: Oxford University Press, 1950. 400 pp.

2461   Rangel, I., "A dinámica da dualidade brasileira" [The dynamics of
        Brazilian duality], Rev. bras. Ciênc. soc. 2:2 (July 1962), 215-235.

2462   Rao, M. S. A., Social Change in Malabar. Bombay: Popular Book Depot,
       1958.   228 pp.

2463   ------ "Social Stratification and Social Change in South East Asia,"
       Sociol. Bull. 13:1 (Mar. 1964), 22-32.

2464   Reynolds, B., The African: His Position in a Changing Society.
       Livingstone, Zambia: Rhodes-Livingstone Museum, 1963.   46 pp.

2465   Romano, E. M., "Economia humanística.   Caso de Moçambique" [Human
       economy: The case of Mozambique], Bol. Soc. Estud. Moçambique 32:134
       (Jan.-Mar. 1963), 5-30.

2466   Rondot, P., "Les Musulmans et l'Islam devant la technique" [The Mus-
       lims and Islam faced with technology], Rev. Déf. natn. 16 (June 1960),
       1011-1027.

2467   ------ "Les Musulmans devant la technique" [The Muslims faced with
       technology], Cah. Inst. Sci. écon. 5:2 (Oct. 1960), 37-63.

2468   Rosen, B. C., "Socialization and Achievement Motivation in Brazil,"
       Am. sociol. Rev. 27:5 (Oct. 1962), 612-624.

2469   Rowe, W. L. (ed.), Contours of Culture Change in South Asia.   New
       York: Society for Applied Anthropology, 1963.   104 pp.

2470   Rubin, V. (ed.), "Social and Cultural Pluralism in the Caribbean,"
       Ann. N.Y. Acad. Sci. 83:5 (1960), 761-916.

2471   Sahiar, G. H., "Social Change with Particular Reference to the Parsi
       Community," J. Univ. Bombay 24:48 (Jan. 1956), 47-49.   [Indian State
       of Maharashta]

2472   Sarachandra, Ediriweera R., "Traditional Values and the Modernization
       of a Buddhist Society: The Case of Ceylon," in GEN 4308 (1965), 109-
       123.

2473   Schapera, Isaac, "Economic Changes in South African Native Life,"
       Africa 1 (1928), 170-188.

2474   Service, Elman R., and Helen S. Service, Tobatí: Paraguayan Town.
       Chicago: University of Chicago Press, 1954.   337 pp.

2475   Singh, Amar Kumar, "Hindu Culture and Economic Development in India,"
       Conspectus 1 (1967), 9-32.

2476   Singh, Yogendra, "Processes and Problems of Social Change in India,"
       Am. polit. Sci. Rev. 4:1 (Apr. 1965), 1-11.

2477   Sjoberg, Gideon, "Rural-Urban Balance and Models of Economic Develop-
       ment," in GEN 4381 (1966), 235-261.

2478   Skalnikova, O., "Ethnographical Research into the Present Changes in
       the Mode of Life of Urban Population in Africa," in GEN 4313 (1964),
       286-297.

2479   Skinner, Elliott P., "West African Economic Systems," in GEN 4336
        (1964), 77-99.

2480   Smith, Thomas Lynn, Brazil: People and Institutions. Baton Rouge:
        Louisiana State University Press, 1954. 704 pp.

2481   ------ "Values Held by People in Latin America Which Affect Technical
        Cooperation," Rur. Sociol. 21:1 (Mar. 1956), 68-75.

2482   Soedjatmoko, Economic Development as a Cultural Problem. Ithaca,
        N.Y.: Cornell University Press, 1958. 23 pp. [Indonesia]

2483   Srinivas, M. N., Social Change in Modern India. Berkeley: University
        of California Press, 1966. 194 pp.

2484   Stewart, Charles, "Economic Change in a Plural Society: Morocco since
        1912." Ph.D. dissertation, University of California at Berkeley,
        1956. 333 mim. pp.

2485   Stolper, Wolfgang, "Social Factors in Economic Planning, with Special
        Reference to Nigeria," E. Afr. econ. Rev. 2:1 (June 1964), 1-17.

2486   Thornburg, Max Weston, People and Policy in the Middle East: A Study
        of Social and Political Change as a Basis for United States Policy.
        New York: Norton, 1964. 247 pp.

2487   Tumin, M. M., and A. S. Feldman, Social Class and Social Change in
        Puerto Rico. Princeton: Princeton University Press, 1961. 549 pp.

2488   UNESCO, ECLA, and OAS, "Relatório do grupo de trabalho sobre los
        aspectos sociais do desenvolvimento econômico na América Latina"
        [Report of the working group on social aspects of economic develop-
        ment in Latin America], Rev. bras. Ciênc. soc. 2:1 (Mar. 1962), 251-
        273.

2489   Van der Kroef, Justin M. A., "Economic Development in Indonesia: Some
        Social and Cultural Impediments," Econ. Dev. cult. Change 4:2 (Jan.
        1956), 116-133.

2490   ------ "Religious Organization and Economic Process in Indonesia,"
        Sthwest. soc. Sci. Quart. 39:3 (Dec. 1958), 187-202, bibl.

2491   Vellard, J. A., Civilisations des Andes: Evolution des populations
        du haut-plateau bolivien [Civilization of the Andes: Evolution of
        the peoples of the Bolivian plateau]. Paris: Gallimard, 1963.
        272 pp.

2492   Vidyarthi, Lalita P. (ed.), Aspects of Religion in Indian Society.
        Ranchi, India: Council of Social and Cultural Research, 1961. 358
        pp. Issued as J. Soc. Res. 4:1-2.

2493   Von Bissing, W. M., Ostasiatische Studien zu Wortschaft und Gesell-
        schaft in Thailand, Hong-Kong, und Japan [East Asian studies on economy
        and society in Thailand, Hong Kong, and Japan]. Berlin: Dunker &
        Humblot, 1962. 226 pp.

2494   Wagley, Charles, <u>An Introduction to Brazil</u>. New York: Columbia
        University Press, 1963. 322 pp.

2495   Warriner, Doreen, <u>Contrasts in Emerging Societies.</u> Bloomington:
        Indiana University Press, 1965. 402 pp.

2496   Wertheim, Willem F., <u>Indonesian Society in Transition</u>. New York:
        Institute of Pacific Relations, 1956. 36 pp.

2497   ------ "Die Kulturelle Erneuerung in der Indonesischen Gesellschaft"
        [Cultural renewal in Indonesian society], in GEN 4334 (1962), 473-
        489.

2498   Whetten, N. L., <u>Guatemala: The Land and the People</u>. New Haven:
        Yale University Press, 1961. 399 pp.

2499   Willner, Ann R., "Social Change in Javanese Town-Village Life," <u>Econ.</u>
        <u>Dev. cult. Change</u> 6:3 (Apr. 1958), 229-242.

2500   Wolf, Eric R., <u>Sons of the Shaking Earth</u>. Chicago: University of
        Chicago Press, 1959. 302 pp. [Guatemala]

2501   Yepes del Pozo, Juan, "Sociología económica: La educación y la
        economía" [Economic sociology: Education and the economy], <u>Rev.</u>
        <u>Folkl.</u> 42:4 (Dec. 1955), 95-118.

3. General Bibliographies

3301   Alexander-Frutschi, M. C. (ed.), <u>Human Resources and Economic Growth</u>:
        <u>An International Annotated Bibliography on the Role of Education and</u>
        <u>Training in Economic and Social Development</u>. Menlo Park, Calif.:
        Stanford Research Institute, International Development Center, 1963.
        398 pp.

3302   Balandier, Georges, "Conséquences sociales du progrès techniques dans
        les pays sous-développés" [Social consequences of technical progress
        in the underdeveloped countries], <u>Curr. Sociol</u>. 3:1 (1954), 1-75,
        bibl.

3303   Banks, J. A., "Social Implications of Technological Change," in GEN
        4302 (1962), 61-106, bibl.

3304   Brembeck, Cole S., and Edward W. Weidner, <u>Education and Development</u>
        <u>in India and Pakistan: A Select and Annotated Bibliography.</u> East
        Lansing, Mich.: Michigan State University Press, 1962. 221 pp.

3305   ------, and J. P. Keith, <u>Education in Emerging Africa: A Select and</u>
        <u>Annotated Bibliography</u>. East Lansing, Mich.: Michigan State Univer-
        sity Press, 1962. 153 pp.

3306   Coult, L. H., Annotated Research Bibliography of Studies in Arabic,
        English and French of the Fellah of the Egyptian Nile, 1798-1955.
        Miami, Fla.: University of Miami Press, 1958. 144 pp.

3307   Embree, John F., and Lillian Ota Dotson, Bibliography of the Peoples
        and Cultures of Mainland Southeast Asia. New Haven: Yale University
        Press, 1950. 821 pp.

3308   Friedman, G., "The Social Consequences of Technical Progress," Int.
        soc. Sci. Bull. (J) 4:2 (1952), 243-260.

3309   Halpern, Joel M., An Annotated Bibliography on the Peoples of Laos and
        Northern Thailand. Los Angeles: University of California, Department
        of Anthropology, 1961. 5 mim. pp.

3310   Hart, Donn V., and Quintin A. Eala, An Annotated Guide to Current
        Philippine Periodicals. New Haven: Yale University, Southeast Asia
        Studies, Bibliography Series, 1957. 116 pp.

3311   Hunter, George, The New Societies of Tropical Africa. London: Oxford
        University Press, 1962. 376 pp.

3312   Index to Current Periodicals received in the Library of the Royal
        Anthropological Institute. London: Royal Anthropological Institute,
        quarterly.

3313   Irikura, James K., Southeast Asia: Selected, Annotated Bibliography
        of Japanese Publications. New Haven, Conn.: Human Resources Area
        File, 1956. 537 pp.

3314   Jaspan, M. A., Social Stratification and Social Mobility in Indonesia:
        A Trend Report and Annotated Bibliography. 2nd rev. ed. Djakarta,
        Indonesia: Gunung Agung, 1961. 95 pp.

3315   Neff, K. L., Selected Bibliography on Education in Southeast Asia.
        Washington, D.C.: Government Printing Office, 1963, 16 pp.

3316   Ogburn, W. F., "Social Implications of Technical Advance: A Trend
        Report and Bibliography" [Conséquences sociales du progrès technique.
        Tendances actuelles et bibliographie], Curr. Sociol. 1:4 (1953), 187-
        266.

3317   Piatier, A., Equilibre entre développement économique et développement
        social [Balance between economic and social development]. Paris:
        Editions Genin, 1962. 181 pp., bibl.

3318   ReQua, Eloise, and Jane Statham, The Developing Nations: A Guide to
        Information Sources Concerning Their Economic, Political, Technical,
        and Social Problems. Detroit, Mich.: Gale Research Co., Book Tower,
        1965. 339 pp.

3319   Rogers, Everett M., Bibliography of Research on the Diffusion of
        Innovations. East Lansing: Michigan State University, Department of
        Communication, 1964. 65 mim. pp.

3320   Schapera, Isaac (ed.), Select Bibliography of South African Native

Life and Problems. London: Oxford University Press, 1941. 249 pp.

3321   Shannon, L. W., "Social Factors in Economic Growth: A Trend Report and
       Bibliography" [Les facteurs sociaux du développement économique.
       Tendances de la recherche et bibliographie], Curr. Sociol. 6:3 (1957),
       171-238.

3322   UNESCO, Research Centre on Social and Economic Development in South
       Asia, South Asia Social Science Abstracts, 1952. Calcutta: Research
       Centre on Social and Economic Development in Southern Asia, 1954.
       86 mim. pp. 1953 (1955), 136 mim. pp.; 1954 (1956), 123 mim. pp.;
       1955 (1956), 169 mim. pp.; 1956 (1958), 157 mim. pp.; 1957 (1958),
       147 mim. pp.; 1958 (1959), 150 mim. pp.

3323   ------ Research Centre on Social and Economic Development in South
       Asia, Southern Asia Social Science Bibliography, No. 1, 1952.
       Calcutta: Research Centre on Social and Economic Development in
       Southern Asia, 1954. 176 mim. pp. No. 2, 1953 (1955), 122 mim. pp.;
       No. 3, 1954 (1956), 85 mim. pp.; No. 4, 1955 (1957), 101 mim. pp.;
       No. 5, 1956 (1958), 135 mim. pp.; No. 6, 1957 (1958), 159 mim. pp.;
       No. 7, 1958 (1959), 141 mim. pp.; No. 8 (with annotations and
       abstracts), 1959 (1960), 230 mim. pp.; No. 9 (with annotations and
       abstracts), 1960 (1963), 190 mim. pp.

3324   Van der Kroef, Justin M. A., "Religious Organization and Economic
       Process in Indonesia," Sthwest. soc. Sci. Quart. 39:3 (Dec. 1958),
       187-202, bibl.

                          4.   Repository Articles
                (in books cited elsewhere in the bibliography)

4301   Aspectos sociais do crescimento econômico [Social aspects of economic
       development]. Salvador, Brazil: University of Bahia, 1959. 117 pp.
       See also Aspectos sociales del desarrollo económico. Santiago, Chile,
       1959. 129 pp. Translations in Spanish and Portuguese of GEN 1380.

4302   Balandier, Georges, Economic Development and Its Social Implications:
       Technological Change and Industrialization. Paris: Presses Univer-
       sitaires de France, 1962. 209 pp. See GEN 1307, 1313, 1407; IND
       1307, 1323, 2403, 5314, 5323, 5346; URB 3317; RUR 1387.

4303   ------ (ed.), Social, Economic and Technological Change: A Theoreti-
       cal Approach. Paris: Presses Universitaires de France, 1958. 355 pp.
       See GEN 1357, 1399, 1424.

4304   ------ (ed.), Le "Tiers-Monde': Sous-développement et développement
       [The nonindustrialized world: Underdevelopment and development].
       Paris: Presses Universitaires de France, 1956. 393 pp. See GEN
       1305.

4305   Banton, Michael P. (ed.), The Social Anthropology of Complex
        Societies. New York: Praeger, 1966. 156 pp. See GEN 1473;
        RUR 1305; URB 1327.

4306   Bascom, William R., and Melville J. Herskovitz (eds.), Continuity
        and Change in African Cultures. Chicago: University of Chicago
        Press, 1959. 309 pp. See RUR 4001, 9017, 9021.

4307   Becher, Hans (ed.), Beiträge zur Völkerkunde Südamerikas [Contribu-
        tion to the knowledge of the South American peoples]. Hanover, W.
        Germany: Münstermann, 1964. 374 pp. See RUR 2613, 8520.

4308   Bellah, Robert Neely (ed.), Religion and Progress in Modern Asia.
        New York: Free Press, 1965. 246 pp. See GEN 2364, 2384, 2430,
        2472.

4309   Ben-David, Joseph (ed.), Agricultural Planning and Village Community
        in Israel. Paris: UNESCO, 1964. 159 pp. See RUR 1390, 2607.

4310   Biebuyck, Daniel (ed.), African Agrarian Systems: Studies Presented
        and Discussed at the 2nd International African Seminar, Lovanium
        University, Leopoldville, January, 1960. London: Oxford University
        Press, 1963. 407 pp. See RUR 2044, 3005, 4017, 8333, 9019.

4311   Birket-Smith, Kai, Primitive Man and His Ways: Patterns of Life in
        Some Native Societies. Cleveland, Ohio: World Publishing Co.,
        1960. 247 pp. (Tr. of Fjaerne Folk: Kar og Kultur i Seks Primitive
        Semfand [Copenhagen: Jespersen of Pio, 1957], 215 pp.) See RUR
        1308.

4312   Bohannan, Paul J., and George Dalton, Markets in Africa. Evanston,
        Ill.: Northwestern University Press, 1962. 762 pp. See URB 2024,
        2028, 2032; RUR 6002, 6009, 6013, 6014, 6015, 6020, 6022, 6023,
        6028, 6030, 6033, 6035, 6037, 6038, 6043, 6045, 6052, 6054, 6058,
        6395, 6403, 6416, 6450, 6488.

4313   Bown, Lalage, and Michael Crowder (eds.), The Proceedings of the
        First International Congress of Africanists: Accra, 11th-18th Decem-
        ber 1962. Evanston, Ill.: Northwestern University Press, 1964. 368
        pp. See GEN 1467, 2312, 2478.

4314   Braibanti, R. J. D., and J. J. Spengler (eds.), Tradition, Values and
        Socio-Economic Development. Durham, N.C.: Duke University Press,
        1961. 305 pp. See GEN 1379, 1394, 1427.

4315   Brokensha, David (ed.), Ecology and Economic Development in Tropical
        Africa. Berkeley, Calif.: Institute of International Affairs, Uni-
        versity of California, 1965. 268 pp. See GEN 1407.

4316   Buttrick, John A., and Harold Francis Williamson, Economic Develop-
        ment: Principles and Patterns. New York: Prentice-Hall, 1954.
        576 pp. See GEN 1397.

4317   Colson, Elizabeth, and Max Gluckman (eds.), Seven Tribes of British
        Central Africa. Manchester, England: Manchester University Press,
        1959. 409 pp. See URB 2007.

4318   Congreso Nacional de Sociología VI, Estudios sociologicos. [Socio-
          logical studies], Vol. 6. Mexico City: Congreso Nacional de Sociol-
          ogía, 1955. See URB 4375.

4319   Dalton, George (ed.), Tribal and Peasant Economies: Readings in
          Economic Anthropology. Garden City, N.Y.: Natural History Press,
          1967. 584 pp. See GEN 1455; URB 2349; RUR 1329, 1370, 1391, 5343,
          6306, 6323, 6334, 6335, 6336, 6344, 6410, 6411, 6430, 6456, 6475,
          6490, 7382.

4320   Desai, A. R., Rural Sociology in India: The Indian Society of Agri-
          cultural Economics. 3rd rev. ed. Bombay: Indian Society of Agri-
          cultural Economics, 1961. 730 pp. See RUR 5011.

4321   Dole, G. E., and R. L. Carneiro (eds.), Essays in the Science of
          Culture. In honor of Leslie A. White, in celebration of his sixtieth
          birthday and his thirtieth year of teaching at the University of
          Michigan. New York: Crowell, 1960. 509 pp. See GEN 2452.

4322   Economic and Social Studies Conference Board, Social Aspects of
          Economic Development: A Report of the International Conference on
          Social Aspects of Economic Development held at Istanbul, August 4-24,
          1963, sponsored by the Economic and Social Studies Conference Board.
          Istanbul: Economic and Social Studies Conference Board, 1964. 391
          pp. See GEN 2419; IND 5335; URB 4336.

4323   L'évolution sociale au Maroc [Social evolution in Morocco]. Paris:
          Editions Peyronnet, 1950. 230 pp. See IND 2002; URB 4402.

4324   Firth, Raymond W., and B. S. Yamey, Capital, Saving and Credit in
          Peasant Societies: Studies from Asia, Oceania, the Caribbean, and
          Middle America. Chicago: Aldine, 1964. 393 pp. See RUR 6003,
          6016, 6039, 6041, 6308, 6310, 6312, 6315, 6341, 6354, 6374, 6386,
          6467, 6468, 6476, 6489.

4325   Forde, Daryll (ed.), Social Implications of Industrialization and
          Urbanization in Africa South of the Sahara. Paris: UNESCO, 1956.
          743 pp. See IND 2003, 2033, 2390, 2451, 6331; URB 1303, 1323, 1325,
          1326, 2009, 2039, 2393, 2421, 3013, 3309, 3341, 4304, 4338, 5349,
          5353, 5363; RUR 2467, 3313, 5323.

4326   Garfield, Viola E. (ed.), Symposium on Community Studies in Anthro-
          pology: Proceedings of the 1963 Annual Spring Meeting of the
          American Ethnological Society. Seattle: University of Washington,
          1964. 79 pp. See RUR 1343, 2003, 6010.

4327   ------ Symposium: Patterns of Land Utilization and Other Papers:
          Proceedings of the 1961 Annual Spring Meeting of the American Ethno-
          logical Society. Seattle: University of Washington Press, 1961.
          119 pp. See RUR 1328, 6011, 6040.

4328   General Missionary Conference of South Africa, Report of the Pro-
          ceedings of the Fifth General Missionary Conference of South Africa
          held at Durban, 18th to 22nd July, 1921. Durban: The Commercial
          Printing Co., 1922. 154 pp. See URB 5375.

4329   Gluckman, Max (ed.), Closed Systems and Open Minds: The Limits of
        Naivety in Social Anthropology. Chicago: Aldine, 1964. 274 pp.
        See URB 2342; RUR 8310.

4330   Goodenough, Ward H., Explorations in Cultural Anthropology: Essays in
        Honor of George Peter Murdock. New York: McGraw-Hill, 1964. 635 pp.
        See RUR 2010, 2592, 6029, 9316, 11365.

4331   Gurvitch, Georges, Traité de sociologie [Treatise on sociology].
        Paris: Presses Universitaires de France, 1962. Vol. 1, 514 pp. See
        GEN 1311.

4332   Hauser, Philip M. (ed.), Urbanization in Latin America: Proceedings
        of a Seminar Jointly Sponsored by the Bureau of Social Affairs of
        the United Nations, the Economic Commission for Latin America, and
        UNESCO (in co-operation with the International Labour Organisation
        and the Organization of American States) on Urbanization Problems
        in Latin America, Santiago (Chile), 6 to 18 July 1959. Paris:
        UNESCO, 1961. 331 pp. See URB 2015, 2023, 2025, 2031.

4333   Hauser, Philip M., and Leo F. Schnore (eds.), The Study of Urbani-
        zation. New York: John Wiley, 1966. 554 pp. See URB 1317, 1320,
        1334, 4330, 4348, 4384, 4388.

4334   Heinz, Peter (ed.), Soziologie der Entwicklungsländer: Eine System-
        atische Anthologie [Sociology of developing countries: A systematic
        anthology]. Cologne, West Germany: Kiepenheuer & Witsch, 1962.
        723 pp. See GEN 2497.

4335   Helm, June (ed.), Essays in Economic Anthropology: Proceedings of
        the 1965 Annual Spring Meeting of the American Ethnological Society.
        Seattle: University of Washington Press, 1965. 139 pp. See RUR
        1318, 3007, 6025, 6031, 6047, 6391.

4336   Herskovits, Melville J., and Mitchell Harwitz (eds.), Economic
        Transition in Africa. Evanston, Ill.: Northwestern University
        Press, 1964. 444 pp. See GEN 1355, 2331, 2368, 2395, 2396, 2415,
        2479; RUR 6049, 6465, 10304, 10339, 10354.

4337   Higgins, Benjamin H. (ed.), Entrepreneurship and Labor Skills in
        Indonesian Economic Development: A Symposium. New Haven: South-
        east Asia Studies, Yale University, 1961. 140 pp. See IND 2362;
        URB 2369.

4338   His Royal Highness the Duke of Edinburgh's Study Conference on the
        Human Problems of Industrial Communities within the Commonwealth and
        Empire, Background Papers: Appendixes and Index. London: Oxford
        University Press, 1957. 339 pp. See GEN 2424; IND 2333, 2395, 5371;
        URB 2400; RUR 1327, 3305.

4339   Hoebel, E. A., et al. (eds.), Readings in Anthropology. New York:
        McGraw-Hill, 1955. 417 pp. See RUR 8372.

4340   Hoselitz, Bert F. (ed.), The Progress of Underdeveloped Areas.
        Chicago: University of Chicago Press, 1952. 296 pp. See GEN
        1369, 1413, 1414.

4341   Hunter, Guy (ed.), <u>Industrialisation and Race Relations: A Symposium.</u>
        London: Oxford University Press, 1965. 285 pp. See GEN 2320, 2332,
        2335; IND 5356, 5368, 5375.

4342   Institute of Social Sciences, <u>Seminar on Social Integration in India.</u>
        Agra, India: Institute of Social Sciences, Agra University, 1961.
        140 pp. See RUR 2434.

4343   International Christian University, Social Science Research Institute,
        <u>The Power Structure in a Rural Community: The Case of Mutsuzawa Mura.</u>
        Tokyo: Mitaka, 1960. 45 pp. Translation of summaries of articles
        in Kokusai Chintsu-kyo Daigaku, Noson no Kenkyo-ku Kozo, 1959.
        See RUR 5007, 5009.

4344   International Congress of Americanists, <u>Actas Del XXXIII Congreso</u>
        <u>Internacional de Americanistas: San José, 20-27 Julio 1958</u>, Vol. 1
        [Acts of the 33rd International Congress of Americanists, San José,
        20-27 July 1958]. San José, Costa Rica: Lehmann, 1959. 429 pp.
        See IND 1332; RUR 8084.

4345   ------ <u>XXXV Congreso Internacional de Americanistas: México, 1962;</u>
        <u>Actas y memorias</u>, Vol. 3 [35th International Congress of American-
        ists: Mexico, 1962; Proceedings]. Mexico City: Editorial Libros
        de Mexico, 1964. 507 pp. See RUR 6429.

4346   International Sociological Association, <u>Transactions of the Third</u>
        <u>World Congress of Sociology, Koninklijk Instituut voor de Tropen,</u>
        <u>Amsterdam, 22-29 August, 1956.</u> General Theme: <u>Problems of Social</u>
        <u>Change in the 20th Century. Vol. II. Changes in Economic Structure.</u>
        London: International Sociological Association, 1956. 352 pp.
        See RUR 3326, 4357, 6479.

4347   ------ <u>Transactions of the Third World Congress of Sociology</u>, Vol.
        III. London: International Sociological Association, 1956. 356 pp.
        See RUR 2019, 2369, 2561, 4005, 4327.

4348   ------ <u>Transactions of the Fifth World Congress of Sociology</u>, Wash-
        <u>ington, D.C., 2-8 September 1962. Vol. II. The Sociology of Develop-</u>
        <u>ment.</u> London: International Sociological Association, 1962.
        208 pp. See IND 1313; URB 1329.

4349   Jennings, Jesse D., and E. Adamson Hoebel, <u>Readings in Anthropology.</u>
        New York: McGraw-Hill, 1966. 489 pp. See RUR 1311, 1370, 6323,
        6459, 8372.

4350   Lambert, Richard D., and Bert F. Hoselitz (eds.), <u>The Role of</u>
        <u>Savings and Wealth in Southern Asia and the West.</u> Paris: UNESCO,
        1963. 432 pp. See GEN 2418; RUR 6469; IND 1318, 4350, 5336, 5362,
        5372, 5373, 5378

4351   Manners, Robert A. (ed.), <u>Process and Pattern in Culture: Essays in</u>
        <u>Honor of Julian H. Steward.</u> Chicago: Aldine, 1964. 434 pp. See
        GEN 1361.

4352   Maron, Stanley (ed.), <u>Pakistan: Society and Culture.</u> New Haven:

Conn.:   Human Relations Area Files, Behavior Science Monographs, 1957.   192 pp.   See URB 3001.

4353   Marriott, McKim (ed.), Village India: Studies in the Little Commu-nity. Chicago: University of Chicago Press, 1955.   269 pp.   See RUR 1350, 1358, 2038, 8013, 8020, 8045, 8574, 9358.

4354   Matthews, David, and Raymond Apthorpe, Social Relations in Central African Industry: The 12th Conference Proceedings of the Rhodes-Livingstone Institute for Social Research. Lusaka, Zambia: Rhodes-Livingstone Institute, 1958.   135 pp.   See IND 2034, 2327, 2377, 5352; URB 5321.

4355   "Le Méxique" [Mexico], Tiers-Monde 4:15 (July-Sept. 1963), 3-398. See RUR 2382a.

4356   Meynaud, Jean, Social Change and Economic Development. Paris: UNESCO, 1963.   210 pp.   See GEN 1304, 1359, 1381; IND 2306, 2328, 5357; RUR 2375, 4361, 6322, 6355, 6409, 8067, 9357.

4357   Mills, John E. (ed.), Ethnosociological Reports of Three Korean Villages. San Francisco, Calif.:   U.S. Operations Mission to Korea, Community Development Division, 1958.   87 pp.   See RUR 8070, 8511, 8609.

4358   Minzokugaku Noto: Oka Masao Kyoju Kanreki Kinen Ronbunshu [Essays on ethnology: A collection of papers in commemoration of the sixtieth birthday of Professor Masao Oka]. Tokyo: Heibonsha, 1963. 360 pp.

4359   Morgan, Theodore, George W. Betz, and N. K. Choudhry, Readings in Economic Development. Belmont, Calif.: Wadsworth, 1963.   431 pp. See GEN 1389; RUR 8393.

4360   Nimkoff, M. F., Comparative Family Systems. Boston: Houghton Miff-lin, 1965.   402 pp.   See RUR 7009, 7316, 7344.

4361   Nyirenda, A. A., H. D. Ngwane, and D. G. Bettison, Further Economic and Social Studies, Blantyre-Limbe, Nyasaland. Lusaka, Zambia: Rhodes-Livingstone Institute, 1959.   49 pp.   See RUR 6317, 6345, 7348.

4362   Ogburn, William Fielding, and Alexander Goldenweiser, The Social Sciences and Their Interrelations. Boston: Houghton Mifflin, 1927. 506 pp.   See GEN 1372, 1451, 1474.

4363   Ottenberg, Simon, and Phoebe Ottenberg (eds.), Cultures and Socie-ties of Africa. New York: Random House, 1960.   614 pp., bibl. See URB 2020, 2309, 4361.

4364   Pitt-Rivers, Julian, Mediterranean Countrymen: Essays in the Social Anthropology of the Mediterranean. The Hague: Mouton, 1963, 236 pp. See RUR 2001, 8517, 8576, 10306.

4365   Plantation Systems of the New World: Papers and Discussion Summaries of the Seminar Held in San Juan, Puerto Rico. Washington, D.C.: Pan

American Union, 1959. 212 pp. See RUR 1365, 3301, 3325, 3332, 7373.

4366   Ray, Verne F (ed.), Cultural Stability and Cultural Change: Proceed-
        ings of the 1957 Annual Spring Meeting of the American Ethnological
        Society. Seattle: University of Washington, 1957. 84 pp. See IND
        3001; RUR 1322, 2037, 2411, 2478.

4367   ------ Intermediate Societies, Social Mobility, and Communication:
        Proceedings of the 1959 Annual Spring Meeting of the American Ethno-
        logical Society. Seattle: University of Washington, 1959. 74 pp.
        See RUR 1364, 1382, 6417.

4368   The Relevance of Models for Social Anthropology. London: Tavistock
        Foundation, 1965. 238 pp. See RUR 6452.

4369   Remer, Charles Frederick, Readings in Economics for China. Shanghai:
        Commercial Press, 1922. 685 pp. See IND 2319.

4370   Rowe, W. L.. (ed.), Contours of Culture Change in South Asia. New
        York: Society for Applied Anthropology, 1963. 104 pp. See GEN
        2304; RUR 1355, 2420, 8467.

4371   Sakai, Robert Kenjiro (ed.), Studies on Asia. Omaha: University of
        Nebraska Press, 1960. 97 pp. See RUR 8025, 8430.

4372   Schapera, Isaac (ed.), The Bantu-Speaking Tribes of South Africa: An
        Ethnographical Survey Edited for the [South African] Inter-University
        Committee for African Studies. London: Routledge, 1937. 453 pp.
        See URB 2019; RUR 2022, 2540.

4373   ------ Western Civilization and the Natives of South Africa: Studies
        in Culture Contact. London: Routledge, 1934. 312 pp. See URB 2368,
        2427; RUR 2543, 6448.

4374   Schrieke, Bertram J. O. (ed.), The Effect of Western Influence on
        Native Civilisations in the Malay Archipelago. Batavia, Netherlands
        East Indies, 1929. 247 pp. See RUR 2451, 10355.

4375   Seminar on Social Integration in Guatemala, Integración social en
        Guatemala [Social integration in Guatemala]. 2nd rev. ed. Guatemala
        City: Seminario de Integración Social Guatemalteca, 1956. 479 pp.
        See RUR 6357, 6492.

4376   Seminar on Social Integration in India, Report. Agra, India: Uni-
        versity Press, 1961. 140 pp. [Issued as J. soc. Sci. 3, Suppl.
        (1961).] See RUR 2434.

4377   Shapiro, Harry L. (ed.), Man, Culture and Society. London: Oxford
        University Press, 1956. 380 pp. See RUR 1329.

4378   Siam Society, Felicitation Volumes of Southeast Asian Studies Pre-
        sented to His Highness Prince Dhaninivat Kromamun Bidyalabh Brid-
        hyakorn on the Occasion of His Eightieth Birthday. 2 vols. Bangkok:
        Siam Society, 1965. 349 pp. See RUR 9343.

4379   Singer, Milton B. (ed.), Traditional India: Structure and Change.
         Philadelphia: American Folklore Society, 1959. 332 pp. See IND
         2025; URB 2010, 2037, 2319; RUR 8560, 9006.

4380   Singh, V. B. (ed.), Industrial Labour in India. London: Asia
         Publishing House, 1963. 664 pp. See IND 2343, 2415, 5302, 5367.

4381   Smelser, Neil J., and Seymour Martin Lipset, Social Structure and
         Mobility in Economic Development. Chicago: Aldine, 1966. 399 pp.
         See GEN 1334, 1339, 1365, 1383, 1423, 1452, 1456, 1458, 1470, 2327,
         2388, 2439, 2477; RUR 1344, 1383.

4382   Smith, Robert J., and Richard K. Beardsley, Japanese Culture: Its
         Development and Characteristics. New York: Wenner-Gren Foundation,
         1962. 193 pp. See RUR 2432, 5329.

4383   South African Institute of Race Relations, "Training Africans in
         Industry," Race Relat. 1 (1949), 1-22. See IND 2435, 2446.

4384   Southall, A. W. (ed.), Social Change in Modern Africa. Studies Pre-
         sented and Discussed at the First International African Seminar,
         Makere College, Kampala, January 1959. London: Oxford University
         Press, 1961. 337 pp. See URB 1304, 1316, 2002, 2005, 2016, 2033,
         2036, 2040, 2045, 2301, 3003, 3006, 3009, 3011, 3015, 5304, 5316,
         5328, 5378; RUR 3002, 11305.

4385   Spicer, Edward H. (ed.), Human Problems in Technological Change.
         New York: Russell Sage Foundation, 1952. 301 pp. See IND 3348;
         RUR 4006, 4015, 5372.

4386   Srinivas, M. N., India's Villages. 2nd rev. ed. London: Asia
         Publishing House, 1960. 222 pp. See RUR 4376, 8004, 8011, 8019,
         8065, 8066, 8083, 8339, 8367, 8469, 8491, 8540, 8564, 8573.

4387   Steward, Julian H., et al., The People of Puerto Rico: A Study in
         Social Anthropology. Urbana: University of Illinois Press, 1956.
         540 pp. See URB 2050, 2395; RUR 3008, 3010.

4388   Tax, Sol (ed.), Acculturation in the Americas: Proceedings and
         Selected Papers of the XXIXth International Congress of Americanists.
         Chicago: University of Chicago Press, 1952. 339 pp. See RUR 8014.

4389   Tax, Sol, Horizons of Anthropology. Chicago: Aldine, 1964. 288 pp.
         See RUR 1370.

4390   Theodorson, George A., Studies in Human Ecology. New York: Harper,
         1961. 626 pp. See GEN 2442; URB 2325, 2438, 5312, 5341.

4391   Turner, Roy (ed.), India's Urban Future: Selected Studies from an
         International Conference Sponsored by Kingsley Davis, Richard L.
         Park, and Catherine Bauer Wurster. Berkeley: University of Cali-
         fornia Press, 1962. 470 pp. See URB 2330, 4320, 4351; RUR 2494.

4392   UNESCO, Nomades et nomadisme au Sahara [Nomads and nomadism in the
         Sahara]. Paris: UNESCO, 1963. 195 pp. See RUR 2314, 2315, 2316,
         2317, 2318, 8541, 9020, 9305, 9308, 9312, 9313, 9379, 9389.

4393   ------ Research Center on the Social Implications of Industrialization
          in Southern Asia, The Social Implications of Industrialization and
          Urbanization: Five Studies of Urban Populations of Recent Rural
          Origin in Cities of Southern Asia. Calcutta: UNESCO, 1956. 268 pp.
          See IND 6326; URB 2011, 2034, 2369.

4394   Vu, Quôc Thuc (ed.), Social Research and Problems of Rural Development
          in South-East Asia. Brussels, Belgium: UNESCO, 1963. 268 pp.
          See RUR 1319, 1351, 2358, 2417, 2418, 2498, 4409, 5370, 10368.

4395   Wallace, Anthony F. C. (ed.), Men and Cultures: Selected Papers of
          the Fifth International Congress of Anthropological and Ethnological
          Sciences Philadelphia, September 1-9, 1956. Philadelphia: University
          of Pennsylvania Press, 1960. 810 pp. See GEN 1461, 1462, 2336,
          2630; RUR 1372, 2401, 2403, 2552, 4318.

4396   Wallerstein, Immanuel, Social Change: The Colonial Situation. New
          York: Wiley, 1966. 674 pp. See GEN 2377; URB 2306; RUR 2416, 2566,
          2567, 2596, 5326, 6362, 6406, 10320, 10358.

4397   Weiner, Myron (ed.), Modernization: The Dynamics of Growth. New
          York: Basic Books, 1966. 355 pp. See GEN 1398, 1453; IND 1317;
          URB 1315.

4398   West African Institute of Social and Economic Research, Annual Con-
          ference, Sociology Section, Ibadan, March 1953. Ibadan, Nigeria:
          West Africa Institute of Social and Economic Research, 1953. 205 pp.
          See IND 5310, 5381; URB 2360.

4399   West Bengal Government, Development Department, India's Villages.
          Calcutta: Government Printing Office, 1955. 198 pp. [First edition
          of GEN 4386.]

4400   Zaidi, S. M. Hafeez (ed.), "Rural Social Research," J. Pakistan
          Acad. vill. Dev.,   special issue (July 1962), 122 pp. See RUR 6027.

4401   Zollschan, George K., and Walter Hirsch (eds.), Explorations in Social
          Change. Boston: Houghton Mifflin, 1964. 832 pp. See GEN 1382, 1449;
          RUR 2353, 6368.

PART II.   INDUSTRIALIZATION (IND)

1301-7305

1. The Theory of Industrial Social Change

1301   Balandier, Georges, "Problèmes de désorganisation sociale liés à
        l'industrialisation et à l'urbanisation dans les pays en cours de
        développement économique rapide" [Problems of social disorganization
        connected with industrialization and urbanization in countries in
        the process of rapid economic development], Inform. ISSC 6 (Oct.
        1955), 1-15.

1302   Bendix, R., "Industrialization, Ideologies and Social Structure,"
        Am. sociol. Rev. 24:5 (Oct. 1959), 613-623.

1303   Boeke, J. H. (ed.), Indonesian Economics: The Concept of Dualism
        in Theory and Policy. The Hague: W. van Hoeve, 1961.   446 pp.

1304   Bonazzi, G., "Alcune ipotesi sul rapporto tra reclutamento de mano-
        dopera industriale e processo di acculturazione in comunità
        arretrate" [Some hypotheses concerning the relationship between the
        recruiting of industrial labor and the process of acculturation in
        backward communities], Quad. Sociol. 11:40 (Spring 1961), 160-170.

1305   Devasagayam, A., "A Study of Socio-Economic Problems of Industrial
        Urbanization," Indust. Relat. 11:5 (Sept.-Oct. 1959), 232-237.

1306   Dunning, E. G., and E. I. Hopper, "Industrialization and the
        Problem of Convergence: A Critical Note," Sociol. Rev. 14:2 (July
        1966), 163-195.

1307   Feldman, Arnold S., "The Interpenetration of Firm and Society," in
        GEN 4302 (1962), 179-192.

1308   Froehlich, W. (ed.), Land Tenure, Industrialization and Social
        Stability. Milwaukee, Wis.: Marquette University Press, 1961.
        301 pp.

1309   Gould, H. A., "Some Preliminary Observations Concerning the Anthro-
        pology of Industrialization," East. Anthrop. 14:1 (Jan.-Apr. 1961),
        30-47. [India]

1310   Greenfield, S. M., "Industrialization and the Family in Sociological
        Theory," Am. J. Sociol. 67:3 (Nov. 1961), 312-322.

1311   Hashimoto, M., "Rekishi-teki Hendō ni okeru Kitei insotoshite no
        Shakai Kōzō" [The role of social structure in industrialization],
        Jimbun Gakuho 42 (1959), 89-103.

1312   Hoselitz, Bert F., "The City, the Factory and Economic Growth," Am.
        econ. Rev. 45:2 (May 1955), 166-184.

1313   ------ "The Development of a Labor Market in the Process of Economic
        Growth," in GEN 4348 (1962), 51-71.

1314   ------ "The Role of Incentive in Industrialization," Econ. Wkly.
        15:28-30 (July 1963), 1237-1242.

1315   ------ "Small Industry in Underdeveloped Countries," J. econ. Hist.
        19:4 (Dec. 1959), 600-620, bibl.

1316   ------, and Wilbert E. Moore (eds.), Industrialization and Society:
        Proceedings. Paris: UNESCO, 1963. 437 pp.

1317   Lambert, Richard D., "The Modernization of the Labor Force," in GEN
        4397 (1966), 281-293.

1318   ------, and B. F. Hoselitz, "Southern Asia and the West," in GEN
        4350 (1963), 389-432.

1319   "Method and Approach in a Survey on the Impact of Factory-Employment
        on the Life of the Workers," Sociol. Bull. 9:1 (Mar. 1960), 46-59.

1320   Minkoff, M. F., "Is the Joint Family an Obstacle to Industrializa-
        tion?" Int. J. comp. Sociol. 1:1 (Mar. 1960), 109-118.

1321   Moore, Wilbert E., Industrialization and Labor: Social Aspects of
        Economic Development. Ithaca, N.Y.: Cornell University Press,
        1951. 410 pp.

1322   ------ "Primitives and Peasants in Industry," Soc. Res. 15:1 (Mar.
        1948), 44-81, bibl.

1323   ------ "Technological Change and Industrial Organization," in GEN
        4302 (1962), 199-205.

1324   ------ "Theoretical Aspects of Industrialization," Soc. Res. 15
        (1948), 277-303.

1325   ------, and Arnold S. Feldman (eds.), Labor Commitment and Social
        Change in Developing Areas. New York: Social Science Research
        Council, 1960. 378 pp.

1326   Nash, Manning, "Some Notes on Village Industrialization in South and
        East Asia," Econ. Dev. cult. Change 3:3 (Apr. 1955), 271-277.

1327   Neale, W. C., "Social Effects of Industrialization," Econ. Wkly.
        8:32 (11 Aug. 1956), 951-954.

1328   Nishiyama, M., "Sangyô Shûdan ni Okeru Ningen Kankei" [Human rela-
        tions in the industrial work group], Kôbe Jyogakuin Daigaku Ronshû
        9:22 (1962), 101-152.

1329   Pagès, M., "Sociotherapy of the Enterprise: The Conditions of
        Psychosocial Change in Industrial Concerns and the Role of the
        Social Psychologist as an Agent of Social Change," Hum. Relat. 12:4
        (Winter 1959), 317-334, bibl.

1330   Phillips, Walter, Jr., "La resistenza alle innovazioni tecnologiche
        nel processo di industrializzazione" [Resistance to technological
        innovation in the industrialization process], Inform. Svimez 13:139
        (June 1964), 4935-4942.

1331   ------ "Technological Levels and Labor Resistance to Change in the
        Course of Industrialization," Econ. Dev. cult. Change 9:3, Pt. 1
        (Apr. 1963), 257-266.

1332   Pozas, R., "Los cambios sociales y la industrialización" [Social
        change and industrialization], in GEN 4344 (1959), 373-379.

1333   Shimkin, D. B., "Industrialization: A Challenging Problem for
        Cultural Anthropology," Sthwest. J. Anthrop. 8:1 (Spring 1952), 84-
        91.

1334   Slotkin, James S., From Field to Factory: New Industrial Employees.
        Glencoe, Ill.: Free Press, 1960. 156 pp.

1335   Udy, Stanley H., Jr., Organization of Work: A Comparative Analysis
        of Production Among Non-Industrial Peoples. New Haven, Conn.:
        Human Resources Area File Press, 1959. 182 pp.

1336   Whyte, William F., "Culture, Industrial Relations, and Economic
        Development: The Case of Peru," Indust. Labor Relat. Rev. 16:4
        (July 1963), 583-594.

2. The Industrial Worker

A. Annotated Case Studies

2001   Bose, S. K., "Group Cohesiveness and Productivity," Psychol. Stud.
        3:1 (Jan. 1958), 20-28. [West Bengal State, India]

        Cohesiveness is found to be positively correlated with better
    morale and less anxiety about work in a Calcutta factory.

2002   Delisle, Stéphane, "Le prolétariat marocain de Port-Lyautey" [The
        Moroccan proletariat of Port Lyautey], in GEN 4323 (1950), 109-200.

Ten case studies in which individuals describe the reactions and motivations of Moroccan workers confronting industrial employment.

*2003   Doucy, A., and P. Feldhein, "Some Effects of Industrialization in Two Districts of Equatoria Province (Belgian Congo)," in GEN 4325 (1956), 670-692.

Though Africans are highly attracted to the town, most of them wish to return ultimately to the village. The paternalistic nature of the colonial administration has hindered the native from being influenced by the incentive of cash wages. Prestige in the form of Europeanization is a far stronger motivation.

*2004   Elkan, W., An African Labour Force. Kampala, Uganda: East African Institute of Social Research, 1956. 59 pp.

The workers in the two factories studied have adapted to industrial life by treating the employer as though he were in loco parentis. He is expected to provide food, and if he fails to do so, he creates resentment. There is a high rate of turnover because of the poor understanding between labor and management, neither of which seems to understand its role, and so many workers want to return to the village.

*2005   Gangrade, K. D., "Employee Morale," Indian J. soc. Wk. 15:13 (Dec. 1954), 175-183. [Indian State of Maharashtra]

This study of workers in a Bombay factory indicates that employee morale is related to the extent to which workers are treated as partners and given a sense of responsibility.

*2006   Ganguli, Harish Chandra, "An Enquiry into Incentives for Workers in an Engineering Factory," Indian J. soc. Wk. 15:1 (1954), 30-40. [Indian State of West Bengal]

This study, conducted in a Calcutta factory, concludes that what the workers most desire is an adequate income, a steady job, and opportunity for promotion.

*2007   ------ "A Further Analysis of the Relation of Union-Membership to Attitudes of Industrial Workers," Indian J. Psychol. 30:1-2 (1955), 61-72. [Indian State of West Bengal]

The morale of workers in a Calcutta factory is in inverse proportion to their membership in a union, in which morale is low.

2008   ------ "A Study of the Effect of Union Membership on Industrial Morale," Indian J. Psychol. 29:1-2 (1954), 45-59. [Indian State of West Bengal]

Depicts the low morale among union workers.

2009   ------ and P. R. Chatterjee, "Social Attitudes and Voting Behaviour in Small Industrial Samples," Indian J. soc. Wk. 20:3 (Dec. 1959), 193-199. [Indian State of West Bengal]

Voting is regarded as a social act.

2010   Ganguly, T., "The Workers' Attitude towards the Management," Indian
        J. Psychol. 28:1-4 (1953), 29-37. [Indian State of West Bengal]

        The workers' identification with management in a Tata factory is
        not related to pay alone.

*2011   Guilbot, J., Petite étude sur la main-d'oeuvre à Douala [A short
        study of unskilled workers in Douala]. Douala, Cameroons: Centre
        de l'Institut Fondamental d'Afrique Noire, n.d. 76 pp.

        The workers evince great instability and a high rate of turnover
        because of the difficulty inherent in imposing ways of working not
        adapted to African habits.

**2012 Hellmann, Ellen P., Sellgoods: A Sociological Survey of an African
        Commercial Labour Force. Cape Town: South African Institute of
        Race Relations, 1953. 68 pp. [Republic of South Africa]

        Those workers with records of long employment are also those who
        most cut themselves off from any rural contacts.

*2013   Hendry, J. B., The Work Force in Saigon: A Survey of Some Economic
        and Social Characteristics of Employees in Medium Sized Industry.
        Saigon: Michigan State University Vietnam Advisory Group, 1960.
        178 pp.

        A descriptive study of the reasons for choosing a job, for
        feeling satisfied with a job, and for liking or disliking the
        employer.

**2014 Husain, A. F. A., and A. Farouk, Problems of Social Integration of
        Industrial Workers in Khulna, with Special Reference to the Problem
        of Industrial Unrest. Dacca: Socio-Economic Research Board, Uni-
        versity of Dacca, 1961. 100 pp. [East Pakistan]

        A study of the local influence of a jute mill. Almost all the
        workers have been recruited from outside the district but have not
        brought their families with them. As a result, they are not well
        integrated into the community and feel quite insecure. This
        insecurity is reinforced by the disdainful attitude of the managers
        and their failure to compensate the workers for experience or
        seniority.

**2015 ------ Social Integration of Industrial Workers in Khulna. Dacca:
        Bureau of Economic Research, University of Dacca, 1963. 207 pp.
        [East Pakistan]

        Low wages and unsympathetic management seem to have blocked the
        integration of the workers--most of whom come from outside the city--
        into the local society.

**2016 Japan Cultural Science Society, Construction of the Sakuma Dam for
        the Electric Power Development and Its Effect on Local Communities.
        Tokyo: Japanese National Commission for UNESCO, 1959. 48 pp.
        Summary of IND 2017.

Before the advent of the dam, construction work was done by groups of workers who formed what might be called "baronies." With the coming of the dam, the labor "barons" took up engineering rather than becoming rural leaders who could supply a labor force. Technical ability was considered an important asset for success. See Sakuma Dam.

**2017   ------ Sakuma Dam [The Sakuma Dam]. Tokyo: Tōkyō Daigaku Shuppan-kai, 1958. 640 pp. In Japanese.

*2018   Kahl, Joseph A., "Three Types of Mexican Industrial Workers," Econ. Dev. cult. Change 8:2 (Jan. 1960), 163-169.

Depicts the connection between social and work levels; the middle-level workers are neither "dirty" peasants nor "clean" middle-class.

*2019   Lambert, Richard D., "Factory Workers and the Non-factory Population in Poona," J. Asian Stud. 18:1 (Nov. 1958), 21-42. [Indian State of Maharashta]

A study of the impact of factories on urban areas already in existence. The author attempts to determine whether the factory workers are different because of their having been selected or because of their factory work.

**2020   ------ Workers, Factories, and Social Change in India. Princeton: Princeton University Press, 1963. 247 pp.

This socio-economic survey of five factories includes an analysis of the results of a questionnaire administered to the workers. The social life in the factory tends to reflect the form of the society. Thus the factory is not a good means of transforming the society but is rather a graft onto traditional society.

2021   Montagne, Robert (ed.), Naissance du prolétariat marocain [Birth of the Moroccan proletariat]. Paris: Peyronnet, 1952. 291 pp.

Several case studies of individual workers.

*2022   Moore, Wilbert E., Industrialization and Labor: Social Aspects of Economic Development. Ithaca: Cornell University Press, 1951. 410 pp.

Part II is a case study of workers in a small town east of Mexico City. The author discusses the reasons why workers leave the poor mountain villages to work in factories in the town nearby.

2023   Morgaut, M. E., Cinq années de psychologies africaines [Five years of African psychologies]. Paris: Presses Universitaires de France, 1962. 88 pp.

Describes the tests used by firms to select workers for initial employment or for promotion.

*2024   Natal, University of, Department of Economics, The African Factory
         Worker. London: Oxford University Press, 1950. 220 pp. [Republic
         of South Africa]

              This case study, based on interviews, shows that much of the work
         instability results from both the Africans' lack of qualifications
         and from the employers' preference for young workers.

**2025   Orans, Martin, "A Tribal People in an Industrial Setting," in GEN
         4379 (1959), 216-239. [Indian State of Bihar]

              A study of a Santal group working in the Tata iron and steel
         mills in Jamshedpar. These workers have migrated to the mills for
         economic reasons. Their traditional great fear of illness, which
         modern medical care (obligatory for all workers) has touched but
         slightly, binds these workers to their tribe.

2026   Parthasarathy, V. S., "Caste in a South Indian Textile Mill," Econ.
         Wkly. 10:33 (16 Aug. 1958), 1083-1086. [Indian State of Mysore]

              Although economic conditions have forced all castes to seek work
         in the mill, caste lines are still present.

*2027   Powdermaker, Hortense, Copper Town: Changing Africa. The Human
         Situation on the Rhodesian Copperbelt. New York: Harper, 1962.
         391 pp.

              This study stresses the Africans' widening horizons and heightened
         sense of dignity resulting from their increased contact with industry.

**2028   Rice, Albert Kenneth, Productivity and Social Organization: The
         Ahmedabad Experiment. London: Tavistock Institute, 1958. 298 pp.
         [Indian State of Gujarat]

              A study of the reorganization of work patterns in an Indian
         textile mill. The workers were formed into groups to allow for
         specialization by task. Considerable emphasis was placed on the
         creation of an atmosphere of trust and self-reliance. This kind of
         change seems to have responded to the needs of the Indian workers.

**2029   Savage, Charles H., Jr., Social Reorganization in a Factory in the
         Andes. Ithaca: Society for Applied Anthropology, Cornell Univer-
         sity, 1964. 22 pp.

              A study of a Colombian village factory modernized by city-trained
         engineers. Before its reorganization the forger was supreme, even a
         father figure, in the social structure; but afterward the polisher
         assumed the dominant position, since he could reject the forger's
         work. The engineers thought that pecuniary interest would override
         the social structure and so they stressed impersonal relations. How-
         ever, the strong social cohesiveness of the workers thwarted the
         potential power of the polishers. Advancement was sought only through
         the group, not individually. See also IND 2425.

**2030   Shih, Kuo-heng, China Enters the Machine Age. Cambridge, Mass.:
         Harvard University Press, 1944. 206 pp.

Reactions to factory life and management are given in this study of workers in a displaced factory in Yunnan during the early part of the Sino-Japanese conflict. The factory was manned by a mixture of refugees and local workers. In general they proved not impervious to change, partly because this was a government project in which jobs had the traditionally high status of government bureaucracy.

2031   Sinha, D., "Personal Factors in Absenteeism," Indian J. soc. Wk. 17:2 (Sept. 1956), 86-93. [Indian State of Bihar]

The results of tests given workers in a factory indicate that those with a high degree of absenteeism tend to be either neurotic, or from the villages, or both.

*2032   Sinha, S., "A Survey of Some Factors on the Question of Industriali-sation in India," Indian J. Psychol. 35:1 (1960), 9-16. [Indian State of West Bengal]

A study of Bengali workers showing that their morale is negatively related to their length of service.

*2033   Sofer, C., "Urban African Social Structure and Working Group Behaviour at Jinja (Uganda)," in GEN 4325 (1956), 590-612.

The sharp racial divisions of the community seem to prevent the African from adequately adapting to industrial experience.

2034   Stent, G. E., S. Biesheuvel, G. Clack, and R. V. Sutton, "Personnel Control in Central African Industry," in GEN 4354 (1958), 105-132. [Southern Rhodesia]

Descriptions of nonverbal tests administered to prospective workers.

*2035   Textor, Robert B., From Peasant to Pedicab Driver: A Social Study of Northeastern Thai Farmers Who Periodically Migrated to Bangkok and Became Pedicab Drivers. 2nd ed. New Haven: Yale University Press, 1961. 83 pp.

A general discussion of the sociological changes produced by periodic migration. A reprint of the questionnaire that was to have been used had funds been available is appended.

2036   Trystram, J. P., "Recherches psychotechniques au Maroc. Principes et applications" [Psychotechnical research in Morocco: Principles and applications], Bull. écon. soc. Maroc 57:1 (1953), 219-226.

A theoretical study that includes the results of an inquiry in Morocco on the stability of unskilled workers.

*2037   Whitehill, Arthur Murray, Jr., and S.-I. Takezawa, Cultural Values in Management Worker Relations. Japan: Gimu in Transition. Chapel Hill: University of North Carolina Press, 1961. 113 pp.

A study based on interviews of the modern urban factory worker. The questionnaire used is given and analyzed in detail. The authors

find that specifically Japanese elements (such as Gimu) have
remained with the workers.

B. Other Case Studies

2301   Abegglen, J. C., "Subordination and Autonomy Attitudes of Japanese
        Workers," Am. J. Sociol. 63:2 (Sept. 1957), 181-189, bibl.

2302   Abraham, J. C., Report on Nyasaland Natives in the Union of South
        Africa and in Southern Rhodesia. Zomba, Union of South Africa:
        Government Printer, 1937. 65 pp.

2303   Adams, Richard N., "A Study of Labor Preferences in Peru," Hum.
        Organiz. 10:3 (Summer 1951), 37-38.

2304   Akktar, S. Sultan, and Dinyar Pestonjee, "A Study of Employees' Ad-
        justment Within and Outside the Work Situation," Indian J. soc. Wk.
        23 (Jan. 1963), 327-330.

2305   Balandier, Georges, Les problèmes du travailleur africain au Gabon
        et au Congo [The problems of the African worker in Gabon and in the
        Congo]. Paris: International Bureau of Research on the Social
        Implications of Technical Progress, 1954. 17 mim. pp. [Congo
        (Brazzaville); Gabon]

2306   ------ "The Problems of the African Worker in the Gabon and the
        Congo," in GEN 4356 (1963), 188-196.

2307   Banerjee, Niharika, "Survey of Tribals Employed at Jamshedpur,"
        Patna Univ. J. 18 (July 1963), 255-276. [India]

2308   Bannum, R., "The African as Industrial Worker," Race Relat. 12:2
        (1945).

2309   Bhutani, D. H., "The Socio-economic Background and Productivity,"
        Indian J. soc. Res.   (Apr. 1964), 18-23.

2310   Bonne, A., "The Adjustment of Oriental Immigrants to Industrial
        Employment in Israel," Int. soc. Sci. Bull. 8 (1956), 12-36.

2311   Botha, J. H., Die Arbeidsvraagstuk van Suid-Afrika [The worker
        problem in South Africa]. Amsterdam: H. J. Paris, 1928. 253 pp.

2312   Brandão Lopes, J. R., "Relations industrielles dans deux communautés
        brésiliennes" [Industrial relations in two Brazilian communities],
        Sociol. Trav. 3:4 (1961), 18-32.

2313   Campbell, E., "Industrial Training Methods and Techniques," Soc.
        Econ. Stud. 2:1 (Sept. 1953), 5-101. [Jamaica]

2314   Capelle, M., "The Industrial Employment of Women in the Belgian
        Congo," Afr. Women 3:3 (Dec. 1959), 59-61.

2315   Carson, W. M., "Social History of an Egyptian Factory," Mid. E. J.
        11:4 (Fall 1957), 361-370.

2316   Cholia, C. N., Dock Labourers in Bombay. Calcutta: Longmans, Green,
        1941. 156 pp. [Indian State of West Bengal]

2317   Cian, R., "Riflessi dell' industrializzazione sui lavoratori
        meridionali" [Influence of industrialization on southern workers],
        Quad. Azione Soc. 13:45 (July-Oct. 1962), 847-858. [South Italy]

2318   Clay, H., Report on Industrial Relations in Southern Rhodesia.
        Salisbury: Southern Rhodesian Legislative Assembly, Cmd. Paper 3,
        1930. 43 pp.

2319   Corkery, K. J., "The Chinese Laborer from the Point of View of an
        American Manager," in GEN 4369 (1922), 455-462.

2320   Cortis, L. E., "A Comparative Study of the Attitudes of Bantu and
        European Workers," Psychol. afr. 9 (1962), 148-167. [Republic of
        South Africa]

2321   Dabholkar, Venu, "Life and Labour of Employed Women in Poona," Artha
        Vijnana 3 (Sept. 1961), 181-193. [Indian State of Maharashtra]

2322   Darbel, A., et al., Travail et travailleurs en Algérie [Work and
        workers in Algeria]. The Hague-Paris: Mouton, 1963. 366 pp.

2323   Das, T. C., "Method and Approach in a Survey on the Impact of
        Factory-Employment on the Life of the Workers," Sociol. Bull. 9:1
        (Mar. 1960), 46-59. [Indian State of West Bengal]

2324   Dawson, J. L. M., "Traditional Values and Work Efficiency in a West
        African Mine Labour Force," Occup. Psychol. 37:3 (July 1963), 209-
        218.

2325   De, Nitish R., "Personnel Practices in the Jute Textile Industry,"
        Indian Labour J. 2 (Dec. 1961), 1138-1146. [Indian State of West
        Bengal]

2326   De Brie, H., "Profil des cadres de l'industrie et industrialisation
        africaine" [Profile of industrial foremen and industrialization in
        Africa], Ass. Cadres dir. Ind. B. 189 (Apr. 1964), 146-159.

2327   De Haas, J., and R. M. Bango, "Social Group Relations at the Plant
        Level," in GEN 4354 (1958), 93-104. [Southern Rhodesia]

2328   Doucy, A., "The Unsettled Attitude of Negro Workers in the Belgian
        Congo," in GEN 4356 (1963), 179-187.

2329   Doxey, G. V., The Industrial Colour Bar in South Africa. London:
        Oxford University Press, 1961. 205 pp.

2330   Dubey, S. M., "White-Collar Workers in Gorakhpur, U.P.," Man in India
       45:3 (July-Sept. 1965), 244-246. [Indian State of Uttar Pradesh]

2331   Durand, R., "La formation professionelle et la psychologie des noirs"
       [Professional training and the psychology of Negroes], Probl. Afr.
       Cent. 24 (1954), 102-108. [Central Africa]

2332   Eisenstadt, S. N., "Remarks on the Sociological Aspects of the Problem
       of Productivization of Immigrants," Inform. ISSC 5 (1955), 1-11.
       [Israel]

2333   Elkan, Walter, "Incentives in West Africa," in GEN 4338 (1957), 121-
       128.

2334   ------ Migrants and Proletarians: Urban Labour in the Economic
       Development of Uganda. London: Oxford University Press, 1960.
       149 pp.

2335   "Estudio sobre o absentismo e a instabilidade da Mão-de-obra Africana"
       [Research on absenteeism and instability in the African labor force],
       Estud. polít. soc. 44:3 (1960), 11-262.

2336   Galenson, Walter (ed.), Labor in Developing Economies. Berkeley:
       University of California Press, 1962. 299 pp. [Argentina; Brazil;
       Chile; Indonesia; Israel; Pakistan; and Turkey]

2337   Ganguli, Harish Chandra, "Attitudes of Union and Non-Union Employees
       in a Calcutta Electrical Engineering Factory," J. appl. Psychol.
       40:2 (1956), 78-82.

2338   ------ "A Discussion of Some Variables Affecting the Attitude of
       Industrial Workers," Indian J. Psychol. 32:3-4 (1957), 133-150.
       [Indian State of West Bengal]

2339   ------ "An Enquiry into Incentives for Workers in an Engineering
       Factory," Indian J. soc. Wk. 15:1 (1954).

2340   ------ "Human Engineering Research and the Defence Services," Def.
       Sci. J. (July 1961). [India]

2341   ------ Industrial Productivity and Motivation: A Psychological
       Analysis. Bombay: Asia Publishing House, 1961. 92 pp. [India]

2342   ------ "Isolation of Some Morale Dimensions by Factor Analysis,"
       Sankhya 17:4 (Feb. 1957), 393-400.

2343   ------ "Psychological Research on Labour Problems in India," in GEN
       4380 (1963), 557-600.

2344   ------ "Relation of Union Membership to the Attitude of Industrial
       Workers," Indian J. soc. Wk. 15 (1954), 189-199.

2345   ------ "Some Factors Influencing Income Aspiration," J. appl. Psychol.
       41:1 (1957), 32-36.

2346   ------ "Stimulus-Response Compatibility and Stress Effects in a One-

Dimensional Tracking Task," J. aero-med. Soc. (July 1960).

2347   ------ Structure and Processes of an Organisation. Bombay: Asia
        Publishing House, 1964. 184 pp.

2348   ------ "A Study of the Effect of Union Membership on Industrial
        Morale," Indian J. Psychol. (1954), 29, 45-60.

2349   ------ "A Study of Some Variables Affecting Attitudes of Industrial
        Workers," ibid. 30 (Sept. 1955).

2350   ------ A Study of Supervision in a Government Engineering Factory.
        Kharagpur, India: Indian Institute of Technology, 1957. 63 pp.

2351   ------ and S. Goswami, "Some Characteristics of Effective Supervision
        in a Government Engineering Factory," J. Inst. Engng. 38:9-1 (May
        1958) and 39:4-1 (Dec. 1958).

2352   ------ S. Goswami, and R. Ghosh, "A Railway Study on Differential
        Perception of First-Line Supervisory Practices," Indian J. Psychol.
        32:1-2 (1957), 89-100.

2353   ------ "Study of Differential Perception of First-Line Supervisory
        Practices in a Government Workshop," Indian J. soc. Wk. 18:3 (Dec.
        1957), 191-198.

2354   ------ and M. N. Rao, "Noise and Industrial Efficiency," Arbeitz-
        physiologie 15 (1954), 344-354.

2355   Ganguly, Tapodhan, An Experimental Study on Workers' Morale and
        Productivity. Industrial Health in India Series, No. 77. Calcutta:
        All India Institute of Hygiene and Public Health, n.d. 22 pp.

2356   ------ "Group Participation as an Effective Technique to Improve the
        Industrial Workers' Attitude and Morale: An Experiment," Indian J.
        Psychol. 33:1 (1958), 25-36.

2357   Ghurye, G. S., "Bombay Suburbanites: Some Aspects of Their Working
        Life," Sociol. Bull. 13 (Sept. 1964), 73-83 and 14 (Sept. 1965), 1-8.

2358   Giri, Varahagiri V., Labour Problems in Indian Industry. 2nd rev. ed.,
        Bombay: Asia Publishing House, 1959. 520 pp.

2359   Gould, H. A., "Lucknow Rickshawallas: The Social Organization of an
        Occupational Category," Int. J. comp. Sociol. 6:1 (Mar. 1965), 24-
        47.

2360   Gulliver, P. H., "Incentives in Labor Migration," Hum. Organiz. 19:3
        (Fall 1960), 159-163. [South Africa]

2361   Gussman, Boris W., "Industrial Efficiency and the Urban African,"
        Africa 23:2 (Apr. 1953), 135-144. [Southern Rhodeisa]

2362   Guthrie, Harold W., "The Development of a Skilled Labor Force in
        Indonesia," in GEN 4337 (1961), 98-138.

2363   Harbison, F. H., and I. A. Ibrahim, "Some Labor Problems of Indus-
        trialization in Egypt," Ann. Am. Acad. polit. soc. Sci. 305 (May
        1956), 114-124.

2364   Hooker, J. R., "The African Worker in Southern Rhodesia: Black
        Aspirations in a White Economy, 1927-1936," Race 6:2 (Oct. 1964),
        142-151.

2365   Hudson, W., "Psychological Research on the African Worker," Civili-
        sations 8:2 (May 1958), 193-201.

2366   Huizenga, L. H., "The Training of the Papuan for Employment in Agri-
        culture, Industry, and Trade in Netherlands New Guinea," Nieuw-Guinea
        Stud. 6:1 (Mar. 1962), 13-33.

2367   Hutchinson, B., "Urban Social Mobility Rates in Brazil Related to
        Migration and Changing Occupational Structure," Amér. lat. 6:3 (July-
        Sept. 1963), 47-61.

2368   International Labour Organisation, African Labour Survey. Geneva:
        International Labour Organisation, 1962. 712 pp.

2369   ------ Asian Regional Conference, New Delhi, 1957 (4th Session).
        Report II: Labour and Social Problems of Small-Scale and Handicraft
        Industries in Asian Countries. Geneva: International Labour Organi-
        sation, 1957. 143 pp.

2370   ------ Labour Conditions in the Oil Industry in Iran. Geneva: Inter-
        national Labour Organisation, 1950. 87 pp.

2371   ------ Iron and Steel Committee, Monterrey, 1957 (6th Session).
        Report III: Conditions of Work and Social Problems in the Iron and
        Steel Industry of the Countries in the Course of Industrialisation.
        Geneva: International Labour Organisation, 1957. 125 pp.

2372   James, R. C., "Discrimination Against Women in Bombay Textiles,"
        Indust. Labor Relat. Rev. 15:2 (Jan. 1962), 209-220.

2373   Jaspan, M. A., "Indonesian Worker's Attitudes in Nationalized Indus-
        try," Sci. Soc. 26 (Summer 1962), 257-275.

2374   ------ "Productivity Inhibition Among Workers in a Nationalized Indus-
        try: A Factory Case Study in Java," Anthrop. Forum 1:1 (July 1963),
        98-111.

2375   Joint Commission on Rural Reconstruction in China, A Study on Rural
        Labor Mobility in Relation to Industrialization and Urbanization in
        Taiwan. Taipei, 1964. 19 mim. pp.

2376   Kakade, R. G., The Bombay Cotton Mill Worker. Bombay: Millowner's
        Association, 1957(?). 125 pp. [Indian State of Maharashtra]

2377   Kenny, W. J., C. Collard, E. M. B. West, and E. R. Hester, "Labour
        Policies in Central Africa," in GEN 4354 (1958), 45-55.

2378   Kilby, Peter, "African Productivity Reconsidered," Econ. J. 71

(1962), 273-291.

2379   Knox, J. B., "Absenteeism and Turnover in an Argentine Factory," Am.
         sociol. Rev. 26:3 (June 1961), 424-428.

2380   Kolaja, Jiri, A Polish Factory: A Case Study of Workers' Participa-
         tion in Decision Making. Lexington: University of Kentucky Press,
         1960. 145 pp.

2381   Kundu, S. R., "A Psychological Study of Accidents in a Factory,"
         Educ. Psychol. 4:1 (Mar. 1957), 17-24. [India]

2382   "Labour Conditions in Paper Mill Industry," Indian Labour J. 3:7
         (July 1962), 531-569. [India]

2383   Laksawala, D. T., and B. V. Mehta, "Small and Medium Scale Engineer-
         ing Factories in Bombay City," J. Univ. Bombay 26 (Jan. 1958),
         50-103. [Indian State of Maharashtra]

2384   Lambert, Richard D., "Aspiration Levels Among Workers in Five Fac-
         tories in India," Artha Vijnana 3 (June 1961), 107-115.

2385   ------ "Factory Workers and the Non-Factory Population in Poona," J.
         Asian Stud. 18:1 (Nov. 1958), 21-42. [Indian State of Maharashtra]

2386   ------ "Occupational Rank and Favourableness to the Company in Five
         Factories in Poona," Econ. Wkly. 14:15-16 (14, 21 Apr. 1962), 625-628
         and 661-670.

2387   Leistner, G. M. E., "Patterns of Urban Bantu Labour: Some Findings of
         a Sample Survey in the Metropolitan Area of Pretoria," Afr. J. Econ.
         32:4 (Dec. 1964), 253-277.

2388   Lenhard, R., "Profissão e instrução dos trabalhadores em São José do
         Rio Prêto" [Proficiency and Training of Labourers in São José of Rio
         Prêto], Sociologia 27:3 (1965), 219-239.

2389   Linn, J. M., A. Causy, et al., Du douar à l'usine [From the douar
         (Arab tent village) to the factory]. Paris: Centre des Etudes
         Sociales Nord-Africaines, 1951. 38 pp. [Algeria; North Africa]

2390   McCulloch, Meran, "Survey of Recent and Current Field Studies on the
         Social Effects of Economic Development in Inter-Tropical Africa," in
         GEN 4325 (1956), 53-225.

2391   Mamoria, C. B., and S. L. Uoshi, Labour Problems and Social Welfare
         in India. Bombay: Kitab Mahal, 1958. 439 pp.

2392   Mathur, W. S., "Quelques aspects de l'éducation des travailleurs en
         Inde" [Some aspects of the education of workers in India], Fundl.
         Educ. adult Educ. 7:1 (Jan. 1955), 3-9.

2393   Matsushima, S., Rōmu Kanri no Nihonteki Tokushitu to Hensen [Charac-
         teristics and development of labor management in Japan]. Tokyo:
         Diamond Co., 1962. 490 pp.

2394   Merlo, J. D., "Das Proletariat in Douala: Soziologische Untersuchung
        einer Afrikanischen Hafenstadt" [The proletariat in Douala: Socio-
        logical research in an African port], Neues Afr. 3:8 (Aug. 1961),
        316-319. [Cameroons]

2395   Mitchell, J. Clyde, "Africans in Industrial Towns in Northern
        Rhodesia," in GEN 4338 (1957), Background Papers, 1-10.

2396   Morgaut, M.-E., "Cinq années de psychologies africaines" [Five years
        of African psychologies], Etud. Tiers-Monde (1962), 1-82.

2397   Morris, Morris David, The Emergence of an Industrial Labor in India:
        A Study of the Bombay Cotton Mills, 1854-1947. Berkeley: University
        of California Press, 1965. 263 pp.

2398   ------ "Myth of 'Paradise Lost': UNESCO's Study of Bombay Labour,"
        Econ. Wkly. 9:26-28 (July 1957), 857-862. [Indian State of
        Maharashtra]

2399   Mukerji, Girija Prasad, "On the Efficacy of Economic Incentives and
        Their Effect on Industrial Productivity," Indian J. soc. Wk. 23
        (Apr. 1962), 35-39.

2400   Mwewa, Parkinson B., The African Railway Workers Union, Ndola,
        Northern Rhodesia. Lusaka, Zambia: Rhodes-Livingstone Institute,
        1958. 17 mim. pp.

2401   Nakamoto, Hiromichi, "Labor Consciousness in the Salt-Field Workers:
        Three Cases of the Salt-Farms in Kagawa Prefecture," Shakaigaku
        Hyôron 6:3 (Oct. 1955), 110-115, and 7:1 (Feb. 1956), 60-92. In
        Japanese.

2402   Nash, Manning, "The Recruitment of Wage Labor and Development of New
        Skills," Ann. Am. Acad. polit. soc. Sci. 305 (May 1956), 23-31.

2403   Niddrie, D., "The Road to Work: A Survey of the Influence of Trans-
        port on Migrant Labour in Central Africa," J. Rhodes-Livingst. Inst.
        15 (1954), 31-42.

2404   Niehoff, Arthur H., "Caste and Industrial Organization in North
        India," Admve. Sci. Quart. 3:4 (Mar. 1959), 494-508.

2405   ------ Factory Workers in India. Milwaukee, Wis.: Milwaukee Public
        Museum, 1959. 115 pp. [India; Indian State of Uttar Pradesh]

2406   Noble, Walter James, The Black Trek: From Village to Mine in Africa.
        London: Edinburgh House Press, 1931. 148 pp. [South Africa]

2407   Noon, J. A., Labour Problems of Africa. Philadelphia: University of
        Pennsylvania Press, 1944. 147 pp.

2408   Ōdaka, Kuniō, "An Iron Worker's Community in Japan: A Study in the
        Sociology of Industrial Groups," Am. sociol. Rev. 15:2 (Apr. 1950),
        186-195.

2409   Orde-Browne, Granville St. J., The African Labourer. London: Oxford

University Press, 1933.   248 pp.

2410   ------ Labour Conditions in Northern Rhodesia. Report. Col. 150.
London: HMSO, 1938.   99 pp.

2411   Palacios, L. M., "Encuesta socio-económica de familias de trabajadores
en Arequipa" [Socioeconomic survey of workers' families in Arequipa],
Rev. Fac. Ciênc. econ. coml. 65 (July-Dec. 1962), 165-170.

2412   Pauvert, Jean Claude, "La notion du travail en Afrique noire" [The
idea of work in Black Africa], Présence afr. 13 (1952), 92-107.

2413   Prabhu, Pandharinath, "UNESCO Study of Bombay Labour," Econ. Wkly.
9:36 (7 Sept. 1957), 1157-1158. See IND 2398. [Indian State of
Maharashtra]

2414   Prasad, Kali, Fatigue and Efficiency in Textile Industry: A Psychological Investigation. Lucknow, India: Laboratory of Experimental
Investigation, Lucknow University, Part I, 1950; Part II, 1952.

2415   ------ "Industrial Fatigue, Accidents and Occupational Diseases," in
GEN 4380 (1963), 533-556.

2416   Prothero, R. M., "Migratory Labour from North-Western Nigeria,"
Africa 27 (1957), 251-261.

2417   Raz, S. Mobin Uddin, "Caste Attitudes Among the Industrial Townsmen
and Agricultural Villagers," Patna Univ. J. 17 (July 1962), 158-180.

2418   Read, Margaret, From Field to Factory: An Introductory Study of the
Indian Peasant Turned Factory Hand. London: Student Christian
Movement, 1927.   78 pp.

2419   ------ The Indian Peasant Uprooted: A Study of the Human Machine.
London: Longmans, Green, 1931.   256 pp.

2420   Rice, Albert Kenneth, "The Experimental Reorganization of Non-Auto-
matic Weaving in an Indian Mill. A Further Study of Productivity and
Social Organization," Hum. Relat. 8:3 (Aug. 1955), 199-249.

2421   ------ "Productivity and Social Organization in an Indian Weaving
Mill," ibid. 8:4 (Nov. 1955), 399-428. [Indian State of Gujarat]

2422   ------ "Productivity and Social Organization in an Indian Weaving
Shed," ibid. 6:4 (Nov. 1953), 297-329. [Indian State of Gujarat]

2423   Rimmer, D., "The New Industrial Relations in Ghana," Indust. Labor
Relat. Rev. 14:2 (Jan. 1961), 206-226.

2424   Ryan, J. C., "Industrial and Workers Productive Co-operatives,"
Soc. Action 14:4 (Apr. 1964), 193-199. [India]

2425   Savage, Charles H., Jr., Management Behavior in a Developing Economy.
Cambridge: Sloan School of Industrial Management, Massachusetts Insti-
tute of Technology, 1962.   80 mim. pp. Extract from "Factory in the
Andes: Social Organization in a Developing Economy." DBA dissertation,

Harvard Business School, 1962. [Colombia]

2426   Sheth, N. R., "An Indian Factory: Aspects of Its Social Framework,"
        J. Maharaja Sayajirao Univ. 9:1 (Mar. 1960), 47-66. [India]

2427   ------ "Informal Bonds of Factory Workers," Econ. Wkly. 15:8 (23
        Feb. 1963), 359-360, 362-363.

2428   Shih Kuo-heng, "Social Implications of Tin-Mining in Yunnan," Pacif.
        Aff. 20:1 (Mar. 1947), 53-61. [China]

2429   Singh, Paramjit, and Durganand Sinha, "Job Satisfaction and Absen-
        teeism," Indian J. soc. Wk. 21 (Mar. 1961), 337-343.

2430   Singh, Paras Nath, and Robert J. Wherry, "Ranking Factors by Factory
        Workers in India," Personnel Psychol. 16 (Spring 1963), 29-33.
        [India]

2431   Singh, Paras Nath, Robert J. Wherry, and Sophia C. Huang, "Dimen-
        sions of Industrial Morale in India: A Methodological Comparison
        of Two Types of Measures," ibid. 16 (Summer 1963), 145-150. [India]

2432   Singh, V. B., and A. K. Saran (eds.), Industrial Labour in India.
        Bombay: Asia Publishing House, 1960. 528 pp.

2433   Sinha, Durganand, "Frustrations in Industrial Work," Indian J. soc.
        Wk. 23 (July 1962), 155-166.

2434   ------ "Social and Behavioural Problems in Industry," Indian J. soc.
        Wk. 21:3 (Dec. 1960), 235-245.

2435   Stanton, E. W., "Native Labour on Repetition Work," in GEN 4383
        (1949), 1-14. [Republic of South Africa]

2436   Sur, M., et al., Personnel Management in India: The Practical
        Approach to Human Relations in Industry. New York: Asia Publishing
        House, 1961. 316 pp.

2437   Tang, Chee Hong, "The Cantonese Women Building Labourers: A Study of
        a Group of Sam-Sui Women in the Building Trade." Thesis, Singapore
        University, n.d. [Malaysia]

2438   Tomita, Yoshior, and Shohei Yosoi, "Survey of the Human Relations in
        Two Large Factories in Nagoya: Through Workers' Grievances," Shakai-
        gaku Hyôron 5 (Mar. 1955), 45-57. In Japanese.

2439   Trouillot, Henock, "Les ouvriers de couleur à Saint-Dominique"
        [Colored workers in St. Dominique], Rev. Soc. haïtienne Géogr. 29:101
        (Apr. 1956), 33-60.

2440   Unwalla, D. B., "Delegation of Duties: An Aspect of the Factory
        System," Sociol. Bull. 7:1 (Mar. 1958), 1-22. [India]

2441   Van der Horst, Sheila T., "The African Worker in Urban Areas," Race
        Relat. 29 (1946), 21-31. [Republic of South Africa]

2442   ------ <u>Native Labour in South Africa</u>. London: Oxford University
        Press, 1941. 352 pp. [Republic of South Africa]

2443   ------ "Native Labour and Wages," <u>Race Relat.</u> 4 (1937), 66-70.
        [Republic of South Africa]

2444   Van Goylen, A. J., "Het Inlandse Arbeidersvraagstuk in Belgisch
        Kongo" [The problem of native workers in the Belgian Congo], <u>Econ.
        soc. Tijdschr.</u> 1 (1948), 35-51.

2445   Wells, F. A., and W. A. Warmington, <u>Studies in Industrialization:
        Nigeria and the Cameroons</u>. London: Oxford University Press, 1963.
        266 pp.

2446   Whyte, Q., "Welfare and Efficiency of Industrial Personnel," in GEN
        4383 (1949), 15-22. [Republic of South Africa]

2447   Whyte, William F., "Culture, Industrial Relations, and Economic
        Development: The Case of Peru," <u>Indust. Labor Relat. Rev.</u> 16:4
        (July 1963), 583-594.

2448   Willner, Ann Ruth, "The Adaption of Peasants to Conditions of
        Factory Labor: A Case Study in Java," <u>Asian Surv.</u> 3:11 (Nov. 1963),
        560-571.

2449   ------ "Problems of Management and Authority in a Transitional
        Society: A Study of a Javanese Factory," <u>Hum. Organiz.</u> 22:2
        (Summer 1963), 133-141.

2450   Xydias, Nellie, "Les Africains du Congo Belge: Aptitudes, attitudes
        vis-à-vis du travail" [Africans of the Belgian Congo: Aptitudes,
        attitudes toward work], <u>Trav. hum.</u> 23:1-2 (Jan.-June 1960), 41-45.

2451   ------ "Social Effects of Urbanization in Stanleyville, Belgian
        Congo: Labour conditions, aptitudes, training," in GEN 4325 (1956),
        275-367.

3. The Impact of Industry

A. Annotated Case Study

3001   Stein, William W., "Outside Contact and Cultural Stability in a
        Peruvian Highland Village," in GEN 4366 (1957), 15-19.

        The author finds that extensive migration to work outside the
        village is an "acculturationally irrelevant contact." The Indian
        society, though now geared to accept the use of cash, has remained
        a "sacred" society turned toward the land.

B.   Other Case Studies

3301   Agulla, J. C., "Aspectos sociales del proceso de industrialización
        en una comunidad urbana" [Social aspects of the industrialization
        process in an urban community], Rev. méx. Sociol. 25:2 (May-Aug.
        1963), 747-772. [Argentina]

3302   Akhtar, A. U., "Impact of Industrialisation on Socio-Economic Life
        in the Urban Areas of Pakistan," Pakist. Labour Gaz. 7:1 (Jan.-Mar.
        1959), 18-25.

3303   Balandier, Georges, "Le travail non-salarié dans les 'Brazzavilles
        noires'" [Unsalaried work in the "Black Brazzavilles"], Zaïre 6:7
        (July-Aug. 1952), 675-690.

3304   Balasubramanian, M., "Social Effects of Industrialisation," Indian
        J. Labour Econ. 5 (Jan. 1963), 393-395.

3305   Bourdieu, F., "La hantise du chômage chez l'ouvrier algérien" [The
        obsessive fear of unemployment in the Algerian worker], Sociol. Trav.
        4:4 (Oct.-Dec. 1962), 313-331.

3306   Cardoso, F. E., and O. Ianni, Condiciones y efectos de la industri-
        alización de São Paulo [Conditions and effects of industrialization
        on São Paulo]. Milano: A. Giuffrè, 1961. 842 pp. [Brazil]

3307   Chowdhury, J. K., "New Industrial Township: Nangal," Urban rur.
        Plann. Thought 1:1 (Jan. 1958), 12-27. [India]

3308   Coulter, C. W., "Problems Arising from Industrialization of Native
        Life in Central Africa," Am. J. Sociol. 40 (1935), 582-592.

3309   Das Gupta, Pranab Kumar, "Cultural Factors in Industrialization: A
        Case Study at Chittaranjan, West Bengal," J. soc. Res. 8 (Mar. 1965),
        76-82.

3310   Dholakia, J. L., "Social Effects of Industrialisation," Indian J.
        Labour Econ. 5 (Jan. 1963), 396-400.

3311   Dugal, B. S., "Village Chief in the Indian Construction Industry,"
        Hum. Organiz. 18:4 (Winter 1959-1960), 174-176. [India]

3312   Elkan, W., "Quelques conséquences sociales du développement industriel
        en Afrique orientale" [Some social consequences of industrial develop-
        ment in East Africa], Riv. int. Sci. soc. 16:3 (1964), 423-433.

3313   Fukutake, Tadashi, Man and Society in Japan. Tokyo: Tokyo University
        Press, 1962. 241 pp.

3314   Geiger, Theodore, Business Performance Abroad: The Case Study of
        Agrifor and U.S. Plywood in the Congo. Washington, D.C.: National
        Planning Association, 1965. 76 pp.

3315   Hoyt, E. E., "Voluntary Unemployment and Unemployability in Jamaica

with Special Reference to the Standard of Living," Br. J. Sociol.
11:2 (June 1960), 129-136.

3316   Husain, Mohammad, "The Impact of Industrialisation on Socio-Economic
Life in the Urban Areas of Pakistan," Pakist. Labour Gaz. 7:1 (Jan.-
Mar. 1959), 10-17.

3317   Ianni, Octavio, Industrialização e desenvolvimento social no Brasil
[Industrialization and social development in Brazil]. Rio de
Janeiro: Editôra Civilização Brasileira, 1963. 269 pp.

3318   Japan Cultural Science Society (ed.), Damu Kensetsu no Shakai-teki
Eikyo [Social consequences of the construction of a dam]. Tokyo:
Todai Shuppan kai, 1959. 492 pp. [Japan]

3319   Japan Cultural Science Society, Effect of Modern Industry (Light
Industry) on Regional Communities. Tokyo: Japanese National
Commission for UNESCO, 1955.

3320   ------ Growth of Modern Industry (Heavy Industry) and Its Influence
upon the Local Communities. Tokyo: Japanese National Commission for
UNESCO, 1954.

3321   Kotoki, T., "Kôgyô-ka Katê ni okeru Bunka Dôtai ni tsuite" [Cultural
dynamics and industrialization], Hôgaku Kenkyû 30:4 (1963), 22-57.

3322   Lambiri, J., "The Impact of Industrial Employment on the Position of
Women in a Greek Country Town," Br. J. Sociol. 14:3 (Sept. 1963),
240-247.

3323   Lewis, David M., and Archibald O. Haller, "Rural-Urban Differences
in Pre-Industrial and Industrial Evaluations of Occupations by
Japanese Adolescent Boys," Rur. Sociol. 29 (Sept. 1964), 324-329.

3324   Lux, André, "Industrialisation et dynamique des tensions raciales
et sociales dans l'ancien Congo Belge" [Industrialization and the
dynamics of racial and social tensions in the former Belgian Congo],
Anthropologica 8:2 (1966), 291-314.

3325   McCrory, James T., Small Industry in a North Indian Town: Case
Studies in Latent Industrial Potential. New Delhi: Government of
India, 1956. 145 pp. [Indian State of Uttar Pradesh]

3326   Malhotra, P. C., "Social Effects of Industrialization," Indian J.
Labour Econ. 5 (Jan. 1963), 401-408.

3327   Millen, Bruce H., The Political Role of Labor in Developing
Countries. Washington, D.C.: The Brookings Institution, 1963.
148 pp.

3328   Moore, Wilbert E., The Impact of Industry. Englewood Cliffs, N.J.:
Prentice-Hall, 1965. 117 pp.

3329   ------ "Labor Attitudes toward Industrialization in Underdeveloped
Countries," Am. econ. Rev. 45:2 (May 1955), 156-165.

3330   Moore, Wilbert E., and Arnold S. Feldman (eds.), Labor Commitment
        and Social Change in Developing Areas. New York: Social Science
        Research Council, 1960. 378 pp.

3331   Murteira, M., "Sindicalismo e evolução social na Africa ao sul do
        Sara" [Labor unions and social evolution in Africa south of the
        Sahara], Estud. polít. soc. 30 (1960), 9-120.

3332   Ogbuagu, B., "Enugu, Coal Town," Nigeria 70 (Sept. 1961), 241-252.

3333   Ôhara, M., "Chihô toshi kôgyôka to jûmin ishiki" [The industrializa-
        tion of a city and the social consciousness of the residents], Hôgaku
        Shimpô 69:5 (May 1962), 292-313. [Japan]

3334   Padmanabhan, C. B., "Social Effects of Industrialization-Urbanization,"
        Indian J. Labour Econ. 5 (Jan. 1963), 409-413.

3335   Poupart, R., Première esquisse de l'évolution du syndicalisme au Congo
        [A preliminary sketch of the evolution of labor unions in the Congo].
        Brussels: Editions de l'Institut de Sociologie Solvay, 1960.   235 pp.
        [Congo (Leopoldville)]

3336   Psicologia dello sviluppo economico [Psychology of economic develop-
        ment]. Milan: Associazione per la Psicologia Italiana del Lavoro,
        1964. 146 pp.

3337   Rahim, A. M. A., "Impact of Industrialisation on Socio-Economic Life
        in the Urban Areas of Pakistan," Pakist. Labour Gaz. 7:1 (Jan.-Mar.
        1959), 2-9.

3338   Read, Margaret, "Migrant Labour in Africa and Its Effects on Tribal
        Life," Int. Labour Rev. 45 (1942), 605-631. [Central Africa]

3339   Roy, Biswanath, "A Cross-Cultural Study of Persons within the
        Industrial Belt of Calcutta," J. soc. Psychol. 60 (Aug. 1963), 195-
        201. [Indian State of West Bengal]

3340   Schapera, Isaac, "Labour Migration from a Bechuanaland Reserve," J.
        roy. Afr. Soc. 32 (1933), 386-397; and 33 (1934), 49-58. [Republic
        of South Africa]

3341   Shri Kanwar Sain, I. S. E., "Social Repercussions of Hydraulic
        Projects in India," Civilisations 5:2 (May 1955), 183-191.

3342   Simão, A., "Industrialisation et syndicalisme au Brésil" [Industrial-
        ization and labor unions in Brazil], Sociol. Trav. 3:4 (Oct.-Dec. 1961),
        66-76.

3343   Singh, Amar Kumar, "Industrialization and Its Impact on Indian Social
        Institutions," J. soc. Res. 8 (Mar. 1965), 71-75.

3344   Sperling, Jan Bodo, Die Rourkela-Deutschen [The Rourkela Germans].
        Stuttgart, W. Germany: Deutsche Verlags-Anstalt, 1965. 248 pp.

3345   Spitaels, G., "Considérations sur le chômage à Léopoldville" [Reflec-
        tions on unemployment in Leopoldville], Rev. Inst. Sociol. 1 (1960),
        55-72.

[93]

3346   Takeda, R., "Sangyô to Chiiki Shakai" [Industry and the community],
        Waseda Daigaku Kiyô 9 (1963), 43-59. [Japan]

3347   Touraine, A., "Industrialisation et conscience ouvrière à São Paulo"
        [Industrialization and the class consciousness of the worker in São
        Paulo], Sociol. Trav. 3:4 (Oct.-Dec. 1961), 77-95. [Brazil]

3348   Useem, John, "South Sea Island Strike: Labor-Management Relations in
        the Caroline Islands, Micronesia," in GEN 4385 (1952), 149-164.

3349   Yokoyama, K., "Chihô toshi kôgyô to jûmin soshiki" [Industrialization
        of a city and of its organization residents], Hôgaku Shimpô 69:5 (May
        1962), 314-332.

3350   Yokoyama, Rycichi, "Migration and Industry in a City: A Research in
        Yokkaichi City, Mie Prefecture," Shakaigaku Hyôron 5:1 (Jan. 1955),
        73-95. In Japanese. [Japan]

                            4. Rural Industry

                        A. Annotated Case Studies

4001   Brunet, R., "Un centre minier de Tunisie: Redeyef" [A mining center
        in Tunisia: Redeyef], Ann. Géogr. 67:363 (Sept.-Oct. 1958), 430-446.

        A general study of the human and social transformations ensuing
        from the installation of mines near Redeyef.

**4002 Elder, J. W., "Industrialism in Hindu Society: A Case Study in Social
        Change." Ph.D. dissertation, Harvard University, 1959. 460 mim. pp.
        [Indian State of Uttar Pradesh]

        A study of a village in Uttar Pradesh where a sugar mill was
        installed in 1939. Factory procedures seem to have been adapted to
        the needs or desires of the workers and managers. The effect on
        Hinduism has been in the direction of secularizing or universalizing
        it.

**4003 Fei, Hsiao-t'ung, Peasant Life in China: A Field Study of Country
        Life in the Yangtze Valley. London: Routledge, 1939. 300 pp.

        The author discusses the introduction into this village of a silk-
        processing factory, which was initiated by the local people them-
        selves when the price of unprocessed silk fell in the late 'twenties
        and early 'thirties. The enterprise was a failure as prices con-
        tinued to fall after the factory was established. Its social impact,
        however, was large, since most of its employees were young women.

                                [94]

Their employment tended to foster individualism.

**4004   Fei, Hsiao-t'ung, and Chang Chih-i, Earthbound China: A Study of
          Rural Economy in Yunnan. Chicago: University of Chicago Press,
          1945. 319 pp.

          A socioeconomic study of the impact on two villages of the intro-
          duction of a paper industry and of truck gardening. The authors find
          that these activities tended to depress the older local industries.
          Some description of the social effects.

*4005   France, Organisation Commune des Régions Sahariennes, Les mekhadma.
          Etude sur l'évolution d'un groupe humain dans le Sahara moderne [The
          Makhadma: Study of the evolution of a group of people in modern
          Sahara]. Paris: Arts et Métiers Graphiques, 1960. 236 pp.

          A study conducted by the French Army on the results of the
          discovery of oil in this region of the Algerian Sahara. The book
          has little sociology but presents a good survey of the type of out-
          side or modern employment held by the natives, with their reasons
          for seeking, changing, or leaving their jobs.

**4006   Furushima, Toshio, Sanson no Kōzō [The structure of a mountain
          village]. Tokyo: Nihon Hyoronsha, 1949. 304 pp. [Japan]

          A historical study of the impact on a village in southern Japan
          of the introduction of sericulture and silk weaving in the early
          twentieth century. The author stresses the breakdown this caused
          in the traditional value system and cohesiveness of the village. He
          also discusses the impact of mechanization and the change-over to a
          cash-wage system.

**4007   Nash, Manning, Machine Age Maya: The Industrialization of a Guate-
          malan Community. Glencoe, Ill.: Free Press, 1958. 118 pp.

          A study of the introduction of a large cotton-textile mill into
          a village. The villagers were involved only as workers, which
          appears to have facilitated their adaptation to industrial work.
          All in all, the factory has had few social effects on the
          community.

4008   Peggio, E., Industrializzazione e sottosviluppo [Industrialization
          and underdevelopment]. Turin: Einaudi, 1960. 277 pp.

          An historical-institutional study of the Sicilian province of
          Syracuse, with a case history of a village near Augusta.

**4009   Salz, Beate R., "The Human Element in Industrialization: A Hypo-
          thetical Case Study of Ecuadorean Indians," Econ. Dev. cult. Change
          4:1 (1955), 1-265, bibl.; and Am. Anthrop. 56:6 (1955), 1-265.
          Parts I and II.

          The author is pessimistic about the acculturation of these
          Indians to an industrial state, and finds them much too "down-to-
          earth," a trait discussed with reference to their use of time, their
          motivation, and their incentives.

[95]

B. Other Case Studies

4301   Arias, Magdalena, "The Influence of Cottage Industries on the Socio-Economic Status of the Philippine Rural Areas," Centro Escolar Univ. Stud. 6 (1955), 236-258.

4302   Bose, Nirmal Kumar, "Some Observations on Industrialization and Its Effects on Tribal Life," Man in India 42:1 (Jan.-Mar. 1962), 5-9. [India]

4303   Burridge, Kenelm O. L., "Managerial Influences in a Johore Village," J. roy. Asiat. Soc. (Malayan) 30:1 (1957; actual date 1962), 92-114. [Malaysia]

4304   Dalmasso, E., "Une cité minière du Nord-Sahara: Béchar Djédid" [A mining city in the North Sahara: Béchar Djédid], Méditerranée 3:1 (Jan.-Mar. 1962), 21-50. [Algeria]

4305   Forde, Daryll, "Les aspects sociaux de l'industrialisation en Afrique au sud du Sahara dans les régions rurales" [Social aspects of industrialization in the rural regions of Africa south of the Sahara], Int. soc. Sci. Bull.(J.) 9:3 (1957), 421-435.

4306   Freitas Marcondes, J. V., "A agricultura em tempo parcial no estado de São Paulo e a industrialização" [Part-time agriculture in the State of São Paulo and industrialization], Sociologia 24:1 (Mar. 1962), 29-40. [Brazil]

4307   Hoselitz, Bert F., "Economic Growth and Rural Industrialization," Econ. Wkly. 10:8 (22 Feb. 1958), 291-301.

4308   Kurup, A. M., "Changing Phase of Tribal Economy: A Study of Tribal Coal Miners," Bull. tribal Res. Inst. 3:1 (Apr. 1959), 77-91. [India]

4309   Lazarew, P., "Les villages miniers de la région de Khouribga" [Mining villages of the region of Khouribga], Notes maroc. 14 (1960), 39-58. [Morocco]

4310   "Makatea: Bilan socio-économique d'un demi-siècle d'expérience" [Makatea: The socio-economic results of a half-century of experience], J. Soc. Océanist. 15 (1955), 199-210. [Polynesia]

4311   Nash, Manning, "Some Notes on Village Industrialization in South and East Asia," Econ. Dev. cult. Change 3:3 (Apr. 1955), 271-277.

4312   Omi, T. et al., "Tankô to Chiiki Shakai" [The coal mine and the community], Shakai Kagaku Tôkyû 18:2-3 (1963), 1-345. [Japan]

4313   Orans, M., "A Tribal People in an Industrial Setting," J. Am. Folkl. 7:281 (July-Sept. 1958), 422-445. [Indian State of Bihar]

4314   Piegeay, C., "Industrialisation et habitat" [Industrialization and habitation], Encycl. mens. d'outre-mer 5:59 (July 1955), 325-329. [British Caribbean]

4315   Ritzenthaler, R. E., "The Impact of Small Industry on an Indian
        Community," Am. Anthrop. 55:1 (Feb. 1953), 143-148. [India]

4316   Sadie, J. L., "The Industrialization of the Bantu Areas," J. racial
        Aff. 11:2 (Jan. 1960), 57-116. [Republic of South Africa]

4317   Sato, M., "Shikki Kanai Kôgyô Chiiki ni okeru Shihai Taisei no Hendô-
        Akitaken Okatugun Kawatsura Chiku no Baai" [On the change in authority
        structure in a community of the domestic lacquer industry: Kawatsura
        Area, Akita Prefecture], Shakaigaku Hyôron 11:3-4 (1960), 76-92.
        [Japan]

4318   Seshadri, K., "Administration of Rural Small-Scale Industry Develop-
        ment Schemes in Andhra Pradesh, India," J. local Adm. Overseas 4:4
        (1965), 260-69.

4319   Singh, Gurminder, "Social Factors in Adoption of Rural (Subsidiary)
        Industries," All India Congr. Comm. econ. Rev. 16 (25 Oct. 1964),
        27-28.

4320   Srinivas, M. N., "The Industrialization and Urbanization of Rural
        Areas," Sociol. Bull. 5:2 (Sept. 1956), 79-88. [India]

4321   Stepanek, J. E., and C. H. Prien, "The Role of Rural Industries in
        Underdeveloped Areas," Pacif. Aff. 23:1 (Mar. 1950), 65-76. [Asia]

5. General Studies

5301   Adam, A., "L'Influence de l'industrialisation sur la vie sociale au
        Maroc" [The influence of industrialization on social life in Morocco],
        Way Forum 32 (July 1959), 18-21.

5302   Adler, Franz, "Industrial Sociology," in GEN 4380 (1963), 481-518.

5303   Anfossi, A., "Aspetti sociali dell' industrializzazione del mezzo-
        giorno" [Social aspects of the industrialization of southern Italy],
        Nuovo Oss. 4:10 (Jan. 1963), 22-74 and 4:11 (Feb. 1963), 152-158.

5304   Balandier, Georges, "Le développement industriel et la prolétarisation
        en Afrique noire" [Industrial development and proletarization in
        Black Africa], Afr. Asie 20:4 (1952), 45-53.

5305   Banton, M. P., "Les implications sociales de l'industrialisation en
        Afrique au sud du Sahara" [Social implications of industrialization
        in Africa south of the Sahara], Inform. ISSC 25 (July 1960), 1-6.

5306   Bazzanella, W., "Industrialização e urbanização no Brasil" [Indus-
        trialization and urbanization in Brazil], Amér. lat. 6:1 (Jan.-Mar.
        1963), 3-26.

5307   Berna, J. J., "Industrialization in Underdeveloped Countries," Soc.
        Order 7:1 (Jan. 1957), 14-28.

5308   Binet, J., "Industrialisation et sociétés africaines" [Industrial-
        ization and African societies], Rev. Action pop. 144 (Jan. 1961),
        49-63.

5309   Bogardus, E. S., "Social Change in Lebanon," Sociol. soc. Res. 39
        (Mar. 1955), 254-260, bibl.

5310   Busia, K. A., "The Impact of Industrialism on African Communities,"
        in GEN 4398 (1953), 31-37.

5311   Busino, G., "Aspetti sociali dell' industrializzazione in Asia"
        [Social aspects of industrialization in Asia], Tempi mod. 3:3 (Oct.-
        Dec. 1960), 125-141.

5312   Cabrita, H., "Aspectos humanos e sociais de industrialização na
        Africa Portuguesa" [Human and social aspects of industrialization in
        Portuguese Africa], Bol. geral Ultramar 29:340 (Oct. 1953), 55-80.
        [Angola; Mozambique; Portuguese Guinea]

5313   Cola Alberich, J., "Derivaciones sociológicas de la industrialización
        de Africa" [Sociological consequences of the industrialization of
        Africa], Cuad. Estud. afr. 27:3 (1954), 41-50.

5314   Costa Pinto, L. A., "Economic Development in Brazil: A General View
        of Its Sociological Implications," in GEN 4302 (1962), 131-142.

5315   ------ "Economic Development in Brazil: Its Sociological Implica-
        tions," Int. soc. Sci. Bull.(J.) 11:4 (1959), 589-597.

5316   Datta, A., "Industrialisation and Culture," Econ. Wkly. 9:50 (14 Dec.
        1957), 1595-1597.

5317   Deane, Phyllis, "The Industrial Revolution in British Central
        Africa," Civilisations 12:3 (July 1962), 331-355.

5318   De Boer, D., "De industrialisatie van Taiwan (Formosa) in verband
        met de spreiding van de bevolking," Tijdschr. econ. soc. Geogr. 55
        (Feb. 1964), 29-41; and 56 (Mar. 1964), 70-77.

5319   De Briey, P., "L'industrialisation de l'Afrique Centrale et les
        problèmes sociaux qu'elle pose" [Industrialization of Central Africa
        and the problems it poses], Int. Labour Rev. 63:45 (May 1951), 515-
        549.

5320   De Moraes Filho, E., "Algunas consecuencias de la industrialización
        sobre la estructura y la dinámica de la empresa" [Some consequences
        of industrialization on the structure and dynamics of the enterprise],
        Rev. méx. Sociol. 22:1 (Apr. 1960), 67-75. [Latin America]

5321   Desai, A. R., "Soziologische Probleme der Wirtschaftlichen Entwicklung
        Indiens" [Sociological Problems of the Economic Development of India],

Z. ges. Staatswiss. 113 (1957), 128-132.

5322   Edokpayi, S. I., "Industrialisation in West Africa," Afr. Aff. 56:
        225 (Oct. 1957), 317-324.

5323   El-Saaty, Hassan, "Some Aspects of the Social Implications of Techno-
        logical Change in Egypt, U.A.R.," in GEN 4302 (1962), 153-165.

5324   Ford, E., "Impact of Industry on African Peoples," Afr. Wld.
        (July 1955), 13-14.

5325   Forde, Daryll (ed.), Social Implications of Industrialization and
        Urbanization in Africa South of the Sahara. Paris: UNESCO, 1956.
        743 pp.

5326   Froehlich, W. (ed.), Land Tenure, Industrialization and Social
        Stability. Milwaukee, Wis.: Marquette University Press, 1961.
        301 pp.

5327   Galibert, G., "Problèmes humains et économiques de mise en valeur
        industrielle au Sahara occidental" [Human and economic problems of
        the industrialization of West Sahara], Cah. d'outre-mer 11:42 (Apr.-
        June 1958), 142-172.

5328   Glade, W., "Social Backwardness, Social Reform and Productivity in
        Latin America," Inter-Am. econ. Aff. 15 (Winter 1961), 3-32.

5329   Gore, M. S., "India," in GEN 4350 (1963), 178-218.

5330   Grosskopf, J. F. W., "The Position of the Native Population in the
        Economic System of South Africa," Weltwirtschaftliches Archiv 38
        (1933), 414-441.

5331   Gundappa, D. V., "Industrial Technology and Indian Society," Pacif.
        Spectator 9 (Spring 1955), 199-209.

5332   Gupta, S. S. L., "Industrialisierung und Kastenwesen in Indien"
        [Industrialization and caste in India], Uebersee-Rdsch. 9:2 (1957),
        16-18.

5333   Hennessy, L. F., "Indigenous Industrial Organization in Papua and
        New Guinea," Austr. Territ. 4:1 (Feb. 1964), 4-13.

5334   Holness, J., "The Crisis of Colonial Industrial Technique," Présence
        afr. 14:15 (June-Sept. 1957), 84-106. [Africa]

5335   Hoselitz, Bert F., "Emergence and Development of an Industrial Labor
        Force," in GEN 4322 (1964), 143-158.

5336   Husain, A. F. A., "Pakistan," in GEN 4350 (1963), 245-315.

5337   Ianni, O., "Factores humanos de la industrialización en Brasil"
        [Human factors of industrialization in Brazil], Cienc. polít. soc.
        6:20 (Apr.-June 1960), 325-338.

5338   ------ Industrialização e desenvolvimento social no Brasil

[Industrialization and social development in Brazil]. Rio de Janeiro: Editôra Civilização Brasileira, 1963. 269 pp.

5339   Iutaka, S., "Social Mobility and Differential Occupational Opportunity in Brazil," Hum. Organiz. 25:2 (Summer 1966), 126-130.

5340   Jaffe, A. J., People, Jobs and Economic Development: A Case History of Puerto Rico Supplemented by Recent Mexican Experience. Glencoe, Ill.: Free Press, 1959. 381 pp.

5341   Japan Cultural Science Society, Brief Report of Research on the Effect of Modern Industry on Local Communities in 1956. Tokyo: Japanese National Commission for UNESCO, 1959. 48 pp.

5342   ------ Brief Report of Research on the Effect of Modern Industry on Local Communities in 1957. Tokyo: Japanese National Commission for UNESCO, 1960. 61 pp.

5343   Kerr, Clark et al., Industrialism and Industrial Man: The Problems of Labor and Management in Economic Growth. Cambridge, Mass.: Harvard University Press, 1960. 331 pp.

5344   Kirby, A., "Industrialisation in East Africa," Corona Libr. 13:5 (May 1961), 171-174.

5345   Korner, H., "Zur Industrialisierung in Pakistan" [On the industrialization of Pakistan], Wirtschaftsdienst 43:12 (Dec. 1963), 514-519.

5346   Koyama, Elizo, "Social Implications of Technological Change in Japan," in GEN 4302 (1962), 107-116.

5347   Leduc, G. (ed.), Industrialisation de l'Afrique du Nord [Industrialization of North Africa]. Paris: Armand Colin, 1952. 320 pp.

5348   Manndorff, H., "Auswirkungen der Industrialisierung und Verstädterung auf die indische Kasten-Gesellschaft" [Effects of industrialization and urbanization on Indian caste society], Sociologus 8:1 (Apr. 1958), 40-57.

5349   ------ "Die sozialen und kulturellen Auswirkungen den Industrialisierung auf die indische Kasten-Gesellschaft" [The social and cultural effects of industrialization on Indian caste society], Mitt. anthrop. Ges. Wien 87 (1957), 103-105.

5350   ------ "Soziale Umwandlungsprozesse als Folgeerscheinung der Industrialisierung in Südasien" [Social change as the result of industrialization in South Asia], Sociologus 7 (1957), 181-183.

5351   Massachusetts Institute of Technology, Center for International Studies, Stanvac in Indonesia. Washington, D.C.: National Planning Association, 1957. 118 pp.

5352   Matthews, David, "The Systematic Study of Large-Scale Group Conflict," in GEN 4354 (1958), 57-92. [Zambia]

5353   Moore, J. F., "Some Aspects of Industrialization and Co-operative

Development in Underdeveloped Areas," Indian econ. Rev. 1:4 (Aug. 1953), 1-21.

5354   Moore, Wilbert E., and Arnold S. Feldman, Labor Commitment and Social Change in Developing Areas. New York: Social Science Research Council, 1960. 48 pp.

5355   Morgaut, Marc-Edmond, Un dialogue nouveau: L'Afrique et l'industrie [A new dialogue: Africa and industry]. Paris: Arthème Fayard, 1959. 208 pp.

5356   Morris, Morris David, "The Effects of Industrialisation on 'Race' Relations in India," in GEN 4341 (1965), 141-160.

5357   Motwani, K., "The Impact of Modern Technology on the Social Structures of South Asia," in GEN 4356 (1963), 99-109.

5358   Myers, Charles Andrew, Labor Problems in the Industrialization of India. Cambridge, Mass.: Harvard University Press, 1958. 297 pp.

5359   Nash, Manning, "The Multiple Society in Economic Development: Mexico and Guatemala," Am. Anthrop. 59:5 (Oct. 1957), 825-833.

5360   Nay, R., "The Impact of the Oil Industry on the Persian Gulf Shaykedoms," Mid. E. J. 9:4 (Fall 1955), 361-372. [Iran]

5361   Nolte, Richard H., Social Change and Industrialization in Egypt. New York: American University Field Staff, 1955. 31 pp.

5362   Pal, Agaton P., "The Philippines," in GEN 4350 (1963), 316-360.

5363   Patai, R., "The Dynamics of Westernization in the Middle East," Mid. E. J. 9:1 (Winter 1955), 1-16.

5364   Rama, C. M., "Aspectos sociales de la industrialización en el Uruguay" [Social aspects of industrialization in Uruguay], Sociologia 21:4 (Oct. 1959), 418-433.

5365   ------ "Sociological Aspects of Industrialization in Uruguay," Arch. Rechts- Soz. 48:1-2 (1962), 119-133.

5366   Ribadeau-Dumas, J., "Industrialisation outre-mer et problèmes humains" [Industrialization in (French) overseas territories and human problems], Ass. Cadres dir. Ind. B. 120 (Jan. 1958), 19-26. [Africa]

5367   Saigal, J. P., "Personnel Management," in GEN 4380 (1963), 519-532.

5368   Silcock, T. H., "The Effects of Industrialisation on Race Relations in Malaya," in GEN 4341 (1965), 177-199.

5369   Sperling, J. Bodo, Rourkela. Bonn: Eichholz-Verlag, 1963. 79 pp. [Indian State of West Bengal]

5370   Srinivas, M. N., "The Industrialization and Urbanization of Rural Areas," Sociol. Bull. 5:2 (Sept. 1956), 79-88. [India]

5371   Stevens, Siaka, "The West African Miner," in GEN 4338 (1957), 179-184.

5372   Tambiah, S. J., "Ceylon," in GEN 4350 (1963), 44-125.

5373   Topley, M., "Hong Kong," in GEN 4350 (1963), 126-177.

5374   United Nations, Committee on Information from Non-self-governing Territories, Social Aspects of Industrialization in Africa South of the Sahara in Rural Areas. Paris: UNESCO, 1957. 27 pp.

5375   Van der Horst, Sheila, "The Effects of Industrialisation on Race Relations in South Africa," in GEN 4341 (1965), 97-140.

5376   Van der Kroef, Justus M. A., "Social Movements and Economic Development in Indonesia," Am. J. Econ. Sociol. 14:2 (Jan. 1955), 123-137.

5377   ------ "Social Structure and Economic Development in Indonesia," Soc. Res. 23 (1956), 394-418.

5378   Vu, Quôc Thuc, "Viet-Nam," in GEN 4350 (1963), 361-388.

5379   Wilkinson, Thomas O., "Family Structure and Industrialization in Japan," Am. sociol. Rev. 27:5 (Oct. 1962), 678-682.

5380   ------ "Urban Structure and Industrialization," Am. sociol. Rev. 25:3 (June 1960), 356-363. [Japan]

5381   Williams, P. M., "Social Consequences of Industrialism among the Southwestern Yoruba: A Comparative Study," in GEN 4398 (1953), 21-30. [Nigeria]

5382   Yesufu, T. M., An Introduction to Industrial Relations in Nigeria. London: Oxford University Press, 1962. 190 pp.

6. Socioeconomic Studies

A. Social Aspects

6301   Althabe, Gérard, Le chômage à Brazzaville. Etude psychologique [Unemployment in Brazzaville. Psychological study]. Paris: Office de la Recherche Scientifique et Technique Outre-Mer, 1959. 163 pp.

6302   Bettison, David G., Cash Wages and Occupational Structure, Blantyre-Limbe, Nyasaland. Lusaka, Zambia: Rhodes-Livingstone Institute, 1958. 19 mim. pp. [Malawi]

6303   Blake, Donald J., _Indonesian Labor Productivity Monograph_. Djakarta,
        Indonesia: Fakultas Ekonomi, Lambaga Penjelidikan Ekonomi dan
        Masjarakat, Universitas Indonesia, 1962. 55 pp.

6304   Bridgman, F. B., "Social Conditions in Johannesburg," _Int. Rev._
        Missions 15 (1926), 569-583.

6305   Chadda, Tilak Raj, _Socio-economic Survey of an Urban Working Class:_
        An Enquiry into the Cost and Standard of Living of Industrial Workers
        in Peshawar City. Hyderabad, India: Purohit, 196?. 80 pp. [Pakis-
        tan]

6306   Chattopadhyay, K. P., _Municipal Labour in Calcutta_. Calcutta: Cal-
        cutta University Press, 1947. 36 pp. [Indian State of West Bengal]

6307   Devauges, R., _Le chômage à Brazzaville en 1957. Etude sociologique_
        [Unemployment in Brazzaville in 1957. A sociological study]. Paris:
        Office de la Recherche Scientifique et Technique Outre-Mer, 1958.
        258 pp.

6308   Hellmann, Ellen P., _Sellgoods: A Sociological Survey of an African_
        Commercial Labour Force. Cape Town: South African Institute of
        Race Relations, 1953. 68 pp. [Republic of South Africa]

6309   Husain, A. F. A., and A. Farouk, _Social Integration of Industrial_
        Workers in Khulna. Dacca: Bureau of Economic Research, University
        of Dacca, 1963. 207 pp. [East Pakistan]

6310   Ingram, James C., _Economic Change in Thailand since 1850_. Palo Alto:
        Stanford University Press, 1955. 254 pp.

6311   International Labour Organisation, _African Labour Survey._ Geneva:
        International Labour Organisation, 1962. 712 pp.

6312   Kadri, S. K., "An Inquiry into the Socio-Economic Conditions of
        Employees in the Hair-Cutting Establishments in the City of Bombay,"
        J. Univ. Bombay Pt. 4, 21 (Jan. 1953), 91-93. [Indian State of
        Maharashtra]

6313   Khurana, B. K., "A Socio-Economic Study of Clerks," _Sociol. Bull._
        6:1 (Mar. 1957), 72-79 and 7:2 (Sept. 1958), 134-136. [Indian State
        of West Bengal]

6314   Leistner, G. M. E., "Patterns of Urban Bantu Labour: Some Findings
        of a Sample Survey in the Metropolitan Area of Pretoria," _S. afr. J._
        Econ. 32:4 (1964), 253-257.

6315   Lin, S. H., _Factory Workers in Tangku_. Peiping: China Foundation,
        1928. 128 pp.

6316   Mukerjee, Radhakamal, _The Indian Working Class_. Bombay: Hind Kitabs,
        1945. 336 pp.

6317   Northcott, C. H., _African Labour Efficiency_. London: Colonial
        Research Publications, 1949. 123 pp.

6318   O'Grady-Jones, Lorraine, Labor in Sudan. Washington, D.C.: Bureau
        of Statistics, Department of Labor, 1961. 27 pp.

6319   Palacios, L. M., "Encuesta socio-económica de familias de trabajadores
        en Arequipa" [Socioeconomic survey of workers' families in Arequipa],
        Rev. Fac. Cienc. econ. coml. 65 (July-Dec. 1962), 165-170. [Peru]

6320   Perin-Hockers, Maryse, L'absentéisme des travailleurs africains et
        l'instabilité dans les entreprises de la région d'Elisabethville,
        1957-1958 [Absenteeism of African workers in enterprises in the
        region of Elisabethville, 1957-1958]. Brussels: Université Libre,
        1959. 265 pp.

6321   Prabhu, Pandharinath, "Social Effects of Urbanization on Industrial
        Workers in Bombay," Sociol. Bull. 5:1 (Mar. 1956), 30-50; 5:2 (Sept.
        1956), 127-143; 6:1 (Mar. 1957), 14-33. [Indian State of Maharashtra]

6322   UNESCO, Research Center on Social and Economic Development in Southern
        Asia, Social Aspects of Small Industries in India: Studies in Howrah
        and Bombay. Delhi: Research Center on Social and Economic Develop-
        ment in Southern Asia, UNESCO, 1962. 135 pp. [Indian States of
        Maharashtra and West Bengal]

                        B.   Industrial Surveys

6323   Davis, J. Merle (ed.), Modern Industry and the African. London:
        Macmillan, 1933. 433 pp. [Zambia]

6324   Dhar, P. N., Small-Scale Industries in Delhi: A Study in Investment,
        Output and Employment Aspects. Bombay: Asia Publishing House, 1958.
        277 pp. [Indian State of Uttar Pradesh]

6325   Husain, A. F. A., Human and Social Impact of Technological Change in
        Pakistan: A Report on a Survey Conducted by the University of
        Dacca. 2 vols. Dacca: Oxford University Press, 1956. 404 and 344 pp.
        [East Pakistan]

6326   ------ "Human and Social Impact of Technological Change in East
        Pakistan," in GEN 4393 (1956), 107-142. [East Pakistan]

6327   Japan Cultural Science Society, Effect of Modern Industry (Light
        Industry) on Regional Communities. Tokyo: Japanese National
        Committee for UNESCO, 1955. [Japan]

6328   ------ Gijitsu Kakushin no Shakai-teki Eikyō [The sociological
        impact of technological change]. Tokyo: Tokyo University, 1963.
        523 pp.

            Two studies: (1) Tôta automobile factory; and (2) Eastern High
        Pressure's Shigewara factory.

6329   ------ Growth of Modern Industry (Heavy Industry) and Its Influence
        upon the Local Communities. Tokyo: Japanese National Committee for
        UNESCO, 1954.

6330   Siew, Nim Chee, Labour and Tin Mining in Malaya.   Ithaca, N.Y.:
        Southeast Asia Program, Cornell University, 1953.   48 pp.

6331   Xydias, Nelly, "Social Effects of Urbanization in Stanleyville,
        Belgian Congo. Labor: Conditions, Aptitudes, Training," in GEN
        4325 (1956), 275-367.

                        7. Bibliographies

7301   Balandier, Georges, Conséquences sociales de l'industrialisation
        et problèmes urbains en Afrique [Social consequences of industriali-
        zation and urban problems in Africa].   Paris: International Social
        Science Council, 1954.   77 mim. pp.

7302   Dethine, P., Aspects économiques et sociaux de l'industrialisation
        en Afrique [Economic and social aspects of industrialization in
        Africa].   Belgium: Centre d'Etudes Démographiques, Economiques, et
        Sociales d'Afrique, 1961.   136 pp.

7303   McCulloch, Merran, Industrialization in Africa.   Part I: Digest of
        Information concerning Industrialization in Africa.   Part II:
        Survey of Recent and Current Field Studies on the Social Effects
        of Economic Development in Inter-Tropical Africa.   London: Inter-
        national African Institute, 1954.   Pt. I, 118 mim. pp., and Part II,
        113 mim. pp.

7304   Sufrin, Sidney C., and Frank E. Wagner, A Brief Annotated Bibliography
        on Labor in Emerging Societies.   Syracuse, N.Y.:   Maxwell Graduate
        School, Syracuse University, 1961.   64 pp.

7305   United Nations, Bibliography on Industrialization in Under-developed
        Countries.   New York: United Nations, 1956.

PART III. URBANIZATION (URB)

1301-6308

1. The Theory of Urban Social Change

1301   Abu-Lughod, J., "Urban-rural Differences as a Function of the Demo-
        graphic Transition: Egyptian Data and an Analytical Model," Am. J.
        Sociol. 69:5 (Mar. 1964), 476-490.

1302   Balandier, Georges, "Problèmes de désorganisation sociale liés à
        l'industrialisation et à l'urbanisation dans les pays en cours de
        développement économique rapide" [Problems of social disorganiza-
        tion connected with industrialization and urbanization in countries
        undergoing rapid economic development], Inform. ISSC 6 (Oct. 1955),
        1-15.

1303   ------ "Urbanism in West and Central Africa: The Scope and Aims of
        Research," in GEN 4325 (1956), 495-510.

1304   Banton, Michael P., "The Restructuring of Social Relationships," in
        GEN 4384 (1961), 113-125. [Sierra Leone; Zambia]

1305   Bauer, Catherine, "The Pattern of Urban and Economic Development:
        Social Implications," Ann. Am. Acad. polit. soc. Sci. 305 (May 1956),
        60-69.

1306   Beals, Ralph L., "Urbanism, Urbanization and Acculturation," Am.
        Anthrop. 53:1 (Feb. 1951), 1-10.

1307   Benedict, B., "Stratification in Plural Societies," Am. Anthrop.
        64:6 (Dec. 1962), 1235-1246.

1308   Bopegamage, A., "Demographic Approach to the Study of Urban Ecology,"
        Sociol. Bull. 9:1 (Mar. 1960), 82-93.

1309   Bose, Nirmal Kumar, "The Effect of Urbanization on Work and Leisure,"
        Man in India 37:1 (Jan.-Mar. 1957), 1-9. See URB 1310.

1310   Burman, B. K. R., "Observations on 'The Effect of Urbanization on
        Work and Leisure,'" Man in India 37:3 (July-Sept. 1957), 217-229.
        A critique of URB 1309.

1311   Davis, Kingsley, and H. H. Golden, "Urbanization and the Development
        of Pre-Industrial Area," Econ. Dev. cult. Change 3:1 (Oct. 1954),
        6-26.

1312   Desai, A. R., "Urbanization and Social Stratification," Sociol. Bull.
        9:2 (Sept. 1960), 7-14.

1313   Durand, J., "Quelques problèmes à propos des villes à urbanisation
        rapide dans les pays en voie de développement" [Some problems con-
        cerning cities undergoing rapid urbanization in developing
        countries], C. r. mens. Séanc. Acad. Sci. d'outre-mer 22:3 (Mar.
        1962), 108-114.

1314   Gibbs, J. P., and W. T. Martin, "Urbanization and Natural Resources:
        A Study in Organizational Ecology," Am. sociol. Rev. 23:3 (June
        1958), 266-277, bibl.

1315   Ginsberg, Norton S., "The City and Modernization," in GEN 4397
        (1966), 122-137.

1316   Goldthorpe, J. E., "Educated Africans: Some Conceptual and Termi-
        nological Problems," in GEN 4384 (1961), 145-158.

1317   Hauser, Philip M., "Observations on the Urban-Folk and Urban-Rural
        Dichotomies as Forms of Western Ethnocentrism," in GEN 4333 (1966),
        503-518.

1318   Hoselitz, Bert F., "Cities in Advanced and Underdeveloped
        Countries," Confluence 4 (Oct. 1955), 321-334.

1319   ------ "Generative and Parasitic Cities," Econ Dev. cult. Change
        3:3 (Apr. 1955), 278-294.

1320   Lewis, Oscar, "Further Observations on the Folk-Urban Continuum and
        Urbanization with Special Reference to Mexico City," in GEN 4333
        (1966), 491-502.

1321   ------ "Nuevas observaciones sobre el 'continuum' folk-urbano y
        urbanización con especial referencia a México" [New observations on
        the folk-urban continuum and urbanization, with special reference
        to Mexico], Cienc. polít. soc. 9:31 (Jan.-Mar. 1963), 13-28.

1322   Little, Kenneth L., West African Urbanization: A Study of Volun-
        tary Associations in Social Change. London: Cambridge University
        Press, 1965. 179 pp., bibl.

1323   Malengreau, G., "Observations of the Orientation of Sociological
        Researches in African Urban Centres, with Reference to the Situa-
        tion in the Belgian Congo," in GEN 4325 (1956), 624-638.

1324   Marriott, McKim, "Some Comments on William L. Kolb's 'The Structure
        and Functions of Cities' in the Light of India's Urbanizations,"
        Econ. Dev. cult. Change 3:1 (Oct. 1954), 50-52.

1325   Mercier, P., "An Experimental Investigation into Occupational and
        Social Categories in Dakar," in GEN 4325 (1956), 510-523. [Senegal]

1326   Mersadier, Y., "An Experimental Investigation into Urban African
        Standards of Living in Thiès," in GEN 4325 (1956), 535-545.
        [Senegal]

1327   Mitchell, J. Clyde, "Theoretical Orientations in African Urban
        Studies," in GEN 4305 (1966), 37-68.

1328   Naroll, R., "A Preliminary Index of Social Development," Am Anthrop.
        58:4 (Aug. 1956), 687-715.

1329   Pizzorno, Alessandro, "Développement économique et urbanisation"
        [Economic development and urbanization], in GEN 4348 (1962), 91-123.

1330   Redfield, Robert, and M. B. Singer, "The Cultural Role of Cities,"
        Econ. Dev. cult. Change 3:1 (Oct. 1954), 53-73.

1331   Siegel, Bernard J., "The Role of Perception in Urban-Rural Change:
        A Brazilian Case Study," Econ. Dev. cult. Change 5:3 (Apr. 1957),
        244-256.

1332   Sovani, N. V., "The Analysis of 'Over-urbanization,'" Econ. Dev.
        cult. Change 12:2 (Jan. 1964), 113-122.

1333   Srinivas, M. N., "The Industrialization and Urbanization of Rural
        Areas," Sociol. Bull. 5:2 (Sept. 1956), 79-88.

1334   Thompson, Wilbur R., "Urban Economic Growth and Development in a
        National System of Cities," in GEN 4333 (1966), 431-490.

1335   UNESCO Regional Seminar on Urban-Rural Differences and Relationships
        in Southern Asia, Urban-Rural Differences in Southern Asia; Some
        Aspects and Methods of Analysis: Report. Delhi: UNESCO Research
        Center on Social and Economic Development in Southern Asia, 1964.
        147 pp.

1336   Woortman, J., "Implicaçãoes sociais do desenvolvimento da urbanização"
        [Social implications of development and of urbanization], Educ. Ciênc.
        soc. 10:20 (May-Aug. 1962), 110-119.

                         2. Urban Problems

                      A. Annotated Case Studies

*2001   Althabe, G., Le chômage à Brazzaville: Etude psychologique [Unem-
        ployment in Brazzaville: Psychological study]. Paris: Office de la
        Recherche Scientifique et Technique Outre-Mer, 1959. 163 pp.

        Shows a widespread feeling of revolt against the whites.

                              [109]

*2002   Baeck, Louis, "An Expenditure Study of the Congolese Evolués of
           Leopoldville, Belgian Congo," in GEN 4384 (1961), 159-181.

               The "demonstration effect" is strong among the Westernized natives
           as they spend almost all of their marginal income on consumption.

2003   Balandier, Georges, Sociologie des Brazzavilles noires [Sociology of
           the Black Brazzavillians]. Paris: A. Colin, 1965. 274 pp.

               A study of the adaptation of the West and Equatorial Africans to
           life in a city. The author is particularly interested in the roles
           of the government and the common worker.

2004   Banton, Michael P., "Adaptation and Integration in the Social System
           of Temne Immigrants in Freetown," Africa 26:4 (Oct. 1956), 354-368.
           [Sierra Leone]

               A historical and sociological study showing that while these immi-
           grants as individuals adapt to city life, their tribe is not integrated
           into the urban pattern. This fact proves to be a point of social
           disintegration.

**2005   ------ "The Restructuring of Social Relationships," in GEN 4384
           (1961), 113-125. [Sierra Leone; Zambia]

               A comparison of two urban studies, J. C. Mitchell's Kalela Dance
           and M. P. Banton's West African City: A Study of Tribal Life in Free-
           town. Change is thought to come from the changing obligations of
           individuals. Freetown (a Creole city) has adopted European ways as
           the destruction of the tribal structure has created new obligations
           among individuals. In Northern Rhodesia, the traditional tribal
           obligations have remained--thus there has been little change.

**2006   ------ West African City: A Study of Tribal Life in Freetown.
           London: Oxford University Press, 1957. 228 pp. [Sierra Leone]

               The case of Freetown is unique because of the continued influence
           of the tribal headmen installed in the city by the British. The
           study describes the results of this tribal adaptation to city life
           as opposed to the tribal disorganization usually associated with
           urbanizing Africa.

*2007   Barnes, J. A., "The Fort Jameson Ngoni," in GEN 4317 (1951), 194-252.

               The Ngoni who have migrated to the city are more like other towns-
           men than like their fellow tribesmen in the villages.

2008   Calderón Alvarado, L., Poder retentivo del "área local urbana" en las
           relaciones sociales. Investigación en tres áreas de deferente clase
           social: alta, media y baja, en Bogotá [Retentive power of the "local
           urban area" in social relations. An investigation of three different
           social class areas: upper, middle, and lower in Bogotá]. Fribourg,
           Switzerland: Fédération Européenne de Recherche Economique et Social,
           1963. 216 pp.

**2009   Clément, Pierre, "Social Effects of Urbanization in Stanleyville,
           Belgian Congo: Social Patterns of Urban Life," in GEN 4325 (1956),
           368-492.

           The wealth of voluntary organizations in modern Africa reflects
           the Africans' need for security in an urban environment. These
           associations are very much oriented toward an évolué status.

2010   Cohn, Bernard S., "Changing Traditions of a Low Caste," in GEN 4379
           (1959), 207-215. [North India]

           A study of the Camars of Northern India. Urban contact has
           tended to raise their status through Sanskritization, greater
           participation in Hindu culture, and political action by urban
           college students.

2011   Desmukh, M. B., "A Study of Floating Migration," in GEN 4393 (1956),
           143-226. [Indian State of Uttar Pradesh]

           Migrants tend not to adapt, yet their original reasons for coming
           to the city tend to keep them there.

**2012   Dethier, Robert, Les citadins katangais et leur jardin: Aspects
           psycho-sociaux de la vie en milieu africain urbain [City dwellers
           of Katanga and their garden: Psychosocial aspects of life in an
           urban African milieu]. Liège, Belgium: Imprimerie Vaillant-Carmanne,
           1961. 103 pp. [Congo (Leopoldville)]

           Improvements in the existing garden plots are not being carried
           out for lack of social motivation. Garden cultivation is associated
           with farming and thus with a traditional occupation. Only at a
           higher level does it become socially acceptable.

***2013   ------   Une famille de citadins du Katanga [A family of city
           dwellers in Katanga]. Liège, Beligum: Institut de Sociologie de la
           Faculté de Droit, 1961. 75 pp. [Congo (Leopoldville)]

           A study of an évolué who has been greatly influenced by European
           ways. He resents not being accepted by Europeans, even though he
           has not yet fully adopted their ways. He is an uprooted individual--
           no longer in his tribe but with only a vague image of the life of a
           white man. Despite his lack of contact with the white world and of
           proper school education, he wants to emulate the white man's ways,
           since he considers them more "powerful."

*2014   Devauges, R., Le chômage à Brazzaville en 1957: Etude sociologique
           [Unemployment in Brazzaville in 1957: A sociological study]. Paris:
           Office de la Recherche Scientifique et Technique Outre-Mer, 1958.
           258 pp.

           The author stresses the natives desire to stay in the city, even
           if work is lacking or his salary is lowered.

*2015   Germani, Gino, "Inquiry into the Social Effects of Urbanization in a
           Working-Class Sector of Greater Buenos Aires," in GEN 4332 (1961),
           206-233.

A study conducted by questionnaire. The author thoroughly covers
adaptation both to the job and to the city. He finds a general trend
to demoralization among the migrants.

2016   Gluckman, Max, "Anthropological Problems Arising from the African
        Industrial Revolution," in GEN 4384 (1961), 67-82. [Zambia; S. Rhodesia]

        A summary of work done by the Rhodes-Livingstone Institute, in
        particular, that of A. L. Epstein and J. C. Mitchell (Kalela Dance).
        The emphasis falls on the survival of tribal ties in the towns in a
        form sharper than is to be found in European towns.

2017   Gulliver, P. H., Labour Migration in a Rural Economy--A Study of the
        Ngoni and Ndendeuli of Southern Tanganyika. Kampala, Uganda: East
        African Institute of Social Research, 1955. 48 pp.

        A study of the effects of migration. The author emphasizes the
        lowered morality of the migrants.

2018   Halpern, Joel M., Government, Politics, and Social Structure in Laos:
        A Study of Tradition and Innovation. New Haven: Southeast Asia
        Studies, Yale University, 1964. 184 pp.

        A number of short autobiographies of urban elite and urban
        workers.

**2019   Hellmann, Ellen P., "The Native in the Towns," in GEN 4372 (1937),
        405-434. [Republic of South Africa]

        Though natives are excluded from European society in South
        African tours, cultural change has come about by a fusion of native
        and European elements. This fusion, however, seems to be very fluid
        and insecure.

***2020   ------ Rooiyard: A Sociological Survey of an Urban Slum Yard. Cape
        Town: Oxford University Press, 1948. 125 pp. See also GEN 4363
        (1960), 546-564. [Republic of South Africa]

        A study conducted in Johannesburg in 1935 by means of interviews.
        The European world seems to have had a great attraction for the
        natives, but at the same time it has left them in disorder and chaos.
        They are highly distrustful of Europeans, who seem to have greatly
        mistreated them.

2021   Lambiri, Ioanna, Social Change in a Greek Country Town: The Impact
        of Factory Work on the Position of Women. Athens: Center of
        Planning and Economic Research, 1965. 163 pp.

        Despite early opposition to women's working in a factory, it has
        gradually been accepted.

2022   Little, Kenneth L. West African Urbanization: A Study of Voluntary
        Associations in Social Change. London: Cambridge University Press,
        1965. 180 pp.

        The voluntary associations form a bridge between the urban setting and the formal structure of the tribe.

**2023   Lopes, Juarez Rubens Brandão, "Aspects of the Adjustment of Rural
         Migrants to Urban-Industrial Conditions in São Paulo, Brazil," in GEN
         4332 (1961), 234-248.

         A study of production-line operators from two different rural
         origins: one from a semisubsistence economy (individual males), and
         the other from a rural market economy (nuclear families). The author
         finds that (1) the workers want to return to the countryside as soon
         as they have saved enough money to buy a bit of land; (2) the rural
         control patterns remain in the individual but are weakened by contact
         with others who do not follow these patterns; and (3) these workers do
         no participate in collective action because it has no corollary in
         their rural society and because they do not want to identify themselves
         with the city.

2024   McCall, Daniel F., "The Koforidua Market," in GEN 4312 (1962), 667-
         697.

         A descriptive study of Ghana.

2025   Matos-Mar, J., "Migration and Urbanization: The 'Barriadas' of Lima:
         An Example of Integration into Urban Life," in GEN 4332 (1961), 170-
         190.

         A study of the new slum areas in Lima settled by new immigrants
         to the city. They have come primarily for economic reasons but also
         out of a desire to become more modern.

2026   Mayer, Philip, and I. Mayer, Townsmen or Tribesmen: Conservatism
         and the Process of Urbanization in a South African City. Cape Town:
         Oxford University Press, 1961. 306 pp.

         Town society is divided into three levels of acculturation, each
         forming its own group--a traditional group, a modern rural group,
         and an urban group. A study that is largely descriptive, since the
         authors' white skin blocked a deeper study.

2027   Miner, Horace M., and G. De Vos, Oasis and Casbah: Algerian Culture
         and Personality in Change. Ann Arbor: University of Michigan Press,
         1960. 236 pp.

         A description of the relations between Algerian personality and
         culture under the impact of life in France or in the Algerian cities.

2028   Miracle, Marvin P., "African Markets and Trade in the Copperbelt," in
         GEN 4312 (1962), 698-738.

         The African trader shows sensitivity to conditions of demand and
         supply in so far as he has any knowledge of them.

**2029   Mitchell, J. Clyde, The Kalela Dance. Manchester, Eng.: Manchester
         University Press, 1956. 52 pp., bibl. [Zambia]

         The Kalela dance is performed by teams who are dressed as Europeans and mock other tribes. Tribal attachments have been retained in the city but merely as joking rivalries.

2030   Mukwaya, A. B., "The Marketing of Staple Foods in Kampala, Uganda," in GEN 4312 (1962), 643-666. [Uganda]

    A descriptive study.

2031   Pearse, Andrew, "Some Characteristics of Urbanization in the City of Rio de Janeiro," in GEN 4332 (1961), 191-205.

    An analysis of the shift from rural dependence to urban independence that comes with migration to the city.

**2032   Pizzorno, Alessandro, Comunità e razionalizzazione: Ricerca sociologica su un caso di sviluppo industriale [Community and rationalization: Sociological case study of industrial development]. Turin: Einaudi, 1960. 431 pp.

    A case study, containing many life histories, of a developing town near Milan. The author finds that the strongest resistance is to purely technological changes or to "change out of rhythm." There is a keen desire for house ownership (a sign of the disaggregation of the family) and a tendency for the circoli to die out in favor of individual action.

***2033   Pons, V. G., "Two Small Groups in Avenue 21: Some Aspects of the System of Social Relations in a Remote Corner of Stanleyville, Belgian Congo," in GEN 4384 (1961), 205-216.

    A study in the early 1950's of two reactions to an urban setting, both fairly free of tribalism. One was a formal association of friends, on a European model; the other, a spontaneous grouping of strangers in the local store.

2034   Prabhu, Pandharinath, "A Study on the Social Effects of Urbanization," in GEN 4393 (1956), 49-106. [Indian State of Maharashtra]

    A study of Bombay, presenting many figures but little analysis, that suggests a general weakening of traditional values among migrants to the city.

*2035   Reader, D. H., The Black Man's Portion: History, Demography, and Living Conditions in the Native Locations of East London, Cape Province. Cape Town: Oxford University Press, 1961. 180 pp. [Republic of South Africa]

    This study underlines the intense hostility and the lack of understanding between the Blacks and the Whites. The natives engage in illegal commercial activities, partly out of desperation and partly because their need of money is stronger than their fear of the police.

*2036   Schwab, W. B., "Social Stratification in Gwele," in GEN 4384 (1961), 126-144. [Southern Rhodesia]

    This study derives from a field survey of a town in Southern

Rhodesia. Though tribal affiliations are still strong, the individual is evaluated by Western standards; social stratification is thus based on job categories and other symbols of European origin, such as education. This system applies only to men, as their families are usually left behind in the village.

**2037 Singer, Milton B., "The Great Tradition in a Metropolitan Center: Madras," in GEN 4379 (1959), 141-182. [Indian State of Madras]

Traditional forms are shifting from religious to cultural character. This change signifies not so much a secularization as a democratization.

2038 Sofer, Cyril, and Rhona Sofer, Jinja Transformed. Kampala, Uganda: East African Institute of Social Research, 1955. 120 pp.

A study of a small town in Uganda not yet industrialized. The authors are particularly interested in how the problem of racial harmony affects the residents' adaptation to town life.

*2039 Southall, A. W., "Determinants of the Social Structure of African Urban Populations, with Special Reference to Kampala, Uganda," in GEN 4325 (1956), 557-590.

Here social status is determined largely by influence, for which the essential is chiefly wealth, but also tribal origin.

**2040 ------ "Kinship, Friendship, and the Network of Relations in Kisenyi, Kampala," in GEN 4384 (1961), 217-229. [Uganda]

A study of a section of a Central African town conducted by means of a questionnaire. There seem to be few structural group patterns-- "order" is generally thought to be external to the individual. The two key factors in the social network are tribal affiliation and the women beer sellers, who provide a motive and locale for social contacts.

2041 Sovani, N. V., and K. Pradhan, "Occupational Mobility in Poona City between Three Generations," Indian econ. Rev. 2:4 (Aug. 1955), 23-36. [Indian State of Maharashtra]

Families evince a strong tendency to remain stationary.

2042 Tan, Giok-lan, The Chinese of Sukabumi: A Study in Social and Cultural Accommodation. Ithaca: Modern Indonesia Project, Cornell University, 1963. 314 pp. [Indonesia]

The author finds little social interaction, but nevertheless a considerable acculturation on the part of the Chinese.

***2043 Tardits, Claude, Porto-Novo: Les nouvelles générations africaines entre leurs traditions et l'Occident [Porto-Novo: The new generations of Africans between their traditions and the West]. Paris: Mouton, 1958. 128 pp. [Dahomey]

A study of a society in which modern and traditional patterns coexist. Traditionally, this society has always been competitive, and this characteristic has now been extended to economic matters, in particular, to the pursuit of small businesses and to pressing their demands on the whites. Women and unions are in the forefront of these activities.

2044   Van den Berghe, Pierre L., <u>Caneville: The Social Structure of a South African Town</u>. Middletown: Wesleyan University Press, 1964. 276 pp.

    Acculturation to European urban life has taken place in Caneville, even though the African has no chance of being admitted to European society, which blocks integration.

**2045   Van Velsen, J., "Labour Migration as a Positive Factor in the Continuity of Tonga Tribal Society," GEN 4384 (1961), 230-241. [Malawi]

    A study conducted in Nyasaland in the early 1950's. Traditional values predominate in this region, in spite of a marked tendency to migrate to the nearby towns. One reason for the persistence of traditional values is thought to be the denial to the migrants of a "full" town life, for wages are fixed at a level sufficient only for a bachelor.

*2046   Vilakazi, Absolom, <u>Zulu Transformations: A Study of the Dynamics of Social Change</u>. Pietermaritzburg, South Africa: University of Natal Press, 1962. 168 pp. [Republic of South Africa]

    The urbanized Zulu seems to be far more individualistic than his traditionalist counterpart. Coupled with this individualism is an increasing receptivity to new ideas along with a decreasing emotional security.

2047   Willmott, Donald Earl, <u>The Chinese of Semarang: A Changing Minority Community in Indonesia</u>. London: Oxford University Press, 1961. 374 pp.

    The author finds an "emergent change"--contractual relations are replacing those based on trust--as the scope of economic activity enlarges.

**2048   Wilson, Godfrey, <u>An Essay on the Economics of Detribalization in Northern Rhodesia</u>. Lusaka, Zambia: Rhodes-Livingstone Institute, Vol. 1, 1941; Vol. 2, <u>1942</u>. 71 and 82 pp. [Zambia]

    Low wages and poor conditions allow only the able-bodied young men to stay in Broken Hill, an industrial town. Some young women as well join the men. This emigration of the most able destroys the basis for rural farming and drives more and more individuals to the town. As a result urban wages are law, and gifts to the rural inhabitants do not compensate for the lost labor force.

**2049   Wilson, Monica H., and A. Mafeje, <u>Langa: A Study of the Social Groups in an African Township</u>. Cape Town: Oxford University Press, 1963. 190 pp. [Republic of South Africa]

A study of a Cape Town suburb, in which relationships are based on association rather than on kinship, as in rural areas. Color discrimination exerts a powerful influence that incites the evasion of law and breeds a deepening bitterness.

2050   Wolf, E. R., "San José: Subcultures of a Traditional Coffee Municipality," in GEN 4387 (1956), 171-264. [Puerto Rico]

A study of a medium-sized town with a number of family case histories.

                            B.   Other Case Studies

2301   Abrahams, R. G., "Kahama Township, Western Province, Tanganyika," in GEN 4384 (1961), 242-253.

2302   Abu-Lughod, J., "Urban-rural Differences as a Function of the Demographic Transition: Egyptian Data and an Analytical Model," Am. J. Sociol. 69:5 (Mar. 1964), 476-490. [Egypt]

2303   Back, Kurt W., Slums, Projects, and People: Social Psychological Problems of Relocation in Puerto Rico. Durham, N.C.: Duke University Press, 1962. 123 pp.

2304   Ballinger, M., "Native Life in South African Towns," J. roy. Afr. Soc. 37 (1938), 326-338.

2305   Balsara, J. F., "Urban Community Development," Indian J. soc. Wk. 18:1 (June 1957), 1-6. [Indian State of Maharashtra]

2306   Banton, Michael P., "Adaptation and Integration in the Social System of Temne Immigrants in Freetown," in GEN 4396 (1966), 402-419. [Sierra Leone]

2307   ------ "Economic Development and Social Change in Sierra Leone," Econ. Dev. soc. Change 2:2 (July 1953), 136-138.

2308   Bascom, William R., "Some Aspects of Yoruba Urbanism," Am. Anthrop. 64:4 (Aug. 1962), 699-709. [Nigeria]

2309   ------ "Urbanization among the Yoruba," in GEN 4363 (1960), 255-267. Repr. from Am. J. Sociol. 60 (1955), 446-454. [Nigeria]

2310   Benedict, Burton, Indians in a Plural Society: A Report on Mauritius. London: HMSO, 1961. 168 pp.

2311   Benoist, J., "Les Martiniquais: Anthropologie d'une population métissée" [The residents of Martinique: Anthropology of a hybrid population], Bull. Mém. Soc. Anthrop. Paris 4-9:2 (Apr.-June 1963), 241-432.

2312   Bernus, E., "Note sur l'agglomération d'Abidjan et sa population"
          [Note on the urban area of Abidjan and its population], Bull. Inst.
          fr. Afr. noire 24:1 (Jan.-Apr. 1962), 54-85. [Ivory Coast]

2313   Bonnigue, A., "Banlieu de Bangkok: L'homme dilué" [A Bangkok suburb:
          Man diluted], Rev. Action pop: 168 (May 1963), 595-600. [Thailand]

2314   Bopegamage, A., Delhi: A Study in Urban Sociology. Bombay: University
          of Bombay Press, 1957. 235 pp. [Indian State of Uttar Pradesh]

2315   ------ "Neighbourhood Relations in Indian Cities--Delhi," Sociol.
          Bull. 6:1 (Mar. 1957), 34-43. [Indian State of Uttar Pradesh]

2316   ------ "A Village Within a Metropolitan Area," Sociol. Bull. 5:2
          (Sept. 1956), 102-110. [India]

2317   Bose, Nirmal Kumar, "Effect of Urbanization on Work and Leisure,"
          Man in India 37:1 (Jan.-Mar. 1957), 1-9. [Indian State of West
          Bengal]

              Pages 10-33 contain a report of the field work carried out at
          Amdabad and Panihati by B. Bandopadhyaya.

2318   ------ "Social and Cultural Life in Calcutta," Geogr. Rev. India
          20:1 (1958), 1-46. [Indian State of West Bengal]

2319   ------ "Some Aspects of Caste in Bengal," in GEN 4379 (1959), 191-
          206. [Indian State of West Bengal]

2320   Brisseau, J., "Les 'Barrios' de Petare, faubourgs populaires d'une
          banlieu de Caracas" [The "Barrios" of Petare, the working class
          districts of a Caracas suburb], Cah. d'outre-mer 16:61 (Jan.-Mar.
          1963), 5-42. [Venezuela]

2321   Bruner, E. M., "Urbanization and Ethnic Identity in North Sumatra,"
          Am. Anthrop. 63:3 (June 1961), 508-521, bibl. [Indonesia]

2322   Butterworth, D. S., "A Study of the Urbanization Process among
          Mixtec Migrants from Tilantongo in Mexico City," Amér. indíg. 22:3
          (July 1962), 257-274. [Mexico]

2323   Callaway, A., "Unemployment among African School Leavers," J. mod.
          Afr. Stud. 1:3 (Sept. 1963), 351-371.

2324   Capelle, E., La cité indigène de Léopoldville [The native quarter of
          Leopoldville]. Léopoldville: Centre d'Etudes Sociales Africaines,
          1947. 137 pp. [Congo]

2325   Caplow, Theodore, "The Scoial Ecology of Guatemala City," GEN 4390
          (1961), 331-347.

2326   Caplow, T., S. Stryker, and S. E. Wallace, The Urban Ambience: A
          Study of San Juan, Puerto Rico. Totowa, N.J.: Bedminster Press,
          1964. 243 pp.

2327   Carail, J., "La création urbaine au Sahara pétrolier: Hassi-Messaoud,

1956-1962" [Urban development in the Sahara oil fields, Hassi-
Messaoud, 1956-1962], Vie urbaine 2 (Apr.-June 1964), 113-160 and
3 (July-Sept. 1964), 197-224. [Algeria]

2328   Cardoso, F. E., and O. Ianni, "Conditiones y efectos de la industrial-
izacion de São Paulo" [Conditions and effects of the industrialization
of São Paulo], Cienc. polít. soc. 5:18 (Oct.-Dec. 1959), 577-584.
[Brazil]

2329   Choudhury, Anjana Roy, "Caste and Occupation in Bhowanipur, Calcutta,"
Man in India 44:3 (July-Sept. 1964), 207-220. [Indian State of West
Bengal]

2330   Clinard, Marshall B., and B. Chatterjee, "Urban Community Development
in India: The Delhi Pilot Project," in GEN 4391 (1962), 71-93.
[Indian State of Uttar Pradesh]

2331   Cohen, A., "Politics of the Kola Trade: Some Processes of Tribal
Community among Migrants in West African Towns," Africa 36:1 (Jan.
1966), 18-36.

2332   Comhaire, Jean L., "Some Aspects of Urbanization in the Belgian
Congo," Am. J. Sociol. 62:1 (July 1956), 8-13.

2333   Cruago, Paitoon, "Changing Thai Society: A Study of the Impact of
Urban Cultural Traits and Behavior upon Rural Thailand." Ph.D.
dissertation, Cornell University, 1962. 109 mim. pp.

2334   Daumezon, G. et al., "L'incidence psychopathologique sur une population transplantée d'origine Nord-Africaine" [Psychopathological
incidence among a transplanted population of North African origin],
Monogr. Inst. natn. Hyg. 7 (1955), 83-125. [North Africa]

2335   De Bruyn, J. V., "Urban Local Government in the South Pacific," Mens
en Maatschappij 41:3 (1966), 183-194. [Polynesia]

2336   De Recasens, M. R. M., "Estudio del ritmo de vida en una pequeña
communidad urbana" [Study of the rhythm of life in a small urban
community], Rev. colomb. Antrop. 11 (1962), 189-238. [Colombia]

2337   De Ridder, J. C., The Personality of the Urban African in South
Africa. London: Routledge & Kegan Paul, 1961. 180 pp.

2338   Devanandan, P. D., and M. M. Thomas, Community Development in India's
Industrial Urban Areas. Bangalore, India: Committee for Literature
on Social Concerns, 1958. 151 pp. [India]

2339   Dupon, F., "Tambacounda, capitale du Sénégal oriental" [Tambacounda,
capital of Eastern Senegal], Cah. d'outre-mer 17:66 (Apr.-June 1964),
175-214.

2340   Eames, E., "Some Aspects of Urban Migration from a Village in North
Central India," East. Anthrop. 8:1 (Sept. 1954), 13-26.

2341   Epstein, A. L., Politics in an Urban African Community. Manchester,
England: Manchester University Press, 1960. 254 pp. [Zambia]

2342   ------ "Urban Communities in Africa," in GEN 4329 (1964), 83-102.

2343   Fougeurollas, P., "Phénomènes d'acculturation chez les étudiants
         de la cité universitaire de Dakar" [Acculturation phenomena among
         students in the university living quarters of Dakar], Rev. fr. Sociol.
         4:4 (Oct.-Dec. 1963), 411-423. [Senegal]

2344   Fraenkel, Merran, Tribe and Class in Monrovia. London: Oxford Uni-
         versity Press, 1964. 244 pp.

2345   Franchi, J., "Urbanisation d'un bidonville: Bordj Moulay Omar
         (Meknès)" [Urbanization of a shanty town: Bordj Moulay Omar
         (Meknès)], Bull. econ. soc. Maroc 23:83 (Jan. 1960), 255-291.
         [Morocco]

2346   Fried, Morton H., Fabric of Chinese Society: A Study of the Social
         Life of a Chinese County Seat. New York: Praeger, 1953. 243 pp.

2347   Gamble, Sidney D., and J. S. Burgess, Peking: A Social Survey. New
         York: George H. Doran, 1921. 538 pp.

2348   Gast, Marceau, "Evolution de la vie économique et structure sociale en
         Ahaggar, de 1660 à 1965" [Evolution of economic life and social
         structure in Ahaggar from 1660 to 1965], Trav. Inst. Rech. saharéennes
         24:1-2 (1965), 129-143. [Algeria]

2349   Geertz, Clifford, "Social Change and Economic Modernization in Two
         Indonesian Towns: A Case in Point," in GEN 4319 (1967), 366-394.
         [Indonesia]

2350   ------ The Social History of an Indonesian Town. Cambridge, Mass.:
         M.I.T. Press, 1965. 217 pp.

2351   Ghurye, G. S., "Bombay Suburbanites: Some Aspects of Their Working
         Life," Sociol. Bull. 13:2 (Sept. 1964), 73-83.

2352   Guha, Meera, "Social Institutions in a Municipal Ward in Calcutta,"
         Man in India 42:3 (July-Sept. 1962), 181-194. [Indian State of West
         Bengal]

2353   Grieveson, E. T., "Educational Needs of Urbanised Natives in South
         Africa," J. roy. Afr. Soc. 36 (1937), 321-336.

2354   Guha, Meera, "The Definition of an Indian Urban Neighborhood," Man
         in India 46:1 (Jan.-Mar. 1966), 59-65.

2355   Gussman, Boris W., African Life in an Urban Area. Bulawayo, unknown,
         1952. [Southern Rhodesia]

2356   Gutkind, Peter C. W., "Accommodation and Conflict in an African Peri-
         Urban Area," Anthropologica 4:1 (1962), 163-174. [Uganda]

2357   ------ The Royal Capital of Buganda: A Study of Internal Conflict and
         External Ambiguity. The Hague: Mouton, 1963. 330 pp. [Uganda]

2358   Habibullah, M., Pattern of Urban Savings: A Case Study of Dacca

City. Dacca: Bureau of Economic Research, Dacca University, 1964.
144 pp. [East Pakistan]

2359   Haider, Agha Sajjad, Village in an Urban Orbit: Shah-Di-Khui, A
        Village in Lahore Urban Area. Lahore: Social Science Research
        Council, University of Punjab, 1960. 35 pp. [Indian State of
        Punjab]

2360   Hair, P. E. H., "An Industrial and Urban Community in East Nigeria,
        1914-1953," in GEN 4398 (1953), 143-169.

2361   Hasegawa, A., "Kyotofu-ka Noson no Toshi eno Izon Kankei" [Dependent
        relations of rural communities to urban centers in the Kyoto prefec-
        ture], Kyoto Gakujitsu Hokoku 13 (1961), 1-14. [Japan]

2362   Hellmann, Ellen P., "The Importance of Beer-Brewing in an Urban
        Native Yard," Bantu Stud. 8 (1934), 39-60.

2363   ------ "Native Life in a Johannesburg Slum Yard," Africa 8 (1935),
        34-62. [Republic of South Africa]

2364   Henrard, L., "L'urbanisation de la province" [The urbanization of the
        provinces], Industrie 12:6 (1958), 431-442. [Leopoldville, Congo]

2365   Hollnsteiner, M. R., The Dynamics of Power in a Philippine Munici-
        pality. Quezon City: University of the Philippines, 1963. 227 pp.

2366   Honrao, M. S., "Urban Features of Bijapur," J. Karnatak Univ. (Hum.)
        4 (June 1960), 64-74. [Indian State of Mysore]

2367   Hutchinson, B., "Urban Social Mobility Rates in Brazil Related to
        Migration and Changing Occupational Structure," Amér. lat. 6:3
        (July-Sept. 1963), 47-61.

2368   Hutt, W. H., "The Economic Position of the Bantu in South Africa," in
        GEN 4373 (1934), 195-237.

2369   Institute of Economic and Social Research, "A Study of Urbanization,"
        in GEN 4393 (1956), 227-266. [Indonesia]

2370   Isomura, E., "Koiki Toshi no Keshiki to Mondai" [Some problems of the
        structure of the regional city], Toshi Mondai Kenkyu 15:10 (1963),
        3-13. [Japan]

2371   Jabavu, N., The Ochre People: Scenes from a South African Life. New
        York: St. Martin's Press, 1963. 261 pp.

2372   Kahl, J. A., "Urbanização e mudanças ocupacionais no Brasil" [Urbani-
        zation and occupational change in Brazil], Amér. lat. 5:4 (Oct.-Dec.
        1962), 21-29.

2373   Kaldate, Sudha, "Urbanization and Disintegration of Rural Joint
        Family," Sociol. Bull. 11 (1962), 103-111. [India]

2374   Kapadia, K. M., "The Growth of Townships in South Gujarat: Maroli
        Bazar," Sociol. Bull. 10:2 (Sept. 1961), 69-87. [Indian State of
        Gujarat]

2375   Kay, P., "Aspects of Social Structure in a Tahitian Urban Neighbour-
        hood," J. Polynesian Soc. 72:4 (Dec. 1963), 325-371.

2376   Khin, Ma Lay, "Urban Study of the Sittang Valley," J. Burma Res. Soc.
        45 (Dec. 1962), 163-180. [Burma]

2377   Kinai, Senji, "The Slums of Kamagasaki," Orient/West 7:3 (Mar. 1962),
        69-73. [Japan]

2378   "Kotla Mubarakpur--An Urban Village," Urb. rur. Plann. Thought 1:1
        (Jan. 1958), 41-54. [Indian State]

2379   Kurasawa, S., "Toshi-ka to Chiiki Soshiki" [Urbanization and neighbor-
        hood], Shakai Kyoiku Kenkyujo 18:10 (1963), 8-13. [Japan]

2380   Lai, D. C. Y., and D. J. Dwyer, "Tsuen Wan: A New Industrial Town in
        Hong Kong," Geogr. Rev. 54:2 (Apr. 1964), 151-169.

2381   Laquian, A. A., "Isla de Kokomo: Politics Among Urban Slum Dwellers,"
        Philipp. J. pub. Adm. 8:2 (Apr. 1964), 112-122.

2382   Lee, Sang-Beck, "Social Stratification and Mobility in Three Cities
        of Korea," E. Asian cult. Stud. 4 (Mar. 1965), 127-132.

2383   Lenhard, R., "Actividades económicas na cidade de São José do Rio
        Prêto" [Economic activity in the city of São José do Rio Prêto],
        Sociologia 26:2 (June 1964), 171-182. [Brazil]

2384   ------ "Hierarquias sociais urbanas" [Urban social hierarchies],
        Sociologia 25:3 (Sept. 1963), 253-270. [Brazil]

2385   "Léopoldville et Lagos. Etude comparée des conditions urbaines en
        1960" [Leopoldville and Lagos: Comparative study of urban condi-
        tions in 1960], Bull. écon. Afr. 1:2 (June 1961), 54-70. [Congo
        (Leopoldville); Nigeria]

2386   Leubuscher, C., Die Südafrikanischen Eingeborenen als Industriear-
        beiter und als Stadtbewohner [The South African native as industrial
        worker and city dweller]. Jena, East Germany: Fischer, 1931.
        222 pp.

2387   Little, Kenneth L., "Some Traditionally Based Forms of Mutual Aid in
        West African Urbanization," Ethnology 1:2 (Apr. 1962), 197-211.
        [Sierra Leone]

2388   ------ "Structural Change in the Sierra Leone Protectorate," Africa
        25:3 (July 1955), 217-234.

2389   ------ "The Urban Role of Tribal Associations in West Africa," Afr.
        Stud. 21:1 (March 1962), 1-9.

2390   Lloyd, P. C., "Yoruba Towns," Ibadan 9 (June 1960), 26-29. [Nigeria]

2391   Mabogunje, A. L., Yoruba Towns. Ibadan: Ibadan University Press,
        1962. 22 pp. [Nigeria]

2392   Mabogunje, A. L., and M. O. Oyawoye, "The Problems of the Northern
        Yoruba Towns," Nigerian geogr. J. 4:2 (Dec. 1961), 2-10.

2393   McCulloch, Meran, "Survey of Recent and Current Field Studies on the
        Social Effects of Economic Development in Inter-tropical Africa," in
        GEN 4325 (1956), 53-225.

2394   Mäding, Klaus, Wirtschaftswachstum und Kulturwandel in Hongkong. Ein
        Beitrag zur Wirtschafts- und Sozialpsychologie der Hongkong-Chinesen
        [Economic growth and cultural change: An essay on the economy and
        social psychology of the Hong Kong Chinese]. Cologne: Westdeutscher
        Verlag, 1964. 76 pp. [Hong Kong]

2395   Manners, Robert A., "Tabara: Subcultures of a Tobacco and Mixed Crops
        Municipality," in GEN 4387 (1956), 93-170. [Puerto Rico]

2396   Meillassoux, Claude, "The Social Structure of Modern Bamako," Africa
        35:2 (Apr. 1965), 125-142. [Mali]

2397   Meinkoth, Marian R., "Migration in Thailand with Particular Reference
        to the Northeast," Econ. Busin. Bull. 14 (June 1962), 2-45.

2398   Miner, Horace M., The Primitive City of Timbuctoo. Princeton:
        Princeton University Press, 1953. 334 pp. Rev. ed., paper, New
        York: Doubleday-Anchor, 1965. [The French Sudan]

2399   Minon, P., "Quelques aspects de l'évolution récente de centre extra-
        coûtumier d'Elisabethville" [Some aspects of the recent evolution of
        the nontraditional center of Elisabethville], Bull. trimest. Cent.
        Etud. Probl. 36 (1957), 5-51. [Leopoldville, Congo]

2400   Mitchell, J. Clyde, "Africans in Industrial Towns in Northern
        Rhodesia," in GEN 4338 (1957), 1-9. [Zambia]

2401   ------ African Urbanization in Ndola and Luanshya. Lusaka: Rhodes-
        Livingstone Institute, 1954. 24 pp. [Zambia]

2402   ------ "A Note on the Urbanization of Africans on the Copperbelt,"
        Hum. Probl. B.C.A. 12 (1951), 20-27. [Zambia]

2403   ------ "Social Change and the New Towns of Bantu Africa," in GEN 4302
        (1962), 112-130, bibl. [South Africa]

2404   Mitchell, J. C., and S. H. Irvine, "Social Position and the Grading of
        Occupations," J. Rhodes-Livingst. Inst. 38 (Dec. 1965), 42-54.
        [Zambia]

2405   Mohsin, Mohammad, Chittaranjan: A Study in Urban Sociology. Bombay:
        Popular Prakashan, 1964. 198 pp.

2406   ------ "The Tenor of Indian Urbanism, with Particular Reference to
        Chittaranjan," Sociol. Bull. 12:2 (Sept. 1963), 50-65. [Indian State
        of Assam]

2407   Molina Filho, J., "Absenteísmo e agricultura em tempo parcial no
        município de Rio das Pedras" [Absenteeism and part-time agriculture

in the municipality of Rio das Padras], Sociologia 25:3 (Sept. 1963), 213-232. [Brazil]

2408   Monbeig, P., "Salvador de Bahia: Les paradoxes d'une ancienne capitale brésilienne" [Salvador de Bahia: The paradoxes of an old Brazilian capital], Industrie 14:1 (Jan. 1960),]5-34. [Brazil]

2409   Nagpaul, H., "Sviluppo di comunità in zone urbane dell' India" [Community development in the urban zones of India], Int. Rev. Community Dev. 9 (1962), 95-111.

2410   Narayanan, R., "Urban Fringe Settlement: A Case Study," J. soc. Res. 3 (Mar. 1960), 55-61. [India]

2411   Nathan, Andrew, "The Jurong Story: A Special Survey of Singapore's New Industrial Complex," Far E. econ. Rev. 45 (27 Aug. 1964), 381-396.

2412   Nicolas, J., "Un quartier de Casablanca: Le Maarif" [A section of Casablanca: The Maarif], Cah. d'outre-mer 16:63 (July-Sept. 1963), 281-302. [Morocco]

2413   Ôhara, M., "Chihô toshi kôgyôka to jûmin ishiki" [The industrialization of a city and the social consciousness of its residents], Hôgaku Shimpô 69:5 (May 1962), 292-313. [Japan]

2414   O'Loughlin, C., "Problems in the Economic Development of Antigua," Soc. econ. Stud. 10:3 (Sept. 1961), 237-277. [British Caribbean]

2415   Pacyaya, Alfredo G., "Acculturation and Culture Change in Sagada," Silliman J. 11:1-2 (Mar.-June 1964), 14-25. [Philippines]

2416   Padmanabhan, C. B., "Social Effects of Industrialization-Urbanization," Indian J. Labour Econ. 5 (Jan. 1963), 409-413. [India]

2417   Parkin, D. J., "Urban Voluntary Associations as Institutions of Adaptation," Man 1:1 (Mar. 1966), 90-95. [Uganda]

2418   Patterson, Sheila C., Colour and Culture in South Africa: A Study of the Cape Coloured People within the Social Structure of the Union of South Africa. London: Routledge & Kegal Paul, 1953. 402 pp. [Republic of South Africa]

2419   Phillips, R. E., The Bantu Are Coming: Phases of South Africa's Race Problem. London: Student Christian Movement Press, 1930. 238 pp.

2420   ------ The Bantu in the City: A Study of Cultural Adjustment on the Witwatersrand. Lovedale, Union of South Africa: Lovedale Press, 1938. 452 pp.

2421   Pons, V. G., "Social Effects of Urbanization in Stanleyville, Belgian Congo: The Growth of Stanleyville and the Composition of Its African Population," in GEN 4325 (1956), 229-273.

2422   Porter, Arthur T., Creoledom: A Study of the Development of Freetown Society. London: Oxford University Press, 1963. 151 pp. [Sierra Leone]

2423   Powdermaker, Hortense, "Social Change through Imagery and Values of
        Teen-Age Africans in Northern Rhodesia," Am. Anthrop. 58:5 (Oct.
        1956), 783-813. [Zambia]

2424   Prabhu, Pandharinath, "Social Effects of Urbanization on the
        Industrial Workers of Bombay," Soc. Bull. 5:1 (Mar. 1956), 29-50,
        and 5:2 (Sept. 1956), 127-143. [Indian State of Maharashtra]

2425   ------ "Social Effects of Urbanization on Industrial Workers in Bom-
        bay," Soc. Bull. 6:1 (Mar. 1957), 14-33.

2426   Rajagopalan, C., The Greater Bombay: A Study in Suburban Ecology.
        Bombay: Popular Book Depot, 1962. 211 pp. [Indian State of
        Maharashtra]

2427   Rheinallt-Jones, J. D., "Social and Economic Condition of the Urban
        Native," in GEN 4373 (1934), 159-192. [Republic of South Africa]

2428   Sahara, R., "Tsukuda-shima to sono Shakai, Bunka-teki Henka" [Socio-
        cultural changes of Tsukuda-shima, a unique small community in old
        Tokyo], Keiô Daigaku Kiyô 2 (1963), 1-16.

2429   Sangave, Vilas A., "Changing Pattern of Caste Organisation in Kolhapur
        City," Sociol. Bull. 11:1 (Mar. 1962), 36-61. [Indian State of Maha-
        rashtra]

2430   Sankale, M., and H. Ba, "Introduction aux problèmes d'urbanisation"
        [Introduction to the problems of urbanization], Afr. Docums. 66
        (Jan.-Feb. 1963), 3-24. [Senegal]

2431   Santoro, G., Algunos aspectos de la vida urbana en San José: Tres
        problemas apremiantes [Some aspects of urban life in San José:
        Three pressing problems]. San José: Instituto Centroamericano de
        Investigaciones Sociales y Economicas, 1962. 62 pp. [Costa Rica]

2432   Seck, A., "Dakar," Cah. d'outre-mer 14:56 (Oct.-Dec. 1961), 372-392.
        [Senegal]

2433   Segall, M. H., "Acquiescence and 'Identification with the Aggressor'
        among Acculturating Africans," J. soc. Psychol. 61:2 (Dec. 1963),
        247-262. [Uganda]

2434   Seminar on Social Problems of Urbanization in Pakistan, Social Pro-
        blems of Urbanization in Pakistan: A Report of the Proceedings and
        Recommendations of a Three-Day Seminar, September 7-9, 1962.
        Karachi: Social Services Coordinating Council, 1963. 83 pp.

2435   Simms, Ruth P., Urbanization in West Africa: A Review of Current
        Literature. Evanston, Ill.: Northwestern University Press, 1965.
        109 pp.

2436   Singh, Indera P., and H. L. Harit, "Effects of Urbanisation in a Delhi
        Suburban Village," J. soc. Res. 3 (Mar. 1960), 38-43. [Indian State
        of Uttar Pradesh]

2437   Southall, A. W., and P. C. W. Gutkind, Townsmen in the Making:

Kampala and Its Suburbs. Kampala, Uganda: East African Institute
of Social Research, 1957. 248 pp. [Uganda]

2438   Stanislawski, Dan, "The Anatomy of Eleven Towns in Michoacán," in
        GEN 4390 (1961), 348-354. [Mexico]

2439   Steiner, Jesse F., _Mitaka: From Village to Suburban City: A Study
        of Tokyo's Urban Fringe._ Tokyo: International Christian University,
        Rural Welfare Research Institute, 1957. 39 pp.

2440   Stent, G. E., "Migrancy and Urbanization in the Union of South
        Africa," _Africa_ 18:3 (1948), 161-183.

2441   Suzuki, P., "Village Solidarity among Turkish Peasants Undergoing
        Urbanization," _Science_ 132 (Sept. 1960), 890 pp.

2442   Taieb, J., "Une banlieue de Tunis: L'Ariana" [A suburb of Tunis:
        Ariana], _Cah. Tunisie_ 8:32 (Oct.-Dec. 1960), 33-76.

2443   Tan, Giok-lan, _The Chinese of Sukabumi: A Study in Social and
        Cultural Accommodation._ Ithaca, N.Y.: Cornell University Press,
        1963. 314 pp. [Indonesia]

2444   Torres Restrepo, Camilo, _La proletarización de Bogotá_ [The prole-
        tarization of Bogotá]. Bogotá: Universidad Nacional de Colombia,
        1961. 42 pp.

2445   Van Den Berghe, P. L., and E. Miller, _Caneville: The Social
        Structure of a South African Town._ Middletown, Conn.: Wesleyan
        University Press, 1964. 276 pp.

2446   Vennetier, P., "Banlieue noire de Brazzaville" [Black suburb of
        Brazzaville], _Cah. d'outre-mer_ 10:38 (Apr.-June 1957), 131-157.
        [Congo (Brazzaville)]

2447   ------ "Mvouti, une agglomération semi-urbaine dans la République
        du Congo" [Mvouti: A semi-urban area in the Republic of the Congo],
        Rev. Géogr. Lyon 36:1 (1961), 51-81. [Congo (Brazzaville)]

2448   ------ "L'urbanisation et ses conséquences au Congo (Brazzaville)"
        [Urbanization and its consequences in the Congo (Brazzaville)],
        Cah. d'outre-mer 16:63 (July-Sept. 1963), 263-280.

2449   ------ "La vie agricole urbaine a Pointe-Noire, Congo" [Urban agri-
        cultural life in Pointe-Noire, Congo], _Cah. d'outre-mer_ 14:53 (Jan.-
        Mar. 1961), 60-84. [Congo (Brazzaville)]

2450   Villien-Rossi, M. L., "Bamako, capitale du Mali" [Bamako, capital of
        Mali], _Bull. Inst. fr. Afr. noire_ 28:1-2 (Jan.-Apr. 1966), 249-380.

2451   ------ "Bamako, capitale du Mali" [Bamako, capital of Mali], _Cah.
        d'outre-mer_ 16:64 (Oct.-Dec. 1963), 379-393.

2452   Vyas, N. N., "Kherwara: A Town in a Tribal Setting," _Man in India_
        45:4 (Oct.-Dec. 1965), 296-300. [Indian State of Rajasthan]

2453   Wagley, Charles, <u>Amazon Town: A Study of Man in the Tropics</u>. New
        York: Macmillan, 1953. 305 pp. [Brazil]

2454   Watanabe, Hisata, "A Note on the Amalgamation of Cities and Villages
        in the East and West Tenant Country, Toyama Prefecture: A Comparison
        with 'Gun-go-System,'" <u>Shakaigaku Hyôron</u> 7 (Oct. 1956), 61-81.
        [Japan]

2455   Whiteford, Andrew Hunter, <u>Popayán y Querétaro. Comparación de sus
        clases sociales</u> [Popayán and Querétaro: Comparison of their social
        classes]. Bogotá: Universidad nacional de Colombia, 1963. 283 pp.

2456   ------ <u>Two Cities of Latin America: A Comparative Description of
        Social Classes</u>. Beloit, Wis.: The Logan Museum of Anthropology,
        Beloit College, 1960. 156 pp.

2457   Williamson, Robert C., "Some Factors in Urbanism in a Quasi-Rural
        Setting: San Salvador and San José," <u>Sociol. soc. Res</u>. 47:2 (Jan.
        1963), 187-200. [Costa Rica; San Salvador]

2458   Yokoyama, K., "Chihô toshi kôgyô to jûmin soshiki" [Industrialization
        of a city and organization of the residents], <u>Hôgaku Shimpô</u> 69:5
        (May 1962), 314-332. [Japan]

2459   Yokoyama, Ryuichi, "Migration and Industry in a City: A Research in
        Yokkaichi City, Mie Prefecture," <u>Shakaigaku Hyôron</u> 5 (Jan. 1955),
        73-95. In Japanese. [Japan]

2460   Yonemura, S., "Chôson Gappei to Bunson Mondai" [Issues in the amal-
        gamation of town and village], <u>Okayama Shûruku</u> 15 (1963), 19-37.
        [Japan]

2461   Yuan, Y., and E. G. Stockwell, "The Rural-Urban Continuum: A Case
        Study of Taiwan," <u>Rur. Sociol</u>. 29:3 (Sept. 1964), 247-260.

3. Urban Families

A. Annotated Case Studies

3001   Aird, John, "Bengali Urban Growth and Village Life," in GEN 4352
        (1957), 16-45.

        No change has yet occurred in family life, though there are
        indications of future unrest.

3002   Barnes, J. A., <u>Marriage in a Changing Society</u>. Manchester, England:
        Manchester University Press, 1951. 136 pp.

        In Zambia the divorce rate has increased.

**3003   Bettison, D. G., "Changes in the Composition and Status of Kin Groups
         in Nyasaland and Northern Rhodesia," in GEN 4384 (1961), 273-285.
         [Malawi; Zambia]

         A comparison of Blantyre-Limbe (Malawi) with Lusaka (Zambia), both
         medium-sized cities. Lusaka is physically cut off from the native
         villages by an area of farmland held by whites, but Blantyre is not.
         In Lusaka the native is isolated to an extent not apparent in
         Blantyre. The greater unrest is therefore to be found in Lusaka.

3004   Diop, Abdoulaye Bara, Société Toucouleur et migration [Toucouleur
         society and migration]. Dakar, Senegal: Institut Français
         d'Afrique Noire, 1965. 232 pp.

         In Dakar marriage and family life have become matters of individual
         concern rather than the traditional group concern, yet the strength
         of group interaction remains strong.

**3005   Djamour, Judith, Malay Kinship and Marriage in Singapore. London:
         Athlone Press, 1959. 151 pp. [Malaysia]

         The closest ties are those relating the mother, her married
         children, and her daughters' children. These ties discourage easy
         divorce and serve as a means of security against the vicissitudes of
         individualistic family life.

**3006   Izzett, A., "Family Life among the Yoruba, in Lagos, Nigeria," in
         GEN 4384 (1961), 305-315.

         Marriages frequently fail in Lagos. A major cause is the problem
         of financial support: a wife will leave her husband as soon as he
         is unable to support her. Mobility and lack of family structure
         increase the problem. Parents often reinforce this tendency by
         selling off their daughters.

*3007   Kurian, George, The Indian Family in Transition: A Case Study of
         Kerala Syrian Christians. Paris: Mouton, 1961. 142 pp. [Indian
         State of Kerela]

         Education has diminished rural-urban differences. Urban contacts
         widen horizons and weaken the position of religious and authoritative
         figures. In general, those traditions that remain are neutral with
         regard to "progress."

*3008   Leblanc, Maria, Personnalité de la femme Katangaise: Contribution à
         l'étude de son acculturation [The personality of the Katangese woman:
         A contribution to the study of her acculturation]. Louvain: Publi-
         cations Universitaires, 1960. 403 pp. [Leopoldville, Congo]

         Acculturation is most noticeable in the women's increased capacity
         to recognize sexual conflict.

**3009   McCall, Daniel F., "Trade and the Role of Wife in a Modern West
         African Town," in GEN 4384 (1961), 286-299. [Ghana]

         A survey of a town in Ghana. Its women can be economically

independent because they can engage in marketing, which frees them
from male dominance economically and sexually.

**3010   Marris, P., Family and Social Change in an African City: A Study of
Rehousing in Lagos. London: Routledge & Kegan Paul, 1961. 180 pp.
[Nigeria]

Those families who live in housing developments built outside the
city for reasons of space tend to be isolated from their extended
families. Individualism is admired in these housing units and
encouraged by the developing economic system. Personal power is
accepted, contrary to the traditional attitude. The claims of the
extended family on the successful member represent an acute source of
conflict, from which these housing units offer an escape.

**3011   Mitchell, J. Clyde, "Social Change and the Stability of African
Marriage in Northern Rhodesia," in GEN 4384 (1961), 316-330.
[Zambia]

The divorce rate is related to the prevailing form of rights over
children. Divorce occurs less frequently when the father's group
rights over the children are in force; and most frequently when there
are matrilineal or bilateral rights over them. Though town life tends
to weaken the father's group rights, the family structure remains
stronger than in matrilineal or bilateral rights.

3012   Pauw, B. A., The Second Generation: A Study of the Family among
Urbanized Bantu in East London. Cape Town: Oxford University Press,
1963. 219 pp. [Republic of South Africa]

A description of the breakdown of family life.

3013   Pons, V. G., "The Changing Significance of Ethnic Affiliation and of
Westernization in the African Settlement Patterns in Stanleyville,"
in GEN 4325 (1956), 638-669.   [Congo (Leopoldville)]

The significance of ethnic affiliation is declining.

3014   Ross, Aileen D., The Hindu Family in Its Urban Setting. Toronto:
University of Toronto Press, 1961. 325 pp. [Indian State of Mysore]

A study of Bangalore, where education has diminished family
loyalties to the extended family, thus diminishing economic security.

**3015   Rouch, Jean, "Second Generation Migrants in Ghana and the Ivory
Coast," in GEN 4384 (1961), 300-304.

Rejected by traditional tribal groups, these migrants are forming
their own nontribal society.

**3016   Southall, Aidan W., and Peter C. W. Gutkind, Townsmen in the Making:
Kampala and Its Suburbs. Kampala, Uganda: East African Institute of
Social Research, 1957. 248 pp. [Uganda]

Urban contacts, implying greater economic freedom for women,
coupled with a less rigid definition of their role as wives and

mothers, has made marriage very unstable. New forms of marriage
adapted to the urban multitribal situation are developing, but they
are hampered by a legal system juxtaposing modern Christian law and
native law.

B.   Other Case Studies

3301   Agarwala, A. N., "Nature and Extent of Social Change in a Mobile
         Commercial Community: Study of Change in Family and Marriage
         Patterns," Sociol. Bull. 11 (1962), 141-145. [India]

3302   Aldous, J., "Urbanization, the Extended Family, and Kinship Ties
         in West Africa," Soc. Forces 41:1 (Oct. 1962), 6-11.

3303   Atienza, Maria Fe G., "The Filipino Family: The Impact of New Social
         and Cultural Forces on It," Philipp. educ. Forum 13:3 (Nov. 1964),
         10-14.

3304   Caldwell, J. C., "The Erosion of the Family: A Study of the Fate of
         the Family in Ghana," Popul. Stud. 20:1 (1966), 5-26.

3305   Chabot, H. T., "Jonge Vrouwen in Conflict. Een Studie in Cultuur-
         verandering, aan der Hand ener Vergelijking van Stads-en Plattelands-
         gegevens" [Young women in conflict: Study in cultural change,
         comparing urban and rural regions], Indonésie 8:1 (Feb. 1955),
         40-47. [Indonesia]

3306   Chauhan, I. S., "Three Families in a Small Town: A Study in Social
         Change," J. soc. Res. 8 (Mar. 1965), 83-90.

3307   "Changes in the Family," Int. soc. Sci. Bull. 14 (1962).

3308   Chinn, W. H., "The Family in Areas of Rapid Urbanization," Oversea
         Quart. 2:3 (1960), 75-77.

3309   Clément, Pierre, "Social Effects of Urbanization in Stanleyville,
         Belgian Congo: Social Patterns of Urban Life," in GEN 4325 (1956),
         368-492.

3310   Clignet, Remi, "Urban and Family Structure in the Ivory Coast,"
         Comp. Stud. Soc. Hist. 8:4 (July 1966), 385-401.

3311   Dasgupta, Manisha, "Changes in the Joint Family in India," Man in
         India 45:4 (Oct.-Dec. 1965), 283-288.

3312   Desai, I, P., Some Aspects of Family in Mahuva: A Sociological Study
         of Jointness in a Small Town. Bombay: Asia Publishing House, 1965.
         239 pp. [Indian State of Gujarat]

3313   "Evolution et problèmes de la famille urbaine en Afrique au sud du

Sahara" [The evolution and problems of the urban family in Africa south of the Sahara], Inform. Birispt 18 (1958), 1-30.

3314   Forthomme, G., Mariage et industrialisation: Evolution de la men-
        talité indigène dans une cité de travailleurs d'Elisabethville
        [Marriage and industrialization: Evolution of the indigenous
        mentality in a workers' city, Elizabethville]. Liège: Institut de
        Sociologie de l'Université, 1957. 104 pp. [Leopoldville, Congo]

3315   Gamble, S. P., "The Temne Family in a Modern Town (Lunsar) in Sierra
        Leone," Africa 33:3 (July 1963), 209-226.

3316   Gangrade, K. D., "Conflicting Value System and Social Case Work,"
        Indian J. Soc. Wk. 24 (Jan. 1964), 247-256.

3317   Germani, Gino, "Algunos aspectos de la familia en transición en
        Argentina," in GEN 4302 (1962), 29-44. [A French translation
        follows on pp. 45-60.]

3318   Goode, William J., World Revolution and Family Patterns. New York:
        Free Press of Glencoe, 1963. 432 pp.

3319   Green, T. L., "Evolution de la famille à Ceylon sous l'influence de
        l'instruction et des contacts sociaux" [The evolution of the family
        in Ceylon under the influence of instruction and social contacts],
        Fam. Monde 9:4 (Dec. 1956), 283-298.

3320   Gutkind, Peter C. W., "African Urban Family Life," Cah. Etud. Afr.
        3:10 (1962), 149-217. [Africa; Central Africa]

3321   ------ "African Urban Family Life and the Urban System," J. Asian
        Afr. Stud. 1:1 (Jan. 1966), 35-42.

3322   ------ "African Urban Marriage and Family Life: A Note on Some
        Social and Demographic Characteristics from Kampala, Uganda," Bull.
        Inst. fr. Afr. noire 25:3-4 (July-Oct. 1963), 266-287.

3323   ------ "La famille africaine et son adaptation à la vie urbaine:
        quelques aspects du problème d'après une étude effectuée à Kampala,
        Ouganda, Afrique Orientale Britannique" [The African family and its
        adaptation to urban living: Some aspects of the problem according
        to a study conducted in Kampala, Uganda, British East Africa],
        Diogène 37 (Jan.-Mar. 1962), 93-112. [Uganda]

3324   ------ "Some Problems of African Urban Family Life: An Example from
        Kampala, Uganda, British East Africa," Zaïre 15:1 (Jan. 1961),
        59-74.

3325   Hallenback, W. (ed.), The Baumannville Community: A Study of the
        Family Life of Urban Africans. Durban, South Africa: University of
        Natal Press, 1955. [Republic of South Africa]

3326   Harries-Jones, P., "Marital Disputes and the Process of Conciliation
        in a Copperbelt Town," Hum. Probl. B.C.A. 35 (June 1964), 29-72.
        [Zambia]

3327   Hirabayashi, G. K., and M. Ishaq, "Social Change in Jordan: A
        Quantitative Approach in a Non-Census Area," Am. J. Sociol. 64:1
        (July 1958), 36-40.

3328   Irving, James, "Households and Relationship in a South African Non-
        Industrial Urban Area," Tijdschr. Maat. Navors 6:1 (June 1955),
        5-24.

3329   Jahoda, G., "Love, Marriage and Social Change: Letters to the
        Advice Column of a West African Newspaper," Africa 29 (1959), 177-190.
        [Ghana]

3330   Kennedy, B. C., "Rural-Urban Contrasts in Parent-Child Relations in
        India," Indian J. soc. Wk. 15:3 (Dec. 1954), 162-175.

3331   Krige, Eileen J., "Changing Conditions in Marital Relations and
        Parental Duties among Urbanized Natives," Africa 9 (1936), 1-23.
        [South Africa]

3332   ------ "Some Social and Economic Facts Revealed in Native Family
        Budgets," Race Relat. 1 (1934), 94-108. [South Africa]

3333   Lewis, Oscar, La Vida: A Puerto Rican Family in the Culture of
        Poverty--San Juan and New York. New York: Random House, 1965.
        669 pp.

3334   Little, Kenneth L., "The Changing Position of Women in the Sierra
        Leone Protectorate," Africa 18:1 (Feb. 1948), 1-17.

3335   Marris, Peter, "Slum Clearance and Family Life in Lagos," Hum.
        Organiz. 19:3 (Fall 1960), 123-128. [Nigeria]

3336   Maud, Dorothy, "Daughters of the Golden City," J. Afr. Soc. 32
        (1933), 379-385. [Republic of South Africa]

3337   Mitchell, J. Clyde, "Aspects of African Marriage on the Copperbelt
        of Northern Rhodesia," J. Rhodes-Livingst. Inst. 22 (1957), 1-30.
        [Zambia]

3338   Parkin, D. J., "Types of Urban African Marriage in Kampala," Africa
        36:3 (July 1966), 269-285. [Uganda]

3339   Ross, A. D., The Hindu Family in Its Urban Setting. Bombay: Oxford
        University Press, 1961. 325 pp. [India]

3340   Soenardi, Sosrooetoyo, "Estimating the Income of Low Income Households
        in a Philippine City Using Food Expenditures as Predictors," Phil-
        ippine Stat. 12:1 (Mar. 1963), 23-50.

3341   Sofer, Rhona, "Adaptation Problems of Africans in an Early Phase of
        Industrialization at Jinja (Uganda)," in GEN 4325 (1956), 613-623.

3342   Stephens, W. N., The Family in Cross-Cultural Perspective. New York:
        Holt, Rinehart & Winston, 1963. 460 pp.

3343   Tardits, Claude, "Réflections sur le problème de la scolarisation des

filles au Dahomey" [Reflections on the problem of girls' schooling
in Dahomey], Cah. Etud. afr. 3:10 (1962), 266-281.

3344   Thomas, R. Murray, and Winarno Surachmad, "Social-Class Differences
        in Mothers' Expectations for Children in Indonesia," J. soc. Psychol.
        57 (1962), 303-307.

3345   Thore, Luc, "Mariage et divorce dans la banlieue de Dakar" [Marriage
        and divorce in the suburbs of Dakar], Cah. Etud. afr. 4:4 (1964),
        479-551.

3346   United Nations, Economic Committee for Africa, Les effets de l'urban-
        isation sur la vie familiale en Afrique [The effects of urbanization
        on family life in Africa]. New York: United Nations, 1960. 13 pp.

3347   Vogel, Ezra F., Japan's New Middle Class: The Salary Man and His
        Family in a Tokyo Suburb. Berkeley: University of California Press,
        1963. 336 pp.

3348   Wright, Beryl R., "Social Aspects of Change in the Chinese Family
        Pattern in Hong Kong," J. soc. Psychol. 63:1 (June 1964), 31-39.

                        4. General Studies

4301   Aldous, J., "Urbanization, the Extended Family, and Kinship Ties
        in West Africa," Soc. Forces 41:1 (Oct. 1962), 6-11.

4302   Baeck, Louis, "Le changement social en Afrique centrale" [Social
        change in Central Africa], Bull. Inst. Rech. écon. soc. 25:8 (1959),
        729-768.

4303   Balandier, Georges, "Problèmes du développement économique et social
        de l'Afrique noire" [Problems of economic and social development in
        Black Africa], Rech. Débats 24 (1958), 117-125.

4304   ------ "Urbanism in West and Central Africa: The Scope and Aims of
        Research," in GEN 4325 (1956), 495-510.

4305   Bascom, William R., "The Urban African and His World," Cah. Etud.
        afr. 4:2 (1963), 163-185.

4306   Bataillon, C., "Comunicación de masa y vida urbana en México" [Mass
        communication and urban life in Mexico], Cienc. polít. soc. 6:32
        (Apr.-June 1963), 143-158.

4307   Bazzanella, W., "Industrialização e urbanização no Brasil" [Indus-
        trialization and urbanization in Brazil], Amér. lat. 6:1 (Jan.-Mar.
        1963), 3-26.

4308   Bose, Nirmal Kumar, "Some Problems of Urbanization," Man in India 42:
        4 (Oct.-Dec. 1962), 255-262. [India]

                                [133]

4309   Breese, Gerald, Urbanization in Newly Developing Countries. Engle-
         wood Cliffs, N.J.: Prentice-Hall, 1966. 151 pp.

4310   Brys, A., "Sociale Toestanden en Sociale Actie in Congo" [Social
         conditions and social action in the Congo], Gids Mijk Gebied 44:7-8
         (July-Aug. 1953), 583-621. [Leopoldville, Congo]

4311   Busia, K. A., "Africa in Transition. I. Before European Colonization.
         II. Under European Colonialism. III. Technical Civilization," Pract.
         Anthrop. 6:3 (May-June 1959), 117-123; 6:4 (July-Aug. 1959), 171-178;
         6:5 (Sept.-Oct. 1959), 223-230.

4312   Crane, R. I., "Urbanism in India," Am. J. Sociol. 60:3 (Mar. 1955),
         463-470.

4313   Cressey, Paul Frederick, "Urbanization in the Philippines," Sociol.
         soc. Res. 44 (July 1960), 402-409.

4314   Davis, Kingsley, "Colonial Expansion and Urban Diffusion in the
         Americas," Int. J. comp. Sociol. 1:1 (Mar. 1960), 43-66.

4315   De Briey, Pierre, "Urban Agglomerations and the Modernisation of the
         Developing States," Civilisations 16:1 (Jan. 1966), 2-25.

4316   Descloitres, R., C. Descloitres, and J. C. Reverdy, "Organization
         urbaine et structures sociales en Algérie" [Urban organization and
         social structure in Algeria], Civilisations 12:2 (May 1962), 211-236.

4317   Dobyns, H. F., and M. C. Vasquez (eds.), Migración e integración en el
         Perú [Migration and integration in Peru]. Lima, Peru: Editorial
         Estudios Andinos, 1963. 196 pp.

4318   Dorse Laer, J., and A. Gregory, La urbanización en América Latina.
         Tomo 1. Descripción del fenómeno de urbanización en América Latina
         [Urbanization in Latin America. Vol. 1. A description of the
         phenomenon of urbanization in Latin America]. Bogotá: Oficina
         Internacional de Investigaciones Sociales de Fédération Européenne
         de Recherche Economique et Sociale, 1962. 192 pp.

4319   Dresch, J., "Villes d'Afrique occidentale" [Cities of West Africa],
         Cah. d'outre-mer 11 (July-Sept. 1950), 200-230.

4320   Ellefsen, Richard A., "City-Hinterland Relationships in India," in GEN
         4391 (1962), 94-116.

4321   Fraizier, E. F., "Urbanization and Social Change in Africa," Howard
         Univ. Mag. 2 (Jan. 1960), 8-13.

4322   Fukutake, Tadashi, Gappei Machi-Mura no Jittai [The realities of
         rural-urban union]. Tokyo: Tokyo University Press, 1958. 467 pp.
         [Japan]

4323   Fyfe, C., Sierra Leone Inheritance. London: Oxford University Press,
         1964. 352 pp.

4324   Gangrade, K. D., "Conflicting Value System and Social Case Work,"

Indian J. soc. Wk. 24 (Jan. 1964), 247-256. [India]

4325 Geiger, P. P., and F. Davidovich, "Aspectos do fato urbano no Brasil" [Aspects of urban conditions in Brazil], Rev. bras. Geogr. 23:2 (Apr.-June 1961), 263-362.

4326 Germani, Gino, "El proceso de urbanización en la Argentina" [The urbanization process in Argentina], Rev. interamér. Cienc. soc. 2:3 (1963), 287-345.

4327 ------ "Urbanización, secularización y desarrollo económico" [Urbanization, secularization, and economic development], Rev. mex. Sociol. 25:2 (May-Aug. 1963), 625-646.

4328 Ghose, B., "Colonial Beginnings of Calcutta: Urbanisation without Industrialisation," Econ. Wkly. 12:33 (Aug. 1960), 1255-1260. [Indian State of West Bengal]

4329 Ghurye, G. S., "Cities of India," Sociol. Bull. 2:1 (Mar. 1953), 47-71.

4330 Ginsburg, Norton S., "Urban Geography and 'Non-Western' Areas," in GEN 4333 (1966), 311-346.

4331 Guha, S., "Socio-Economic Impact of Urbanisation," All India Congr. Comm. econ. Rev. 10:3 (1 June 1958), 16-18. [India]

4332 Gutkind, P. C. W., "African Urbanism, Mobility and the Social Network," Int. J. comp. Sociol. 6:1 (Mar. 1965), 48-60.

4333 ------ "The African Urban Milieu: A Force in Rapid Change," Civilisations 12:2 (May 1962), 167-195.

4334 ------ "Congestion and Overcrowding: An African Urban Problem," Hum. Organiz. 19:3 (Fall 1960), 129-134.

4335 Hanks, L. M., Jr., "Merit and Power in the Thai Social Order," Am. Anthrop. 64:6 (Dec. 1962), 1247-1261.

4336 Hart, C. W. M., "Peasants Come to Town," in GEN 4322 (1964), 58-71.

4337 Hauser, Philip M. (ed.), Urbanization in Asia and the Far East. Calcutta: UNESCO, 1957. 286 pp. [Asia; East Asia; South Asia; Southeast Asia]

4338 Hellmann, Ellen P., "The Development of Social Groupings among Urban Africans in the Union of South Africa," in GEN 4325 (1956), 724-743.

4339- Herskovits, Melville J., "Traditions et bouleversements de la
4340 culture en Afrique" [Traditions and cultural upheavals in Africa], Présence afr. 34-35 (Oct. 1960-Jan. 1961), 124-131.

4341 Hoselitz, Bert F., "Urbanization and Economic Growth in Asia," Econ. Dev. cult. Change 6:1 (Oct. 1957), 42-54.

4342 ------ "Urbanization in India," Kyklos 13:3 (1960), 361-372.

4343   Hunt, C. L., "The 'Americanization' Process in the Philippines," India Quart. 12:1 (1956), 117-130.

4344   Institut d'Etude du Développement Economique et Social, "La société urbaine égyptienne" [Egyptian urban society], Tiers-Monde 2:2 (1961), 183-234.

4345   International Institute of Differing Institutions, L'attraction exercée par les centres urbains et industriels dans les pays en voie d'industrialisation [The attraction exercised by urban and industrial centers in countries on the way to industrialization]. Brussels: International Institute of Differing Institutions, 1952. 662 pp.

4346   Kamian, B., "Les villes dans les nouveaux états d'Afrique occidentale" [The cities in the new states of West Africa], Tiers-Monde 4:13-14 (Jan.-June 1963), 65-80.

4347   Kayser, B., Géographie humaine de la Grèce. Eléments pour l'étude de l'urbanisation [Human geography of Greece: Elements of a study of urbanization]. Paris: Presses Universitaires de France, 1964. 149 pp.

4348   Keyfitz, Nathan, "Political-Economic Aspects of Urbanization in South and Southeast Asia," in GEN 4333 (1966), 265-310.

4349   Kuper, Hilda (ed.), Urbanization and Migration in West Africa. Berkeley: University of California Press, 1965. 227 pp.

4350   Kurasawa, S., "Nihon Toshi no Sôgô Bunrui to Kêsê Katê" [Types and the formation process of the Japanese city], Toshi Mondai Kenkyû 15:9 (1963), 73-92.

4351   Lambert, Richard D., "The Impact of Urban Society upon Village Life," in GEN 4391 (1962), 117-140. [India]

4352   Lancksweirt, F., "La détribalisation des noirs dans les villes d'Afrique" [Detribalization of the Black native in the cities of Africa], Cah. Bruges 4:1 (Apr. 1954), 23-41.

4353   LeTourneau, R., "Social Change in the Muslim Cities of North Africa," Am. J. Sociol. 60:6 (May 1955), 527-535.

4354   Little, Kenneth L., "Some Social Consequences," Afr. Aff. 65:259 (1966), 160-169. [West Africa]

4355   ------ "The Study of Social Change in British West Africa," Africa 23:4 (Oct. 1953), 274-284.

4356   ------ "Urbanism in West Africa," Sociol. Rev. 7:1 (July 1959), 5-13.

4357   ------ "La ville dans l'ouest africain" [The city in West Africa], Diogène 29:1 (1960), 20-37.

4358   Lombard, J., "Acculturation et affaiblissement des pouvoirs traditionelles en Afrique Occidentale Française" [Acculturation and

the weakening of traditional powers in French West Africa], Bol.
cult. Guiné port. 12:45 (Jan. 1957), 7-20.

4359   Longmore, C., "African Poverty and Social Unrest," Afr. Aff. 57:229
        (Oct. 1958), 291-294. [Republic of South Africa]

4360   Mabogunje, A. L., Yoruba Towns. Ibadan, Nigeria: Ibadan University
        Press, 1962. 22 pp. [Nigeria]

4361   McCall, D. F., "Dynamics of Urbanization in Africa," in GEN 4363
        (1960), 522-535. See also Ann. Am. Acad. polit. soc. Sci. 298 (1955),
        151-160.

4362   Makulu, H. F., "Patterns of Rural-Urban Development in Africa," Bull.
        Res. Grp. Migration Probl. 8:3 (July-Sept. 1960), 57-62.

4363   Manndorff, H., "Auswirkungen der Industrialisierung und Verstädterung
        auf die Indische Kasten-Gesellschaft" [Consequences of industrialization
        and urbanization on Indian caste society], Sociologus 8:1 (1958),
        40-57.

4364   Mayer, Philip, "Migrancy and the Study of Africans in Towns," Am.
        Anthrop. 64:3, Pt. 1 (June 1962), 576-592.

4365   Milone, P. D., "Contemporary Urbanization in Indonesia," Asian Surv.
        4:8 (Aug. 1964), 1000-1012.

4366   Molohan, M. J. B., Detribalization. Dar-es-Salaam, Tanganyika:
        publisher unknown, 1957. 94 pp. [Africa]

4367   Nagpaul, Hans, "Sviluppo de comunità in zone urbane dell'India"
        [Community development in the urban zones of India], Int. Rev.
        Community Dev. 9 (1962), 95-111.

4368   Nair, B. N., "Urbanization and Corruption," Sociol. Bull. 9:2 (Sept.
        1960), 15-33. [India]

4369   Narain, D., "Urbanization and Some Social Problems," Sociol. Bull.
        9:2 (Sept. 1960), 1-6.

4370   Okigbo, Pius, "Social Consequences of Economic Development in West
        Africa," Ann. Am. Acad. polit. soc. Sci. 305 (May 1956), 125-133.

4371   Panchanadikar, K. C., and Jalu M. Panchanadikar, "Process of Social
        Change in India under the Colonial and Decolonial Era: An Analysis
        of Changing Rural-Urban Complex," Sociol. Bull. 14 (Sept. 1965), 9-26.

4372   Phillips, Walter, Jr., "Urbanization and Social Change in Pakistan,"
        Phylon 25:1 (Spring 1964), 33-43.

4373   Ray Burman, B. K., "Observations on the Effect of Urbanization on
        Work and Leisure," Man in India 37:3 (July-Sept. 1957), 217-229.

4374   Rayner, William, The Tribe and Its Successors: An Account of
        African Traditional Life and European Settlement in Southern
        Rhodesia. London: Faber & Faber, 1962. 239 pp.

4375   Recasens Siches, Luis, "El problema de la adaptación de las gentes
        de origén rural que migran en las grandes ciudades o centros
        industriales" [The adaptation problems of rural migrants to large
        cities or industrial centers], in GEN 4318 (1955), 361-377. [Latin
        America]

4376   Rheinallt-Jones, J. D., "The Effects of Urbanization in South and
        Central Africa," Afr. Aff. 52:206 (Jan. 1953), 37-44.

4377   Riggs, Frederick W., "Public Administration: A Neglected Factor in
        Economic Development," Ann. Am. Acad. polit. soc. Sci. 305 (May
        1956), 70-80.

4378   Robinson, R. D., "Turkey's Agrarian Revolution and the Problem of
        Urbanization," Pub. Opin. Quart. 22:3 (Fall 1958), 397-405, bibl.

4379   Russinger, A., "La municipalisation en Grande Kabylie" [Urbanization
        in the Grande Kabylie], Rev. algér. tunis. maroc. 76:3 (1960), 80-88.
        [Algeria]

4380   Ruytinx, J., "Ethique indigène et problèmes d'acculturation en Afrique
        centrale belge" [Indigenous ethics and the problems of acculturation
        in Belgian Central Africa], Rev. Inst. Sociol. 2 (1958), 309-334.

4381   Rycroft, W. Stanley, and Myrtle M. Clemmer, A Study of Urbanization
        in Latin America. New York: Commission on Ecumenical Mission and
        Relations, The United Presbyterian Church in the U.S.A., 1963.
        150 pp.

4382   Sautter, G., "Aperçu sur les villes 'africaines' du Moyen-Congo"
        [African cities of the Middle Congo: An over-all view], Afr. Asie
        14:2 (Apr.-June 1951), 34-53. [Congo (Leopoldville)]

4383   Saxena, D. P., "Emigration and Rural Social Change," Ind. sociol.
        Bull. 1:4 (July 1964), 20-23.

4384   Schnore, Leo F., "On the Spatial Structure of Cities in the Two
        Americas," in GEN 4333 (1966), 347-398.

4385   Seklani, M., "Villes et campagnes en Tunisie. Evaluation et
        prévisions" [Cities and countryside in Tunisia: Evaluation and fore-
        casts], Population 15:3 (June-July 1960), 485-511.

4386   Selosoemardjan, Social Changes in Jogjakarta. Ithaca, N.Y.:
        Cornell University Press, 1962. 440 pp. [Indonesia]

4387   Shakai Kagaku Kenkyujo, Local Community and Urbanization. Tokyo:
        International Christian University, 1963. 39 pp. [Japan]

4388   Sjoberg, Gideon, "Cities in Developing and in Industrial Societies:
        A Cross-cultural Analysis," in GEN 4333 (1966), 213-264.

4389   Southall, A. W., "Introductory Summary," in GEN 4384 (1961), 1-66.

4390   Sovani, N. V., Urbanization and Urban India. Bombay: Asia
        Publishing House, 1966. 160 pp.

4391   Spate, Oskar H. K., "Aspects of the City in South Asia," Confluence
        7 (Spring 1958), 16-28. [South Asia]

4392   Srinivas, M. N., "The Industrialization and Urbanization of Rural
        Areas," Sociol. Bull. 5:2 (Sept. 1956), 79-88. [India]

4393   Sundrum, R. M., "Urbanisation: The Burmese Experience," J. Burma
        Res. Soc. 40 (1957), 105-127.

4394   The, Siauw Giap, "Urbanisatie Problemen in Indonesie" [Problems of
        urbanization in Indonesia], Bijdr. Taal- Land- Volk. 115 (1959),
        249-276.

4395   Thomas, L. V., "Acculturation et déplacements de populations en
        Afrique de l'ouest" [Acculturation and population movements in West
        Africa], Rev. Psychol. Peuples 16:1 (1961), 49-76.

4396   "Urbanism in West Africa," Sociol. Rev. 7 (July 1959), 15-122, bibl.

4397   Van der Kroef, J. M. A., "The Changing Class Structure of Indonesia,"
        Am. sociol. Rev. 21:2 (Apr. 1956), 138-148.

4398   ------ "Structural Change in Indonesian Society," Econ. Dev. cult.
        Change 1:3 (Oct. 1952), 216-228.

4399   Vennetier, P., "L'urbanisation et ses conséquences au Congo
        (Brazzaville)" [Urbanization and its consequences in the Congo
        (Brazzaville)], Cah. d'outre-mer 16:63 (July-Sept. 1963), 263-280.

4400   Verlinden, C., "Acculturatieproblemen in Belgisch Kongo" [Problems
        of acculturation in the Belgian Congo], Tijdschr. soc. Wet. 4:4
        (1959), 341-351.

4401   Versluys, J. D. N., "Urbanization in Southeast Asia," Int. J. comp.
        Soc. 4 (1963), 140-151.

4402   Villème, Louis, "L'évolution de la vie citadine au Maroc" [Evolution
        of city life in Morocco], in GEN 4323 (1950 or 1951).

4403   Wertheim, Willem F., and Siauw Giap The, "Social Change in Java,
        1900-1930," Pacif. Aff. 35 (Fall 1962), 223-247. [Indonesia]

4404   Wilkinson, T. O., "Urban Structure and Industrialization," Am.
        sociol. Rev. 25:3 (June 1960), 356-363. [Japan]

                    5. Socioeconomic Studies

5301   Acharya, Hemalata, "Urbanizing Role of a One-Lakh City," Sociol.
        Bull. 5:2 (Sept. 1956), 89-101. [India]

                              [139]

5302   Acquah, Ione, <u>Accra Survey</u>. London: University of London Press,
        1958. 176 pp. [Ghana]

5303   Baeck, Louis, <u>Etude socio-économique du centre extra-coutumier</u>
        <u>d'Usumbura</u> [Socioeconomic study of the nontraditional urban center of
        Usumbura]. Brussels: Académie Royale des Sciences Coloniales, 1957.
        156 pp. [Congo (Leopoldville)]

5304   ------ "An Expenditure Study of the Congolese Evolués of Leopoldville,
        Belgian Congo," in GEN 4384 (1961), 159-181.

5305   ------ "Quelques aspects sociaux de l'urbanisation au Ruanda-Urundi"
        [Some social aspects of urbanization in Ruanda-Urundi], <u>Zaïre</u> 10:2
        (Feb. 1956), 115-146.

5306   ------ "Socio-économie de l'agglomération de Léopoldville" [Socio-
        economic aspects of Leopoldville as an urban center], <u>Industrie</u> 12:6
        (1958), 443-449.

5307   Benedict, Burton, <u>Indians in a Plural Society: A Report on Mauritius</u>.
        London: HMSO, 1961. 168 pp.

5308   Bettison, D. G., and P. J. Rigby, <u>Patterns of Income and Expenditure</u>,
        <u>Blantyre-Limbe, Nyasaland</u>: Part I, <u>The Peri-Urban Villages</u>; Part II,
        <u>The Urban Households</u>. Lusaka, Zambia: Rhodes-Livingstone Institute,
        1961. 153 mim. pp. [Malawi]

5309   Bharat Sevak Samaj, <u>Slums of Old Delhi: Report of the Socio-Economic</u>
        <u>Survey of the Slum Dwellers of the Old Delhi City</u>. Delhi: Atma Ram
        & Sons, 1958. 239 pp. [Indian State of Uttar Pradesh]

5310   Bloemfontein Joint Council of Europeans and Bantu, "The Cost of
        Living in a Native Urban Community," <u>Soc. indust. Rev</u>. 6 (1928),
        528-532. [Republic of South Africa]

5311   Bon Espasandin, M., "Aspectos socio-económicos del Cantegril" [Socio-
        economic aspects of the Cantegril], <u>Sociologia</u> 24:2 (June 1962), 107-
        115. [Uruguay]

5312   Caplow, Theodore, "The Social Ecology of Guatemala City," in GEN
        4390 (1961), 331-347.

5313   Chadda, Tilak Raj, <u>Socio-economic Survey of an Urban Working Class</u>:
        <u>An Enquiry into the Cost and Standard of Living of Industrial</u>
        <u>Workers in Peshawar City</u>. Hyderabad, India: Purohit, 196-? 80 pp.

5314   Denis, Jacques, <u>Le phénomène urbain en Afrique centrale</u> [The urban
        phenomenon in Central Africa]. Paris: Académie Royale de Sciences
        Coloniales, Vol. 19, Pt. 1, 1958. 407 pp.

5315   De Thier, Franz M., <u>Le centre extra-coutumier de Coquilhatville</u> [The
        nontraditional urban center at Coquilhatville]. Brussels: Univer-
        sité Libre, 1956. 143 pp. [Congo (Leopoldville)]

5316   Devauges, R., "Mieux-être et promotion sociale chez les salariés
        africains de Brazzaville" [Improved standard of living and social

advancement among the African workers of Brazzaville], in GEN 4384
(1961), 182-204.

5317   Dhekney, B. R., Hubli City: A Study in Urban Economic Life.
        Dharwar, Mysore: Karnatak University Press, 1959. 281 pp. [Indian
        State of Mysore]

5318   Diop, Abdoulaye Bara, Société Toucouleur et Migration [Toucouleur
        society and migration]. Dakar, Senegal: Institut Français d'Afrique
        Noire, 1965. 232 pp.

5319   Diziain, R., and A. Cambon, Etude sur la population du quartier New-
        Bell à Douala [Study of the population of the New-Bell section in
        Douala]. Yaoundé: Institut de Recherches Scientifiques du Cameroun,
        1962. 210 pp. [Cameroons]

5320   Dollfuse, O., "Conakry en 1951-1952: Etude humaine et économique"
        [Conakry in 1951-1952: A human and economic study], Etud guiné. 10-11
        (1952), 3-109. [Guinea]

5321   Fosbrooke, H. A., et al., "The Impact of Administrative Decisions on
        Social and Economic Development," in GEN 4354 (1958), 4-23.
        [Zambia]

5322   Fournier, H., "Tanarive: Etude d'économie urbaine" [Tanarive: A
        study in urban economics], Mém. Inst. sci. Madagascar 1:1 (1952),
        29-157. [Madagascar]

5323   Fukutake, Tadashi, Gappei Machi-Mura no Jittai [The realities of
        rural-urban union]. Tokyo: Tokyo University Press, 1958. 467 pp.
        [Japan]

5324   ------ Man and Society in Japan. Tokyo: Tokyo University Press,
        1962. 241 pp.

5325   Gadgil, D. R., Poona: A Socio-economic Survey. Poona, India:
        Gokhale Institute of Politics and Economics, 1945; 1952. Pt. 1,
        300 pp.; Pt. 2, 324 pp. [Indian State of Maharashtra]

5326   ------ Sholapur City: Socio-Economic Studies. Poona, India: Gokhale
        Institute of Politics and Economics, 1965. 337 pp.

5327   Garbett, Kingsley G., Growth and Change in a Shona Ward. Salisbury,
        Southern Rhodesia: University College of Rhodesia and Nyasaland,
        1960. 100 pp.

5328   Gouellain, R., "Parenté et affinités ethniques dans l'écologie du
        'Grand Quartier' de New-Bell, Douala" [Parentage and ethnic affinity
        in the ecology of the "Grand Quartier" of New-Bell, Douala], in GEN
        4384 (1961), 254-272. [Cameroons]

5329   Grevisse, F., Le centre extra-coutumier d'Elisabethville. Quelques
        aspects de la politique indigène du Haut-Katanga Industriel [The new
        city of Elisabethville: Some aspects of the treatment of natives in
        the industrial regions of Upper Katanga]. Brussels: Institut Royal
        Colonial Belge, 1951. 448 pp. [Congo (Leopoldville)]

5330   Gupta, S. C., and B. G. Prasad, "A Note on the Living and Working
         Conditions of the Sweeper Community in Lucknow," East. Anthrop. 18:3
         (Sept.-Dec. 1965), 177-185.

5331   Gutkind, P. C. W., "African Urban Marriage and Family Life: A Note on
         Some Social and Demographic Characteristics from Kampala, Uganda,"
         Bull. Inst. fr. Afr. noire 25:3-4 (July-Oct. 1963), 266-287.

5332   Heeren, H. J. (ed.), "The Urbanization of Djakarta," Ekon. Keuangan
         Indonesia 8:11 (Nov. 1955), 1-43.

5333   Hellmann, Ellen P., "Native Life in a Johannesburg Slum Yard," Africa
         8 (1935), 34-62. [Republic of South Africa]

5334   Herrick, Bruce H., Urban Migration and Economic Development in Chile.
         Cambridge, Mass.: M.I.T. Press, 1965. 126 pp.

5335   Houghton, D. H., Some Economic Problems of the Bantu in South Africa.
         Johannesburg: South African Institute of Race Relations, 1938.
         55 pp. [Republic of South Africa]

5336   Indian Institute of Economics, Report on a Socio-Economic and Health
         Survey of Street Beggars in Hyderabad-Secunderabad City Area.
         Hyderabad, India: Government Press, 1956. 175 pp. [Indian State
         of Andhra]

5337   Kay, George, A Social and Economic Study of Fort Roseberry. Part I:
         The Township. Part II: The Peri-urban Area. Lusaka, Zambia:
         Rhodes-Livingstone Institute, 1960. 55 and 75 pp. [Zambia]

5338   Kaye, B., Upper Nankin Street: A Sociological Study of Chinese
         Households Living in a Densely Populated Area. Singapore: Univer-
         sity of Malaya, 1960. 439 pp. [Malaysia]

5339   Khan, Fazie Karim, and Mohammad Masood, "Urban Structure of Comilla
         Town," Orient. Geogr. 6 (July 1962), 109-138. [East Pakistan]

5340   Kuper, Leo, Hilstan Watts, and Ronald Davies, Durban: A Study in
         Racial Ecology. New York: Columbia University Press, 1958. 221 pp.

5341   ------ "Durban: A Study in Racial Ecology," in GEN 4390 (1961),
         304-316. [Republic of South Africa]

5342   Leslie, J. A. K., A Survey of Dar es Salaam. London: Oxford Uni-
         versity Press, 1963. 305 pp. [Tanzania]

5343   Leubuscher, Charlotte, Der sudafrikanische Eingeborene als Industri-
         arbeiter und als Stadtbewohner [The South African native as industri-
         al worker and city dweller]. Jena, E. Germany: G. Fischer, 1931.
         222 pp. [Republic of South Africa]

5344   McCulloch, Merran, A Social Survey of the African Population of
         Livingstone. Manchester, England: Manchester University Press,
         1956. 82 pp. [Zambia]

5345   McLoughlin, P. F. M., "The Sudan's Three Towns: A Demographic and

Economic Profile of an African Urban Complex," Econ. Dev. cult.
Change 12:1 (Oct. 1963), 70-83; 12:2 (Jan. 1964), 158-173; 12:3
(Apr. 1964), 286-304.

5346   Majumdar, Dhirendra Nath, Social Contours of an Industrial City:
Social Survey of Kanpur, 1954-1956. Bombay: Asia Publishing House,
1960. 247 pp. [Indian State of Uttar Pradesh]

5347   Malhotra, P. C., Socio-Economic Survey of Bhopal City and Bairagarh.
New York: Asia Publishing House, 1964. 404 pp. [Indian State of
Madhya Pradesh]

5348   Malkani, H. C., A Socio-economic Survey of Baroda City. Baroda,
India: University of Baroda Press, 1958. 179 pp. [Indian State of
Gujarat]

5349   Massé, L., "Preliminary Results of Demographic Surveys in the Urban
Centres of Senegal," in GEN 4325 (1956), 523-535.

5350   Mehta, Aban B., The Domestic Servant Class. Bombay: Popular Book
Depot, 1960. 324 pp. [India]

5351   Misra, B. R., Report of Socio-economic Survey of Jamshedpur City.
2 vols. Patna, India: Patna University Press, 1959. 174 and 34 pp.
[Indian State of Bihar]

5352   ------ "Socio-Economic Survey of Jamshedpur," Econ. Pap. 2:2 (Nov.
1957), 1-26. [Indian State of Bihar]

5353   Mitchell, J. Clyde, "Urbanization, Detribalization and Stabilization
in Southern Africa: A Problem of Definition and Measurement," in
GEN 4325 (1956), 693-711.

5354   Mukerjee, Radhakamal, and Baljit Singh, A District Town in Transition:
Social and Economic Survey of Gorakhpur. Bombay: Asia Publishing
House, 1965. 187 pp. [Indian State of Uttar Pradesh]

5355   ------ Social Profiles of a Metropolis: Social and Economic Structure of Lucknow, Capital of Uttar Pradesh, 1954-1956. London: Asia
Publishing House, 1961. 210 pp. [Indian State of Uttar Pradesh]

5356   Mukherjee, S. B., "Urbanization in Burdwan Division," Calcutta
Statist. Ass. Bull. 6:21 (Mar. 1955), 1-16. [Indian State of West
Bengal]

5357   Natal, Government of, Regional Survey, Small Towns of Natal: A
Socio-Economic Sample Survey. Pietermaritzburg, South Africa:
University of Natal Press, 1953. 113 pp. [Republic of South
Africa]

5358   National Council of Applied Economic Research, Techno-economic Survey
of Goa, Daman, and Diu. New Delhi: National Council of Applied
Rconomic Research, 1964. 275 pp. [Indian State of Madhya Pradesh]

5359   Nyirenda, A. A., H. D. Ngyane, and D. G. Pettison, Further Economic
and Social Studies, Blantyre-Limbe, Nyasaland· Lusaka, Zambia :

Rhodes-Livingstone Institute, 1959. 49 pp. [Malawi]

5360   Oberg, Kalervo, Toledo, A Municipio on the Western Frontier of the
        State of Parana. Rio de Janeiro: United States Overseas Mission,
        1957. 87 pp. [Brazil]

5361   Palmer, Mabel, "Notes on Some Native Budgets Collected in Durban,"
        S. Afr. J. Sci. 25 (1928), 499-506. [Republic of South Africa]

5362   Phillips, R. E., The Bantu in the City: A Study of Cultural Adjust-
        ment on the Witwatersrand. Lovedale, South Africa: Lovedale Press,
        1938. 452 pp. [Republic of South Africa]

5363   Pons, V. G., "Social Effects of Urbanization in Stanleyville, Belgian
        Congo: The Growth of Stanleyville and the Composition of Its African
        Population," in GEN 4325 (1956), 229-273.

5364   Rajagopalan, C. "Bombay: A Study in Urban Demography and Ecology,"
        Sociol. Bull. 9 (Mar. 1960), 16-38. [Indian State of Maharashtra]

5365   Rao, V. K. R. V., and P. B. Desai, Greater Delhi: A Study in Urbani-
        zation, 1940-1957. New York: Asia Publishing House, 1965. 479 pp.
        [Indian State of Uttar Pradesh]

5366   Reader, D. H., The Black Man's Portion: History, Demography, and
        Living Conditions in the Native Locations of East London, Cape
        Province. Cape Town, South Africa: Oxford University Press, 1961.
        180 pp. [Republic of South Africa]

5367   Rycroft, W. Stanley, and Myrtle M. Clemmer, A Study of Urbanization
        in Latin America. New York: Commission on Ecumenical Mission and
        Relations, The United Presbyterian Church in the U.S.A., 1963.
        150 pp.

5368   Sariola, S., Análisis socio-económico del barrio Sagrada Familia,
        area recién urbanizada de San José, Costa Rica [Socioeconomic
        analysis of the Sagrada Familia district, a recently urbanized area
        of San José, Costa Rica]. San José, Costa Rica: Escuela Superior
        de Administración Pública de América Central, 1961. 104 pp.

5369   Sastry, D. U., "Some Aspects of Economic Life in Davangere: A Study
        in Urbanisation," Asian econ. Rev. 2:4 (Aug. 1960), 467-489. [Indian
        State of Mysore]

5370   Sebag, Paul, Un faubourg de Tunis: Saida Manoubia [Saida Manoubia:
        A suburb of Tunis]. Paris: Presses Universitaires de France, 1960.
        92 pp.

5371   Sen, Saurendra Nath, The City of Calcutta: A Socio-economic Survey,
        1954-1955 to 1957-1958. Calcutta: Bookland Private, 1960(?).
        271 pp. [Indian State of West Bengal]

5372   Sovani, N. V., The Social Survey of Kolhapur City. I. Population and
        Fertility. II. Industry, Trade, and Labour. III. Family Living and
        Social Life. Poona, India: Gokhale Institute of Politics and
        Economics, I, 1949; II, 1951; III, 1952. [Indian State of Maharashtra]

5373   Sovani, N. V., D. P. Aple, and R. G. Pendse, Poona: A Re-survey:
          The Changing Pattern of Employment and Earnings. Poona, India:
          Gokhale Institute of Politics and Economics, 1956. 555 pp.
          [Indian State of Maharashtra]

5374   Tao, L. K., Livelihood in Peking: An Analysis of the Budgets of 60
          Families. Peking: China Foundation for the Promotion of Education
          and Culture, 1928. 158 pp. [China]

5375   Taylor, J. D., and A. W. Cragg, "Report of the Social and Economic
          Condition of the Natives in Natal, with Special Reference to the
          Conditions Prevailing in Durban and Maritzburg," in GEN 4328 (1922),
          73-95. [Republic of South Africa]

5376   Venkatarayappa, K. N., Bangalore: A Socio-ecological Study. Bombay:
          University of Bombay Press, 1957. 157 pp. [Indian State of Mysore]

5377   Vietnam, Vien Quoc-gia Thong-ke, Enquête démographique à Saigon en
          1962 [Demographic inquiry in Saigon, 1962]. Saigon: Institut
          National de la Statistique, 1963. 232 pp. [Vietnam]

5378   Wilson, Gordon, "Mombasa: A Modern Colonial Municipality," in GEN
          4384 (1961), 98-112. [Tanzania]

6. Bibliographies

6301   Comhaire, Jean L., Urban Conditions in Africa. London: Oxford
          University Press, 1952. 48 pp.

6302   International Social Science Council, Conséquences sociales de
          l'industrialisation et problèmes urbains en Afrique [Social conse-
          quences of industrialization and urban problems in Africa]. Paris:
          International Social Science Council, 1954. 77 mim. pp.

6303   Jaspan, M. A., Social Stratification and Social Mobility in
          Indonesia: A Trend Report and Annotated Bibliography. Djakarta:
          n.p., 1959. 76 pp. [Indonesia]

6304   Lorenz, Robert, Paul Meadows, and Warner Bloomberg, Jr., A World of
          Cities: A Cross-Cultural Urban Bibliography. Syracuse, N.Y.:
          Syracuse University Press, 1964. 150 pp.

6305   Simms, Ruth P., Urbanization in West Africa: A Review of Current
          Literature. Evanston, Ill.: Northwestern University Press, 1965.
          109 pp.

6306   UNESCO, New Towns. Paris: UNESCO, 1960. 82 pp.

6307   "Urbanism in West Africa," Sociol. Rev. 7 (July 1959), 15-122,
          bibl.

6308   Verhaegen, P., <u>L'urbanisation de l'Afrique noire: Son cadre, ses</u>
        <u>causes et ses conséquences économiques, sociales et culturelles</u>
        [Urbanization of Black Africa: Its environment, its causes and its
        economic, social, and cultural consequences]. Brussels: Centre
        d'Etudes Démographiques, Economiques et Sociales d'Afrique, 1962.
        387 pp.

PART IV.   RURAL MODERNIZATION (RUR)

1301-12304

1. Theory of Rural Social Change

1301   Adams, D. W., "The Use of Socio-Economic Research in Developing a
        Strategy of Change for Rural Communities: A Colombian Example,"
        Econ. Dev. cult. Change 14:2 (Jan. 1966), 204-216.

1302   Balandier, Georges, "Structures sociales traditionelles et change-
        ments économiques" [Traditional social structures and economic
        change], Rev. Inst. sociol. 1 (1959), 27-40.

1303   ------ "Structures sociales traditionelles et changements économiques"
        [Traditional social structures and economic change], Cah. Etud. afr.
        1:1 (Jan. 1960), 1-14.

1304   Barber, William J., "Economic Rationality and Behavior Patterns in
        an Underdeveloped Area: A Case Study of African Economic Behavior
        in the Rhodesias," Econ. Dev. cult. Change 8:3 (Apr. 1960), 237-251.
        [Zambia; Rhodesia]

1305   Benedict, Burton, "Sociological Characteristics of Small Territories
        and Their Implications for Economic Development, in GEN 4305 (1966),
        23-36.

1306   Berliner, J. S., "The Feet of the Natives Are Large," Curr. Anthrop.
        3 (1962), 47-61.

1307   Bessaignet, Pierre, Principes de l'ethnologie économique: Une
        théorie de l'économie des peuples primitifs [Principles of economic
        ethnology: A theory of the economics of primitive peoples]. Paris:
        Librairie Générale de Droit et de Jurisprudence, 1966. 190 pp.

1308   Birket-Smith, K., "Adaptation and Cultural Development," in GEN
        4311 (1960), 236-239.

1309   Boeke, J. H., Economics and Economic Policy of Duel Societies as
        Exemplified by Indonesia. New York: Institute of Pacific Relations,
        1953. 324 pp.

1310   Bose, Santi Paiya, "Peasant Values and Innovation in India," Am. J.
        Sociol. 67:5 (Mar. 1962), 552-560.

[147]

1311-   Burling, Robbins, "Maximization Theory and the Study of Economic
1312   Anthropology," Am. Anthrop. 64:4 (Aug. 1962), 802-821. Also in GEN
          4349 (1966), 396-403.

1313   Cancian, Frank, "Maximization as Norm, Strategy, and Theory: A
          Comment on Programmatic Statements in Economic Anthropology," Am.
          Anthrop. 68:2, Pt. 1 (Apr. 1966), 465-470.

1314   Chiva, I., Rural Communities: Problems, Methods and Types of
          Research. Paris: UNESCO, 1959. 52 pp.

1315   Cook, Scott, "The Obsolete 'Anti-Market' Mentality: A Critique of
          the Substantive Approach to Economic Anthropology," Am. Anthrop.
          68:2, Pt. 1 (Apr. 1966), 323-345.

1316-   Dalton, George, "Economic Theory and Primitive Society," Am. Anthrop.
1317   63:1 (Feb. 1961), 1-25. See RUR 1349 (1962).

1318   ------ "Primitive, Archaic, and Modern Economies: Karl Polanyi's
          Contribution to Economic Anthropology and Comparative Economy," in
          GEN 4335 (1965), 1-24.

1319   De Clerck, M., "Education for Community Development," in GEN 4394
          (1963), 112-135.

1320   Dhoquois, Guy, "Le mode de production asiatique" [The Asian mode of
          production], Cah. int. Sociol. 41 (July-Dec. 1966), 83-92.

1321   Diégues Júnior, M., Establecimentos rurais na América latina.
          Ensaio de sugestães sôbre sua tipologia e suas caracteristicas
          econômicas e sociais [Rural establishments in Latin America:
          Suggestions on their typology and on their economic and social
          characteristics]. Geneva: Comissão Internacional Catolica de
          Migrações, 1963. 128 pp.

1322   Dohrenwend, Bruce P., and Robert J. Smith, "A Suggested Framework
          for the Study of Acculturation," in GEN 4366 (1957), 76-84.

1323   Doob, L. W., Becoming More Civilized. New Haven: Yale University
          Press, 1960. 333 pp.

1324   Finney, Ben R., "Resource Distribution and Social Structure in
          Tahiti," Ethnology 5:1 (Jan. 1966), 80-86.

1325-   Firth, Raymond W., Primitive Polynesian Economy. London: Routledge
1326   & Kegan Paul, 1939. 387 pp. 2nd ed. 1964. 385 pp.

1327   ------ "Work and Community in a Primitive Society," in GEN 4338
          (1957), 103-114. [Polynesia]

1328   Fitchen, Janet Mathew, "'Peasantry' as a Social Type," in GEN 4327
          (1961), 114-119.

1329   Forde, Daryll, and Mary Douglas, "Primitive Economics," in GEN 4377
          (1956), 330-344. Also in GEN 4319 (1967), 13-28.

1330-   Foster, George M., "The Dyadic Contract: A Model for the Social
1331   Structure of a Mexican Peasant Village," Am. Anthrop. 63:6 (Dec. 1961),
          1173-1192; and 65:6 (Dec. 1963), 1280-1294.

1332   ------ "Peasant Society and the Image of Limited Good," Am. Anthrop.
          67:2 (Apr. 1965), 293-315.

1333   ------ "What Is Folk Culture?" Am. Anthrop. 55:2 (Apr. 1953), 159-
          173.

1334   Fox, R. B., "The Study of Filipino Society and Its Significance to
          Programs of Economic and Social Development," Philipp. sociol. Rev.
          7:1-2 (Jan.-Apr. 1959), 2-15.

1335   Fraser, Thomas M., Jr., "Sociocultural Parameters in Directed
          Change," Hum. Organiz. 22:1 (Spring 1963), 95-104. [Mexico]

1336   Fukutake, Tadashi, "Change and Stagnation in Indian Village
          Society," Dev. Econ. 2:2 (June 1964), 125-146. [North India]

1337-   Gluckman, Max, Analysis of a Social Situation in Modern Zululand.
1338   Manchester, England: Manchester University Press, 1958. 77 pp.
          Also in Bantu Stud. 14:2 (1940), 91-146. [Republic of South Africa]

1339   Goodenough, Ward Hunt, Cooperation in Change: An Anthropological
          Approach to Community Development. New York: Russell Sage
          Foundation, 1963. 593 pp.

1340   Gosselin, G., "Pour une anthropologie du travail rural en Afrique
          noire" [Toward an anthropology of rural labor in Black Africa],
          Cah. Etud. afr. 3:4 (Oct. 1963), 511-550.

1341   Hadji-Dimou, Pierre, "Sobre la necesidad de clarificación conceptual
          en el domínio de las structural sociales 'in Fieri'" [On the
          necessity of conceptual clarification in the domain of "in Fieri"
          social structures], Rev. mex. Sociol. 21:2 (May-Aug. 1959), 493-
          536. [Mexico]

1342   Herskovits, Melville J., Economic Anthropology: A Study in Compara-
          tive Economics. 2nd ed. New York: Knopf, 1952. 547 pp.

1343   Hickman, John M., "An Approach to the Study of the Assimilation
          Process," in GEN 4326 (1964), 72-79.

1344   Hoselitz, Bert F., "Interaction between Industrial and Pre-Industrial
          Stratification Systems," in GEN 4381 (1966), 177-193.

1345   Katsumata, T., "Nihon Sonraku no Shakai Kôzô-ron ni tsuite" [The
          theory of social structure in the Japanese village], Kaiho 9 (1959),
          11-15.

1346   Kinoshita, K., "Sonraku Kōzō-ron no Kihon-teki Shiten" [A comment on
          the theories of Japanese village structure], Shakaigaku Hyôron
          12:3-4 (1961), 17-30.

1347   Krishnamurthy, L., "Status and Levels of Living: A Methodological

Study," Indian J. agric. Econ. 18 (Jan. 1963), 270-278.

1348   Kunkel, J. H., "Economic Autonomy and Social Change in Mexican
        Villages," Econ. Dev. cult. Change 10:1 (Oct. 1961), 51-63.

1349   LeClair, Edward E., Jr., "Economic Theory and Economic Anthropology,"
        Am. Anthrop. 64:6 (Dec. 1962), 1179-1203. A reply to RUR 1317.

1350   Lewis, Oscar, "Peasant Culture in India and Mexico: A Comparative
        Analysis," in GEN 4353 (1955), 145-170. [Indian State of Uttar
        Pradesh; Mexico]

1351   Lindstrom, D. E., "The Communication of New Techniques and Ideas,"
        in GEN 4394 (1963), 74-94.

1352   Lionberger, H. F., Adoption of New Ideas and Practices: A Summary
        of the Research Dealing with the Acceptance of Technological Change
        in Agriculture, with Implications for Action in Facilitating Such
        Change. Iowa City: Iowa State University Press, 1960. 164 pp.

1353   Lockwood, W. G., "The Market Place as a Social Mechanism in Peasant
        Society," Kroeber Anthrop. Soc. Pap. 32 (1965), 47-67. [Yugoslavia]

1354   Loomis, Charles P. et al. (eds.), Turrialba: Social Systems and
        the Introduction of Change. Glencoe., Ill.: Free Press, 1953.
        288 pp. [Costa Rica]

1355   Luschinsky, Mildred, "Problems of Culture Change in the Indian
        Village," Hum. Organiz. 22:1 (Spring 1963), 66-74.

1356   Maahs, A. M., A Social Interpretation of the Cargo Cult of New Guinea
        and Selected Comparable Phenomena in Other Areas of the World. Ann
        Arbor, Mich.: University Microfilms, 1956. 137 pp.

1357   Malinowski, Bronislaw, Argonauts of the Western Pacific: An Account
        of Native Enterprise and Adventure in the Archipelagos of Melanesian
        New Guinea. London: Routledge and Kegan Paul, 1922. 527 pp.

1358   Marriott, McKim, "Little Communities in an Indigenous Civilization,"
        in GEN 4353 (1955), 171-222. [Indian State of Uttar Pradesh]

1359   ------ "Technological Change in Overdeveloped Rural Areas," Econ.
        Dev. cult. Change 1:4 (Dec. 1952), 261-272.

1360   Matsubara, H., "Nômin Ishiki eno Shakaigaku-Teki Approach" [A socio-
        logical approach to the social consciousness of the peasantry],
        Shakaigaku Hyôron 11:3-4 (1960), 138-143. [Japan]

1361   Meillassoux, C., "Essai d'interprétation du phénomène économique
        dans les sociétés traditionelles d'autosubsistence" [An interpre-
        tative essay on the economic phenomenon in traditional subsistence
        societies], Cah. Etud. afr. 1:1 (Jan. 1960), 38-67.

1362   Meister, Albert, Desarrollo comunitario y cambio social: Investi-
        gación acerca de los factores favorables y las resistencias al
        cambio social en una zona de la Argentina [Community development and

social change: Investigation of the factors favorable to and
resistant to change in a district of Argentina]. Buenos Aires:
Departamento de Sociología, Universidad de Buenos Aires, 1961.
194 mim. pp. (An outline of the project with a copy of the
questionnaire.)

1363   Mintz, Sidney W., "The Folk-Urban Continuum and the Rural Prole-
       tarian Community," Am. J. Sociol. 59:1 (July 1953), 136-143.

1364   ------ "Internal Market Systems as Mechanisms of Social Articula-
       tion," in GEN 4367 (1959), 20-30.

1365   ------ "The Plantation as a Socio-Cultural Type," in GEN 4365 (1959),
       42-49.

1366   ------ "On Redfield and Foster," Am. Anthrop. 56:1 (Feb. 1954),
       87-92.

1367   Mousinho Guidi, M. L., "Elementos de análise des 'Estudos de
       comunidades' realizados no Brasil e publicados de 1948 a 1960"
       [Analytical elements of "Community Studies" conducted in Brazil
       and published from 1948 to 1960], Educ. Ciênc. soc. 10:9 (Jan.-
       Apr. 1962), 45-87.

1368   Mukherjee, Ramkrishna, Economic Surveys in Underdeveloped Countries:
       A Study in Methodology. Bombay: Asia Publishing House, 1959.
       263 pp. [India]

1369   ------ Dynamics of a Rural Society. Berlin: Akademie Verlag, 1957.
       134 pp. [Indian State of West Bengal]

1370   Nash, Manning, "The Organization of Economic Life," in GEN 4389
       (1964), 171-180. Also in GEN 4319 (1967), 3-12; and GEN 4349 (1966),
       384-388.

1371   ------ Primitive and Peasant Economic Systems. San Francisco:
       Chandler, 1966. 166 pp.

1372   Orenstein, Henry, "Irrigation, Settlement Pattern, and Social
       Organization," in GEN 4395 (1960), 318-323. [India]

1373   Pauvert, J.-Cl., "Note sur quelques aspects de développement commu-
       nautaire" [Note on some aspects of community development], in GEN
       4302 (1962), 143-152.

1374   Ramakrishnam Raju, B., "Innovations: Their Acceptance and
       Rejection," J. Karnatak Univ. (Hum.) 8 (1964), 317-322. [India]

1375   Raval, Indubhai B., "Sociology of Tribal Economic Development,"
       Indian J. soc. Wk. 25 (Apr. 1964), 43-51. [India]

1376   Redfield, Robert, The Folk Culture of Yucatan. Chicago: University
       of Chicago Press, 1941. 416 pp. [Mexico]

1377   ------ Peasant Society and Culture. Chicago-London: University of
       Chicago Press, 1956. 163 pp.

1378   ------ The Primitive World and Its Transformations. Ithaca, N.Y.:
          Cornell University Press, 1957. 185 pp.

1379   Sahlins, Marshall D., Social Stratification in Polynesia. Seattle:
          University of Washington Press, 1958. 306 pp.

1380   Schwartz, J., "Systems of Areal Integration: Some Considerations
          Based on the Admiralty Islands of Northern Melanesia," Anthrop.
          Forum 1:1 (July 1963), 56-97.

1381   Shea, T. W., Jr., "Barriers to Economic Development in Traditional
          Societies: Malabar, A Case Study," J. econ. Hist. 19:4 (Dec. 1959),
          504-522. [Indian State of Kerela]

1382   Silverman, Sydel F., "Some Cultural Correlates of the Cyclical
          Market," in GEN 4367 (1959), 31-36.

1383   Smith, Michael G., "Pre-Industrial Stratification Systems," in GEN
          4381 (1966), 141-176.

1384   Stinchcombe, A. L., "Agricultural Enterprise and Rural Class
          Relations," Am. J. Sociol. 67:2 (Sept. 1961), 165-176.

1385   Takeda, T., "'Mura' ni okeru kyodotaiteki kōzō no Hen'i" [Change in
          community structure in the "village"], Kyôdôtai No Hikaku Kenkyû 1
          (1964), 1-8.

1386   UNESCO, Cultural Patterns and Technical Change. Paris: UNESCO,
          1953. 348 pp.

1387   Vakil, C. N., "Social Implications of Technological Change at the
          Level of the Community," in GEN 4302 (1962), 167-178.

1388   Van de Moosdijk, T., "Een Evaluatie van het 'Rural-urban Continuum'"
          [An Evaluation of the "rural-urban continuum"], Mens en Maatschappij
          41:1 (1966), 20-27.

1389   Walker, K. F., "The Study of Primitive Economics," Oceania 13:2
          (Dec. 1942), 131-142.

1390   Weintraub, Dov, and Moshe Lissak, "Social Integration and Change,"
          in GEN 4309 (1964), 129-159.

1391   Wolf, Eric R., "Types of Latin American Peasantry," Am. Anthrop.
          57:3, Pt. 1 (June 1955), 452-471. Also in GEN 4319 (1967), 501-
          523.

1392   Wolfe, A. W., In the Ngombe Tradition: Continuity and Change in
          the Congo. Evanston, Ill.: Northwestern University Press, 1961.
          167 pp. [Congo (Leopoldville)]

2. Modernization of the Rural Sector

A. Annotated Case Studies

2001   Abou-Zaid, A. M., "Migrant Labour and Social Structure in Kharga
Oasis," in GEN 4364 (1963), 41-53. [Egypt]

The introduction of cash (brought in by the migrants) into the
Oasis has tended to obviate the traditional power structure and to
integrate the individual into the national economy.

2002   Bailey, Frederick G., "Economic Innovation," J. Maharaja Sayajirao
Univ. 3:1 (Mar. 1954), 13-27. [Indian State of Gujarat]

The introduction of the wage system has allowed the landless to
better their social and political position, even to the point of
altering patterns of caste.

2003   Beardsley, Richard K., "Ecological and Social Parallels between
Rice-growing Communities of Japan and Spain," in GEN 4326 (1964),
51-63.

Even though the villages are highly integrated in the monetary
economy and have extensive outside contacts, the communal structure
has remained active and vigorous.

**2004   Belshaw, Cyril S., In Search of Wealth: A Study of the Emergence
of Commercial Operations in the Melanesian Society of Southeastern
Papua. Menasha, Wis.: American Anthropological Association, 1955.
84 pp.

The author stresses the compatibility of the traditional social
structure and modern economic development. The close kinship
system, for instance, proves to be more effective as a base for
"incorporation" than does the traditional impersonal Western
corporate structure. The still traditional nonmonetized sector
provides a cushion against a recession in the monetary sector.
With development, of course, the goods of the monetary sector no
longer are luxuries; and this tends to increase mobility by freeing
the individual both from the land and from the wider forms of the
family. This should lead to greater trade and a concomitant rise
in demand. Meeting this demand may be difficult, since the
administration (and therefore the banks) insists on Western
organizational methods that are often unsuitable, thus limiting
the availability of investment funds.

2005   Boeke, J. H., Dorp en Desa [Village and desa]. Leiden: H. E.
Stenfert Kroese, 1934. 73 pp. [Indonesia]

A general account of Javanese village society under the impact
of modern capitalism.

2006   Burridge, Kenelm O. L., <u>Mambu: A Melanesian Millennium.</u> London:
          Methuen, 1960.   296 pp.

             The "Cargo" movement (the belief that modern commodities will be
          sent from Heaven) represents an attempt to bridge the gap between the
          known traditional way of life and the European, as yet barely per-
          ceived.   The expansion of traditional trading is not enough to
          enable the inhabitants to make the long cultural leap, and so this
          accounts for the "Cargo" myth-dream.

2007   Damle, Y. B., <u>The Communication of Modern Ideas and Knowledge in
          Indian Villages</u>. Cambridge, Mass.: Center for International
          Studies, Massachusetts Institute of Technology, 1955.   28 pp.
          [Indian State of Maharashtra]

             A study of seven villages near Poona, Maharashtra, showing that
          communication, in the sociological sense, is not based merely on
          physical contiguity.

2008   De Waal Malefijt, Annemarie, <u>The Javanese of Surinam: Segment of a
          Plural Society</u>. Assen, Netherlands: Van Gorcum, 1963.   206 pp.

             Faced with a totally new situation upon their arrival in Surinam,
          the Javanese chose to turn inward upon their own society.   However,
          as this society has no function in the new situation, the end result
          has been the isolation of the group as well as a strengthened sense
          of solidarity.

2009   Eames, E., "Some Aspects in Urban Migration from a Village in North-
          Central India," <u>East. Anthrop</u>. 8:1 (Sept.-Nov. 1954), 18-26.
          [Indian State of Madhya Pradesh]

             Migration has yet to cause many changes in the village.   The
          author stresses the differential migratory patterns of upper and
          lower castes--the upper castes migrating for education, the lower
          for work.

2010   Ember, Melvin, "Commercialization and Political Change in American
          Samoa," in GEN 4330 (1964), 95-110.

             Commercialization and change in the political structure of the
          village are closely related.

2011   Fei, Hsiao-tung, <u>China's Gentry: Essays in Rural-Urban Relations</u>.
          Chicago: Chicago University Press, 1954.   290 pp.

             Several case studies of individuals who have been affected by
          urban contacts.

**2012   Finney, Ben R., "Polynesian Peasants and Proletarians: Socio-
          Economic Change among the Tahitians of French Polynesia," <u>J. Poly-
          nesian Soc</u>. 74:3 (Sept. 1965), 269-328.

             A study of an isolated community that has turned to cash crop-
          ping and of a peri-urban community that has turned to wage labor.
          In response to outside economic stimuli, both communities have

shifted from traditional subsistence activities to a "rational" exploitation of the new choices available to them. These new modes of livelihood have been accompanied by the dissolution of the extended family in favor of the nuclear family. The author finds that economic change is ipso facto social change, and vice versa.

2013   Garbett, Kingsley G., Growth and Change in a Shona Ward. Salisbury: University College of Rhodesia and Nyasaland, 1960. 100 pp. [Rhodesia]

Despite an increased tendency to emigrate, men still cling to their holdings of land.

**2014   Geertz, Clifford, Peddlers and Princes: Social Development and Economic Change in Two Indonesian Towns. Chicago: University of Chicago Press, 1963. 162 pp.

Though economic development has a relation to the social structure, this is not an all-inclusive one. The entrepreneurial group, while homogeneous, is distinguishable from the rest of the society, for it is likely to have had long-standing contacts beyond the village. In the cases here studied, this innovative group feels responsible for reshaping and ameliorating the rest of the society. Their primary role is to introduce new techniques and get them accepted.

*2015   Go, Gien Tjwan, Eenheid in Verscheidenheid in een Indonesisch Dorp [Unity in diversity in an Indonesian village]. Amsterdam: Socio-Historical Seminary for Southeast Asia, University of Amsterdam, 1966. 267 mim. pp.

Agricultural progress is blocked by the high cost of improved methods. Though outwardly they seem assimilated, the descendants of Chinese immigrants have acted as middlemen and traders between the village and the outside world. This has enabled them to escape the poverty of the village, but by the same token it has enhanced racial division.

*2016   Goldsen, R. K., and M. Ralis, Factors Related to Acceptance of Innovations in Bang Chan, Thailand: Analysis of a Survey Conducted by the Cornell Cross-Cultural Methodology Project, May 1955. Ithaca: Cornell University Press, 1957. 72 pp.

The new techniques that require more capital seem equally to exact more risk and a greater commitment to innovation. There appears to be a high correlation between literary and urban contacts and the acceptance of innovation.

*2017   Hart, Donn Vorhis, The Philippine Plaza Complex: A Focal Point in Culture Change. New Haven: Southeast Asia Studies, Yale University, 1955. 57 pp.

The role of religious celebrations in diffusing urban characteristics: the peasants are ridiculed into dressing and acting like urban dwellers.

2018   Herskovits, Melville J., <u>Life in a Haitian Valley</u>. New York:
          Octagon Books, 1937. 350 pp.

              Though the origins of the voodoo cult are African, much of the
          social structure in Haiti derives from Europe.

2019   Hirabayashi, G. K., and L. Armstrong, "Social Structure and Differen-
          tiation in Rural Lebanon," in GEN 4347 (1956), 349-356.

              There is a marked differentiation at all levels of income in the
          rural area.

**2020   Holas, B., <u>Changements sociaux en Côte d'Ivoire</u> [Social changes on
          the Ivory Coast]. Paris: Presses Universitaires de France, 1961.
          117 pp.

              Coffee growing has brought about marked changes in the status of
          women. As they handle the crop, they have become economically
          valuable. Thus the traditional sexual license after an initiation
          ceremony has been restricted.

*2021   Howarth, David A., <u>The Shadow of the Dam</u>. New York: Macmillan,
          1961. 175 pp. [Zambia]

              A study of the opposition by the primitive Tonga of Northern
          Rhodesia to being moved before the dam flooded their villages, and
          of the problems of their relocation. The natives were generally
          unable to understand the rationale of the dam and the consequent
          flood.

*2022   Hunter, Monica, "The Bantu on European-owned Farms," in GEN 4372
          (1937), 389-404. [Republic of South Africa]

              The Bantu farm communities are extremely conservative; they
          follow traditional practices even when these no longer correspond
          to present-day realities.

**2023   Jayawardena, C., <u>Conflict and Solidarity in a Guianese Plantation</u>.
          London: Athlone Press, 1963. 159 pp. [British Guiana]

              An attempt at intervention in a dispute by a third party, known
          as an "eye-pass," is socially unacceptable; unlike other labor-
          management confrontations, it is met with violence. The "eye-pass"
          is one means of assuring equality among workers, and thus it hinders
          individual socioeconomic improvement.

2024   Jones, William O., "Manioc: An Example of Innovation in African
          Economies," <u>Econ. Dev. cult. Change</u> 5:2 (Jan. 1957), 97-117.
          [West Africa]

              The introduction of manioc into Africa before the coming of the
          Europeans illustrates native resourcefulness.

**2025   Maher, Robert F., <u>New Men of Papua: A Study of Culture Change</u>.
          Madison: University of Wisconsin Press, 1961. 148 pp. [New
          Guinea]

    This tribe has passed within forty years from cannibalism to a
commercial economy. A comparison of the present situation with
that of the early 1920's shows that a change in one aspect of a
society causes change elsewhere in the social structure, and that
the degree of alteration is relative to the importance of what has
changed. In this case, cannibalism was centrally important to the
society, and its disappearance has led to the dislocation of the
village and probably to a decline in population. The following
cultural periods are distinguished: (1) the acceptance of steel
knives and other tools; (2) the labor for Europeans during World
War II; (3) general Europeanization; (4) and withdrawal, as
Europeanization seems a failure (this last is the author's
speculation).

2026   Mathur, J. C., and Paul M. Neurath, An Indian Experiment in Farm
        Radio Forums. Paris: UNESCO, 1959. 132 pp. [Indian State of
        Maharashtra]

        These forums do communicate new methods of farming.

2027   Mathur, J. C., and H. P. Saksena, TV for Better Citizenship. Report
        of an AIR-UNESCO Project on Adult Education through TV. 2 vols.
        New Delhi: UNESCO, 1962. 113 and 105 pp. [Indian State of
        Maharashtra]

        Communication via TV is less effective than via the radio forum,
for TV is so much of a novelty that it is distracting.

2028   Morton-Williams, P., Cinema in Rural Nigeria: A Field Study of the
        Impact of Fundamental-Education Films on Rural Audiences in Nigeria.
        Lagos, Nigeria: Federal Information Service, 195?. 195 pp.

        Reports of specific cases.

2029   Nash, Manning, The Golden Road to Modernity. New York: Wiley, 1965.
        333 pp. [Burma]

        A study of two villages, with many miscellaneous facts gathered
from direct observation.

*2030   Neurath, Paul M., "The Radio Farm Forum as a Tool of Change in
        Indian Villages," Econ. Dev. cult. Change 10:3 (Apr. 1962), 275-
        283. [Indian State of Maharashtra]

        A study of the effects of a series of broadcasts by Radio Poona
on agricultural techniques. The study groups of farmers organized
around these broadcasts were generally successful, especially in
generating their desire to participate in the debate.

*2031   Niehoff, Arthur H., and Juanita Niehoff, East Indians in the West
        Indies. Milwaukee, Wis.: Olsen Publishing Co., 1960. 192 pp.
        [Trinidad and Tobago]

        While caste has all but disappeared among the East Indians, the
joint family has survived. In general the family has adapted to
the new environment in so far as this was requisite for economic
reasons, but it has resisted any changes in the structure of the
family.

**2032   Redfield, Robert, <u>The Folk Culture of Yucatan</u>. Chicago: University of Chicago Press, 1941. 416 pp.

    As the contacts between village and city multiply, they become more complex; the division of labor is more defined, individualism is the stronger, and the family the weaker. These changes are examined primarily in forms of exchange rather than in attitudes as motives.

*2033   Rowley, Charles, <u>The New Guinea Villager: The Impact of Colonial Rule on Primitive Society and Economy</u>. New York: Praeger, 1966. 240 pp.

    The New Guinea villager envies the white man and equally hates him. The villager responds to economic incentive, but he is often hampered by his lack of critical skills. In general urban influence is a disruptive force in New Guinea. The natives' wages are extremely low, for they are based on a single man's subsistence level--insufficient to support a family in an urban area. As a result, urban groups are unstable, being composed primarily of males.

**2034   Sahlins, Marshall D., <u>Social Stratification in Polynesia.</u> Seattle: University of Washington Press, 1958. 306 pp.

    The author relates economic productivity to the degree of social stratification. This relationship derives from the fact that the cultures are redistributive: surplus production is eventually redistributed by the social hierarchy. The Polynesian subcultures have adapted their social system (the form and degree of stratification) to their local environment.

*2035   Salim, S. M., <u>Marsh Dwellers of the Euphrates Delta</u>. London: Athlone Press, 1962. 157 pp. [Iraq]

    A study of a Bedouin group that was previously a despotic sheikdom. The tribesmen had been driven into the swamps and eventually brought under foreign control. The sheikdom has now disappeared, and greater economic equality is found; but social status is not yet accorded on the basis of wealth; commercial activities are considered unworthy of a "warrior" Bedouin.

*2036   Smith, M. G., <u>Stratification in Granada</u>. Berkeley: University of California Press, 1965. 271 pp. [British Caribbean]

    Granada is a plural society in which social structure has no consensus. Such a society is a viable one, but the process of change is likely to be particularly difficult because of the underlying strains in the system.

2037   Snyder, Joan, "The Changing Context of an Andean Community," in GEN 4366 (1957), 20-29.

    Because the Indians are blocked from rising in the local class structure, increasing acculturation leads to increasing emigration and enhanced individuality.

2038   Steed, Gitel P., "Notes on an Approach to a Study of Personality
        Formation in a Hindu Village in Gujarat," in GEN 4353 (1955), 102-
        144. [India]

            A case study of an "overlord" in an isolated feudal village.

2039   Swift, M. G., Malay Peasant Society in Jelebu. New York: Humanities
        Press, 1965. 181 pp.

            The introduction of rubber plantations seems to have furthered
        the weakening of village and kinship ties.

*2040   Trent, S., "Impact of Money Economy and Adult Suffrage on a Mysore
        Village," Econ. Wkly. 8:3-5 (Jan. 1956), 101-104. [Indian State of
        Mysore]

            Economic prosperity has not changed the internal credit system.
        Thus the introduction of adult suffrage (voting by a show of hands)
        has not been effective.

2041   ------ "Irrigation and Socio-Economic Change in a Mysore Village,"
        Econ. Wkly. 7:37 (19 Sept. 1955), 1091-1094. [Indian State of
        Mysore]

            The villagers are eager for change. The caste system has been
        modified, but is still strong enough to keep the economic forces
        evolutionary instead of revolutionary.

2042   Tumin, Melvin M., Caste in a Peasant Society: A Case Study in the
        Dynamics of Caste. Princeton: Princeton University Press, 1952.
        300 pp. [Guatemala]

            Prejudice against the Indian has kept him in his place despite
        any ability or desire he might have to rise in the caste order.

2043   UNESCO, Rural Television in Japan. A Report on an Experiment in
        Adult Education. Paris: UNESCO, 1960. 198 pp.

            A study of the effects of a special program series for farmers
        given in 1956-1957.

**2044 Vanderlinden, Jacques, "Problèmes posés par l'introduction de
        nouveaux modes d'usage des terres chez les Zande Vungara du Congo
        Belge" [Problems brought about by the introduction of new methods
        of land exploitation among the Zande Vungara of the Belgian Congo],
        in GEN 4310 (1963), 331-347.

            A study of a remote section of the Belgian Congo. At first the
        new method of growing cotton was not adopted, since it required
        much more work than did the old method, without any concomitant
        economic reward. The new cotton was better, but there was little
        demand for it on the local market. The change was finally effected
        by buying off the chiefs and by other forms of coercion.

*2045   Watson, William, Tribal Cohesion in a Money Economy: A Study of
        the Mambwe People of Northern Rhodesia. Manchester, England:

Manchester University Press, 1958.   246 pp. [Zambia]

The tribal ownership of land has tended to keep the individual attached to the tribe and to preserve its institutions, despite the influx of money earned by working in the mines. Land is a social and economic force in stabilizing the society.

*2046   Willems, Emelio, Uma vila brasileira: Tradição e transição [A Brazilian village: Tradition and transition]. São Paulo: Difusão Européia do Livro, 1961. 222 pp.

The traditional culture is undergoing dissolution, since the once oppressed rural groups are now able to migrate to the city. This process has been slowed, however, by the relative isolation of the village and by the traditional lack of emphasis on economic activity.

2047   Worsley, Peter, The Trumpet Shall Sound: A Study of Cargo Cults in Melanesia. London: MacGibbon and Kee, 1957.   290 pp.

The author believes that the New Guinea natives' enthusiastic response to the idea that the whites would bring vast riches results from the excessive tension between the native standard of living and the wealth of the whites. Too great a stimulation can be destructive in the end.

*2048   Young, Frank W., and Ruth C. Young, "Social Integration and Change in 24 Mexican Villages," Econ. Dev. cult. Change 8:4, Pt. 1 (July 1960), 366-377. See also ibid. 8:3 (Apr. 1960), 257-264.

A determination of the absolute and relative degrees of change from 1950 to 1958. The authors treat the community as a "social fact" that responds as a whole to various outside influences. They find that communities are the more likely to accept change as their wealth increases or as they develop more outside contacts.

B.   Other Case Studies

2301   Abrahams, R. G., "Neighbourhood Organisation: A Major Subsystem among the Northern Nyamwezi," Africa 35:2 (Apr. 1965), 168-186. [Tanzania]

2302   Ahmed, Zahir, Dusk and Dawn in Village India. New York: Praeger, 1966.   144 pp. [Indian State of Andhra]

2303   Ainsworth, M. D., and L. H. Ainsworth, "Acculturation in East Africa. I. Political Awareness and Attitudes toward Authority. II. Frustra- tion and Aggression. III. Attitudes toward Parents, Teachers, and Education. IV. Summary Discussion," J. Soc. Psychol. 57:2 (Aug. 1962), 391-432.

2304   Akhauri, N., "Socio-Cultural Barriers to Rural Change in an East
        Bihar Community," East. Anthrop. 11:3-4 (Mar.-Aug. 1958), 212-219.
        [Indian State of Bihar]

2305   Alers-Montalvo, Manuel, "Cultural Change in a Costa Rican Village,"
        Hum. Organiz. 15:4 (Winter 1957), 2-7.

2306   ------ "Cultural Change in a Costa Rican Village." Ph.D. disser-
        tation, Michigan State University, 1963.

2307   Altekar, M. D., "Caste System and Its Relation to Social and
        Economic Life," Ann. Am. Acad. polit. soc. Sci. 233 (May 1944),
        183-187. [India]

2308   Anzola Gómez, G., Cómo llegar hasta los campesinos por medio de
        la educación: Resultados de una experiencia en el CREFAL [How to
        reach the peasants through education: Results of an experience in
        CREFAL (Regional Center for Fundamental Education in Latin
        America, Pátzcuaro, Mexico)]. Bogotá: Ministerio de Educación
        Nacional, 1962. 398 pp. [Colombia]

2309   Aoyagi, K., "Trinidad Shakai no Kaiso to Shudan" [Status and group
        in Trinidad society], Kaigaijijô Hôkoku 1 (1964), 3-8.

2310   Arya, Y. C., "Rural Attitude to Change," Rur. India 22:6 (June
        1959), 213-216. [India]

2311   Baer, G., "The Dissolution of the Egyptian Village Community," Wld.
        Islam 6:1-2 (1959), 56-70.

2312   Balsara, Jal F., "Nature and Extent of Social Change in Rural
        Society," Sociol. Bull. 11 (1962), 166-172. [India]

2313   Barennes, Y., La modernisation rurale au Maroc [Rural modernization
        in Morocco]. Paris: Librairie Générale de Droit et de Juris-
        prudence, 1948. 152 pp.

2314   Bataillon, C., "Modernisation du nomadisme pastoral" [Modernization
        of pastoral nomadism], in GEN 4392 (1963), 165-178. [Sahara Region]

2315   ------ "Relations extérieurs des nomades" [External relations of the
        nomads], in GEN 4392 (1963), 43-50. [Sahara Region]

2316   ------ "Résistance ou décadence du nomadisme"[Resistance or decay of
        nomadism], in GEN 4392 (1963), 143-152. [Sahara Region]

2317   ------ "Valeurs et attitudes du monde nomade" [Values and attitudes
        of the nomad world], in GEN 4392 (1963), 37-42. [Sahara Region]

2318   Bataillon, C., and Ch. Verlaque, "Nomadisme et économie moderne"
        [Nomadism and modern economy], in GEN 4392 (1963), 153-164.
        [Sahara Region]

2319   Bausch, G. E. J.-B., "Problèmes du travail au Gezira" [Problems of
        work in Gezira], Civilisations 13:3 (July 1963), 250-266. [Sudan]

2320   Beckett, Jeremy, "Social Change in Pukapuka," J. Polynesian Soc.
        73:3 (Dec. 1964), 411-430.

2321   Bennett, John W., and Iwao Ishino, Paternalism in the Japanese
        Economy: Anthropological Studies of Oyabun-Kobun Patterns.
        Minneapolis: University of Minnesota Press, 1963. 307 pp.

2322   Bergmann, Theodor, "Problems of Mechanization in Indian Agriculture,"
        Indian J. agric. Econ. 18 (Oct. 1963), 20-31.

2323   Berndt, C. H., "Mateship or Success: An Assimilation Dilemma,"
        Oceania 33:2 (Dec. 1962), 71-89. [New Guinea]

2324   ------ "Social and Cultural Change in New Guinea: Communication
        and Views About 'Other People,'" Sociologus 7:1 (Apr. 1957), 38-57.

2325   Bernus, E., Quelques aspects de l'évolution des Touareg de l'ouest
        de la République du Niger [Some aspects of the evolution of the
        Touareg in the western part of the Republic of Nigeria]. Niamey:
        Institut Fondamental d'Afrique Noire, 1963. 87 pp. [Nigeria]

2326   Berreman, G. D., "Effects of a Technological Change in an Aleutian
        Village," J. Arctic Inst. No. Am. 7:2 (1954), 102-107.

2327   Bessac, Frank B., "Some Social Effects on Land Reform in a Village
        on the Taichung Plain," J. China Soc. 4 (1964), 15-28. [Taiwan]

2328   Beteille, André, "Class and Caste: A Rejoinder," Man in India
        46:2 (Apr.-June 1966), 172-176. [India]

2329   Beuchelt, E., "Cheju-do: Wandlungen in der Gesellschaftsordnung
        einer koreanischen Inselkultur" [Changes in the social order of a
        Korean island culture], Sociologus 13:2 (1963), 150-168.

2330   Blacking, John, Black Background: The Childhood of a South
        African Girl. New York: Abelard-Schuman, 1964. 207 pp.

2331   Blair, Th. L., "Social Structure and Information Exposure in Rural
        Brazil," Rur. Sociol. 25:1 (June 1960), 65-75.

2332   Bose, A. B., and N. S. Jodha, "The Jajmani System in a Desert
        Village," Man in India 45:2 (Apr.-June 1965), 105-126. [Indian
        State of Punjab]

2333   Bose, A. B., and S. P. Malhotra, "Studies in Agricultural Sociology
        at the Central Arid Zone Research Institute: Some Characteristics
        of Lower, Middle and Upper Class Farmers," Indian J. Soc. Res.
        (Aug. 1964), 201-212. [North India]

2334   Bose, A. B., and P. C. Saxena, "The Diffusion of Innovations in a
        Village of Western Rajasthan," East. Anthrop. 18:3 (Sept.-Dec.
        1965), 138-151. [Indian State of Rajasthan]

2335   Bose, Santi Priya, "Characteristics of Farmers Who Adopt Agricul-
        tural Practices in Indian Villages," Rur. Sociol. 26:1 (June 1961),
        138-145. [India]

2336   ------ "The Diffusion of a Farm Practice in Indian Villages," Rur.
        Sociol. 29:1 (Mar. 1964), 53-66.

2337   ------ "Peasant Values and Innovation in India," Am. J. Sociol. 67:5
        (Mar. 1962), 552-560.

2338   Bourdieu, P., and A. Sayad, "Paysans déracinés: Bouleversements
        morphologiques et changements culturels en Algérie" [Uprooted
        peasants: Morphological and cultural changes in Algeria], Etud.
        rur. 12 (Jan.-Mar. 1964), 56-94.

2339   Brausch, G. E., "Transformations et continuité dans la région de
        la Gezireh au Soudan" [Transformations and continuity in the Gezireh
        region of the Sudan], Rev. int. Sci. soc. 16:3 (1964), 371-386.

2340   Burke, Jean T., A Study of Existing Social Conditions in the Eight
        Townships of the Shihmen Reservoir Area Including a Brief Analysis
        of the Impact of Irrigation and Benchmarks for Measuring Social
        Change. Lungtan, Taoyuan, Taiwan: Joint Commission on Rural
        Reconstruction in China, 1962. 114 pp. [Taiwan]

2341   Burns, William (ed.), Sons of the Soil: Studies of the Indian
        Cultivator. Delhi: Manager of Publications, 1941. 128 pp.
        [India]

2342   Capot-Rey, R., "Les problèmes du nomadisme au Sahara" [The problems
        of nomadism in the Sahara], Rev. int. Trav. 90:5 (Nov. 1964), 531-
        546.

2343   Caso, A., "Renaissance économique des communautés indigènes du
        Méxique" [Economic renaissance of indigenous communities in Mexico],
        Diogène 43 (July-Sept. 1963), 64-79.

2344   Caviedes, H., "El desarrollo espontáneo de la comunidad indígena
        de Bolivia" [Spontaneous development of the Indian community in
        Bolivia], Amér. indíg. 24:2 (2nd Quarter 1964), 123-128.

2345   Chandra, P., "Communication of Some New Ideas in a Madhya Pradesh
        Village: A Sociological Study Conducted in a Mixed Village,"
        East. Anthrop. 17:3 (Sept.-Dec. 1964), 183-214. [Indian State of
        Madhya Pradesh]

2346   Chapuis, E., "Conditionnement socio-culturel de l'économie dans la
        région de Tuléar (Madagascar)" [Sociocultural impact on the economy
        of the Tulear (Madagascar) region], Cah. Inst. Sci. écon. 145, series
        5:7 (Jan. 1964), 199-226.

2347   Chatterji, A., and P. Maitreya, "Some Aspects of Regional Variations
        in Agricultural Productivity and Development in West Bengal,"
        Indian J. agri. Econ. 19:1 (Jan. 1964), 207-212. [Indian State of
        West Bengal]

2348   Chattopadhyay, K. P. (ed.), Study of Changes in Traditional Culture.
        Calcutta: University of Calcutta, 1957. 132 pp. [India]

2349   Chauhan, Brij Raj, "A Cash Crop in a Village Community: A Case

Study," J. soc. Res. 3 (Mar. 1960), 16-20. [Indian State of Gujarat]

2350   Christiansen, S., "Koraløen Ahus: En melanesisk handelsnation" [The coral island Ahus: A Melanesian commercial nation], Geogr. Tidsskr. 62 (1963), 24-33.

2351   Clauzel, J., "L'évolution contemporaine de l'économie et de la société chez les Touaregs" [Contemporary evolution of the economy and the society among the Touaregs], Actual. d'outre-mer 24 (July 1963), 5-24. [Chad]

2352   Clay, Horace F., "Some Effects of Cultural Factors on Adult Educational Processes: A Comparison of Cooperative Extension Techniques as They Apply to Small Farm Operators in Costa Rica, Guatemala and Hawaii." Ph.D. dissertation, University of Chicago, 1950. Microfilm 6114 LC.

2353   Cohen, Ronald, "Conflict and Change in a Northern Nigerian Emirate," in GEN 4401 (1964), 495-521.

2354   Colson, Elizabeth, "Social Change and the Gwembe Tonga," Hum. Probl. B.C.A. 35 (June 1964), 1-13. [Zambia]

2355   "Como trabalha uma equipe de missão rural da C.N.E.R." [How a rural working group of the national campaign for rural education functions], Rev. Campanha nac. Educ. rur. 2:2 (1956), 98-119. [Brazil]

2356   Cornell, John B., "Ainu Assimilation and Cultural Extinction: Acculturation Policy in Hokkaido," Ethnol. 3:3 (July 1964), 287-304. [Japan]

2357   ------ "Outcaste Relations in a Japanese Village," Am. Anthrop. 63:2 (Apr. 1961), 282-296.

2358   Dalisay, A. M., "Economic Research and Agricultural Extension Work: A Philippine Experience," in GEN 4394 (1963), 181-188.

2359   Dalton, G., "Le développement des économies de subsistance et des économies paysannes en Afrique" [The development of subsistence and peasant economies in Africa], Riv. int. Sci. soc. 16:3 (1964), 409-422.

2360   Darling, Malcolm Lyall, The Punjab Peasant in Prosperity and Debt. London: Oxford University Press, 1925. 298 pp. [Indian State of Punjab]

2361   Das, N., "Changing Pattern of a Koraput Village," Vanyajati 8:2 (Apr. 1960), 65-76. [Indian State of Orisa]

2362   Dasgupta, Satadal, "Communication and Innovation in Indian Villages," Soc. Forces 43:3 (Mar. 1965), 330-337.

2363   Deschamps, Hubert J., Les migrations intérieures à Madagascar [Internal migrations in Madagascar]. Paris: Berger-Levrault, 1959. 283 pp.

2364   Dhillon, S. H. S., Leadership and Groups in a South Indian Village.
        New Delhi: Government of India Press, 1955.

2365   Diégues Júnior, M., "Transformações na communidade rural da América
        latina" [Transformations in the Latin American rural community],
        Amér. lat. 7:3 (July-Sept. 1964), 25-36.

2366   Doutreloux, Albert, "Tenure foncière et valeurs socio-culturelles
        dans un groupe africain" [Land tenure and socio-cultural values in
        an African group], Anthropologica 8:2 (1966), 217-234. [West Africa]

2367   Driver, Edwin D., "Caste and Occupational Structure in Central
        India," Soc. Forces 41:1 (Oct. 1962), 26-31.

2368   Dubbeldam, L. F. B., "The Devaluation of the Kapauku Cowrie as a
        Factor of Social Disintegration," Am. Anthrop. 66:4, Pt. 2 (Aug.
        1964), 293-303. [New Guinea]

2369   Dube, S. C., "Social Structure and Change in Indian Peasant Commu-
        nities," in GEN 4347 (1956), 259-266.

2370   Du Bois, Cora Alice, The People of Alor: A Social-Psychological
        Study of an East Indian Island. Minneapolis: University of Minne-
        sota Press, 1944. 654 pp. [Indian State of Andaman Islands]

2371   Dunn, Stephen P., "The Transformation of Economy and Culture in the
        Soviet North," Arctic Anthrop. 1:2 (irregular 1963), 1-28.

2372   Dyson-Hudson, N., "Factors Inhibiting Change in an African Pastoral
        Society: The Karimojong of Northeast Uganda," Trans. N.Y. Acad.
        Sci. 24:7 (May 1962), 771-801.

2373   Eglar, Zekiye S., "Vartan Bhanji: Institutionalized Reciprocity in
        a Changing Punjab Village." Ann Arbor, Mich.: University Micro-
        films, 1958. [Indian State of Punjab]

2374   Eisenstadt, S. N., "Israel: Traditional and Modern Social Values
        and Economic Development," Ann. Am. Acad. polit. soc. Sci. 305 (May
        1956), 145-156.

2375   Elkin, A. P., "Western Technology and the Australian Aborigines,"
        in GEN 4356 (1963), 146-156. [Melanesia]

2376   Epstein, A. L., "The Economy of Modern Matupit: Continuity and
        Change on the Gazelle Peninsula, New Britain," Oceania 33:3 (Mar.
        1963), 182-215. [Melanesia]

2377   Epstein, T. Scarlett, "A Note on Regional Development and Social
        Change," J. Asian Afr. Stud. 1:1 (Jan. 1966), 63-67. [Indian State
        of Madhya Pradesh]

2378   Erasmus, Charles J., "Agricultural Changes in Haiti: Patterns of
        Resistance and Acceptance," Hum. Organiz. 2:4 (Winter 1952),
        20-26.

2379   ------ "Culture Structure and Process. The Occurrence and

Disappearance of Reciprocal Farm Labor," Sthwest. J. Anthrop. 12:4 (Winter 1956), 444-470. [Haiti]

2380   Etienne, P., "Phénomènes religieux et facteurs socio-économiques dans un village de la région de Bouaké (Côte d'Ivoire)" [Religious phenomena and socio-economic factors in a village in the Bouaké region (Ivory Coast)], Cah. Etud. afr. 6:3 (Oct. 1966), 367-401.

2381   Faure, H., "Quelques obstacles sociaux au développement de l'économie traditionnelle" [Some social obstacles to the development of the traditional economy], Cah. Sociol. écon. 9 (Nov. 1963), 105-123.

2382   Fautz, Bruno, Sozialstruktur und Bodennutzumg in der Kulturland- schaft des Swat [Social structure and land use in the cultural land- scape of the Swat]. Giessen, W. Germany: W. Schmitz, 1963. 119 pp. [Indian State of Gujarat]

2382a   Favre, Henri, "L'intégration socio-économique des Indiens au Méxique" [The socioeconomic integration of the Indians in Mexico], in GEN 4355 (1963), 453-469.

2383   Feder, E., "Feodalismo y desarrollo agrícola: El papel del credito controlado en la agricultura chilenna" [Feudalism and agricultural development: The role of controlled credit in Chilean agriculture], Rev. mex. Sociol. 22:1 (Jan.-Apr. 1960), 39-65.

2384   Finney, B. R., "Polynesian Peasants and Proletarians: Socio- economic Change among the Tahitians of French Polynesia," J. Poly- nesian Soc. 74:3 (Sept. 1965), 269-328.

2385   Foster, G. M., Traditional Cultures and the Impact of Technological Change. New York: Harper and Row, 1962. 292 pp.

2386   Fountain, O. C., "Religion and Economy in Mission Station-Village Relationships," Pract. Anthrop. 13:2 (1966), 49-58. [New Guinea]

2387   Fraenkel, Merran, "Social Changes on the Kru Coast of Liberia," Africa 36:2 (Apr. 1966), 154-172.

2388   Fujimoto, I., "The Process of Community Differentiation: An Insight into Development," Philipp. sociol. Rev. 13:4 (1965), 199- 210.

2389   Fukutake, Tadashi, "Post-War Democratization in Japan: Rural Society," Int. soc. Sci. J. 13 (1961), 65-77.

2390   Friedrich, P., "The External Relations of an Open, Corporate Village," Kroeber anthrop. Soc. Pap. 27 (Fall 1962), 27-44. [Mexico]

2391   Gaudry, M., La société féminine au Djebel Amour et au Ksel. Etude de sociologie rurale Nord-Africaine [The world of women in the Djebel Amour and at Ksel: A study of rural North-African sociology]. Algiers: Société Algérienne d'Impressions Diverses, 1961. 529 pp. [Algeria]

2392   Geddes, W. R., "Acceleration of Social Change in a Fijian Community,"
        Oceania 16:1 (Sept. 1945), 1-14.

2393   Geertz, Clifford, "Ritual and Social Change: A Javenese Example,"
        Am. Anthrop. 59:2 (Feb. 1957), 32-54.

2394   ------ The Social History of an Indonesian Town. Cambridge, Mass.:
        M.I.T. Press, 1965. 217 pp.

2395   Georges, M., "La vie rurale chez les Banda" [Rural life among the
        Banda], Cah. d'outre-mer 16:64 (Oct.-Dec. 1963), 321-359. [Central
        African Republic]

2396   Gerlach, L. P., "Traders on Bicycle: A Study of Entrepreneurship and
        Culture Change among the Digo and Duruma of Kenya," Sociologus 13:1
        (1963), 32-49.

2397   Ghosh, Madan Gopal, and Nripendranath Bandyopadhyay, "A Comparative
        Study of Some Aspects of Agricultural Development in Two States of
        Eastern Zone: West Bengal and Orissa," Indian J. agric. Econ. 19
        (Jan. 1964), 212-219.

2398   Gluckman, Max, Analysis of a Social Situation in Modern Zululand.
        Manchester, England: Manchester University Press, 1958. 77 pp. See
        also Bantu Stud. 14:2 (1940), 91-146.

2399   ------ "How the Bemba Make Their Living: An Appreciation of
        Richard's Land, Labor, and Diet in Northern Rhodesia," Am. Anthrop.
        47:1 (Jan. 1945), 57-75. [Zambia]

2400   Goddard, S., "Town-Farm Relationships in Yorubaland: A Case Study
        from Oyo," Africa 35:1 (Jan. 1965), 21-29. [Nigeria]

2401   Goldman, Irving, "The Evolution of Status Systems in Polynesia," in
        GEN 4395 (1960), 255-260.

2402   Green, James W., "Success and Failure in Technical Assistance: A
        Case Study," Hum. Organiz. 20:1 (Spring 1961), 2-10.

2403   Guiart, Jean, "Les tendances modernes de l'évolution des sociétés
        Mélanésiennes (Nouvelles-Hébrides et Nouvelle-Calédonie)" [Modern
        evolutionary tendencies in Melanesian societies (New Hebrides and
        New Caledonia)], in GEN 4395 (1960), 261-269.

2404   Guillard, J., "Les sous-secteur de modernisation rurale du pays
        Toupouri (Nord-Cameroun)" [The subsector of rural modernization of the
        Toupouri region, North Cameroons], Sols afr. 4:2 (1956), 31-64.

2405   Guiteras-Holmes, C., Perils of the Soul: The World View of a Tzotzil
        Indian. New York: Free Press of Glencoe, 1961. 371 pp. [Mexico]

2406   Gumperz, John J., "Religion and Social Communication in a Village
        in North India," J. Asian Stud. 23:3 (June 1964), 89-97.

2407   Halpern, Joel M., "Yugoslav Peasant Society in Transition: Stability
        in Change," Anthrop. Quart. 36:3 (July 1963), 156-182.

2408   Hammel, E. A., "Social Rank and Evolutionary Position in a Coastal
        Peruvian Village," Sthwest. J. Anthrop. 18:3 (Autumn 1962), 199-215.

2409   Hanawa, R., "Nishi-Nihon ni okeru Nôgyô-keitai to Nômin-sô Bunkai"
        [Agricultural structure and the differentiation of peasantry in
        Western Japan], Tochiseido Shigaku 18 (Jan. 1963), 1-25.

2410   Hancock, Richard H., The Role of the Bracero in the Economic and
        Cultural Dynamics of Mexico: A Case Study of Chihuahua. Stanford,
        Calif.: Hispanic American Society, 1959. 146 pp.

2411   Hanks, Lucian M., Jr., "Five Generalizations on the Structure of
        Foreign Contact: A Comparison of Two Periods in Thai History," in
        GEN 4366 (1957), 72-75.

2412   ------ "Indifference to Modern Education in a Thai Farming Commu-
        nity," Pract. Anthrop. 7 (1960), 18-29.

2413   ------ "A Note on Psycho-Social Tensions in a Thai Village after
        the Advent of Occidental Technology," Econ. Dev. cult. Change 1:5
        (Feb. 1953), 394-396.

2414   Hara, H., "Kinkô Nôson ni okeru Kengyô Nôka no Tenkai" [A report on
        change among part-time farmers], Shakaigaku Hyôron 11:3-4 (1960),
        62-75. [Japan]

2415   ------ "Sonraku Shakaigaku no Jisshô Kenkyû ni tsuite" [Practical
        studies in rural sociology], Kenkyû Tsûshin 15 (1963), 11-16.
        [Japan]

2416   Harris, M., "Labor Emigration among the Moçambique Thonga: Cultural
        and Political Factors," in GEN 4396 (1966), 91-106. [Mozambique]

2417   Hayashi, Jun'ichi, "Sociological Problems of Introducing New Agri-
        cultural Practices: A Japanese Experience," in GEN 4394 (1963),
        160-171.

2418   Henry, R. N., "Participation and Initiative of the Local People,"
        in GEN 4394 (1963), 199-212. [Southeast Asia]

2419   Herradura, Elma Sison, "The Ideals and Values of Filipino
        Adolescents." Ph.D. dissertation, University of California at
        Berkeley, 1962. 173 mim. pp.

2420   Hitchcock, John T., "Some Effects of Recent Change in Rural Nepal,"
        Hum. Organiz. 22:1 (Spring 1963), 75-82.

2421   Hogbin, H. Ian, "Culture Change in the Solomon Islands," Oceania
        4 (1934), 233-267. [Melanesia]

2422   Honigmann, J. J., "Education and Career Specialization in a West
        Pakistan Village of Renown," Anthropos 55:5-6 (1960), 825-840.

2423   Hopper, W. D., "Seasonal Labour Cycles in an Eastern Uttar Pradesh
        Village," East. Anthrop. 8:3-4 (Mar.-Aug. 1955), 141-150. [Indian
        State of Uttar Pradesh]

2424   Howard, Alan, "Land Tenure and Social Change in Rotuma," J. Poly-
        nesian Soc. 73:1 (Mar. 1964), 26-52. [Polynesia]

2425   Hsieh, Sam-Chung, "Socio-economic Surveying in China: The Experience
        of Rural Taiwan," in GEN 4394 (1963), 172-180.

2426   Hunter, Monica, "The Effects of Contact with Europeans on the Status
        of Pondo Women," Africa 6 (1933), 259-276. [Republic of South Africa]

2427   Hutchinson, Harry W., Village and Plantation Life in Northeastern
        Brazil. Spokane: University of Washington Press, 1957. 199 pp.

2428   Huzioka, Yosinaru, "Rorschach Test in Farming Villages of North
        Thailand," Nat. Life S.E. Asia 2 (1962), 139-273.

2429   Ilo, P., "Réalisations faites par des indigènes non-éduqués en vue
        d'un début de développement économique des Nouvelles-Hébrides"
        [Achievements of noneducated natives toward a beginning of economic
        development in the New Hebrides], Etud. mélanés. 8 (Dec. 1954), 103-
        108. [Melanesia]

2430   International Labour Organisation, Why Labour Leaves the Land: A
        Comparative Study of the Movement of Labour out of Agriculture.
        Geneva: International Labour Organisation, 1960. 229 pp. [India;
        Pakistan; Japan; Brazil; Africa; Turkey]

2431   Ishida, Y., "Mukyokai: Indigenous Movement in Japan," Pract. Anthrop.
        10:1 (Jan.-Feb. 1963), 21-26.

2432   Ishino, Iwao, "Social and Technological Change in Rural Japan:
        Continuities and Discontinuities," in GEN 4382 (1962), 100-112.

2433   Ishwaran, K., "Goldsmith in a Mysore Village," J. Asian afr. Stud.
        1:1 (Jan. 1966), 50-62. [Indian State of Mysore]

2434   ------ "Caste and Social Tension in South India," in GEN 4376 (1961),
        97-107.

2435   Japan Cultural Science Society (ed.), Damu Kensetsu no Shakai-teki
        Eikyō [Social consequences of the construction of a dam]. Tokyo:
        Tōdai Shuppan kai, 1959. 492 pp. [Japan]

2436   ------ Effect of the Construction of a Multi-Purpose Dam on the
        Social, Cultural, and Economic Interests of the Local Community.
        Tokyo: Japanese National Committee for UNESCO, 1960. 61 pp.

2437   Jarre, R., "Notes sur les changements survenus dans les coutumes
        Fidjiennes depuis l'occupation européenne" [Notes on the changes that
        have occurred in Fijian customs since the European occupation], J.
        Soc. Océan. 11 (1955), 15-36.

2438   Joglekar, N. M., "Study of Crop Patterns on an Urban Fringe," Indian
        J. agric. Econ. 18:1 (Jan. 1963), 84-90. [Indian State of Madhya
        Pradesh]

2439   Johnson, E., "Perseverance through Orderly Change: The 'Traditional'

Buraku in a Modern Community," Hum. Organiz. 22:3 (Fall 1963), 218-223. [Japan]

2440   Joshi, Vidya, "Attitude towards Reception of Technology," J. soc. Psychol. 58 (Oct. 1962), 3-7. [Indian State of Uttar Pradesh]

2441   Judd, Laurence Cecil, "Chao Rai: Dry Rice Farmers in Northern Thailand." Ph.D. dissertation, Cornell University, 1961. 381 mim. pp.

2442   Kagaya, H., "Iran no Shuzoku Shakai no Kindaiteki Hatten" [Modernization of an Iranian tribal society], Asia Keizai 5:5 (1964). [Iran]

2443   Kaneta, H., "Nōson ni okeru 'Shakaitekijōshō-kōbai' no Sokutei" [Measurement of the social rising gradient in the rural community], Hōkeikai Ronsō 14 (Oct. 1955), 80-103. [Japan]

2444   Karpat, Kemal H., "Social Effects of Farm Mechanization in Turkish Villages," Soc. Res. 27:1 (Spring 1960), 83-103.

2445   Katsube, K., "Suiden Tansaku Chitai ni okeru Sangyo Kumiai no Keiei: Hikawa-Mura Hisagi Chiku ni tsuite" [Management of a farmers' cooperative in the rice crop area: The case of the Village Hisagi, Hikawa Area], Shimane Daigaku Ronshû 5 (1959), 53-72. [Japan]

2446   Khare, R. S., "A Study of Social Resistance to Sanitation Programmes in Rural India," East. Anthrop. 17:2 (May 1964), 86-94.

2447   Kingon, J. R. L., "The Transition from Tribalism to Individualism," S. Afr. J. Sci. 16 (1920), 113-157. [Republic of South Africa]

2448   Knowles, William H., "Social Consequences of Economic Change in Jamaica," Ann. Am. Acad. polit. soc. Sci. 305 (May 1956), 134-144.

2449   Koch, G., "Kulturwandel bei den Polynesiern des Ellice-Archipels" [Cultural change among the Polynesians of the Ellice Archipelago], Sociologus 12:2 (1962), 128-141. [Polynesia]

2450   Koentjaraningrat, Some Social-Anthropological Observations on Gotong-Rojong Practices in Two Villages of Central Java. Ithaca: Cornell University Press, 1961. 67 pp. [Indonesia]

2451   Kruyt, A. C., "The Influence of Western Civilisation on the Inhabitants of Poso (Central Celebes)," in GEN 4374 (1929), 1-9. [Indonesia]

2452   Kuper, H., Indian People in Natal. Natal, Republic of South Africa: The University Press, 1960. 296 pp. [Republic of South Africa]

2453   Lakshmana Rao, Y. V., "Communication and Development: A Study of Two Indian Villages." Ph.D. dissertation, University of Minnesota, 1963. 324 mim. pp.

2454   Landy, D., "Tropical Childhood: Cultural Transmission and Learning in a Rural Puerto Rican Village," Am. Sociol. Rev. 25:5 (Oct. 1960), 775-776.

2455   Lasswell, H. D., "Integrating Communities into Inclusive Systems,"
         Hum. Organiz. 21:2 (Summer 1962), 116-124. [Peru]

2456   Launay, M., Paysans algériens [Algerian peasants]. Paris: Le Seuil,
         1963. 428 pp.

2457   Lauria, A., Jr., "'Respeto,' 'Relajo' and Inter-personal Relations
         in Puerto Rico," Anthrop. Quart. 37:2 (Apr. 1964), 53-67.

2458   Lawrence, P., "Religion: Help or Hindrance to Economic Development
         in Papua and New Guinea," Mankind 6:1 (May 1963), 3-11.

2459   Lebra, W. P., and T. W. Maretzki, "The Community Cooperative in
         Northern Okinawa," Econ. Dev. cult. Change 3 (1963), 225-238.

2460   Leighton, Alexander H., et al., Psychiatric Disorder among the Yoruba:
         A Report from the Cornell-Aro Mental Health Research Project in the
         Western Region, Nigeria. Ithaca: Cornell University Press, 1963.
         413 pp.

2461   Lewis, I. N., A Pastoral Democracy: A Study of Pastoralism and
         Politics among the Northern Somali of the Horn of Africa. London:
         Oxford University Press, 1961. 320 pp. [Somali Republic]

2462   Lewis, Oscar, "The Effects of Technical Progress on Mental Health in
         Rural Populations," Amér. indíg. 12:4 (Oct. 1952), 299-307. [Latin
         America]

2463   ------ "Social and Economic Changes in a Mexican Village, Tepoztlan,"
         Amér. indíg. 4:2 (Apr. 1944), 281-314.

2464   Long, Jancis F., et al., "Economic and Social Conditions among
         Farmers in Changwad Khonkaen." Bangkhen, Bangkok: Faculty of
         Economics and Cooperative Science, Kasetsart University, 1963.   164
         mim. pp. [Thailand]

2465   Lord, R. F., Economic Aspects of Mechanised Farming at Nachingwea,
         Tanganyika. London: H.M.S.O., 1963. 191 pp.

2466   McCulloch, Meran, "Les conséquences sociales du développement
         économique dans les régions rurales de l'Afrique Orientale et
         Centrale" [The social consequences of economic development in the
         rural regions of East and Central Africa], Inform. ISSC 14 (Oct.
         1957), 1-17. [East and Central Africa]

2467   ------ "Survey of Recent and Current Field Studies on the Social
         Effects of Economic Development in Inter-tropical Africa," in GEN
         4325 (1956), 53-225. [Central Africa]

2468   McLane, John R., Social Change in Burdwan District. Berkeley:
         Center for South Asia Studies, University of California, 1964(?).
         15 mim. pp. [West Bengal]

2469   Maher, Robert F., "Social Structure and Cultural Change in Papua,"
         Am. Anthrop. 62:4 (Aug. 1960), 593-603. [New Guinea]

2470   Majumdar, D. N., "Rural Life and Communication," East. Anthrop. 11:1-
        3 (Mar.-Aug. 1958), 175-188. [North India]

2471   Majumdar, D. N., M. C. Pradham, C. Sen, and S. Misra, "Inter-caste
        Relations in Gohanakallan: A Village near Lucknow," East. Anthrop.
        8:3-4 (May-Aug. 1955), 191-214. [Indian State of Uttar Pradesh]

2472   Makino, Y., "Nashi-saibai no Fukyû to Sonraku Kôzô: Aichi-ken
        Nishio-shi Yokote-cho" [On a diffusion process in the technique of
        pearl culture and social structure], Nôgyo Gijitsu Kenkyû (1963),
        99-116. [Japan]

2473   Malya, M. Meenakshi, "Urbanisation and Cropping Pattern," Indian J.
        agric. Econ. 18:1 (Jan. 1963), 90-96. [India]

2474   Mangin, William P., "The Role of Regional Associations in the
        Adaptation of Rural Population in Peru," Sociologus 9:1 (1959), 12-22.

2475   Mann, R. S., "Attitude of Minas towards Improved Agricultural Prac-
        tices," Man in India 46:2 (Apr.-June 1966), 131-134. [India]

2476   Marinho, A., "Técnicas de construção de jangada: Um estudo de
        mudança cultural" [Construction techniques used to build rafts: A
        study in cultural change], Sociologia 27:3 (1965), 241-247. [Brazil]

2477   Marriott, McKim, "Technological Change in Overdeveloped Rural Areas,"
        Econ. Dev. cult. Change 1:4 (Dec. 1952), 261-272.

2478   Mason, Leonard, "Ecologic Change and Culture Pattern in the Resettle-
        ment of Bikini Marshallese," in GEN 4366 (1957), 1-6. [Melanesia]

2479   Maude, H. E., "The Evolution of the Gilbertese Boti. An Ethno-His-
        torical interpretation," J. Polynesian Soc. 35 Suppl. (1963), 68 pp.
        [Polynesia]

2480   Mayer, A. C., Indians in Fiji. London: Oxford University Press,
        1963. 142 pp.

2481   Mdhluli, S. V. H., The Development of the African. Natal, Union of
        South Africa: Mariannhill Mission Press, 1933. 64 pp. [Republic of
        South Africa]

2482   Méndez-Arocha, A., La pesca en la isla de Margarita, Venezuela
        [Fishing on Margarita Island, Venezuela]. Caracas: Fundación La
        Salle de Ciencias Naturales, 1963. 267 pp. [Venezuela]

2483   Middleton, J., "Social Change in Northern Uganda," Contemp. Rev.
        1112 (Aug. 1958), 92-96.

2484   Miner, Horace M., "Culture Change under Pressure: A Hausa Case,"
        Hum. Organiz. 19:3 (Fall 1960), 164-167. [Nigeria]

2485   Mitani, T., "Rito Noson ni okeru Kazoku rui to Seisanruikei" [Types
        of family and production in agricultural villages of an isolated
        island], Shakaigaku Hyôron 15:1 (1964), 14-28. [Japan]

2486   Moerman, Michael Harris, "Farming in Ban Phaed: Technological
        Decisions and Their Consequences for the External Relations of a
        Thai-Lue Village." Ph.D. dissertation, Yale University, 1964.
        371 mim. pp. [Thailand]

2487   Moreira, J. R., "Rural Education and Socio-Economic Development in
        Brazil," Rur. Sociol. 25:1 (Mar. 1960), 38-50.

2488   Morrison, W. A., "Knowledge of Political Personages Held by the Male
        Villagers of Badlapur," Sociol. Bull. 12:1 (Mar. 1963), 1-17. [India]

2489   Mukherji, P., "Gramdan in Village Berain: Sociological Analysis,"
        Hum. Organiz. 25:1 (Spring 1966), 33-41. [India]

2490   Nakamura, R., "Gyujutsu Henka to Sonraku Shakai. Bunka Yōso no Chi-
        kan ni kansuru Mondai o meguru Jinrui-gaku-teki Kosatsu" [Dynamics of
        technical change in a village community: Problem of the transposition
        of cultural elements], Jinruigaku Zasshi 66:3 (Mar. 1958), 37-43.
        [Japan]

2491   Nandi, S. B., "Cultural Changes in an Oraon Village," Vanyajati 8:1
        (Jan. 1960), 12-20.

2492   Nash, Manning, "The Social Context of Economic Choice in a Small
        Society," Man 61:11 (Nov. 1961), 186-191. [Mexico]

2493   Nath, Kamla, "Women in the New Village," Econ. Wkly. 17:20 (15 May
        1965), 813-816. [India]

2494   Nath, V., "The Village and the Community," in GEN 4391 (1962), 141-
        154. [India]

2495   "Native Loans Board of the Territory of Papua and New Guinea,"
        Austr. Territ. 3:2 (Mar. 1963), 13-18.

2496   Nesson, Claude, "Structure agraire et évolution sociale dans les
        oasis de l'Oued Righ" [Agricultural structure and social evolution
        in the Righ Oued Oasis], Trav. Inst. Rech. saharéennes 24:1-2
        (1965), 85-129.

2497   Netting, Robert McC., "Household Organization and Intensive Agri-
        culture: The Kofyas Case," Africa 35:4 (Oct. 1965), 422-429.
        [Nigeria]

2498   Nguyen, Cao Hách, "Some Obstacles to the Application of New
        Techniques of Production in South-East Asia," in GEN 4394 (1963),
        189-198.

2499   Niehoff, Arthur H., and Juanita Niehoff. East Indians in the West
        Indies. Milwaukee, Wis.: Milwaukee Public Museum, 1960. 192 pp.
        [Trinidad; Tobago]

2500   Oberg, K., "The Marginal Peasant in Rural Brazil," Am. Anthrop.
        67:6 (Dec. 1965), 1417-1427.

2501   ------ Kalervo, and F. Van Dijk, The Fishermen of Surinam.

Paramaribo: Surinam-American Technical Cooperative Service, 1960.
58 pp. [British Caribbean]

2502   O'Brien, Denise, and Anton Ploeg, "Acculturation Movements among the
        Western Dani," Am. Anthrop. 66:4, Pt. 2 (Aug. 1964), 281-292. [New
        Guinea]

2503   Okigbo, Pius, "Social Consequences of Economic Development in West
        Africa," Ann. Am. Acad. polit. soc. Sci. 305 (May 1956), 125-133.

2504   Oliver, Symmes C., "Individuality, Freedom of Choice, and Cultural
        Flexibility of the Kamba," Am. Anthrop. 67:2 (Apr. 1965), 421-428.
        [Kenya]

2505   Ortega Mata, R., "La electrificación planificada y sus consecuencias
        sociales en los países poco y subdesarrollados de Latino-América"
        [Planned electrification and its social consequences in the small
        underdeveloped countries of Latin America], Rev. Cienc. soc. 8:1
        (Mar. 1964), 79-102.

2506   "Our Changing Values: A Symposium on the Problems of Change in a
        Traditional Society," Seminar 64 (Dec. 1964), 10-52. [India]

2507   Pal, Agaton P., The Resources, Levels of Living, and Aspirations of
        Rural Households in Negros Oriental. Quezon City, Philippines:
        Community Development Research Council, University of the Philippines,
        1963. 429 pp. [Philippines]

2508   Papanek, Hanna, "The Woman Field Worker in a Purdah Society," Hum.
        Organiz. 23:2 (Summer 1964), 160-163. [Pakistan]

2509   Patterson, H. O. L., "Slavery, Acculturation and Social Change: The
        Jamaican Case," Br. J. Sociol. 17:2 (1966), 151-164.

2510   Paulme, Denise, Une société du côte d'Ivoire hier et aujourd'hui:
        Les Bété [An Ivory Coast society yesterday and today: The Bété].
        The Hague: Mouton, 1962. 204 pp.

2511   Phillips, Herbert Phineas, Thai Peasant Personality: The Patterning
        of Interpersonal Behavior in the Village of Bang Chan. Berkeley:
        University of California Press, 1964. 231 pp. [Thailand]

2512   Pospisil, L., "Social Change and Primitive Law: Consequences of a
        Papuan Legal Case," Am. Anthrop. 60:5 (Oct. 1958), 832-837. [New
        Guinea]

2513   Pouwer, Jan, "A Social System in the Star Mountains: Toward a
        Reorientation of the Study of Social Systems," Am. Anthrop. 66:4,
        Pt. 2 (Aug. 1964), 133-161. [Indonesia]

2514   Powdermaker, Hortense, "Social Change Through Imagery and Values of
        Teen-age Africans in Northern Rhodesia," Am. Anthrop. 58:5 (Oct.
        1956), 783-813. [Zambia]

2515   Prakasha, V., "A Socio-Educational Study of Rural Life in Rajasthan,"
        J. Educ. Psychol. 13:4 (Jan. 1956), 183-200. [Indian State of Rajas-
        than]

2516   Quint, M. N., "The Idea of Progress in an Iraqi Village," Mid. E. J.
        12:4 (Autumn 1956), 369-384.

2517   Rabello, O., "Algunos aspectos sociais da educação no meio rural
        paulista" [Some social aspects of education in the São Paulo rural
        milieu], Sociologia 25:1 (Mar. 1963), 65-76. [Brazil]

2518   Rahim, S. A., The Diffusion and Adoption of Agricultural Practices:
        A Study in a Village in East Pakistan. Comilla, Pakistan: Pakistan
        Academy of Village Development, 1961. 76 pp.

2519   Rayner, W., The Tribe and Its Successors: An Account of African
        Traditional Life and European Settlement in Southern Rhodesia.
        London: Faber and Faber, 1962. 239 pp.

2520   Raz, S. Mobin Uddin, "Caste Attitudes among the Industrial Townsmen
        and Agricultural Villagers," Patna Univ. 17 (July 1962), 158-180.
        [India]

2521   Read, Margaret, Native Standards of Living and African Culture
        Change Illustrated by Examples from the Ngoni Highlands of Nyasa-
        land. London: Institute for African Language and Culture, 1938.
        56 pp. [Malawi]

2522   Reddy, N. S., "Community-Conflict among the Depressed Castes of
        Andhra," Man in India, 30:4 (Oct.-Dec. 1950), 1-12. [Indian State of
        Andhra]

2523   ------ "Functional Relationship of Lohars in a North Indian Village,"
        East. Anthrop. 8:3-4 (Mar.-Aug. 1955), 129-140. [India]

2524   Redfield, Robert, "Culture Change in Yucatan," Am. Anthrop. 36 (1934),
        57-69.

2525   Reichel-Dolmatoff, Gerardo, Contactos y cambios culturales en la
        Sierra Nevada de Santa Maria [Cultural contact and change in the
        Sierra Nevada de Santa Maria]. Bogotá: Antares Imprenta-Editorial,
        1953. 122 pp. [Colombia]

2526   Reynolds, Barrie, The African: His Position in a Changing Society.
        Livingstone: Rhodes-Livingstone Museum, 1963. 46 pp. [Zambia]

2527   Richards, Audrey I. (ed.), Economic Development and Tribal Change:
        A Study of Immigrant Labour in Buganda. Cambridge, England:
        Heffers, 1954. 300 pp. [Uganda]

2528   Rodríguez Sala de Gomez Gil, M. L., "Incremento de las comunicaciones
        en México y algunos de sus efectos económico-sociales" [Increase of
        communications in Mexico and some of its economic and social effects],
        Rev. mex. Sociol. 25:1 (Jan.-Apr. 1963), 189-202.

2529   Romanucci Schwartz, L., "Conflits fonciers à Mokerang, village
        Matankor des Iles de l'Amirauté" [Land conflicts in Mokerang, Matankor
        Village of the Admiralty Islands], Homme 6:2 (1965), 423-432.
        [Micronesia]

2530   Rondot, P., "L'adaptation de l'esprit tribal aux institutions
        modernes" [The adaptation of the tribal mentality to modern insti-
        tutions], Rev. int. Ethnopsychol. 1:1 (1956), 59-78. [North Africa]

2531   Ruel, M. J., "The Modern Adaptation of Associations among the
        Banyang of the West Cameroon," Sthwest. J. Anthrop. 20:1 (Spring
        1964), 1-14.

2532   Ryan, D., "The Toaripi Association: Some Problems of Economic
        Development in Papua," Mankind 6:1 (May 1963), 11-15. [New Guinea
        (Irian and Papua)]

2533   Saber, Mamitua, "Some Observations on Maranao Social and Cultural
        Transition," Philipp. sociol. Rev. 11:1 (Jan.-Apr. 1963), 51-56.

2534   Sachchidananda, Cultural Change in Tribal Bihar: Munda and Oraon.
        Calcutta: Bookland, 1964. 158 pp. [Indian State of Bihar]

2535   Saito, Hiroshi, "A Japanese Co-Operative Society in Brazil: A Case
        Study on the Progress of Cultural Transplantation," Int. econ. Rev.
        9 (Mar. 1959), 109-147.

2536   Saitô, S., Tetsudô husetsu ni tomonau Kindai-ka no Kenkyû: Shizuoda-
        ken Kamo-gun Shimoda-chô no Baai [A study of modernization through
        the construction of a railroad: A research project in Shimoda].
        Tokyo: Nihon Daigaku Bunrigakubu Shakaigaku Kenkyû-shitsu, 1963.
        55 pp. [Japan]

2537   Sapre, S. G., "Changes in Land Utilization and in Cropping Pattern in
        an Irrigated Village over Two Decades Ending in 1960," Artha Vijnana
        6 (June 1964), 106-115. [India]

2538   Sarker, S. C., "Stability and Change in Rural Life," Mod. Rev. 116:4
        (Oct. 1964), 277-283. [India]

2539   Sarveswara Rao, B., The Economic and Social Effects of Zamindari
        Abolition in Andhra. Delhi: Manager of Publications, 1964. 100
        pp. [Indian State of Andhra]

2540   Schapera, Isaac, "Cultural Changes in Tribal Life," in GEN 4372
        (1937), 357-388. [Republic of South Africa]

2541   ------ "Economic Changes in South African Native Life," Africa 1
        (1928), 170-188.

2542   ------ "Economic Conditions in a Bechuanaland Native Reserve," S.
        Afr. J. Sci. 30 (1933), 633-655. [Botswana]

2543   ------ "Present-Day Life in the Native Reserves," in GEN 4373
        (1934), 39-62. [Botswana]

2544   Schoorl, Johan Willem, "Kultuur en Kultuurveranderingen in het
        Moejoe-gebied" [Culture and cultural change in the Muyu Region].
        Ph.D. dissertation, University of Leiden, 1957. 298 pp. [New
        Guinea (Irian and Papua)]

2545   Schuman, Howard, "Social Change and the Validity of Regional Stereo-
       types in East Pakistan," Sociometry 29:4 (Dec. 1966), 428-440.

2546   Segall, M. H., "Acquiescence and 'Identification with the Aggressor'
       among Acculturating Africans," J. soc. Psychol. 61:2 (Dec. 1963),
       247-262. [Uganda]

2547   Sen, Sachin, "Impact of Modern Forces on Castes and Tribes," J. soc.
       Res. 7:1-2 (Mar.-Sept. 1964), 113-118. [India]

2548   Shack, W. A., "Religious Ideas and Social Action in Gurage Bond-
       Friendship," Africa 33:3 (July 1963), 198-208. [Ethiopia]

2549   Sharma, K. N., "Occupational Mobility of Castes in a North Indian
       Village," Sthwest. J. Anthrop. 17:2 (Summer 1961), 146-164. [India]

2550   Shri Kanwar Sain, I. S. E., "Social Repercussions of Hydraulic
       Projects in India," Civilisations 5:2 (May 1955), 183-191. [India]

2551   Silla, Ousmane, "Persistance des castes dans la société Wolof con-
       temporaine" [The persistence of castes in contemporary Wolof society],
       Bull. Inst. fr. Afr. noire 28:3-4 (July-Oct. 1966), 731-770. [West
       Africa; Senegal; Mali]

2552   Simpson, George Eaton, "The Acculturative Process in Jamaican
       Revivalism," in GEN 4395 (1960), 332-341.

2553   ------ "The Acculturative Progress in Trinidadian Shango," Anthrop.
       Quart. 37:1 (Jan. 1964), 16-27.

2554   Singer, Milton B., "Cultural Values in India's Economic Development,"
       Ann. Am. Acad. polit. soc. Sci. 305 (May 1956), 81-91.

2555   Singh, Amar Kumar, "Some Socio-psychological Implications of
       Changing Caste-values," J. soc. Res. 7 (Mar.-Sept. 1964), 136-138.
       [Indian States of Andhra and Bihar]

2556   Singh, Baljit, and Shridhar Misra, A Study of Land Reforms in Uttar
       Pradesh. Calcutta: Oxford Book Co., 1964. 266 pp. [Indian State
       of Uttar Pradesh]

2557   Singh, Dool, Land Reforms in Rajasthan: A Study of Evasion, Imple-
       mentation and Socio-Economic Effects of Land Reforms. New Delhi:
       Research Programmes Committee, Planning Commission, Government of
       India, 1964. 452 pp. [Indian State of Rajasthan]

2558   Singh, D. P., "Caste Dynamics: A Case from Uttar Pradesh," Man in
       India 40 (Jan.-Mar. 1960), 19-29.

2559   Singh, Gurdit, and Swarn Singh, Effects of Bhakra Dam Irrigation on
       the Economy of the Barani Villages in the Hissar District, 1960-61.
       Chandigarh: Statistical Organisation, Government of Punjab, 1963.
       260 pp.

2560   Singh, Tarlok, "Agricultural Policy and Rural Economic Progress,"
       Indian J. agric. Econ. 18:1 (Jan. 1963), 10-23. [India]

2561   ------ "The Landless Labourer and the Pattern of Social and Economic
        Change," in GEN 4347 (1956), 278-288. [India]

2562   Singh, Yogendra, "Land Reform and Social Tension in Villages," J.
        soc. Sci. 1:2 (July 1958), 89-103. [India]

2563   ------ "Social Change and Social Problems: The Case Study of Crime
        Incidence in Six Villages of Uttar Pradesh," J. soc. Sci. 2 (July
        1960), 31-46.

2564   Sinha, D. P., "Caste Dynamics: A Case from Uttar Pradesh," Man in
        India 40:1 (Jan.-Mar. 1960), 19-29. [Indian State of Uttar Pradesh]

2565   Sinha, S., "Levels of Economic Initiative and Ethnic Groups in
        Pargana Barabhum," East. Anthrop. 16:2 (May-Aug. 1963), 65-74.
        [India]

2566   Skinner, E. P., "Labour Migration and Its Relationship to Socio-
        Cultural Change in Mossi Society," in GEN 4396 (1966), 137-157.
        [Upper Volta; Ivory Coast; Ghana]

2567   Skinner, G. W., "The Nature of Loyalties in Rural Indonesia," in GEN
        4396 (1966), 265-277.

2568   Smith, Michael G., "Short Range Prospects in the British Caribbean,"
        Soc. econ. Stud. 11:4 (Dec. 1962), 392-408.

2569   Smith, T. L., "Social Control in a Southern Ryukyuan Village," Res.
        Stud. 29:2 (June 1961), 51-76; 29:3 (Sept. 1961), 151-174; 29:4
        (Dec. 1961), 175-209. [Japan]

2570   Soares Barata, O., "As Implicações sociais dos grandes projectos na
        Africa aõ sul do Sahara" [Social implications of the great projects
        in Africa south of the Sahara], Estud. ultramarinos 2 (1960), 119-139.
        [Mosambique; Angola; Portuguese Guinea]

2571   Sonoda, K., "Nōmin no Shakai Ishiki" [The social consciousness of the
        peasantry], Shakaigaku Hyōron 11:3-4 (1960), 100-114. [Japan]

2572   Sonraku Shakai Kenkyukai, Sengo Nōson no Henbō [The nature of change
        in the postwar farming community]. Tokyo: Jichō Sha, 1958. 257 pp.
        [Japan]

2573   Srinivas, M. N., "A Caste Dispute among Washermen of Mysore," East.
        Anthrop. 7:3-4 (Mar.-Aug. 1954), 149-168. [Indian State of Mysore]

2574   Stabler, George M., "Bejucal: Social Values and Changes in Agri-
        cultural Practices in a Cuban Urban Community." Ph.D. disserta-
        tion, Michigan State University, 1958.

2575   Starr, B. W., "Levels of Communal Relations," Am. J. Sociol. 60:2
        (Sept. 1954), 125-135. [Mexico]

2576   Stavenhagen, R., "Desarrollo agrícola y classes sociales en África"
        [Agricultural development and social classes in Africa], Foro int.
        3:4 (Apr.-June 1963), 508-530.

2577   Steinzor, L. V., "Individualistic and Cooperative Attitudes among
        Farmers in a Land Reform Project," J. soc. Psychol. 59:2 (Apr. 1963),
        221-238.

2578   Straus, M. A., "Cultural Factors in the Functioning of Agricultural
        Extension in Ceylon," Rur. Sociol. 18:3 (Sept. 1953), 249-256.

2579   Sturtevant, D. R., Philippine Social Structure and Its Relation to
        Agrarian Unrest. Ann Arbor, Mich.: University Microfilms, 1959.
        241 mim. pp.

2580   Suzuki, P., "Encounters with Istanbul: Urban Peasants and Village
        Peasants," Int. J. comp. Sociol. 5:2 (1964), 208-216. [Turkey]

2581   Takes, C. A. P., Socio-economic Factors Affecting the Productivity
        of Agriculture in Okigwi Division: Preliminary Report. I. Eastern
        Region. II. Western Region. Ibadan, Nigeria: Institute of Social
        and Economic Research, 1963. 67 pp. [Nigeria]

2582   Takeuchi, T. (ed.), Tôhoku Nôson no Shakai Hendô. Shinshûdan no
        Seisei to Sonraku Taisei [Social changes in villages of the Tôhoku
        district in Japan: Formation of new groups and a village system].
        Tokyo: Tokyo Daigaku Syuppan-kai, 1963. 373 pp.

2583   Tardits, Claude, Contribution à l'étude des populations: Bamiléké
        de l'Ouest Cameroun [Contribution to the study of populations:
        Bamiléké of West Cameroon]. Paris: Berger-Levrault, 1960. 135 pp.

2584   Tax, Sol, "World View and Social Relations in Guatemala," Am.
        Anthrop. 43:1 (Feb. 1951), 27-42.

2585   Taylor, Robert B., "Conservative Factors in the Changing Culture of
        a Zapotec Town," Hum. Organiz. 25:2 (Summer 1966), 116-121.
        [Mexico]

2586   Teulières, R., "Les paysans viêtnamiens et la réforme rurale au Sud
        Viêt-Nam" [Vietnamese peasants and rural reform in South Vietnam],
        Cah. d'outre-mer 15:57 (Jan.-Mar. 1962), 47-84.

2587   Thelin, Mark, and Li Wen-lang, "Religion in Two Taiwanese Villages," J.
        China Soc. 3 (1963), 44-57.

2588   Thomas, L. V., "Economie et ostentation chez les Diola" [Thrift and
        ostentation among the Diola], Notes afr. 98 (Apr. 1963), 33-39.
        [Senegal]

2589   Thurnwald, R. C., "Soziologische Forschungen über Veränderungen in
        Leben des Afrikaners unter den Einworkungen der Europäischen Zivili-
        sation" [Sociological research on the changes in the life of the
        Africans under the influence of European civilization], Forschn.
        Fortschr. 7 (1931). [Republic of South Africa]

2590   Tirayakian, "Work Partner Choice in a Philippine Village," Silliman
        J. 4 (1957), 196-206.

2591   Trent, S., "Irrigation and Socio-Economic Change in a Mysore Village,"

Econ. Wkly. 7:37 (10 Sept. 1955), 1091-1094. [Indian State of
Mysore]

2592   Underwood, Frances W., "Land and Its Manipulation among the Haitian
Peasantry," in GEN 4330 (1964), 469-482.

2593   Van Amelsvoort, V., Culture, Stone Age and Modern Medicine. Assen,
Netherlands: Van Gorcum, 1964. 245 pp. [New Guinea]

2594   Van Den Ban, A. W., "Cultural Change: The Basis for Increasing
Agricultural Productivity," Int. Rev. Community Dev. 12 (1963), 67-
78.

2595   Van Der Kroef, J. M. A., "Land Tenure and Social Structure in Rural
Java," Rur. Soc. 25:4 (Dec. 1960), 414-430. [Indonesia]

2596   Van Velsen, J., "Labor Migration as a Positive Factor in the Continuity of Tonga Tribal Society," in GEN 4396 (1966), 158-168.
[Malawi]

2597   Varma, Baidya N., Communication and Social Change in Rural India.
Ann Arbor, Mich.: University Microfilms, 1959. [India]

2598   Velásquez, R., "Gentilicios africanos del occidente de Colombia"
[African "knights" of West Colombia], Rev. colomb. Folkl. 3:7
(1962), 107-148.

2599   Vellard, J. A., "La réforme agraire dans les pays andins" [Agricul-
tural reform in the Andes], Rev. Trav. Acad. Sci. mor. polit. 116:4
(1 Sept. 1963), 38-51. [Colombia; Peru; Bolivia]

2600   Verschueren, J., "Om Een Nieuwe Wereld: Bijdrag" [Problems of
cultural contact in New Guinea], Bijdr. Taal- Land- Volk. 113:3
(1957), 209-237.

2601   Versluys, J. D. N., "Some Notes on the Social and Economic Effects
of Rural Electrification in Burma," J. Asian Afr. Stud. 1:3 (July
1966), 220-236.

2602   Vogt, Evon Z., "Structural and Conceptual Replication in Zinacantan
Culture," Am. Anthrop. 67:2 (Apr. 1965), 342-353. [Mexico]

2603   Vu, Quoc Thuc, Social Research and Problems of Rural Development in
South-East Asia. Paris: UNESCO, 1963. 300 pp.

2604   Watson, J. B., "Caste as a Form of Acculturation," Sthwest. J.
Anthrop. 19:4 (Winter 1963), 356-379.

2605   Watson, V. D., "An Example of Rural Brazilian Acculturation," Acta
am. 3:3 (1945), 152-162.

2606   Weintraub, D., and F. Bernstein, "Social Structure and Modernization:
A Comparative Study of Two Villages," Am. J. Sociol. 71:5 (Mar. 1966),
509-521. [Israel]

2607   Weintraub, Dov, and Moshe Lissak, "Social Integration and Change," in

GEN 4309 (1964), 129-159. [Israel]

2608   Welikala, George H. F., "An Analysis of the Adoption of Some Agri-
        cultural, Medical, Public Health and Cooperative Practices in Six
        Selected Villages of Ceylon." M.A. thesis, Michigan State Univer-
        sity, 1959.

2609   Wertheim, Willem F., Sociological Aspects of Inter-Island Migration
        in Indonesia. Amsterdam: Sociologisch-Histroisch Seminarium voor
        Zuidoost Azie, Universiteit van Amsterdam, 1960(?). 19 pp.

2610   Whiteman, J., "Change and Tradition in an Abelam Village," Oceania
        36:2 (Dec. 1965), 102-120. [New Guinea]

2611   Wikkramatileke, R., "Variable Ethnic Attributes in Malayan Rural
        Land Development," Pacif. Viewpoint 5:1 (May 1964), 35-50.
        [Malaysia]

2612   Willems, Emilio, "Problemas de Aculturação no Brasil Meridionial"
        [Problems of acculturation in Southern Brazil[, Acta am. 3:3 (1945),
        145-151.

2613   ------ "San Andrés: Continuity and Change in the Culture of a
        Caribbean Island," in GEN 4307 (1964), 315-328. [Colombia]

2614   Williams, M., The Stone Age Island: New Guinea Today. Garden City,
        N.Y.: Doubleday, 1964. 342 pp.

2615   Wilson, Monica Hunter, Reaction to Conquest: Effects of Contact with
        Europeans of the Pondo of South Africa. London: Oxford University
        Press, 1936. 582 pp.

2616   Winner, I., "Some Problems of Nomadism and Social Organization among
        the Recently Settled Kazakhs," Cent. Asian Rev. 11:3 (1963), 246-
        267. [Central Asia]

2617   Wolf, Eric R., Peasants. Englewood Cliffs, N.J.: Prentice-Hall,
        1966. 116 pp.

2618   Yamaoka, Euchi, "Nōmin Ishiki no Henbō" [The transformation of the
        social attitudes of farmers], Shimane Daigaku Ronshû 5 (1959), 88-
        104. [Japan]

2619   Yescas Peralta, P., "Teotitlan del Valle: Muestra en el proceso de
        transculturación" [Teotitlan del Valle: An example of the process of
        cultural change], Rev. mex. Sociol. 16:3 (Sept.-Dec. 1954), 397-408.
        [Mexico]

2620   Young, Frank W., and Ruth C. Young, "Individual Commitment to Indus-
        trialization in Rural Mexico," Am. J. Sociol. 71:4 (Jan. 1966),
        373-383.

2621   Yoshida, Teigo, "Cultural Integration and Change in Japanese Villages,"
        Am. Anthrop. 65:1 (Feb. 1963), 102-116.

2622   Yuan, D. Y., "The Rural-Urban Continuum: A Cast Study of Taiwan,"

Rur. Sociol. 29:3 (Sept. 1964), 247-260.

3. Industrial Agriculture

A. Annotated Case Studies

3001   Ankara University, Faculty of Political Science, Economic and Social
          Aspects of Farm Mechanization in Turkey. Ankara: Ankara University,
          1953. 105 pp.

              Largely a study of the economic effect of the introduction of
          tractors into Turkey. The social impact seems to have driven tenants
          and sharecroppers off the land.

**3002   Ardener, E. W., "Social and Demographic Problems of the Southern
          Cameroons Plantation Area," in GEN 4384 (1961), 83-97.

              This area is found to have the same problems as a new African
          city, where the problems, though many, are not related to size. In
          the plantation area the main causes of distress are the instability,
          the low economic level, and the heterogeneity of the population.

*3003   Clerc, Joseph, P. Adam, and C. Tardits, Société paysanne et problèmes
          fonciers de la palmeraie dahoméenne. Etude sociologique et cada-
          strale [Peasant society and land problems of the Dahomean palm plan-
          tations: A sociological and cadastral study]. Paris: Office de
          la Recherche Scientifique et Technique d'Outre-Mer, 1956. 147 pp.

              This study stresses the increasing role of women in commerce and
          the disappearance of the large family. The economic independence of
          women has led to extreme instability in the family.

3004   Geertz, Clifford, The Impact of Capital-Intensive Agriculture on
          Peasant Social Structure: A Case Study. Cambridge, Mass.: Center
          for International Studies, M.I.T., 1956. 20 pp. [Indonesia]

              A summary of part of "The Social Context of Economic Change": a
          study of a sugarcane plantation in Central Java, from a political
          and economic standpoint.

*3005   Hill, Polly, "Three Types of Southern Ghanaian Cocoa Farmer," in
          GEN 4310 (1963), 203-223.

              A description of the beginning of cocoa cultivation by migrating
          farmers who cleared unused forest lands. This migratory movement
          was once very strong, but low prices have caused it to slow down.
          The three types of farmers are (1) groups of patrilinears who bought
          the land jointly but who cultivate separately; (2) a matrilineage
          buying and cultivating the land as a unit; (3) natives of the area

who transformed the land themselves (this last of minor importance).

**3006 Hammel, Eugene A., <u>Wealth, Authority and Prestige in the Ica Valley,</u> <u>Peru</u>. Albuquerque, N.M.: University of New Mexico Press, 1962. 110 pp.

The introduction of deep-well irrigation at first benefited only the rich, but as the water level dropped, necessitating deeper wells too expensive even for the rich, the poorer farmers were urged to form cooperatives to dig the wells. In addition, new means of communication have introduced Euro-American criteria of prestige, and this allows the lower classes a means of escaping from traditional hierarchy.

3007 Lang, Norris G., "Stratification and Industrialization: A Case Study of an Ecuadorean Sugar Plantation," in GEN 4335 (1965), 130-139.

Economic pressures have led to the emergence of a tri-class struc- ture not unlike that of the West.

3008 Mintz, Sidney W., "Cañamelar: The Subculture of a Rural Sugar Plan- tation Proletariat," in GEN 4387 (1956), 314-417.

A study of the introduction of large-scale mechanized sugar pro- duction, but with little discussion of the effects on the individuals involved.

***3009 Norbeck, Edward, <u>Pineapple Town, Hawaii</u>. Berkeley: University of California Press, 1959. 159 pp.

A study of a Hawaiian town on an outer island, where the workers represent a mixture of varying cultures. They are under pressure to conform to the demands of industrial techniques on the plantation, since those who do not conform are discharged. The result is the retention of only those customs that do not conflict with the indus- trial process--largely, those focused on the family. While these family cultural traits are emphasized, the disappearance of external differences has tended toward greater cross-cultural mobility. Wherever cultural traits have no functional purpose in the society, the author believes they will soon fade.

3010 Seda, Elena Padilla, "Nocora: The Subculture of Workers on a Govern- ment-Owned Sugar Plantation," in GEN 4387 (1956), 265-313. [Puerto Rico]

A study of a medium-sized town, with some case studies. The plan- tation has not stimulated much modernization in the town.

B. Other Case Studies

3301 Adams, Richard N., "On the Relation between Plantation and 'Creole Cultures,'" in GEN 4365 (1959), 73-82. [Latin America]

3302   Andrews, J., "Commercial Agriculture and the Papua in New Guinea
        Economy," Austr. Geogr. 6:5 (1956), 21-28.

3303   Ardener, E. W., S. Ardener, and W. A. Warmington, Plantation and
        Village in the Cameroons: Some Economic and Social Studies. London:
        Oxford University Press, 1960. 435 pp.

3304   Benitez, Fernando, Ki: El drama de un pueblo y de una planta [Ki:
        Drama of a people and of a crop]. Mexico City: Fondo de Cultura
        Económica, 1956. 291 pp. [Mexico]

2205   Choudhury, H. K., "The Plantation Workers of Malaya," in GEN 4338
        (1957), 171-178.

3306   Crist, R. E., "The Indian in Andean America. I. From Encomienda to
        Hacienda. II. The Basis for Development and Hemispheric Solidarity,"
        Am. J. econ. Sociol. 23:2 (Apr. 1964), 131-143 and 23:2 (July 1964),
        303-313. [Peru]

3307   Cumper, G. E., "A Modern Jamaican Sugar Estate," Soc. econ. Stud.
        3:2 (Sept. 1954), 119-160.

3308   Das, Amal Kumar, and Hemendra Nath Banerjee, Impact of the Tea Indus-
        try on the Life of the Tribals of West Bengal. Calcutta: Tribal
        Welfare Department, Cultural Research Institute, Government of West
        Bengal, 1964. 88 pp. [Indian State of Uttar Pradesh]

3309   Eisenstadt, S. N., "Sociological Aspects of the Economic Adaptation
        of Oriental Immigrants in Israel: A Case Study in the Problem of
        Modernization," Econ. Dev. cult. Change 4:3 (Apr. 1956), 269-278.

3310   García, A., "Estructura de una hacienda señorial en la sierra
        ecuatoriana. Análisis y proyecto de recolonización dentro de un
        esquema de reforma agraria" [Plan of a manorial hacienda in the
        Ecuadorian mountains: Analysis and project of recolonization with-
        in an agrarian reform scheme], Cienc. polít. soc. 9:33 (July-Sept.
        1964), 359-453.

3311   Geertz, Clifford, "Capital-Intensive Agriculture in Peasant Society:
        A Case Study," Soc. Res. 23:4 (Winter 1956), 433-439. [Indonesia]

3312   Haouat, H., "De quelques aspects sociaux de la mécanisation agricole
        en Tunisie" [On some social aspects of agricultural mechanization in
        Tunisia], Bull. écon. soc. Tunisie 77 (June 1953), 80-87.

3313   Hauser, A., "The Mechanization of Agriculture in Tropical Africa," in
        GEN 4325 (1956), 546-556. [West and Central Africa]

3314   Hill, Polly, Gold Coast Cocoa Farmer. London: Oxford University
        Press, 1956. 139 pp. [Ghana]

3315   Holas, B., "Le paysannat africain devant le problème des cultures
        industrielles. L'exemple des Oubi (Côte d'Ivoire)" [The African
        peasantry faced with the problem of industrial cultures: The example
        of the Oubi (Ivory Coast)], Rev. Inst. Sociol. 2 (1957), 219-233.

3316   Houghton, D. H., "Keiskammahoek Rural Survey: A Study of the
        Failure of Social Adaptation," Econ. Dev. cult. Change 1:5 (Feb.
        1953), 350-359. [Republic of South Africa]

3317   India, Labour Bureau of, "Family Living of the Tea Plantation
        Workers in Tripura," Publication No. 64. Delhi: Manager of Publi-
        cations, 1964. 92 pp. [Indian State of Andhra]

3318   Jayawardena, C., "Family Organisation in Plantations in British
        Guiana," Int. J. comp. Sociol. 3:1 (Sept. 1962), 43-64.

3319   Kobben, A. J. F., "Le planteur noir. Essai d'une ethnographie
        d'aspect" [The black planter: A proposed ethnography of external
        forms], Etud. éburn. 5 (1956), 7-190. [Ivory Coast]

3320   Labisa, A. S., "Algunas problemas de produção e mão-de-obra indígenas
        em Angola" [Some problems relating to production and local manpower
        in Angola], Estud. ultramarinos 4 (1959), 75-116.

3321   Lajberich, C. M., and N. Thoai, "Factores favorables y desfavorables
        para la mecanización agrícola en la mentalidád campenisa de Tonkin y
        de Francia" [Favorable and unfavorable factors for agricultural
        mechanization in the mentality of Tonkin and Francia peasants],
        Estud. soc. (1955), 169-180. [Vietnam]

3322   Marthelot, P., "Juxtaposition en Tunisie d'une économie de type
        traditionnel et d'une économie de type moderne" [The juxtaposition
        of a traditional economy and a modern economy in Tunisia], Inst.
        Belles Lettres arabes 18:72 (1955), 481-502.

3323   Parmer, J. N., Colonial Labor Policy and Administration: A History
        of the Rubber Plantation Industry in Malaya, c. 1910-1941. Locust
        Valley, N.Y.: J. J. Augustin, 1960. 294 pp. [Malaysia]

3324   Pelzer, K. J., "Western Impact on East Sumatra and North Tapanuli:
        The Roles of the Planter and the Missionary," J. S. E. Asian Hist.
        2:2 (July 1961), 66-71. [Indonesia]

3325   Thompson, Edgar T., "The Plantation as a Social System," in GEN 4365
        (1959), 26-36. [Latin America]

3326   Ülken, H. Z., "La répercussion sociale de l'agriculture mécanisée
        en Turquie" [The social repercussion of mechanized agriculture in
        Turkey], in GEN 4346 (1956), 319-325.

3327   Vincent, J.-F., La culture du cacao et son retentissement social dans
        la région de Souanké [The cultivation of cocoa and its social reper-
        cussions in the Souanké Region]. Brazzaville, Congo: Institut de
        Recherches Scientifiques au Congo, 1961. 106 pp. [Congo (Leopold-
        ville)]

3328   Watters, R. F., "The Development of Agricultural Enterprise in Fiji,"
        J. Polynesian Soc. 74:4 (Dec. 1965), 490-502.

3329   Wauthion, R., "Pour le développement d'une économie rurale indigène
        dans l'hinterland des grand centres industriels du Haut-Katanga"

[Toward the development of a native rural economy in the hinterland
of the big industrial centers of Upper Katanga], Bull. trimest. Cent.
Etud. Probl. 34 (Sept. 1956), 5-20. [Congo (Leopoldville)]

3330   Wells, F. A., and W. A. Warmington, Studies in Industrialization:
        Nigeria and the Cameroons. London: Oxford University Press, 1963.
        266 pp.

3331   Williamson, K. R., "The Tolai Cocoa Project," S. Pacif. 9:13 (July-
        Aug. 1958), 593-600. [New Guinea]

3332   Wolf, Eric R., "Specific Aspects of Plantation Systems in the New
        World: Community Sub-Cultures and Social Class," in GEN 4365 (1959),
        136-145. [Latin America]

3333   Zayas, Alvarado E., Worker in the Cane: A Puerto Rican Life History.
        New Haven: Yale University Press, 1960. 288 pp. A life story as
        told to S. W. Mintz.

                        4. Community Development

                        A. Annotated Case Studies

*4001   Baldwin, K. D. S., The Niger Agricultural Project: An Experiment
        in African Development. Cambridge, Mass.: Harvard University
        Press, 1957. 221 pp. [Niger]

            An account of a project that failed. The lack of rising incomes
        destroyed the only factor that held the new communities together.

**4002 Dube, S. C., India's Changing Villages: Human Factors in Community
        Development. London: Routledge & Kegan Paul, 1958. 230 pp.
        [Indian State of Uttar Pradesh]

            A study of a village in a development block. The villages
        readily undertook the cultivation of a new cash crop, but they
        resisted an improved variety of wheat that offered no immediate
        monetary gain. They adopted many projects for the sake of prestige,
        without their fully realizing the continued effort needed to make
        them effective. One reason for this was that many projects were
        poorly planned by the government officials. The peasants' main
        motives for cooperating with a project were economic advantage,
        prestige, novelty, and compliance with authority. The main obstacles
        were apathy, suspicion of government officials, lack of communication
        between the leaders and the peasants, and tradition. Appendix II
        gives a minute account of ten days in the work of a Village Level
        Worker, which brings out the peasant's rooted skepticism and
        hostility to change.

                                [186]

4003   Gamble, Sidney David, <u>Ting Hsien, A North China Rural Community</u>.
New York: Institute of Pacific Relations, 1954. 472 pp.

A general prewar study of the effectiveness of a rural-education
program.

**4004-   Hammond, Peter B., "Economic Change and Mossi Acculturation," in
GEN 4306 (1959), 238-256. [Upper Volta]

A study of a Mossi group of farmers according to tradition, who
were resettled in a government development area, where they were
expected to use new techniques. The administrators of the project
retained the traditional social structure in order to stabilize the
way of life, but the result has been the opposite. The young, who
could best be trained in the new methods, are prevented from rising,
since they have no place in the traditional system. The result is
that life on the project is considered a temporary means of acquiring
extra income.

*4005   Heeren, H. J., "Some Problems of Rural Collective Settlements in
Indonesia," in GEN 4347 (1956), 302-308.

A study of a group that immigrated to Sumatra. After several
years, no assimilation has taken place because of language barriers,
lack of administrative help and understanding, and the hostility of
an extremely conservative native group.

**4006   Holmberg, Allan R., "An Attempt to Establish a Stable Water Supply
in Viru Valley, Peru," in GEN (1952), 113-124.

A description of an abortive attempt by the government to develop
a supply of water for a part of the valley. The government found
water, but it had to abandon the project because of local resistance.
The government seems to have taken no account of local leaders or
conditions. As a result, the villagers regarded the project as an
intrusion into their affairs.

4007   Honigmann, John J., "A Case Study of Community Development in
Pakistan," <u>Econ. Dev. cult. Change</u> 8:3 (Apr. 1960), 288-303. [West
Pakistan]

A study that demonstrates how a development project that has been
inadequately explained to the villagers may meet with apathy or even
antagonism, if its significance is not understood.

4008   India, Government of, Planning Commission, <u>Leadership and Groups in
a South Indian Village</u>. New Delhi: Government Printing Office,
1955. 148 pp. [Indian State of Mysore]

A study of a village in Mysore, in which the Village Extension
Worker (a government employee) was ineffectual, as he was exploited
by one faction of the village to further its own aims.

*4009   Madigan, F. C., <u>The Farmer Said No: A Study of Background Factors
Associated with Dispositions to Cooperate with or Be Resistant to
Community Development Projects</u>. Quezon City: University of the

Philippines, Community Development Council, 1962. 359 pp. [Philippines]

The author relates individual cooperation in community development projects (as measured verbally) with a number of explanatory variables. The most important explanatory variables are the level of education and the kind of leadership desired (that is, strong rather than weak).

4010   Mayer, Albert et al., Pilot Project, India: The Story of Rural Development at Etawah, Uttar Pradesh. Berkeley: University of California Press, 1958. 367 pp. [Indian State of Uttar Pradesh]

A study of the techniques of implementing a project.

*4011   Miner, Horace M., "Culture Change under Pressure: A Hausa Case," Hum. Organiz. 19:3 (Fall 1960), 164-167. [Nigeria]

A study of the effectiveness of community development in Northern Nigeria. The British introduction of non-native forms of political hierarchy was gradually accepted because of the economic advantages of cooperation. However, this acceptance was never more than partial, since it had no roots in the traditional culture.

*4012   Reining, Conrad C., The Zande Scheme: An Anthropological Case Study of Economic Development in Africa. Evanston, Ill.: Northwestern University Press, 1966. 255 pp. [Sudan]

Both the natives and the British officials desired economic development. The scheme failed, however, since neither group understood the other. Its development was decentralized so as to minimize urban growth, and therefore the natives were insulated from the economic incentives of higher prices for cotton. Therefore they became convinced that they were being exploited, and consequently they lost interest.

4013   Sangave, V. A., "Community Development Programme in Kolhapur Project," Sociol. Bull. 7:2 (Sept. 1958), 97-111. [Indian State of Mahashtra]

A study of a project that ultimately led to the villagers' almost total disappointment.

**4014   Schuman, Howard, Economic Development and Individual Change: A Social-Psychological Study of the Comilla Experiment in Pakistan. Cambridge: Center for International Affairs, Harvard University, 1967. 59 pp. [East Pakistan]

The author has sampled villages from within the Comilla community development area and from villages just outside this area. He finds little difference in these two categories with respect to ultimate goals. However, he finds a difference in certain traits that enable the individual to reach these goals. In general, the inhabitants of the community development villages seem more satisfied and less frustrated than do those living outside those villages.

4015   Singh, Rudra Datt, "An Introduction of Green Manuring in Rural

India," in GEN 4385 (1952), 55-68. [Indian State of Uttar Pradesh]

A case study of successful innovations in a village in Uttar Pradesh, illustrating the necessity of the administrators' working with and trusting the villagers if acceptance is to be gained.

***4016   Weingrod, Alex, Reluctant Pioneers: Village Development in Israel. Ithaca, N.Y.: Cornell University Press, 1966. 213 pp.

Two essential elements for a successfully directed innovation are the guarantee of economic security and the incorporation of the traditional family structure. A key factor is the intermediation by the native village leadership between the outside authority and the village. This leadership must implement the directives from above, and get them modified whenever they are inacceptable to the village. The ability to maneuver between these requirements is essential to successful leadership.

**4017   Zahan, Dominique, "Problèmes sociaux posés par la transplantation des Mossi sur les terres irriguées de l'Office du Niger" [Social problems brought about by moving the Mossi onto the irrigated lands of the Niger Office], in GEN 4310 (1963), 392-403.

From 1937 on the Mossi were brought in from the Upper Volta. They came largely to escape the authority of their chiefs. Nevertheless, the extended family organization was not weakened, whereas the new villages in the Niger were. Recently this situation has begun to change, partly because the government is now delegating the powers of the family chief to the new villages, and partly because those villages are breaking away from the tribal form of society and are turning to Islam. The disintegration of the extended family has been furthered also by the increasing financial independence of the farmers and by the vastly different agricultural techniques required in farming the new lands. New social classes based on economic factors are being formed.

B. Other Case Studies

4301   Ahmed, Firoza, "The Concept of Community Development with Special Reference to Its Present and Future Applications in Pakistan." Thesis, Florida State University, 1963. 344 mim. pp. [Pakistan]

4302   Antoine, Charles, Quelques considérations sur le milieu rural à Deseaux: Une expérience de développement communautaire dans la vallée de l'Artibonite [Some thoughts on the rural milieu at Deseaux: An experience in community development in the Valley of the Artibonite]. Port-au-Prince: Théodore, n.d. 59 pp. [Haiti]

4303   Arcarya, H., "Some Observations on Community Projects," Sociol. Bull. 8:2 (Sept. 1959), 19-31. [India]

4304   Aziz, Ungku A., "Poverty and Rural Development in Malaysia," Kajian
        Ekonomi Malaysia 1:1 (June 1964), 70-105.

4305   Balakrishnan, T., "Sentimental Content in Community Development," J.
        nat. Acad. Adm. 8 (Apr. 1963), 41-58. [India]

4306-7 Balsara, J. F., "Community Development Programme in India: The Social
        Impact of Community Development and Other Projects on Rural Life,"
        Sociol. Bull. 7:2 (Sept. 1958), 81-97.

4308   Basinski, J. J., "Some Problems of Agricultural Development in the
        Southern Provinces of the Sudan," Sudan Notes Rec. 38:1-2 (1957),
        21-46.

4309   Bathgate, John, "Christian Participation in Rural Development in
        India," Int. Rev. Missions 52 (July 1963), 289-299.

4310   Bathgate, John (ed.), Experiment in Extension: The Gaon Sathi.
        Bombay: Oxford University Press, 1956. 240 pp. [Indian State of
        Uttar Pradesh]

4311   ------ "Some Christian Efforts in Rural Reconstruction in India: A
        Study in the Problem of Missions and Social Change." Thesis, Union
        Theological Seminary, 1962. 723 mim. pp.

4312   Batten, T. R., Communities and Their Development: An Introductory
        Study with Special Reference to the Tropics. London: Oxford Uni-
        versity Press, 1957. 248 pp.

4313   Belshaw, Michael, "Aspects of Community Development in Rural Mexico,"
        Inter-Am. Econ. Aff. 15:4 (Spring 1962), 71-94.

4314   ------ "Community Development in the Nimboran," S. Pacif. Comm.
        quart. Bull. 8:1 (Jan. 1958), 53-57. [New Guinea]

4315   Bhattacarya, S. N., Village on the March. Delhi: Metropolitan Book
        Co., n.d. 67 pp. [India]

4316   Board, C., "The Rehabilitation Programme in the Bantu Areas and Its
        Effect on the Agricultural Practices and Rural Life of the Bantu in
        the Eastern Cape," S. Afr. J. Econ. 32:1 (Mar. 1964), 36-52.
        [Republic of South Africa]

4317   ------ "A Sample Survey to Assess the Effect on Bantu Agriculture of
        the Rehabilitation Programme," S. Afr. J. Sci. 60:7 (Aug. 1964),
        229-235. [Republic of South Africa]

4318   Brausch, G. E. J. B., "Applied Anthropology in the Belgian Terri-
        tories in Africa: An Experience of Integration of the Tribal Insti-
        tutions into the Pattern of the New Social Action in Central
        Africa," in GEN 4395 (1960), 755-763. [Congo (Kinshasa); Rwanda-
        Urundi]

4319   Campos, C. M., and J. Arroyo Riestra, Desarrollo de las communidades
        rurales [Development of rural communities]. Mexico City: B. Costa
        Amic, 1963. 159 pp. [Mexico]

4320   Carley, Verna A., and Elmer A. Starch, Report on Community Develop-
        ment Programs in Jamaica, Puerto Rico, Bolivia, and Peru. Washington:
        Government Printing Office, 1955. 76 pp. [Jamaica; Puerto Rico;
        Bolivia; Peru]

4321   Casewa, Gangalal, "Obstacles to Development of Cooperative
        Marketing," Indian coop. Rev. 2 (Oct. 1964), 7-12. [India]

4322   Chapekar, L. N., "Community Development Project Blocks in Badlapur,"
        Sociol. Bull. 7:2 (Sept. 1958), 111-122. [India]

4323   Condominas, Georges, Fokon'olona et collectivités rurales au Imerina
        [Fokon'olona and rural collectivities in Imerina]. Paris: Berger-
        Levrault, 1960. 234 pp. [Madagascar]

4324   Dalisay, Amando M., "Assessing the Contribution of Investment in
        Human Resources to Agricultural and Community Development," Philipp.
        econ. Bull. 2:6 (July-Aug. 1964), 5-28. [Philippines]

4325   Datta, A. K., "Some Aspects of Social Change in Rural India and the
        Role of the Community Development Programme," Indonesië 10:2 (Apr.
        1957), 89-108.

4326   Desai, A. R., "Community Development Projects: A Sociological
        Analysis," Sociol. Bull. 7:2 (Sept. 1958), 152-166. [India]

4327   ------ "Impact of the Measures Adopted by the Government of the
        Indian Union on the Life of the Rural People," in GEN 4347 (1956),
        267-277. [India]

4328   Deshpande, A. R., "Education sociale et développement communautaire
        en Inde" [Social education and community development in India], Fundl.
        Educ. adult Educ. 10:2 (1958), 80-90.

4329   Dey, Surendra Kumar, Community Development. 2 vols. Allahabad: Kitab
        Mahal, 1960. [India]

4330   ------ Community Development: A Bird's Eye View. New York: Asia
        Publishing House, 1964. 104 pp. [India]

4331   ------ Nilokheri. New York: Asia Publishing House, 1962. 128 pp.
        [India]

4332   Domínguez, O., El condicionamiento de la reforma agraria: Estudio de
        los factores económicos, demográficos y sociales que determinan la
        promoción del campesino chileno [The conditioning of the agrarian
        reform: A study of the economic, demographic, and social factors that
        determine the advance of the Chilean peasant]. Louvain: E. Warny,
        1963. 220 pp. [Chile]

4333   Doshi, S. L., "Village Traditions and Community Development," Econ.
        Wkly. 16:4-6 (25 Jan. 1964), 117, 119-120. [India]

4334   Dube, S. C., "Cultural Factors in Rural Community Development," J.
        Asian Stud. 15:1 (Nov. 1956), 19-30. [India]

4335   Dube, S. C., "Some Problems of Communication in Rural Economic
        Development," Econ. Dev. cult. Change 5:2 (Jan. 1957), 129-146.
        [Indian State of Uttar Pradesh]

4336   Dubey, D. C., and Willis A. Sutton, Jr., "A Rural 'Man in the
        Middle': The Indian Village Level Worker in Community Development,"
        Hum. Organiz. 24:2 (Summer 1965), 148-151.

4337   Dubey, D. C., Willis A. Sutton, Jr., and Gladys Gallup, Village
        Level Workers: Their Work and Result Demonstrations. Delhi:
        Manager of Publications, 1962. 167 pp. [India]

4338   Dunn, Stephen P., "Directed Culture Change in the Soviet Union: Some
        Soviet Studies," Am. Anthrop. 64:2 (Apr. 1962), 328-339.

4339   Dupree, Louis B., "The Comilla Experiment: A Scheme for Village
        Development in East Pakistan," Am. Univ. Field Staff: S. Am. 8:2
        (1964), 20 pp.

4340   Du Sautoy, P., Community Development in Ghana. London: Oxford Uni-
        versity Press, 1958. 209 pp.

4341   Duynstee, S., "Développement communautaire à Palma di Montechiaro,
        Sicile" [Community development in Palma di Montechiaro, Sicily],
        Int. Rev. Community Dev. 12 (1963), 109-118; Centro Soc. 10:53-54
        (1963), 109-118. [South Italy]

4342   Einsiedel, Luz A., Success and Failure in Selected Community
        Development Projects in Batangas. Study Series No. 3. Quezon
        City, Philippines: Community Development Research Council, Uni-
        versity of the Philippines, 1960. 125 pp. [Philippines]

4343   Espiritu, Socorro C., and Chester L. Hunt, Social Foundations of
        Community Development: Readings on the Philippines. Manila: R.
        M. García, 1964. 684 pp. [Philippines]

4344   Farmer, Bertram Hughes, Pioneer Peasant Colonization in Ceylon: A
        Study in Asian Agrarian Problems. London: Oxford University Press,
        1957. 387 pp.

4345   Fisher, Glen, Directed Culture Change in Nayarit, Mexico: Analysis
        of a Pilot Project in Basic Education. New Orleans: Tulane Uni-
        versity Press, 1953. 111 pp.

4346   Friends, American Society of, A Village Development Project in Jordan
        Final Report to the Ford Foundation. Philadelphia: American Society
        of Friends, 1958. 2 vols., 109 pp. and 105 pp.

4347   Gallin, Bernard, "Rural Development in Taiwan: The Role of the
        Government," Rur. Sociol. 29:3 (Sept. 1964), 313-323.

4348   Ghose, Samir Kumar, The Community Development Project in India: A
        Critical Survey of the Movement from 1952 to 1958. Basel, Switzer-
        land: Buchdruckerei Gasser, 1963. 144 pp.

4349   Grader, Charles J., Rural Organization and Village Revival in

Indonesia. Ithaca: Southeast Asia Program, Cornell University, 1952. 15 pp.

4350   Guérin, M., "Une expérience de modernisation rurale dans l'extrême sud de Madagascar" [An experiment in rural modernization in the extreme south of Madagascar], Cah. Inst. Sci. écon. 145, suppl., series 5:7 (Jan. 1964), 227-255.

4351   Gupta, Ranjit, Community Development Co-operation and Panchayati raj in Alipore: A Pilot Survey. New Delhi: Indian Cooperative Union, 1964. 30 pp. [Indian State of Andhra]

4352   Gupta, S. K., "Dandakaranya: A Survey of Rehabilitation," Econ. Wkly. 17 (2 Jan. 1965), 15-17 ff.; (9 Jan. 1965), 59-65; (16 Jan. 1965), 89 ff. [India]

4353   Halcrow, Magnus, Recent Advances in the Northern and Luapula Provinces of Northern Rhodesia: A Report on Intensive Rural Development. Lusaka: Northern Rhodesian Government Press, 1959. 12 pp. [Zambia]

4354   Hancock, R. N., "Routes, rizières et développement rural dans le district de Madang en Nouvelle-Guinée" [Roads, rice fields and rural development in the Madang District in New Guinea], S. Pacif. Comm. quart. Bull. 4:4 (Oct. 1954), 44-56.

4355   Hayden, Howard, "Community Development on Moturiki Fiji," Oversea Educ. 24:4 (Jan. 1953), 2-12.

4356   ------ Moturiki: Un projet pilote de développement communautaire [Moturiki: A pilot project in community development]. Nouméa, New Caledonia: Commission du Pacifique-Sud, 1956. 182 pp. [Fiji]

4357   Heeren, H. J., "Some Problems of Rural Collective Settlements in Indonesia," in GEN 4346 (1956), 302-308.

4358   Holmberg, A. R., H. F. Dobyns, et al., "Community and Regional Development: The Joint Cornell-Peru Experiment," Hum. Organiz. 21:2 (Summer 1962), 107-115.

4359   Holz, V. R., "Community Development Needs in Uruguay," Int. Rev. Community Dev. 112 (1963), 113-143.

4360   Honigmann, John J., "Relocation of a Punjab Pakistan Community," Mid. E. J. 8:4 (Nov. 1954), 429-444. [West Pakistan]

4361   Hourani, C., "The Arab Development Society's Project in Jericho, Jordan," in GEN 4356 (1963), 197-202.

4362   Huizer, G., "A Community Development Experience in a Central American Village," Int. Rev. Community Dev. 12 (1963), 161-178.

4363   Hussein, Ahmed, and Carl C. Taylor, Report of the Mission on Rural Community Organization and Development in the Caribbean and Mexico. New York: United Nations, 1953. 45 pp.

4364   India, Government of, Ministry of Community Development, <u>Evolution of Community Development Programme in India</u>. Delhi: Government of India, 1963. 104 pp.

4365   India, Government of, Ministry of Food and Agriculture, <u>Extension Education in Community Development</u>. New Delhi: Government of India, 1961. 458 pp.

4366   Jackson, I. C., <u>Advance in Africa: A Study of Community Development in Eastern Nigeria</u>. London: Oxford University Press, 1956. 110 pp.

4367   Jain, Hari Kishore, <u>Community Development Programme in India.</u> Bangalore, India: Bangalore Publishing Co., 1962. 128 pp.

4368   Jocano, F. Landa, "Social Structure and the Program of Directed Change: A Case Study from Western Visayas, Philippines," <u>Sci. Rev.</u> 4 (Nov. 1963), 8-13.

4369   Junod, V. I., "An Urban African Community (pilot) Project," <u>Hum. Organiz.</u> 23:1 (Spring 1964), 28-35. [Republic of South Africa]

4370   Kahn, A. Z. M. Obaidullah, <u>The Comilla District Development Project</u>. Comilla, Pakistan: Pakistan Academy fur Rural Development, 1964. 59 pp. [East Pakistan]

4371   Kaufman, Harold F., "Rural Community Development in India," <u>Int. Rev. Community Dev.</u> 9 (1962), 77-94.

4372   Khare, R. S., "A Study of Social Resistance to Sanitation Programmes in Rural India," <u>East. Anthrop.</u> 17:2 (May-Aug. 1964), 86-94.

4373   Langworthy, Russell L., "Some Economic and Sociological Issues of Cooperative Farming in India," <u>J. Asian Afr. Stud.</u> 1:2 (Apr. 1966), 100-117. [North India]

4374   Madan, G. R., <u>The Changing Pattern of Indian Villages: With Special Reference to Community Development</u>. 2nd ed. rev. and enl. Delhi: S. Chand, 1964. 509 pp.

4375   Malhotra, S. P., "Bihar Resettlement Schemes," <u>J. soc. Res.</u> 3:2 (Sept. 1960), 69-81. [Indian State of Bihar]

4376   Mandelbaum, David G., "Social Organization and Planned Cultural Change in India," in GEN 4386 (1960), 15-20.

4377   Mayer, A. C., "Development Projects in an Indian Village," <u>Pacif. Aff.</u> 29:1 (Mar. 1956), 37-45. [Indian State of Uttar Pradesh]

4378   ------ "An Indian Community Development Block Revisited," <u>Pacif. Aff.</u> 30:1 (Mar. 1957), 35-46. [Indian State of Uttar Pradesh]

4379   Mehta, Ratilal, "Rural Reconstruction around Santiniketan," <u>Mod. Rev.</u> 114:6 (Dec. 1963), 421-426. [India]

4380   Mertin, J., <u>Das Dorfentwicklungsprogram als Methode des</u>

Wirtschaftsausbaus für das ländliche Indien [The program of community development as a method of economic construction for peasant
India]. Stuttgart: G. Fischer, 1962. 151 pp.

4381   Mezirow, J. F., and F. A. Santopolo, "Community Development in
        Pakistan: The First Five Years," Int. soc. Sci. J. 12:3 (1960),
        394-405.

4382   Morales, Julio O., Community Development Program: Program and
        Objectives. Turrialba, Costa Rica: The Inter-American Institute of
        Agricultural Sciences, 1953. [Costa Rica]

4383   Mukerji, Brahmadeva, Community Development in India. Bombay: Orient
        Longmans, 1962. 312 pp.

4384   Nanavati, Manilal Balabhai, Fifty Years of Co-operation in Kodinar
        Taluka: A Case Study. Bombay: Indian Society of Agricultural
        Economics, 1964. 37 pp. [Indian State of Gujarat]

4385   Nanjundappa, D. M., Community Development and Employment. Dharwar,
        India: Karnatak University, 1963. 89 pp. [India]

4386   Neisser, Charlotte S., "Community Development and Mass Education in
        British Nigeria," Econ. Dev. cult. Change 3:4 (July 1955), 352-365.

4387   Niehoff, Arthur H. (ed.), A Casebook of Social Change. Chicago:
        Aldine, 1966. 305 pp.

4388   Pal, Agaton Palen, "A Philippine Barrio: A Study of Social Organiza-
        tions in Relation to Planned Cultural Change," J. E. Asiat. Stud. 5:4
        (Oct. 1956), 333-486.

4389   Panchanadikar, J. M., "Indian Rural Society under the Impact of
        Planned Development: A Sociological Analysis," Sociol. Bull. 11
        (1962), 173-198.

4390   Patnaik, N., "Digging Wells in Barpali, Orissa: An Experience in
        Rural Reconstruction," Man in India 41:2 (Jan. 1961), 83-99. [Indian
        State of Orissa]

4391   Pin, E., "Effetti psicosociologici della riforma agraria" [Psycho-
        logical effects of agrarian reform], Riv. Sociol. 2:4 (May-Aug.
        1964), 79-102. [South Italy]

4392   Plant, H. T., "Local Government and Community Development in Rural
        Areas of Papua and New Guinea," Austr. Territ. 2:2 (Mar. 1962), 4-12.

4393   Prasad, Brahmanand, "Evaluation of Community Development Programmes,"
        Patna Univ. J. 18 (Jan. 1963), 118-128. [India]

4394   Prasad, Narmadeshwar, "Factions in Tribal and Rural Settings and
        Community Development Movement," Patna Univ. J. 18 (July 1963),
        241-254. [India]

4395   Quirino-Lanhounemy, J., "Le développement communautaire en Afrique
        Noire: Leçons d'une expérience au Dahomey" [Community development

in Black Africa: The lesson of an experiment in Dahomey], <u>Polit.</u> <u>étrang.</u> 29:2 (1964), 161-180.

4396   Rahudkar, W. B., "The Relationship of Certain Factors to the Success of Village Level Workers," <u>Rur. Sociol</u>. 27:4 (Dec. 1962), 418-427. [India]

4397   Renier, M., "L'installation de paysannats indigènes en savanes du Congo" [The installation of a native peasant society in the savannahs of the Congo], <u>Bull. trimest. Cent. Etud. Probl. soc. indig</u>. 39 (1957), 5-26.

4398   Ruopp, E. (ed.), <u>Approaches to Community Development: A Symposium</u> <u>Introduction to Problems and Methods of Village Welfare in Under-</u> <u>developed Areas.</u> The Hague: W. Van Holve, 1953. 352 pp.

4399   Ryan, D., "The Yoaripi Association: Some Problems of Economic Development in Papua," <u>Mankind</u> 6:1 (May 1963), 11-15. [New Guinea]

4400   Sachchidananda, "Community Development and the Tribals," <u>J. soc.</u> <u>Res</u>. 7:1-2 (Mar.-Sept. 1964), 70-78. [Indian State of Bihar]

4401   Saksena, R. N., "Sociology of Community Development," <u>J. soc. Sci</u>. 3 (1962), 47-67. [India]

4402   Sariola, S., "A Colonization Experiment in Bolivia," <u>Rur. Sociol</u>. 25:1 (Mar. 1960), 76-90.

4403   Sarkar, Subhash Chandra, "Rural Development in India: A Historical Perspective," <u>Indo-Asian Cult</u>. 11 (Apr. 1963), 306-322.

4404   Schweng, L. D., "An Indian Community Development Project in Bolivia," <u>Amér. indíg</u>. 22:2 (Apr. 1962), 155-169.

4405   Selosoemardjan, <u>The Dynamics of Community Development in Rural Central</u> <u>and West Java: A Comparative Report.</u> Ithaca: Modern Indonesia Project, Cornell University, 1963. 162 pp.

4406   ------ <u>The Dynamics of Community Development in Rural Central and</u> <u>West Java</u>. Ithaca: Cornell University Press, 1963. 40 pp.

4407   Shah, C. H., and Tara Shukla, "Impact of a Community Development Project," <u>J. Univ. Bombay</u> 26:4 (Jan. 1958), 18-31. [India]

4408   Sibley, William Elbridge, "Social Structures and Planned Change: A Case Study from the Philippines," <u>Hum. Organiz</u>. 19:4 (Winter 1960-1961), 209-211.

4409   Silcock, T. H., "Some Economic Aspects of Extension Work," in GEN 4394 (1963), 136-148. [Southeast Asia]

4410   Singh, Baljit, <u>Next Step in Village India. A Study of Land Reforms</u> <u>and Group Dynamics.</u> Bombay: Asia Publishing House, 1961. 135 pp.

4411   Singh, Baljit, and Shridhar Misra, <u>A Study of Land Reforms in Uttar</u> <u>Pradesh</u>. Calcutta: Oxford Book Co., 1964. 266 pp.

4412   Singh, Dool, Land Reforms in Rajasthan. A Study of Evasion, Imple-
        mentation and Socio-Economic Effects of Land Reforms. New Delhi:
        Research Programmes Committee, Planning Commission, Government of
        India, 1964. 452 pp.

4413   Singh, Tarlok, Poverty and Social Change: A Study on the Economic
        Reorganization of Indian Rural Society. London-New York-Bombay:
        Longmans, Green, 1945. 200 pp. [Indian State of Punjab]

4414   Singh, Umrao, Community Development in India: Evaluation and
        Statistical Analysis. Kanpur, India: Kitab Ghar, 1962. 304 pp.

4415   Sivaswamy, K. G., "Community Projects and Rural Welfare Centres in
        South Kanara," Econ. Wkly. 5:43 (24 Oct. 1953), 1175-1178. [India]

4416   Srivastava, S. K., "An Experiment: The Village Teacher as VLW,"
        Indian J. adult Educ. 22 (Sept. 1961), 11-15. [India]

4417   Stanner, W. E. H., The South Seas in Transition: A Study of Post-War
        Rehabilitation and Reconstruction in Three British Pacific Dependen-
        cies. Sydney: Australasian Publishing Co., 1953. 448 pp.
        [Melanesia; Micronesia]

4418   Tartib Prawirohardjo, and T. Krishnamurthy, Community Education in
        Indonesia. Djakarta, Indonesia: Community Education Department,
        Ministry of Education, 1960. 189 pp.

4419   Thanom Kittikachon, Trends in Community Development. Bangkok,
        Thailand: Community Development Department, Ministry of Interior,
        1964. 30 pp. [Thailand]

4420   Thorner, Daniel, Agricultural Cooperatives in India: A Field Report.
        New York: Asia Publishing House, 1964. 119 pp.

4421   Tomasetti, W. E., "Aspects of Community Development in New Guinea,"
        Pub. Adm. 22:4 (Dec. 1963), 379-394.

4422   Turner, Damon A., "An Analysis of Conflict and Accommodation between
        Vested Interests in Eight Case Examples of Consciously Planned Social
        Change." Ph.D. dissertation. Ann Arbor, Mich.: University Micro-
        films, 1959.

4423   United Nations, Economic Commission for Asia and the Far East,
        Community Development. Part II A: A Case Study of the Ghosi
        Community Development Block, Uttar Pradesh, India. Bangkok, Thailand:
        United Nations, 1960. 100 pp.

4424   United Nations, Economic Commission for Asia and the Far East,
        Planning for Social and Economic Development in India with Reference
        to the Damodar Valley Project Area: A Case Study. New Delhi:
        UNESCO, 1959. 43 pp. [Indian State of West Bengal]

4425   Villanueva, Buenaventura M., The Philippine Rural Reconstruction Move-
        ment. I: Non-governmental Programs in Community Development. Quezon
        City, Philippines: Special Study Series No. 9, Community Development
        Research Council, University of the Philippines, 1962. 147 mim. pp.

4426   Waring, P. A., "An Experiment in Development: Rural India," Man in
        India 46:2 (Apr.-June 1966), 108-113.

4427   Watson, R. G. T., Tongaati: An African Experiment. London:
        Hutchinson, 1960. 260 pp. [Republic of South Africa]

4428   Weitz, Raanan (ed.), Rural Planning in Developing Countries: Report
        on the Second Rehovoth Conference: Israel, August 1963. London:
        Routledge & Kegan Paul, 1965. 443 pp.

4429   White, Gilbert Fowler, et al., Economic and Social Aspects of the
        Lower Mekong Development: A Report to the Committee for Co-ordina-
        tion of Investigations of the Lower Mekong Basin. Bangkok, Thai-
        land, 1962. 106 pp. [Vietnam]

4430   Wikkramatileke, R., "Variable Ethnic Attributes in Malayan Rural Land
        Development," Pacif. Viewpoint 5:1 (May 1964), 35-50. [Malaysia]

4431   Winniw, W. W., Jr., "The Papaloapan Project: An Experiment in
        Tropical Development," Econ. Geogr. 34:3 (July 1958), 227-248.
        [Mexico]

4432   Yang, Martin C., "Land Reform and Community Development in Taiwan,"
        J. China Soc. 3 (1963), 65-75.

5. Rural Leadership

A. Annotated Case Studies

5001   Bailey, Frederick George, Politics and Social Change: Orissa in
        1959. Berkeley: University of California Press, 1963. 241 pp.

        A study of the 1957 campaign in the Indian State of Orissa and
        specifically in two villages, showing the relationship of politi-
        cal expression to the social structure.

*5002   Beidelman, Thomas O., A Comparative Analysis of the Jajmani System.
        Locust Valley, N.Y.: Augustin, 1959. 86 pp. [North India]

        The widening of the economic sphere of the village to include
        markets outside its immediate area has freed the peasant from the
        rule of the Jajman, without as yet giving the peasant any real
        economic security in return. The result has been increased tension
        with no real means of preserving village cohesion.

**5003 Béteille, André, Caste, Class and Power: Changing Patterns of Strati-
        fication in a Tanjore Village. Berkeley: University of California
        Press, 1965. 238 pp. [Indian State of Madras]

The increase in exterior economic opportunities has tended to loosen the tight relationship between caste and class. While the lines between the classes have become blurred, those between castes have been strengthened, particularly as regards political power. This situation may be only temporary, however, for caste may not survive without corresponding divisions of class and power.

5004   Firmalino, Tito G., Political Activities of Barrio Citizens in Iloilo as They Affect Community Development: A Research Study. Quezon City: Community Development Research Council, University of the Philippines, 1959. 266 pp.

A series of case studies of local leaders. The citizens tend to look to government for everything they need. Consequently, they are beginning to understand how government may be influenced.

5005   Goethals, Peter R., Aspects of Local Government in a Sumbawan Village (Eastern Indonesia). Ithaca: Cornell University Press, 1961. 143 pp.

The village has remained a closed corporate entity despite its considerable material progress.

5006   Hollnsteiner, M. R., "The Development of Political Parties on the Local Level: A Social Anthropological Case Study of Hulo Municipality, Bulcaan," Philipp. J. Publ. Adm. 4:2 (Apr. 1960), 111-131.

Political parties are polarized around family lines and feuds.

5007   Ide, Yoshinori, Hiroshi Hokama, Shoichi Izumi, and Hachiro Nakamura, "Structure of Local Administration," in GEN 4343 (1960), 32-42. [Japan]

A study of the influence of self-government on the village. This change from the previous feudal structure was resisted, but it was also aided by the merger of several villages and towns into a larger unit.

5008   Jay, Robert R., Religion and Politics in Rural Central Java. New Haven: Southeast Asia Studies, Yale University, 1963. 117 pp.

The author finds a great increase in religious functionalism in recent years.

5009   Niimaku, Noboru, "Changes in Economic Structure in Farming Villages after the War and Their Relation to the Political Process," in GEN 4343 (1960), 20-31. [Japan]

Land reform has not eliminated the political power of the former landlords, for they are more experienced and better educated than the peasants, whose outlook remains traditional.

5010   Retzloff, Ralph H., A Case Study of Panchayats in a North Indian Village. A paper presented before the South Asia Colloquium, February 1959. Berkeley: University of California Press, 1959. 126 pp. [Indian State of Uttar Pradesh]

The Panchayat elections have tended to destroy village unity.

5011   Singh, Yogendra, "The Changing Power Structure of the Village
        Community: A Case Study of Six Villages in Eastern Uttar Pradesh,"
        in GEN 4320 (1961), 669-688. [Indian State of Uttar Pradesh]

        A study of the changes ensuing from the demise of the Zamindari
        system. Such changes have been more legal than actual.

*5012   Smith, Michael Garfield, The Economy of Hausa Communities in Zaria.
        Colonial Research Studies 16. London: HMSO, 1955. 264 pp.
        [Nigeria]

        The British ruled this part of Northern Nigeria through the local
        chiefs, who were formerly slaveholders and slave dealers. Even
        though slavery was banned at the turn of the century, these nobles
        have retained their social position by adapting to the British
        indirect rule.

**5013 ------ "Kagoro Political Development," Hum. Organiz. 19:3 (Fall 1960),
        137-149. [Nigeria]

        The British, by imposing an alien system of power on the Kagoro,
        eventually succeeded in altering the structure of their society.
        Their internal status was changed to meet external conditions. Thus
        new and acceptable modes of competing were developed that preserved
        as far as possible the essential elements of the old modes.

*5014   Whitten, Norman E., Jr., Class, Kinship, and Power in an Ecuadorian
        Town: The Negroes of San Lorenzo. Stanford, Calif.: Stanford
        University Press, 1965. 238 pp.

        Adaptability among these people is related to a strong kinship
        structure. It is a trait found primarily in their ability to exploit
        economic possibilities outside the community. Internal change tends
        to undermine the traditional social framework, in which graft plays
        an extensive role.

*5015   Van Velsen, J., The Politics of Kinship: A Study of Social
        Manipulation among the Lakeside Tonga of Nyasaland. Manchester,
        England: Manchester University Press, 1964. 338 pp.

        Tonga society is highly egalitarian, and authority is diffuse.
        The British administration, however, was hierarchical and authori-
        tarian. Despite close contact between these two modes of govern-
        ment and the fact that many Tonga men work in industrial concerns,
        the Tonga still find their ultimate security within the tribal
        system.

B.   Other Case Studies

5301   Ainsworth, M. D., and L. H. Ainsworth, "Acculturation in East
        Africa: I. Political Awareness and Attitudes toward Authority;
        II. Frustration and Aggression; III. Attitudes toward Parents,
        Teachers, and Education; IV. Summary Discussion," J. soc. Psychol.
        57:2 (Aug. 1962), 391-432.

5302   Alexandre, P., "Organisation politique des Kotokoli du Nord Togo"
        [Political organization of the Kotokoli of North Togo], Cah. Etud.
        afr. 4:2 (May 1963), 223-274.

5303   Apter, D. E., The Political Kingdom in Uganda: A Study in Bureau-
        cratic Nationalism. Princeton: Princeton University Press, 1961.
        498 pp.

5304   Bailey, F. G., "Political Change in the Kondmals," East. Anthrop.
        11:2 (Dec. 1957-Feb. 1958), 88-106. [Indian State of Orissa]

5305   Baker, Richard St. Barbe, Kabongo: The Story of a Kikuyu Chief.
        New York: Barnes and Noble, 1955. [Kenya]

5306   Balandier, Georges, "Réflexions sur le fait politique: Le cas des
        sociétés africaines" [Reflections on political reality: The case of
        the African societies], Cah. int. Sociol. 2:37 (July-Dec. 1964), 23-50.

5307   Bardier. C. H., "La formation des cadres intermédiaires dans les pays
        en voie de développement" [Formation of intermediate cadres in the
        developing countries], Int. Rev. Community Dev. 12 (1963), 21-52.

5308   Barnes, James A., Politics in a Changing Society: A Political History
        of the Fort Jameson Ngoni. Cape Town, South Africa: Oxford Univer-
        sity Press, 1954. 220 pp. [Zambia]

5309   Barth, Fredrik, Political Leadership among Swat Pathans. London:
        Athlone Press, 1959. 143 pp. [Afghanistan]

5310   Beals, Alan R., "The Government in the Indian Village," Econ. Dev.
        cult. Change 2:5 (June 1954), 397-407.

5311   Beattie, J. H. M., "Bunyoro: An African Feudality?" J. afr. Hist.
        5:1 (1964), 25-36. [Uganda]

5312   Befu, Hirofumi, "Political Complexity and Village Community: Test
        of an Hypothesis," Anthrop. Quart. 39:2 (Apr. 1966), 43-52.

5313   Bhouraskur, K. M., "Leadership in a Tribal Village," Man in India
        44:4 (Oct.-Dec. 1964), 329-340. [Indian State of Madhya Pradesh]

5314   Bose, A. B., and S. P. Malhotra, "Studies in Group Dynamics I:
        Factionalism in a Desert Village," Man in India 44 (Oct. 1964),
        311-328. [India]

5315   Bose, A. B., and P. C. Saxena, "Opinion Leaders in a Village in
        Western Rajasthan," Man in India 46:2 (Apr. 1966), 121-130. [Indian
        State of Rajasthan]

5316   Busia, Kofi A., The Position of the Chief in the Modern Political
        System of Ashanti: A Study of the Influence of Contemporary Social
        Changes on Ashanti Political Institutions. London: Oxford Univer-
        sity Press, 1951. 233 pp. [Ghana]

5317   Buxton, J. C., Chiefs and Strangers: A Study of Political Assimi-
        lation among the Mandari. Oxford: Clarendon Press, 1963. 167 pp.
        [Sudan]

5318   Chaudhuri, Ranjit, "Pattern of Leadership in a West Bengal Village,"
        Econ. Wkly. 16:14 (4 Apr. 1964), 641, 643-644. [Indian State of West
        Bengal]

5319   Cowan, L. Gray, Local Government in West Africa. New York: Columbia
        University Press, 1958. 292 pp.

5320   Dubey, S. M., "Role of Kinship and Ideology in Rural Factionalism: A
        Study of Factions in a Village of Eastern Uttar Pradesh, with Special
        Reference to the Role of Patti," East. Anthrop. 18 (Jan. 1965),
        22-33.

5321   Encarnación, Vicente, Jr., "Leadership in a Benguet Village,"
        Philipp. Stud. 9:4 (1961), 571-583. [Philippines]

5322   ------ "Types of Authority in a Benguet Village," Phillip. J. pub.
        Adm. 1:4 (Oct. 1957), 379-391. [Philippines]

5323   Epstein, A. L., "An Outline of the Political Structure of an African
        Urban Community of the Copperbelt of Northern Rhodesia," in GEN 4325
        (1956), 711-724. [Zambia]

5324   Epstein, A. L., and J. Clyde Mitchell, "Power and Prestige among
        Africans in Northern Rhodesia: An Experiment," Rhod. Sci. Ass.
        45 (1957), 13-26. [Zambia]

5325   Erasmus, Charles J., "The Leader vs. Tradition: A Case Study," Am.
        Anthrop. 54:2 (Pt. 1) (1952), 168-178. [Mexico]

5326   Fallers, L. A., "The Predicament of the Modern African Chief: An
        Instance from Uganda," in GEN 4396 (1966), 232-248.

5327   Fayyaz, Muhammad, "Reference Individuals in Pakistani Rural Setting."
        Ph.D. thesis, Cornell University, 1964.

5328   Freed, R. S., and S. A. Freed, "Unity in Diversity in the Celebration
        of Cattle-curing Rites in a North Indian Village: A Study in the
        Resolution of Conflict," Am. Anthrop. 68:3 (June 1966), 673-692.

5329   Fukutake, Tadashi, "Village Community (Buraku) in Japan and Its
        Democratization," in GEN 4382 (1962), 86-90.

5330   Galjart, B., "Class and 'Following' in Rural Brazil," Amér. lat. 7:3
        (July-Sept. 1964), 3-24.

5331   Gould, H. A., "A Jajmani System of North India: Its Structure,
        Magnitude, and Meaning," Ethnology 3 (1964), 12-41.

5332   Gray, R. F., "Political Parties in New African Nations: An Anthro-
        pological View," Comp. Stud. Soc. Hist. 5:4 (July 1963), 449-461.

5333   Green, M. M., Ibo Village Affairs. New ed. New York: Praeger,
        1964. 262 pp. [Nigeria]

5334   Gullick, J. M., Indigenous Political Systems of Western Malaya.
        London: Athlone Press, 1958. 151 pp.

5335   Harries-Jones, P., and J. C. Chiwale, "Kasaka: A Case Study in
        Succession and Dynamics of a Bembe Village," Hum. Probl. B.C.A. 33
        (June 1963), 1-67. [Southern Rhodesia]

5336   Hirabayashi, G. K., and M. Fathalla el Khatib, "Communication and
        Political Awareness in the Villages of Egypt," Pub. Opin. Quart. 22
        (1958), 357-362.

5337   Holmes, L. D., "Decision Making in a Samoan Village," Anthropologica
        7:2 (1965), 229-238.

5338   International Christian University, Social Service Division, Nôson
        no Kenkyoku Kôzô [Power structure in a rural community]. Tokyo:
        International Christian University, 1959. 515 pp. [Japan]

5339   John, P. V., "Changing Pattern of Leadership in a Village in Madhya
        Pradesh," Sociol. Bull. 12:1 (Mar. 1963), 32-38. [Indian State of
        Madhya Pradesh]

5340   Kapferer, Bruce, Co-operation, Leadership, and Village Structure: A
        Preliminary Economic and Political Study of Ten Bisa Villages in the
        Northern Province of Zambia. Manchester, England: Manchester Univer-
        sity Press, 1967. 77 pp.

5341   Keesing, F. M., Modern Samoa: Its Government and Changing Life. Stan-
        ford, Calif.: Stanford University Press, 1934. 506 pp.

5342   Khare, R. S., "Group Dynamics in a North Indian Village," Hum.
        Organiz. 21:3 (Fall 1962), 201-213.

5343   Kolenda, Pauline Mahar, "Toward a Model of the Hindu Jajmani System,"
        Hum. Organiz. 22:1 (Spring 1963), 11-31. Also in GEN 4319 (1967),
        285-332. [North India]

5344   Langness, L. L., "Notes on the Bena Council, Eastern Highland,"
        Oceania 33:3 (Mar. 1963), 151-170. [New Guinea]

5345   Liebenow, G. J., Jr., "Responses to Planned Political Change in a
        Tanganyika Tribal Group," Am. polit. Sci. Rev. 50:2 (June 1956),
        442-461.

5346   Little, Kenneth L., "Mende Political Institutions in Transition,"
        Africa 17:1 (1947), 8-23. [Sierra Leone]

5347   Low, D. A., "The Advent of Populism in Buganda," Comp. Stud. Soc.
        Hist. 6:4 (July 1964), 424-444. [Uganda]

5348   McCormack, William C., "Changing Leadership of a Mysore Village."
        Ph.D. dissertation, University of Chicago, 1956. [Indian State of
        Mysore]

5349   Mathur, P. C., "Sociological Dimensions of Panchayati Raj," Indian
        J. pub. Adm. 10:1 (Jan.-Mar. 1964), 58-72. [India]

5350   Mitchell, J. Clyde, "The Political Organisation of the Yao of
        Southern Nyasaland," Afr. Stud. 8:3 (Mar. 1949). [Malawi]

5351   Moore, C. H., "Politics in a Tunisian Village," Mid. E. J. 17:5
        (Autumn 1963), 527-540.

5352   Nader, L., and D. Metzger, "Conflict Resolution in Two Mexican
        Communities," Am. Anthrop. 65:3 (June 1963), 584-592.

5353   Nayacakalou, R. R., "Les cadres traditionnels et modernes et les
        problèmes de développement économique aux Iles Fidji" [Traditional
        and modern cadres and the problems of economic development in the Fiji
        Islands], Rev. int. Sci. soc. 16:2 (1964), 285-296.

5354   Nishikawa, T., and T. Masuda, "Nômin no seiji ishiki to seikatsu
        ishiki. Hyôgo-ken Hikami-chô oyobi Yashiro-chô ni okeru jittai
        chôsa" [The mental attitudes of the farming classes toward politics
        and life: A field study in Hikami-chô and Yashiro-chô, Hyôgo
        Prefecture], Kôbe Hôgaku 12:4 (Mar. 1963), 468-525. [Japan]

5355   North, A. C., "Rural Local Government Training in Northern Rhodesia,"
        J. afr. Adm. 13:2 (Apr. 1961), 67-77. [Zambia]

5356   Orenstein, H., "Exploitation or Function in the Interpretation of
        Jajmani," Sthwest. J. Anthrop. 18 (1962), 302-316. [India]

5357   Pauvert, J. C., "L'évolution politique des Ewe" [The political
        evolution of the Ewe], Cah. Etud. afr. 2 (May 1960),161-192. [Togo]

5358   Plant, H. T., "Local Government and Community Development in Rural
        Areas of Papua and New Guinea," Austr. Territ. 2:2 (Mar. 1962),
        4-12.

5359   Rahudkar, W. B., "Local Leaders and the Adoption of Farm Practices,"
        Nagpur agric. Col. Mag. 34 (1960), 1-13. [India]

5360   Rao, A. V. Raman, Structure and Working of Village Panchayats: A
        Survey Based on Case Studies in Bombay and Madras. Poona, India:
        Gokhale Institute of Politics and Economics, 1954. 218 pp. [Indian
        States of Madras and Maharashtra]

5361   Rastogi, P. N., "Factionalism, Politics and Crime in an Uttar
        Pradesh Village," East. Anthrop. 17:3 (Sept.-Dec. 1964), 168-184.

5362   ------ "Factions in Kurnipur," Man in India 45:4 (Oct.-Dec. 1965),
        289-295. [Indian State of Uttar Pradesh]

5363   Retzlaff, Ralph H., Village Government in India: A Case Study.
        New York: Asia Publishing House, 1962. 140 pp.

5364   Richards, Audrey Isabel (ed.), East African Chiefs: A Study of
        Political Development in Some Uganda and Tanganyika Tribes. London:
        Faber and Faber, 1960. 419 pp.

5365   Rogers, Everett M., and Johannes C. van Es, Opinion Leadership in
        Traditional and Modern Colombian Peasant Communities. East Lansing,
        Mich.: Department of Communication, Michigan State University, 1964.

5366   Sachchidananda, "Leadership and Culture Change in Kullu," Man in
        India 44:2 (Apr. 1964), 116-131. [Indian State of Bihar]

5367   Saikia, P. D., "Village Leadership in North-east India: Assessment
        and Conclusion on Case Studies in Six Villages," Man in India 43:2
        (Apr. 1963), 92-99. [Indian State of West Bengal]

5368   Seshaiah, S., "Post-war Reforms and Changes in the Leadership
        Structure of Village Japan: A Case Study," East. Anthrop. 19:1
        (Jan.-Apr. 1966), 1-28.

5369   Seyliowicz, J. S., "The Political Dynamics of Rural Turkey," Mid.
        E. J. 16:4 (Autumn 1962), 430-442.

5370   Sharp, Lauriston, "Local Initiative and Central Government in Thai-
        land," in GEN 4394 (1963), 95-111.

5371   Sirsikar, V. M., "Leadership Patterns in Rural Maharashtra," Asian
        Surv. 4:7 (July 1964), 929-939. [Indian State of Maharashtra]

5372   Skinner, E. P., The Mossi of the Upper Volta: The Political Develop-
        ment of the Sudanese People. Stanford, Calif.: Stanford University
        Press, 1964. 236 pp.

5373   Skinner, George W. (ed.), Local Ethnic and National Loyalties in
        Village Indonesia: A Symposium. New Haven: Southeast Asia Studies,
        Yale University, 1959. 68 pp.

5374   Solenberger, R. R., "Continuity of Political Institutions in the
        Marianas," Hum. Organiz. 23:1 (Spring 1964), 53-60. [Micronesia]

5375   Somjee, A. H., Village Leadership in Transition: A Case Study.
        Contribution to the Bombay Round Table, January 4-10, 1964. Paris:
        International Political Science Association, 1964. 17 pp. [India]

5376   Sonraku Shakai Kenkyû kai (ed.), Nominsô Bunkai to Soshiki [Social
        differentiation and the organization of the peasantry]. Tokyo:
        Jochôsha, 1963. 261 pp. [Japan]

5377   Southwold, Martin, Bureaucracy and Chiefship in Buganda. Kampala,
        Uganda: East African Institute of Social Research, n.d. 20 pp.
        [Uganda]

5378   Suzuki, E., "Chôsen no Kei to Pumashi" [The Kei and Pumashi associa-
        tions in the Korean rural community], Minzokugaku Kenkyû 27:3 (1963),
        22-28.

5379   Suzuki, M., "Polynesia ni okeru kokkakeisei no mondaiten: Tahiti no
         baai" [Problems in the formation of a state society: A case study of
         Tahiti], Minzokugaku Kenkyû 27:2 (31 Mar. 1963), 30-50.

5380   Thorner, Daniel, "The Village Panchayat as a Vehicle of Change," Econ.
         Dev. cult. Change 2:3 (Oct. 1953), 209-215. [India]

5381   Tinker, H., "Authority and Community in Village India," Pacif. Aff.
         32:4 (Dec. 1959), 354-375.

5382   Useem, John, "The Development of Democratic Leadership in the Micro-
         nesian Islands," in GEN 4385 (n.d.), 261-280.

5383   Valentine, C. A., "Social Status, Political Power, and Native
         Responses to European Influence in Oceania," Anthrop. Forum 1:1
         (July 1963), 3-5. [Polynesia]

5384   Van der Kroef, J. M. A., "Collectivitism in Indonesian Society," Soc.
         Res. 20:2 (Summer 1953), 193-209.

5385   Warriner, C. K., "Traditional Authority and the Modern State: The
         Case of the Mananao of the Philippines," Soc. Probl. 12:1 (Summer
         1964), 51-56.

5386   Winans, Edgar V., "The Political Context of Economic Adaptation in the
         Southern Highlands of Tanganyika," Am. Anthrop. 67:2 (Apr. 1965),
         435-441.

5387   Woodruff, Lloyd Wilbur, The Study of a Vietnamese Rural Community:
         Administrative Activity. 2 vols. Saigon: Michigan State University
         Vietnam Advisory Group, 1960. 308 and 50 pp.

5388   Wraith, R., Local Government in West Africa. London: Allen and
         Unwin, 1964. 184 pp.

6. Rural Economy

A. Annotated Case Studies

*6001   Althabe, Georges, "Problèmes socio-économiques du Nord Congo" [Eco-
         nomic and social problems of the North Congo], Cah. Inst. Sci. écon.
         series 5:5 (Nov. 1962), 187-282.

         A study of a village into which the cultivation of coffee was
         introduced by the government with the aid of a strong local chief,
         Three years later these communal plantings were abandoned in favor
         of meager individual ones. The market for coffee was controlled by
         the government, which dictated prices and conditions to the peasants.
         Consequently they had no enthusiasm for communal plantings.

6002   Ames, David, "The Rural Wolof of the Gambia," in GEN 4312 (1962),
          29-60.

              The introduction of money into this subsistence economy has
          tended to increase social mobility.

*6003   Bailey, F. G., "Capital, Saving and Credit in Highland Orissa
          (India)," in GEN 4324 (1964), 104-132.

              The introduction of a commercial economy has enabled nonruling
          castes to free themselves of caste limitations. The society
          esteems wealth, but those who accumulate it are despised and an
          effort is made to reduce them to poverty. Although the higher
          caste Oriyas could earn more by cultivating turmeric than by selling
          it, they do not grow it. The lower caste Konds do grow the root,
          but they use the profits only for personal expenses, not for further
          economic gain. The only successful entrepreneurs are the brokers who
          act as liaison between the individual and the government in the
          distribution of funds for development.

*6004   Bastide, R., and P. Verger, "Contribution à l'étude sociologique des
          marchés Nagô du Bas Dahomey" [Contribution to the sociological study
          of the Nagô markets in the Lower Dahomey], Cah. Inst. Sci. écon.
          series 5:1 (Nov. 1959), 33-64.

              The building of roads has reinforced traditional individualism and
          has also produced middle men who are eliminating the previous direct
          selling by the producer. The industrialization of palm-oil production
          has tended to group the sales of palm nuts, but the natives have yet
          to learn to budget the proceeds over the year. When their money
          runs out, the women leave home to sell goods in the cities.

**6005   Belshaw, Cyril S., In Search of Wealth: A Study of the Emergence of
          Commercial Operations in the Melanesian Society of Southeastern
          Papua. Menasha, Wis.: American Anthropological Association, 1955.
          84 pp.

              The author stresses the compatibility between the traditional
          social structure and modern economic development. The close kinship
          system, for instance, proves to be more effective as a base for
          "incorporation" than does the traditional Western impersonal corpor-
          ation. The nonmonetized sector provides a cushion against a recession
          in the monetary sector. With further development, the goods of the
          monetary sector will no longer be luxuries. This tends to increase
          mobility by freeing the individual both from the land and from the
          wider forms of the family. This should lead to expanded trade and
          concomitantly a rise in demand. To meet this demand may be difficult,
          since the administration (and through it the banks) insist on Western
          organizational methods that are often inappropriate, thus blocking
          the availability of investment funds.

**6006   ------ Under the Ivy Tree: Society and Economic Growth in Rural Fiji.
          Berkeley: University of California Press, 1964. 336 pp.

              Though individual Fijians show considerable entrepreneurial
          ability, the rigidity of the social system holds them back, for the
          contemporary system does not encourage adaptability as much as the

[207]

traditional one does. There is no coordination in the Fijian political hierarchy, nor capital for proceeding individually. The Fijians
are highly price sensitive, but this may not be enough to overcome the
lack of social overhead--particularly in the area of marketing
procedure.

6007   Boeke, J. H., "Three Forms of Disintegration in Dual Societies,"
        Indonesië 4 (Apr. 1954), 278-296. [Indonesia]

        A study of the capitalist closed economy of the desa.

6008   Brelsford, W. V., Fishermen of the Bangweulu Swamps: A Study of the
        Fishing Activities of the Unga Tribe. Livingstone, Zambia: The
        Rhodes-Livingstone Institute, 1946. 169 pp. [Zambia]

        Contains a section on the economics of decision making in this
        Northern Rhodesian tribe.

6009   Colson, Elizabeth, "Trade and Wealth among the Tonga," in GEN 4312
        (1962), 601-616. [Zambia]

        Though the Tonga are heavily engaged in the market economy intro-
        duced by the British, they still operate in the market only when they
        need some item to be found there. Commerce for the sake of accruing
        wealth has not found a place in Tonga society.

6010   Comitas, Lambros, "Occupation Multiplicity in Rural Jamaica," in GEN
        4326 (1964), 41-50.

        Occupational multiplicity builds a complex set of social obliga-
        tions that are needed to fill the void left by a weak family
        structure.

*6011   Davenport, William H., "When a Primitive and a Civilized Money Meet,"
        in GEN 4327 (1961), 64-77. [Melanesia]

        Australian money, being more stable and more widely in use, is
        driving the traditional feather currency out of the market. Feather
        currency is hoarded, since its value appreciates as the production
        of such currency decreases.

6012   Dean, Edwin R., "Social Determinants of Price in Several African
        Markets," Econ. Dev. cult. Change 11:3, Pt. 1 (Apr. 1963), 239-256.
        [Malawi]

        The results of a controlled experiment in Nyasaland analyzed
        statistically, with inconclusive results. There is some indication
        that prices are not determined by whether the buyer originates
        from one group or another.

6013   Dorjahn, Vernon R., "African Traders in Central Sierra Leone," in
        GEN 4312 (1962), 61-88.

        Trade relationships tend to follow social patterns and to be
        influenced by them. Kinship obligations tend to limit an individual
        trader's independence.

**6014   Douglas, Mary, "Lele Economy Compared with the Bushong: A Study of Economic Backwardness," in GEN 4312 (1962), 211-236.

By reinforcing the insecurity of feuding villages and generations, the Lele seem to have voluntarily cut themselves off from the greater economic achievements of the Bushong on the other side of the river. This refusal to adopt better techniques is owing to Lele social institutions, which tend to reinforce and perpetuate the initial conditions that lead to insecurity.

6015   Dupire, Marguerite, "Trade and Markets in the Economy of the Nomadic Fulani of Niger (Bororo)," in GEN 4312 (1962), 335-364.

The development of markets may be detrimental to a nomadic tribe, since it is likely to upset the careful traditional balance between their needs and their environment.

**6016   Epstein, T. Scarlett, "Personal Capital Formation among the Tolai of New Britain," in GEN 4324 (1964), 53-68. [Melanesia]

A study of a matrilineal people whose mode of life is being changed by the introduction of cash cropping (sons help their father in his gardening, but the wife's brother's sons may not). Though cash is needed for the purchase of European goods, shell currency is also used, for it occupies a central place in the social system. These two monetary systems are not considered interchangeable even when the exchange rate would make such interchanges profitable. The author traces the career of an individual entrepreneur and shows how he has gradually changed from a matrilineal system of holding capital to an individual one. He is blocked from further expansion, not for lack of desire, but by restrictions on credit imposed on the natives by the European government.

*6017   Firth, Raymond W., Malay Fishermen: Their Peasant Economy. London: Kegan Paul, Trench, Trubner, 1946. 2nd ed. Hamden, Conn.: Archon Books, 1966. 354 and 398 pp. [Malaysia]

The introduction of large-scale nets in the 1960's has greatly changed the social structure of this village. Extensive credit is needed not only for the nets but also for the transportation and the ice supply required by the larger catches. The terms of the credit from the net dealers and the increased capitalization of fishing has shifted the control of fishing from the fishermen to the fish-dealers. All credit payments and other capital expenses are now met first, with any remainder being distributed among the men who worked with the nets. As a result, the distribution of wealth has become less uniform than in the 1940's. The author finds that social factors have not inhibited the rise of native entrepreneurs.

**6018   ------ Primitive Polynesian Economy. 2nd ed. London: Routledge & Kegan Paul, 1964. 385 pp. 1st ed. 1939, 387 pp.

While the author finds that this primitive economy is basically a rational one, its economic ties are more detached from personal relations than is true in the West. The Tikopia native is a realist, but he gives a less dominant place to the pursuit of economic ends than does the Westerner.

[209]

*6019   Foster, George M., A Primitive Mexican Economy. New York: J. J.
         Augustin, 1942. 115 pp.

            Author finds this primitive economy is roughly similar to that in
         the West. Market activities are conducted in cash, coffee is sold to
         the outside world, but there does not seem to be any considerable
         source of credit.

6020   Gibson, Gordon D., "Bridewealth and Other Forms of Exchange among the
         Herero," in GEN 4312 (1962), 617-642.   Republic of South Africa]

            Bridewealth payments have not changed with the advent of a market
         economy among the Herero. This fact is ascribed to the ritual,
         rather than to the economic, importance of bridewealth.

6021   Gluckman, Max, Economy of the Central Barotse Plain. The Rhodes-
         Livingstone Papers, No. 7. Lovedale, Union of S. Africa: The Love-
         dale Press, 1941. 122 pp.

            Though the political relations between natives and whites seem
         satisfactory, the growing monetization of the native economy has
         tended to increase the distance between the ruling hierarchy and the
         ordinary people. The hierarchy can now use their position to trade
         for money and thus accumulate wealth, whereas perishable goods if
         traded cannot be accumulated.

6022   Gray, Robert F., "Economic Exchange in a Sonjo Village," in GEN
         4312 (1962), 469-492. [Tanganyika]

            An exchange system may develop out of a social structure as well
         as out of a mode of production. In this case, market exchange seems
         to have come about from the need for external goods for acquiring
         land (on an individual basis), for bride-price payments, and for
         the purchase of water rights.

6023   Gulliver, P. H., "The Evolution of Arusha Trade," in GEN 3212 (1962),
         431-456. [Tanganyika]

            The Arusha did not accept the possibilities of the market fostered
         by the coming of the Europeans until their shortage of land forced
         them to turn away from their traditional economic pursuits.

6024   Halpern, Joel Martin, "Trade Patterns in Northern Laos," East.
         Anthrop. 12:2 (Dec. 1958-Feb. 1959), 119-124.

            The increase in modern communications and the availability of
         goods are drawing the tribes of this area more and more into the
         modern world.

6025   Harding, Thomas G., "Trade and Politics: A Comparison of Papuan and
         New Guinea Traders," in GEN 4335 (1965), 46-53.

            Trade tends to be dominated by the political-social structure of
         the society, and is carried on not so much for economic benefit as
         to gain culturally recognized power.

*6026   Haswell, M. R., Economics of Agriculture in a Savannah Village:
         Report on Three Years' Study in Genieri Village and Its Lands. The

<u>Gambia</u>. Colonial Research Studies 8.   London: HMSO, 1953.   142 pp.

   The possibility of cash work in the town has lured many to it,
thus inducing the disintegration of the family, which has been the
prime means of cohesion in the village. The young prefer outside
employment to subordination in the family. An experiment in mechanization has produced much lower yields than native techniques have produced. This may be a result of the multi-family approach necessitated
by the scale of operations and the consequent lack of personal
incentive.

6027   Hendry, James B., "Economic Rationality and Innovational Response in
        Rural Areas: A Case Study of Some Examples in Vietnam," in GEN 4401
        (1962), 80-90.

           The villagers are willing to adopt such new ideas as demonstrate
        convincing proof of their economic merit.

6028   Hodder, B. W., "The Yoruba Rural Market," in GEN 4312 (1962), 103-117.
        [Nigeria]

           A description of several rural markets.

6029   Hoffmann, Hans, "Money, Ecology, and Acculturation among the Shipibo
        of Peru," in GEN 4330 (1964), 259-276.

           This tribe has adapted to the introduction of a money economy by
        assuming the role of intermediary between the external suppliers of
        goods and the needs of the local populace.

6030   Horner, George R., "The Bulu Response to European Economy," in GEN
        4312 (1962), 170-189.   [Cameroons]

           Since wealth confers social status, the Bulu have simply adopted
        the cash market as a new but "traditional" way to gain social
        prestige.

6031   Hunt, Robert, "The Developmental Cycle of the Family Business in Rural
        Mexico," in GEN 4335 (1965), 54-79.

           Business tends to be run by individual heads of families, not only
        for economic reasons but also because social pressures encourage
        families to create an authoritarian hierarchy.

*6032   Izikowitz, Karl Gustav, <u>Lamet: Hill Peasants in French Indochina</u>.
        Göteborg, Sweden: Etnografiska Museet, 1951.   375 pp.   [Laos]

           Rice is grown both as a dietary staple and as a medium of exchange.
        Wealth is estimated both in masculine forms (buffaloes) and feminine
        (silks, etc.). Extensive trading has always been carried on so as to
        procure these forms of wealth and also the iron implements needed in
        the forest. However, many villagers have recently gone to work for
        cash wages in the plantations and town of Siam. This has brought them
        a degree of independence of traditional means of exchange, since cash
        is more suitable for accumulation either in itself or in the form of
        traditional wealth. When the workers return to the village, their
        prestige is enhanced by having been away and by having accumulated

                                   [211]

cash. Thus an economic class structure is developing in the village.

6033   LeVine, Robert A., "Wealth and Power in Gusiiland," in GEN 4312
          (1962), 520-536. [Kenya]

          The traditional relationship between wealth and political power
          has created both powerful chief-traders and nonchief bureaucrat-
          traders, who rise in the bureaucracy because of their education.

6034   Malinowski, Bronislaw, Argonauts of the Western Pacific: An Account
          of Native Enterprise and Adventure in the Archipalagos of Melanesian
          New Guinea. London: Routledge, 1922. 527 pp. [New Guinea]

          Trade in this society is dominated by its social-psychological
          "function."

6035   Manners, R. A., "Land Use, Trade and the Growth of Market Economy in
          Kipsigis Country," in GEN 4312 (1962), 493-519. [Kenya]

          A description of markets in an area dominated by tea and coffee
          plantations.

*6036   Mayer, Philip, Two Studies in Applied Anthropology in Kenya. Part 1:
          Agricultural Co-operation by Neighbourhood Groups among the Gush.
          Colonial Research Studies 3. London: HMSO, 1951. 18 pp.

          Even where farmers have adopted modern farming methods (plowing),
          neighborhood work parties paid with beer still provide temporary
          labor. This traditional practice is effective in a modernized
          context, wherever other sources of temporary labor are either
          unavailable or too costly.

*6037   Meillassoux, Claude, "Social and Economic Factors Affecting Markets
          in Guro Land," in GEN 4312 (1962), 279-298. [Ivory Coast]

          Markets tend to develop at points of contact between zones having
          complementary goods. Such markets promote integration of zones, and
          also disruption, by introducing new goods and new ways of achieving
          status.

6038   Middleton, John, "Trade and Markets among the Lugbara of Uganda," in
          GEN 4312 (1962), 561-580.

          The advent of markets has provided women with a means of escape
          from traditional social bonds. These markets have also given rise to
          a wealthy class of "new people," whose conspicuous consumption of
          market goods exhibits their improved status.

*6039   Mintz, Sidney W., "The Employment of Capital by Market Women in
          Haiti," in GEN 4324 (1964), 256-286.

          A large segment of the population is engaged in marketing because
          of the highly diversified nature of local farming. The market women
          show a firm grasp of economic factors, but they are blocked in their
          efforts to expand their operations by governmental restrictions and by
          other outside forces.

*6040   ------ "Pratik: Haitian Personal Economic Relationships," in GEN
         4327 (1961), 54-63.

         The Haitian custom of reserving merchandise for an established
         buyer (a form of contractual relation) shows a basic understanding
         of the Haitian economy. The highly volatile supply of most of the
         goods traded makes a guaranteed trading relation a valuable
         stabilizing factor.

6041   Nash, Manning, "Capital, Saving and Credit in a Guatemalan and a
         Mexican Indian Peasant Society," in GEN 4324 (1964), 287-304.

         The Mexican village is little integrated with the outside world
         because of its physical isolation and its lack of contacts with
         non-Indians. The Indian mores discourage savings (kinship obliga-
         tions have a leveling influence); furthermore the non-Indian society
         tends to exclude Indians.

*6042   Nicolas, G., "Aspects de la vie économique dans un canton du Niger:
         Kantché" [Aspects of economic life in a canton of Niger: Kantché],
         Cah. Inst. Sci. écon. Series 5:5 (Nov. 1962), 105-186.

         There is an interaction between the Islamic society and the newly
         introduced modern economy. On the one hand, the ease with which a
         divorce may be had has pushed women to strive for positions of eco-
         nomic independence. Religious groups have been strengthened, since
         they are in a position to profit from economic opportunities that
         demand more than one individual can handle. On the other hand,
         economic values have begun to replace the traditional warrior values,
         and the influence of the traditional liens (cheffery) of the extended
         family have waned.

6043   Ottenberg, Simon, and Phoebe Ottenberg, "Afikpo Markets: 1900-1960,"
         in GEN 4312 (1962), 118-169. [Nigeria]

         Despite a growing market and an increase in economic activity
         outside the market, many traditional trading aspects have remained,
         such as bargaining, women traders, and the role of the market as a
         social center.

6044   Palmer, Mabel, "Some Problems of the Transition from Subsistence to
         Money Economy," S. Afr. J. Sci. 27 (1930), 117-125. [Republic of
         South Africa]

         Discusses the advantages of tribal land tenure and labor migration
         to native agricultural development.

*6045   Reining, Conrad C., "Zande Markets and Commerce," in GEN 4312 (1962),
         537-560. [Sudan]

         After forty years of contact with a monetary economy, the Zande
         still have only a rough idea of monetary operations. The reasons are
         the isolation of the region and the consequent lack of commercial
         contacts and of credit. Commercial operations are all the harder for
         the Zande, since the non-Zande who now control them do not wish to
         relinquish their monopoly.

6046   Richards, A. I., <u>Land, Labour and Diet in Northern Rhodesia: An</u>
            <u>Economic Study of the Bemba Tribe</u>. London: Oxford University Press,
            1939. 423 pp. [Zambia]

            The Bemba reliance on mutual support tends to limit the development
            of trading patterns. This contrasts with the neighboring Bisa
            (fishermen), who are more individualistic and are very sharp traders.

*6047   Sahlins, Marshall D., "Exchange-Value and the Diplomacy of Primitive
            Trade," in GEN 4335 (1965), 95-129. [Polynesia]

            The exchange ratios are differentially responsive to changes in
            long-term supply and demand. The nature of either the social
            relation or the exchange contract between the traders seems to dampen
            the fluctuations in demand and supply.

***6048   Salisbury, R. F., <u>From Stone to Steel: Economic Consequences of a</u>
            <u>Technological Change in New Guinea</u>. Victoria, Australia: Melbourne
            University Press, 1962. 237 pp. bibl.

            The change-over from stone to steel represents, not more capital
            investment, but rather an increased output of subsistence goods per
            unit of input. Rather than producing more subsistence goods for
            which there is no market, the people began to produce more luxury
            or prestige goods. This has increased the wealth of the community,
            particularly that of those already rich. Eventually this increase in
            wealth changed consumption patterns in favor of a greater consumption
            of subsistence goods. This economic development, which underlies
            social transformations, is inevitable, since goods in one category
            cannot be exchanged for goods in another: only the production time
            can be shifted.

6049   Schneider, Harold K., "Economics in East African Aboriginal
            Societies," in GEN 4336 (1964), 53-76.

            In many East African primitive societies, cattle are used as a
            monetary unit. The difference between these primitive economies and
            a modern economy is only one of degree, not of kind.

*6050   Schoorl, Johan Willem, "Kultuur en Kultuurveranderingen in het
            Moejoe Gebied" [Culture and cultural change in the Muja region].
            Ph.D. dissertation, University of Leiden, 1957. 298 pp. [New
            Guinea]

            The cultural elements of the West have been readily accepted,
            since Western goods can be easily assimilated to the traditional
            forms of wealth. The accumulation of wealth is a strong tradition
            in the society, so that the impetus to Westernization has had a
            marked effect. The natives have turned from a developing interest
            in Western forms of wealth to the accumulation of money and to a
            realization that greater wealth can be had only by adopting Western
            practices.

6051   Schultz, Theodore W., <u>Transforming Traditional Agriculture</u>. New
            Haven: Yale University Press, 1964. 212 pp. [Guatemala; India]

            An economic analysis of Sol Tax's <u>Penny Capitalism: A Guatemalan</u>

Indian Economy (1953) and W. David Hopper's The Economic Organization
of a Village in North Central India. The cost of agricultural
improvement is very high, since technical education and also capital
investment are required.

6052   Skinner, Elliott P., "Trade and Markets among the Mossi People," in
        GEN 4312 (1962), 237-278. [Upper Volta]

        A historical and descriptive study.

*6053   Smith, Michael Garfield, The Economy of Hausa Communities in Zaria.
        Colonial Research Studies 16. London: HMSO, 1955. 264 pp.
        [Nigeria]

        The British ruled through the local chiefs, a closed class of
        former slave dealers who considered themselves above manual work.
        This situation considerably slowed down the introduction of modern
        economy on the coast. Since only those who were not nobles needed to
        or could profit from economic innovation or technical education,
        modernization conferred but little social prestige.

*6054   ------ "Exchange and Marketing among the Hausa," in GEN 4312 (1962),
        299-334. [Nigeria]

        Owing to the traditional diversity of the Hausa economy of
        subsistence and exchange, the advent of the British had little
        influence on the Hausa, except in the area of village trading, which
        is still a not very large part of the local economy.

*6055   Tardits, Claude, and Claudine Tardits, "Traditional Market Economy
        in the South Dahomey," in GEN 4312 (1962), 89-102.

        As all trading is traditionally handled by women, the advent of
        the modern market has turned women into bankers, who finance the
        irregular expenses of the men who farm. The market is relatively
        free from social influences; prices, for instance, are determined
        solely by supply and demand, coupled with oligopolistic tendencies.

*6056   Underwood, Frances W., The Marketing System in Peasant Haiti. New
        Haven: Department of Anthropology, Yale University, 1960. 33 pp.

        The Haitian peasant society is closely integrated with the
        marketing system, which forms a vehicle of acculturation. However,
        the distrust and haggling that characterize the marketplace tend to
        hinder progress.

6057   Van Dooren, P. J., De sociaal-economische Ontwikkeling van de
        inheemse Samenleving in Uganda [The socio-economic development of the
        indigenous society in Uganda]. Maastricht, Netherlands: E. Van
        Aelst, 1954. 197 pp.

        A study of the clash of capitalist and precapitalist systems in
        Uganda and the resulting changes.

6058   Vansina, Jan, "Trade and Markets among the Kuba," in GEN 4312 (1962),

190-210. [Congo]

A description of the market.

B. Other Case Studies

6301   Abdul Aziz, Ungku, <u>Some Aspects of the Malayan Rural Economy Related</u>
        <u>to Measures for Mobilizing Rural Savings</u>. New York: United Nations,
        1954. [Malaysia]

6302   Alers-Montalvo, Manuel, "Social Systems Analysis of Supervised Agri-
        cultural Credit in an Andean Community," <u>Rur. Sociol</u>. 25:1 (Mar.
        1960), 51-64. [Peru]

6303   Amunugama, Sarath, "Rural Credit in Ceylon: Some Ideological Obser-
        vations," <u>Ceylon J. hist. soc. Stud</u>. 7:3 (July 1964), 135-143.

6304   Apti, D. P., "Uncertainties in Agriculture and Decisions of the
        Cultivators Regarding the Crops To Be Cultivated," <u>Indian J. agric.</u>
        <u>Econ</u>. 19 (Jan. 1964), 109-114. [India]

6305   Ardener, S., "The Comparative Study of Rotating Credit Associations,"
        <u>J. roy. Anthrop. Inst</u>. 94:2 (July-Dec. 1964), 201-229.

6306   Armstrong, W. E., "Rossel Island Money: A Unique Monetary System,"
        <u>Econ. J</u>. 34:135 (Sept. 1924), 423-429. Also in GEN 4319 (1967),
        246-253. [Melanesia]

6307   Barber, W. J., <u>The Economy of British Central Africa: A Case Study</u>
        <u>of Economic Development in a Dualistic Society</u>. Stanford, Calif.:
        Stanford University Press, 1961. 271 pp. [Zambia; Southern
        Rhodesia]

6308   Barić, Lorraine, "Some Aspects of Credit, Saving and Investment in a
        'Non-Monetary' Economy (Rossel Island)," in GEN 4324 (1964), 35-52.
        [Melanesia]

6309   Barrau, J. D., and H. S. McKee, "From Subsistence Gardening to Cash
        Crops," <u>S. Pacif. Comm. quart. Bull</u>. 6:4 (1956), 14-15ff. [Melanesia]

6310   Barth, Fredrik, "Capital, Investment and the Social Structure of a
        Pastoral Nomad Group in South Persia," in GEN 4324 (1964), 69-81.
        [Iran]

6311   Bauer, Peter, <u>West African Trade</u>. London: Cambridge University
        Press, 1954. 450 pp. [West Africa]

6312   Belshaw, Cyril S., "Institutions for Capital Formation and Distribu-
        tion among Fijians," in GEN 4324 (1964), 187-206.

6313   ------ "Port Moresby Canoe Traders," Oceania 23:1 (Sept. 1952),
        26-39. [New Guinea]

6314   Belshaw, Michael, A Village Economy: Land and People of Huecorio.
        New York: Columbia University Press, 1967. 448 pp. [Mexico]

6315   Benedict, Burton, "Capital, Saving and Credit among Mauritian
        Indians," in GEN 4324 (1964), 330-346. [Mauritius]

6316   Bergmann, Theodor, "Problems of Mechanization in Indian Agriculture,"
        Indian J. agric. Econ. 18:4 (Oct. 1963), 20-31. [India]

6317   Bettison, David G., "Price Changes in African Markets, Blantyre-Limbe,
        Nyasaland," in GEN 4361 (1959), 35-49. [Malawi]

6318   Bhowmick, P. K., "Economic Life of the Lodhas," East. Anthrop. 13
        (Mar.-May 1960), 105-120. [India]

6319   Binet, Jacques. "Les budgets familiaux africains" [African family
        budgets], Cah. Inst. Sci. écon. series 5:5 (Nov. 1962), 61-84.
        [West Africa]

6320   ------ "Marchés africains" [African markets], Cah. Inst. Sci. écon.
        series 5:1 (Nov. 1959), 65-84. [West Africa]

6321   ------ "Marchés en pays soussou" [Markets in the Soussou country-
        side], Cah. Etud. afr. 3:1 (Jan. 1962), 104-114. [Guinea]

6322   Boeke, J. H., "Capitalist Development in Indonesia and in Uganda: A
        Contrast," in GEN 4356 (1963), 90-98.

6323   Bohannan, Paul J., "The Impact of Money on an African Subsistence
        Economy," J. econ. Hist. 19:4 (Dec. 1959), 491-503. Also in GEN
        4319 (1967), 123-135, and GEN 4349 (1966), 389-396. [Nigeria]

6324   ------ "Some Principles of Exchange and Investment among the Tiv,"
        Am. Anthrop. 57:1 (Feb. 1959), 60-70. [Nigeria]

6325   Bose, Saradindu, "Economy of the Onge of Little Andaman," Man in
        India 44:4 (Oct.-Dec. 1964), 298-310. [Indian State of West Bengal]

6326   Boulanger, A., "Evolution économique d'un milieu rural en district de
        Kabinda" [Economic evolution of a rural milieu in the district of
        Kabinda], Bull. trimest. Cent. Probl. soc. indig. 36 (1957), 52-85.
        [Congo (Leopoldville)]

6327   Chatterji, A., and P. Maitreya, "Some Aspects of Regional Variations
        in Agricultural Productivity and Development in West Bengal," Indian
        J. agric. Econ. 19 (Jan. 1964), 297-212. [Indian State of West
        Bengal]

6328   Christiansen, S., "Kopraproductionen; Bismarck arkipelet" [The copra
        production of the Bismarck Archipelago], Geogr. Tidsskr. 62 (1963),
        47-55. [Melanesia]

6329   ------ "Koraløen Ahus: En melanesisk handelsnation" [The coral

island Ahus: A Melanesian commercial nation], Geogr. Tidsskr. 62
(1963), 24-33. [Melanesia]

6330   Clauzel, J., "L'évolution contemporaine de l'économie et de la
        société chez les Touaregs" [Contemporary evolution of the economy
        and the society among the Tuaregs], Actual. d'outre-mer 24 (July
        1963), 5-24. [Chad]

6331   Cohen, Abner, "The Social Organization of Credit in a West African
        Cattle Market," Africa 35:1 (Jan. 1965), 8-19. [Nigeria]

6332   Colson, Elizabeth, "Marketing of Cattle among the Plateau Tonga,"
        Hum. Probl. B.C.A. 37 (June 1965), 42-50. [Zambia]

6333   Cumper, G. E., "The Differentiation of Economic Groups in the West
        Indies," Soc. econ. Stud. 11:4 (Dec. 1962), 319-332. [British
        Caribbean]

6334   Dalton, George, "The Development of Subsistence and Peasant
        Economies in Africa," Int. soc. Sci. J. 16:3 (1964), 378-389. Also
        in GEN 4319 (1967), 155-170.

6335   ------ "Primitive Money," Am. Anthrop. 67:1 (Feb. 1965), 44-65. Also
        in GEN 4319 (1967), 254-281, and GEN 4349 (1966), 371-383.

6336   ------ "Traditional Production in Primitive Africain Economies,"
        Quart. J. Econ. 76:3 (Aug. 1962), 360-378. Also in GEN 4319 (1967),
        61-80.

6337   DaSilva, L., "Embarcações e utensilos de pesca dòa Ilheus de Luanda"
        [Boats and fishing implements of the Luanda Islanders], Estud.
        etnog. 1 (1960), 1-119. [Angola]

6338   Davenport, William H., "A Comparative Study of Two Jamaican Fishing
        Communities." Ph.D. dissertation, Yale University, 1956.

6339   Dean, E. R., "Studies in Price Formation in African Markets," Hum.
        Probl. B.C.A. 31 (June 1962), 1-20. [Zambia; Southern Rhodesia]

6340   De Schlippe, Pierre, Shifting Cultivation in Africa: The Zande
        System of Agriculture. London: Routledge and Kegan Paul, 1956.
        304 pp. [Sudan; Congo (Leopoldville)]

6341   Dewey, Alice G., "Capital, Credit and Saving in Javanese Marketing,"
        in GEN 4324 (1964), 230-255. [Indonesia]

6342   ------ Peasant Marketing in Java. New York: Free Press of Glencoe,
        1962. 238 pp. [Indonesia]

6343   ------ "Trade and Social Control in Java," J. roy. Anthrop. Inst. 92
        (1962), 177-190. [Indonesia]

6344   Douglas, Mary, "Raffia Cloth Distribution in the Lele Economy,"
        Africa 28:2 (Apr. 1958), 109-122. Also in GEN 4319 (1967), 103-122.
        [Congo]

6345   Dubbeldam, L. F. B., "The Devaluation of the Kapauku Cowrie as a
        Factor of Social Disintegration," Am. Anthrop. 66:4, Pt. 2 (Aug.
        1964), 293-303. [New Guinea]

6346   Eames, E., "Population and Economic Structure of an Indian Rural
        Community," East. Anthrop. 8:3-4 (Mar.-Aug. 1955), 173-181. [India]

6347   Ehrenfels, U. R., "Consumption and Prosperity: Comparative Data
        from East Africa," Int. J. comp. Sociol. 2:1 (Mar. 1961), 59-64.

6348   Elvery, A. W., "Savings and Loan Societies in the Territory of Papua
        and New Guinea," Austr. Territ. 2:2 (Mar. 1962), 25-31.

6349   Epstein, A. L., "The Economy of Modern Matupit: Continuity and
        Change on the Gazelle Peninsula, New Britain," Oceania 33:3 (Mar.
        1963), 182-215. [Melanesia]

6350   Epstein, Trude Scarlett, "European Contact and Tolai Economic
        Development: A Schema of Economic Growth," Econ. Dev. cult. Change
        11:3 (Apr. 1963), 289-307. [Melanesia]

6351   ------ "A Study of Rabaul Market," Austr. J. agric. Econ. 5:1 (June
        1961), 1-18. [Melanesia]

6352   Erasmus, Charles J., "Work Patterns in a Mayo Village," Am. Anthrop.
        57:2 (Apr. 1955), 322-334. [Mexico]

6353   Falcon, Walter P., "Farmer Response to Price in a Subsistence
        Economy: The Case of West Pakistan," Am. econ. Rev. 54:2 (May 1964),
        580-591.

6354   Firth, Raymond W., "Capital, Saving and Credit in Peasant Societies:
        A Viewpoint from Economic Anthropology," in GEN 4324 (1964), 15-34.

6355   ------ "Money, Work and Social Change in Indo-Pacific Economic
        Systems," in GEN 4356 (1963), 79-89.

6356   ------ "Social Changes in the Western Pacific," J. roy. Soc. Arts
        101:4909 (Oct. 1953), 803-819. [Melanesia]

6357   Foster, George M., "Comentario" (on an article by Sol Tax), in GEN
        4375 (1956), 129-136: (2nd ed. 1959), 65-80. [Guatemala]

6358   ------ "The Folk Economy of Rural Mexico with Special Reference to
        Marketing," J. Marketing (Oct. 1948), 153-162.

6359   Galletti, R., K. D. S. Baldwin, and I. O. Dina, Nigerian Cocoa
        Farmer: An Economic Survey of Yoruba Cocoa Farming Activities.
        London: Oxford University Press, 1956. 774 pp. [Nigeria]

6360   Geertz, Clifford, Agricultural Involution: The Processes of Ecological
        Change in Indonesia. Berkeley: University of California Press, 1963.
        176 pp.

6361   ------ "Capital-Intensive Agriculture in Peasant Society: A Case
        Study," Soc. Res. 23:4 (1956), 433-450. [Indonesia]

6362   ------ "The Rotating Credit Association: A 'Middle Rung' in Develop-
        ment," in GEN 4396 (1966), 420-446.

6363   Gerlach, L. P., "Traders on Bicycle: A Study of Entrepreneurship and
        Culture Change among the Digo and Duruma of Kenya," Sociologus 13:1
        (1963), 32-49. [Kenya]

6364   Ghosh, Madan Gopal, and Nripendranath Bandyopadhyay, "A Comparative
        Study of Some Aspects of Agricultural Development in Two States of
        Eastern Zone: West Bengal and Orissa," Indian J. agric. Econ. 19:1
        (Jan. 1964), 212-219.

6365   Ghosh, S., Monetization of an Economy. Calcutta: World Press,
        1964. 82 pp. [India]

6366   Goodfellow, David Martin, Principles of Economic Sociology: The
        Economics of Primitive Life as Illustrated from the Bantu Peoples of
        South and East Africa. London: George Routledge, 1939. 289 pp.
        2nd ed. New York: Humanities Press, 1950.

6367   Govil, Madhu, "Contribution of Women to Rural Economy," Agra Univ.
        J. Res. 12 (Jan. 1964), 123-129. [India]

6368   Greenfield, Sidney M., "Stocks, Bonds, and Peasant Canes in Barbados:
        Some Notes on the Use of Land in an Overdeveloped Economy," in GEN
        4402 (1964), 619-650. [British Caribbean]

6369   Grove, J. M., "Some Aspects of the Economy of the Volta Delta
        (Ghana)," Bull. Inst. fr. Afr. noire 28:1-2 (Jan.-Apr. 1966), 381-
        432.

6370   Guillaume, Albert, L'évolution économique de la société rurale
        marocaine [The economic evolution of Moroccan rural society]. Paris:
        Librairie Générale de Droit et de Jurisprudence, 1955. 168 pp.

6371   Guy, G. S.-C., "The Economic Life of the Mountain Tribes of Northern
        Luzon, Philippines," J. E. Asiat. Stud. 7 (1958), 1-88.

6372   Haines, E. S., "The Transkei Trader," S. Afr. J. Econ. 1 (1933), 201-
        216. [South Africa]

6373   Halpern, Joel Martin, Capital, Savings, and Credit among Lao and Serb
        Peasants: A Contrast in Cultural Values. Los Angeles: Department of
        Anthropology, University of California, 1961. 19 mim. pp. [Laos;
        Yugoslavia]

6374   ------ "Capital, Saving and Credit among Lao Peasants," in GEN 4324
        (1964), 82-103.

6375   ------ "The Economics of Lao and Serb Peasants: A Contrast in
        Cultural Values," Sthwest. J. Anthrop. 17:2 (Summer 1962), 165-177.
        [Laos; Yugoslavia]

6376   Hamilton, J. W., "Effects of the Thai Market on Karen Life," Pract.
        Anthrop. 10:5 (Sept.-Oct. 1963), 209-215. [Thailand]

6377   Handler, J. S., "Small-scale Sugar Cane Farming in Barbados,"
        Ethnology 5:3 (July 1966), 264-283. [British Caribbean]

6378   Harper, E. B., "Two Systems of Economic Exchange in Village India
        (The Jajmani System)," Am. Anthrop. 61:5 (Oct. 1959), 760-778, bibl.

6379   Harris, J. S., "Some Aspects of the Economics of Sixteen Ibo Indi-
        viduals," Africa 14 (1944), 302-335. [Nigeria]

6380   Harris, M., "The Economy Has No Surplus? (Operational Framework of
        Economic Anthropology," Am. Anthrop. 61:2 (Apr. 1959), 185-199.

6381   Hill, Polly, "Landlords and Brokers: A West Africn Trading System,"
        Cah. Etud. afr. 6:3 (Oct. 1966), 349-366. [Ghana]

6382   ------ "Markets in Africa," J. mod. Afr. Stud. 1:4 (Dec. 1963), 441-
        453.

6383   ------ "Notes on Traditional Market Authority and Market Periodicity
        in West Africa," J. afr. Hist. 7:2 (1966), 295-311. [Ghana; West
        Africa]

6384   Hirsch, Leon V., Marketing in an Underdeveloped Economy: The North
        Indian Sugar Industry. Englewood Cliffs, N.J.: Prentice-Hall, 1961.
        392 pp.

6385   Hopper, W. David, "The Economic Organization of a Village in North
        Central India." Ph.D. dissertation, Cornell University, 1957.
        [India]

6386   Hoselitz, Bert F., "Capital Formation, Saving, and Credit in Indian
        Agricultural Society," in GEN 4324 (1964), 347-375.

6387   Hoyt, Elizabeth E., "The Impact of a Money Economy on Consumption
        Patterns," Ann. Am. Acad. polit. soc. Sci. 305 (May 1956), 12-22.

6388   Husain, A. F. A., "Aspects of Agricultural Development in Pakistan,"
        Pakistan econ. J. 12 (Sept. 1962), 1-18.

6389   Hussain, Mushtaq, "A Note on Farmer Response to Price in East
        Pakistan," Pakistan Dev. Rev. 4 (Spring 1964), 93-106.

6390   Janlekha, Kamol, A Study of the Economy of a Rice Growing Village in
        Central Thailand. Bangkok, Thailand: Ministry of Agriculture, 1955.
        196 pp.

6391   Kaplan, David, "The Mexican Marketplace Then and Now," in GEN 4335
        (1965), 80-94.

6392   Kay, George, "Sources and Uses of Cash in Some Ushi Villages, Fort
        Rosebery District," Hum. Probl. B.C.A. 35 (June 1964), 14-28.
        [Zambia]

6393   Kay, P., "A Guttman Scale of Tahitian Consumer Behavior," Sthwest.
        J. Anthrop. 20:2 (Summer 1964), 160-167.

6394   Khuri, Fuad I., "Kinship, Emigration, and the Trade Partnership among
        the Lebanese of West Africa," Africa 35:4 (Oct. 1965), 385-395.

6395   Kluckhohn, Richard, "The Konso Economy of Southern Ethiopia," in GEN
        4312 (1962), 409-430.

6396   Kobben, A. J. F., "The Development of an Under-Developed Territory,"
        Sociologus 8:1 (1958), 29-40. [Ivory Coast]

6397   Krishna, Raj, "Farm Supply Response in the Punjab (India-Pakistan): A
        Case Study of Cotton." Ph.D. dissertation, University of Chicago,
        1961. [Indian State of Punjab; West Pakistan]

6398   Kuls, W., "Land, Wirtschaft und Siedlung der Gumuz im Westen von
        Godjam, Äthiopien" [Land, economy, and settlement of the Gumuz in the
        West of Godjam, Ethiopia], Paideuma 8:1 (1962), 45-61.

6399   Lall, R. B., "Changing Economy of the Orasons," J. soc. Res. 3:2 (Sep
        (Sept. 1960), 82-92. [Indian State of Orissa]

6400   Lancaster, L., "Crédit, épargne et investissement dans une économie
        non-monétaire" [Credit, savings, and investment in a nonmonetary
        economy], Eur. J. Sociol. 3 (1962), 149-164.

6401   Lembezat, B., "Marchés du Nord Cameroun" [Markets of the Northern
        Cameroons], Cah. Inst. Sci. écon. series 5:5 (Nov. 1962), 85-104.

6402   Leuva, K. K., "Graingolas in Bihar: A Critical Review about Their
        Working," J. soc. Res. 3 (Sept. 1960), 121-127. [Indian State of
        Bihar]

6403   Lewis, I. M., "Trade and Markets in Northern Somaliland," in GEN
        4312 (1962), 365-385.

6404   Lewis, Oscar, "Aspects of Land Tenure and Economics in a North Indian
        Village," Econ. Dev. cult. Change 4:3 (Apr. 1956), 279-302. [India]

6405   ------ "Wealth Differences in a Mexican Village," Sci. Mon. 15:2
        (1947), 127-132.

6406   Lloyd, P. C., "Craft Organization in Yoruba Towns," in GEN 4396
        (1966), 383-401. [Nigeria]

6407   Lord, R. F., Economic Aspects of Mechanised Farming at Nachingwea,
        Tanganyika. London: HMSO, 1963. 191 pp.

6408   MacDonald, J. S., and L. MacDonald, "Institutional Economics and
        Rural Development: Two Italian Types," Hum. Organiz. 23:2 (Summer
        1964), 113-118. [Italy]

6409   Madan, B. K., "The Economics of the Indian Village and Its Implica-
        tions in Social Structure," in GEN 4356 (1963), 110-118.

6410   Malinowski, Bronislaw, "Kula: The Circulating Exchange of Valuables
        in the Archipelagoes of Eastern New Guinea," Man 20:51 (July 1920),
        97-105. Also in GEN 4319 (1967), 171-184.

6411   ------ "Tribal Economics in the Trobriands," in GEN 4319 (1967),
        185-223. [Melanesia]

6412   Marroquin, Alejandro D., "Consideraciones sobre el problema económico
        de la región tzeltal-tzotzil" [Considerations on the economic problem
        of the Tzeltal-Tzotzil region], Amér. indíg. 16:3 (June 1956), 191-
        203. [Mexico]

6413   Martin, A., The Marketing of Minor Crops in Uganda. London: HMSO,
        1963. 78 pp.

6414   Mathur, K. S., "An Aspect of Village Economy in Malwa," East. Anthrop.
        17 (May 1964), 98-113. [India]

6415   Mayer, E., "R. F. Salisbury's Model Applied to Epstein's Material from
        India," Anthropology 1 (1966), 5-9. [Indian State of Madras]

6416   Messing, Simon D., "The Abyssinian Market Town," in GEN 4312 (1962),
        386-408.

6417   Mintz, Sidney W., "Internal Marketing Systems as Mechanisms of Social
        Articulation," in GEN 4367 (1959), 20-30. [Haiti; Jamaica]

6418   ------ "The Jamaican Internal Marketing Pattern: Some Notes and
        Hypotheses," Soc. econ. Stud. 4:1 (March 1955), 95-103.

6419   ------ "Peasant Markets," Sci. Am. 203:2 (Aug. 1960), 112-118ff.
        [Haiti; Jamaica; British Caribbean]

6420   ------ "The Role of the Middleman in the Internal Distribution System
        of a Caribbean Peasant Economy," Hum. Organiz. 15:2 (Summer 1956),
        18-23. [Haiti]

6421   ------ "Standards of Value and Units of Measure in the Fond des
        Nègres Market Place, Haiti," J. roy. Anthrop. Inst. 91 (1961), 23-38.

6422   ------ "A Tentative Typology of Eight Haitian Market Places," Rev.
        Cienc. Soc. 4:1 (Mar. 1960), 15-57. [Puerto Rico]

6423   Mintz, S. W., and D. Hall, "The Origins of the Jamaican Internal
        Marketing System," Yale Univ. Pub. Anthrop. 57 (1960), 3-26.

6424   Misra, S., "Earnings of Village Servants in UP," East. Anthrop.
        5:2-3 (1952), 96-100. [Indian State of Uttar Pradesh]

6425   Mukherjee, P. K., and S. C. Gupta, A Pilot Survey of 14 Villages in UP
        and Punjab: A Study in Methodology of Research in Rural Change.
        Bombay: Asia Publishing House, 1960. 195 pp. [Indian States of
        Uttar Pradesh and Punjab]

6426   Mukherjee, Ramkrishna, "Economic Structure of Rural Bengal," Am.
        sociol. Rev. 13:6 (Dec. 1948), 660-672. [Indian State of West
        Bengal and East Pakistan]

6427   Mukhtyar, Gatoobal Chhaganbal, Life and Labour in a South Gujarat
        Village. Calcutta: Longmans, Green, 1930. 303 pp. [Indian State
        of Gujarat]

6428   Mylius, K., "Wirtschaftsformen auf den Nikobaren-Inseln" [Economic forms on the Nicobar Islands], Z. Ethnol. 87:1 (1962), 39-50. [Andaman Islands]

6429   Nash, Manning, "The Indian Economies of Middle America," in GEN 4345 (1964), 299-311. [Guatemala; Mexico]

6430   ------ "The Social Context of Economic Choice in a Small Society," Man 61 (Nov. 1961), 186-191. Also in GEN 4319 (1967), 524-538. [Mexico]

6431   National Council of Applied Economic Research, Rehabilitation and Development of Basti District: A Case Study in the Economics of Depressed Areas. Bombay: Asia Publishing House, 1959. 151 pp. [Indian State of Uttar Pradesh]

6432   "Native Loans Board of the Territory of Papua and New Guinea," Austr. Territ. 3:2 (Mar. 1963), 13-18.

6433   "Note on the Weekly Market at Gokulpeth (Nagpur)," East. Anthrop. 16:2 (May-Aug. 1963), 148-150. [Indian State of Madhya Pradesh]

6434   Nyirenda, A. A., "African Market Vendors in Lusaka: With a Note on the Recent Boycott," Hum. Probl. B.C.A. 22 (1957), 31-63. [Zambia]

6435   ------ "Markets and Price Fixing in Blantyre-Limbe," in GEN 4361 (1959), 1-22. [Malawi]

6436   Obayashi, T., "Hokusei Tai, Lawazoku no keizai seikatsu oboegaki" [Notes on the economic life of the Lawa in North Thailand], Hitotsubashi Ronsô 51:6 (Dec. 1964), 49-54.

6437   Orans, Martin, "Surplus," Hum. Organiz. 25:1 (Spring 1966), 24-32. [Polynesia; Melanesia]

6438   Orenstein, H., "Notes on the Ecology of Irrigation Agriculture in Contemporary Peasant Societies," Am. Anthrop. 67:6 (Dec. 1965), 1529-1532.

6439   Ottino, P., Les économies paysannes malgaches du Bas Mangoky [Peasant economies of the Lower Mangoky, Malagasy]. Paris: Editions Levrault, 1963. 375 pp.

6440   Pal, Agaton P., "Barrio Institutions and Their Economic Implications," Philipp. sociol. Rev. 7:1-2 (Jan.-Apr. 1959), 51-65. [Philippines]

6441   Pankhurst, R., "Primitive Money in Ethiopia," J. Soc. Afric. 32:2 (1962), 213-248.

6442   Pfanner, David E., and Jasper Ingersoll, "Theravada Buddhism and Village Economic Behavior, a Burmese and Thai Comparison," J. Asian Stud. 21 (May 1962), 341-361.

6443   Polanyi, Karl, Conrad M. Arensberg, and Harry W. Pearson, Trade and Market in the Early Empires: Economies in History and Theory. Glencoe, Ill.: Free Press, 1957. 382 pp. [India; West Africa; Near East; Mexico; Dahomey]

6444   Porter, Philip W., "Environmental Potentials and Economic Opportuni-
        ties: A Background for Cultural Adaptation," Am. Anthrop. 67:2 (Apr.
        1965), 409-420. [Kenya]

6445   Pospisil, Leopold, Kapauku Papuan Economy. New Haven: Yale Univer-
        sity Publications in Anthropology, No. 67, 1963. 502 pp. [New
        Guinea]

6446   Rao, M. M., "Some Economic Aspects of an Andhra Village," Rur. India
        21:1-2 (Jan.-Feb. 1958), 31-39. [Indian State of Andhra]

6447   Ray, Siddheswar, "A Method to Find Out the Extent of Non-monetisation
        of Our Rural Economy," Econ. Aff. 9 (Sept. 1964), 429-432. [India]

6448   Robertson, H. M., "The Economic Condition of the Rural Natives," in
        GEN 4373 (1934), 143-155. [Republic of South Africa]

6449   Robolos, Zenaida M., "Promissory and Debt Aspects of the Folk Ritual
        in Misamis Oriental," Philipp. sociol. Rev. 12 (Jan.-Apr. 1964), 95-
        101. [Philippines]

6450   Rotberg, Robert I., "Rural Rhodesian Markets," in GEN 4312 (1962),
        581-600. [Zambia]

6451   Ryan, D., "The Yoaripi Association: Some Problems of Economic
        Development in Papua," Mankind 6:1 (May 1963), 11-15. [New Guinea]

6452   Sahlins, Marshall D., "On the Sociology of Primitive Exchange," in
        GEN 4368 (1965), 139-236.

6453   Sanghi, Upendra, "Income, Expenditure and Consumption Patterns: A
        Rural Study, Jaipur District," All India Congr. Comm. econ. Rev. 16
        (25 Aug. 1964), 19-22. [Indian State of Rajasthan]

6454   Sapre, S. G., "Changes in Land Utilization and in Cropping Pattern in
        an Irrigated Village Over Two Decades Ending in 1960," Artha Vijnana
        6 (June 1964), 106-115. [India]

6455   Saxena, Ranvir Prakash, Tribal Economy in Central India. Calcutta:
        Mukhopadhyay, 1964. 312 pp. [India]

6456   Schapera, Isaac, "Economic Changes in South African Native Life,"
        Africa 1 (1928), 170-188. Also in GEN 4319 (1967), 136-154.

6457   Sengupta, A. K., "Economic Organisation of an Oraon Village,"
        Vanyajati 13 (Apr. 1965), 41-45. [Indian State of Orissa]

6458   Setonaikai Sogo Kenkyukai, Nōsōn no seikatsu [The life of an agri-
        cultural village]. Okayama, Japan: Setonaikai, 1951. 236 pp.
        [Japan]

6459   Sharp, Lauristan, "Steel Axes for Stone-Age Australians," Hum.
        Organiz. 11:2 (Summer 1952), 17-22. Also in GEN 4349 (1966), 342-
        347. [Melanesia]

6460   Silva Fuenzalida, I., "Aspectos de la organización económica de las comunidades rurales de la provincia de Nuble" [Aspects of the economic organization of the rural communities of the province of Nuble], Economía 20:75-76 (July-Dec. 1962), 65-86. [Chile]

6461   Singaravelu, S., "The Origin and Development of Barter Trade," Tamil Cult. 11:4 (Oct.-Dec. 1964), 317-328. [Indian State of Madras]

6462   Singh, Tarlok, "Agricultural Policy and Rural Economic Progress," Indian J. agric. Econ. 18:1 (Jan. 1963), 10-23. [India]

6463   Sinha, S., "Levels of Economic Initiative and Ethnic Groups in Pargana Barabhum," East. Anthrop. 16 (1963), 65-74. [India]

6464   Siverts, H., "Some Economic Implications of Plural Society in Highland Chiapas, Mexico," Folk 7 (1965), 153-162.

6465   Skinner, Elliott P., "West African Economic Systems," in GEN 4336 (1964), 77-98.

6466   Smelser, Neil J., "A Comparative View of Exchange Systems," Econ. Dev. cult. Change 7:2 (Jan. 1959), 173-182. A review of RUR 6443.

6467   Smith, Raymond T., "Ethnic Difference and Peasant Economy in British Guiana," in GEN 4324 (1964), 305-329. [British Guiana]

6468   Swift, M. G., "Capital, Saving and Credit in a Malay Peasant Economy," in GEN 4324 (1964), 133-156. [Malaysia]

6469   ------ "Malay Peasants," in GEN 4350 (1963), 219-244.

6470   Tagumpay-Castillo, Gelia, "Sociological Factors in Savings and Capital Accumulation: Some Research Findings," Philipp. econ. J. 3:2 (1964), 189-197. [Philippines]

6471   Tax, Sol, "Changing Consumption in Indian Guatemala," Pract. Anthrop. 9:1 (Jan.-Feb. 1962), 15-26.

6472   ------ "Los indios en la economía de Guatemala" [Indians in the Guatemalan economy], in GEN 4375 (1956), 107-128. 2nd ed., 59-64.

6473   Temple, P. H., "Nakasero Market, Kampala," Uganda J. 28:2 (Sept. 1964), 165-178. [Uganda]

6474   Thurnwald, Richard C., Economics in Primitive Communities. London: Oxford University Press, 1932. 314 pp. [Polynesia]

6475   ------ "Pigs and Currency in Buin: Observations about Primitive Standards of Value and Economics," Oceania 5:2 (Dec. 1934), 119-141. Also in GEN 4319 (1967), 224-245. [New Guinea]

6476   Topley, Marjorie, "Capital, Saving and Credit among Indigenous Rice Farmers and Immigrant Vegetable Farmers in Hong Kong's New Territories," in GEN 4324 (1964), 157-186.

6477   Troin, J. F., "Observations sur les souks de la région d'Azrou et de Khénifra" [Observations of the bazaars in the Azrou region and Khénifra], Rev. Géogr. maroc. 3-4 (1963), 109-120. [Morocco]

6478   Tubiana, M.-J., "Le marché de Hili-ba: Moutons, mil, sel et contre-
        bande" [The market at Hili-ba: Sheep, Millet, Salt and Contraband],
        Cah. Etud. afr. 2:2 (May 1961), 196-243. [Chad]

6479   Twum-Barima, K., "Some Problems of Agricultural Evolution in the Akan
        Community of the Gold Coast," in GEN 4346 (1956), 309-318. [Ghana]

6480   Van der Kroef, J. M. A., "Problems of Economic Motivation and Develop-
        ment in Rural Indonesia," Soc. econ. Stud. 7:4 (Dec. 1958), 193-209.

6481   Vu, Quoc Thuc, "L'économie communaliste du Viet-Nam. Essai d'une
        explication sociologique de l'économie vietnamienne" [The communal
        economy of Vietnam. A sociological explanation of the Vietnamese
        economy]. Ph.D. dissertation, University of Paris, 1957. 554 mim.
        pp.

6482   Wagley, Charles, Economics of a Guatemalan Village. Menasha, Wis.:
        American Anthropological Association, 1941. 87 pp.

6483   Wagner, Gunter, "Aspects of Conservatism and Adaptation in the
        Economic Life of the Herero," Sociologia 2:1 (1952), 1-26. [Brazil]

6484   Warmington, W. A., "Saving and Indebtedness among Cameroons Planta-
        tion Workers," Africa 28 (1958), 329-343.

6485   White, C. M. N., A Preliminary Survey of Luvale Rural Economy.
        Manchester, England: Manchester University Press, 1959. 58 pp.
        [Zambia]

6486   Wilson, Godfrey, An Essay on the Economics of Detribalization in
        Northern Rhodesia. 2 vols. Livingstone, Zambia: The Rhodes-Living-
        stone Institute, 1941 and 1942. 71 and 82 pp.

6487   Winter, Edward H., Bwamba Economy: The Development of a Primitive
        Subsistence Economy in Uganda. Kampala, Uganda: East African Insti-
        tute of Social Research, 1955. 43 pp.

6488   ------ "Livestock Markets among the Iraqw of Northern Tanganyika," in
        GEN 4312 (1962), 457-468.

6489   Yamey, B. S., "The Study of Peasant Economic Systems: Some Conclu-
        ding Comments and Questions," in GEN 4324 (1964), 376-386.

6490   Yang, Martin C., "The Family as a Primary Economic Group (China)," in
        GEN 4319 (1967), 333-346.

6491   Young, Frank W., and Ruth C. Young, "Two Determinants of Community
        Reaction to Industrialization in Rural Mexico," Econ. Dev. cult. Change
        8:3 (Apr. 1960), 257-264.

7. Rural Families

A. Annotated Case Studies

7001   Cohen, Y. A., "Structure and Function: Family Organization and
        Socialization in a Jamaican Community," Am. Anthrop. 58:4 (Aug.
        1956), 664-686, bibl.

        The author finds very little sense of family solidarity, and he
        traces this lack to historical sources.

7002   Dasgupta, Manisha, "Changes in the Joint Family in India," Man in
        India 45:4 (Oct.-Dec. 1965), 283-288.

        Author finds that "implanted" industrial development need not
        accelerate social change. In some cases, as in India, industrial
        development may lead to social disintegration due to the gap
        between industrialization and traditionalism.

7003   Ferrari, Alfonso Trujillo, "A familia em Potengi" [The family in
        Potengi], Sociologia 17:2 (May 1955), 147-162. [Brazil]

        A study of family structure in a rural community of highly migrant
        workers.

7004   Graham, Henry M., Some Changes in Thai Family Life. Bangkok: Insti-
        tute of Public Administration, Thaumasat University, 1958. 55 mim. pp.

        Rapidly changing values and economic roles have made the family
        unstable and in search of its new role.

*7005   Kaberry, Phyllis M., Women of the Grassfields: A Study of the Eco-
        nomic Position of Women in Bamenda, British Cameroons. London:
        HMSO, 1952. 220 pp.

        Since women produce the crops and therefore control land rights,
        their status is not low despite the traditional polygamy.

7006   Levy, Marion J., Jr., The Family Revolution in Modern China. Cam-
        bridge, Mass.: Harvard University Press, 1949. 390 pp.

        A comparison of family structure in traditional China and in the
        transitional China of modern times. A general study of the effects
        of modernization on kinship structure.

7007   Morrison, W. A., "Family Types in Badlapur: An Analysis of a Changing
        Institution in a Maharashtrian Village," Sociol. Bull. 8:2 (Sept.
        1959), 45-67. [Indian State of Maharashtra]

        The nuclear family is found among both the upper and lower castes.
        Among the upper castes it reflects the new urban-industrial values,
        while among the lower, it manifests the effects of poverty.

*7008   Smith, Raymond Thomas, The Negro Family in British Guiana: Family
        Structure and Social Status in the Villages. London: Routledge and

Kegan Paul, 1956.   282 pp.   [British Guiana]

A study of an area that has no self-contained villages. The villagers are only part-time farmers. To get additional work, they take part in an area-wide labor pool.

7009   Talmon, Yonina, "The Family in a Revolutionary Movement: The Case of the Kibbutz in Israel," in GEN 4360 (1965), 259-286.

Despite the early emphasis on collectivity and a reduced differentiation of roles, the family has tended to reassert itself.

B.   Other Case Studies

7301   Araujo, Alceu Maynard, "A familia numa comunidade alagoana" [The family in an Alagoan community], Sociologia 17:2 (May 1955), 113-131. [Brazil]

7302   Atienza, Maria Fe G., "The Filipino Family: Impact of New Social and Cultural Forces on It," Philipp. educ. Forum 13:3 (Nov. 1964), 10-14.

7303   Berndt, C. H., "Mateship or Success: An Assimilation Dilemma," Oceania 33:2 (Dec. 1962), 71-89. [New Guinea]

7304   Burling, R., Rengsanggri: Family and Kinship in a Garo Village. Philadelphia: University of Pennsylvania Press, 1963. 377 pp. [India]

7305   Chao, J., "Sozialer Wandel und Familie in China" [Social change and the family in China], Kölner Z. Soziol. Sozialps. 14:4 (1962), 645-672.

7306   Clarke, Edith, "Land Tenure and the Family in Four Selected Communities in Jamaica," Soc. econ. Stud. 1:4 (Aug. 1953), 81-117.

7307   ------ My Mother Who Fathered Me: A Study of the Family in Three Selected Communities in Jamaica. London: Allen and Unwin, 1957. 215 pp.

7308   Cohen, Y. A., "Structure and Function: Family Organization and Socialization in a Jamaican Community," Am. Anthrop. 58:4 (Aug. 1956), 664-686, bibl.

7309   Comhaire, Jean L., "Economic Change and the Extended Family," Ann. Am. Acad. polit. soc. Sci. 305 (May 1956), 45-52.

7310   Costa, Esdras Borges, "Relações de familia em Cerrado e Retiro" [Family relationships in Cerrado and Retiro], Sociologia 17:2 (May 1955), 132-146. [Brazil]

7311   Cumper, G. E., "The Jamaican Family: Village and Estate," Soc. econ.

Stud. 7:1 (Mar. 1958), 76-107.

7312   Das, P., "Women under India's Community Development Programme," Int.
        Labour Rev. 80:1 (July 1959), 26-45.

7313   Desai, I. P., "The Joint Family in India: An Analysis," Sociol.
        Bull. 5:2 (Sept. 1956), 144-156.

7314   De Vos, G., and H. Wagatsuma, "Value Attitudes toward Role Behavior of
        Women in Two Japanese Villages," Am. Anthrop. 63:6 (Dec. 1961), 1204-
        1230, bibl.

7315   Epstein, Trude Scarlett, "Economic Development and Peasant Marriage in
        South India," Man in India 40:3 (July-Sept. 1960), 192-232. [Indian
        State of Madras]

7316   Firth, Raymond W., "Family in Tikopia," in GEN 4360 (1965), 105-120.
        [Polynesia]

7317   Fonsecca, M. B., "Family Disorganization and Divorce in Indian
        Communities," Sociol. Bull. 12:2 (Sept. 1963), 14-33.

7318   Forde, Daryll, Marriage and the Family among the Yakö in South-
        Eastern Nigeria. London: London School of Economics, 1941. 121 pp.

7319   Fox, R. B., "The Study of Filipino Society and Its Significance to
        Programs of Economic and Social Development," Philipp. sociol. Rev.
        7:1-2 (Jan.-Apr. 1959), 2-15.

7320   Geertz, H., The Javanese Family: A Study of Kinship and Socialization.
        New York: Free Press of Glencoe, 1961. 176 pp. [Indonesia]

7321   Gonzalez, P. A., "Changes in the Filipino Family," Philipp. sociol.
        Rev. 3:2 (Apr. 1955), 15-17.

7322   Goode, William J., World Revolution and Family Patterns. New York:
        Free Press of Glencoe, 1963. 432 pp.

7323   Gray, R. F., and P. H. Gulliver (eds.), The Family Estate in Africa:
        Studies in the Role of Property in Family Structure and Lineage
        Continuity. Boston: Boston University Press, 1964. 265 pp.

7324   Greenfield, Sidney M., English Rustics in Black Skin: A Study of
        Modern Family Forms in a Pre-Industrial Society. New Haven: College
        and University Press, 1966. 208 pp. [British Caribbean]

7325   Gupta, T. R., "Rural Family Status and Migration: Study of a Punjab
        Village," Econ. Wkly. 13:41 (14 Oct. 1961), 1597-1603.

7326   Gutiérrez de Pineda, Virginia, La Familia en Colombia: Estudio
        antropológico [The family in Colombia: Anthropological study].
        Bogotá: Fédération Européenne de Recherche Economique et Sociale,
        1962. 86 pp.

7327   Hogbin, H. Ian, Kinship and Marriage in a New Guinea Village.
        London: Athlone Press, 1963. 177 pp.

7328   Iwai, H., "Kindai Gijitsu no Kazoku Seikatsu ni ataeru Kinpaku" [The impact of modern technique on the Japanese family], Jimbun Gakuhŏ 21 (1959), 135-202.

7329   Jayawardena, C., "Family Organization in Plantations in British Guiana," Int. J. comp. Sociol. 3:1 (Sept. 1962), 43-64.

7330   Jha, Jai Chand, and Bishwa Bandhu Chatterjee, "The Changing Family in a Polyandrous Community," East. Anthrop. 18:2 (May 1965), 64-72. [India]

7331   Kapadia, K. M., "Rural Family Patterns," Sociol. Bull. 5:2 (Sept. 1956), 111-126. [Indian State of Maharashtra]

7332   Khaing, Mi Mi, Burmese Family. 2nd rev. ed. Bloomington: Indiana University Press, 1962. 200 pp.

7333   Knak, D. S., "Einflusse der europaïschen Zivilisation auf das Familienleben der Bantu" [Influence of European civilization on the Bantu family], Africa 4 (1931), 178-201. [Republic of South Africa]

7334   Kochar, V. K., "Fission and Segmentation Process in the Joint-Families of a Tharu Village," Vanyajati 13 (Jan. 1965), 3-8. [Indian State of Rajasthan]

7335   ------ "Nuclear Units in the Domestic Groups of a Santal Village," East. Anthrop. 18 (Jan. 1965), 17-21. [India]

7336   Koyano, Shogo, "Changing Family Behavior in Four Japanese Communities," J. Marr. Fam. Living 26:2 (May 1964), 149-159.

7337   Launay, M., Paysans algériens [Algerian peasants]. Paris: Le Seuil, 1963. 428 pp.

7338   Lewis, I. M., Marriage and the Family in Northern Somaliland. Kampala, Uganda: East African Institute of Social Research, 1962. 51 pp.

7339   Lewis, Oscar, The Children of Sanchez: Autobiography of a Mexican Family. New York: Random House, 1961. 499 pp.

7340   ------ Five Families: Mexican Case Studies in the Culture of Poverty. New York: Basic Books, 1959. 351 pp.

7341   ------ Pedro Martinez: A Mexican Peasant and His Family. New York: Random House, 1964. 507 pp.

7342   Mayer, A. C., "Fiji Indian Kin Groups: An Aspect of Change in an Immigrant Society," Oceania 24:3 (Mar. 1954), 161-171.

7343   Mencher Joan P., "Changing Familial Roles among South Malabar Nayars," Sthwest. J. Anthrop. 18:3 (Aug. 1962), 230-245. [Indian State of Kerela]

7344   ------ "The Nayars of South Malabar," in GEN 4360 (1965), 163-191. [Indian State of Kerela]

7345   Mitani, T., "Ritô Nôson ni okeru Kazoku rui to Seisanruikei" [Types
        of family and production in the agricultural villages of an isolated
        island], Shakaigaku Hyôron 15:1 (1964), 14-28.

7346   Mitchell, J. C., "Marriage, Matriliny and Social Structure among the
        Yao of Southern Nyasaland," Int. J. comp. Sociol. 3:1 (Sept. 1962),
        29-42. [Malawi]

7347   Nash, J., and M. Nash, "Marriage, Family and Population Growth in
        Upper Burma," Sthwest. J. Anthrop. 19:3 (Autumn 1963), 251-266.

7348   Ngwane, H. D., "Some Aspects of Marriage in Peri-Urban Villages,
        Blantyre-Limbe, Nyasaland," in GEN 4361 (1959), 23-33. [Malawi]

7349   Nimkoff, M. F., "Some Problems Concerning Research on the Changing
        Family in India," Sociol. Bull. 8:2 (Sept. 1959), 32-38.

7350   Ninomiya, T., "Dōzoku Soshiki no Seiritsu Hatten oyobi Hōkai Katai-
        Hokensei to Dōzokusei" [The process of establishment, growth, and
        disorganization of the extended family system], Shakaigaku Hyôron 32
        (1958), 37-59. [Japan]

7351   Nurge, Ethel, Life in a Leyte Village. Seattle: University of
        Washington Press, 1965. 157 pp. [Philippines]

7352   Nwogugu, E. I., "Matrilineal Family Law and Custom in Malawi: A
        Comparison of Two Systems," J. Afr. Law 8:2 (Summer 1964), 91-105.

7353   Oyama, H., "Okinawa no Kazoku Sêdo no Kenkyû" [A study of the family
        system in Okinawa], Kagoshima Hôkoku 10 (1963), 153-199.

7354   Pakrasi, Kanti, "On Some Aspects of Family Structures of the Refugees
        of West Bengal, 1947-48," Sociol. Bull. 14 (Mar. 1965), 13-20.

7355   Pal, Agaton P., The Resources, Levels of Living, and Aspirations of
        Rural Households in Negros Oriental. Quezon City, Philippines:
        Community Development Research Council, University of the Philippines,
        1963. 429 pp. [Philippines]

7356   Queen, Stuart A., Robert W. Habenstein, and John B. Adams, The Family
        in Various Cultures. Philadelphia: J. B. Lippincott, 1961. 314 pp.

7357   Quisumbing, Lourdes R., "Characteristic Features of Cebuano Family
        Life amidst a Changing Society," Philipp. sociol. Rev. 11 (Jan.-Apr.
        1963), 135-141. [Philippines]

7358   Reuter, A., Native Marriages in South Africa according to Law and
        Custom. Münster, W. Germany: Aschendorff, 1963. 376 pp. [Republic
        of South Africa]

7359   Richards, Audrey I., Bemba Marriage and Present Economic Conditions.
        Lusaka, Zambia: Rhodes-Livingstone Institute, 1940. 123 pp. [Zambia]

7360   Roberts, S., "Matrilineal Family Law and Custom in Malawi: A
        Comparison of Two Systems," J. Afr. Law 8:2 (Summer 1964), 77-90.

7361   Ross, A. D., "Education and Family Change," Sociol. Bull. 8:2 (Sept. 1959), 39-44.

7362   Rowe, W. L., "Marriage Network and Structural Change in a North Indian Village," Sthwest. J. Anthrop. 16:3 (Fall 1960), 299-311.

7363   Rosenfeld, H., "Processes of Structural Change Within the Arab Village Extended Family," Am. Anthrop. 60:6 (Dec. 1958), 1127-1139. [Near East]

7364   St. Erlich, Vera, Family in Transition: A Study of 300 Yugoslav Villages. Princeton: Princeton University Press, 1966. 469 pp.

7365   Sarma, Jyotirmoyee, "The Nuclearization of Joint Family Households in West Bengal," Man in India 44:3 (July-Sept. 1964), 193-206.

7366   Schapera, Isaac, "Premarital Pregnancy and Native Opinion: A Note on Social Change," Africa 6 (1933), 59-89. [Botzwama]

7367   Sen, Lalit Kumar, "Family in Four Indian Villages," Man in India 45:1 (Jan.-Mar. 1965), 1-16. [Indian State of West Bengal]

7368   Sengupta, Sunil C., "Family Organisation in West Bengal, Its Nature and Dynamics," Econ. Wkly. 10:11 (15 Mar. 1958), 384-389.

7369   Shah, Vimal P., "Attitudinal Change and Traditionalism in the Hindu Family," Sociol. Bull. 14:1 (Mar. 1965), 77-89.

7370   Smith, Michael G., Kinship and Community in Carriacou. New Haven: Yale University Press, 1962. 347 pp. [British Caribbean]

7371   Smith, M. G., West Indian Family Structure. Seattle: University of Washington Press, 1962. 311 pp. [British Caribbean]

7372   Smith, Raymond T., "Culture and Social Structure in the Caribbean: Some Recent Work on Family and Kinship Studies," Comp. Stud. Soc. Hist. 6:1 (Oct. 1963), 24-46.

7373   ------ "Family Structure and Plantation Systems in the New World," in GEN 4365 (1959), 148-159.

7374   Stephens, W. N., The Family in Cross-Cultural Perspective. New York: Holt, Rinehart and Winston, 1963. 460 pp.

7375   Suginohara, J., "Fatuhiba To no Kazoku ni kansuru Jakkan no Oboegaki" [Some notes on the families of Fatuhiba Island], Kenkyû 34 (1964), 102-116. [Japan]

7376   Tachi, I., "Toshi ni okeru Kazoku Seikatsu no Jittai" [A field study of family life in a mountain village], Meiji Gakuin Ronsô 52:1 (1959), 35-63. [Japan]

7377   Takeda, T., Minzoku Kanko to Shite no Inkyo no Kenkyû [A study of the "Inkyo" system as a folk custom]. Tokyo: Miraisha, 1964. 500 pp. [Japan]

7378   Tsukamoto, Tetsundo, "The Extended Family System of 'Honke' and the

Structure of Rural Community: The Analysis of Case Studies in Two
Rural Communities," Shakaigaku Hyôron 5 (Jan.-Mar. 1955), 23-44 and
47-72. [Japan]

7379   Van Velsen, J., The Politics of Kinship: A Study of Social Manipu-
        lation among the Lakeside Tonga of Nyasaland. Manchester, England:
        Manchester University Press, 1964. 338 pp. [Malawi]

7380   Wagner, G., "The Changing Family among the Bantu Kacirondo," Africa
        12:1, suppl. (1939). [Republic of South Africa]

7381   Watanabe, Y., "Ie no Kaitai to sono Hakkaku--Nōson no Kurasa to
        Akarusa" [The disintegration of the family system and its revival:
        The bright and dark sides of a rural community], Sekai 142 (Oct.
        1957), 115-127. [Japan]

7382   Yang, Martin C., "The Family as a Primary Economic Group (China)," in
        GEN 4319 (1967), 333-346.

7383   Yim, Seong-hi, Die Grundlage und die Entwicklung der Familie in Korea
        [The foundation and development of the family in Korea]. Cologne, W.
        Germany: W. Kleipkampl, 1961. 181 pp.

7384   Zeghari, M., "Evolution des structures familiales dans les pays en voie
        de transformation sociale, économique, politique et institutionnelle"
        [Evolution of family structure in countries undergoing social,
        economic, political, and institutional transformation], Fam. Monde
        15:3-4 (Sept.-Dec. 1962), 132-149. [Morocco]

8. Villages

A. Annotated Case Studies

*8001   Adams, Richard N., A Community in the Andes: Problems and Progress
        in Muquiyauyo. Seattle: University of Washington Press, 1959. 251
        pp. [Peru]

        A detailed account based on historical and survey material, of the
        acceptance of change. This mestizo-Indian village in Peru has
        accepted (and initiated) a great deal of innovation, depending on cul-
        tural conditioning. The villagers have been willing to accept change
        whenever it could be shown that it would better their position in
        terms of their own values.

8002   Ammar, Hamid Mustafa, Growing Up in an Egyptian Village: Silwa,
        Province of Aswan. London: Routledge & Kegan Paul, 1954. 316 pp.
        [Egypt]

        This study treats of the changes that have come to this village

since the late 1930's. The author is particularly interested in the
effects of education and new practices in child-rearing. He finds
that the widening contacts of these villages have tended to weaken the
pattern of authority in the family, but the over-all family picture
has not changed. One reason is that the modern education the children
receive does not train them for jobs to which they can aspire.

8003   Ayabe, Tsuneo, The Village of Ban Pha Khao, Vientiane Province: A
        Preliminary Report. Los Angeles: Department of Anthropology, Uni-
        versity of California, 1959. 55 pp. [Laos] See also: Nihon
        Minzokugaku 23 (1959).

        A study of a loosely organized social unit near Vientiane. The
        population is still primarily agricultural despite its high degree of
        mobility, and the introduction of automobiles and battery-operated
        radios.

8004   Bailey, Frederick George, "An Oriya Hill Village," in GEN 4386 (1960),
        122-146. [Indian State of Orissa]

        The author finds that caste lines are altered by changes in wealth
        of each caste.

**8005 ------ Caste and the Economic Frontier. Manchester, England: Man-
        chester University Press, 1957. 292 pp. [Indian State of Orissa]

        This study of a village in an isolated part of the Indian province
        of Orissa is a striking example of what change has brought. The area
        is highly suited to the production of a valuable industrial crop that
        is easily transported through the jungle and over mountains. This has
        brought wealth into the village, but it has not changed the agricul-
        tural system. As there is much free land in the jungle that can be
        used for the production of this marketable crop, money has become
        available to almost anyone willing to work hard. The lower castes in
        particular have profited from this situation to gain money and buy
        land. As this is not an area with a tradition of education, all
        government administrators come from the outside and tend to look down
        on the natives. The villagers in turn distrust them and avoid them.
        Nevertheless, the lower castes have begun to turn to the administra-
        tors in an attempt to break out of the bonds of the caste system.

*8006   Balandier, Georges, and J. C. Pauvert, Les villages gabonais. Aspects
        démographiques, économiques, sociologiques. Projets de modernisation
        [Gabonese villages. Demographic, economic, and sociological aspects.
        Projects for modernization]. Brazzaville, Congo: Mémoires de
        l'Institut d'Etudes Centrafricaines, 1952. 90 pp., bibl. [Gabon]

        An interesting but loosely organized study of the effect of the
        modern market economy on these villages. The basic unit is not the
        village but the family. The market economy has raised the position of
        women (they can trade in the market) and has given the young more inde-
        pendence.

*8007   Banfield, Edward C., The Moral Basis of a Backward Society. Glencoe,
        Ill.: Free Press, 1958. 204 pp. [South Italy]

        A study of the resistance to economic improvements on the part of

a South Italian community. The author contends that the "moral basis
of the society"--in this case a family-centered ethos--can be a major
limitation to economic change. The moral basis of this village
society is characterized as "amoral familism," based on the supposition
that one should make the most of the short-run, material benefits of
the nuclear family. An exceptional fear of death and deprivation
seems to have produced this cynical view. Whatever the cause, this
attitude has made any form of cooperation or village improvement
impossible.

8008   Barclay, Harold B., Buurri al Lamaab, a Surburban Village in the
        Sudan. Ithaca: Cornell University Press, 1964. 296 pp.

        The village shows an increasing secularization and a decreasing
        sense of identity.

8009   Bardin, P., La vie d'un douar. Essai sur la vie rurale dans les
        grandes plaines de la Haute Medjerda, Tunisie [Life in a douar.
        Essay on rural life on the vast plains of the High Medjerda, Tunisia].
        The Hague: Mouton, 1965. 148 pp.

        Life in this Arab tent village appears unchanged, despite the
        advent of nationalism and mechanization. The villagers cling to
        their old ways, while the young leave for the city.

8010   Beaglehole, Ernest, Social Change in the South Pacific: Rarotonga
        and Aitutaki. London: Allen & Unwin, 1957. 268 pp. [Polynesia]

        The social changes described have been initiated primarily by
        governmental authority rather than through contact with the outside
        world.

8011   Beals, Alan R., "Change in the Leadership of a Mysore Village," in
        GEN 4386 (1960), 147-160. [Indian State of Mysore]

        Many villagers had educated themselves and then found outside
        employment during World War II. These men were then able to oppose
        the effort of the traditional dominant caste to reimpose its feudal
        rule.

8012   ------ Gopalpur: A South Indian Village. New York: Holt, Rinehart
        & Winston, 1962. 99 pp. [Indian State of Mysore]

        A study of a village at some distance from a large city. Although
        new agricultural techniques have been introduced, these have not been
        successful. The Village Level Worker is a city person and looks down
        on the villagers, who in turn do not respect him. In addition, there
        is no market for the small farmer, who cannot raise enough produce to
        make a shipment to the city worth while. Even though the government
        officials are contemptuous of the mores of the villagers (and vice
        versa), still they have managed to change the traditional social
        hierarchy, but they have offered no replacement. This village is
        compared with another village in the same region but quite close to
        the city. The proximity of the city has caused this other village to
        change radically. Cash cropping is feasible since the produce can be
        sold in the city.

8013   ------ "Interplay among Factors of Change in a Mysore Village," in
            GEN 4353 (1955), 78-101. [Indian State of Mysore]

            Modernization began after World War I with expanded education and
            the entry of many villagers into government service. World War II
            brought prosperity and widespread Westernization. The author indi-
            cates the effect of major calamities or outside events on the pace of
            change, but he gives little specific information on social changes
            in the village.

*8014   Beals, Ralph L., "Acculturation, Economy and Social Change in an
            Ecuadorean Village," in GEN 4388 (1952), 67-73.

            A study of an Indian village near Quito, describing the following
            changes in the village in recent times: the weakening of family
            ties, the reorganization of political ties, the secularization of
            fiestas, and an increase in formal education.

*8015   Beardsley, R. K., J. W. Hall, and R. E. Ward, Village Japan.
            Chicago: University of Chicago Press, 1959. 408 pp.

            The village investigated is on Honshu on the Inland Sea. It is
            considered a pacesetter in agricultural innovation and well oriented
            to a cash-crop economy. Though village affairs are kept within the
            village, many residents work in the nearby city, and much machinery
            is now used. The effects of this have been that (1) youth has tended
            to become more prominent through their new skill with machines, (2)
            there is less cooperative work, and (3) villagers who work in the
            city can now cultivate their fields on Sunday, thus regaining their
            full place in the village.

**8016   Belshaw, C. S., The Great Village. London: Routledge & Kegan Paul,
            1957. 302 pp. [New Guinea]

            The New Guinea village has rejected its traditional economic
            forms, but it is hampered by the lack of funds for capital investment
            --commercial credit has been blocked by the colonial government--as
            well as by the lack of education. Though all the villagers are now
            wage earners, the kinship system has not been changed, for it
            provides strength and stability and is not incompatible with a modern
            economy. The traditional religion has been replaced by Christianity,
            but the old elaborate ceremonies have been kept--further cutting down
            on the funds available for investment. Yet, the author concludes, the
            elimination of these ceremonies might lead to apathy rather than to
            the freeing of funds for investment. Natives will not work for other
            natives--"bossmanship" is for the whites--and the courts are not
            effective in protecting the native, though they do look after the
            whites.

8017   Brokensha, David, Social Change at Larteh, Ghana. London: Clarendon
            Press, 1966. 294 pp.

            Economic change in this village has taken place within the tradi-
            tional framework. Social change has taken the form of adaptation and
            accommodation rather than conflict.

*8018   Cancian, Frank, Economics and Prestige in a Maya Community: The

                                    [237]

Religious Cargo System in Zincantan. Stanford: Stanford University
Press, 1965. 238 pp. [Mexico]

Economic expansion has brought more wealth and a larger population.
Both these factors undermine the social integration of the village.
The cargos form a rigid hierarchy of position that cannot be expanded
to match the growing affluence of the villagers. The results are
frustration and the dissolution of the bonds that held the community
together.

8019   Carstairs, G. Morris, "A Village in Rajasthan," in GEN 4386 (1960),
        36-41. [Indian State of Rajasthan]

The author describes how this village has been changed by the
disappearance of the former ruler and his court and by the return of
workers to the village.

*8020   Cohn, Bernard S., "The Changing Status of a Depressed Caste," in GEN
        4353 (1955), 53-77. [Indian State of Uttar Pradesh]

A description of a village in Uttar Pradesh in which outside
employment is beginning to take effect. While the upper castes are
being Westernized, the lower castes are being Hinduized. These
latter have used outside legal and political means to overthrow the
upper castes, but they have been unable to consolidate their gains.

8021   Consejo de Bienestas Rural, Problemas económicos y sociales de los
        Andes venezolanos [Economic and social problems in the Venezuelan
        Andes]. Part 2. Caracas: Consejo de Bienestas Rural, 1956(?).
        136 pp.

Part 2 is a general sociological survey of a very poor farming
area. A few selected villages were studied in detail and the
impressions of the observers are given here. (Part 1 is an economic
survey.)

*8022   Cornell, John B., and Robert J. Smith, Two Japanese Villages:
        Matsunagi, a Japanese Mountain Community. Kurusu, a Japanese
        Agricultural Community. Ann Arbor: University of Michigan Press,
        1956. 232 pp.

Cornell describes a village on Honshu on the Inland Sea. Electricity was introduced in 1923 and modern transportation in the
'thirties. Although the village is oriented to cash crops and uses
much machinery, the household structure seems to have been unaffected.

Smith describes a village in Shikoku that was greatly influenced
by World War II and by the land reform of the early 'fifties. He
finds a marked trend toward individualism and away from religion.

8023   Danielsson, Bengt, Work and Life on Raroia: An Acculturation Study
        from the Tuamotu Group, French Oceania. Uppsala: Almqvist & Wik-
        sells, 1955. 244 pp. [Caledonia]

The changes observed in this study result from the new authority
structure of the inhabitants of Raroia and not from the introduction
of industry.

[238]

8024   Desai, Madkukar N., <u>The Life and Living in the Rural Karnatak</u> (with <u>reference to Gokak Taluka</u>). Poona, India: Gokhale Institute of Politics and Economics, 1945. 347 + 62 pp. [Indian State of Gujarat]

     A description of the wartime increase in cash cropping.

8025   Downs, R. E., "A Rural Community in Kelantan, Malaya: A Brief Account of Its Socio-Economic Organization and Regional Setting," in GEN 4371 (1960), 51-62. [Malaysia]

     A study of a village developing its contacts with the outside world through the cash cropping of rubber.

**8026   Dube, Shyama Charan, <u>Indian Village</u>. London: Routledge & Kegan Paul, 1955. 248 pp. [Indian State of Andhra]

     A study of a village in Hyderabad (Andhra), where the caste system has been undisturbed by modern influences, for there is always a "poor" cousin to replace the son gone off to the city. In general, the village has remained traditional, but it is willing to accept such changes as represent a pecuniary gain, as mill cloth, cash crops, and so forth.

     The following table shows the significant lines of variation in social organization, with special reference to family, caste, and village council.

I. FAMILY

Then	Now
1. Insistence on family solidarity and cohesion	1. Growth of individualism
2. Greater attachment to the soil and the settlement	2. Migrations more frequent
3. Intrafamily relations governed by regard for age and kinship status	3. Less regard for these traditional principles

II. CASTE

Then	Now
1. Occupational specialization based on caste	1. Caste no longer the only determinant of occupation
2. Prohibition of interdining with some equal castes and with all lower castes	2. Rules of interdining less rigid
3. Hierarchy and permanent distance among different castes	3. Mild protest against social hierarchy; some modification in actual practice

III. VILLAGE COUNCIL

Then

1. Constituted on hereditary
   principles
2. Little outside intervention

3. Decisions generally accepted

Now

1. Also admits people with
   "achieved status"
2. Considerable outside
   pressure
3. Defiance or avoidance
   possible.

8027   Dupree, Louis B., "The Changing Character of South Central Afghanistan Villages," Hum. Organiz. 14:4 (Winter 1956), 26-29.

A study of a village in which land has been freely sold for the
last century. This has led to village disintegration, since it has
weakened the force of the clans.

8028   Eglar, Zekiye Suleyman, A Punjabi Village in Pakistan. New York:
Columbia University Press, 1960. 240 pp. [West Pakistan]

The village craftsmen have become more specialized and have moved
to the cities to practice their trades.

*8029   Embree, John F., A Japanese Village: Suye Mura. Chicago: University
of Chicago Press, 1939. 354 pp.

A study of a village in southern Kyushu, in which increasing
external contacts (political and transportational) have weakened the
traditional village system. Cooperation has tended to disappear as
new social classes based on money and occupational status emerge.
See RUR 8095 for a later study of the same village.

***8030 Epstein, Trude S., Economic Development and Social Change in South
India. Manchester, England: Manchester University Press, 1962.
353 pp. [Indian State of Mysore]

A study of two villages in Mysore--one that had had irrigation
introduced into it in 1939; and another, just beyond the level of
irrigation, in the same district. Irrigation brought prosperity to the
"wet" village, but the traditional social structure has remained in-
tact. However, the introduction of a cash crop (sugar cane) has tended
to free money from traditional restrictions, thus allowing women to
engage in commerce; consequently they have gained status and increased
freedom. The general prosperity has factionalized the village to some
extent, but the factions seem to be separated on all issues and not
to be topical. The "dry" village has been changed far more by the
introduction of irrigation into the neighboring village. Its population has become economically diversified and mobile. Status is now
achieved by leaving the village or by breaking traditional bonds by
going into a new business, such as milling, machine-shop work, and so
forth. One faction in the village is attempting to rise outside the
village rather than through ritual status, as happens in the "wet"
village.

**8031   Fals-Borda, Orlando, <u>Peasant Society in the Colombian Andes: A
           Sociological Study of Saucio</u>. Gainesville: University of Florida
           Press, 1955.   277 pp.

           A study of a village near Bogotá. The peasant society described
           seems to be dominated by the political parties of the country. Each
           peasant is attached to a specific party and waits passively for his
           party to come to power, at which time he reaps the spoils of
           victory. The author suspects that the advent of outside employment,
           the return of émigrés, and increasing education may change this
           system.

**8032   Firth, Raymond W., <u>Social Change in Tikopia: Re-Study of a
           Polynesian Community after a Generation</u>. London: Allen & Unwin,
           1959.   360 pp.   [Polynesia]

           This study of the change in a small island between 1928 and
           1952 treats the theory of change induced by the introduction of
           money and modern transport in relation to the author's observations
           of this community. The strongest impact seems to have been on the
           organization of the society, but the structure of the society was
           also beginning to change in 1952. The author finds a tendency to
           individualism, a growing divergence between wealth and status, a
           waning of traditional authority, and an enlarging of the natives'
           view of the world.

***8033   Fraser, T. M., <u>Rusembilan: A Malay Fishing Village in Southern
           Thailand</u>. Ithaca: Cornell University Press, 1960.   281 pp.

           Author studied a village whose economy has changed from a rice
           and fish subsistence to commercial fishing. The change was induced
           by the needs of an increasing populace. The villagers are individ-
           ualistic in economic affairs but are still communalistic in reli-
           gious matters. However, individualism seems to be self-reinforcing,
           for it is receptive to change, which further develops economic inde-
           pendence. Innovations have become such prestige symbols that in
           one case an innovation was adopted that was not wise in any economic
           sense. The very low margin of profit from the larger-sized fishing
           operations has tended to put the hiring of labor on strict economic
           terms with no reference to kinship, as was previously the case.

**8034   Fukutake, Tadashi, <u>Amerika Mura</u> [American village]. Tokyo: Tôdai
           Shuppan Kai, 1953.   550 pp.   [Japan]

           A study of a village founded by returned emigrants to the United
           States.

*8035   ------ <u>Man and Society in Japan</u>. Tokyo: Tokyo University Press,
           1962.   241 pp.

           Part II is composed of two case studies. The second discusses
           the impact of returning emigrants on a village in southern Japan.

**8036   ------ <u>Nihon Sonraku no Shakaikôzô</u> [The social structure of Japa-
           nese villages]. Tokyo: Tokyo University Press, 1959.   589 pp.

This study is based on a series of case studies carried out under the author's direction. He is particularly interested in the changes in the social structure brought about by land reform, health campaigns, and other governmentally induced reforms.

**8037   Fukutake, T., and T. Tsukamoto, Nihon Nōmin no Shakaiteki Seikaku [Social character of the Japanese farmer]. Tokyo: Yuhikaku, 1954. 313 pp.

A study of two villages in southern Japan, one in the populated plain, and the other isolated in the mountains. The villages are described in detail. Selected heads of family were interviewed by means of an extensive questionnaire, which is appended to the text. The authors analyze changes desired and the reactions to previous changes. The farmers seem not bound by tradition but receptive to innovation.

**8038   Fukutake, T., Tsutomu Ouchi, and Chie Nakane, The Socio-Economic Structure of the Indian Village: Surveys of Villages in Gujarat and West Bengal. Tokyo: Institute of Asian Economic Affairs, 1964. 174 pp.

A study of two villages, one in a dry farming area, and the other in a wet farming area. The first village has extensive contacts with the city, but this is true of the richer farmers and cotton merchants, who are very commercially minded. The village is being secularized, and political offices are increasingly allotted on the basis of ability or function. The people have been more successful in fulfilling their political aspirations than their economic ones. This may be a future source of conflict. Because of the relative isolation of the wet farming village, it has not retained its upper caste groups, and this has helped to weaken the caste system there, except for the untouchables. Though the government has worked with the latter, they have not responded, partly because they are so dominated and partly because there is no city-oriented upper-caste group to emulate.

*8039   Fuller, Anne H., Buarij: Portrait of a Lebanese Muslim Village. Cambridge, Mass.: Harvard University Press, 1961. 98 pp.

A prewar study of a mountain village located near the highway from Beirut to Damascus. The author finds the village quite conservative and resistant to change, though it is used by city Muslims as a summer resort. There is an extensive description of the villagers' attitudes toward the world outside the village and beyond.

*8040   Gallin, Bernard, Hsin Hsing, Taiwan: A Chinese Village in Change. Berkeley: University of California Press, 1966. 324 pp.

The increasing population puts a pressure on owning land, and new economic opportunities in the urban centers have weakened both the joint family and the village social structure. These have been replaced by the reenforcement of wider kinship groups and the creation of voluntary associations cutting across kinship lines. The traditional attachment to the land seems to have been greatly weakened. Some families have sold their family lands and migrated

[242]

permanently to the cities. Others have gone to the cities then
returned to the village in order to develop modern commercial agriculture. The result of all these changes has been to fragment the
village and push the villager to rely more on outside contacts for
his economic security.

8041   Geddes, W. R., Deuba: A Study of a Fijian Village. Wellington, New
        Zealand: Polynesian Society, 1945. 70 pp.

        The impact of wartime contacts with Europeans has both weakened
        the old societies and fostered a resentful nationalism.

8042   Gillin, John P., The Culture of Security in San Carlos: A Study of
        a Guatemalan Community of Indians and Ladinos. New Orleans: Middle
        American Research Institute, Tulane University, 1951. 128 pp.
        [Guatemala]

        A study of a relatively isolated village. Much of its insecurity
        results from the introduction of modern (Latin American) culture and
        power.

8043   Glacken, Clarence J., The Great Loochoo: A Study of Okinawan Village
        Life. Berkeley: University of California Press, 1955. 324 pp.

        A study of three villages, primarily from a historical viewpoint.
        The author places little emphasis on the sociology of economic
        change, though many of the younger villagers have worked or are now
        working outside the community.

8044   Goldkind, Victor, "Social Stratification in the Peasant Community:
        Redfield's Chan Kom Reinterpreted," Am. Anthrop. 67:4 (Aug. 1965),
        863-884. [Mexico]

        The author on re-examining Redfield's data suggests that instead
        of the classless homogeneity the latter found, Chan Kom has a
        Weberian heterogeneity of social classes. See RUR 8533.

8045   Gough, E. Kathleen, "The Social Structure of a Tanjore Village," in
        GEN 4353 (1955), 36-52. See also: Econ. Wkly. 4:21 (24 May 1952),
        531-536; and GEN 4386 (1960), 90-102. [Indian State of Madras]

        The land in this village was once owned by the local Brahman caste,
        but it has gradually been sold to outsiders from the nearby city. As
        a result, the power of this caste has declined. At the same time there
        has been a rise in Communist activity (anticaste movements) in the
        village.

*8046   Gulick, John, Social Structure and Culture Change in a Lebanese
        Village. New York: Wenner-Gren Foundation, 1955. 191 pp.

        A study of a Maronite mountain community with a strong tradition
        of migration from and return to the village. There seems to be great
        resistance to social change, despite the economic innovations caused
        by the massive emigration and the influx of summer residents.

*8047   Halpern, Joel Martin, A Serbian Village. New York: Columbia

University Press, 1958.   325 pp.   [Yugoslavia]

A historical-descriptive study of a village in a country that lost
its professional and commercial strata with the departure of the
Turks in the nineteenth century.   To fill the void, former peasants
have established closer ties with the urban areas.   This has caused
a decline in the extended family, though the presence of a modern
coal mine near the village has apparently stabilized the peasant
culture.

**8048   Hendry, James B., The Small World of Khanh Hau.   Chicago: Aldine,
1964.   312 pp.   [Vietnam]

A study of the economics of the village based on a questionnaire.
The author finds that the economic activity of the peasant is based
above all on economic criteria and only slightly on the social
structure of the community.   Although the villager is quite conservative, he is acutely interested in any new technique that will, in his
context, make him richer.   The author believes that the problem
centers not on getting the villager to accept innovations but rather
on finding innovations that will in fact be profitable for him.

8049   Herskovits, Melville J., and Frances S. Herskovits, Trinidad
Village.   New York: Knopf, 1947.   351 pp.

The many Africanisms that have survived in this village have
generally been relegated to the margin of the society, or adapted to
the dominant European mode of life.

8050   Hickey, Gerald Cannon, The Study of a Vietnamese Rural Community-
Sociology.   Saigon: Michigan State University Vietnam Advisory Group,
1960.   266 pp.

A study of a village south of Saigon that has had much French
influence and urban integration, but the author does not analyze
the impact of these factors.

8051   ------ Village in Vietnam.   New Haven: Yale University Press, 1964.
325 pp.

The impact of economic change seems to be confined to the more
well-to-do classes, who readily accept an innovation once it has been
shown to be profitable.   The village has remained traditional, however, perhaps because the turmoil and insecurity from the present war
allow   only the rich to profit from change.

*8052   Holmes, L. D., Ta'u: Stability and Change in a Samoan Village.
Wellington, New Zealand: Polynesian Society, 1958.   87 pp.

A study of a very isolated island that has hardly changed its
customs, despite the considerable change in the material aspects
of life and, in particular, the commercialization of copra cultivation.

**8053   Kaufman, Howard Keva, Bangkhuad: A Community Study in Thailand.
Locust Valley, N.Y.:   J. J. Augustin, 1960.   235 pp.

A study of a village near Bangkok that has changed (1) from a simple subsistence economy to a complex one; (2) from a noncompetitive economy to a competitive one; (3) from barter to cash; (4) from the extended family to the nuclear family; (5) from nonmechanical to mechanical irrigation; (6) from a sedentary to a migratory population; and (7) from a local to a national orientation. The increasing demand for rice to export has heightened the value of land, and therefore it is no longer given to the young, who are sent to the city to work. The latter's adaptation to city life has been difficult because of their insufficient schooling. The introduction of compulsory nationalized education has undermined religion and increased consciousness of nationality, which is not incompatible with a mania for Westernization.

8054   Kawashima, Tetsurô, Kôchi-ken no Shakai [The sociology of Kôchi Prefecture]. Kôchi, Japan: Kôchi Public Library, 1958. 269 pp. [Japan]

Some description of the effects of the introduction of tobacco cultivation.

*8055   Kingshill, Konrad, Ku Daeng, The Red Tomb: A Village Study in Northern Thailand. Chiangmai, Thailand: Prince Royal's College, 1960. 310 pp.

A study of a village close to railroad and bus facilities. Although the villagers do not tend to travel beyond the local market town, Western styles are rapidly assimilated.

*8056   Leach, E. R., Pul Eliya: A Village in Ceylon: A Study of Land Tenure and Kinship. Cambridge, England: Cambridge University Press, 1961. 244 pp.

The author is chiefly concerned with showing that locality (in this case the form or change in land tenure) is part and parcel of the society (kinship or change in family relationships).

**8057 Leslie, Charles M., Now We Are Civilized: A Study of the World View of the Zapotec Indians of Mitla, Oaxaca. Detroit, Mich.: Wayne State University Press, 1960. 108 pp. [Mexico]

In comparison with the prewar state of the town as described by Talcott Parsons, the natives are more in touch with the outside world and more money oriented. Nevertheless, they still hold to their old beliefs in the supernatural.

*8058   Lewis, Oscar, Group Dynamics in a North-Indian Village: A Study of Factions. New Delhi: Government of India Planning Commission, 1954. 48 pp. [Indian State of Uttar Pradesh] See also: Econ. Wkly. 6:15 (10 Apr. 1954), 423-425; 6:16 (17 Apr. 1954), 445-451; 6:17 (24 Apr. 1954), 477-482; 6:18 (1 May 1954), 501-506.

Factions follow caste and kinship lines but are altered by education and economic development.

*8059   ------ Life in a Mexican Village: Tepoztlán Revisited. Urbana: University of Illinois Press, 1951. 512 pp.

Despite modern innovations such as new roads and schools, the author finds little change in the personality traits of the villagers.

8060   ------ Tepoztlán, Village in Mexico. New York: Holt, Rinehart & Winston, 1960. 104 pp.

Many economic changes have already occurred, such as the introduction of electricity and the cinema, and though the number of laborers leaving for the United States has greatly increased, the author does not analyze the effects on the society.

**8061   Lewis, O., and V. Barnouw, Village Life in Northern India: Studies in a Delhi Village. Urbana: University of Illinois Press, 1958. 384 pp. [Indian State of Uttar Pradesh]

A study of a village that has had a great deal of contact with the city. This contact has begun to upset the traditional economic structure. The untouchables have grown independent and look to the courts for protection. Consequently many of the higher castes have taken over the untouchables' menial jobs, and this has been economically detrimental to the untouchables. The authors compare the changes here with those in Tepoztlán in Mexico.

*8062   McCormack, W. C., "Mysore Villager's View of Change," Econ. Dev. cult. Change 5:3 (Apr. 1957), 257-262.

The author stresses the factors blocking change: the "ideal of village unity" and factionalism. This is a case study of how these elements blocked the introduction of a school.

*8063   Madge, Charles, Survey Before Development in Thai Villages. New York: United Nations, 1957. 90 pp.

The basic interest of this study is the use of fundamental education in the process of economic development. The author has included several rather interesting case studies of individuals and the effect of education on them.

8064   Majumdar, D. N., Caste and Communication in an Indian Village. Bombay: Asia Publishing House, 1958. 358 pp. [Indian State of Uttar Pradesh]

A study of a village near Lucknow. The author has given little space to the effect of the city on the villagers and changes in the village, though his study is otherwise comprehensive.

**8065   Mandelbaum, David G., "Technology, Credit and Culture in a Nilgiri Village," in GEN 4386 (1960), 103-105. [Indian State of Kerela]

The author describes the breakdown of the interdependence of two castes as a result of economic changes over the last twenty-five years. One group rendered services to the other in return for grain. Now the grain-growing group can sell its crop and buy these services, and this has forced the other group to grow a cash crop also. This in turn has tended to destroy the unity of the village, for by growing a cash crop one can be independent of the village.

**8066   Marriott, McKim, "Social Structure and Change in a U.P. [Uttar

Pradesh] Village," in GEN 4386 (1960), 106-121. See also: Econ.
Wkly. 4:34 (23 Aug. 1952), 869-874.

 The new tenancy laws seem to have broken up many of the previously
interdependent groupings: tenants are now secure, but subtenants are
now impelled to move with great frequency so as to prevent their
becoming tenants in terms of the law. The war has fostered the
destruction of the power of many landlords, through inflation and
through the introduction by the government of the present stricter
tenancy laws. Thus wealth and social rank have become less correlated,
and intravillage cooperation has declined. This friction within the
village is exploited by the government to achieve its ends.

**8067 Matos Mar, J., "Three Indian Communities in Peru," in GEN 4356
    (1963), 130-138.

 A study of two isolated villages and a third that attempted to
modernize itself. This latter failed because of anti-Indian prejudice
and inadequate cultural preparation for the introduction of industry.

*8068 Mayer, Adrian C., Caste and Kinship in Central India: A Village and
    Its Region. Berkeley: University of California Press, 1960. 295
    pp. [Indian State of Madhya Pradesh]

 The author points out that there is now a new capacity for change
stemming from the possibility of defying traditional authority by
appealing to outside forces.

8069 Mendras, Henri, Six villages d'Epire: Problèmes de développement
    socio-économique [Six villages of Epirus: Problems of socio-eco-
    nomic development]. UNESCO Mission Reports, No. 11. Paris: UNESCO,
    1961. 92 pp. [Greece]
 While the villagers of the plains see some future in farming, the
mountain villagers wish to emigrate to the cities, for they think
that industry alone can offer them any possibilities.

8070 Nam, Kyu Back, "Nopunto," in GEN 4357 (1958), 43 pp. [Korea]

 Describes the leveling effect of postwar inflation. A case study
of one family.

**8071 Norbeck, Edward, Takeshima, a Japanese Fishing Community. Salt Lake
    City: University of Utah Press, 1954. 231 pp.

 A study of a village on the Inland Sea that is still without
electricity. The economy has changed from barter to cash fishing.
Other innovations are: a growing specialization, status that is
based primarily on money, weakening family ties, and a rage for
Americanisms.

*8072 Orenstein, Henry, Gaon: Conflict and Cohesion in an Indian Village.
    Princeton: Princeton University Press, 1965. 351 pp. [Indian State
    of Maharashtra]

 In the not too distant past this village was a markedly self-
centered social group, despite a high level of conflict. Recent
efforts by the central government to rationalize governmental contacts

and to help the lower castes have encouraged individuals to break
away from the village structure. The result has been a disintegration of the village in favor of caste groupings that are often
stronger than ever.

8073   Patnaik, N., "Service Relationship between Barbers and Villagers in a
        Small Village in Ranpur," Econ. Wkly. 12:20 (14 May 1960), 737-742.
        [Indian State of Orissa] See also: "Barbers and Their Clients in an
        Orissan Village," Man in India 40:2 (Apr.-June 1960), 109-115.

        The traditional service ties of the barbers are dying out because
        of the weakening of the caste assembly of barbers.

*8074   Phillips, Herbert P., Thai Peasant Personality: The Patterning of
        Interpersonal Behavior in the Village of Bang Chan. Berkeley:
        University of California Press, 1965. 231 pp.

        Relying on sentence-completion tests, the author finds the Thai
        personality to be characterized by the anxiety about poverty and a
        recognition of the inherent loneliness of existence.

8075   Raper, A. F., et al., The Japanese Village in Transition. Tokyo:
        Natural Resources Section, General Headquarters, Supreme Command for
        the Allied Powers, 1950. 272 pp.

        A survey of thirteen villages throughout Japan, giving considerable
        data on the effects of land reforms and other postwar improvements.

8076   Ravicz, Robert S., Organización social de los Mixtecos [Social organi-
        zation of the Mixtecans]. Mexico City: Instituto Nacional Indigen-
        ista, 1965. 281 pp.

        The Mixtec villages differ in their social structure. These dif-
        ferences are ascribable to the extent of the contacts a village has
        with European culture, and to the predominantly racial form of these
        contacts rather than to the impact of its economic relations.

**8077 Redfield, Robert, Tepoztlán, a Mexican Village: A Study of Folk
        Life. Chicago: University of Chicago Press, 1930. 247 pp.

        Education has been a strong influence in orienting one part of the
        village toward the city. The other part has remained staunchly
        traditionalist.

***8078 Reichel-Dolmatoff, Gerardo, and Alicia Reichel-Dolmatoff, The People
        of Aritama: The Cultural Personality of a Colombian Mestizo Village.
        London: Routledge & Kegan Paul, 1961. 483 pp.

        While the lowland Creole society has become very materialistic and
        hedonistic, the village in the mountains has not. Since the intro-
        duction of modern communications in the 1940's, cash cropping has
        replaced subsistence farming in the village. At present the village
        is in transition. Its people's greatest fear is to lack prestige or
        to be taken for an Indian, a fear augmented by suspicion and hostility
        toward the government.

*8079   Reina, Ruben E., Chinautla: A Guatemalan Indian Community. A Study
          in the Relationship of Community Culture and National Change. Publi-
          cation 24. New Orleans: American Research Institute, Tulane Univer-
          sity, 1960, 55-130.

              The degree of cultural continuity and stability in this village is
          very high despite its proximity to the capital.

*8080   Rubio Orbe, Gonzalo, Punyaro: Estudio de antropología social y
          cultural de una comunidad indígena y mestiza [Punyaro: A study of
          the social and cultural anthropology in a native and in a mestizo
          community]. Quito: Editorial Casa de la Cultura Ecuadoriana, 1956.
          422 pp.

              There is very little evidence of assimilation among the villagers,
          for two reasons: the Indian culture is very strong and xenophobic,
          and the Indians are badly treated by the Spanish-speaking classes.

*8081   Ryan, B., et al., Sinhalese Village. Coral Gables, Fla.: University
          of Miami Press, 1958. 229 pp. [Ceylon]

              A study of a village in Ceylon near Colombo. Rubber plantations
          were introduced into the area at the turn of the century. The author
          is particularly interested in secularization, which he finds proceed-
          ing slowly and without too much disorganization of the peasant
          society. This village seems to have been particularly affected by
          the Buddhist idea of detachment and by its unstructured form of
          society.

*8082   Sahlins, Marshall D., Moala: Culture and Nature on a Fijian Island.
          Ann Arbor: University of Michigan Press, 1962. 453 pp.

              The author finds that the traditional forms of economic relations
          (such as unrestricted access to relatives' property) are gradually
          being transformed as certain native products become marketable out-
          side the island. For the moment, however, the conflict between
          sharing and acquisition for sale has not been resolved so as to per-
          mit the accumulation of wealth.

8083   Sarma, Jyotirmoyee, "A Village in West Bengal," in GEN 4386 (1960),
          180-201. [Indian State of West Bengal]

              A general study of a village whose inhabitants frequently work
          or trade in Calcutta.

**8084   Sibley, W. E., "The Maintenance of Unity and Distinctiveness by a
          Philippine Peasant Village," in GEN 4344 (1960), 506-512.

              A study of a village on Negros Island. The author finds that
          cash payments have increased individualism but the local city market,
          although visited by the villagers, seems to have had little effect
          on their traditional ways.

*8085   Sivertsen, D., When Caste Barriers Fall: A Study of Social and
          Economic Change in a South Indian Village. New York: Humanities
          Press, 1963. 141 pp.

Although the upper castes are no longer conceded the moral supremacy they once had, their economic position still assures them a dominant social status. However, the weakening of personal ties and the tighter group cohesiveness of the lower castes have made the position of the upper castes much less secure.

*8086   Spoehr, A., Majuro: A Village in the Marshall Islands. Chicago: Chicago Natural History Museum, 1949. 266 pp. [Micronesia]

The author finds that these villagers readily accept change despite the fact that they evince a solid core of cultural self-identity.

*8087   Stein, William W., Hualcan: Life in the Highlands of Peru. Ithaca: Cornell University Press, 1961. 383 pp.

Work outside the village has had little effect on the local society because of its rigid class structure. The local value system has remained unchanged, though the inflow of money from workers has had a material effect.

8088   Stirling, Paul, Turkish Village. London: Weidenfeld & Nicolson, 1965. 316 pp.

The social distance between village and town is very great and is only gradually being broken down by increased rural-urban contacts. However, this contact also serves to weaken village solidarity.

**8089   Tax, Sol, Penny Capitalism: A Guatemalan Indian Economy. Washington: Smithsonian Institution, 1953. 230 pp.

A detailed study of a village, whose smallness may in part account for the lack of wealth-tied social classes, as seen in other Indian villages.

**8090   Touma, Toufic, Un village de montagne au Liban (Hadeth el-Jobbé) [A mountain village in Lebanon (Hadeth el-Jobbé)]. Paris: Mouton, 1958. 151 pp.

A study of a Maronite village, in which emigration has long been traditional. The village is strongly united despite this emigration and the fact that it is a summer resort area.

8091   Tumin, Melvin M., Caste in a Peasant Society: A Case Study in the Dynamics of Caste. Princeton: Princeton University Press, 1952. 300 pp. [Guatemala]

While the Indians aspire to the culture and status of the "Ladinos," the rigid caste system has allowed them no means of realizing these aspirations without concealing their Indian origins. The author sees little resentment of this situation among the Indians, though he compares this caste system to its counterpart in the South of the United States. For another view of this village, see RUR 8042 (1951), 128 pp.

**8092   Van Stone, James W., "A Successful Combination of Subsistence and Wage Economies on the Village Level," Econ. Dev. cult. Change 8:2

(Jan. 1960), 174-191.

A study of an essentially forward-looking fishing village in Alaska. It has combined the use of modern implements with its traditional subsistence economy.

*8093   Willems, Emelio, Cunha: Tradição e transição em uma cultura rural do Brasil [Cunha: Tradition and transition in a rural society in Brazil]. São Paulo: Secretaria de Agricultura, Directoria de Publicada Agricola, 1947. 240 pp.

A study of a rural area near São Paulo that has been greatly influenced by the growth of the cities in southern Brazil. As a result the agriculture of the area has turned to cash cropping. There are detailed descriptions of the economic and social changes that have taken place, but no analysis of their causes or relationships.

**8094   Willems, E., and G. Mussolini, Buzios Island: A Caiçara Community in Southern Brazil. Locust Valley, N.Y.: J. J. Augustin, 1953. 116 pp.

A study of an extremely isolated island off the coast of southern Brazil. The villagers show great mobility and alertness to economic opportunities. Those who are dissatisfied with the island leave very readily. The introduction of a cash economy has impoverished the islanders by lessening their inclination to cooperative work.

**8095   Yoshino, I. Roger, Study of Suye Mura: An Investigation of Social Change. Pullman: State College of Washington, 1956. 182 pp. [Japan] See RUR 8029 on the same village before the war.

Study of the impact of the reforms introduced in Japan by the American occupation. The author finds that the family structure is quite resistant to these changes. The youth, on the other hand, seem to be ready to accept more individualism than the older generation.

B.   Other Case Studies

8301   Abdul Rahman bin Ahmad, "The Island Malays; A Study of a Group of Malays in an Island off Singapore: Their Life, Customs, Beliefs, and the Degree to Which They Communicate with Other Places to Meet Their Various Needs." Social Studies thesis, Singapore City University, 1960. [Malaysia]

8302   Adams, John B., "Culture and Conflict in an Egyptian Village," Am. Anthrop. 59:2 (Apr. 1957), 225-235.

8303   Afsaruddin, Mohammad, Rural Life in East Pakistan: A Study of Five Selected Villages. E. Pakistan: Department of Sociology, University of Dacca, 1964. 82 pp.

8304   Ahmed, N. U., "La comunidad Laua" [The Laua community], Rev. mex.
        Sociol. 25:1 (Jan.-Apr. 1963), 215-234. [East Pakistan]

8305   Akhauri, N., "Socio-Cultural Barriers to Rural Change in an East-
        Bihar Community," East. Anthrop. 11:3-4 (Mar.-Aug. 1958), 212-219.
        [Indian State of Bihar]

8306   Armstrong, L., and G. K. Hirabayashi, "Social Differentiation in
        Selected Lebanese Villages," Am. sociol. Rev. 21:4 (Aug. 1956),
        425-434.

8307   Atarashi, M., "Shakai Kôzô: Tottori-ken Ichi-gyoson ni okeru" [The
        social structure of a fishing village in the Tottori prefecture],
        Sochioroji 9:4 (1963), 38-81. [Japan]

8308   Ayabe, Tsuneo, "Teichi Lao-Zoku no Sonraku-Kôzô: Pha Khao Buraku,
        Ban Pha Khao no Baai" [The village structure of lowland Lao: A case
        study of Ban Pha Khao], Minzokugaku Kenkyû 23 (1959), 87-117.
        [Laos]

8309   Baden-Powerll, Baden Henry, The Indian Village Community. New Haven:
        Human Relations Area Files Press, 1957. 456 pp.

8310   Bailey, F. G., "Two Villages in Orissa (India)," in GEN 4329 (1964),
        52-82. [Indian State of Orissa]

8311   Balandier, Georges, "Problèmes économiques et problèmes politiques
        au niveau du village Fang" [Economic and political problems at the
        level of the Fang village], Bull. Inst. Stud. centrafr. 1 (1950),
        49-64. [Gabon]

8312   Banerjee, Hemendra Nath, "Community Structure in an Artisan Village
        of Pargannah Barabhum," J. soc. Res. 3 (Mar. 1960), 68-79. [India]

8313   Banks, E. P., "A Carib Village in Dominica," Soc. econ. Stud. 5:1
        (Mar. 1956), 74-86.

8314   Barnabas, A. P., "Social Change in a North Indian Village." Ph.D.
        dissertation, Cornell University, 1960. [India]

8315   Barnett, Homer G., Palauan Society: A Study of Contemporary Native
        Life in the Palau Islands. Eugene: University of Oregon Press,
        1949. 223 pp. [Micronesia]

8316   Basu, Tara Krishna, The Bengal Peasant from Time to Time. Calcutta:
        Statistical Publishing Society, 1962. 205 pp. [Indian State of Uttar
        Pradesh]

8317   Batista, D., W. R. Oliveira, et al., "Codajás: Comunidade amazônica.
        Estudo médico-social de um a população da hinterlândia amazônica"
        [Codajás: Amazon community. Medicosocial study of a population of
        the Amazon hinterland], Rev. bras. Geogr. 22:3 (July-Sept. 1960),
        321-342. [Brazil]

8318   Beaglehole, E., and P. Beaglehole, "Pangai: A Village in Tonga,"
        Polynesian Soc. Mem. 18 (1941). [Polynesia]

8319   Beals, Ralph L., Cheran: A Sierra Tarascan Village. Washington:
        Smithsonian Institution, 1946. 225 pp. [Mexico]

8320   Befu, Harumi, "The Hamlet in a Nation: The Place of Three Japanese
        Rural Communities in Their Broader Social Context." Ph.D. disserta-
        tion, University of Wisconsin, 1962. 315 mim. pp.

8321   Bennett, J. W., amd I. Ishino, "Futomi: A Case Study of the Social-
        Economic Adjustments of a Marginal Community in Japan," Rur. Sociol.
        20:1 (Mar. 1955), 41-50.

8322   Berque, Jacques, Histoire sociale d'un village égyptien au XXe siècle
        [The social history of an Egyptian village in the 20th century].
        Paris-La Haye: Mouton, 1957. 87 pp.

8323   ------ "Sur la structure sociale de qualques villages égyptiens"
        [The social structure of some Egyptian villages], Ann. Univ. Paris
        10:2 (June 1955), 199-215.

8324   Berreman, Gerald D., Hindus of the Himalayas. Berkeley: University
        of California Press, 1963. 430 pp. [India]

8325   Beteille, André, "Sripuram: A Village in Tanjore District," Econ.
        Wkly. 14:4-6 (Feb. 1962), 141-146. [India]

8326   Beuchelt, E., "Cheju-do: Wandlungen in der Gesellschaftsordnung einer
        koreanischen Inselkultur" [Cheju-do: Social change in an islands
        culture of Korea], Sociologus 13:2 (Sept. 1963), 150-168.

8327   Bhowmick, P. K., "Caste and Service in a Bengal Village," Man in
        India 43:4 (Oct.-Dec. 1963), 277-327. [Indian State of West Bengal]

8328   ------ "Kasba Narayangarh: A Muslim Village," Man in India 45:3
        (July-Sept. 1965), 201-222. [Indian State of West Bengal]

8329   Bose, A. B., "Society, Economy and Change in a Desert Village," Ann.
        arid Zone 1:1 (Dec. 1962), 1-15. [Indian State of Rajasthan]

8330   Bose, A. B., and S. P. Malhotra, "Studies in Group Dynamics. I,
        Factionalism in a Desert Village," Man in India 44:4 (Oct.-Dec.
        1964), 311-328. [Indian State of Rajasthan]

8331   Bose, Nirma Kumer, "Types of Villages in West Bengal: A Study in
        Social Change," Econ. Wkly. 10:4-6 (Jan. 1958), 149-152.

8332   Bourricaud, F., Changements à Puno. Etude de sociologie andine
        [Changes in Puno. A study in Andean sociology]. Paris: Institut
        des Hautes Etudes de l'Amérique Latine, 1962. 241 pp. [Peru]

8333   Boutillier, Jean Louis, "Les rapports du système foncier Toucouleur
        et de l'organisation sociale et économique traditionnelle. Leur
        évolution actuelle" [The relationship of the Toucouleur land system
        and the traditional social and economic organization: Their present
        evolution], in GEN 4310 (1963), 116-136. [West Africa]

8334   Brand, Donald D., Quiroga: A Mexican Village. Washington: Smithsonian
        Institution, 1951. 242 pp.

                                [253]

8335   Bretones, G. J., "Expériences de développement communautaire en Haïti"
        [Experiences of community development in Haiti], Int. Rev. Community
        Dev. 10 (1962), 75-88.

8336   Buitrón, A., "Panorama de la aculturación en Otavalo, Ecuador"
        [Panorama of Acculturation in Otavalo, Ecuador], Amér. indíg. 22:4
        (Oct. 1962), 313-322.

8337   Bunzel, Ruth Leah, Chichicastenango: A Guatemalan Village. Locust
        Valley, N.Y.: J. J. Augustin, 1952. 438 pp.

8338   Carroll, John, "Notes on the Bisaya in the Philippines and Borneo,"
        J. E. Asiat. Stud. 8:1-2 (Jan.-Apr. 1959), 42-72.

8339   Carstairs, G. Morris, "Bhil Villages of Western Udaipur: A Study
        in Resistance to Social Change," in GEN 4386 (1960), 68-76. [Indian
        State of Rajasthan]   See also Econ. Wkly. 4:9 (1 Mar. 1952), 231-
        233.

8340   Chandra, Prabhat, "Communication of Some New Ideas in a Madhya
        Pradesh Village: A Sociological Study Conducted in a Mixed Village,"
        East. Anthrop. 17:3 (Sept. 1964), 183-214. [Indian State of Madhya
        Pradesh]

8341   Chattopadhyay, Gouranga, Ranjana: A Village in West Bengal.
        Calcutta: Bookland, 1964. 262 pp.

8342   Chaves, M., "La Guajira: Una región y una cultura de Colombia" [The
        Guajira: A region and a culture of Colombia], Rev. colomb. Antrop.
        1:1 (June 1953), 123-195.

8343   Chiba, Hiromi, "The Japanese Farming Community and the Life of Farm
        Households," Asian Aff. 6:2 (Mar. 1962), 68-100.

8344   Clauzel, J., "Les hiérarchies sociales en pays touareg" [The social
        hierarchies of the Touareg country], Trav. Inst. Rech. saharéennes
        21 (Jan.-June 1962), 120-175. [Algeria]

8345   Cohen, Abner, Arab Border-villages in Israel: A Study of Continuity
        and Change in Social Organization. Manchester, England: Manchester
        University Press, 1965. 194 pp.

8346   Cohen, R., "The Success That Failed: An Experiment in Culture Change
        in Africa," Anthropologica 3:1 (1961), 21-36. [Nigeria]

8347   Cohen, Y. A., "The Social Organization of a Selected Community in
        Jamaica," Soc. econ. Stud. 2:4 (Mar. 1954), 104-133.

8348   Cohn, B. S., "Madhopur Revisited," Econ. Wkly. 11:28-30 (11, 18, 25
        July 1959), 963-966. [Indian State of Bihar]

8349   Collier, John, Jr., and Anibal Buitrón, The Awakening Valley.
        Chicago: University of Chicago Press, 1949. 199 pp. [Ecuador]

8350   Collin Delavaud, C., "Les communautés de petits cultivateurs
        indigènes sur la côte nord du Pérou" [Communities of small native

cultivators on the north coast of Peru], J. Soc. Amér. 54:2 (1965), 239-246.

8351   Cornejo Cabera, E., "Necesidad de enmarcar los programas de mejoramiento agrario en una planaficación regional. El caso de los ejidos veracruzanos" [The necessity of including programs for agrarian improvement in a regional plan: The case of the Vera Cruz Ejidos], Rev. mex. Sociol. 24:2 (May-Aug. 1962), 401-436. [Mexico]

8352   Cornell, John B., "Dozoku: An Example of Evolution and Transition in Japanese Village Society," Comp. Stud. Soc. Hist. 6:4 (July 1964), 449-480.

8353   ------ "Local Group Stability in the Japanese Community," Hum. Organiz. 22:2 (Summer 1963), 113-125.

8354   Cotler, Julio, Los cambios en la propiedad, la comunidad y la familia en San Lorenzo de Quinti [Changes in property, community, and family in San Lorenzo de Quinti]. Lima: Impreso de la Universidad Nacional Mayor de San Marco, 1950. 92 pp. [Peru]

8355   Cuisenier, J., "Le sous-développement économique dans un groupement rural: Le Djebel Lansarine" [Economic underdevelopment in a rural grouping: Mount Anssarine (Jabal al Anṣārīn)], Cah. Tunisie 6:23-24 (1958), 219-26 . [Tunisia]

8356   Darling, Malcolm Lyall, Wisdom and Waste in the Punjab Village. London: Oxford University Press, 1934. 368 pp. [Indian State of Punjab]

8357   Debunne, O., "Sirsod, village indien dans un monde en transition" [Sirsod: An Indian village in a world in transition], Int. soc. Wk. 6 (Mar. 1960), 48-52. [India]

8358   De Planhol, X., Nouveaux villages algérois: Atlas Blidéen, Chenoua, Mitidja Occidentale [New villages in Algeria: The Blidean Atlas, Chenoua, Western Mitidja]. Paris: Presses Universitaires de France, 1961. 124 pp.

8359   ------ "Les nouveaux villages de l'Atlas Blidéen, du Chenoua et de la Mitidja Occidentale" [The new villages of the Blidean Atlas, of Chenoua, and of Western Mitidja], Rev. afr. 105:1-2 (1961), 5-48. [Algeria]

8360   ------ "Un village de montagne de l'Azerbaidjan iranien: Lighwan" [A mountain village of the Iranian Azerbaidjan: Lighwan], Rev. Géogr. Lyon 35:4 (1960), 395-418. [Iran]

8361   De Young, John E., Village Life in Modern Thailand. Berkeley: University of California Press, 1955. 224 pp.

8362   Diaz, May N., "Opposition and Alliance in a Mexican Town," Ethnology 3:2 (Apr. 1964), 179-184.

8363   ------ Tonala: Conservatism, Responsibility, and Authority in a Mexican Town. Berkeley: University of California Press, 1966. 234 pp.

[255]

8364   Diskalkar, P. D., <u>Resurvey of a Deccan Village: Pimple Saudagar.</u>
        Bombay: Indian Society of Agricultural Economics, 1960. 152 pp.
        [Indian State of Maharashtra] See RUR 8464 for an earlier treatment
        of the same village.

8365   Donoghue, John D., and Vo Hong-Phuc, <u>My-Thuan: The Study of a Delta
        Village in South Vietnam.</u> Saigon: Michigan State University Vietnam
        Advisory Group, 1961. 65 pp.

8366   Donoghue, John D., et al., <u>Cam An: A Fishing Village in Central Viet
        Nam.</u> Local Administration Series Vol. 6. Saigon: Michigan State
        University Advisory Group, National Institute of Administration, 1962.
        123 pp.

8367   Dube, S. C., "A Deccan Village," in GEN 4386 (1960), 202-215. [Indian
        State of Maharashtra]

8368   ------ "Shamirpet: The Social Structure of an Indian Village," <u>Man in
        India</u> 32:1 (Jan.-Mar. 1952), 17-22. [Indian State of Andhra]

8369   Ducommun, Dolores, "Sisangat: A Fishing Community of Sulu," <u>Philipp.
        sociol. Rev.</u> 10 (July-Oct. 1962), 91-107. [Philippines]

8370   Dupree, Louis B., "The Changing Character of South-Central Afghanistan
        Villages," <u>Hum. Organiz.</u> 14:4 (Winter 1956), 26-29.

8371   ------ "The Disintegration of the Clan Village in Badwan, a Pathan
        Farming Village in Southwest Afghanistan," <u>J. Ala. Acad. Sci.</u> 26 (Dec.
        1954).

8372   Eggan, F. R., "Some Aspects of Culture Change in the Northern
        Philippines," in GEN 4339 (1955), 343-349. See also <u>Am. Anthrop.</u>
        43:1 (Feb. 1941), 11-18; and GEN 4349 (1966), 322-326.

8373   Epstein, Trude Scarlett, "Economic Development and Peasant Marriage in
        South India," <u>Man in India</u> 40 (July-Sept. 1960), 192-232. [Indian
        State of Mysore] See also RUR 8030 (1962).

8374   Fals Borda, Orlando, <u>Campesinos de los Andes. Estudio sociológico de
        Saucío</u> [Peasants of the Andes: Sociological study of Saucío].
        Bogotá: Universidad Nacional de Colombia, 1961. 340 pp. [Colombia]
        Translation in RUR 8031 (1955).

8375   Ferrer Faria, Ivan, <u>Ensayo sociológico de un medio rural concentrado
        venezolano</u> [Sociological experiment in a rural area of average
        population in Venezuela]. Maracaibo: Tipográfico Cervantes, 1957.
        141 pp. [Venezuela]

8376   Forde, C. D., "Social Change in a West African Community," <u>Man</u> 5
        (1937).

8377   Foster, George M., "The Dyadic Contract: A Model for the Social
        Structure of a Mexican Peasant Village," <u>Am. Anthrop.</u> 63:6 (Dec.
        1961), 1173-1192 and 65:6 (Dec. 1963), 1280-1294.

8378   ------ <u>Empire's Children: The People of Tzintzuntzan.</u> Mexico City:
        Imprenta Nuevo Mundo, 1948. 297 pp.

8379   Freedman, M., "A Note on Social Organisation in a Rural Area of Greater Djakarta," Man 60 (1960), 82-84. [Indonesia]

8380   Fried, J., "Social Organization and Personal Security in a Peruvian Hacienda Indian Community," Am. Anthrop. 64:4 (Aug. 1962), 771-780.

8381   Friedl, E., Vasilika: A Village in Modern Greece. New York: Holt, Rinehart & Winston, 1962. 110 pp.

8382   Friedrich, P., "Naranja y el mundo exterior" [Naranja and the external world], Rev. interamer. Cienc. soc. 2:3 (1963), 346-375. [Mexico]

8383   Fujiki, Michiko, "Engan Sho-gyoson ni okeru Gyogyo Keitai no Hensen to Sonraku Kōzō: Oshika-Hantō Gobuura no Jirei" [Changes in fishing methods and in village structure: A case study of Gobuura on Ojika Peninsula], Kenkyû Nempô 6 (1958), 6-8. [Japan]

8384   Fujiki, Michiko, and Hajime Fujii, "A Monograph of a Fishing Village of the Ojika Peninsula," Shakaigaku Hyôron 8:4 (1958), 85-102. In Japanese.

8385   Fukutake, Tadashi, Chukoku Nōson Shakai no Kōzō [The social structure of the Chinese farm village]. Tokyo: Daiga Dō, 1946. 507 pp.

8386   ------ "India Sonraku no Shakai Kôzô" [Social structure of the Indian village], Asia Keizai 3:8 (1962), 16-24.

8387   ------ Nihon Nōson no Shakaiteki Seikaku [The sociological character of the Japanese farm village]. Tokyo: Tokyo University Press, 1949. 298 pp.

8388   ------ Nihon Nōson Shakai no Kōzō Bunseki--Sonraku no Shakai Kōzō to Nōsei Shintō [An essay on the social structure of the Japanese farm village: A look into the social structure and government of the village]. Tokyo: Tokyo University Press, 1954. 504 pp.

8389   Fuse, T., "Sonraku Shakai Kōzō Bunseki Hōhō" [An analysis of the social structure of the Japanese village], Shakaigaku Hyôron 13:2 (Aug. 1962), 2-26.

8390   Gaitskell, A., Gezira: A Story of Development in the Sudan. London: Faber & Faber, 1959. 373 pp.

8391   Gamo, M., et al., "Aogashima no Shakai to Minzoku" [Society and folk culture of Aogashima], in GEN 4358 (1963), 13-62.

8392   Geertz, Clifford, "Form and Variation in Balinese Village Structure," Am. Anthrop. 61:5 (Oct. 1959), 991-1012. [Indonesia]

8393   ------ "Religious Belief and Economic Behavior in a Central Javanese Town: Some Preliminary Considerations," Econ. Dev. cult. Change 4:2 (Jan. 1956), 134-158. See also GEN 4359 (1963).

8394   ------ The Social Context of Economic Change: An Indonesian Case Study. Cambridge: Center for International Studies, Massachusetts Institute of Technology, 1956. 179 pp. [Indonesia] See also RUR 3004.

8395   ------ "Tihingan: A Balinese Village," Bijdr. Taal- Land- Volk. 120:1
        (1964), 1-33. [Indonesia]

8396   Gidal, S., and T. Gidal, My Village in India. New York: Pantheon,
        1956. 75 pp.

8397   Gillain, H., "Promotion du paysannat" [The rise of the peasantry],
        Arch. int. Sociol. Coop. 8 (Jan.-June 1961), 69-92. [Madagascar]

8398   Gillin, John P., Moche: A Peruvian Coastal Community. Washington:
        Smithsonian Institution, 1946. 166 pp.

8399   Goswami, M. C., "The Social Structure of an Assamese Village," Man
        Art 22 (Feb. 1954). [Indian State of Assam]

8400   Gotô, K., Nagoya-shi Shin-shiiki ni okeru Nôgyô Shûraku no Kôzô [The
        structure of agricultural villages in the suburban districts of
        Nagoya City]. Nagoya, Japan: Shiyakusho, 1959. 95 pp. [Japan]

8401   Guillard, Joanny, Golonpoui: Analyse des conditions de modernisation
        d'un village du Nord-Cameroun [Golonpoui: Analysis of the conditions
        of modernization in a village of North Cameroon]. The Hague: Mouton,
        1965. 502 pp.

8402   Gulick, J., "Conservatism and Change in a Lebanese Village," Mid. E.
        J. 8:3 (Summer 1954), 295-307.

8403   ------ "The Lebanese Village: An Introduction," Am. Anthrop. 55:3
        (Aug. 1953), 367-372.

8404   Hakoyama, K., "Koidamura-Sonraku Kyôdôtai no Suii" [Changes in the
        village community: Koida Village], Nihon Minzokugaku 19 (1961),
        21-28. [Japan]

8405   Halpern, Joel Martin, Aspects of Village Life and Culture Change in
        Laos: Special Report. New York: Council on Economic and Cultural
        Affairs, 1958. 143 pp.

8406   ------ Social and Cultural Change in a Serbian Village. New Haven:
        Human Relations Area Files Press, 1956. 619 pp. [Yugoslavia]

8407   Hansen, H. H., "Innovationsproblemet Belyst ved en Undersøgelse
        af Forholdene i en Muhammedansk Landsby på øen Bahrain i den
        Persiske Golf" [Problems of innovation in the light of field
        research on conditions in a Mohammedan village on the island of
        Bahrain in the Persian Gulf], Sociol. Meddr. 8:1 (1963), 3-27.
        [Arabian Peninsula]

8408   Hara, H., "Tsushima Sonraku Shakai Kōzō no Shō-danmen" [Brief report
        of village social structure on Tsushima Island], Orio Koto Gakko
        Kiyô 3 (1959), 29-44. [Japan]

8409   Harrison-Church, R. J., "Port Etienne: A Mauritanian Pioneer Town,"
        Geogr. J. 128:4 (Dec. 1962), 498-504.

8410   Hart, Donn V., Barrio Caticugan: A Visayan Filipino Community. Ann

Arbor, Mich.:   University Microfilms, 1954.   769 mim. pp.

8411   Heeren, H. J., "The Indonesian Village: Its Change and Future,"
        Civilisations 3 (1953), 853-914.

8412   Herskovits, Melville J., Life in a Haitian Valley. New York:
        Octagon Books, 1937. 350 pp.

8413   Hogbin, H. Ian, Transformation Scene: The Changing Culture of a New
        Guinea Village. London: Routledge & Kegan Paul, 1951.   326 pp.

8414   Honigmann, John J., Three Pakistani Villages. Chapel Hill: Institute
        for Research in Social Science, University of North Carolina, 1958.

8415   Horne, B. C., Un ensayo social agrario: La colonia San José, Entre
        Ríos, 1857-1957, con una introducción sobre el estado actual del
        problema agrario y dos estudios de sociología rural [A social
        agrarian experiment: The San José Settlement, Entre Ríos, 1857-1957,
        with an introduction to the present state of the agrarian problem and
        some rural sociological studies]. Buenos Aires: Ediciones Leviatán,
        1957. 142 pp. [Argentina]

8416   Hoshino, H., "Hibikinada-shima no Shakai Kôzô" [A study of the social
        structure in the Hibikinada Island villages], Shakaigaku Hyôron 13:4
        (1963), 82-137. [Japan]

8417   Huizer, G., "Some Observations on a Central American Village,"
        Amér. indíg. 23:3 (July-Sept. 1963), 211-224. [San Salvador]

8418   Huke, R., "Maloco: A Representative Aklan Barrio," Philipp. sociol.
        Rev. 4:2-3 (Apr.-July 1956), 23-29. [Philippines]

8419   Ishihara, J., "Mura no naka no sho-shudan ni tsuite" [On small
        communal groups in the village], Jinbun Chiri 16:2 (1964), 102-110.
        [Japan]

8420   Ishwaran, K., Tradition and Economy in Village India. London: Rout-
        ledge & Kegan Paul, 1966. 169 pp.

8421   Isoda, S., Sonraku Kōzō no Kenkyū--Tokushima-Ken Kiyahira-Mura [Study
        of a village structure: Tokushima Prefecture, Kiyahira-Mura]. Tokyo:
        Tokyo Daigaku Syuppankai, 1955. 305 pp. [Japan]

8422   Izard-Heritier, F., and M. Izard, Bouna: Monographie d'un village
        Pana de la Vallée du Sourou (Haute-Volta) [Bouna: Monograph on a
        Pana village in the Sourou Valley (Upper Volta)]. Bordeaux:
        Institut des Sciences Humaines Appliquées de l'Université de Bordeaux,
        1958. 184 pp. [Upper Volta]

8423   Jaulin, R., "Note sur Marabé, le village Mara" [Note on Marabe, the
        village of Mara], Cah. Etud. afr. 4:4 (Dec. 1960), 85-98. [Chad]

8424   John, P. V., and Lal Chand Gupta, "A Comparative Study of Some
        Aspects of the Levels of Living in Two Villages [in Madhya Pradesh],"
        Indian J. agric. Econ. 18 (Jan. 1963), 324-327.

8425   Kapferer, Bruce, Co-operation, Leadership, and Village Structure: A
        Preliminary Economic and Political Study of Ten Bisa Villages in the
        Northern Province of Zambia. Manchester, England: Manchester Uni-
        versity Press, 1967. 77 pp.

8426   Karve, Irawati, and Yashwant Bhaskar Damle, Group Relations in a
        Village Community. Poona, India: Deccan College Post-graduate and
        Research Institute, 1963. 483 pp. [India]

8427   Katiyar, T. S., Social Life in Rajasthan: A Case Study. Allahabad,
        India: Kitab Mahal, 1964. 127 pp.

8428   Kattenburg, Paul M., A Central Javanese Village in 1950. Ithaca:
        Southeast Asia Program, Cornell University, 1951. 17 pp. [Indonesia]

8429   Kaufman, Howard K., Village Life in Vientiane Province, 1956-57. Los
        Angeles: University of California Press, 1958. 82 pp. [Laos]

8430   Kaut, Charles, "Process and Social Structure in a Philippine Lowland
        Settlement," in GEN 4371 (1960), 35-50.

8431   Kawagoe, J., "Shima Gyoson no Kenkyu-1-" [Study of a fishing community
        in the Shima Peninsula-I], Aichidaigaku Ronsô 27 (1964), 1-20.
        [Japan]

8432   Kawamura, N., and O. Hasumi, "Kindai Nihon ni okeru Sonraku Kōzō
        no Tenkai-katei" [The process of development of the village struc-
        ture in modern Japan], Shisō 407 (1958), 55-73, and 408 (1958),
        87-102.

8433   Khare, R. S., "Group Dynamics in a North Indian Village," Hum.
        Organiz. 21:3 (Fall 1962), 201-213. [India]

8434   Kiba, S., "Un village de Haute-Volta" [A village of Upper-Volta],
        Rev. Action pop. 39 (June 1960), 757-766.

8435   Kitahara, Machiko, "A Report on Nakayama Village, Shiga Prefecture:
        An Instance of Dual System," Shiron 4 (1956), 223-238. [Japan]

8436   Kitamura, T., "Hatasaku, Raku-Nōson no Shakai Kōzō" [The social
        structure of a dry-farming and dairy village], Hokkaidō Gakugei
        Daigaku Kiyō 9:1 (1958), 137-144. [Japan]

8437   ------ "Sengo Kaitaku Hekichi no Shakai Kōzō" [The social structure
        of a remote postwar rehabilitated village], Hekichi Kyoiku Kenkyû
        6:3 (1959), 22-38. [Japan]

8438   Konig, R., "Eine Gemeindestudie aus der Turkei" [Study of a Turkish
        community], Kölner Z. Soziol. Sozialps. 7:4 (1955), 601-610.

8439   Kostić, C., "Changement de structure du village en Yougoslavie"
        [Change in the structure of the village in Yugoslavia], Cah. int.
        Sociol. 23 (July-Dec. 1957), 142-156.

8440   Krishnamurthy, L., "Pathikonda: A Study of the Social Structure of
        a Backward Village," All India Congr. Comm. econ. Rev. 13 (7 Oct.
        1961), 16-22. [India]

8441   Kuchira, Masuo, "A Typology of Desa: A Comparative Study of Village
       Structure and Leadership in Java, 1954-1955." M.A. thesis, Cornell
       University, 1962. 147 mim. pp. [Indonesia]

8442   Le Blanc, C., "Un village de la vallée du Sénégal: Amadi-Ounaré"
       [A village in the Senegal valley: Amadi-Ounaré], Cah. d'outre-mer
       17:66 (Apr.-June 1964), 117-148.

8443   Lewis, Oscar, "La cultura campesina en la India y en México.
       Análisis comparativo" [Peasant society in India and in Mexico: A
       comparative analysis], Cienc. polít. soc. 6:34 (Aug. 1955), 194-218.
       [Indian State of Uttar Pradesh; Mexico]

8444   Leynaud, E., "Ligwa, un village Zande de la RCA" [Ligwa, a Zande
       village of the Central African Republic], Cah. Etud. afr. 3:3 (1963),
       318-390. [Central African Republic]

8445   Lindstrom, D. E., Community Development in Seki-Mura. Urbana:
       Department of Agricultural Economics, College of Agriculture, Univer-
       sity of Illinois, 1960. 92 pp. [Japan]

8446   Loomis, Charles P., et al. (eds.), Turrialba: Social Systems and the
       Introduction of Change. Glencoe, Ill.: Free Press, 1953. 288 pp.
       [Costa Rica]

8447   Lubin, M. A., "Quelques aspects des communautés rurales d'Haïti"
       [Some aspects of rural communities in Haiti], Bull. Amér. lat. 5:1-2
       (Jan.-June 1962), 3-22.

8448   Lux, Thomas E., "Mango Village: Northeastern Thai Social Organization,
       Ethos, and Factionalism." M.A. thesis, University of Chicago, 1962.
       114 mim. pp. [Thailand]

8449   McCormack, William C., "Changing Leadership of a Mysore Village."
       Ph.D. dissertation, University of Chicago, 1956. [Indian State of
       Mysore]

8450   McCurdy, David Whitwell, "A Bhil Village of Rajasthan." Ph.D.
       dissertation, Cornell University, 1964. 510 mim. pp. [Indian State
       of Rajasthan]

8451   Majumdar, D. N., "A Little Community," Indian Sociol. 1:1 (1956-
       1957), 1-9. [Indian State of Uttar Pradesh]

8452   Makal, Mahmut, A Village in Anatolia. London: Vallentine, Mitchell,
       1954. 190 pp. [Turkey]

8453   Malhotra, S. P., "Socio-economic Differences of Population Inhabiting
       an Arid and Semi-arid Tract of Western Rajasthan," J. soc. Res. 7:1-2
       (Mar.-Sept. 1964), 87-103. [Indian State of Rajasthan]

8454   Mallart, J., "Un exemple des implications sociales du progrès
       technique" [An example of the social implications of technical
       progress], Trav. hum. 20:3-4 (July-Dec. 1957), 305-312.

8455   Mandal, G. C., and Sunil C. Sengupta, A Report on Re-Survey of a
       Village. Santiniketan, India: Agro-Economic Research Centre,

Visva-Bharati, 1962. 104 pp. [India]

8456   Mandelbaum, D. G., "Technology, Credit and Culture in an Indian
         Village," Econ. Wkly. 4:32-33 (15 Aug. 1952), 827-828. [Indian State
         of Kerela]

8457   Manndorff, H., "Sozialökonomische Struktur und Kulturwandel in
         Südindischen Dorfern" [Socioeconomic structure and cultural change in
         South Indian villages], Sociologus 5:2 (1955), 157-178.

8458   Maretzki, Thomas W., and Hatsumi Maretzki, Taira: An Okinawan Village.
         New York: John Wiley & Sons, 1966. 176 pp.

8459   Marriott, McKim, "Social Change in an Indian Village," Econ. Dev.
         cult. Change 1:2 (June 1952), 144-155. [Indian State of Uttar
         Pradesh]

8460   Mason, L., "Kili Community in Transition," S. Pacif. Comm. quart.
         Bull. 8:2 (Apr. 1958), 32-35ff. [Melanesia]

8461   Mathur, Kripa Shanker, Caste and Ritual in a Malwa Village. London:
         Asia Publishing House, 1964. 215 pp. [India]

8462   ------ "Occupational Structure of a Malwa Village," East. Anthrop.
         12 (1960). [India]

8463   Mayer, Adrian C., "Change in a Malwa Village," Econ. Wkly. 7:39
         (24 Sept. 1955), 1147-1149. [India]

8464   Mann, Harold Hart, Land and Labour in a Deccan Village. Bombay:
         Oxford University Press, 1917. 184 pp. [Indian State of Andhra]
         See RUR 8364 (1960).

8465   Mann, H. H., and N. V. Kanitkar, Land and Labour in a Deccan Village:
         Study No. 2. Bombay: Oxford University Press, 1921. 182 pp.
         [Indian State of Andhra]

8466   Meenakshi Malaya, M., "Pallipuram: A Suburban Village in Kerela,"
         All India Congr. Comm. econ. Rev. 13 (7 Aug. 1963), 19-24. [Indian
         State of Kerela]

8467   Mencher, Joan P., "Growing Up in South Malabar," Hum. Organiz. 22:1
         (Spring 1963), 54-65. [Indian State of Kerela]

8468   Menicías Chávez, J., Riobama, Ecuador; Estudio de la elevación socio-
         cultural y religiosa del Indio [Riobama, Ecuador: A study of the
         sociocultural and religious advancement of the Indian]. Fribourg,
         Switzerland: Oficina Internacional de Investigaciones Sociales de
         la Fédération Européenne de Recherche Economique et Sociale, 1962.
         154 pp.

8469   Miller, Eric J., "Village Structure in North Kerela," in GEN 4386
         (1960), 42-55. [Indian State of Kerela]

8470   Miller, W. C., "Hosseinabad: A Persian Village," Mid. E. J. 18:4
         (Autumn 1964), 483-498. [Iran]

8471   Misra, Bidyadhar, L. K. Pati, and A. K. Mitra, "A Study of Levels of
        Living in a Village in Orissa," Indian J. agric. Econ. 18:1 (Jan.
        1963), 333-340. [Indian State of Orissa]

8472   Mitsuyoshi, T., "India Sonraku Kenkyû" [A study of the Indian village],
        Shakaigaku Hyôron 12:1 (1961), 105-115.

8473   Miyagi, H., "Gendai India no Sonraku to Caste Sei" [The modern Indian
        village and caste], Soshioroji 8:2 (1960), 1-28.

8474   Miyamoto, T., "Tsushima Tsutsu no Sonraku-kōzō" [The village structure
        of Tsutsu of Tsushima Island], Nihon Minzokugaku 7 (July 1959), 1-13;
        8 (Aug. 1959), 1-9; 9 (Oct. 1959), 37-47. [Japan]

8475   Mizoguchi, Y., "Tahichi-tō ni okeru Shoki no Bunka-sesshoku-henrdō"
        [The early stage of acculturation in Tahiti], Kôbe Jyogakuin Daigaku
        Ronshû 3:3 (Feb. 1957), 75-92.

8476   ------ "Hiji-shotō ni okeru Shoki no Bunka-sesshoku-hendō" [The early
        stage of acculturation in the Fiji Islands], Kôbe Jyogakuin Daigaku
        Ronshû 4:1 (June 1957), 1-19.

8477   Modjtabawi, Ak Akbar, Gesellschaft und Wirtschaft in Manutschehrabad:
        Studie über eine junge Dorfgemeinschaft in Luristan (Südwest-Iran)
        [The society and economy of Manuchehrabad: A study of a new village
        in Lauristan, Southwest Iran]. Cologne, W. Germany: Cologne Univer-
        sity, 1961. 146 pp. [Iran]

8478   Moerman, Michael H., A Memorandum: A Northern Thai Village. Bangkok:
        Regional Research Office, United States Information Service, 1961.
        19 mim. pp. [Thailand]

8479   Morrill, W. T., "Socio-Cultural Adaptation in a West African Lebanese
        Community," Anthrop. Quart. 35:4 (Oct. 1962), 143-157.

8480   Morris, H. S., Report on a Melanau Sago Producing Community in
        Sarawak. London: HMSO, 1953. 184 pp. [Malaysia]

8481   Mukherjee, Ramkrishna, "The Economic Structure and Social Life in
        Six Villages of Bengal," Am. sociol. Rev. 14:3 (June 1949), 415-425.
        [Indian State of West Bengal]

8482   Muratake, S., et al., "Izu Niijima Wakago no Shakai Soshiki" [Social
        organization of a fishing village: Niijima Island, Izu Province,
        Japan], Minzokugaku Kenkyû 22:3-4 (1959), 48-88. [Japan]

8483   Muthiah, C., "Levels of Living in Four Villages of Rural Bhopal,"
        Indian J. agric. Econ. 18:1 (Jan. 1963), 327-333. [Indian State of
        Madhya Pradesh]

8484   Najafi, Najmeh, Reveille for a Persian Village. London: Gollancz,
        1958. 273 pp. [Iran]

8485   Nakada, E., "Sanson no Henbô" [The transformation of a mountain
        village. An example from the Chichibu district], Shien 23:2 (1963),
        38-58. [Japan]

8486   Nakamura, M., "Higonokuni Amakusa-tô ni okeru Gyoson no Sôritsu to
        Tenkai" [Formation and development of the fishing villages in the
        Amakusa Islands of Higo Province], Kyûshû Daigaku Ronbunshû 8:9
        (1961), 143-162. [Japan]

8487   Nakano, T., "Gyogyô e peguru Sonraku Shakai no Henka" [The process
        of change in a fishing community], Jinrui Kagaku 15 (1963), 292-318.
        [Japan]

8488   Nanavati, Manilal Balabhai, Fifty Years of Co-operation in Kodinar
        Taluka: A Case Study. Bombay: Indian Society of Agricultural
        Economics, 1964. 37 pp. [Indian State of Gujarat]

8489   ------ "A Village in Gujarat: A Study," Indian J. agric. Econ. 16:2
        (Apr. 1961), 1-11. [Indian State of Gujarat]

8490   Nath, Y. V. S., "Bhils of Ratanmal: An Analysis of the Social Struc-
        ture of a West Indian Community." M.S. thesis, University of Baroda,
        1960. 229 mim. pp. [Indian State of Maharashtra]

8491   Newell, William Harc, "Goshen: A Gaddi Village in the Himalayas," in
        GEN 4386 (1960), 56-67. [Indian State of Uttar Pradesh]

8492   Newnham, T. O., Lake Village in Cambodia. Melbourne, Australia:
        Longmans, 1965. 23 pp.

8493   ------ South Indian Village. Melbourne, Australia: Longmans, 1965.
        22 pp.

8494   Niangoran-Bouah, G., "Le village Abouré" [The village of Abouré],
        Cah. Etud. afr. 1:2 (May 1960), 113-127. [Ivory Coast]

8495   Nicholas, Ralph W., "Ecology and Village Structure in Deltaic West
        Bengal," Econ. Wkly. 15:28-30 (July 1963), 1185-1186ff.

8496   Nicolas, G., "Un village Bouzou du Niger. Etude d'un terroir" [A
        Bouzou village of Niger: An area study], Cah. d'outre-mer 15:58
        (Apr.-June 1962), 138-165.

8497   ------ "Un village Haoussa de la République de Niger: Tassao-
        Hassoua" [A Haoussa village of the Republic of Niger: Tassao-
        Hassoua], Cah. d'outre-mer 13:52 (Oct.-Dec. 1960), 421-450.

8498   Nihon University, Department of Sociology, Sonraku Shakai no Jittai:
        Izu Ihama oyobi Inazusa Chiku Ochiai no Chôsa [A Japanese village
        community in Izu Peninsula]. Tokyo: Nihon University Press, 1961.
        54 pp. [Japan]

8499   Nitisastro, W., and J. E. Ismael, The Government, Economy, and Taxes
        of a Central Javanese Village. Ithaca: Southeast Asia Program,
        Cornell University, 1959. 37 pp. [Indonesia]

8500   Nyce, Ray, The New Villages of Malaya: A Community Study. Hartford,
        Conn.: Hartford Seminary, 1962. 437 mim. pp. [Malaysia]

8501   Nydegger, William F., and Corinne Nydegger, Tarong: An Ilocos

Barrio in the Philippines. New York: John Wiley & Sons, 1966.
180 pp.

8502   Oberg, K., "Aspectos sociais da vida do pescador de Surinam" [Social
        aspects of the life of a Surinam fisherman], Sociologia 23:3 (Sept.
        1961), 239-251. [British Caribbean]

8503   Opler, Marris E., "Technological Change and Social Organization in a
        Village of North India," Anthrop. Quart. 32:3 (July 1959), 127-133.
        [Indian State of Uttar Pradesh]

8504   ------ "The Extensions of an Indian Village," J. Asian Stud. 16:1
        (Nov. 1956), 5-9. [Indian State of Uttar Pradesh]

8505   Opler, M. E., and Rudra Dutt Singh, "Economic, Political and Social
        Change in a Village in North Central India," Hum. Organiz. 2:2
        (Summer 1952), 5-12. [Indian State of Uttar Pradesh]

8506   ------ "Two Villages in Eastern Uttar Pradesh, India: An Analysis
        of Similarities and Differences," Am. Anthrop. 54:2 (Apr. 1952),
        179-190.

8507   Osgood, C., Village Life in Old China; A Community Study of Kao Yao,
        Yunnan. New York: Ronald Press, 1963. 401 pp.

8508   Pandey, H. N., "Social Interaction in a Bastar Village," Vanyajati 10
        (Jan. and Apr. 1962), 17-23; 54-60. [India]

8509   Paques, V., "Technique et religion dans un village du Soudan" [Tech-
        nology and religion in a village of the Sudan], Prod. fr. 19-20
        (July-Aug. 1953), 44-47. [Chad]

8510   Pareek, Udai, and T. K. Moulik, "Sociometric Study of a North Indian
        Village," Int. J. Sociom. Sociat. 3 (Mar.-June 1963), 6-17. [India]

8511   Park, Joon, "Hasin Village," in GEN 4357 (1958), 25 pp.
        [Korea]

8512   Parker, S., "Ethnic Identity and Acculturation in Two Eskimo
        Villages," Am. Anthrop. 66:2 (Apr. 1964), 325-340.

8513   Parsons, Elsie Clews, Mitla, Town of the Souls. Chicago: University
        of Chicago Press, 1936. 590 pp. [Mexico]

8514   Parthasarathy, G., "A South Indian Village after Two Decades:
        Vadamalaipuram," Econ. Wkly. 15:2 (12 Jan. 1963), 49-55.

8515   Patel, S. D., "Rural Community of South Gujarat," J. Gujarat Res.
        Soc. 27 (Jan. 1965), 52-62.

8516   Pereira de Queiroz, M. I., "De l'organisation des petites communes
        brésiliennes" [On the organization of small Brazilian communities],
        Cah. int. Sociol. 28 (Jan.-June 1960), 159-173.

8517   Peters, Emrys L., "Aspects of Rank and Status among Muslims in a
        Lebanese Village," in GEN 4364 (1963), 159-200.

8518   Pierce, J. E., _Life in a Turkish Village_. New York: Holt, Rinehart
        & Winston, 1964. 102 pp.

8519   Pierson, D., _Cruz das Almas: A Brazilian Village_. Washington: U.S.
        Government Printing Office, 1951. 226 pp.

8520   ------ "Life in a Brazilian Village," in GEN 4307 (1964), 249-259.

8521   Pittman, G. P., _Village India_. London: Marshall, Morgan & Scott,
        1951. 158 pp.

8522   Planck, U., _Die sozialen und ökonomischen Verhältnisse in einem
        iranischen Dorf_ [Social and economic relations in an Iranian village].
        Cologne, W. Germany: Westdeutscher Verlag, 1962. 135 pp.

8523   Plummer, John Frederick, "Oya, a Village of Northeast Japan." Ph.D.
        dissertation, University of Michigan, 1963. 318 mim. pp.

8524   Polson, Robert A., and Agaton P. Pal, "The Influence of Isolation on
        the Acceptance of Technological Changes in the Dumaguete City Trade
        Area, Philippines," _Silliman J_. 2 (1956), 149-159.

8525   ------ The Status of Rural Life in the Dumaguete City Trade Area,
        Philippines, 1952. Ithaca: Southeast Asia Program, Cornell Univer-
        sity, 1956. 108 pp.

8526   Potter, Jack Michael, "P'ing Shan: The Changing Economy of a Chinese
        Village in Hong Kong." Ph.D. dissertation, University of California,
        1964. 401 mim. pp.

8527   Pozas, R., _Chamula, un pueblo indio de Los Altos de Chiapas_ [Chamula,
        an Indian village in Los Altos de Chiapas]. Mexico City: Ediciones
        del Instituto Nacional Indigenista, 1959. 207 pp. [Mexico]

8528   Quain, Buell Halvor, _Fijian Village_. Chicago: University of Chicago
        Press, 1948. 459 pp.

8529   Qubain, F. I., "Social Classes and Tensions in Bahrain," _Mid. E. J._
        9:3 (Summer 1955), 269-280. [Arabian Peninsula]

8530   Rajapurohit, A. R., "Business Organization, Caste and Technical
        Change in a Fishing Community," _Artha Vijnana_ 5 (June 1963), 112-131.
        [India]

8531   Ravault, F., "Kanel: L'exode rural dans un village de la vallée du
        Sénégal" [Kanel: The rural exodus in a village in the Senegal
        Valley], _Cah. d'outre-mer_ 17:65 (Jan.-Mar. 1964), 58-80.

8532   Raynal, R., "La terre et l'homme en Haute Moulouya: Quelques
        exemples d'évolution récente des genres de vie" [Land and man in
        Upper Moulouya: Some examples of recent evolution in ways of
        living], _Hesperis_ 39:3-4 (1952), 487-500. [Morocco]

8533   Redfield, Robert, _A Village That Chose Progress: Chan Kom Revisited_.
        Chicago: Chicago University Press, 1950. 187 pp. [Mexico] See
        RUR 8044.

8534   Redfield, R., and Alfonso Villa Rojas, Chan Kom: A Maya Village.
        Washington: Carnegie Institute Publications, 1934. 387 pp. [Mexico]

8535   Reina, Ruben E., Continuidad de la cultura indígena en una comunidad
        Guatemalteca [Continuity of native culture in a Guatemalan community].
        Guatemala: Editorial del Ministerio de Educación Publica "José de
        Pineda Ibarra," 1959. 28 pp. Also in Rev. Cienc. soc. 2:2 (June
        1958). See RUR 8079.

8536   Rhodesia, Northern, Report on Intensive Rural Development in the
        Northern and Luapula Provinces of Northern Rhodesia, 1957-1961.
        Lusaka, Zambia: Government of Northern Rhodesia, 1961. 42 pp.

8537   Richardson, E. M., Aushi Village Structure in the Fort Rosebery
        District of Northern Rhodesia. Lusaka, Zambia: Rhodes-Livingstone
        Institute, 1951. 36 mim. pp.

8538   Ritzenthaler, Robert E., and P. Ritzenthaler, Cameroons Village: An
        Ethnography of the Bafut. Milwaukee, Wis.: Public Museum, 1962.
        147 pp.

8539   Rosenfeld, H., "Social Change in an Arab Village," New Outlook 2:6
        (Feb. 1959), 37-42 and 2:7 (Mar.-Apr. 1959), 14-23. [Near East]

8540   Rosser, Colin A., "Hermit Village in Kulu," in GEN 4386 (1960),
        77-89. [India]

8541   Rovillois-Brigol, Madeleine, "La sédentarisation autour d'Ouargla"
        [Sedentation around Ouargla], in GEN 4392 (1963), 135-142.
        [Algeria]

8542   Ryan, B., and C. Arulgragasam, "The Agricultural System of a Ceylon
        Jungle Village," East. Anthrop. 8:3-4 (Mar.-Aug. 1955), 151-160.

8543   Sabogal Wiesse, J. R., "La comunidad andina de Pucara" [The Andean
        community of Pucara], Amér. indíg. 21:1 (Jan. 1961), 39-42. [Peru]

8544   Saffa, Samir, "Exploitation économique et agricole d'un domaine rural
        égyptien" [The economic and agricultural exploitation of a rural
        Egyptian estate], Egypte contemp. 40:251-252 (Apr.-May 1949), 277-
        452.

8545   Saito, H., Donan Gyōson no Kōzō to Hensen [Structure and transfor-
        mation in a fishing village in Southern Hokkaido]. Sapporo, Japan:
        Hokkaido kaihatsu kyoku, 1956. 137 pp. [Japan]

8546   Saito, Hyoichi, "The Sociology of a Fishing Community," Shakaigaku
        Hyôron 5 (Mar.-Apr. 1955), 1-22, 33-54. [Japan] In Japanese.

8547   Sakamoto, T., "Indo Nōson-Shakai Kindai-ka no Katei" [Modernization
        of rural societies in Coorg and Malabar, South India], Nōgyo Sōgō
        Kenkyū 9:2 (Apr. 1955), 233-304. [Indian State of Kerela]

8548   Sanders, Irwin T., Balkan Village. Lexington: University of
        Kentucky Press, 1949. 291 pp. [Bulgaria]

8549   Sarker, Subhash Chandra, "Stability and Change in Rural Life: Village
        Survey Findings," Mod. Rev. 116 (Oct. 1964), 277-283. [India]

8550   Saxena, J. C., "Profile of a Village in a Semi-Arid Part of
        Rajasthan," East. Anthrop. 17:1 (Jan. 1964), 49-61.

8551   Seki, K., Kaihatsu Jigyo Koka no Sokute ni Kansuru Kenkyu [Pilot farm
        construction and change in the local community]. Hokkaido, Japan:
        Kaihatsukyoku, 1959. 95 pp. [Japan]

8552   ------   "Kaitaku Shūraku no Shakai Kôzô to Kazoku Ruikê" [Social
        structure and family patterns in an agricultural community],
        Shakaigaku Hyôron 13:4 (1963), 2-22. [Japan]

8553   Sengupta, Sunil C., "Levels of Living in Three Villages of West
        Bengal: A Cross-Sectional Study," Indian J. agric. Econ. 18:1 (Jan.
        1963), 278-287.

8554   Sharp, Lauriston, and Robert J. Smith, "Strategy of Research in Longi-
        tudinal Community Studies: The Case of a Thai Rice Village," Asian
        Cult. 2:2 (Apr.-June 1960), 133-145.

8555   Shimamoto, A., "Shima Gyôson Hamajima ni okeru Gyôgyô Seisan Kôzô no
        Henyo" [Change in fishing villages: A study of Hamajima in the Shima
        Peninsula], Aichidaigaku Ronsô 27 (1964), 21-58. [Japan]

8556   Shimamoto, H., "India Sonraku no Shakai Kōzō to Sonmin no Kachi Shikō
        ni tsuite no Oboegaki" [A note on the social structure and value
        orientation of Indian villages], Aichi Daigaku Kiyō 28 (1959),
        53-68.

8557   Sibley, Willis E., "Social Structures and Planned Change: A Case
        Study from the Philippines," Hum. Organiz. 19:2 (Summer 1960),
        9-211.

8558   Singer, Milton B., M. E. Opler, R. D. Singh, and S. C. Dube, "The
        Indian Village: A Symposium," J. Asian Stud. 16:1 (Nov. 1956),
        3-30.

8559   Singh, Indra P., "A Sikh Village," J. Am. Folkl. 7 (July-Sept.
        1958), 479-503. [Indian State of Punjab]

8560   ------ "A Sikh Village," in GEN 4379 (1959), 273-297. [Indian State
        of Punjab]

8561   Singh, R. D., "The Unity of an Indian Village," J. Asian Stud. 16:1
        (Nov. 1956), 10-18. [Indian State of Punjab]

8562   Slater, Gilbert (ed.), Some South Indian Villages. Madras: Oxford
        University Press, 1918. 265 pp.

8563   Smith, Marion W., "The Misal: A Structural Village Group of India
        and Pakistan," Am. Anthrop. 54:1 (Feb. 1952), 41-56. [Indian State
        of West Bengal; East Pakistan]

8564   ------ "Social Structure in the Punjab," in GEN 4386 (1960), 161-179.

8565   ------ "Village Notes from Bengal," Am. Anthrop. 48:4 (Aug. 1946), 574-592.

8566   Smith, Michael G., "Community Organization in Rural Jamaica," Soc. econ. Stud. 5:3 (Sept. 1956), 295-312.

8567   Smith, R. J., and E. P. Reyes, "Community Interrelations with the Outside World: The Case of a Japanese Agricultural Community," Am. Anthrop. 59:3 (June 1957), 463-472.

8568   Smith, Robert J., "A Comparative Study of the Shift in Six Selected Villages from Economic Self-Sufficiency to Dependence on the Larger Unit." M.A. thesis, Cornell University, 1951. [Japan]

8569   ------ "The Japanese Rural Community: Norms, Sanctions and Ostracism," Am. Anthrop. 63:3 (June 1961), 522-533.

8570   Smith, William Charles, "The People of La Pacenda: Social Organization and Social Change in a Tarascan Village." Ph.D. dissertation, University of California (Berkeley), 1965. [Mexico]

8571   Smyly, William J., "Tsuen Wan Township," Far E. econ. Rev. 33 (1961), 395-421. [T'aiwan]

8572   Soares, Rebelo, D. J., "Breves apontamentos sobre um grupo de Indianos em Moçambique. A comunidade ismailia maometana" [Brief notes on a group of Indians in Mozambique: An Ismailian Mohammedan community], Bol. Soc. Estud. Moçambique 30:128 (July-Sept. 1961), 83-91.

8573   Srinivas, M. N., "The Social Structure of a Mysore Village," in GEN 4386 (1960), 21-35.

8574   ------ "The Social System of a Mysore Village," in GEN 4353 (1955), 1-35.

8575   Sternberg-Sarel, B., "Les oasis de Djerid" [The oases of Djerid], Cah. int. Sociol. 30 (1961), 131-145. [Tunisia]

8576   Stirling, Paul, "The Domestic Cycle and the Distribution of Power in Turkish Villages," in GEN 4364 (1963), 201-216.

8577   Sweet, Louise E., Tell Toqaan: A Syrian Village. Ann Arbor: University of Michigan Press, 1960. 280 pp.

8578   Takeda, T., "Mura' ni okeru kyôdôtaiteki kôzô no Hen'i" [Change of community structure in the village], Kyôdôtai No Hikaku Kenkyû 1 (1964), 1-8. [Japan]

8579   Tannous, A. I., "Emigration: A Force of Social Change in an Arab Village," Rur. Sociol. 7:1 (Mar. 1942), 62-74. [Lebanon]

8580   ------ "Social Change in an Arab Village," Am. sociol. Rev. 6:5 (Oct. 1941), 650-662. [Lebanon]

8581   Tonegawa, M., "Sanson ni okeru Sonraku Shakai no Tenkai Katei"

[Village structure in a mountain area], <u>Shakai Kagaku Kenkyū</u> 16 (1959), 41-58. [Japan]

8582   Thomas, Parakunnel Joseph, and K. R. Ramakrishnan, <u>Some South Indian Villages: A Resurvey</u>. Madras: University of Madras Press, 1940. 460 pp.

8583   Toupet, C., "Agrarian and Social Transformations in the Tamourt Valley, Mauretania," <u>Malayan J. trop. Geogr.</u> 8 (1956), 82-86.

8584   Tripathi, C. B., "Some Notes on a Central Javanese Village," <u>East. Anthrop.</u> 10:3-4 (Mar.-May; June-Aug. 1957), 155-172. [Indonesia]

8585   Trujillo Ferrari, Alfonso, "Lunahuana: Una comunidad Yunga en el Peru" [Lunahuana: A Yunga community in Peru], <u>Rev. Mus. nac.</u> 21 (1952), 197-296.

8586   ------ "Situação actual dos Kiriri de Porto Real do Colegio" [The present situation of the Kiriri of Porto Real of Colegio], <u>Sociologia</u> 19:1 (1957), 17-35. [Brazil]

8587   Ullah, Inayat, "Caste, Patti and Faction in the Life of a Punjab Village," <u>Sociologus</u> 8 (1958), 170-186.

8588   Ushiomi, Toshitaka, <u>Forestry and Mountain Village Communities in Japan: A Study of Human Relations</u>. Tokyo: Kokusai Bunka Shinkokai, 1964. 107 pp.

8589   Van Nieuwenjuijze, C. A. O., "The Near Eastern Village: A Profile," <u>Mid. E. J.</u> 16:3 (Summer 1962), 295-308.

8590   Vasquez, M. C., "Cambios en la estratificación social en una hacienda andina del Peru" [Changes in the social stratification of an Andean farm in Peru], <u>Peru indíg.</u> 6:14-15 (1957), 67-87. See also <u>Rev. Mus. nac.</u> 24 (1955), 190-209.

8591   Vyas, K. C., "Avidha: A Narration of Changing Life in a Gujarat Village," <u>Sociol. Bull.</u> 2:1 (Mar. 1953), 19-34.

8592   Wagley, Charles, <u>The Social and Religious Life of a Guatemalan Village.</u> Menasha, Wis.: American Anthropological Association, 1949. 150 pp.

8593   Weingrod, A., "Change and Continuity in a Moroccan Immigrant Village in Israel," <u>Mid. E. J.</u> 14:3 (Summer 1960), 277-291.

8594   ------ "Reciprocal Change: A Case Study of a Moroccan Immigrant Village in Israel," <u>Am. Anthrop.</u> 64:1, Pt. 1 (Feb. 1962), 115-131.

8595   Westphal-Hellbusch, S., "Einige Nomadengruppen West-Pakistans in der Anpassung an die moderne Zeit" [Some nomadic groups of West Pakistan in their adapting to modern times], <u>Sociologus</u> 12:2 (1962), 97-112.

8596   Wikkramatileke, R., "Hambegamuwa Village: An Example of Rural Settlement in Ceylon's Dry Zone," <u>Econ. Geogr.</u> 33:4 (Oct. 1957), 362-373.

8597   ------ "Trends in Settlement and Economic Development in Eastern
        Malaya: A Study of Mukims Padang Endau and Triang," Pacif. View-
        point 3:1 (Mar. 1962), 27-50. [Malaysia]

8598   Wilson, Monica H., et al., Keiskammahoek Rural Survey. Vol. 3, Social
        Structure. Pietermaritzburg, Union of South Africa: Shuter &
        Shooter, 1952. 220 pp. [Republic of South Africa]

8599   Wiser, Charlotte, Behind Mud Walls, 1930-1960. Berkeley: University
        of California Press, 1963. 249 pp. [India]

8600   Wiser, William Henricks, The Hindu Jajmani System: A Socio-economic
        System Interrelating Members of a Hindu Village Community in
        Services. 2nd ed. Lucknow: Lucknow Publishing House, 1958.
        160 pp. [India]

8601   ------ "Social Institutions of a Hindu Village in North India." Ph.D.
        dissertation, Cornell University, 1933.

8602   Yamamoto, N., and R. Nakajima, "Mikaihô Buraku no Seikatsu Kôzô" [Life
        structure in the village of Mikaihô], Jimbun Kenkyû 12:10 (1961),
        1-86. [Japan]

8603   Yamaoka, Euchi, "Gyoson-Shakai no Henbō-Katei" [The process of trans-
        formation of fishing villages], Shimane Daigaku Ronshū 1 (Feb. 1955),
        91-111. [Japan]

8604   ------ "Gyoson no Shakai Kêzaishi-teki Kenkyû: Ooura no Baai" [Socio-
        economic research in a fishing village: A case study of Oura],
        Shimane Kiyô 4 (1963), 1-34. [Japan]

8605   ------ Sanin Nôson no Shakai Kôzô [The social structure of rural
        society in the Sanin District]. Tokyo: Todai Shuppankai, 1959.
        400 pp. [Japan]

8606   Yang, C. K., A Chinese Village in Early Communist Transition.
        Cambridge, Mass.: Harvard University Press, 1959. 284 pp.

8607   Yang, Martin C., A Chinese Village: Taitou, Shantung Province. New
        York: Columbia University Press, 1947. 275 pp.

8608   Yatsushiro, Toshio, "Some Aspects of Village Life in Northeast Thai-
        land," Comm. Dev. Bull. 3:8 (Aug. 1964), 1-34. In Thai and English.

8609   Yoon, Eul Byung, "Naejongja," in GEN 4357 (1958), 19 pp.
        [Korea]

8610   Yoshi, T., "Sanson no Shakai-Tôgô to Sanson-Min no Kôdô" [Social
        integration and social behavior in a mountain village], Jimbun
        Kenkyū 13:9 (1962), 42-66. [Japan]

8611   Yoshida, T., "Cultural Integration and Change in Japanese Villages,"
        Am. Anthrop. 65:1 (Jan. 1963), 102-116.

8612   ------ "Social Conflict and Cohesion in a Japanese Rural Community,"
        Ethnology 3:3 (July 1964), 219-231.

8613   Younes, S., "Un village du Maten libanais" [A village of the Maten
        region of Mount Lebanon], Ann. Géogr. 70:378 (Mar.-Apr. 1961),
        145-161.

9. Tribal Factors

A. Annotated Case Studies

*9001   Bailey, Frederick G., Tribe, Caste and Nation: A Study of Political
        Activity and Political Change in Highland Orissa. Manchester,
        England: Manchester University Press, 1960. 279 pp.

           A study of a semi-Hindu tribe in Orissa, and of how an "unclean"
        caste is trying to break free of the bonds of caste by appealing to
        a wider political entity than the village.

*9002   Balandier, Georges, Sociologie actuelle de l'Afrique noire.
        Dynamique des changements sociaux en Afrique centrale. [The present
        sociology of Black Africa: The dynamics of social change in Central
        Africa]. Paris: Presses Universitaires de France, 1955. 511 pp.
        [Congo (Brazzaville); Gabon]

           A study of the Fang in the Gabon and of the Ba-kongo in the Congo
        (Brazzaville), with emphasis on the intercommunication of economic and
        social structures. The widening of the economic horizon tends to
        destroy primitive authority and thus to bring disorder.

9003   Barnett, H. G., Being a Palauan. New York: Henry Holt, 1960. 87
        pp. [Micronesia]

           A general study, with several case histories of natives who have
        broken away from the islands. Also contains a brief analysis of the
        effects of the occupation of the islands by the Germans, Japanese,
        and Americans.

*9004   Edwards, A. C., The Ovimbundu under Two Sovereignties: A Study of
        Social Control and Social Change among a People of Angola. London:
        Oxford University Press, 1962. 169 pp.

           Rubber production and the slave trade (both introduced in the nine-
        teenth century) brought a temporary prosperity that has now died out.
        The Ovimbundu tribe is highly Europeanized, and traditional authority
        is very weak. For resolving disputes it applies to European authori-
        ties. It avoids direct contact with the Angola government, but when
        necessary it appeals to white missionaries as "patrons." As a result
        there is no native government but only squabbling.

9005   Girling, F. K., The Acholi of Uganda. London: HMSO, 1960. 238 pp.

A study conducted in 1950 on a tribe whose main activity is the cultivation of cotton for commerce. Old traditions are being abandoned as national consciousness develops and a new class based on wealth emerges.

*9006   Gough, E. Kathleen, "Cults of the Dead among the Nayars," in GEN 4379 (1959), 240-272. [Indian State of Madras]

The decline of communal responsibility under law has caused a decline in the belief in communal responsibility for the appearance of ghosts. The increasing closeness of the nuclear family has decreased the belief that the ghosts of parents are punitive.

9007   Gulliver, P. H., Land Tenure and Social Change among the Nyakusa: An Essay in Applied Anthropology in South-West Tanganyika. Kampala, Uganda: East African Institute of Social Research, 1958. 47 pp. [Malawi]

The traditional social structure has been reinforced by the population pressure on the land.

*9008   Herskovits, Melville J., Dahomey: An Ancient West African Kingdom. 2 vols. New York: J. J. Augustin, 1938. 402 and 407 pp.

The French introduced currency into the area as a nonperishable medium of exchange and put an end to slavery. Slaves were useful above all in promoting the accumulation of wealth through cultivating large tracts of land and storing the produce. When slavery was done away with, it was no longer possible to accumulate great wealth in a short period, whereas the introduction of a storable form of wealth (money) meant that wealth might still be accumulated, though more slowly than before.

*9009   Hogbin, H. Ian, Experiements in Civilization. London: Routledge & Kegan Paul, 1939. 268 pp. [Melanesia]

A study of the Solomon Islands showing that the elders' authority has been undermined by the young peoples' superior knowledge of European ways.

*9010   Huntingford, G. W. B., Nandi Work and Culture. London: HMSO, 1950. 126 pp. [Kenya]

Though the Nandi were exposed to European contacts for half a century, they have been but little influenced by them. Their value system, based on cattle, does not admit the incentives of cash goods the Europeans have to offer, except in forms that have no effect on Nandi culture.

*9011   Kouwenhoven, William J. H., Nimboran: A Study of Social Change and Social-Economic Development in a New Guinea Society. The Hague: J. N. Voorhoeve, 1956. 238 pp.

The principal economic changes are an increased circulation of money and the marketing of local produce. The result is an estrangement of generations, a decline in group solidarity, and new approaches to the concept of family and the relations between men and women.

9012   Lehman, F. K., The Structure of Chin Society: A Tribal People of
        Burma Adapted to a Non-Western Civilization. Urbana: University of
        Illinois Press, 1963. 244 pp.

        A description of the cash economy and the resultant desire for
        money.

*9013   Lesne, Marcel, Les Zemmour: Evolution d'un groupement berbère [The
        Zemmour: The evolution of a Berber group]. Rabat: Ecole du Livre,
        1959. 472 pp. [Morocco]

        A study of a tribe of shepherds settled in the lowlands. They
        have had considerable contact with modern agricultural enterprises,
        yet they have resisted sedentation. They use modern goods, but also
        their traditional individualism is increasing. The young, however,
        seem to be more Arabized than ever.

*9014   Little, Kenneth L., The Mende of Sierra Leone: A West African People
        in Transition. London: Routledge & Kegan Paul, 1951. 307 pp.

        A new class structure has grown out of the Mende's contacts with
        Europeans. Their social structure is nontribal and lacks cohesiveness.

*9015   Mead, Margaret, New Lives for Old: Cultural Transformation--Manus,
        1928-1953. New York: Morrow, 1956. 548 pp. [New Guinea]

        A description of the passage of this tribe from a primitive state
        to the apperception of civilization.

9016   Middleton, John, The Lugbara of Uganda. New York: Holt, Rinehart
        and Winston, 1965. 96 pp.

        The introduction of cash cropping and outside work has tended to
        atomize family structure. A class of "new men" has developed, in
        which status is based solely on monetary gain.

9017   Ottenberg, Simon, "Ibo Receptivity to Change," in GEN 4306 (1959),
        130-143. [Nigeria]

        A study of a Nigerian tribe that has found a place in the British
        system because of its traditional emphasis on individualism. There
        is little information on the extent of economic change.

*9018   Reader, D. H., Zulu Tribe in Transition: The Makhanya of Southern
        Natal. Manchester, England: Manchester University Press, 1966.
        363 pp.

        The author points out that "social values of a political charac-
        ter," that is, the native reaction to white paternalism, tend to
        dampen the response of the native to economic incentives. Moderniza-
        tion is channeled through the schools into an urban context, only to
        be reflected in a longing for the rural, since no place is assigned
        the native in the white man's urban environment. Traditional members
        of the tribe are often unwilling to use money to purchase food. This

is not the case for the "school" or Christianized tribals. However, both groups are highly sensitive to small differences in prices of nonfood items. The main effect of the extensive contacts with urban industrial jobs is the detribalization of the family and the social structure.

*9019   Richards, Audrey I., "Some Effects of the Introduction of Individual Freehold into Buganda," in GEN 4310 (1963), 267-280. [Uganda]

    The English introduced the individual ownership of land, the cultivation of cotton and coffee, and the railroad. These changes have brought about the growth of an independent landowning class and the weakening of the authority of the chiefs, the fractionizing of land holdings, the raising of landholding to a supreme goal, so that factory work is looked down on, and the development of commercial agriculture.

**9020   Rognon, P., "Problèmes des Touaregs du Hoggar" [Problems of the Touaregs of Hoggar], in GEN 4392 (1963), 59-66. [Algeria]

    The Touaregs appear blocked from adapting to modern ways by their aristocratic traditions, while the noirs, previously their servants, are becoming richer than the Touaregs through working in the mines.

*9021   Schneider, H. K., "Pakot Resistance to Change," in GEN 4306 (1959), 144-167. [Kenya]

    This tribe is extremely resistant to change, largely because of a "cattle complex," plus their addiction to a pastoral life that precludes cash-cropping.

9022   Schoorl, J. W., Kultuur en Kultuurveranderingen in het Moejoe-Gebied [Culture and cultural change in the Muju area]. Leiden: University of Leiden Press, 1957. 299 pp. [New Guinea]

    A descriptive study of the reaction of a primitive tribe to the introduction of a commercial economy.

9023   Southall, Aidan William, Alur Society: A Study in Processes and Types of Domination. Cambridge, England: Heffer, 1956. 397 pp. [Uganda]

    A detailed description of the seemingly marked economic changes since World War II, with but little sociological analysis.

B.   Other Case Studies

9301   Armstrong, W. E., Rossel Island. Cambridge, England: Cambridge University Press, 1928. 274 pp. [Melanesia]

9302   Aurora, G. S., "Economy of a Tribal Village," Econ. Wkly. 16:39 (26
        Sept. 1964), 1557. [India]

9303   Bailleul, H., "Les Bayaka. Aperçu de l'évolution économique et
        politique de leur pays jusqu'en 1958" [The Bayaka: A general view of
        the economic and political evolution of their country up to 1958],
        Zaïre 13:8 (1959), 823-842. [Congo (Kinshasa)]

9304   Barwell, C. W., "A Note on Some Changes in the Economy of the Kipsigis
        Tribe," J. Afr. Adm. 8:2 (Apr. 1956), 95-101. [Kenya]

9305   Bataillon, C., "Les Rebaia: Semi-nomades du Souf" [The Rebaia: Semi-
        Nomads of the Souf], in GEN 4392 (1963), 113-122. [Algeria]

9306   Beattie, John H. M., Bunyoro: An African Kingdom. New York: Holt,
        Rinehart & Winston, 1960. 86 pp. [Uganda]

9307   Beuchelt, E., Kulturwandel bei den Bambara von Ségou. Gesellschafts-
        ordnung, Weltanschauung, Sozialweihen [Cultural change among the Bam-
        bara of Ségou: Social order, philosophy, social initiation rites].
        Bonn: Schroeder, 1962. 426 pp. [Mali]

9308   Bisson, J., "Nomadisation chez les Reguibat L'Gouacem" [Nomadization
        among the Reguibat L'Gouacem], in GEN 4392 (1963), 51-58.
        [Mauretania]

9309   Bose, Saradindu, "Economy of the Onge of Little Andaman," Man in
        India 44 (Oct. 1964), 298-310. [Andaman Islands]

9310   Bottomley, A., "Economic Growth in a Semi-Nomadic Herding Community,"
        Econ. Dev. cult. Change 11:4 (July 1963), 407-419. [Sahara Region]

9311   Brookfield, H. C., and P. Brown, Struggle for Land: Agriculture and
        Group Territories among the Chimbu of the New Guinea Highlands.
        Melbourne-New York: Oxford University Press, 1963. 193 pp.

9312   Capot-Rey, R., "Le nomadisms des Toubous" [The nomadism of the
        Toubous], in GEN 4392 (1963), 81-92. [Sahara Region]

9313   Cauneille, A., "Le semi-nomadism dans l'ouest Libyen: Fezzan,
        Tripolitaine" [Seminomadism in Western Libya: Fezzan, Tripolitaine],
        in GEN 4392 (1963), 101-112. [Libya]

9314   Das, Amal Kumar, and Manis Kumar Raha, The Oraons of Sunderban.
        Calcutta: Special Series No. 3, Bulletin of the Cultural Research
        Institute, Tribal Welfare Department, Government of West Bengal,
        1963. 476 pp. [India]

9315   Das, T. C., "Nature and Extent of Social Change in a Tribal Society
        of Eastern India," Sociol. Bull. 11 (1962), 221-238. [India]

9316   Davenport, William H., "Social Structure of Santa Cruz Island," in
        GEN 4330 (1964), 57-93. [Melanesia]

9317   De Garine, I., Les Massa du Cameroun. Vie économique et sociale [The
        Massa of the Cameroons: Economic and social life]. Paris: Presses
        Universitaires de France, 1964. n.p.

9318   Di Martino, A., Tra i Wahehe (Tanganika): Un passo alla volta
        [Among the Wahehe (Tanganyika): A step toward change]. Turin:
        Mission   consolata, 1963. 222 pp.

9319   Douglas, Mary, The Lele of the Kasai. London: Oxford University
        Press, 1963. 271 pp. [Congo]

9320   Fallers, Lloyd A., Bantu Bureaucracy: A Study of Integration and
        Conflict in the Political Institutions of an East African People.
        Cambridge, England: Heffer, 1956. 283 pp. [Uganda]

9321   Faron, L. C., Mapuche Social Structure: Institutional Reintegration
        in a Patrilineal Society of Central Chile. Urbana: University of
        Illinois Press, 1961. 247 pp.

9322   Faure, H., "Quelques obstacles sociaux au développement de l'économie
        traditionelle" [Some social obstacles to the development of a tradi-
        tional economy], Cah. Sociol. écon. 9:9 (Nov. 1963), 105-123.
        [Mexico]

9323   Forno, M., "Richerche sull' acculturamento dei Ghivaro" [Research on
        the acculturation of the Jivaro], Ann. lateran. 28 (1964), 151-178.
        [Brazil]

9324   Fortune, R. F., Sorcerers of Dobu: The Social Anthropology of the
        Dobu Islanders of the Western Pacific. Rev. ed. New York: E. P.
        Dutton, 1963. 326 pp. [Melanesia]

9325   Frémont, A., "Un petit regroupement des hautes plaines constanti-
        noises" [A tribal subgroup of the Constantine plateau], Cah. Sociol.
        écon. 4 (May 1961), 93-105. [Algeria]

9326   Friedländer, M.,"Zur Frage der Klassenverhältnisse der Ewe unter dem
        Einfluss der Kolonisation" [On the problem of Ewe social stratifica-
        tion under the influence of colonization]. Thesis, The Free Univer-
        sity of Berlin, 1962. 165 mim. pp. [Togo]

9327   Garg, R. P., The Dacoit Problem in Chambal Valley: A Sociological
        Study. Varanasi, India: Gandhian Institute of Studies, 1965. 78 pp.
        [India]

9328   Gray, R. F., The Sonjo of Tanganyika: An Anthropological Study of
        an Irrigation-Based Society. London-New York: Oxford University
        Press, 1963. 181 pp.

9329   Hammond-Tooke, W. D., Bhaca Society: A People of the Transkeian
        Uplands, South Africa. Cape Town: Oxford University Press, 1962.
        325 pp. [Republic of South Africa]

9330   Herzog, R., "Veränderungen und Auflösungerscheinungen in Nordafrikan-
        ischen Nomadentum" [Transformations and signs of dissolution in North
        African nomadism], Paideuma 6:4 (Nov. 1956), 210-223. [Sahara]

9331   Hinners, David G., "Developments in the Political and Social System
        of Tribal Thai Groups in Northern Indochina since World War II."
        M.A. thesis, Cornell University, 1961. 50 mim. pp. [Thailand]

9332   Hogbin, H. Ian, A Guadalcanal Society: The Kaoka Speakers. New York:
        Holt, Rinehart & Winston, 1964. 103 pp. [Melanesia]

9333   Holas, Bohumel, "Le Nya: Changements spirituels modernes d'une
        société Ouest-Africaine" [The Nya: Modern spiritual changes in a
        West African society], Acta Trop. 12:2 (1955), 97-122. [Ivory
        Coast]

9334   Hurault, J., Les Indiens de Guyane française. Problèmes pratiques
        d'administration et de contacts de civilisation [Indians of French
        Guiana: Practical problems of administration and cultural contacts].
        The Hague: M. Nijhoff, 1963. 102 pp.

9335   ------ La structure sociale des Bamiléké [The social structure of
        the Bamiléké]. Paris and The Hague: Mouton, 1962. 133 pp.
        [Senegal]

9336   Iijima, Shigeru, "Cultural Change among the Hill Karens in Northern
        Thailand," Asian Surv. 5:8 (Aug. 1965), 417-423.

9337   Iwata, Keiji, Ethnic Groups in the Valley of the Nam Song and the Nam
        Lik: Their Geographical Distribution and Some Aspects of Social
        Change. A Preliminary Report. Los Angeles: Department of Anthropo-
        logy, University of California, 1960. 30 mim. pp. [Laos]

9338   ------ "Indochina Hantô Hokubu ni okeru Thai Gôzoku no Kazoku to
        Shinzoku" [A comparative study of the social organization of three
        Thai groups, Thai Yai, Thai Lu, and Thai Neua], Minzokugaku Kenkyû
        29:1 (1964), 1-31. [Thailand]

9339   ------ "Muang no Bunka" [Muang culture], Kaigaijijo Kenkyûsho Hôkoku
        12:10 (1964), 53-61.

9340   Junod, Henri A., The Life of a South African Tribe. Vol. 1, rev. ed.
        New York: University Books, 1962. 559 pp. [Republic of South
        Africa]

9341   Kagaya, H., "Iran no Shuzoku Shakai no Kindaiteki Hatten" [The
        Modernization of Iranian tribal society], Asia Keizai 5:5 (1964).
        [Iran]

9342   Kandre, Peter K., Autonomy and Integration of Social Systems: The Iu
        Mien ("Yao" or "Man") Mountain Population and Their Neighbors. N.p.,
        1965. 72 pp. [Thailand]

9343   Kandre, Peter K., and Lej Tsan Kuej, "Aspects of Wealth-Accumulation,
        Ancestor Worship and Household Stability among the Iu Mien-Yao," in
        GEN 4378 (1965), 127-148. [Thailand]

9344   Keuning, Johannes, The Toba Batal Formerly and Now. Translated by
        Claire Holt. Ithaca: Modern Indonesia Project, Department of Far
        Eastern Studies, Cornell University, 1958. 24 pp. [Indonesia] See
        also Indonesie 6:2 (Sept. 1952).

9345   Koch, G., "Kulturwandel bei den Polynesiern des Ellice-Archipels"
        [Cultural change among the Polynesians of the Ellice Archipelago],
        Sociologus 12:2 (1962), 128-140.

9346   Kohler, O., "The Stage of Acculturation in South West Africa,"
        Sociologus 6:2 (1956), 138-153. [Republic of South Africa]

9347   Kucher, W., "Europaische Einflüsse in der Landwirtschaft und im
        Bauerntum der südafrikanischen Bantu" [European influences in agri-
        culture and among the peasantry of the South African Bantu], Z.
        Agrargesch. Agrarsoziol. 4:1 (Apr. 1956), 69-85.

9348   Lang, G. O., and M. B. Lang, "Problems of Social and Economic Change
        in Sukumaland, Tanganyika," Anthrop. Quart. 35:2 (Apr. 1962), 86-101.

9349   Laroche, M. C., "La vie dans les tribus calédoniennes en 1954. Notes
        pour une ethnologie de l'acculturation" [Life among the Caledonian
        tribes in 1954: Notes for an ethnology of acculturation], J. Soc.
        Océan. 10 (1954), 77-90. [Polynesia]

9350   Lawrance, J. C. D., The Iteso: Fifty Years of Change in a Nilo-
        Hamitic Tribe of Uganda. London: Oxford University Press, 1957.
        280 pp.

9351   Lewis, Diane Katherine, "The Manangkabau Malay of Negri Sembilan: A
        Study of Socio-Cultural Change." Ph.D. dissertation, Cornell Univer-
        sity, 1962. 375 mim. pp. [Malaysia]

9352   Loeb, E. M., In Feudal Africa. Bloomington: Research Center in
        Anthropology, Folklore and Linguistics, Indiana University, 1962.
        383 pp. [Angola]

9353   Mahapatra, L. K., "The Cerenga Kulha of Bonai, Orissa: Their
        Changing Economy," Baessler-Archiv 11 (Apr. 1964), 347-359.

9354   Maher, R. F., "Varieties of Change in Koriki Culture," Sthwest. J.
        Anthrop. 17:1 (Spring 1961), 28-49. [Melanesia]

9355   Majumdar, Dhirendra Nath, "Onge Culture in Transition," Bull. Inst.
        tradit. Cult. (1957), 7-10. [Indian State of Andaman Islands]

9356   ------ The Santal. A Study in Culture Change. Calcutta: Department
        of Anthropology, Government of India, 1956. 150 pp. [India]

9357   ------ "Tribal Rehabilitation in India," in GEN 4356 (1963), 119-129.

9358   Mandelbaum, David G., "The World and the World View of the Kota,"
        in GEN 4353 (1955), 223-254. [Indian State of Madras]

9359   Middelkoop, P., "Spontane Acculturatie op Timor" [Spontaneous accul-
        turation on Timor], Heerbaan 2 (1962), 50-72. [Indonesia]

9360   Middleton, J., "The Impact of the West and Social Change in East
        Africa," Kula 2:3 (Dec. 1961), 40-47. [Kenya]

9361   ------ "Social Change among the Lugbara of Uganda," Civilisations
        10:4 (Oct. 1960), 446-454.

9362   Mitchell, J. Clyde, Tribalism and the Plural Society. London:
        Oxford University Press, 1960. 36 pp. [Africa]

9363   ------ The Yao Village: A Study in the Social Structure of a Nyasa-
         land Tribe. Manchester, England: Manchester University Press, 1956.
         235 pp. [Malawi]

9364   Mitchell, J. C., and J. A. Barnes, The Lamba Village: Report of a
         Social Survey. Capetown: School of African Studies, University of
         Cape Town, 1950. 69 pp. [Zambia]

9365   Nader, Luisa, "Talea and Juquila: A Comparison of Zapotec Social
         Organization," Pub. Am. Archeol. Ethnogr. 48:3 (1964), 195-295.
         [Mexico]

9366   Nakane, C., and S. H. Wang, "Taiwan Yami-zoku no shakai soshiki ni
         tsuite--Wei Hweilin Liu Pin-hsing no chôsa hôkoku o chûshin to shite"
         [On the social organization of the Yam, Formosa--The report of Wei
         Hwei-lin and Liu-Pin-hsiung], Minzokugaku Kenkyû 27:4 (30 Nov.
         1963), 59-62. [Taiwan]

9367   Newman, Philip L., Knowing the Gururumba. New York: Holt, Rinehart
         & Winston, 1965. 110 pp. [New Guinea]

9368   Nicolaisen, J., Structures politiques et sociales des Touareg de
         l'Air et de l'Ahaggar [Political and social structures of the
         Touareg of the Air and the Ahaggar]. Niamey, Senegal: Institut
         Fondamental d'Afrique Noire, 1963. 109 pp. [Algeria; Sahara; Nigeria

9369   N'Sougan Agblemagnon, F., "Le concept de crise appliqué à une
         société africaine: Les Ewes" [The concept of crisis applied to an
         African society: The Ewe], Cah. int. Sociol. 23 (July-Dec. 1957),
         157-166. [Togo]

9370   Oración, Timoteo S., "Notes on the Social Structure and the Social
         Change of the Negritos on Negros Islands," Philipp. soc. Rev. 11:1
         (Jan.-Apr. 1963), 57-67. [Philippines]

9371   Paulme, Denise, Une societe de Côte d'Ivoire, hier et aujourd'hui.
         Les Bété [A society of the Ivory Coast, yesterday and today: The
         Bété]. Paris: Mouton, 1962. 205 pp.

9372   Richards, Audrey I., Hunger and Work in a Savage Tribe: A Functional
         Study of Nutrition among the Southern Bantu. London: George Routledg
         1932. 238 pp. [Republic of South Africa]

9373   Sachchidananda, "Community Development and the Tribals," J. soc. Res.
         7:1-2 (Mar.-Sept. 1964), 70-78. [India]

9374   ------ Cultural Change in Tribal Bihar: Munda and Oraon. Calcutta:
         Bookland, 1964. 158 pp. [Indian State of Bihar]

9375   Sadie, J. L., "The Social Anthropology of Economic Underdevelopment,"
         Econ. J. 70 (1960), 278ff. [East Africa; South Africa]

9376   Saha, Niranjan, "Human Factor in Agricultural Development: Study of
         a Tribal Community," Econ. Wkly. 15:38 (28 Sept. 1963), 1641-1643.
         [India]

9377   Salisbury, R. F., "Changes in Land Use and Tenure among the Siane of
         the New Guinea Highlands, 1952-1961," Pacif. Viewpoint 5:1 (May
         1964), 1-10.

9378   Sangree, W. H., "Structural Continuity and Change in a Bantu Tribe:
         The Nature and Development of Contemporary Tiriki Social Organization."
         Ph.D. dissertation, University of Chicago, 1959.   267 mim. pp. [Kenya]

9379   Sarel-Sternberg, Benno, "Semi-nomades du Nefzaoua" [Seminomads of
         the Nefzaoua], in GEN 4392 (1963), 123-134.   [Tunisia]

9380   Sarkar, Sourindranath, Psycho-dynamics of Tribal Behaviour. Calcutta:
         Bookland, 1965.   167 pp.   [India]

9381   Saxena, Ranvir Prakash, Tribal Economy in Central India. Calcutta:
         Firma K. L. Mukhopadhyay, 1964.   312 pp.

9382   Schaden, E., "Aculturação indígena: Ensaio sôbre fatôres e tendências
         da mudança cultural de tribos índias em contacto com o mundo dos
         brancos" [Indigenous acculturation: An essay on the factors of and
         the tendencies to cultural change among Indian tribes in contact with
         the world of the whites], Rev. Antrop. 13:1-2 (1965), 5-315. [Brazil]

9383   Schapera, Isaac, Migrant Labour and Tribal Life: A Study of Condi-
         tions in Bechuanaland Protectorate.   London: Oxford University Press,
         1947.   248 pp.   [Republic of South Africa]

9384   Scheffler, Harold W., Choiseul Island Social Structure.   Berkeley:
         University of California Press, 1965.   322 pp.   [Melanesia]

9385   Schmitz, C. A., "Gesellschaftsordnung und Wandel in einer Bergbauern-
         kultur in Nordost-Neuguinea" [Social order and change in a mountain
         peasant culture in northeastern New Guinea], Kölner Z. Soziol.
         Sozialps. 9:2 (1957), 258-282.

9386   Serpenti, L. M., Cultivators in the Swamps: Social Structure and
         Horticulture in a New Guinea Society.   Assen, Netherlands: Van
         Gorcum, 1965.   308 pp.

9387   Shah, P. G., Tribal Life in Gujarat: An Analytical Study of the
         Cultural Changes with Special Reference to the Dhanka Tribe. New
         Delhi: Bharatiya Vidya Bhawan, 1964.   344 pp.   [Indian State of
         Gujarat]

9388   Srinivas, M. N., Religion and Society among the Coorgs of South
         India.   Bombay: Asia Publishing House, 1965.   269 pp.

9389   Toupet, Ch., "L'évolution de la nomadisation en Mauritanie Sahélienne"
         [The evolution of nomadization in Sahelien Mauritania], in GEN 4392
         (1963), 67-80.

9390   ------ "La vallée de la Tamourt: Transformations agraires et sociales"
         [The Tamourt Valley: Agrarian and social transformations], Bull. Inst.
         fr. Afr. noire 18:3-4 (July-Oct. 1956), 509-513.   [Mauretania]

9391   Turri, E., "Un genere di vita in trasformazione: Il nomadismo" [A type

of life in transformation: Nomadism], <u>Universo</u> 40:1 (Jan.-Feb.
1960), 33-70. [Sahara Region]

9392   Van Amelsvoort, V., <u>Culture, Stone Age and Modern Medicine</u>. Assen,
        Netherlands: Van Gorcum, 1964. 245 pp. [New Guinea]

9393   Vidyarthi, L. P., "The Changing Face of Tribal Bihar: Some Prelimi-
        nary Observations on the Concept of Detribalisation," <u>J. soc. Res.</u>
        7:1-2 (Mar.-Sept. 1964), 53-61. [Indian State of Bihar]

9394   Vogt, E. Z., and A. Ruz Lhuillier (eds.), <u>Desarrollo cultural de los</u>
        <u>Mayas</u> [Cultural development of the Mayas]. Mexity City: Universidad
        Nacional Autónoma de México, 1964. 405 pp. [Mexico; Guatemala]

9395   Volchok, B. Ya., "The Interaction of Castes and Tribal Communities in
        Central India," <u>J. soc. Res.</u> 7:1-2 (Mar.-Sept. 1964), 104-112.

9396   Wagley, C., <u>Os Indios Tenetehara: Uma cultura em transição</u> [The
        Tenetehara Indians: A culture in transition]. Rio de Janeiro:
        Ministério da Educação e Cultura, Serviço de Documentação, 1961.
        235 pp. A revised translation of <u>The Tenetehara Indians of Brazil</u>:
        <u>A Culture in Transition.</u> New York: Columbia University Press,
        1949.

9397   Warren, Charles P., <u>The Batak of Palawan: A Culture in Transition</u>.
        Research Series No. 3. Chicago: Philippine Studies Program, Depart-
        ment of Anthropology, University of Chicago, 1964. 130 mim. pp.

9398   Williams, Thomas Rhys, <u>The Dusun: A North Borneo Society</u>. New York:
        Holt, Rinehart & Winston, 1965. 100 pp. [Malaysia]

9399   Winter, E. H., <u>Bwamba: A Structural-Functional Analysis of a Patri-</u>
        <u>lineal Society</u>. Cambridge, England: Heffer, 1956. 252 pp. [Zambia]

9400   Wolfe, Alvin W., <u>In the Ngombe Tradition: Continuity and Change in</u>
        <u>the Congo</u>. Evanston, Ill.: Northwestern University Press, 1961.
        167 pp.

9401   Yengoyan, Aram A., "Environment, Shifting Cultivation and Social
        Organization among the Mandaya of Eastern Mindanao, Philippines."
        Thesis, University of Chicago, 1964. 214 mim. pp.

10. General Studies

10301   Allen, Harold Boughton, <u>Rural Reconstruction in Action: Experience</u>
        <u>in the Near and Middle East</u>. Ithaca: Cornell University Press,
        1953. 204 pp.

10302   Arméstar, V. M. A., <u>La tierra y el hombre: Visión panorámica del</u>
        <u>problema agrario-social del Perú y su estrecha relación con el</u>

capital [Land and man: A panoramic view of the socio-agrarian
problem in Peru and its close relation with capital]. Lima:
Imprenta y Litografía Salesiana, 1963. 174 pp.

10303   Ayrout, H. H., The Egyptian Peasant. Rev. ed. Boston: Boston
University Press, 1963. 167 pp. A translation of Moeurs et coutumes
des Fellahs (1938).

10304   Bohannan, Paul J., "Land Use, Land Tenure and Land Reform," in GEN
4336 (1964), 133-151.

10305   Bose, T. K., H. A. Ali, and J. Talukdar, The Bengal Peasant from
Time to Time. New York: Asia Publishing House, 1963. 205 pp.
[Indian State of West Bengal]

10306   Bourdieu, Pierre, "The Attitude of the Algerian Peasant toward
Time," in GEN 4364 (1963), 55-72.

10307   Bui-Dang-Ha-Doa, J., "Les paysans vietnamiens et le développement
economique" [The Vietnamese peasants and economic development], Rev.
Sud-Est asiat. 4 (1962), 75-88.

10308   Bull, G. T., Coral in the Sand. London: Hodder & Stoughton, 1962.
125 pp. [Malaysia]

10309   Burling, Robbins, Hill Farms and Padi Fields: Life in Mainland
Southeast Asia. Englewood Cliffs, N.J.: Prentice-Hall, 1965.
180 pp.

10310   Campos, C. M., J. Arroyo Riestra, and F. Vargas, La vida del
campesino [The peasant's life]. Mexico City: B. Costa-Amic, 1963.
240 pp.

10311   Clayton, E. S., Agrarian Development in Peasant Economies: Some
Lessons from Kenya. London: Pergamon Press, 1964. 154 pp.

10312   Comte, J., Les communes malgaches [Malagasy communities]. Tana-
narive: Edition de la Librairie de Madagascar, 1963. 176 pp.

10313   Dez, V., "Développement économique et tradition à Madagascar" [Eco-
nomic development and tradition in Madagascar], Cah. Inst. Sci. econ.
129, Suppl., Series 5:4 (Sept. 1962), 79-108.

10314   Diégues Júnior, M., Establecimentos rurais na América latina.
Ensaio de sugestoes sôbre sua tipologia e suas características
económicas e sociais [Rural establishments in Latin America:
Suggestions on their typology and their economic and social charac-
teristics]. Geneva, Switzerland: Comissão Internacional Catolica
de Migrações, 1963. 128 pp.

10315   Fukutake, Tadashi, "Change and Stagnation in Indian Village
Society," Dev. Econ. 2:2 (June 1964), 125-146.

10316   Galloy, P., et al., Nomades et paysans d'Afrique noire occidentale
[Nomads and peasants of West Black Africa]. Nancy: Université de
Nancy, 1963. 243 pp.

10317   Gatheru, R. Mugo, Child of Two Worlds: A Kikuyu's Story. New York:
          Praeger, 1964. 216 pp. [Kenya]

10318   Gaudio, A., "Aspetti economici e sociali della Mauritania" [Economic
          and social aspects of Mauritania], Universo 43:4 (July-Aug. 1963),
          701-718.

10319   Ghurye, G. S., "Social Change in Maharashtra," Sociol. Bull. 3:1
          (Mar. 1954), 41-60. [Indian State of Maharashtra]

10320   Gluckman, M., "Tribalism in Modern British Central Africa," in GEN
          4396 (1966), 251-264.

10321   Goodfriend, Arthur, Rice Roots. New York: Simon & Schuster, 1958.
          209 pp. [East Asia]

10322   Holleman, J. F. (ed.), Experiment in Swaziland: Report of the Swazi-
          land Sample Survey 1960 by the Institute for Social Research, Uni-
          versity of Natal for the Swaziland Administration. Cape Town, South
          Africa: Oxford University Press, 1964. 352 pp.

10323   Houghton, D. Hobart, Life in the Ciskei: A Summary of the Findings
          of the Keiskammahoek Rural Survey, 1947-1951. Johannesburg: South
          African Institute of Race Relations, 1955. 72 pp. [Republic of
          South Africa] See RUR 8598 and RUR 11349 for details.

10324   Huitron, Antonio, Metepec: Miseria y grandeza del barro [Metepec:
          The misery and grandeur of the artisan]. Mexico City: Instituto
          de Investigaciones Sociales de la Universidad Nacional, 1962.
          188 pp.

10325   Hunter, D. A., "Bantu Industries," S. Afr. J. Sci. 18 (1922), 183-
          194. [Republic of South Africa]

10326   Ishwaran, K., Tradition and Economy in Village India. London:
          Routledge & Kegan Paul, 1966. 169 pp. [Indian State of Mysore]

10327   Isnard, H., "Disparités régionales et unité à Madagascar" [Regional
          disparities and unity in Madagascar], Cah. int. Sociol. 9:32 (Jan.-
          June 1962), 25-42.

10328   Kajubi, W. Senteza, "Coffee and Prosperity in Buganda: Some Aspects
          of Economic and Social Change," Uganda J. 29:2 (1965), 135-148.

10329   Kiener, A., Poissons, pêche et pisciculture à Madagascar [Fish,
          fishing, and fish breeding in Madagascar]. Madagascar: Centre
          Technique Forestier Tropical, 1963. 243 pp.

10330   Last, Jef, Bali in de Kentering [Bali in transition]. Amsterdam:
          De Bezige Bij, 1955. 207 pp. [Indonesia]

10331   Launay, Michel, Paysans algériens. La terre, la vigne et les hommes
          [Algerian peasants: The land, the wine, and the men]. Paris:
          Editions du Seuil, 1963. 431 pp.

10332   LeVine, Robert A., "Sex Roles and Economic Change in Africa,"
          Ethnology 5:2 (Apr. 1966), 186-193.

10333   Mayer, Adrian C., <u>Land and Society in Malabar</u>. London: Oxford
         University Press, 1952. 158 pp. [Indian State of Kerela]

10334   ------ <u>Peasants in the Pacific: A Study of Fiji Indian Rural
         Society</u>. Berkeley: University of California Press, 1961. 202 pp.

10335   Mencher, Joan P., "Growing Up in South Malabar," <u>Hum. Organiz</u>. 22:1
         (Spring 1963), 54-65. [Indian State of Kerela]

10336   ------ "Kerala and Madras: A Comparative Study of Ecology and Social
         Structure," <u>Ethnology</u> 5:2 (Apr. 1966), 135-171.

10337   Menezes, Djacir, "Desenvolvimento cultural, industrialización y
         humanismo: Notas sobre la vida brasileña" [Cultural development,
         industrialization and humanism: Notes on Brazilian life], <u>Rev. mex.
         Sociol</u>. 26:2 (May-Aug. 1964), 425-438.

10338   Métraux, A., and M. Gutelman, "Les communautés rurales du Pérou" [The
         rural communities of Peru], <u>Etud. rur</u>. 10 (July-Sept. 1963), 5-25.

10339   Moore, Wilbert E., "The Adaptation of African Labor Systems to
         Social Change," in GEN 4336 (1964), 277-299.

10340   Moral, Paul, <u>Le paysan haïtien: Etude sur la vie rurale en Haïti</u>
         [The Haitian peasant: Study of rural life in Haiti]. Paris:
         Maisonneuve et Larose, 1961. 375 pp.

10341   Moreira, J. M., "Estrutura das comunidades rurais da Guiné Portu-
         guesa. Sua promoção e integração no complexo social Português"
         [The structure of rural communities of Portuguese Guinea: Their
         promotion and integration into the Portuguese social system], <u>Bol.
         cult. Guiné port</u>. 17:67 (July 1962), 459-472.

10342   Nair, Kusum, <u>Blossoms in the Dust</u>. New York: Praeger, 1962. 201
         pp. [India]

10343   Nath, V., "The New Village," <u>Econ. Wkly</u>. 17:13-16 (17, 24 Apr., 1, 8
         May 1965), 679-684, 713-719, 745-750, and 777-780. [India]

10344   Norbeck, Edward, "Postwar Cultural Change and Continuity in North-
         eastern Japan," <u>Am. Anthrop</u>. 63:2, Pt. 1 (Apr. 1961), 297-321.

10345   Perez Ramirez, G., <u>El campesinado colombiano. Un problema de
         estructura</u> [The Colombian countryside: A problem of structure].
         Bogotá: Oficina Internacional de Investigaciones Sociales de la
         Fédération Européenne de Recherche Economique et Sociale, 1962.
         188 pp.

10346   Pohl, V., <u>The Dawn and After</u>. London: Faber & Faber, 1964. 157 pp.
         [Republic of South Africa]

10347   Poncet, J., <u>Paysages et problèmes ruraux en Tunisie</u> [Rural land-
         scape and problems in Tunisia]. Paris: Presses Universitaires de
         France, 1963.

10348   Rajamani, A. N., "Agricultural Sociology," <u>Rur. India</u> 22:1 (Jan.
         1959), 16-35. [India]

10349   Reader, D. H., "A Survey of Categories of Economic Activities among
         the Peoples of Africa," Africa 34:1 (Jan. 1964), 28-45.

10350   Redinha, José, Etnossociología do nordeste de Angola [The ethno-
         sociology of Northeast Angola]. Lisbon: Agencial-Geral do Ultra-
         mar, 1958.   247 pp.

10351   Rourke, Robert J., Rural Development in a Communal Society. Ithaca:
         Graduate School of Business and Public Administration, Cornell Uni-
         versity, 1965.   42 mim. pp.

10352   Roy Burman, B. K., "Cultural Factors in Economic Development and
         Technological Change in Tribal India," J. sociol. Res. 8 (Mar.
         1965), 21-32.   Also published in Vanyajati 13 (July 1965), 102-113.

10353   Sanders, Irwin T., Rainbow in the Rock: The People of Rural Greece.
         Cambridge, Mass.: Harvard University Press, 1962.   363 pp.

10354   Schneider, Harold K., "Economics in East African Aboriginal
         Societies," in GEN 4336 (1964), 53-77.

10355   Schrieke, Bertram J. O., "Native Society in the Transformation
         Period," in GEN 4374 (1929), 237-247.   [Indonesia]

10356   Scott, J. G., The Burman: His Life and Notions.   New York: Norton,
         1963.   609 pp.

10357   Skinner, E. P., The Mossi of the Upper Volta: The Political
         Development of the Sudanese People.   Stanford, Calif.:   Stanford
         University Press, 1964.   236 pp.

10358   Sklar, R. L., "The Contribution of Tribalism to Nationalism in
         Western Nigeria," in GEN 4396 (1966), 290-300.

10359   Smith, M. G., The Plural Society in the British West Indies.
         Berkeley: University of California Press, 1965.   359 pp.   [British
         Caribbean]

10360   Solari, A. E., Sociología rural latinoamericana [Rural sociology in
         Latin America]. Buenos Aires: Editorial Universitaria de Buenos
         Aires, 1963.   93 pp.

10361   Stavenhagen, R., "Aspectos sociales de la estructura agraria en
         México" [Social aspects of the structure of agriculture in Mexico].
         Amér. lat. 9:1 (1966), 3-19.

10362   Taylor, Carl C., et al., Experience with Human Factors in Agricultural
         Areas of the World.   Washington: U.S. Department of Agriculture
         Extension Service, 1949.

10363   Terra, G. J. A., "Some Sociological Aspects of Agriculture in S.E.
         Asia," Indonesië 6:4 (1953), 297-463.

10364   Thomas, L. V., "Brève typologie des déplacements de populations au
         Sénégal" [Short typology of population movements in the Senegal],
         Cah. Sociol. écon. 10 (May 1964), 247-284.

10365   Tomasevich, Jozo, Peasants, Politics, and Economic Change in Yugo-
          slavia. Stanford, Calif.: Stanford University Press, 1955. 743 pp.

10366   UNESCO, Cultural Patterns and Technical Change. Paris: UNESCO,
          1953. 348 pp.

10367   Vellard, J. A., Civilisations des Andes. Evolution des populations
          du Haut-Plateau Bolivien [Civilizations of the Andes: The evolu-
          tion of the populations of the Upper Bolivian Plateau]. Paris:
          Gallimard, 1963. 272 pp.

10368   Vu, Quôc Thuc, "The Rural Problem in the Countries of South-East
          Asia," in GEN 4394 (1963), 61-73.

10369   Wulker, G., In Asien und Afrika. Soziale und soziologische Wand-
          lungen [In Asia and Africa: Social and sociological changes].
          Stuttgart, W. Germany: Kreun, 1962. 120 pp.

10370   Yudelman, M., Africans on the Land: Economic Problems of African
          Agricultural Development in Southern, Central, and East Africa,
          with Special Reference to Southern Rhodesia. Cambridge, Mass.:
          Harvard University Press, 1964. 288 pp.

                        11. Socioeconomic Factors

11301   Aguilar García, L., "El trabajo rural. Sus caracteristicas socio-
          econômicas" [Rural labor: Its socioeconomic characteristics],
          Estud. polít. soc. 12 (1961), 171-184.

11302   Ali, Hashim Amir, Then and Now, 1933-1958: A Study of Socio-Eco-
          nomic Structure and Change in Some Villages Near Visva-Bharati
          University, Bengal. London: Asia Publishing House, 1961. 124 pp.
          [Indian State of West Bengal]

11303   Althabe, G., "Problèmes socio-économiques du Nord Congo" [Economic
          and social problems of the North Congo], Cah. Inst. Sci. écon.
          Series 5:5 (Nov. 1962), 187-282.

11304   Andrews, H. T., et al., South Africa in the Sixties: A Socio-eco-
          nomic Survey. Johannesburg: The South Africa Foundation, 1962.
          216 pp.

11305   Ardener, E. W., "Social and Demographic Problems of the Southern
          Cameroons Plantation Area," in GEN 4384 (1961), 83-97.

11306   Baeck, Louis, "Une societe rurale en transition: Etude socio-éco-
          nomique de la région de Thysville" [A rural society in transition:
          A socioeconomic study of the Thysville region], Zaïre 11:2 (1957),
          115-186. [Congo (Leopoldville)]

11307   Beckett, W. H., Akokoaso: A Survey of a Gold Coast Village. London:
          P. Lund, Humphries, 1944. 95 pp. [Ghana]

11308   Belshaw, Cyril S., In Search of Wealth: A Study of the Emergence of
          Commercial Operations in the Melanesian Society of Southeastern
          Papua. Menasha, Wis.: American Anthropological Association, 1955.
          84 pp. [New Guinea]

11309   Binet, Jacques, Budgets familiaux des planteurs de cacao au Cameroun
          [Family budgets of cacao planters in the Cameroons]. Paris: Office
          de la Recherche Scientifique et Technique Outre-Mer, 1956. 154 pp.

11310   Bohannan, Paul J., Tiv Farm and Settlement. Colonial Research
          Studies 15. London: HMSO, 1954. 87 pp. [Nigeria]

11311   Bose, Anil Baran, Economic and Living Conditions of Harijans in
          Uttar Pradesh. Lucknow: J. K. Institute of Sociology and Human
          Relations, 1957. 117 mim. pp.

11312   Boutillier, J. L., and J. Causse, Bongouanou, Côte d'Ivoire: Etude
          socio-économique d'une subdivision [Bongouanou, Ivory Coast: Socio-
          economic study of a subdivision]. Paris: Berger-Levrault, 1960.
          224 pp.

11313   Boutillier, J.-L., et al., La moyenne vallée du Sénégal: Etude
          socio-économique [The middle reaches of the Senegal: A socioeco-
          nomic study]. Paris: Presses Universitaires de France, 1962.
          369 pp.

11314   Brant, Charles S., Tadagale: A Burmese Village in 1950. Ithaca:
          Southeast Asia Program, Cornell University, 1954. 41 pp.

11315   Brown, David W., "A Reconnaissance Study of Farming Organization in
          a Coastal Area of West Johore: A Preliminary Report." Thesis,
          University of Malaya, 1960. [Malaysia]

11316   Bruyns, L., De Social-Economische Ontwikkeling van de Bakongo:
          Gewest Inkisi [The social and economic development of the Bakongo,
          West Inkisi]. Brussels: Institut Royal Colonial Belge, 1951.
          343 pp. [Congo (Leopoldville)]

11317   Camara, Fernando, Chacaltianguis: Comunidad rural en la ribera del
          Papaloapan [Chacaltianguis: A rural community on the Papaloapan
          River]. Veracruz, Mexico: Gobierno del Estado de Veracruz, 1952.
          170 pp. [Mexico]

11318   Campos, C. M., and A. Arredondo, "Las condiciones de vida del
          campesino dominicano" [The living conditions of a Dominican peasant],
          Panorama 1:4 (July-Aug. 1963), 81-110.

11319   Chang, Han-yu, "T'aiwan Nungmin Shengchi chih Yenchia" [A study of
          the livelihood of peasant farmers in Taiwan], Shehui K'ohsueh
          Luents'ung 6 (May 1955), 185-228.

11320   Chapuis, E., "Conditionnement socio-culturel de l'économie dans la
          région de Tuléar (Madagascar)" [Sociocultural influences on the

economy of the Tulear region of Madagascar], <u>Cah. Inst. Sci. écon.</u>
145, Series 5:7 (Jan. 1964), 199-226.

11321 Chattopadhyay, Kumarananda, and Suraj Bandyopadhyay, "A Note on
Variations in the Level of Living in Rural Areas," <u>Indian J. agric.</u>
<u>Econ.</u> 18:1 (Jan. 1963), 238-242. [India]

11322 Delvert, Jean, <u>Le paysan cambodgien</u> [The Cambodian peasant]. Paris:
Mouton, 1961. 740 pp.

11323 Desai, Maganlal Bhagwanji, <u>The Rural Economy of Gujarat</u>. Bombay:
Oxford University Press, 1948. 352 pp.

11324 Diaz, Ralph C., and H. and J. von Oppenfeld, <u>Case Studies of Farm</u>
<u>Families, Laguna Province, Philippines</u>. Manila: University of the
Philippines, 1961. 92 pp.

11325 Diop, Abdoulaye Bara, <u>Société Toucouleur et migration</u> [Toucouleur
society and migration]. Dakar, Senegal: Institut Français d'Afrique
Noire, 1965. 232 pp.

11326 Dupire, M., and J.-L. Boutillier, "Le pays Adioukrou et sa palmeraie:
Etude socio-économique" [The Adioukrou country and its palm-growing
area: A socioeconomic study], <u>Homme d'outre-mer</u> 4 (1958), 5-100.
[Dahomey]

11327 Eames, E., "Population and Economic Structure of an Indian Rural
Community," <u>East. Anthrop.</u> 8:3-4 (n.d.), 173-181.

11328 Fearn, Hugh, <u>An African Economy: A Study of the Economic Develop-</u>
<u>ment of the Nyanza Province of Kenya, 1903-1953</u>. London: Oxford
University Press, 1961. 284 pp.

11329 Forde, Daryll, and Richenda Scott, <u>The Native Economies of Nigeria.</u>
London: Faber & Faber, 1946. 312 pp.

11330 Fortes, M., <u>et al.</u>, "The Ashanti Surveys, 1945-46: An Experiment
in Social Research," <u>Geogr. J.</u> 110:4-6 (Oct.-Dec. 1947), 149-179.
[Ghana]

11331 France, Institut National de Statistiques et d'Etudes Economiques,
<u>Enquête budgétaire dans le delta central nigérien</u> [Budget study of
the Central Nigerian Delta]. Paris: INSEE, 1961. 130 pp.

11332 ------ <u>Une enquête de ménage en pays Lobi (Haute Volta), 1956-57</u>
[A family budget study in the Lobi area, Upper Volta, 1956-57].
Paris: INSEE, 1961. 23 mim. pp.

11333 ------ <u>Enquête socio-économique des Comores</u> [Socioeconomic study of
the Comores]. 2 vols. Paris: INSEE, 1962, 1963. 41 and 73 pp.
[Madagascar]

11334 Gadgil, Dhanonjaya Ramchandra, and V. R. Gadgil, <u>A Survey of Farm</u>
<u>Business in Wai Taluka</u>. Poona, India: Gokhale Institute of Poli-
tics and Economics, 1940. 136 pp. [Indian State of Gujarat]

11335   Gamble, D. P., Contributions to a Socio-Economic Survey of the
         Gambia. London: HMSO, 1949. [Senegal]

11336   Gamble, S. D., North China Villages: Social, Political and Economic
         Activities before 1933. Berkeley: University of California Press,
         1963. 352 pp.

11337   Garbett, G. Kingsley, Growth and Change in a Shona Ward. Salisbury,
         Southern Rhodesia: University College of Rhodesia and Nyasaland,
         1960. 100 pp. [Southern Rhodesia]

11338   Ghilain, J., et al., Le revenu des populations indigènes du Congo-
         Léopoldville. Etude élaborée par le Groupe de l'Economie Africaine
         [The income of the native populations of the Congo-Leopoldville: A
         study conducted by the African Economy Group]. Brussels: Institut
         de Sociologie de l'Université Libre, 1963. 95 pp.

11339   Grad, Andrew J., Land and Peasant in Japan. New York: Institute of
         Pacific Relations, 1952. 262 pp.

11340   Guhl, E., et al., Indios y blancos en la Guajira: Estudio socio-
         económico [Indians and Whites in Guajira: A socioeconomic study].
         Bogotá: Ediciones Tercer Mundo, 1963. 319 pp. [Colombia]

11341   Guillard, Joanny, Golonpoui: Analyse des conditions de moderni-
         sation d'un village du Nord-Cameroun [Golonpaui: Analysis of the
         conditions of modernization of a village in the North Cameroons].
         The Hague: Mouton, 1965. 502 pp.

11342   Gupta, Satish Chandra, An Economic Survey of Shamaspur Village.
         Bombay: Asia Publishing House, 1959. 148 pp. [Indian State of
         Uttar Pradesh]

11343   Halpern, Joel M., Economic and Related Statistics Dealing with Laos.
         Los Angeles: Department of Anthropology, University of California,
         1961. 40 mim. pp. [Laos]

11344   Haswell, M. R., Economics of Agriculture in a Savannah Village:
         Report on Three Years Study in Genieri Village and Its Lands, the
         Gambia. Research Publication 8. London: HMSO, 1953. 142 pp.
         [Gambia]

11345   Hayashi, Magumi, Chûshi Konan Nôson Shakaiseidô Kenkyu [The social
         system of rural communities in central China]. Tokyo: Yuhikaku,
         1953. 250 pp.

11346   Hendry, James B., The Study of a Vietnamese Rural Community:
         Economic Activity. Saigon: Michigan State University Viet Nam
         Advisory Group, 1959. 370 pp.

11347   Holleman, J. F. (ed.), Experiment in Swaziland: Report of the Swazi-
         land Sample Survey, 1960. Cape Town, South Africa: Oxford Univer-
         sity Press, 1964. 352 pp.

11348   Houghton, D. Hobart (ed.), Economic Development in a Plural Society:
         Studies in the Border Region of the Cape Province. Cape Town, South
         Africa: Oxford University Press, 1960. 401 pp.

11349   Houghton, D. Hobart, and E. M. Walton, Keiskammahoek Rural Survey.
        Vol. 2, The Economy of a Native Reserve. Pietermaritzburg, Republic
        of South Africa: Shuter & Shooter, 1952. 194 pp. [Republic of
        South Africa]

11350   Hussain, Matlub, A Socio-Economic Survey of Village Baffa in the
        Hazara District of the Peshawar Division. Pakistan: Peshawar
        University, 1958. 393 pp. [West Pakistan]

11351   Indian Society of Agricultural Economics, Bhadkad: Social and Eco-
        nomic Survey of a Village. A Comparative Study (1915 and 1955).
        Bombay: Indian Society of Agricultural Economics, 1957. 71 pp.
        [Indian State of Maharashtra]

11352   ------ Economic and Social Survey of Meksana District. Bombay:
        Indian Society of Agricultural Economics, 1954. 213 pp. [Indian
        State of Gujarat]

11353   Iyengar, S. K., Rural Economic Enquiries in the Hyderabad State:
        1949-51. Andhra Pradesh, India: Hyderabad Government Press, 1951.
        658 pp. [Indian State of Andhra]

11354   Jack, J. C., The Economic Life of a Bengal Village. London:
        Clarendon Press, 1916. 158 pp.

11355   Jagalpure, L. B., and K. D. Kale, Sarola Kasar: Study of a Deccan
        Village in the Famine Zone. Ahmednager, India: Mihan Press, 1938.
        464 pp. [Indian State of Maharashtra]

11356   Japan Cultural Science Society, Brief Report of Research on Social
        Implications of the Comprehensive Development Programme along the
        Kitakami River. Tokyo: Japanese National Committee for UNESCO,
        1960. 49 pp. [Japan]

11357   Jha, Satish Chandra, "Levels of Living in Rural Households," Indian
        J. agric. Econ. 18:1 (Jan. 1963), 311-316.

11358   Jiménez Paniagua, J., "Sobre la estructura socio-económica de las
        Indios Tzeltales" [On the socioeconomic structure of the Tzeltal
        Indians], Rev. Econ. 26:1 (Jan. 1963), 57-63, and 26:2 (Feb. 1963),
        27-33. [Mexico]

11359   John, P. V., and Lal Chand Gupta, "A Comparative Study of Some
        Aspects of the Levels of Living in Two Villages [in Madhya Pradesh],"
        Indian J. agric. Econ. 18:1 (Jan. 1963), 324-327.

11360   Kaberry, Phyllis M., Women of the Grassfields: A Study of the
        Economic Position of Women in Bamenda, British Cameroons. Colonial
        Research Study 14. London: HMSO, 1952. 220 pp.

11361   Kakade, R. G., A Socio-Economic Survey of Weaving Communities in
        Sholapur. Poona, India: Gokhale Institute of Politics and Eco-
        nomics, 1947. 221 pp. [Indian State of Maharashtra]

11362   Kale, D. N., Agris--A Socio-Economic Survey. Bombay: Asia
        Publishing House, 1952. 411 pp. [Indian State of Maharashtra]

11363   Kay, George, Chief Kalaba's Village: A Preliminary Survey of Eco-
          nomic Life in an Ushi Village, Northern Rhodesia. The Rhodes-Living-
          stone Papers No. 35. Manchester, England: Manchester University
          Press, 1964. 92 pp. [Zambia]

11364   Kumarappa, J. C., A Survey of Matar Taluka, Kaira District. Ahmeda-
          bad, India: Gujarat Vidyapith, 1931. 179 pp. [Indian State of
          Gujarat]

11365   LeBar, Frank M., "A Household Survey of Economic Goods on Romonum
          Island, Truk," in GEN 4330 (1964), 335-349. [Polynesia]

11366   McLoughlin, P. F. M., "The Gash-Tokar Economic Region: Some Aspects
          of Its Labour Force and Income," Sudan Notes Rec. 46 (1965), 67-83.

11367   Mann, Harold Hart, et al., Land and Labour in a Deccan Village.
          Study No. 1, Pimple Saudagar. Bombay: Oxford University Press,
          1917. 184 pp. [Indian State of Maharashtra]

11368   Meade, J. E., et al., The Economic and Social Structure of Mauritius:
          Report to the Governor of Mauritius. London: Methuen, 1961.
          246 pp.

11369   Mehra, Jagdish, "A Socio-Economic Survey of Khedla Village in
          Rajasthan," Mod. Rev. 108:2 (Aug. 1960), 132-139.

11370   Misra, Bidyadhar, L. K. Pati, and A. K. Mitra, "A Study of Levels of
          Living in a Village of Orissa," Indian J. agric. Econ. 18:1 (Jan.
          1963), 333-340.

11371   Morris, H. S., Report on a Melanau Sago Producing Community in
          Sarawak. London: HMSO, 1953. 184 pp. [Malaysia]

11372   Muthiah, C., "Levels of Living in Four Villages of Rural Bhopal,"
          Indian J. agric. Econ. 18 (Jan. 1963), 327-333. [Indian State of
          Madhya Pradesh]

11373   Naik, T. B. (ed.), The Abujhmarhias: Socio-economic Aspects of a
          Little Known Culture. Chhindwara, India: Tribal Research Institute,
          1963. 167 pp. [Indian State of Madhya Pradesh]

11374   Nicolas, G., "Aspects de la vie économique dans un canton du Niger:
          Kantché" [Aspects of economic life in a canton of Niger: Kantché],
          Cah. Inst. Sci. écon. Series 5:5 (Nov. 1962), 105-186.

11375   Nishihira, S., "La mobilité sociale au Japon" [Social mobility in
          Japan], Ann. Inst. Statist. math. 14:3 (1963), 269-278.

11376   Nishikiori, Hideo, Togo-mura, A Village in Northern Japan. New York:
          Institute of Pacific Relations, 1945. 114 pp.

11377   Nitisastro, W., "Some Data on the Population of Djabres: A Village
          in Central Java," Ekon. Keuangan Indonesia 8 (n.d.), 759-784.

11378   Nurge, Ethel, Life in a Leyte Village. Seattle: University of
          Washington Press, 1965. 157 pp.

11379   Oberg, Kalervo, Chomin de Cima: A Rural Community in Minas Gerais,
         Brazil. Rio de Janeiro: United States Overseas Mission, 1956.
         205 pp.

11380   Pal, Agaton P., The Resources, Levels of Living, and Aspirations of
         Rural Households in Negros Oriental. Quezon City, Philippines:
         Community Development Research Council, University of the Philippines,
         1963. 429 pp.

11381   Pande, Jugal Kishore, Agricultural Economy in Village Chitra, Agra
         District. Allahabad, India: Uttar Pradesh Printing and Stationery
         Office, 1958. 190 pp.

11382   ------ "Levels of Living in Rural Areas of Uttar Pradesh," Indian J.
         agric. Econ. 18 (Jan. 1963), 256-261.

11383   Pandit, D. P., Earning One's Livelihood in Mahuva. Bombay: Asia
         Publishing House, 1965. 96 pp. [Indian State of Maharashtra]

11384   Patnaik, N., "A Survey of the Economic and Social Conditions of the
         Chamars of Barpali in Orissa," Econ. Wkly. 5:37 (12 Sept. 1953),
         1003-1005; 5:38 (19 Sept. 1953), 1034-1036; 5:39 (26 Sept. 1953),
         1065-1066.

11385   Pelissier, P., Les pays du Bas-Ouémé. Une région témoin du Dahomey
         méridional [The lands of the Bas-Ouémé: A sample region of Southern
         Dahomey]. Dakar, Senagal: Faculté des Lettres et Sciences Humaines,
         1963. 175 pp.

11386   Pi Hugarte, Renzo, and German Wettstein, Rasgos actuales de un
         ranchero uruguayo [Present-day glimpses of a Uruguayan ranchero].
         Montevideo: Facultad de Derecho y Ciencias Sociales, Universidad
         de Montevideo, 1955. 190 pp.

11387   Read, Margaret, Native Standards of Living and African Culture Change
         Illustrated by Examples from the Ngoni Highlands of Nyasaland.
         London: Institute of African Language and Culture, 1938. 56 pp.
         [Malawi]

11388   Richards, Audrey I., Land, Labour and Diet in Northern Rhodesia.
         London: Oxford University Press, 1939. 423 pp. [Zambia]

11389   Richardson, E. M., and G. R. Collins, Economic and Social Survey of
         the Rural Areas of the Colony of Sierra Leone. London: HMSO, 1953.

11390   Rivera, G., and R. T. McMillan, An Economic and Social Survey of
         Rural Households in Central Luzon. Manila: U.S. Operations
         Mission to the Philippines, 1954. 179 pp.

11391   Sankaranarayanan, U., "Levels of Living in Rural Areas," Indian J.
         agric. Econ. 18:1 (Jan. 1963), 341-348. [India]

11392   Sarkar, N. K., and S. J. Tambiah, The Disintegrating Village: A
         Socio-Economic Survey Conducted by the University of Ceylon. Part I.
         Colombo: Ceylon University Press, 1957. 83 pp.

11393   Sarker, Subhash Chandra, "Stability and Change in Rural Life: Village
         Survey Findings," Mod. Rev. 116:4 (Oct. 1964), 277-283. [India]

11394   Schapera, Isaac, "Economic Conditions in a Bechuanaland Native
         Reserve," S. Afr. J. Sci. 30 (1933), 633-655.

11395   Sengupta, Sunil C., "Levels of Living in Three Villages of West
         Bengal: A Cross-sectional Study," Indian J. agric. Econ. 18:1
         (Jan. 1963), 278-287.

11396   Setonaikai Sôgô Kenkyukai, Gyoson no Seikatsu [Life in a fishing
         village]. Okayama: Chûkoku Insatsu Kabushiki-kaisha, 1954. 424
         pp. [Japan]

11397   ------ Sanson no Seikatsu [Life in a mountain village]. Okayama:
         Chûkoku Insatsu Kabushiki-kaisha, 1955. 432 pp. [Japan]

11398   Shah, C. H., Conditions of Economic Progress of Farmers: An
         Analysis of 36 Case Studies. Bombay: Indian Society of Agricultural
         Economics, 1960. 129 pp. [Indian State of Gujarat]

11399   ------ Problems of Small Farmers: Report on an Enquiry into Problems
         of Low-Income Farmers in Kodinar Toluka. Bombay: Indian Society of
         Agricultural Economics, 1958. 164 pp. [Indian State of Gujarat]

11400   Shah, S. A., and I. S. Bedi, "Levels of Living in Rural Areas: A
         Perspective of Four Case Studies," Indian J. agric. Econ. 18:1 (Jan.
         1963), 349-355. [India]

11401   Shah, Vimal, Bhuvel: Socio-economic Survey of a Village. Bombay:
         Vora, 1949. 154 pp. [Indian State of Gujarat]

11402   Shastri, C. P., "Levels of Living in Rural Areas in Bihar," Indian
         J. agric. Econ. 18:1 (Jan. 1963), 302-310.

11403   Shukla, J. B., Study in Indian Economics: Life and Labour in
         Gujarat Taluka. Calcutta: Longmans, Green, 1937. 291 pp.

11404   Singh, R. D., "Socio-Economic Study of Village Sherpur," All India
         Congr. Comm. econ. Rev. 13 (22 Aug. 1961), 28-31. [Indian State of
         Uttar Pradesh]

11405   Singh, Umrao, "Community Development in India: Evaluation and Statis-
         tical Analysis." Thesis, Agra University, 1962. 304 mim. pp.

11406   Smith, Michael Garfield, The Economy of Hausa Communities in Zaria.
         Colonial Research Studies 16. London: HMSO, 1955. 264 pp.
         [Nigeria]

11407   Snapper, F., "Minimum Wages in Netherlands New Guinea. A Statis-
         tical Comparison with International Standards," Nieuw-Guinea Stud.
         6:3 (July 1962), 219-229.

11408   Tardits, Claude, Contribution à l'étude des populations: Bamiléké
         de l'Ouest Cameroun [Contribution to the study of populations:
         Bamiléké of West Cameroon]. Paris: Berger-Levrault, 1960. 135 pp.

Socioeconomic Factors

RUR 12304

11409 Thailand, Krom Prachasongkhro, Report on the Socio-economic Survey of the Hill Tribes in Northern Thailand. Bangkok: Department of Public Welfare, Ministry of the Interior, 1962. 111 pp.

11410 Thoré, L., "Dagondane-Pikine: Etude démographique et sociologique" [Dagondane-Pikine: A sociological and demographic study], Bull. Inst. fr. Afr. Noire 24:1-2 (Jan.-Apr. 1962), 155-198. [Senegal]

11411 T'ien, Ju-K'ang, The Chinese of Sarawak: A Study of Social Structure. London: Department of Anthropology, London School of Economics and Political Science, 1953. 91 pp. [Malaysia]

11412 Umaña, Salvador C., "A General Socio-economic Survey of the Province of Antique," Contemp. Stud. 1 (Mar. 1964), 45-62. [Philippines]

11413 Velásquez, R., "Apuntes socio-económicos del Atrato Medio" [Socio-economic study of Central Atrato], Rev. colomb. Antrop. 10 (1961), 157-226. [Colombia]

11414 Verin, P., "Notes socio-économiques sur l'île de Rurutu, Polynésie française" [Socioeconomic notes on Rurutu Island in French Polynesia], Cah. Inst. Sci. écon. 145, Suppl., Series 5:7 (Jan. 1964), 99-134.

11415 Wilson, D., "Economic Survey of a Native Village," S. Afr. Outlook 61 (1931), 6-8. [Republic of South Africa]

11416 Yenching University, Ching Ho: The Report of the Preliminary Survey of the Town of Ching Ho, Hopei, North China. Peking: Yenching University Press, 1931. 146 pp.

11417 Yeshwanth, T. S., "Income and Levels of Living in Some South Indian Villages," Indian J. agric. Econ. 18:1 (Jan. 1963), 261-270.

12. Bibliographies

12301 Hart, Donn V., and Paul Meadows, Selected Abstracts in Development Administration: Field Reports of Directed Social Change. Syracuse: Maxwell Graduate School, Syracuse University, 1962. 199 pp.

12302 Keesing, Felix M., Culture Change: An Analysis and Bibliography of Anthropological Sources to 1952. Stanford, Calif.: Stanford University Press, 1953. 242 pp.

12303 United Nations, Department of Economic and Social Affairs, UN Series on Community Development. Selective Book List. New York: United Nations, 1960. 15 pp.

12304 von Fuerer-Haimendorf, An Anthropological Bibliography of South Asia, together with a Directory of Recent Anthropological Field Research. Paris: Mouton, 1958. 748 pp.

[295]

INDEX BY AUTHOR

References are given by section and order within the section. The number in parentheses is the year of publication of the book or article.

Ainsworth, M. D.
  RUR 2303('62), 5301('62)

Aird, J.
  URB 3001('57)

Akhauri, N.
  RUR 2304('58), 8305('58)

Akhtar, A. U.
  IND 3302('59)

Akktar, S.S.
  IND 2304('63)

Aldous, J.
  URB 3302('62), 4301('62)

Alers-Montalvo, M.
  RUR 2305('57), 2306('63), 6302('60)

Alexander-Frutschi, M. C.
  GEN 3301('63)

Alexandre, P.
  RUR 5302('63)

Ali, H. A.
  RUR 10305('63), 11302('61)

Allen, H. B.
  RUR 10301('53)

Almond, G. A.
  GEN 2303('63)

Altekar, M.D.
  RUR 2307('44)

Althabe, G.
  IND 6301('59)
  URB 2001('59)
  RUR 6001('62)

American Society of Friends: see
  Friends

Ames, D.
  RUR 6002('62)

Ames, M.
  GEN 2304('63)

Ammar, H. M.
  RUR 8002('54)

Amunugama, S.
  RUR 6303('64)

Anderson, J. C.
  GEN 1434('64)

Andrews, J.
  RUR 3302('56)

Andrews, H. T.
  RUR 11304('62)

Anfossi, A.
  IND 5303('63)

Ankara University, Fac. Pol. Sci.
  RUR 3001('53)

Antoine, C.
  RUR 4302(n.d.)

Anzola Gomez, G.
  RUR 2308('62)

Aoyagi, K.
  RUR 2309('64)

Aple, D. P.
  URB 5373('56)

Apter, D. E.
  GEN 2305('55)
  RUR 5303('61)

Apthorpe, R.
  GEN 4354('58)

Apti, D. P.
  RUR 6304('64)

Arasteh, J. D.
  GEN 2306('60)

Araujo, A. M.
  RUR 7301('55)

Arcarya, H.
  RUR 4303('59)

Baldwin, K. D. S.
  RUR 4001('57), 6359('56)

Balkrishna, R.
  GEN 1312('60)

Ballinger, M.
  URB 2304('38)

Balsara, J. F.
  URB 2305('57)
  RUR 2312('62), 4306('58), 4307('58)

Bandyopadhyay, N.
  RUR 2397('64), 6364('64)

Bandyopadhyay, S.
  RUR 11321('63)

Banerjee, H. N.
  RUR 3308('64), 8312('60)

Banerjee, N.
  IND 2307('63)

Banfield, E. C.
  RUR 8007('58)

Bango, R. M.
  IND 2327('58)

Banks, E. P.
  RUR 8313('56)

Banks, J. A.
  GEN 1313('62), 3303('62)

Bannum, R.
  IND 2308('45)

Banton, M. P.
  GEN 2318('61), 4305('66)
  IND 5305('60)
  URB 1304('61), 2004('56), 2005('61)
      2006('57), 2306('66), 2307('53)

Barber, W. J.
  RUR 1304('60), 6307('61)

Barbosa Da Silva, J. F.
  GEN 2319('62)

Barclay, H. B.
  RUR 8008('64)

Bardier, C. H.
  RUR 5307('63)

Bardin, P.
  RUR 8009('65)

Barennes, Y.
  RUR 2313('48)

Barić, L.
  RUR 6308('64)

Barnabas, A. P.
  RUR 8314('60)

Barnes, J. A.
  URB 2007('51), 3002('51)
  RUR 5308('54), 9364('50)

Barnett, H. G.
  GEN 1314('53)
  RUR 8315('49), 9003('60)

Barnouw, V.
  RUR 8061('58)

Barrau, J. D.
  RUR 6309('56)

Barth, F.
  RUR 5309('59), 6310('64)

Barwell, C. W.
  RUR 9304('56)

Bascom, W. R.
  GEN 4306('59)
  URB 2308('62), 2309('60), 4305('63)

Basinski, J. J.
  RUR 4308('57)

Bastide, R.
  GEN 2320('65)
  RUR 6004('59)

Basu, T. K.
  RUR 8316('62)

Bataillon, C.
  URB 4306('63)
  RUR 2314('63), 2315('63), 2316('63)
      2317('63), 2318('63), 9305('63)

Bergmann, T.
  RUR 2322('63), 6316('63)

Berliner, J. S.
  GEN 1321('62)
  RUR 1306('62)

Berna, J. J.
  IND 5307('57)

Bernard, S.
  GEN 1322('56), 1399('58)

Berndt, C. H.
  RUR 2323('62), 2324('57), 7303('62)

Bernstein, F.
  RUR 2606('66)

Bernus, E.
  URB 2312('62)
  RUR 2325('63)

Berque, J.
  GEN 2329('63)
  RUR 8322('57), 8323('55)

Berreman, G. D.
  RUR 2326('54), 8324('63)

Bertolino, A.
  GEN 1323('57)

Bessac, F. B.
  RUR 2327('64)

Bessaignet, P.
  RUR 1307('66)

Beteille, A.
  GEN 2330('64)
  RUR 2328('66), 5003('65), 8325('62)

Bettison, D. G.
  GEN 4361('59)
  IND 6302('58)
  URB 3003('61), 5308('61), 5359('59)
  RUR 6317('59)

Betz, G. W.
  GEN 4359('63)

Beuchelt, E.
  RUR 2329('63), 8326('63), 9307('62)

Bharat Sevak Samaj
  URB 5309('58)

Bhattacharya, S. N.
  RUR 4315(n.d.)

Bhouraskur, K. M.
  RUR 5313('64)

Bhowmick, P. K.
  RUR 6318('60), 8327('63), 8328('65)

Bhutani, D. H.
  IND 2309('64)

Bicanič, R.
  GEN 1324('64)

Biebuyck, D.
  GEN 2331('64), 4310('63)

Biesheuvel, S.
  IND 2034('58)

Binet, J.
  IND 5308('61)
  RUR 6319('62), 6320('59), 6321('62)
    11309('59)

Birket-Smith, K.
  GEN 4311('60)
  RUR 1308('60)

Bisson, J.
  RUR 9308('63)

Blacking, J.
  RUR 2330('64)

Blair, A. P.
  GEN 2332('65)

Blair, R. V. V.
  GEN 2333('65)

Blair, T. L.
  RUR 2331('60)

Blake, D. J.
  IND 6303('62)

Bloemfontein Joint Council
  URB 5310('28)

Breese, G.
  URB 4309('66)

Brelsford, W. V.
  RUR 6008('46)

Brembeck, C. S.
  GEN 3304('62), 3305('62)

Bretones, G. J.
  RUR 8335('62)

Bridgman, F. B.
  IND 6304('26)

Brisseau, J.
  URB 2320('63)

Brokensha, D.
  GEN 4315('65)
  RUR 8017('66)

Brookfield, H. C.
  RUR 9311('63)

Brown, D. W.
  RUR 11315('60)

Brown, P.
  RUR 9311('63)

Brozen, Y.
  GEN 1326('49)

Bruner, E. M.
  URB 2321('61)

Brunet, R.
  IND 4001('58)

Bruyns, L.
  RUR 11316('51)

Brys, A.
  URB 4310('53)

Bui-Dang-Ha-Doa, J.
  RUR 10307('62)

Buitron, A.
  RUR 8336('62), 8349('49)

Bull, G. T.
  RUR 10308('62)

Bunzel, R. L.
  RUR 8337('52)

Burgess, J. S.
  URB 2347('21)

Burke, J. T.
  RUR 2340('62)

Burling, R.
  GEN 1327('62)
  RUR 1311('62), 1312('66), 7304('63)
        10309('65)

Burman, B. K. R.
  URB 1310('57)

Burns, W.
  RUR 2341('41)

Burridge, K. O. L.
  IND 4303('62)
  RUR 2006('60)

Busia, K. A.
  IND 5310('53)
  URB 4311('59)
  RUR 5316('51)

Busino, G.
  IND 5311('60)

Butterworth, D. S.
  URB 2322('62)

Buttrick, J. A.
  GEN 4316('54), 4400('54)

Buxton, J. C.
  RUR 5317('63)

Cabrita, H.
  IND 5312('53)

Calderón Alvarado, L.
  URB 2008('63)

Caldwell, J. C.
  URB 3304 ('66)

Callaway, A.
  URB 2323('63)

Chatterjee, B.
  URB 2330('62)

Chatterjee, B. B.
  RUR 7330('65)

Chatterji, A.
  RUR 2347('64), 6327('64)

Chattopadhyay, G.
  RUR 8341('64)

Chattopadhyay, K.
  RUR 11321('63)

Chattopadhyay, K. P.
  IND 6306('47)
  RUR 2348('57)

Chaudhuri, R.
  RUR 5318('64)

Chauhan, B. R.
  RUR 2349('60)

Chauhan, I. S.
  URB 3306('65)

Chaves, M.
  RUR 8342('53)

Chen, C. S.
  GEN 2342('65)

Chen, S. H.
  GEN 2343('56)

Chiba, H.
  RUR 8343('62)

Chin, R.
  GEN 2450('63)

Chinn, W. H.
  URB 3308('60)

Chiva, I.
  RUR 1314('59)

Chiwale, J. C.
  RUR 5335('63)

Cholia, C. N.
  IND 2316('41)

Choudhry, N. K.
  GEN 4359('63)

Choudhury, A. R.
  URB 2329('64)

Choudhury, H. K.
  RUR 3305('57)

Chowdhury, J. K.
  GEN 1330('60)
  IND 3307('58)

Christensen, J. B.
  GEN 2344('57)

Christiansen, S.
  RUR 2350('63), 6328('63)
      6329('63)

Cian, R.
  IND 2317('62)

Clark, G.
  IND 2034('58)

Clarke, E.
  RUR 7306('53), 7307('57)

Clauzel, J.
  RUR 2351('63), 6330('63)
      8344('62)

Clay, H.
  IND 2318('30)

Clay, H. F.
  RUR 2352('50)

Clayton, E. S.
  RUR 10311('64)

Clemens, R.
  GEN 2345('53)

Clément, P.
  URB 2009('56), 3309('56)

Clemmer, M. M.
  URB 4381('63), 5367('63)

Clerc, J.
  RUR 3003('56)

Clignet, R.
  URB 3310('66)

Clinard, M. B.
  URB 2330('62)

Cohen, A.
  URB 2331('66)
  RUR 6331('65), 8345('65)

Cohen, R.
  RUR 2353('64), 8346('61)

Cohen, Y. A.
  RUR 7001('56), 7308('56), 8347('54)

Cohn, B. S.
  URB 2010('59)
  RUR 8020('55), 8348('59)

Cola Alberich, J.
  IND 5313('54)

Collard, C.
  IND 2377('58)

Collier, J. Jr.
  RUR 8349('49)

Collin Delavaud, C.
  RUR 8350('65)

Collins, G. R.
  RUR 11389('53)

Colson, E.
  GEN 2346('62), 4317('59)
  RUR 2354('64), 6009('62), 6332('65)

Comhaire, J. L.
  URB 2332('56), 6301('52)
  RUR 7309('56)

Comitas, L.
  RUR 6010('64)

Comte, J.
  RUR 10312('63)

Condominas, G.
  RUR 4323('60)

Congreso Nacional de Sociología
  GEN 4318('55)

Consejo de Bienestas Rural
  RUR 8021('56)

Cook, S.
  RUR 1315('66)

Corkery, K. J.
  IND 2319('22)

Cornejo Cabera, E.
  RUR 8351('62)

Cornell, J. B.
  RUR 2356('64), 2357('61), 8022('56)
    8352('64), 8353('63)

Cortis, L. E.
  IND 2320('62)

Costa, E. B.
  RUR 7310('55)

Costa Pinto, L. A.
  GEN 1332('63), 2347('58)
  IND 5314('62), 5315('59)

Cotler, J.
  RUR 8354('59)

Coult, L. H.
  GEN 3306('58)

Coulter, C. W.
  IND 3308('35)

Cowan, L. G.
  RUR 5319('58)

Cragg, A. W.
  URB 5375('22)

Crane, R. I.
  GEN 2348('54)
  URB 4312('55)

Crespi, P.
  GEN 1333('63)

Cressey, P. F.
  URB 4313('60)

Crist, R. E.
  RUR 3306('64)

Devanandan, P. D.
  URB 2338('58)

Devasagayam, A.
  IND 1305('59)

Devauges, R.
  IND 6307('58)
  URB 2014('58), 5316('61)

De Vos, G.
  URB 2027('60)
  RUR 7314('61)

De Vries, E.
  GEN 2358('63)

De Waal Malefijt, A.
  RUR 2008('63)

Dewey, A. G.
  RUR 6341('64), 6342('62), 6343('62)

Dey, S. K.
  RUR 4329('60), 4330('64), 4331('62)

De Young, J. E.
  RUR 8361('55)

Dez, V.
  GEN 2359('62)
  RUR 10313 ('62)

Dhar, P. N.
  IND 6342('58)

D'Haucourt, G. M.
  GEN 2360('60)

Dhekney, B. R.
  URB 5317('59)

Dhillon, S. H. S.
  RUR 2364('55)

Dholakia, J. L.
  IND 3310('63)

Dhoquois, G.
  RUR 1320('66)

Diaz, M. N.
  RUR 8362('64), 8363('66)

Diaz, R. C.
  RUR 11324('61)

Diégues Júnior, M.
  RUR 1321('63), 2365('64), 10314('63)

Di Martino, A.
  RUR 9318('63)

Dina, I. O.
  RUR 6359('56)

Diop, A. B.
  URB 3004('65), 5318('65)
  RUR 11325('65)

Diskalkar, P. D.
  RUR 8364('60)

Diziain, R.
  URB 5319('62)

Djamour, J.
  URB 3005('59)

Dobyns, H. F.
  URB 4317('63)
  RUR 4358('62)

Dohrenwend, B. P.
  RUR 1322('57)

Dole, G. E.
  GEN 4321('60)

Dollfuss, O.
  URB 5320('52)

Dominguez, O.
  RUR 4332('63)

Donoghue, J. D.
  RUR 8365('61), 8366('62)

Doob, L. W.
  GEN 1338('61)
  RUR 1323('60)

Dorjahn, V. R.
  RUR 6013('62)

Dorse Laer, J.
  URB 4318('62)

Doshi, S. L.
  RUR 4333('64)

Dosser, D. G. M.
  GEN 2318('61)

Dotson, L. O.
  GEN 3307('50)

Doucy, A.
  GEN 2361('57)
  IND 2003('56), 2328('63)

Douglas, M.
  RUR 1329('56), 6014('62), 6344('58)
    9319('63)

Doutreloux, A.
  RUR 2366('66)

Eggan, F. R.
  RUR 8372('55)

Eglar, Z. S.
  RUR 2373('58), 8028('60)

Ehrenfels, U. R.
  GEN 1342('58)
  RUR 6347('61)

Einsiedel, L. A.
  RUR 4342('60)

Eisenstadt, S. N.
  GEN 1343('54), 1344('64), 1345('65)
      1346('56), 1347('64), 1348('64)
      1349('63), 1350('66), 1351('64)
      1352('64), 1353('65), 2365('54)
      2366('65)
  IND 2332('55)
  RUR 2374('56), 3309('56)

Elder, J. W.
  IND 4002('59)

Elkan, W.
  IND 2004('56), 2333('57), 2334('60)
      3312('64)

Elkin, A. P.
  RUR 2375('63)

Ellefsen, R. A.
  URB 4320('62)

El-Saaty, H.
  IND 5323('62)

Elvery, A. W.
  RUR 6348('62)

Ember, M.
  RUR 2010('64)

Embree, J. F.
  GEN 3307('50)
  RUR 8029('39)

Encarnación, V. Jr.
  RUR 5321('61), 5322('57)

Epstein, A. L.
  URB 2341('60), 2342('64)
  RUR 2376('63), 5323('56), 5324('57)
      6349('63)

Epstein, T. S.
  GEN 1354(64)
  RUR 2377('66), 6016('64), 6350('63)
      6351('61), 7315('60), 8030('62)
      8373('60)

Erasmus, C. J.
  RUR 2378('52), 2379('56), 5325('52)
      6352(55)

Espiritu, S. C.
  RUR 4343('64)

Etienne, P.
  RUR 2380('66)

Etzioni, A.
  GEN 2367('64)

Etzioni, E.
  GEN 2367('64)

Falcon, W. P.
  RUR 6353('64)

Fallers, L. A.
  GEN 1355('64), 2368('64)
  RUR 5326('66), 9320('56)

Fals-Borda, O.
  GEN 2369('62), 2370('59), 2371(61)
  RUR 8031('55), 8374('61)

Farmer, B. H.
  RUR 4344('57)

Faron, L. C.
  RUR 9321('61)

Farouk, A.
  IND 2014('61), 2015('63), 6309('63)

Fathalla el Khatib, M.
  RUR 5336('58)

Faure, H.
  RUR 2381('63), 9322('63)

Fautz, B.
  RUR 2382('63)

Favre, H.
  RUR 2382a('63)

[313]

France, Organisation Commune des
  Régions Sahariennes
  IND 4005('60)

Franchi, J.
  URB 2345('60)

Frankel, S. H.
  GEN 1359('63)

Franzoi, A.
  GEN 2376('61)

Fraser, T. M.
  GEN 1360('63)
  RUR 1335('63), 8033('60)

Freed, R. S.
  RUR 5328('66)

Freed, S. A.
  RUR 5328('66)

Freedman, M.
  RUR 8379('60)

Freeman, M.
  GEN 2377('66)

Freitas Marcondes, J. V.
  IND 4306('62)

Fremont, A.
  RUR 9325('61)

Fried, J.
  RUR 8380('62)

Fried, M. H.
  GEN 1361('64)
  URB 2346('53)

Friedl, E.
  RUR 8381('62)

Friedlander, M.
  RUR 9326('62)

Friedlander, S. L.
  GEN 2378('65)

Friedman, G.
  GEN 3308('52)

Friedmann, F. G.
  GEN 1362('56)

Friedrich, P.
  RUR 2390('62), 8382('63)

Friends, American Society of
  RUR 4346(58)

Froehlich, J. C.
  GEN 2379('63), 2380('63)

Froehlich, W.
  IND 1308('61), 5326('61)

Fujii, H.
  RUR 8384('58)

Fujiki, M.
  RUR 8383('58), 8384('58)

Fujimoto, I.
  RUR 2388('65)

Fukutake, T.
  GEN 1363('62)
  IND 3313('62)
  URB 4322('58), 5323('58), 5324('62)
  RUR 1336('64), 2389('61), 5329('62)
      8034('53), 8035('62), 8036('59)
      8037('54), 8038('64), 8385('46)
      8386('62), 8387('49), 8388('54)
      10315('64)

Fuller, A. H.
  RUR 8039('61)

Furnivall, J. S.
  GEN 2381('39)

Furushima, T.
  IND 4006('49)

Fuse, T.
  RUR 8389('62)

Fyfe, C.
  URB 4323('64)

Gadgil, D. R.
  URB 5325('52), 5326('65)
  RUR 11334('40)

Gadgil, V. R.
  RUR 11334('40)

Gaitskell, A.
  RUR 8390('59)

Galenson, W.
  IND 2336('62)

Galibert, G.
  IND 5327('58)

Galjart, B.
  RUR 5330('64)

Galletti, R.
  RUR 6359('56)

Gallin, B.
  RUR 4347('64), 8040('66)

Galloy, P.
  RUR 10316('63)

Gallup, G.
  RUR 4337('62)

Gamble, D. P.
  RUR 11335('49)

Gamble, S. D.
  URB 2347('21)
  RUR 4003('54), 11336('63)

Gamble, S. P.
  URB 3315('63)

Gamo, M.
  RUR 8391('63)

Gangrade, K. D.
  IND 2005('54)
  URB 3316('64), 4324('64)

Ganguli, H. C.
  IND 2006('54), 2007('55), 2008('54)
    2009('59), 2337('56), 2338('57)
    2339('54), 2340('61), 2341('61)
    2342('57), 2343('63), 2344('54)
    2345('57), 2346('60), 2347('64)
    2348('54), 2349('55), 2350('57)
    2351('58), 2352('57), 2353('57)
    2354('54)

Ganguly, T.
  IND 2010('53), 2355(n.d.), 2356('58)

Garbett, K. G.
  URB 5327('60)
  RUR 2013('60), 11337('60)

García, A.
  RUR 3310('64)

García-Figueras, T.
  GEN 2382('56)

Garfield, V. E.
  GEN 4326('64), 4327('61)

Garg, R. P.
  RUR 9327('65)

Gast, M.
  URB 2348('65)

Gatheru, R. M.
  RUR 10317('64)

Gaudio, A.
  RUR 10318('63)

Gaudry, M.
  RUR 2391('61)

Geddes, W. R.
  RUR 2392('45), 8041('45)

Geertz, C.
  GEN 2383('56), 2384('65), 2385('63)
  URB 2349('67), 2350('65)
  RUR 2014('63), 2393('57), 2394('65)
    3004('56), 3311('56), 6360('63)
    6361('56), 6362('66), 8392('59)
    8393('56), 8394('56), 8395('64)

Geertz, H.
  RUR 7320('61)

Geiger, P. P.
  URB 4325('61)

Geiger, T.
  IND 3314('65)

Gendarme, R.
  GEN 2386('59)

General Missionary Conference of
  South Africa
  GEN 4328('22)

Georges, M.
  RUR 2395('63)

Gerlach, L. P.
  RUR 2396('63), 6363('63)

Germani, G.
  GEN 1364('63), 1365('66), 2387('62)
    2388('66)

  URB 2015('61), 3317('62), 4326('63)
    4327('63)

Ghilain, J.
  RUR 11338('63)

Ghose, B.
  URB 4328('60)

Ghose, S. K.
  RUR 4348('63)

Ghosh, D.
  GEN 1366('60)

Ghosh, M. G.
  RUR 2397('64), 6364('64)

Ghosh, R.
  IND 2352('57), 2353('57)

Ghosh, S.
  RUR 6365('64)

Ghurye, G. S.
  IND 2357('65)
  URB 2351('64), 4329('53)
  RUR 10319('54)

Gibbs, J. P.
  URB 1314('58)

Gibson, G. D.
  RUR 6020('62)

Gidal, S.
  RUR 8396('56)

Gidal, T.
  RUR 8396('56)

Gillain, H.
  RUR 8397('61)

Gillin, J. P.
  RUR 8042('51), 8398('46)

Ginsberg, N. S.
  URB 1315('66)

Ginsburg, N. S.
  URB 4330('66)

Giri, V. V.
  IND 2358('59)

Girling, F. K.
  RUR 9005('60)

Girod, R.
  GEN 1367('59)

Glacken, C. J.
  RUR 8043('55)

Glade, W.
  GEN 2389('61)
  IND 5328('61)

Gluckman, M.
  GEN 4317('59), 4329('64)
  URB 2016('61)
  RUR 1337('40), 1338('58), 2398('40)
    2399('45), 6021('41), 10320('66)

Go, G. T.
  RUR 2015('66)

Goddard, S.
  RUR 2015('66)

Godelier, M.
  GEN 1368('65)

Goethals, P. R.
  RUR 5005('61)

Golden, H. H.
  URB 1311('54)

Goldenweiser, A.
  GEN 4362('27)

Goldkind, V.
  RUR 8044('65)

Guha, M.
  URB 2352('62), 2354('66)

Guha, S.
  URB 4331('58)

Guhl, E.
  RUR 11340('63)

Guiart, J.
  RUR 2403('60)

Guilbot, J.
  IND 2011(n.d.)

Guillard, J.
  RUR 2404('56), 8401('65), 11341('65)

Guillaume, A.
  RUR 6370('55)

Guiteras-Holmes, C.
  RUR 2405('61)

Gulick, J.
  RUR 8046('55), 8402('54), 8403('53)

Gullick, J. M.
  RUR 5334('58)

Gulliver, P. H.
  IND 2360('60)
  URB 2017('55)
  RUR 6023('62), 7323('64), 9007('58)

Gumperz, J. J.
  RUR 2406('64)

Gundappa, D. V.
  IND 5331('55)

Gupta, B. L.
  GEN 2434('64)

Gupta, L. C.
  RUR 8424('63), 11359('63)

Gupta, R.
  RUR 4351('64)

Gupta, S. C.
  URB 5330('65)
  RUR 6425('60), 11342('59)

Gupta, S. K.
  RUR 4352('65)

Gupta, T. R.
  RUR 7325('61)

Gurvitch, G.
  GEN 4331('62)

Gussman, B. W.
  IND 2361('53)
  URB 2355('52)

Gutelman, M.
  RUR 10338('63)

Guthrie, H. W.
  IND 2362('61)

Gutierrez de Pineda, V.
  RUR 7326('62)

Gutkind, P. C. W.
  URB 2356('62), 2357('63), 2437('57)
       3016('57), 3320('62), 3321('66)
       3322(63), 3323('62), 3324('61)
       4332('65), 4333('62), 4334('60)
       5331('63)

Guy, G. S. C.
  RUR 6371('58)

Habibullah, M.
  URB 2358('64)

Hadji-Dimou, P.
  RUR 1341('59)

Hagen, E. E.
  GEN 1374('62)

Haider, A. S.
  URB 2359('60)

Haines, E. S.
  RUR 6372('33)

Hair, P. E. H.
  URB 2360('53)

Hakoyama, K.
  RUR 8404('61)

Halcrow, M.
  RUR 4353('59)

Hall, D.
  RUR 6423('60)

Hall, J. W.
  RUR 8015('59)

Hallenback, W.
  URB 3325('55)

Haller, A. O.
  IND 3323('64)

Halperin, M.
  GEN 2392('55)

Halpern, J. M.
  GEN 2393('64), 2394(n.d.), 3309('61)
  URB 2018('64)
  RUR 2407('63), 6024('59), 6373('61)
      6374('64), 6375('62), 8047('58)
      8405('58), 8406('56), 11343('61)

Hamilton, J. W.
  RUR 6376('63)

Hammel, E. A.
  RUR 2408('62), 3006('62)

Hammond, P. B.
  RUR 4004('59)

Hammond-Tooke, W. D.
  RUR 9329('62)

Hanawa, R.
  RUR 2409('63)

Hancock, R. H.
  RUR 2410('59)

Hancock, R. N.
  RUR 4354('54)

Handler, J. S.
  RUR 6377('66)

Hanks, L. M. Jr.,
  URB 4335('62)

Hanks, L. M. Jr.
  RUR 2411('57), 2412('60), 2413('53)

Hansen, H. H.
  RUR 8407('63)

Haouat, H.
  RUR 3312('53)

Hara, H.
  RUR 2414('60), 2415('63), 8408('59)

Harbison, F. H.
  IND 2363('56)

Harding, T. G.
  RUR 6025('65)

Harit, H. L.
  URB 2436('60)

Harper, E. B.
  RUR 6378('59)

Harries-Jones, P.
  URB 3326('64)
  RUR 5335('63)

Harris, J. S.
  RUR 6379('44)

Harris, M.
  RUR 2416('66), 6380('59)

Harrison-Church, R. J.
  RUR 8409('62)

Hart, C. W. M.
  URB 4336('64)

Hart, D. V.
  GEN 3310('57)
  RUR 2017('55), 8410('54), 12301('62)

Harwitz, M.
  GEN 2395('64)

Hasegawa, A.
  URB 2361('61)

Hashimoto, M.
  IND 1311('59)

Hasumi, O.
  RUR 8432('58)

Haswell, M. R.
  RUR 6026('53), 11344('53)

Hauser, A.
  RUR 3313('56)

Hauser, P. M.
  GEN 4332('61), 4333('66)
  URB 1317('66), 4337('57)

Hawley, A. H.
  GEN 1375('50)

Hayashi, J.
  RUR 2417('63)

Hayashi, M.
  RUR 11345('53)

Hayden, H.
  RUR 4355('53), 4356('56)

Hays, H. R.
  GEN 1376('58)

Heeren, H. J.
  URB 5332('55)
  RUR 4005('56), 4357('56), 8411('53)

Hegba, M.
  GEN 1377('64)

Heinz, P.
  GEN 4334('62)

Hellmann, E. P.
  IND 2012('53), 6308('53)
  URB 2019('37), 2020('48), 2362('34)
    2363('35), 4338('56), 5333('35)

Helm, J.
  GEN 4335('65)

Hendry, J. B.
  IND 2013('60)
  RUR 6027('62), 8048('64), 11346('59)

Hennessy, L. F.
  IND 5333('64)

Henrard, L.
  URB 2364('58)

Henry, R. N.
  RUR 2418('63)

Herradura, E. S.
  RUR 2419('62)

Herrick, B. H.
  URB 5334('65)

Herskovits, F. S.
  RUR 8049('47)

Herskovits, M. J.
  GEN 1378('64), 1379('61), 1380('54)
    1381('63), 2396('64), 2397('52)
    2398('62), 4306('59), 4336('64)
  URB 4339('60), 4340('61)
  RUR 1342('52), 2018('37), 8049('47)
    8412('37), 9008('38)

Herzog, R.
  RUR 9330('56)

Hester, E. R.
  IND 2377('58)

Hickey, G. C.
  RUR 8050('60), 8051('64)

Hickman, J. M.
  RUR 1343('64)

Higgins, B. H.
  Gen 4337('61)

Hill, P.
  RUR 3005('63), 3314('56), 6381('66)
    6382('63), 6383('66)

Hinners, D. G.
  RUR 9331('61)

Hirabayashi, G. K.
  URB 3327('58)
  RUR 2019('56), 5336('58), 8306('56)

Hirsch, A. R.
  GEN 2399('65)

Hirsch, L. V.
  RUR 6384('61)

Hirsch, W.
  GEN 4402('64)

Hitchcock, J. T.
  RUR 2420('63)

Hodder, B. W.
  RUR 6028('62)

Huizenga, L. H.
  IND 2366('62)

Huizer, G.
  RUR 4362('63), 8417('63)

Huke, R.
  RUR 8418('56)

Hunt, C. L.
  GEN 2401('62), 2402('66)
  URB 4343('56)
  RUR 4343('64)

Hunt, R.
  RUR 6031('65)

Hunter, D. A.
  RUR 10325('22)

Hunter, G.
  GEN 2403('62), 3311('62), 4341('65)

Hunter, M.
  RUR 2022('37), 2426('33)

Huntingford, G. W. B.
  RUR 9010('50)

Hurault, J.
  RUR 9334('63), 9335('62)

Husain, A. F. A.
  IND 2014('61), 2015('63), 5336('63)
    6309('63), 6325('56), 6326('56)
  RUR 6388('62)

Husain, I. Z.
  GEN 2404('64)

Husain, M.
  IND 3316('59)

Hussain, M.
  RUR 6389('64), 11350('58)

Hussein, A.
  RUR 4363('53)

Hutchinson, B.
  IND 2367('63)
  URB 2367('63)

Hutchinson, H. W.
  RUR 2427('57)

Hutt, W. H.
  URB 2368('34)

Huzioka, Y.
  RUR 2428('62)

Ianni, O.
  IND 3306('61), 3317('63), 5337('60)
    5338('63)
  URB 2328('59)

Ibrahim, I. A.
  IND 2363('56)

Ide, Y.
  RUR 5007('60)

Iijima, S.
  RUR 9336('65)

Ilo, P.
  RUR 2429('54)

India, Labour Bureau
  RUR 3317('64)

India, Ministry of Community
  Development
  RUR 4364('63)

India, Ministry of Food and
  Agriculture
  RUR 4365('61)

India, Planning Commission
  RUR 4008('55)

Indian Institute of Economics
  URB 5336('56)

Indian Society of Agricultural
  Economics
  RUR 11351('57), 11352('54)

Ingersoll, J.
  RUR 6442('62)

Ingram, J. C.
  IND 6310('55)

Inkeles, A.
  GEN 1398('66), 1457('66)

Jackson, I. C.
  RUR 4366('56)

Jaffe, A. J.
  IND 5340('59)

Jagalpure, L. B.
  RUR 11355('38)

Jahoda, G.
  URB 3329('59)

Jain, H. K.
  RUR 4367('62)

James, R. C.
  IND 2372('62)

Janlekha, K.
  RUR 6390('55)

Janne, H.
  GEN 1399('58)

Jantzen, G.
  GEN 2406('62)

Japan Cultural Science Society
  IND 2016('59), 2017('58), 3318('59)
    3319('55), 3320('54), 5341('59)
    5342('60), 6327('55), 6328('63)
    6329('54)
  RUR 2435('59), 2436('60), 11356('60)

Jarre, R.
  RUR 2437('55)

Jaspan, M. A.
  GEN 3314('61)
  IND 2373('62), 2374('63)
  URB 6303('59)

Jaulin, R.
  RUR 8423('60)

Jay, R. R.
  RUR 5008('63)

Jayawardena, C.
  RUR 20239'63), 3318('62), 7329('62)

Jennings, J. D.
  GEN 4349('66)

Jha, J. C.
  RUR 7330('65)

Jha, S. C.
  RUR 11357('63)

Jiménez Paniagua, J.
  RUR 11358('63)

Jocano, F. L.
  RUR 4368('63)

Jodha, N. S.
  RUR 2332('65)

Joglekar, N. M.
  RUR 2438('63)

John, P. V.
  RUR 5339('63), 8424('63), 11359('63)

Johnson, E.
  RUR 2439('63)

Johnson, G.
  GEN 2407('64)

Joint Commission on Rural
  Reconstruction in China
  IND 2375('64)

Jones, W. O.
  GEN 1400('65)
  RUR 2024('57)

Jones-Quartey, K. A. B.
  GEN 2458('63)

Joshi, V.
  RUR 2440('62)

Judd, L. C.
  RUR 2441('61)

Junod, H. A.
  RUR 9340('62)

Junod, V. I.
  RUR 4369('64)

Kaberry, P. M.
  RUR 7005('52), 11360('52)

Kay, P.
  URB 2375('63)
  RUR 6393('64)

Kaye, B.
  URB 5338('60)

Kayser, B.
  URB 4347('64)

Keesing, F. M.
  RUR 5341('34), 12302('53)

Keith, J. P.
  GEN 3305('62)

Kennedy, B. C.
  URB 3330('54)

Kenny, W. J.
  IND 2377('58)

Kerr, C.
  IND 5343('60)

Keuning, J.
  RUR 9344('58)

Keyfitz, N.
  URB 4348('66)

Khaing, M. M.
  RUR 7332('62)

Khan, F. K.
  URB 5339('62)

Khare, R. S.
  RUR 2446('64), 4372('64), 5342('62)
      8433('62)

Khatri, A. A.
  GEN 2416('61)

Khin, M. L.
  URB 2376('62)

Khurana, B. K.
  IND 6313('58)

Khuri, F. I.
  RUR 6394('65)

Kiba, S.
  RUR 8434('60)

Kiener, A.
  RUR 10329('63)

Kilby, P.
  IND 2378('62)

Kinai, S.
  URB 2377('62)

Kindermann, G. K.
  GEN 1405('62)

Kingon, J. R. L.
  RUR 2447('20)

Kingshill, K.
  RUR 8055('60)

Kinoshita, K.
  RUR 1346('61)

Kirby, A.
  IND 5344('61)

Kitahara, M.
  RUR 8435('56)

Kitamura, T.
  RUR 8436('58), 8437('59)

Kluckhohn, R.
  RUR 6395('62)

Knak, D. S.
  RUR 7333('31)

Knowles, W. H.
  RUR 2448('56)

Knox, J. B.
  IND 2379('61)

Kobben, A. J. F.
  RUR 3319('56), 6396('58)

Koch, G.
  RUR 2449('62), 9345('62)

Kochar, V. K.
  RUR 7334('65), 7335('65)

Koentjaraningrat
  RUR 2450('61)

Lambiri, I.
  URB 2021('65)

Lambiri, J.
  IND 3322('63)

Lancaster, L.
  RUR 6400('62)

Lancksweirt, F.
  URB 4352('54)

Landy, D.
  RUR 2454('60)

Lang, G. O.
  RUR 9348('62)

Lang, M. B.
  RUR 9348('62)

Lang, N. G.
  RUR 3007('65)

Langness, L. L.
  RUR 5344('63)

Langworthy, R. L.
  RUR 4373('66)

Lapiere, R. T.
  GEN 1408('65)

Laquian, A. A.
  URB 2381('64)

Laroche, M. C.
  RUR 9349('54)

Lasswell, H. D.
  RUR 2455('62)

Last, J.
  RUR 10330('55)

Launay, M.
  RUR 2456('63), 7337('63), 10331('63)

Lauria, A. Jr.
  RUR 2457('64)

Lawrance, J. C. D.
  RUR 9350('57)

Lawrence, P.
  RUR 2458('63)

Lazarew, P.
  IND 4309('60)

Leach, E. R.
  RUR 8056('61)

Lebar, F. M.
  RUR 11365('64)

Le Blanc, C.
  RUR 8442('64)

LeBlanc, M.
  URB 3008('60)

Lebra, W. P.
  RUR 2459('63)

Lebret, L. J.
  GEN 1409('61)

Leclair, E. E. Jr.
  GEN 1410('62)
  RUR 1349('62)

Leduc, G.
  IND 5347('52)

Lee, S. B.
  URB 2382('65)

Lehman, F. K.
  RUR 9012('63)

Leighton, A. H.
  RUR 2460('63)

Leistner, G. M. E.
  IND 2387('64), 6314('64)

Lekachman, R.
  GEN 1436('64), 2453('64)

Lembezat, B.
  RUR 6401('62)

Lenhard, R.
  IND 2388('65)
  URB 2383('64), 2384('63)

Lerner, D.
  GEN 2419('64), 2420('58)

Leslie, C. M.
  RUR 8057('60)

Leslie, J. A. K.
  URB 5342('63)

Lesne, M.
  RUR 9013('59)

Letourneau, R.
  URB 4353('55)

Leubuscher, C.
  URB 2386('31), 5343('31)

Leuva, K. K.
  RUR 6402('60)

Levine, D. N.
  GEN 2421('65)

Levine, R. A.
  RUR 6033('62), 10332('66)

Lévi-Strauss, C.
  GEN 1411('63)

Levy, M. J. Jr.
  GEN 1412('62), 1413('52), 2422('62)
    2423('66)
  RUR 7006('49)

Lewis, D. K.
  RUR 9351('62)

Lewis, D. M.
  IND 3323('64)

Lewis, I. M.
  RUR 2461('61), 6403('62), 7338('62)

Lewis, O.
  URB 1320('66), 1321('63), 3333('65)
  RUR 1350('55), 2462('52), 2463('44)
    6404('56), 6405('47), 7339('61)
    7340('59), 7341('64), 8058('54)
    8059('51), 8060('60), 8061('58)
    8443('55)

Lewis, W. A.
  GEN 2424('57)

Leynaud, E.
  RUR 8444('63)

Li, W. L.
  RUR 2587('63)

Liebenow, G. J. Jr.
  RUR 5345('56)

Lin, S. H.
  IND 6315('28)

Lindstrom, D. E.
  RUR 1351('63), 8445('60)

Linn, J. M.
  IND 2389('51)

Linton, R.
  GEN 1414('52)

Lionberger, H. F.
  RUR 1352('60)

Lipset, S. M.
  GEN 1415('64), 1456('66), 4381('66)

Lissak, M.
  RUR 1390('64)

Little, K. L.
  GEN 2425('53)
  URB 1322('65), 2022('65), 2387('62)
    2388('55), 2389('62), 3334('48)
    4354('66), 4355('53), 4356('59)
    4357('60)
  RUR 5346('47), 9014('51)

Lloyd, P. C.
  URB 2390('60)
  RUR 6406('66)

Locher, G. W.
  GEN 1416('63)

Lockwood, W. G.
  RUR 1353('65)

Loeb, E. M.
  RUR 9352('62)

Lombard, J.
  URB 4358('57)

Long, J. F.
  RUR 2464('63)

Longmore, C.
  URB 4359('58)

Loomis, C. P.
  RUR 1354('53), 8446('53)

Lopes, J. R. B.
  URB 2023('61)

Lord, R. F.
  RUR 2465('63), 6407('63)

Lorenz, R.
  URB 6304('64)

Low, D. A.
  RUR 5347('64)

Lubin, M. A.
  RUR 8447('62)

Luschinsky, M.
  RUR 1355('63)

Lux, A.
  IND 3324('66)

Lux, T. E.
  RUR 8448('62)

McCall, D. F.
  URB 2024('62), 3009('61), 4361('60)

McCormack, W. C.
  RUR 5348('56), 8062('57), 8449('56)

McCrory, J. T.
  IND 3325('56)

McCulloch, M.
  IND 2390('56), 7303('54)
  URB 2393('56), 5344('56)
  RUR 2466('57), 2467('56)

McCurdy, D. W.
  RUR 8450('64)

MacDonald, J. S.
  RUR 6408('64)

MacDonald, L.
  RUR 6408('64)

McKee, H. S.
  RUR 6309('56)

McLane, J. R.
  RUR 2468('64)

McLoughlin, P. F. M.
  URB 5345('64)
  RUR 11366('65)

McMillan, R. T.
  RUR 11390('54)

MacRae, D. G.
  GEN 1357('58)

McWilliam, M. D.
  GEN 2426('63)

Maahs, A. M.
  RUR 1356('56)

Mabogunje, A. L.
  URB 2391('62), 2392('61), 4360('62)

Madan, B. K.
  RUR 6409('63)

Madan, G. R.
  RUR 4374('64)

Madge, C.
  RUR 8063('57)

Madigan, F. C.
  GEN 2427('59)
  RUR 4009('62)

Mading, K.
  URB 2394('64)

Mafeje, A.
  URB 2049('63)

Mahapatra, L. K.
  RUR 9353('64)

Maher, R. F.
  RUR 2025('61), 2469('60), 9354('61)

Mair, L.
  GEN 1417('65)

Maitreya, P.
  RUR 2347('64), 6327('64)

Martin, A.
  RUR 6413('63)

Martin, W. T.
  URB 1314('58)

Martin de Nicolas, J.
  GEN 1419('63)

Mason, L.
  RUR 2478('57), 8460('58)

Masood, M.
  URB 5339('62)

M.I.T. Center for International
  Studies
  IND 5351('57)

Masse, L.
  URB 5349('56)

Masuda, T.
  RUR 5354('63)

Mathur, A. S.
  GEN 2434('64)

Mathur, J. C.
  RUR 2026('59), 2027('62)

Mathur, K. S.
  RUR 6414('64), 8461('64), 8462('60)

Mathur, P. C.
  RUR 5349('64)

Mathur, V. S.
  IND 2392('55)

Matiba, J. I.
  GEN 2435('63)

Matos-Mar, J.
  GEN 2436('64)
  URB 2025('61)
  RUR 8067('63)

Matsubara, H.
  RUR 1360('60)

Matsushima, S.
  IND 2393('62)

Matthews, D.
  GEN 4354('58)
  IND 5352('58)

Maud, D.
  URB 3336('33)

Maude, H. E.
  RUR 2479('63)

Mayer, A.
  RUR 4010('58)

Mayer, A. C.
  RUR 2480('63), 4377('56), 4378('57)
    7342('54), 8068('60), 8463('55)
    10333('52), 10334('61)

Mayer, E.
  RUR 6415('66)

Mayer, I.
  URB 2026('61)

Mayer, P.
  URB 2026('61), 4364('62)
  RUR 6036('51)

Mdhluli, S. V. H.
  RUR 2481('33)

Mead, M.
  GEN 1420('64)
  RUR 9015('56)

Meade, J. E.
  RUR 11368('61)

Meadows, P.
  URB 6304('64)
  RUR12301('62)

Meenakshi Malaya, M.
  RUR 8466('63)

Mehra, J.
  RUR 11369('60)

Mehta, A. B.
  GEN 2437('60)
  URB 5350('60)

Mehta, B. V.
  IND 2383('58)

Mehta, R.
  RUR 4379('63)

Meillassoux, C.
  URB 2396('65)
  RUR 1361('60), 6037('62)

Meinkoth, M. R.
  URB 2397('62)

Meister, A.
  RUR 1362('61)

Mencher, J. P.
  RUR 7343('62), 7344('65), 8467('63)
    10335('63), 10336('66)

Mendez-Arocha, A.
  RUR 2482('63)

Mendras, H.
  RUR 8069('61)

Menezes, D.
  RUR 10337('64)

Menicias Chavez, J.
  RUR 8468('62)

Mercier, P.
  URB 1325('56)

Merlo, J. D.
  IND 2394('61)

Mersadier, Y.
  URB 1326('56)

Mertin, J.
  RUR 4380('62)

Messing, S. D.
  RUR 6416('62)

Métraux, A.
  RUR 10338('63)

Metzger, D.
  RUR 5352('63)

Meynaud, J.
  GEN 4356('63)

Mezerik, A. G.
  GEN 1421('59)

Mezirow, J. F.
  RUR 4381('60)

Middelkoop, P.
  RUR 9359('62)

Middleton, J.
  RUR 2483('58), 6038('62), 9016('65)
    9360('61), 9361('60)

Middleton, R.
  GEN 1435('60)

Millen, B. H.
  IND 3327('63)

Miller, E.
  URB 2445('64)

Miller, E. J.
  RUR 8469('60)

Miller, W. C.
  RUR 8470('64)

Mills, J. E.
  GEN 4357('58)

Milone, P. D.
  URB 4365('64)

Miner, H. M.
  URB 2027('60), 2398('53)
  RUR 2484('60), 4011('60)

Minkoff, M. F.
  IND 1320('60)

Minon, P.
  URB 2399('57)

Mintz, S. W.
  RUR 1363('53), 1364('59), 1365('59)
    1366('54), 3008('56), 6039('64)
    6040('61), 6417('59), 6418('55)
    6419('60), 6420('56), 6421('61)
    6422('60), 6423('60)

Miracle, M. P.
  URB 2028('62)

Misra, B.
  RUR 8471('63), 11370('63)

Misra, B. R.
  URB 5351('59), 5352('57)

Misra, S.
  RUR 2471('55), 2556('64), 4411('64)
      6424('52)

Mitani, T.
  RUR 2485('64), 7345('64)

Mitchell, H.
  GEN 4336('64)

Mitchell, J. C.
  IND 2395('57)
  URB 1327('66), 2029('56), 2400('56)
      2401('54), 2402('51), 2403('62)
      2404('65), 3011('61), 3337('57)
      5353('56)
  RUR 5324('57), 5350('49), 7346('62)
      9362('60), 9363('56), 9364('50)

Mitra, A. K.
  RUR 8471('63), 11370('63)

Mitsuyoshi, T.
  RUR 8472('61)

Miyagi, H.
  RUR 8473('60)

Miyamoto, T.
  RUR 8474('59)

Mizoguchi, Y.
  RUR 8475('57), 8476('57)

Modjtabawi, A. A.
  RUR 8477('61)

Moerman, M. H.
  RUR 2486('64), 8478('61)

Mohsin, M.
  URB 2405('64), 2406('63)

Molina Filho, J.
  URB 2407('63)

Molnos, A.
  Gen 2438('65)

Molohan, M. J. B.
  URB 4366('57)

Monbeig, P.
  URB 2408('60)

Montagne, R.
  IND 2021('52)

Mookherjee, D.
  GEN 1422('64)

Moore, C. H.
  RUR 5351('63)

Moore, J. F.
  IND 5353('53)

Moore, W. E.
  GEN 1395('63), 1423('66), 1424('58)
      1425('63), 1426('52), 1427('61)
      2439('66),
  IND 1321('51), 1322('48), 1323('62)
      1324('48), 1325('60), 2022('50)
      3328('65), 3329('55), 3330('60)
      5354('60)
  RUR 10339('64)

Moral, P.
  RUR 10340('61)

Morales, J. O.
  RUR 4382('53)

Moreira, J. M.
  RUR 10341('62)

Moreira, J. R.
  GEN 2440('60)
  RUR 2487('60)

Morgan, J. N.
  GEN 1428('64)

Morgan, T.
  GEN 4359('63)

Morgaut, M. E.
  IND 2023('62), 2396('62), 5355('59)

Moribura, M.
  GEN 2441('63)

Morrill, W. T.
  RUR 8479('62)

Morris, H. S.
  RUR 8480('53), 11371('53)

Morris, M. D.
  IND 2397('65), 2398('57), 5356('65)

Morrison, W. A.
  RUR 2488('63), 7007('59)

Morton-Williams, P.
  RUR 2028(n.d.)

Moshe, L.
  RUR 2607('64)

Motwani, K.
  IND 5357('63)

Moulik, T. K.
  RUR 8510('63)

Mousinho Guidi, M. L.
  RUR 1367('62)

Mukerjee, R.
  GEN 2442('61), 2443('65), 2444('56),
    2445('62)
  IND 6316('45)
  URB 5354('65), 5355('61)

Mukerji, B.
  RUR 4383('62)

Mukerji, G. P.
  IND 2399('62)

Mukherjee, P. K.
  RUR 6425('60)

Mukherjee, R.
  RUR 1368('59), 1369('57), 6426('48)
    8481('49)

Mukherjee, S. B.
  URB 5356('55)

Mukherji, P.
  RUR 2489('66)

Mukhtyar, G. C.
  RUR 6427('30)

Mukwaya, A. B.
  URB 2030('62)

Muratake, S.
  RUR 8482('59)

Murdock, P. G.
  GEN 1429('65)

Murteira, M.
  IND 3331('60)

Mussolini, G.
  RUR 8094('53)

Muthiah, C.
  RUR 8483('63), 11372('63)

Mwewa, P. B.
  IND 2400('58)

Mya, M.
  GEN 2446('64)

Myers, C. A.
  IND 5358('58)

Mylius, K.
  RUR 6428('62)

Nader, L.
  RUR 5352('63), 9365('64)

Nagpaul, H.
  URB 2409('62), 4367('62)

Naik, T. B.
  RUR 11373('63)

Nair, B. N.
  URB 4368('60)

Nair, K.
  RUR 10342('62)

Najafi, N.
  RUR 8484('58)

Nakada, E.
  RUR 8485('63)

Nakajima, R.
  RUR 8602('61)

Nakamoto, H.
  IND 2401('56)

Nakamura, H.
  RUR 5007('60)

Nakamura, M.
  RUR 8486('61)

Nakamura, R.
  RUR 2490('58)

Nakane, C.
  RUR 8038('64), 9366('63)

Nakano, T.
  RUR 8487('63)

Nam, K. B.
  RUR 8070('58)

Nanavati, M. B.
  RUR 4384('64), 8488('64), 8489('61)

Nandi, S. B.
  RUR 2491('60)

Nanjundappa, D. M.
  RUR 4385('63)

Naraghi, E.
  GEN 2447('59)

Narain, D.
  URB 4369('60)

Narayanan, R.
  URB 2410('60)

Naroll, R.
  GEN 1430('56)
  URB 1328('56)

Nash, J.
  RUR 7347('63)

Nash, M.
  GEN 1431('59), 2448('57), 2449('64)
    2450('63)
  IND 1326('55), 2402('56), 4007('58)
    4311('55), 5359('57)
  RUR 1370('64), 1371('66), 2029('65)
    2492('61), 6041('64), 6429('64)
    6430('61), 7347('63)

Natal, Government Of
  URB 5357('53)

Natal, University Of
  IND 2024('50)

Nath, K.
  RUR 2493('65)

Nath, V.
  RUR 2494('62), 10343('65)

Nath, Y. V. S.
  RUR 8490('60)

Nathan, A.
  URB 2411('64)

National Council of Applied
  Economic Research
  URB 5358('64)
  RUR 6431('59)

Nay, R.
  IND 5360('55)

Nayacakalo, R. R.
  RUR 5353('64)

Neale, W. C.
  IND 1327('56)

Neff, K. L.
  GEN 3315('63)

Neisser, C. S.
  RUR 4386('55)

Nelson, L.
  GEN 2451('60)

Nesson, C.
  RUR 2496('65)

Netting, R. M.
  RUR 2497('65)

Nettl, J. P.
  GEN 1432('66)

Neurath, P. M.
  RUR 2026('59), 2030('62)

Newell, W. H.
  RUR 8491('60)

Newman, P. L.
  RUR 9367('65)

Nydegger, W. F.
  RUR 8501('66)

Nyirenda, A. A.
  GEN 4361('59)
  URB 5359('59)
  RUR 6434('57), 6435('59)

Obayashi, T.
  RUR 6436('64)

Oberg, K.
  URB 5360('57)
  RUR 2500('65), 2501('60), 8502('61)
    11379('56)

O'Brien, D.
  RUR 2502('64)

O'Grady-Jones, L.
  IND 6318('61)

O'Loughlin, C.
  URB 2414('61)

Odaka, K.
  IND 2408('50)

Ogbuagu, B.
  IND 3332('61)

Ogburn, W. F.
  GEN 3316('53), 4362('27)

Ôhara, M.
  IND 3333('62)
  URB 2413('62)

Okigbo, P.
  URB 4370('56)
  RUR 2503('56)

Oliveira, W. R.
  RUR 8317('60)

Oliver, S. C.
  RUR 2504('65)

Omi, T.
  IND 4312('63)

Opler, M. E.
  RUR 8503('59), 8504('56), 8505('52)
    8506('52), 8558('56)

Oración, T. S.
  RUR 9370('63)

Orans, M.
  GEN 1437('66)
  IND 2025('59), 4313('58)
  RUR 6437('66)

Orde-Browne, G. S. J.
  IND 2409('33), 2410('38)

Orenstein, H.
  RUR 1372('60), 5356('62), 6438('65)
    8072('65)

Organization of American States
  GEN 2488('62)

Ortega Mata, R.
  RUR 2505('64)

Osgood, C.
  RUR 8507('63)

Otani, Y.
  GEN 2454('64)

Ottenberg, P.
  GEN 4363('60)
  RUR 6043('62)

Ottenberg, S.
  GEN 4363('60)
  RUR 6043('62), 9017('59)

Ottino, P.
  RUR 6439('63)

Ouchi, T.
  RUR 8038('64)

Oyama, H.
  RUR 7353('63)

Oyawoye, M. O.
  URB 2392('61)

Pacyaya, A. G.
  URB 2415('64)

Padmanabhan, C. B.
  IND 3334('63)
  URB 2416('63)

Pauw, B. A.
  URB 3012('63)

Pearse, A.
  URB 2031('61)

Pearson, H. W.
  GEN 1442('57)
  RUR 6443('57)

Peggio, E.
  IND 4008('60)

Pelissier, P.
  RUR 11385('63)

Pelzer, K. J.
  RUR 3324('61)

Pendse, R. G.
  URB 5373('56)

Pereira de Queiroz, M. I.
  RUR 8516('60)

Perez Ramirez, G.
  RUR 10345('62)

Perin-Hockers, M.
  IND 6320('59)

Pestonjee, D.
  IND 2304('63)

Peters, E. L.
  RUR 8517('63)

Pfanner, D. E.
  RUR 6442('62)

Phillips, H. P.
  RUR 2511('64), 8074('65)

Phillips, R. E.
  URB 2419('30), 2420('38), 5362('38)

Phillips, W. Jr.
  IND 1330('64), 1331('63)
  URB 4372('64)

Pi Hugarte, R.
  RUR 11386('55)

Piatier, A.
  GEN 1440('62), 3317('62)

Piegeay, C.
  IND 4314('55)

Pierce, J. E.
  RUR 8518('64)

Pierson, D.
  RUR 8519('51), 8520('64)

Pimpley, P. N.
  GEN 1441('64)

Pin, E.
  RUR 4391('64)

Pittman, G. P.
  RUR 8521('51)

Pitt-Rivers, J.
  GEN 4364('63)

Pizzorno, A.
  URB 1329('62), 2032('60)

Planck, U.
  RUR 8522('62)

Plant, H. T.
  RUR 4392('62), 5358('62)

Ploeg, A.
  RUR 2502('64)

Plummer, J. F.
  RUR 8523('63)

Pohl, V.
  RUR 10346('64)

Polanyi, K.
  GEN 1442('57)
  RUR 1318('65), 6443('57)

Polson, R. A.
  RUR 8524('56), 8525('56)

Poncet, J.
  RUR 10347('63)

Pons, V. G.
  URB 2033('61), 2421('56), 3013('56)
    5363('56)

Porter, A. T.
  URB 2422('63)

Porter, P. W.
  RUR 6444('65)

Pospisil, L.
  RUR 2512('58), 6445('63)

Potter, J. M.
  RUR 8526('64)

Poupart, R.
  IND 3335('60)

Pouwer, J.
  GEN 1443('64)
  RUR 2513('64)

Powdermaker, H.
  IND 2027('62)
  URB 2423('56)
  RUR 2514('56)

Pozas, R.
  IND 1332('59)
  RUR 8527('59)

Prabhu, P.
  IND 2413('57), 6321('57)
  URB 2034('56), 2424('56), 2425('57)

Pradham, M. C.
  RUR 2471('55)

Pradhan, K.
  URB 2041('55)

Prakasha, V.
  RUR 2515('56)

Prasad, B.
  RUR 4393('63)

Prasad, B. G.
  URB 5330('65)

Prasad, K.
  IND 2414('52), 2415('63)

Prasad, N.
  RUR 4394('63)

Prien, C. H.
  IND 4321('50)

Prothero, R. M.
  IND 2416('57)

Pullman, D. R.
  GEN 1444('66)

Quain, B.
  RUR 8528('48)

Qubain, F. I.
  RUR 8529('55)

Queen, S. A.
  RUR 7356('61)

Quint, M. N.
  RUR 2516('56)

Quirino-Lanhounemy, J.
  RUR 4395('64)

Quisumbing, L. R.
  RUR 7357('63)

Rabello, O.
  RUR 2517('63)

Radcliffe-Brown, A. R.
  GEN 2460('50)

Raha, M. K.
  RUR 9314('63)

Rahim, A. M. A.
  IND 3337('59)

Rahim, S. A.
  RUR 2518('61)

Rahadkar, W. B.
  RUR 4396('62), 5359('60)

Rajagopalan, C.
  URB 2426('62), 5364('60)

Rajamani, A. N.
  RUR 10348('59)

Rajapurohit, A. R.
  RUR 8530('63)

Ralis, M.
  RUR 2016('57)

Rama, C. M.
  IND 5364('59), 5365('62)

Ramakrishnan, J.
 RUR 8582('40)

Ramakrishnan, K. R.
 RUR 8582('40)

Ramakrishnam Raju, B.
 RUR 1374('64)

Ramsey, C. E.
 GEN 2451('60)

Rangel, I.
 GEN 2461('62)

Rao, A. V. R.
 RUR 5360('54)

Rao, M. M.
 RUR 6446('58)

Rao, M. N.
 IND 2354('54)

Rao, M. S. A.
 GEN 2462('58), 2463('64)

Rao, V. K. R. V.
 URB 5365('65)

Raper, A. F.
 RUR 8075('50)

Rastogi, P. N.
 RUR 5361('64), 5362('65)

Raval, I. B.
 RUR 1375('64)

Ravault, F.
 RUR 8531('64)

Ravicz, R. S.
 RUR 8076('65)

Ray, S.
 RUR 6447('64)

Ray, V. F.
 GEN 4366('57), 4367('59)

Ray Burman, B. K.
 URB 4373('57)

Raynal, R.
 RUR 8532('52)

Rayner, W.
 URB 4374('62)
 RUR 2519('62)

Raz, S. M. U.
 IND 2417('62)
 RUR 2520('62)

Read, M.
 IND 2418('27), 2419('31), 3338('42)
 RUR 2521('38), 11387('38)

Reader, D. H.
 GEN 1445('64)
 URB 2035('61), 5366('61)
 RUR 9018('66), 10349('64)

Recasens Siches, L.
 URB 4375('55)

Reddy, N. S.
 RUR 2522('50), 2523('55)

Redfield, R.
 URB 1330('54)
 RUR 1376('41), 1377('56), 1378('57)
  2032('41), 2524('34), 8077('30)
  8533('50), 8534('34)

Redinha, J.
 RUR 10350('58)

Reichel-Dolmatoff, A.
 RUR 8078('61)

Reichel-Dolmatoff, G.
 RUR 2525('53), 8078('61)

Reina, R. E.
 RUR 8079('60), 8535('58)

Reining, C. C.
 RUR 4012('66), 6045('62)

Remer, C. F.
 GEN 4369('22)

Renier, M.
 RUR 4397('57)

Requa, E.
  GEN 3318('65)

Retzlaff, R. H.
  RUR 5363('62)

Retzloff, R. H.
  RUR 5010('59)

Reuter, A.
  RUR 7358('63)

Reyes, E. P.
  RUR 8567('57)

Reynolds, B.
  GEN 2464('63)
  RUR 2526('63)

Rheinallt-Jones, J. D.
  URB 2427('34), 4376('53)

Rhodesia, Northern
  RUR 8536('61)

Ribadeau-Dumas, J.
  IND 5366('58)

Rice, A. K.
  IND 2028('58), 2420('55), 2421('55)
    2422('53)

Richards, A. I.
  RUR 2527('54), 5364('60), 6046('39)
    7359('40), 9019('63), 9372('32)
    11388('39)

Richardson, E. M.
  RUR 8537('59), 11389('53)

Rigby, P. J.
  URB 5308('61)

Riggs, F. W.
  GEN 1446('58)
  URB 4377('56)

Rimmer, D.
  IND 2423('61)

Ritzenthaler, P.
  RUR 8538('62)

Ritzenthaler, R. E.
  IND 4315('53)
  RUR 8538('62)

Rivera, G.
  RUR 11390('54)

Roberts, S.
  RUR 7360('64)

Robertson, H. M.
  RUR 6448('34)

Robertson, R.
  GEN 1432('66)

Robinson, R. D.
  URB 4378('58)

Robolos, Z. M.
  RUR 6449('64)

Rodriguez Sala de Gomez Gil, M.
  RUR 2528('63)

Rogers, E. M.
  GEN 1447('58), 1448('62), 3319('64)
  RUR 5365('64)

Rognon, P.
  RUR 9020('63)

Rojas, A. V.
  RUR 8534('34)

Romano, E. M.
  GEN 2465('63)

Romanucci Schwartz, L.
  RUR 2529('65)

Rondot, P.
  GEN 2466('60), 2467('60)
  RUR 2530('56)

Rosen, B. C.
  GEN 2468('62)

Rosenberg, N.
  GEN 1449('64)

Rosenfeld, H.
  RUR 7363('58), 8539('59)

Ross, A. D.
  URB 3014('61), 3339('61)
  RUR 7361('59)

Rosser, C. A.
  RUR 8540('60)

Rotberg, R. I.
  RUR 6450('62)

Rouch, J.
  URB 3015('61)

Rourke, R. J.
  RUR 10351('65)

Rovillois-Brigol, M.
  RUR 8541('63)

Rowe, W. L.
  GEN 2469('63), 4370('63)
  RUR 7362('60)

Rowley, C.
  RUR 2033('66)

Roy, B.
  IND 3339('63)

Roy Burman, B. K.
  RUR 10352('65)

Rubin, V.
  GEN 2470('60)

Rubio Orbe, G.
  RUR 8080('56)

Ruel, M. J.
  RUR 2531('64)

Ruopp, E.
  RUR 4398('53)

Russinger, A.
  URB 4379('60)

Ruytinx, J.
  URB 4380('58)

Ruz Lhuillier, A.
  RUR 9394('64)

Ryan, B.
  RUR 8081('58), 8542('55)

Ryan, D.
  RUR 2532('63), 4399('63), 6451('63)

Ryan, J. C.
  IND 2424('64)

Rycroft, W. S.
  URB 4381('63), 5367('63)

Saber, M.
  RUR 2533('63)

Sabogal Wiesse, J. R.
  RUR 8543('61)

Sachchidananda
  RUR 2534('64), 4400('64), 5366('64)
      9373('64), 9374('64)

Sadie, J. L.
  IND 4316('60)
  RUR 9375('60)

Saffa, S.
  RUR 8544('49)

Saha, N.
  RUR 9376('63)

Sahara, R.
  URB 2428('63)

Sahiar, G. H.
  GEN 2471('56)

Sahlins, M. D.
  GEN 1450('60)
  RUR 1379('58), 2034('58), 6047('65)
      6452('65), 8082('62)

Saigal, J. P.
  IND 5367('63)

Saikia, P. D.
  RUR 5367('63)

St. Erlich, V.
  RUR 7364('66)

Saito, H.
  RUR 2535('59), 8545('56), 8546('55)

Saito, S.
  RUR 2536('63)

Sakai, R.
  GEN 4371('60)

Schapera, I.
  GEN 2473('28), 3320('41), 4372('37)
      4373('34)
  IND 3340('34)
  RUR 2540('37), 2541('28), 2542('33)
      2543('34), 6456('28), 7366('33)
      9383('47), 11394('33)

Scheffler, H. W.
  RUR 9384('65)

Schmitz, C. A.
  RUR 9385('57)

Schneider, H. K.
  RUR 6049('64), 9021('59), 10354('64)

Schnore, L. F.
  GEN 4333('66)
  URB 4384('66)

Schoorl, J. W.
  RUR 2544('57), 6050('57), 9022('57)

Schrieke, B. J. O.
  GEN 4374('29)
  RUR 10355('29)

Schultz, T. W.
  RUR 6051('64)

Schuman, H.
  RUR 2545('66), 4014('67)

Schwab, W. B.
  URB 2036('61)

Schwartz, J.
  RUR 1380('63)

Schweng, L. D.
  RUR 4404('62)

Scott, J. G.
  RUR 10356('63)

Scott, R.
  RUR 11329('46)

Sebag, P.
  URB 5370('60)

Seck, A.
  URB 2432('61)

Seda, E. P.
  RUR 3010('56)

Segall, M. H.
  URB 2433('63)
  RUR 2546('63)

Seki, K.
  RUR 8551('59), 8552('63)

Seklani M.
  URB 4385('60)

Selosoemardjan
  URB 4386('62)
  RUR 4405('63), 4406('63)

Seminar on Social Integration   in
  Guatemala
  GEN 4375('59)

Seminar on Social Integration in
  India
  GEN 4376('61)

Seminar on Social Problems of
  Urbanization
  URB 2434('63)

Sen, C.
  RUR 2471('55)

Sen, L. K.
  RUR 7367('65)

Sen, S.
  RUR 2547('64)

Sen, S. N.
  URB 5371('60)

Sengupta, A. K.
  RUR 6457('65)

Sengupta, S. C.
  RUR 7368('58), 8455('62), 8553('63)
      11395('63)

Serpenti, L. M.
  RUR 9386('65)

Service, E. R.
  GEN 2474('54)

Service, H. S.
  GEN 2474('54)

Simms, R. P.
  URB 2435('65), 6305('65)

Simpson, G. E.
  RUR 2552('60), 2553('64)

Singaravelu, S.
  RUR 6461('64)

Singer, M. B.
  GEN 4379('59)
  URB 1330('54), 2037('59)
  RUR 2554('56), 8558('56)

Singh, A. K.
  GEN 2475('67)
  IND 3343('65)
  RUR 2555('64)

Singh, B.
  URB 5354('65), 5355('61)
  RUR 2556('64), 4410('61), 4411('64)

Singh, D.
  RUR 2557('64), 4412('64)

Singh, D. P.
  RUR 2558('60)

Singh, G.
  IND 4319('64)
  RUR 2559('63)

Singh, I. P.
  URB 2436('60)
  RUR 8559('58), 8560('59)

Singh, P.
  IND 2429('61)

Singh, P. N.
  IND 2430('63), 2431('63)

Singh, R. D.
  RUR 4015('52), 8505('52), 8506('52)
    8558('56), 8561('56), 11404('61)

Singh, S.
  RUR 2559('63)

Singh, T.
  RUR 2560('63), 2561('56), 4413('45)
    6462('63)

Singh, U.
  RUR 4414('62), 11405('62)

Singh, V. B.
  GEN 4380('63)
  IND 2432('60)

Singh, Y.
  GEN 2476('65)
  RUR 2562('58), 2563('60), 5011(61)

Sinha, D.
  IND 2031('56), 2429('61), 2433('62)
    2434('60)

Sinha, D. P.
  RUR 2564('60)

Sinha, S.
  IND 2032('60)
  RUR 2565('63), 6463('63)

Sirsikar, V. M.
  RUR 5371('64)

Sivaswamy, K. G.
  RUR 4415('53)

Siverts, H.
  RUR 6464('65)

Sivertsen, D.
  RUR 8085('63)

Sjoberg, G.
  GEN 1452('66), 2477('66)
  URB 4388('66)

Skalnikova, O.
  GEN 2478('64)

Skinner, E. P.
  GEN 2479('64)
  RUR 2566('66), 5372('64), 6052('62)
    6465('64), 10357('64)

Skinner, G. W.
  RUR 2567('66), 5373('59)

Sklar, R. L.
  RUR 10358('66)

Slater, G.
  RUR 8562('18)

Slotkin, J. S.
  IND 1334('60)

Smelser, N. J.
  GEN 1453('66), 1454('63), 1455('67)
    1456('66), 4381('66)
  RUR 6466('59)

Smith, D. H.
  GEN 1457('66)

Smith, M. G.
  GEN 1458('66)
  RUR 1383('66), 2036('65), 2568('62)
    5012('55), 5013('60), 6053('55)
    6054('62), 7370('62), 7371('62)
    8566('56), 10359('65),11406('55)

Smith, M. W.
  RUR 8563('52), 8564('60), 8565('46)

Smith, R. J.
  GEN 1459('57), 4382('62)
  RUR 1322('57), 8022('56), 8554('60)
    8567('57), 8568('51), 8569('61)

Smith, R. T.
  RUR 6467('64), 7008('56), 7372('63)
    7373('59)

Smith, T. L.
  GEN 2480('54), 2481('56)
  RUR 2569('61)

Smith, W. C.
  RUR 8570(65)

Smyly, W. J.
  RUR 8571('61)

Snapper, F.
  RUR 11407('62)

Snyder, J.
  RUR 2037('57)

Soares Barata, O.
  RUR 2570('60)

Soares Rebelo, D. J.
  RUR 8572('61)

Soedjatmoko,
  GEN 2482('58)

Soenardi, S.
  URB 3340('63)

Sofer, C.
  IND 2033('56)
  URB 2038('55)

Sofer, R.
  URB 2038('55), 3341('56)

Solari, A. E.
  RUR 10360('63)

Solenberger, R. R.
  RUR 5374('64)

Somjee, A. H.
  RUR 5375('64)

Sonoda, K.
  RUR 2571('60)

Sonraku Shakai Kenkyukai
  RUR 2572('58), 5376('63)

South African Institute of Race
Relations
  GEN 4383('49)

Southall, A. W.
  GEN 4384('61)
  URB 2039('56), 2040('61), 2437('57)
    3016('57), 4389('61)
  RUR 9023('56)

Southwold, M.
  RUR 5377(n.d.)

Sovani, N. V.
  URB 1332('64), 2041('55), 4390('66)
    5372('52), 5373('56)

Spate, O. H. K.
  URB 4391('58)

Spengler, J. J.
  GEN 4314('61)

Sperling, J. B.
  IND 3344('65), 5369('63)

Spicer, E. H.
  GEN 4385('52)

Spitaels, G.
IND 3345('60)

Spoehr, A.
RUR 8086('49)

Srinivas, M. N.
GEN 2483('66), 4386('60)
IND 4320('56), 5370('56)
URB 1333('56), 4392('56)
RUR 2573('54), 8573('60), 8574('55)
9388('65)

Srivastava, S. K.
RUR 4416('61)

Stabler, G. M.
RUR 2574('58)

Stanislawski, D.
URB 2438('61)

Stanner, W. E. H.
RUR 4417('53)

Stanton, E. W.
IND 2435('49)

Starch, E. A.
RUR 4320('55)

Starr, B. W.
RUR 2575('54)

Statham, J.
GEN 3318('65)

Stavenhagen, R.
RUR 2576('63), 10361('66)

Steed, G. P.
RUR 2038('55)

Stein, W. W.
IND 3001('57)
RUR 8087('61)

Steiner, J. F.
URB 2439('57)

Steinzor, L. V.
RUR 2577('63)

Stent, G. E.
IND 2034('58)
URB 2440('48)

Stepanek, J. E.
IND 4321('50)

Stephens, W. N.
URB 3342('63)
RUR 7374('63)

Sternberg-Sarel, B.
RUR 8575('61)

Stevens, S.
IND 5371('57)

Steward, J. H.
GEN 4387('56)

Stewart, C.
GEN 2484('56)

Stinchcombe, A. L.
RUR 1384('61)

Stirling, P.
RUR 8088('65), 8576('63)

Stockwell, E. G.
URB 2461('64)

Stolper, W.
GEN 2485('64)

Straus, M. A.
RUR 2578('53)

Stryker, S.
URB 2326('64)

Sturtevant, D. R.
RUR 2579('59)

Sufrin, S. C.
IND 7304('61)

Suginohara, J.
RUR 7375('64)

Sundrum, R. M.
URB 4393('57)

Sur, M.
IND 2436('61)

Thanom Kittikachon
  RUR 4419('64)

The, S. G.
  URB 4394('59), 4403('62)

Thelin, M.
  RUR 2587('63)

Theodorson, G. A.
  GEN 4390('61)

Thoai, N.
  RUR 3321('55)

Thomas, L. V.
  URB 4395('61)
  RUR 2588('63), 10364('64)

Thomas, M. M.
  URB 2338('58)

Thomas, P. J.
  RUR 8582('40)

Thomas, R. M.
  URB 3344('62)

Thompson, E. T.
  RUR 3325('59)

Thompson, L.
  GEN 1462('60)

Thompson, W. R.
  URB 1334('66)

Thore, L.
  URB 3345('64)
  RUR 11410('62)

Thornburg, M. W.
  GEN 2486('64)

Thorner, D.
  RUR 4420('64), 5380('53)

Thorsrud, E.
  GEN 1463('52)

Thurnwald, R. C.
  RUR 2589('31), 6474('32), 6475('34)

T'ien, J.
  RUR 11411('53)

Tinker, H.
  RUR 5381('59)

Tirayakian
  RUR 2590('57)

Tomasetti, W. E.
  RUR 4421('63)

Tomasevich, J.
  RUR 10365('55)

Tomita, Y.
  IND 2438('55)

Tonegawa, M.
  RUR 8581('59)

Topley, M.
  IND 5373('63)
  RUR 6476('64)

Torres Restrepo, C.
  URB 2444('61)

Touma, T.
  RUR 8090('58)

Toupet, C.
  RUR 8583('56), 9389('63), 9390('56)

Touraine, A.
  IND 3347('61)

Trent, S.
  RUR 2040('56), 2041('55), 2591('55)

Tripathi, C. B.
  RUR 8584('57)

Troin, J. F.
  RUR 6477('63)

Trouillot, H.
  IND 2439('56)

Trujillo Ferrari, A.
  RUR 8585('52), 8586('57)

Trystram, J. P.
  IND 2036('53)

Tsukamoto, T.
  RUR 7378('55), 8037('54)

Tubiana, M. J.
  RUR 6478('61)

Tumin, M. M.
  GEN 2487('61)
  RUR 2042('52), 8091('52)

Turner, R.
  GEN 4391('62)

Turner, D. A.
  RUR 4422('59)

Turri, E.
  RUR 9391('60)

Twum-Barima, K.
  RUR 6479('56)

Udy, S. H.
  IND 1335('59)

Ulken, H. Z.
  RUR 3326('56)

Ullah, I.
  RUR 8587('58)

Umana, S. C.
  RUR 11412('64)

Underwood, F. W.
  RUR 2592('64), 6056('60)

UNESCO
  GEN 2488('62), 3322(n.d.), 3323(n.d.)
    4392('63), 4393('56)
  IND 6322('62)
  URB 1335('64), 6306('60)
  RUR 1386('53), 2043('60), 10366('53)

United Nations
  IND 5374('57), 7305('56)

United Nations, Department of
  Economics
  RUR 12303('60)

United Nations, ECA
  URB 3346('60)

United Nations, ECAFE
  RUR 4423('60), 4424('59)

United Nations, ECLA
  GEN 2488('62)

Unwalla, D. B.
  IND 2440('58)

Uoshi, S. L.
  IND 2391('58)

Useem, J.
  IND 3348('52)
  RUR 5382(n.d.)

Ushiomi, T.
  RUR 8588('64)

Vakil, C. N.
  RUR 1387('62)

Valentine, C. A.
  RUR 5383('63)

Van Amelsvoort, V.
  RUR 2593('64), 9392('64)

Van De Moosdijk, J.
  RUR 1388('66)

Van Den Berghe, P. L.
  URB 2044('64), 2445('64)

Van Den Ban, A. W.
  RUR 2594('63)

Van Der Horst, S. T.
  IND 2441('46), 2442('41), 2443('37)
    5375('65)

Van Der Kroef, J. M. A.
  GEN 1464('58), 1465('62), 2489('56)
    2490('58), 3324('58)
  IND 5376('55), 5377('56)
  URB 4397('56), 4398('52)
  RUR 2595('60), 5384('53), 6480('58)

Vanderlinden, J.
  RUR 2044('63)

Van Dijk, F.
  RUR 2501('60)

Van Dooren, P. J.
  RUR 6057('54)

Van Es, J. C.
  RUR 5365('64)

Van Goylen, A. J.
  IND 2444('48)

Van Nieuwenhuijze, C. A. O.
  RUR 8589('62)

Vansina, J.
  RUR 6058('62)

Van Stone, J. W.
  RUR 8092('60)

Van Velsen, J.
  URB 2045('61)
  RUR 2596('66), 5015('64), 7379('64)

Vargas, F.
  RUR 10310('63)

Varma, B. N.
  RUR 2597('59)

Vasquez, M. C.
  URB 4317('63)
  RUR 8590('55)

Velasquez, R.
  RUR 2598('62), 11413('61)

Vellard, J. A.
  GEN 2491('63)
  RUR 2599('63), 10367('63)

Vellas, P.
  GEN 1466('64)

Venkatarayappa, K. N.
  URB 5376('57)

Vennetier, P.
  URB 2446('57), 2447('61), 2448('63)
    2449('61), 4399('63)

Verba, S.
  GEN 2303('63)

Verger, P.
  RUR 6004('59)

Verhaegen, P.
  URB 6308('62)

Verin, P.
  RUR 11414('64)

Verlaque, C.
  RUR 2318('63)

Verlinden, C.
  URB 4400('59)

Verner, C.
  GEN 2451('60)

Verschueren, J.
  RUR 2600('57)

Versluys, J. D. N.
  URB 4401('63)
  RUR 2601('66)

Vidyarthi, L. P.
  GEN 2492('61)
  RUR 9393('64)

Vietnam, Vien Quocgia Thongke
  URB 5377('62)

Vilakazi, A. L.
  GEN 1467('64)

Vilakazi, A.
  URB 2046('62)

Villanueva, B. M.
  RUR 4425('62)

Villeme, L.
  URB 4402(n.d.)

Villien-Rossi, M. L.
  URB 2450('66), 2451('63)

Vincent, J. F.
  RUR 3327('61)

Vo, H. P.
  RUR 8365('61)

Vogel, E. F.
  URB 3347('63)

Vogt, E. Z.
  RUR 2602('65), 9394('64)

Volchok, B. Y.
  RUR 9395('64)

Weitz, R.
  RUR 4428('65)

Welikala, G. H. F.
  RUR 2608('59)

Wells, F. A.
  IND 2445('63)
  RUR 3330('63)

Wertheim, W. F.
  GEN 1468('61), 1469('60), 2496('56)
      2497('62)
  URB 4403('62)
  RUR 2609('60)

West, E. M. B.
  IND 2377('58)

West African Institute of Social and
  Economic Research
  GEN 4398('53)

West Bengal, Government of
  GEN 4399('55)

Westphal-Hellbusch, S.
  RUR 8595('62)

Wettstein, G.
  RUR 11386('55)

Wherry, R. J.
  IND 2430('63), 2431('63)

Whetten, N. L.
  GEN 2498('61)

White, C. M. N.
  RUR 6485('59)

White, G. F.
  RUR 4429('62)

Whiteford, A. H.
  URB 2455('63), 2456('60)

Whitehill, A. M.
  IND 2037('61)

Whiteman, J.
  RUR 2610('65)

Whitten, N. E. Jr.
  RUR 5014('65)

Whyte, Q.
  IND 2446('49)

Whyte, W. F.
  IND 1336('63), 2447('63)

Wikkramatileke, R.
  RUR 2611('64), 4430('64), 8596('57)
      8597('62)

Wilensky, H. L.
  GEN 1470('66)

Wilkinson, T. O.
  IND 5379('62), 5380('60)
  URB 4404('60)

Willems, E.
  RUR 2046('61), 2612('45), 2613('64)
      8093('47), 8094('53)

Williams, M.
  RUR 2614('64)

Williams, P. M.
  IND 5381('53)

Williams, T. R.
  RUR 9398('65)

Williamson, H. F.
  GEN 4316('54), 4400('54)

Williamson, K. R.
  RUR 3331('58)

Williamson, R. C.
  URB 2457('63)

Willis, A. S. Jr.
  RUR 4336('65), 4337('62)

Willmott, D. E.
  URB 2047('61)

Willner, A. R.
  GEN 2499('58)
  IND 2448('63), 2449('63)

Wilson, D.
  RUR 11415('31)

Yokoyama, R.
  IND 3350('55)
  URB 2459('55)

Yonemura, S.
  URB 2460('63)

Yoon, E. B.
  RUR 8609('58)

Yoshi, T.
  RUR 8610('62)

Yoshida, T.
  RUR 2621('63), 8611('63), 8612('64)

Yoshino, I. R.
  RUR 8095('56)

Yosoi, S.
  IND 2438('55)

Younes, S.
  RUR 8613('61)

Young, F. W.
  RUR 2048('60), 2620('66), 6491('60)

Young, R. C.
  RUR 2048('60), 2620('66), 6491('60)

Yuan, D. Y.
  RUR 2622('64)

Yuan, Y.
  URB 2461('64)

Yudelman, M.
  RUR 10370('64)

Zahan, D.
  RUR 4017('63)

Zaidi, S. M. H.
  GEN 4401('62)

Zayas, A. E.
  RUR 3333('60)

Zeghari, M.
  RUR 7384('62)

Zollschan, G. K.
  GEN 4402('64)

INDEX BY AREA

References are given by section and order within the section. The
number in parentheses is the year of publication of the book or article.

Afghanistan
  RUR 5309('59), 8027('56), 8370('56), 8371('54)

Africa
  GEN 1338('61), 1353('65), 1355('64), 1467('64), 1472('39), 2312('64)
      2313('57), 2314('51), 2316('63), 2318('61), 2321('60), 2322('62)
      2333('65), 2346('62), 2350('64), 2356('64), 2357('63), 2376('61)
      2385('63), 2390('63), 2395('64), 2396('64), 2398('62), 2403('62)
      2405('64), 2406('62), 2408('64), 2433('63), 2435('63), 2454('64)
      2458('63), 2460('50), 2464('63), 2478('64), 3305('62)
  IND 2023('62), 2308('45), 2326('64), 2335('60), 2365('58), 2368('62)
      2378('62), 2390('56), 2396('62), 2412('52), 3331('60), 4305('57)
      5304('52), 5305('60), 5308('61), 5310('53), 5313('54), 5324('55)
      5325('56), 5334('57), 5355('59), 5366('58), 5374('57), 6311('62)
      7301('54), 7302('61), 7303('54)
  URB 1316('61), 1327('66), 2323('63), 2342('64), 3313('58), 3320('62)
      3321('66), 3346('60), 4303('58), 4305('63), 4311('59), 4321('60)
      4332('65), 4333('62), 4334('60), 4339('60), 4340('61), 4352('54)
      4361('60), 4362('60), 4364('62), 4366('57), 6301('52), 6302('54)
      6308('62)
  RUR 1340('63), 2359('64), 2430('60), 2526('63), 2576('63), 5306('64)
      5332('63), 6334('64), 6336('62), 6382('63), 7323('64), 9362('60)
      10332('66), 10339('64), 10349('64), 10369('62)

Africa, Central
  GEN 1310('63), 2310('59), 2336('60), 2352('62), 3311('62)
  IND 2331('54), 2377('58), 2403('54), 3308('35), 3338('42), 5317('62)
      5319('51)
  URB 1303('56), 2003('55), 2393('56), 3320('62), 3321('66), 4302('59)
      4304('56), 4376('53), 5314('58)
  RUR 2466('57), 2467('56), 3313('56), 10320('66), 10370('64)

Africa, East
  GEN 1371('39), 2417('62), 2428('56)
  IND 3312('64), 5344('61)
  RUR 2303('62), 2466('57), 5301('62), 6049('64), 6347('61), 6366('39)
      9375('60), 10354('64), 10370('64)

Africa, North
  GEN 1442('57), 2329('63)
  IND 2389('51), 5347('52)
  URB 2334('55), 4353('55)
  RUR 2530('56), 6443('57)

Africa, South
  GEN 1371('39), 1445('64)
  IND 2406('31), 2407('44), 2409('33), 6317('49)
  URB 2403('62), 4376('53), 5353('56)
  RUR 6366('39), 9375('60), 10370('64)

Africa, West
  GEN 2375('53), 2379('63), 2425('53), 2479('64)
  IND 2324('63), 2333('57), 5322('57), 5371('57)
  URB 1303('56), 1322('65), 2003('55), 2022('65), 2331('66), 2387('62)
      2389('62), 2435('65), 3302('62), 4301('62), 4304('56), 4319('50)
      4346('63), 4349('65), 4354('66), 4355('53), 4356('59), 4357('60)
      4358('57), 4370('56), 4395('61), 4396('59), 6305('65), 6307('59)
  RUR 2024('57), 2366('66), 2503('56), 2551('66), 3313('56), 5319('58)
      5388('64), 6311('54), 6319('62), 6320('59), 6383('66), 6394('65)
      6465('64), 8333('63), 8376('37), 8479('62), 10316('63)

Algeria
  GEN 2328('64), 2386('59)
  IND 2322('63), 2389('51), 3305('62), 4304('62)
  URB 2027('60), 2348('65), 4316('62), 4379('60)
  RUR 2338('64), 2391('61), 2456('63), 2496('65), 7337('63), 8344('62)
      8358('61), 8359('61), 8541('63), 9020('63), 9305('63), 9325('61)
      9368('63), 10306('63), 10331('63)

America, Latin
  GEN 2302('62), 2340('64), 2354('63), 2358('63), 2371('61), 2389('61)
      2392('55), 2449('64), 2481('56), 2488('62)
  IND 5320('60), 5328('61)
  URB 4314('60), 4318('62), 4375('55), 4381('63), 4384('66), 5367('63)
  RUR 1321('63), 1391('55), 2365('64), 2462('52), 2505('64), 3301('59)
      3325('59), 3332('59), 7373('59), 10314('63), 10360('63)

Angola
  GEN 2353('62)
  IND 5312('53)
  RUR 2570('60), 3320('59), 6337('60), 9004('62), 9352('62), 10350('58)

Arabian Peninsula
  RUR 8407('63), 8529('55)

Argentina
  GEN 2372('61)
  IND 2336('62), 2379('61), 3301('63)
  URB 2015('61), 3317('62), 4326('63)
  RUR 1362('61), 8415('57)

[361]

Burma
  GEN 2446('64)
  URB 2376('62), 4393('57)
  RUR 2029('65), 2601('66), 6442('62), 7332('62), 7347('63), 9012('63)
      10356('63), 11314('54)

Caledonia (French Oceania)
  RUR 8023('55)

Cambodia
  RUR 8492('65), 11322('61)

Cameroons
  IND 2011(n.d.), 2394('61)
  URB 5319('62), 5328('61)
  RUR 2404('56), 2531('64), 2583('60), 3002('61), 3303('60), 3330('63)
      6030('62), 6401('62), 6484('58), 7005('52), 8401('65), 8538('62)
      9317('64), 11305('61), 11309('56), 11341('65), 11360('52), 11408('60)

Caribbean, British
  GEN 2335('65), 2470('60)
  IND 4314('55)
  URB 2414('61)
  RUR 2036('65), 2501('60), 2568('62), 4363('53), 6333('62), 6368('64)
      6377('66), 6419('60), 7324('66), 7370('62), 7371('62), 7372('63)
      8313('56), 8502('61), 10359('65)

Caribbean, French
  IND 5366('58)
  URB 2311('63)

Central African Republic
  RUR 2395('63), 8444('63)

Ceylon
  GEN 2304('63), 2472('65)
  IND 5372('63)
  URB 3319('56)
  RUR 2578('53), 2608('59), 4344('57), 6303('64), 8056('61), 8081('58)
      8542('55), 8596('57), 11392('57)

Chad
  URB 2398('53)
  RUR 2351('63), 6330('63), 6478('61), 8423('60), 8509('53)

Chile
  IND 2336('62)
  URB 5334('65)
  RUR 2383('60), 4332('63), 6460('62), 9321('61)

China
  GEN 1361('64), 1412('62), 2422('62)
  IND 2030('44), 2319('22), 2428('47), 4003('39), 4004('45), 6315('28)
  URB 2346('53), 2347('21), 5374('28)
  RUR 2011('54), 4003('54), 6490('67), 7006('49), 7305('62), 7382('67)
      8385('46), 8507('63), 8606('59), 8607('47), 11336('63), 11345('53)
      11416('31)

Colombia
  GEN 1374('62), 2369('62), 2370('59)
  IND 2029('64), 2425('62)
  URB 2008('63), 2336('62), 2455('63), 2456('60)
  RUR 1301('66), 2308('62), 2525('53), 2598('62), 2599('63), 2613('64)
      5365('64), 7326('62), 8031('55), 8078('61), 8342('53), 8374('61)
      10345('62), 11340('63), 11413('61)

Congo (Brazzaville)
  IND 2305('54), 2306('63), 3303('52), 6301('59), 6307('58)
  URB 2001('59), 2014('58), 2446('57), 2447('61), 2448('63), 2449('61)
      4399('63)
  RUR 9002('55)

Congo (Kinshasa)
  GEN 2311('59), 2361('57)
  IND 2003('56), 2314('59), 2328('63), 2444('48), 2450('60), 2451('56)
      3314('65), 3324('66), 3335('60), 3345('60), 6320('59), 6331('56)
  URB 1323('56), 2002('61), 2003('55), 2009('56), 2012('61), 2013('61)
      2028('62), 2033('61), 2324("47), 2332('56), 2364('58), 2385('61)
      2399('57), 2421('56), 3008('60), 3013('56), 3309('56), 3314('57)
      4310('53), 4380('58), 4382('51), 4400('59), 5303('57), 5304('61)
      5306('58), 5315('56), 5316('61), 5329('51), 5363('56)
  RUR 1392('61), 2044('63), 3327('61), 3329('56), 4318('60), 4397('57)
      6001('62), 6014('62), 6058('62), 6326('57), 6340('56), 6344('58)
      9303('59), 9319('63), 9400('61), 11303('62), 11306('57), 11316('51)
      11338('63)

Costa Rica
  URB 2431('62), 2457('63), 5368('61)
  RUR 1354('53), 2305('57), 2306('63), 2352('50), 4382('53), 8446('53)

Cuba
  RUR 2574('58)

Dahomey
  GEN 1442('57)
  URB 2043('58), 3343('62)
  RUR 3003('56), 4395('64), 6004('59), 6055('62), 6443('57), 9008('38)
      11326('58), 11385('63)

Dominican Republic
  RUR 11318('63)

Ecuador
  IND 4009('55)
  RUR 3007('65), 3310('64), 5014('65), 8014('52), 8080('56), 8336('62)
      8349('49), 8468('62)

Egypt
  GEN 3306('58)
  IND 2315('57), 2363('56), 5323('62), 5361('55)
  URB 1301('64), 2302('64), 4344('61)
  RUR 2001('63), 2311('59), 5336('58), 8002('54), 8302('57), 8322('57),
      8323('55), 8544('49), 10303('63)

Ethiopia
  GEN 2421('65)
  RUR 2548('63), 6395('62), 6398('62), 6416('62), 6441('62)

Fiji
  RUR 2392('45), 2437('55), 2480('63), 3328('65), 4355('53), 4356('56)
      5353('64), 6006('64), 6312('64), 7342('54), 8041('45), 8082('62)
      8476('57), 8528('48), 10334('61)

French Guiana
  RUR 9334('63)

Gabon
  IND 2305('54), 2306('63)
  RUR 8006('52), 8311('50), 9002('55)

Gambia
  RUR 6002('62), 6026('53), 11344('53)

Ghana
  GEN 2305('55)
  IND 2423('61)
  URB 2024('62), 3009('61), 3015('61), 3304('66), 3329('59), 5302('58)
  RUR 2566('66), 3005('63), 3314('56), 4340('58), 5316('51), 6369('66)
      6381('66), 6383('66), 6479('56), 8017('66), 8337('52), 11307('44)
      11330('47)

Greece
  IND 3322('63)
  URB 2021('65), 4347('64)
  RUR 8069('61), 8381('62), 10353('62)

Guatemala
  GEN 2448('57), 2498('61), 2500('59)
  IND 4007('58), 5359('57)
  URB 2325('61), 5312('61)
  RUR 2042('52), 2352('50), 2584('51), 6041('64), 6051('64), 6357('56)
      6429('64), 6471('62), 6472('56), 6482('41), 8042('51), 8079('60)
      8089('53), 8091('52), 8535('58), 8592('49), 9394('64)

India, North
  IND 2020('63), 2384('61), 2404('59)
  URB 2010('59)
  RUR 1336('64), 2333('64), 2406('64), 2470('58), 4373('66), 5002('59)
      5343('63), 6384('61)

India, South
  GEN 1354('64)
  RUR 2364('55), 2434('61), 8457('55), 8562('18), 8582('40)

Indian States

            Andhra

  IND 4318('65)
  URB 5336('56)
  RUR 2302('66), 2522('50), 2539('64), 3317('64), 4351('64), 6446('58)
      8026('55), 8368('52), 8464('17), 8465('21), 11353('51)

            Assam

  URB 2406('63)
  RUR 8399('54)

            Bihar

  IND 2025('59), 2031('56), 2307('63), 4308('59), 4313('58)
  URB 5351('59), 5352('57)
  RUR 2304('58), 2534('64), 2555('64), 4375('60), 4400('64), 5366('64)
      6402('60), 8305('58), 8348('59), 9374('64), 9393('64), 11402('63)

            Gujarat

  IND 2028('58), 2420('55), 2421('55), 2422('53)
  URB 2374('61), 3312('65), 5348('58)
  RUR 2002('54), 2038('55), 2349('60), 2382('63), 4384('64), 6427('30)
      8024('45), 8038('64), 8488('64), 8489('61), 8515('65), 8591('53)
      9387('64), 11323('48), 11334('40), 11352('54), 11364('31), 11398('60)
      11399('58), 11401('49), 11403('37)

            Kerela

  GEN 2462('58)
  URB 3007('61)
  RUR 1381('59), 7343('62), 7344('65), 8065('60), 8456('52), 8466('63)
      8467('63), 8469('60), 8547('55), 9388('65), 10333('52), 10335('63)
      10336('66)

            Madhya Pradesh

  URB 5347('64), 5358('64)
  RUR 2009('54), 2345('64), 2377('66), 2438('63), 5313('64), 5339('63)
      5359('60), 6433('63), 8068('60), 8340('64), 8424('63), 8483('63)
      11359('63), 11372('63), 11373('63)

Uttar Pradesh (continued)

RUR 1350('55), 1358('55), 2423('55), 2440('62), 2471('55), 2556('64)
2558('60), 2563('60), 2564('60), 4002('58), 4010('58), 4015('52)
4310('56), 4335('57), 4377('56), 4378('57), 4411('64), 4423('60)
5010('59), 5011('61), 5320('65), 5361('64), 5362('65), 6404('56)
6424('52), 6425('60), 6431('59), 8020('55), 8058('54), 8061('58)
8064('58), 8066('60), 8073('60), 8324('63), 8443('55), 8451('57)
8459('52), 8491('60), 8503('59), 8504('56), 8505('52), 8506('52)
8540('60), 11311('57), 11342('59), 11381('58), 11382('63), 11404('61)

West Bengal

IND 2001('58), 2006('54), 2007('55), 2008('54), 2009('59), 2010('53)
2032('60), 2316('41), 2323('60), 2325('61), 2337('56), 2338('57)
2339('54), 3309('65), 3339('63), 3344('65), 5369('63), 6306('47)
6313('58), 6322('62)
URB 2317('57), 2318('58), 2319('59), 2329('64), 2352('62), 2405('64)
4328('60), 5356('55), 5371('60)
RUR 1369('57), 2347('64), 2397('64), 2468('64), 3308('64), 4424('59)
5318('64), 5367('63), 6327('64), 6364('64), 6426('48), 7354('65)
7365('64), 7367('65), 7368('58), 8038('64), 8083('60), 8316('62)
8327('63), 8328('65), 8331('58), 8341('64), 8481('49), 8495('63)
8553('63), 8563('52), 8565('46), 10305('63), 11302('61), 11354('16)
11395('63)

Andaman Islands

RUR 2370('44), 6325('64), 6428('62), 9309('64), 9355('57)

Unknown Indian State

IND 2342('57), 2344('54), 2345('57), 2346('60), 2347('64), 2348('54)
2349('55), 2350('57), 2351('58), 2352('57), 2353('57), 2354('54)
2355(n.d.), 2356('58), 2381('57), 2382('62), 2384('61), 2399('62)
2417('62), 2426('60), 2427('63), 2429('61), 2430('63), 2431('63)
2433('62), 2440('58), 3307('58), 3311('60), 4315('53)
URB 2378('58), 2410('60), 3301('62), 3306('65), 5301('56)
RUR 2310('59), 2335('61), 2367('62), 2453('63), 2475('66), 2488('63)
2489('66), 2493('65), 2520('62), 2523('55), 2537('64), 2549('61)
2550('55), 2565('63), 2597('59), 4322('58), 4336('65), 4352('65)
4372('64), 4379('63), 4407('58), 4414('62), 4415('53), 4416('61)
5314('64), 5328('66), 5331('64), 5342('62), 5375('64), 6051('64)
6318('60), 6346('55), 6385('57), 6414('64), 6454('64), 6455('64)
6463('63), 7304('63), 7330('65), 7335('65), 7362('60), 8312('60)
8314('60), 8357('60), 8426('63), 8433('62), 8440('61), 8455('62)
8461('64), 8462('60), 8463('55), 8493('65), 8508('62), 8510('63)
8514('63), 8530('63), 8549('64), 8562('18), 8582('40), 8601('33)
9302('64), 9314('63), 9315('62), 9327('65), 9356('56), 9376('63)
9380('65), 9381('64), 9395('64), 10352('65), 11327(n.d.), 11400('63)
11417('63)

Indonesia
GEN 1443('64), 1464('58), 1465('62), 2381('39), 2383('56), 2384('65)
2455('60), 2482('58), 2489('56), 2490('58), 2496('56), 2497('62)
2499('58), 3314('61), 3324('58), 4338('57)

Indonesia (continued)
  IND 1303('61), 2336('62), 2362('61), 2373('62), 2374('63), 2448('63)
      2449('63), 5351('57), 5376('55), 5377('56), 6303('62)
  URB 2042('63), 2047('61), 2321('61), 2349('67), 2350('65), 2369('56)
      2443('63), 3305('55), 3344('62), 4308('62), 4365('64), 4386('62)
      4394('59), 4397('56), 4398('52), 4403('62), 5332('55), 6303('59)
  RUR 1309('53), 2005('34), 2008('63), 2014('63), 2015('66), 2393('57)
      2394('65), 2450('61), 2451('29), 2513('64), 2567('66), 2595('60)
      2609('60), 3004('56), 3311('56), 3324('61), 4005('56), 4349('52)
      4357('56), 4405('63), 4406('63), 4418('60), 5005('61), 5008('63)
      5373('59), 5384('53), 6007('54), 6322('63), 6341('64), 6342('62)
      6343('62), 6360('63), 6361('56), 6480('58), 7320('61), 8379('60)
      8392('59), 8393('56), 8394('56), 8395('64), 8411('53), 8428('51)
      8441('62), 8499('59), 8584('57), 9344('58), 9359('62), 10330('55)
      10355('29), 11377(n.d.)

Iran
  GEN 2306('60), 2447('59)
  IND 2370('50), 5360('55)
  RUR 2442('64), 6310('64), 8360('60), 8470('64), 8477('61), 8484('58)
      8522('62), 9341('64)

Iraq
  RUR 2035('62), 2516('56)

Israel
  GEN 1343('54), 1346('56), 2365('54), 2366('65)
  IND 2310('56), 2332('55), 2336('62)
  RUR 2374('56), 2606('66), 2607('64), 3309('56), 4016('66), 7009('65)
      8345('65), 8593('60), 8594('62)

Italy, South
  IND 2317('62), 4008('60), 5303('63)
  URB 2032('60)
  RUR 4341('63), 4391('64), 6408('64), 8007('58)

Ivory Coast
  GEN 2355('62), 2399('65)
  URB 2312('62), 3015('61), 3310('66)
  RUR 2020('61), 2380('66), 2510('62), 2566('66), 3315('57), 3319('56)
      6037('62), 6396('58), 8494('60), 9333('55), 9371('62), 11312('60)

Jamaica
  IND 2313('53), 3315('60)
  RUR 2448('56), 2509('66), 2552('60), 3307('54), 4320('55), 6010('64)
      6338('56), 6417('59), 6418('55), 6419('60), 6423('60), 7001('56)
      7306('53), 7307('57), 7308('56), 7311('58), 8347('54), 8566('56)

Japan
  GEN 1317('58), 1363('62), 1374('62), 1412('62), 2325('62), 2327('66)
      2422('62), 2452('60), 2493('62)

Japan (continued)
IND 1328('62), 2016('59), 2017('58), 2037('61), 2301('57), 2393('62)
     2401('56), 2408('50), 2438('55), 3313('62), 3318('55), 3319('55)
     3320('54), 3321('63), 3323('64), 3333('62), 3346('63), 3349('62)
     3350('55), 4006('49), 4312('63), 4317('60), 5341('59), 5342('60)
     5346('62), 5379('62), 5380('60), 6327('55), 6328('63), 6329('54)
URB 2361('61), 2370('63), 2377('62), 2379('63), 2413('62), 2428('63)
     2439('57), 2454('56), 2458('62), 2459('55), 2460('63), 3347('63)
     4322('58), 4350('63), 4387('63), 4404('60), 5323('58), 5324('62)
RUR 1345('59), 1346('61), 1360('60), 2003('64), 2043('60), 2321('63)
     2356('64), 2357('61), 2389('61), 2409('63), 2414('60), 2415('63)
     2417('63), 2430('60), 2431('63), 2432('62), 2435('59), 2436('60)
     2439('63), 2443('55), 2445('59), 2472('63), 2485('64), 2490('58)
     2536('63), 2569('61), 2571('60), 2572('58), 2582('63), 2618('59)
     2621('63), 5007('60), 5009('60), 5329('62), 5338('59), 5354('63)
     5368('66), 5376('63), 6458('51), 7314('61), 7328('59), 7336('64)
     7345('64), 7350('58), 7375('64), 7376('59), 7377('64), 7378('55)
     7381('57), 8015('59), 8022('56), 8029('39), 8034('53), 8035('62)
     8036('59), 8037('54), 8043('55), 8054('58), 8071('54), 8075('50)
     8095('56), 8307('63), 8320('62), 8321('55), 8343('62), 8352('64)
     8353('63), 8383('58), 8384('58), 8387('49), 8388('54), 8389('62)
     8391('63), 8400('59), 8404('61), 8408('59), 8416('63), 8419('64)
     8421('55), 8431('64), 8432('58), 8435('56), 8436('58), 8437('59)
     8445('60), 8474('59), 8482('59), 8485('63), 8486('61), 8487('63)
     8498('61), 8523('63), 8545('56), 8546('55), 8551('59), 8552('63)
     8555('64), 8567('57), 8568('51), 8569('61), 8578('64), 8581('59)
     8588('64), 8602('61), 8603('55), 8604('63), 8605('59), 8610('62)
     8611('63), 8612('64), 10344('61), 11339('52), 11356('60),
     11375('63), 11376('45), 11396('54), 11397('55)

Jordan
URB 3327('58)
RUR 4346('58), 4361('63)

Kenya
GEN 2426('63), 2438('65)
RUR 2396('63), 2504('65), 5305('55), 6033('62), 6035('62), 6036('51)
     6363('63), 6444('65), 9010('50), 9021('59), 9304('56), 9360('61)
     9378('59), 10311('64), 10317('64), 11328('61)

Korea
URB 2382('65)
RUR 2329('63), 5378('63), 7383('61), 8070('58), 8326('63), 8511('58)
     8609('58)

Laos
GEN 2393('64), 2394(n.d.), 3309('61)
URB 2018('64)
RUR 6024('59), 6032('51), 6373('61), 6374('64), 6375('62), 8003('59)
     8308('59), 8405('58), 8429('58), 9337('60), 9339('64), 11343('61)

Lebanon
  IND 5309('55)
  RUR 2019('56), 8039('61), 8046('55), 8090('58), 8306('56), 8402('54)
      8403('53), 8517('63), 8579('42), 8580('41), 8613('61)

Liberia
  URB 2344('64)
  RUR 2387('66)

Libya
  RUR 9313('63)

Madagascar
  GEN 2359('62)
  URB 5322('52)
  RUR 2346('64), 2363('59), 4323('60), 4350('64), 6439('63), 8397('61)
      10312('63), 10313('62), 10327('62), 10329('63), 11320('64), 11333('63)

Malawi
  IND 6302('58)
  URB 2007('51), 2045('61), 3003('61), 5308('61), 5359('59)
  RUR 2521('38), 2596('66), 5015('64), 5350('49), 6012('63), 6317('59)
      6435('59), 7346('62), 7348('59), 7352('64), 7360('64), 7379('64)
      9007('58), 9363('56), 11387('38)

Malaysia
  GEN 2377('66)
  IND 2437(n.d.), 4303('62), 5368('65), 6330('53)
  URB 3005('59), 5338('60)
  RUR 2039('65), 2611('64), 3305('57), 3323('60), 4304('64), 4430('64)
      5334('58), 6017('66), 6301('54), 6468('64), 6469('63), 8025('60)
      8033('60), 8301('60), 8338('59), 8480('53), 8500('62), 8597('62)
      9351('62), 9398('65), 10308('62), 11315('60), 11371('53), 11411('53)

Mali
  URB 2396('65), 2450('66), 2451('63)
  RUR 2551('66), 9307('62)

Mauretania
  RUR 8583('56), 9308('63), 9389('63), 9390('56), 10318('63)

Mauritius
  URB 2310('61), 5307('61)
  RUR 6315('64), 8409('62), 11368('61)

Melanesia
  GEN 1318('54), 1437('66), 2326('54)
  RUR 1357('22), 1380('63), 2006('60), 2047('57), 2350('63), 2375('63)
      2376('63), 2403('60), 2421('34), 2429('54), 2478('57), 4417('53)
      6011('61), 6016('64), 6306('24), 6308('64), 6309('56), 6328('63)
      6329('63), 6349('63), 6350('63), 6351('61), 6356('53), 6411('67)
      6437('66), 6459('52), 8460('58), 9009('39), 9301('28), 9316('64)
      9324('63), 9332('64), 9332('64), 9354('61), 9384('65)

Mexico
  GEN 1401('59), 1442('57), 2303('63), 2339('62), 2412('64), 2448('57)
  IND 2018('60), 2022('51), 5359('57)
  URB 1320('66), 1321('63), 2322('62), 2438('61), 4306('63)
  RUR 1330('61), 1331('63), 1332('65), 1335('63), 1341('59), 1348('61)
      1350('55), 1376('41), 2032('41), 2048('60), 2343('63), 2382a('63)
      2390('62), 2405('61), 2410('59), 2463('44), 2492('61), 2524('34)
      2528('63), 2575('54), 2585('66), 2602('65), 2619('54), 2620('66)
      3304('56), 4313('62), 4319('63), 4345('53), 4363('53), 4431('58)
      5325('52), 5352('63), 6019('42), 6031('65), 6314('67), 6352('55)
      6358('48), 6391('65), 6405('47), 6412('56), 6429('64), 6430('61)
      6443('57), 6464('65), 6491('60), 7339('61), 7341('64), 8018('65)
      8044('65), 8057('60), 8059('51), 8060('60), 8076('65), 8077('30)
      8319('46), 8334('51), 8351('62), 8362('64), 8363('66), 8377('61)
      8378('48), 8382('63), 8443('55), 8513('36), 8527('59), 8533('50)
      8534('34), 8570('65), 9322('63), 9365('64), 9394('64), 10310('63)
      10324('62), 10361('66), 11317('52), 11358('63)

Micronesia
  GEN 2373('53)
  IND 3348('52)
  RUR 2529('65), 4417('53), 5374('64), 5382(n.d.), 8086('49), 8315('49)
      9003('60)

Morocco
  GEN 2382('56), 2484('56)
  IND 2002('51), 2021('52), 2036('53), 4309('60), 5301('59)
  URB 2345('60), 2412('63), 4402(n.d.)
  RUR 2313('48), 6370('55), 6477('63), 7384('62), 8532('52), 9013('59)

Mozambique
  GEN 2353('62), 2465('63)
  IND 5312('53)
  RUR 2416('66), 2570('60), 8572('61)

Near East
  GEN 1442('57), 2301('62), 2324('57), 2345('53), 2420('58), 2459('62)
      2466('60), 2467('60), 2486('64)
  IND 5363('55)
  RUR 6443('57), 7363('58), 8539('59), 8589('62), 10301('53)

Nepal
  RUR 2420('63)

New Guinea (Irian and Papua)
  IND 2366('62), 5333('64)
  RUR 1356('56), 2004('55), 2025('61), 2033('66), 2323('62), 2324('57)
      2368('64), 2386('66), 2458('63), 2469('60), 2495('63), 2502('64)
      2512('58), 2532('63), 2544('57), 2593('64), 2600('57), 2610('65)
      2614('64), 3302('56), 3331('58), 4314('58), 4354('54), 4392('62)
      4399('63), 4421('63), 5344('63), 5358('62), 6005('55), 6025('65)
      6034('22), 6048('62), 6050('57), 6313('52), 6345('64), 6348('62)
      6410('20), 6432('63), 6445('63), 6451('63), 6475('34), 7303('62)

New Guinea (Irian and Papua) (continued)
      7327('63), 8016('57), 8413('51), 9011('56), 9015('56), 9022('57)
      9311('63), 9367('65), 9377('64), 9385('57), 9386('65), 9392('64)
      11308('55), 11407('62)

Niger
  RUR 2325('63), 4001('57), 4017('63), 6015('62), 6042('62), 8496('62)
      8497('60), 9368('63), 11331('61), 11374('62)

Nigeria
  GEN 2485('64)
  IND 2416('57), 2445('63), 3332('61), 5381('53), 5382('62)
  URB 2308('62), 2309('60), 2360('53), 2385('61), 2390('60), 2391('62)
      2392('61), 3006('61), 3010('61), 3335('60), 4360('62)
  RUR 2028(n.d.), 2353('64), 2400('65), 2460('63), 2484('60), 2497('65)
      2581('63), 4011('60), 4366('56), 4386('55), 5012('55), 5013('60)
      5333('64), 6028('62), 6043('62), 6053('55), 6054('62), 6323('59)
      6324('59), 6331('65), 6359('56), 6379('44), 6406('66), 7318('41)
      8346('61), 9017('59), 10358('66), 11310('54), 11329('46), 11406('55)

Okinawa
  RUR 2459('63), 7353('63), 8458('66)

Pakistan
  GEN 2349('60), 2413('56), 3304('62)
  IND 2336('62), 3302('59), 3316('59), 3337('59), 5336('63), 5345('63)
      6305(n.d.)
  URB 2434('63), 4372('64)
  RUR 2430('60), 2508('64), 4301('63), 4381('60), 6388('62), 8414('58)

Pakistan, East
  IND 2014('61), 2015('63), 6309('63), 6325('56), 6326('56)
  URB 2358('64), 3001('57), 5339('62)
  RUR 2518('61), 2545('66), 4014('67), 4339('64), 4370('64), 6389('64)
      6426('48), 8303('64), 8304('63), 8563('52)

Pakistan, West
  URB 5313(n.d.)
  RUR 2422('60), 4007('60), 4360('54), 5327('64), 6353('64), 6397('61)
      8028('60), 8595('62), 11350('58)

Paraguay
  GEN 2474('54)

Peru
  GEN 2436('64)
  IND 1336('63), 2303('51), 2411('62), 2447('63), 3001('57), 6319('62)
  URB 2025('61), 4317('63)
  RUR 2037('57), 2408('62), 2455('62), 2474('59), 2599('63), 3006('62)
      3306('64), 4006('52), 4320('55), 4358('62), 6029('64), 6302('60)
      8001('59), 8067('63), 8087('61), 8332('62), 8350('65), 8354('59)
      8380('62), 8398('46), 8543('61), 8585('52), 8590('55), 10302('63)
      10338('63)

Philippines

    GEN 1446('58), 2307('59), 2401('62), 2427('59), 2430('65), 2432('60)
       3310('57)
    IND 4301('55), 5362('63)
    URB 2365('63), 2381('64), 2415('64), 3303('64), 3340('63), 4313('60)
       4343('56),
    RUR 1334('59), 2017('55), 2358('63), 2419('62), 2507('63), 2533('63)
       2579('59), 2590('57), 4009('62), 4324('64), 4342('60), 4343('64)
       4368('63), 4388('56), 4408('61), 4425('62), 5004('59), 5006('60)
       5321('61), 5322('57), 5385('64), 6371('58), 6440('59), 6449('64)
       6470('64), 7302('64), 7319('59), 7321('55), 7351('65), 7355('63)
       7357('63), 8084('60), 8338('59), 8369('62), 8372('55), 8410('54)
       8418('56), 8430('60), 8501('66), 8524('56), 8525('56), 8557('60)
       9370('63), 9397('64), 9401('64), 11324('61), 11378('65), 11380('63)
       11390('54), 11412('64)

Poland
    IND 2380('60)

Polynesia
    GEN 1437('66), 2323('48)
    IND 4310('55)
    URB 2335('66)
    RUR 1325('39), 1326('64), 1379('58), 2012('65), 2034('58), 2320('64)
       2401('60), 2424('64), 2449('62), 2479('63), 5383('63), 6018('64)
       6047('65), 6437('66), 6474('32), 7316('65), 8010('57), 8032('59)
       8318('41), 9345('62), 9349('54), 11365('64), 11414('64)

Portugese Guinea
    GEN 2337('62), 2353('62)
    IND 5312('53)
    RUR 2570('60), 10341('62)

Puerto Rico
    GEN 1419('63), 2487('61)
    IND 5340('59)
    URB 2050('56), 2303('62), 2326('64), 2395('56), 3333('65)
    RUR 2454('60), 2457('64), 3008('56), 3010('56), 3333('60), 4320('55)
       6422('60)

Rhodesia, Southern
    GEN 1471('45), 2457('60)
    IND 2027('62), 2034('58), 2302('37), 2318('30), 2327('58), 2361('53)
    URB 2016('61), 2355('52), 4374('62), 5327('60)
    RUR 1304('60), 2013('60), 2519('62), 5335('63), 6307('61), 6339('62)
       11337('60)

Rwanda-Urandi
    URB 5305('56)
    RUR 4318('60)

Sahara Region
  IND 4005('60), 5327('58)
  URB 2327('64)
  RUR 2314('63), 2315('63), 2316('63), 2317('63), 2318('63), 2342('64)
    9310('63), 9312('63), 9330('56), 9368('63), 9391('60)

Samoa
  RUR 2010('64), 5337('65), 5341('34), 8052('58)

San Salvador
  URB 2457('63)
  RUR 8417('63)

Senegal
  GEN 2399('65)
  URB 1325('56), 1326('56), 2339('64), 2343('63), 2430('63), 2432('61)
    3004('65), 3345('64), 5318('65), 5349('56)
  RUR 2551('66), 2588('63), 8442('64), 8531('64), 9335('62), 10364('64)
    11313('62), 11325('65), 11335('49), 11410('62)

Sierra Leone
  URB 1304('61), 2004('56), 2005('61), 2006('57), 2022('65), 2306('66)
    2307('53), 2387('62), 2388('55), 2389('62), 2422('63), 3315('63)
    3334('48), 4323('64)
  RUR 5346('47), 6013('62), 9014('51), 11389('53)

Singapore
  URB 2411('64)

Somali
  RUR 2461('61), 6403('62), 7338('62)

South Africa, Republic of
  GEN 1336('63), 1371('39), 2473('28), 3320('41)
  IND 2012('53), 2024('50), 2302('37), 2311('28), 2320('62), 2329('61)
    2360('60), 2364('64), 2387('64), 2435('49), 2441('46), 2442('41)
    2443('37), 2446('49), 3340('34), 4316('60), 5330('33), 5375('65)
    6304('26), 6308('53), 6314('64)
  URB 2019('37), 2020('48), 2026('61), 2035('61), 2036('61), 2044('64)
    2046('62), 2049('63), 2304('38), 2337('61), 2353('37), 2362('34)
    2363('35), 2368('34), 2371('63), 2386('31), 2403('62), 2418('53)
    2419('30), 2420('38), 2427('34), 2440('48), 2445('64), 3012('63)
    3325('55), 3328('55), 3331('36), 3332('34), 3336('33), 4338('56)
    4359('58), 5310('28), 5333('35), 5335('38), 5340('58), 5341('61)
    5343('31), 5357('53), 5361('28), 5362('38), 5366('61), 5375('22)
  RUR 1337('40), 1338('58), 2022('37), 2330('64), 2398('40), 2426('33)
    2447('20), 2452('60), 2481('33), 2540('37), 2541('28), 2589('31)
    2615('36), 3316('53), 4316('64), 4317('64), 4369('64), 4427('60)
    6020('62), 6044('30), 6366('39), 6372('33), 6448('34), 6456('28)
    7333('31), 7358('63), 7380('39), 8598('52), 9018('66), 9329('62)
    9340('62), 9346('56), 9347('56), 9372('32), 9383('47), 10323('55)
    10325('22), 10346('64), 11304('62), 11348('60), 11349('52)
    11415('31)

Sudan
  IND 6318('61)
  URB 5345('64)
  RUR 2319('63), 2339('64), 4012('66), 4308('57), 5317('63), 6045('62)
      6340('56), 8008('64), 8390('59), 11366('65)

Swaziland
  RUR 10322('64), 11347('64)

Syria
  RUR 8577('60)

Tahiti
  URB 2375('63)
  RUR 1324('66), 2384('65), 5379('63), 6393('64), 8475('57)

T'aiwan
  GEN 2342('65), 2343('56), 2400('63)
  IND 2375('64), 5318('64)
  URB 2461('64)
  RUR 2327('64), 2340('62), 2425('63), 2587('63), 2622('64), 4347('64)
      4432('63), 8040('66), 8571('61), 9366('63), 11319('55)

Tanzania
  GEN 2438('65)
  URB 2017('55), 2301('61), 5342('63), 5378('61)
  RUR 2301('65), 2465('63), 5345('56), 5364('60), 5386('65), 6022('62)
      6023('62), 6407('63), 6488('62), 9318('63), 9328('63), 9348('62)

Thailand
  GEN 2493('62), 3309('61)
  IND 2035('61), 6310('55)
  URB 2313('63), 2333('62), 2397('62), 4335('62)
  RUR 2016('57), 2411('57), 2412('60), 2413('53), 2428('62), 2441('61)
      2464('63), 2486('64), 2511('64), 4419('64), 5370('63), 6376('63)
      6390('55), 6436('64), 6442('62), 7004('58), 8053('60), 8055('60)
      8063('57), 8074('65), 8361('55), 8448('62), 8478('61), 8554('60)
      8608('64), 9331('61), 9336('65), 9338('64), 9339('64), 9342('65)
      9343('65), 11409('62)

Togo
  GEN 2380('63)
  RUR 5302('63), 5357('60), 9326('62), 9369('57)

Trinidad and Tobago
  RUR 2031('60), 2309('64), 2553('64), 8049('47)

Tunesia
  IND 4001('58)
  URB 2442('60), 4385('60), 5370('60)
  RUR 3312('53), 3322('55), 5351('63), 8009('65), 8355('58), 8575('61)
      9379('63), 10347('63)

Zambia (continued)
   RUR 1304('60), 2021('61), 2045('58), 2354('64), 2399('45), 2514('56)
        4353('59), 5308('54), 5323('56), 5324('57), 5340('67), 5355('61)
        6008('46), 6009('62), 6021('41), 6046('39), 6307('61), 6332('65)
        6339('62), 6392('64), 6434('57), 6450('62), 6485('59), 6486('41)
        7359('40), 8425('67), 8536('61), 8537('59), 9364('50), 9399('56)
        11363('64), 11388('39)